ORACLE®   *Oracle Press*™

Oracle8i DBA Handbook

ORACLE®   *Oracle Press*™

Oracle8i DBA Handbook

Kevin Loney
Marlene Theriault

Osborne/McGraw-Hill

Berkeley New York St. Louis San Francisco
Auckland Bogotá Hamburg London Madrid
Mexico City Milan Montreal New Delhi Panama City
Paris São Paulo Singapore Sydney Tokyo Toronto

Osborne/McGraw-Hill
2600 Tenth Street
Berkeley, California 94710
U.S.A.

For information on translations or book distributors outside the U.S.A., or to arrange bulk purchase discounts for sales promotions, premiums, or fund-raisers, please contact Osborne/McGraw-Hill at the above address.

Oracle8i DBA Handbook

1234567890 DOC DOC 019876543210

ISBN 0-07-212188-2

Publisher
Brandon A. Nordin

Associate Publisher and Editor-in-Chief
Scott Rogers

Acquisitions Editor
Jeremy Judson

Project Editor
Mark Karmendy

Editorial Assistant
Monika Faltiss

Technical Editor
Ian Fickling

Copy Editor
Dennis Weaver

Proofreader
John Gildersleeve

Indexer
Rebecca Plunkett

Computer Designers
Jani Beckwith
Ann Sellers

Illustrators
Brian Wells
Beth Young

Series Design
Jani Beckwith

This book was composed with Corel VENTURA™ Publisher.

About the Authors

Kevin Loney (Wilmington, DE) is a veteran Oracle developer and DBA. He is the author of the best-selling *Oracle8 DBA Handbook*, and co-author of *Oracle8 Advanced Tuning & Administration* and *Oracle8: The Complete Reference*. He frequently makes presentations at Oracle conferences and contributes to *Oracle Magazine*.

Marlene Theriault (Vienna, VA) has been an Oracle DBA for over 15 years and is Senior DBA at The John Hopkins University Applied Physics Laboratory. She has been published in several magazines and conference proceedings throughout the world.

To my parents,
and to Sue, Emily, and Rachel

—K.L.

To the two most important men in my life:
Marc Goodman and Nelson Cahill

—M.T.

Contents At A Glance

PART III
Networked Oracle

PART IV
Appendices

Contents

PART I
Database Architecture

PART II
Database Management

PART III

Networked Oracle

PART IV
Appendices

Acknowledgments

As always, this has been a joint effort. Thanks to Marlene Theriault and Ian Fickling, who contributed so much to this edition. Writing is frequently a learning process, and they have been excellent teachers.

Thanks to the folks at Osborne/McGraw-Hill who guided this product through its stages: Scott Rogers, Mark Karmendy, Monika Faltiss, Dennis Weaver, Michelle Galicia, and the others at Osborne. Thanks also to the "Oracle" component of Oracle Press, including Julie Gibbs and Leslie Steere.

Thanks to those who suggested topics, changes, or corrections. Thanks to Eyal Aronoff, Noorali Sonawalla, and Rachel Carmichael, among others, for their advice, comments, corrections, and friendship.

Thanks to the writers and friends along the way. This effort would not have been possible without the help of many.

If you have comments regarding the book or are looking for additional DBA materials, please see my site, http://www.kevinloney.com. As additional ORACLE8i features become available and mature, articles about them will be published on my site.

Kevin Loney

My thanks go first and foremost to Kevin Loney for inviting me to be a part of this venture and for having the unending patience to guide me through this edition's update, gently but firmly. I have learned an astonishing amount while participating in this project—both technically and personally. My thanks go also to Ian Fickling who provided the technical review for this book. His comments were always insightful and accurate.

I'd like to echo Kevin's thanks to the entire staff at Osborne/McGraw Hill for their outstanding effort in helping to put this edition together.

There are no words that can express my thanks to Nelson Cahill for his quiet support and encouragement throughout this process. His belief that I could do this helped me to believe I could.

Special thanks to Carl Dudley for his assistance with Recovery Manager.

I want to thank Rachel Carmichael for her help and support as my friend, longtime writing and presenting partner, and technical guru. And I thank all of the people who have been there for me throughout my life—work associates, friends, and family.

Marlene Theriault

Introduction

hether you're an experienced DBA, a new DBA, or an application developer, you need to know how the internal structures of the ORACLE8 database work and interact. Properly managing the database's internals will allow your database to meet two goals: it will work, and it will work *well*.

In this book, you'll find the information you need to achieve both of these goals. The emphasis throughout is on managing the database's capabilities in an effective, efficient manner to deliver a quality product. The end result will be a database that is dependable, robust, secure, extensible, and designed to meet the objectives of the applications it supports.

Several components are critical to these goals, and you'll see that all of them are covered here in depth. A well-designed logical and physical database architecture will improve performance and ease administration by properly distributing database objects. Determining the correct number and size of rollback segments will allow your database to support all of its transactions. You'll also see appropriate monitoring, security, and tuning strategies for stand-alone and networked databases. Optimal backup and recovery procedures are also provided to help ensure the database's recoverability. The focus in all of these sections is on the proper planning and management techniques for each area.

You'll also find information on how to manage specific problems, such as dealing with very large databases or very high availability requirements.

Networking issues and the management of distributed and client/server databases are thoroughly covered. SQL*Net (now known as Net8), networking configurations, snapshots, location transparency, and everything else you need to successfully implement a distributed or client/server database are described in detail in Part III of this book. You'll also find real-world examples and for every major configuration.

In addition to the commands needed to perform DBA activities, you will also see the Oracle Enterprise Manager screens that perform similar functions. In addition to descriptions of the ORACLE8i features, you will also see sections that compare prior releases to ORACLE8i, to facilitate your migration path. "Solutions" sections throughout the book offer common solutions to the most frequently encountered problems.

By following the techniques in this book, you'll no longer have to worry about disasters striking your databases. Your systems can be designed and implemented so well that tuning efforts will be minimal. Administering the database will become easier as the users get a better product, while the database works—and works well.

PART
I

Database
Architecture

CHAPTER
1

Getting Started with the
ORACLE Architecture

ith every release, ORACLE adds new features or changes existing features. With the release of ORACLE8i, many new features and functionality changes have been added. At the same time, ORACLE has added new tools to simplify database administration tasks. In this part of this book, you will see an overview of the ORACLE architecture and its implementation. You will also see the steps required to create an ORACLE database.

In the second part of this book, you will see specific guidelines for managing aspects of an ORACLE database—such as managing rollback segments and establishing passwords. The third section of the book deals with using ORACLE in a networked environment. The final section of the book contains the command syntax for the most-used SQL commands and a guide to the initialization parameter changes in different ORACLE versions.

This section provides the big picture of the ORACLE architecture and the steps you need to follow in order to create a database. In this chapter, you'll see examples of the components of an ORACLE database and the basic implementation concepts that guide their usage. Administering an ORACLE database requires knowing how these different components interact, where they fit in the big picture, and how to best customize the system to meet your needs. In many ways, this chapter is a road map to the detailed discussions of database administration in the rest of the book.

An Overview of Databases and Instances

Two basic concepts have to be understood in order to make any sense out of the ORACLE architecture: databases and instances. In the following two major sections, you will see descriptions of both of these concepts and their implementation in ORACLE.

Databases

A *database* is a set of data. ORACLE provides the ability to store and access data in a manner consistent with a defined model known as the relational model. Because of this, ORACLE is referred to as a relational database management system (RDBMS). Most references to a "database" refer not only to the physical data but also to the combination of physical, memory, and process objects described in this chapter.

Data in a database is stored in tables. Relational tables are defined by their *columns*, and are given a name. Data is then stored as *rows* in the table. Tables can be related to each other, and the database can be used to enforce these relationships. A sample table structure is shown in Figure 1-1.

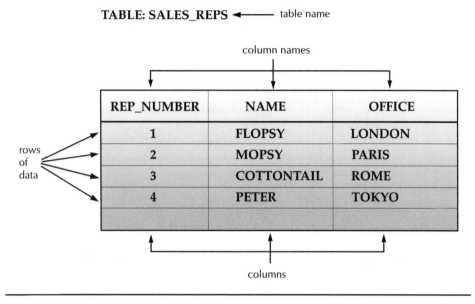

FIGURE 1-1. *Sample table structure*

In addition to storing data in relational format, ORACLE (as of ORACLE8) supports object-oriented (OO) structures such as abstract datatypes and methods. Objects can be related to other objects, and objects can contain other objects. As you will see in Chapter 5, you can use object views to enable OO interfaces to your data without making any modifications to your tables.

Whether you use relational structures or OO structures, an ORACLE database stores its data in files. Internally, there are database structures that provide a logical mapping of data to files, allowing different types of data to be stored separately. These logical divisions are called tablespaces. The next subsections describe tablespaces and files.

Tablespaces

A *tablespace* is a logical division of a database. Each database has at least one tablespace (called the *SYSTEM* tablespace). You can use additional tablespaces to group users or applications together for ease of maintenance and for performance benefits. Examples of such tablespaces would be USERS for general use and RBS for rollback segments (which will be described later in this section). A tablespace can belong to only one database.

Files

Each tablespace is constituted of one or more files, called *datafiles,* on a disk. A datafile can belong to one and only one tablespace. As of ORACLE7.2, datafiles can be resized after their creation. Creating new tablespaces requires creating new datafiles.

Once a datafile has been added to a tablespace, the datafile cannot be removed from the tablespace, and it cannot be associated with any other tablespace.

If you store database objects in multiple tablespaces, then you can physically separate them at the physical level by placing their respective datafiles on separate disks. This separation of data is an important tool in planning and tuning the way in which the database handles the I/O requests made against it. The relationship among databases, tablespaces, and datafiles is illustrated in Figure 1-2.

Instances

In order to access the data in the database, ORACLE uses a set of background processes that are shared by all users. In addition, there are memory structures

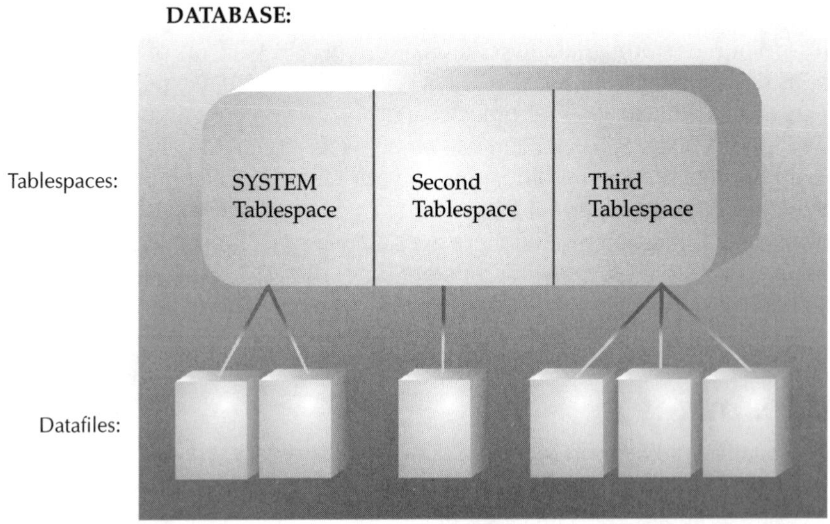

FIGURE 1-2. *Relationship among databases, tablespaces, and datafiles*

(collectively known as the System Global Area, or SGA) that store the most recently queried data from the database. The largest of the SGA sections, the data block buffer cache and the Shared SQL Pool, typically constitute over 95 percent of the memory allocated to the SGA. These memory areas help to improve database performance by decreasing the amount of I/O performed against the datafiles.

A database *instance* (also known as a *server*) is a set of memory structures and background processes that access a set of database files. It is possible for a single database to be accessed by multiple instances (this is the ORACLE Parallel Server option). The relationship between instances and databases is illustrated in Figure 1-3.

The parameters that determine the size and composition of an instance are stored in a file called init.ora. The init.ora file is read during instance startup and may be modified by the DBA. Any modifications made to the init.ora file will not take effect until the next startup. The name of an instance's init.ora file usually includes the name of the instance; if the instance is named ORCL, the init.ora file will usually be named initorcl.ora. A second configuration file, config.ora, stores the settings of variables that do not change after database creation (such as the database block size). The name of an instance's config.ora file usually includes the name of the instance; if the instance is named ORCL, the config.ora file will usually be named configorcl.ora. In order for the config.ora settings to be used, the file must be listed as an included file via the IFILE parameter in the instance's init.ora file.

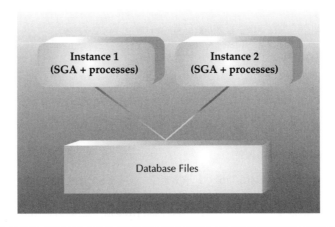

FIGURE 1-3.   *Instances and datafiles in ORACLE*

Internal Database Structures

Given the preceding overview of databases and instances, ORACLE's database structures can be divided among three categories:

- Those that are internal to the database (such as tables)
- Those that are internal to memory areas (including shared memory areas and processes)
- Those that are external to the database

In the following sections, you will find descriptions of each of the elements within each category. The categories will be presented in the order listed above.

In the next section, you will see descriptions of those elements that are internal to the database. These include the following:

- Tables, columns, constraints, and datatypes (including abstract datatypes)
- Partitions and subpartitions
- Users and schemas
- Indexes, clusters, and hash clusters
- Views
- Sequences
- Procedures, functions, packages, and triggers
- Synonyms
- Privileges and roles
- Database links
- Segments, extents, and blocks
- Rollback segments
- Snapshots and materialized views

In the following sections, you will see descriptions of each of these elements.

Tables, Columns, and Datatypes

Tables are the storage mechanism for data within an ORACLE database. As shown previously in Figure 1-1, tables contain a fixed set of columns. The columns of a table describe the attributes of the entity being tracked by the table. Each column has a name and specific characteristics.

A column has a *datatype* and a *length*. For columns using the NUMBER datatype, you can specify their additional characteristics of precision and scale. *Precision* determines the number of significant digits in a numeric value. *Scale* determines the placement of the decimal point. A specification of NUMBER (9,2) for a column has a total of nine digits, two of which are to the right of the decimal point. The default precision is 38 digits, which is also the maximum precision.

The available datatypes are listed in Table 1-1.

In addition to the datatypes listed in Table 1-1, ORACLE provides alternatives for ANSI standard datatypes. For ANSI datatypes CHARACTER and CHAR, use ORACLE's CHAR datatype. For the ANSI datatypes CHARACTER VARYING and CHAR VARYING, use ORACLE's VARCHAR2 datatype. For the ANSI NUMERIC, DECIMAL, DEC, INTEGER, INT, and SMALLINT datatypes, use ORACLE's NUMBER datatype. For the ANSI standard FLOAT, REAL, and DOUBLE PRECISION datatypes, ORACLE supports a FLOAT datatype within PL/SQL.

You can create your own abstract datatypes beginning with ORACLE8. You can also use special REF datatypes that reference row objects elsewhere in the database (see Chapter 5).

The tables owned by the users SYS and SYSTEM are called the *data dictionary tables*. The data dictionary tables provide a system catalog that the database uses to manage itself. The data dictionary is created by a set of catalog scripts provided by ORACLE. Each time you install or upgrade a database, you will need to run scripts that either create or modify the data dictionary tables. When you install a new option in your database, you may need to run additional catalog scripts.

Tables are related to each other via the columns they have in common. You can require the database to enforce these relationships via *referential integrity*. If you use ORACLE's object-oriented features, rows may be related to each other via internal references called object IDs (OIDs). Referential integrity is enforced at the database level via constraints.

Constraints

You can create *constraints* on the columns of a table; when a constraint is applied to a table, every row in the table must satisfy the conditions specified in the

Datatype	Description
CHAR	A fixed-length character field, up to 2,000 bytes in length.
NCHAR	A fixed-length field for multibyte character sets. Maximum size is 2,000 characters or 2,000 bytes, depending on the character set.
VARCHAR2	A variable-length character field, up to 4,000 characters in length.
NVARCHAR2	A variable-length field for multibyte character sets. Maximum size is 4,000 characters or 4,000 bytes, depending on the character set.
DATE	A fixed-length, 7-byte field used to store all dates. The time is stored as part of the date. When queried, the date will be in the format DD-MON-YY, as in 13-APR-99 for April 13, 1999, unless you override the date format by setting the NLS_DATE_FORMAT init.ora parameter.
NUMBER	A variable-length number column. Allowed values are zero and positive and negative numbers. NUMBER values are usually stored in 4 or fewer bytes.
LONG	A variable-length field, up to 2GB in length.
RAW	A variable-length field used for binary data up to 2,000 bytes in length.
LONG RAW	A variable-length field used for binary data up to 2GB in length.
MLSLABEL	For Trusted ORACLE only. This datatype uses between 2 and 5 bytes per row.
BLOB	Binary large object, up to 4GB in length.
CLOB	Character large object, up to 4GB in length.
NCLOB	CLOB datatype for multibyte character sets, up to 4GB in length.
BFILE	External binary file; size is limited by the operating system.
ROWID	Binary data representing a RowID. Value will be 10 bytes for ORACLE8 RowID values, 6 bytes for the restricted RowID format used in ORACLE7.
UROWID	Binary data used for data addressing, up to 4,000 bytes in length.

TABLE 1-1. *ORACLE Datatypes*

constraint definition. In the following **create table** command, an EMPLOYEE table is created with several constraints:

```
create table EMPLOYEE
(EmpNo            NUMBER(10)     PRIMARY KEY,
 Name            VARCHAR2(40)    NOT NULL,
 DeptNo          NUMBER(2)       DEFAULT 10,
 Salary          NUMBER(7,2)     CHECK (salary<1000000),
 Birth_Date      DATE,
 Soc_Sec_Num     CHAR(9)         UNIQUE,
 foreign key (DeptNo) references DEPT(DeptNo))
tablespace USERS;
```

First, note that the table is given a name (EMPLOYEE). Each of its columns is named (EmpNo, Name, etc.). Each column has a specified datatype and length. The EmpNo column is defined as a NUMBER datatype, with no scale—this is the equivalent of an integer. The Name column is defined as a VARCHAR2(40); this will be a variable-length column up to 40 characters in length.

The *primary key* of the table is the column or set of columns that make every row in that table unique. A primary key column will be defined within the database as being **NOT NULL**—this means that every row that is stored in that table must have a value for that column; it cannot be left **NULL**. The **NOT NULL** constraint can be applied to the columns in the table, as used for the Name column in the above example.

A column can have a *DEFAULT* constraint. A DEFAULT constraint will generate a value for a column when a row is **insert**ed in a table but no value is specified for a column.

The *CHECK* constraint ensures that values in a specified column meet a certain criterion (in this case, that the Salary column's value is less than 1,000,000). A CHECK constraint cannot reference a separate table. A NOT NULL constraint is treated by the database as a CHECK constraint.

Another constraint, *UNIQUE*, guarantees uniqueness for columns that should be unique but are not part of the primary key. In this example, the Soc_Sec_Num column has a UNIQUE constraint, so every record in this table must have a unique value for this column.

A *foreign key* constraint specifies the nature of the relationship between tables. A foreign key from one table references a primary key that has been previously defined elsewhere in the database.

For example, if a table called DEPT had a primary key of DeptNo, then the records in DEPT would list all of the valid DeptNo values. The DeptNo column in the EMPLOYEE table shown in the preceding listing *references* that DEPT.DeptNo column. By specifying EMPLOYEE.DeptNo as a foreign key to DEPT.DeptNo, you guarantee that no DeptNo values can be entered into the EMPLOYEE table unless those values already exist in the DEPT table.

The constraints in the database help to ensure the *referential integrity* of the data. Referential integrity provides assurance that all of the references within the database are valid and all constraints have been met.

Abstract Datatypes

As of ORACLE8, you can define your own datatypes. For example, you may create a datatype that contains the multiple parts of a person's name—first name, last name, middle initial, suffix, etc.—as a single datatype. In the following listing, the NAME_TY datatype is created:

```
create type NAME_TY as object
(First_Name      VARCHAR2(25),
Middle_Initial   CHAR(1),
Last_Name        VARCHAR2(30),
Suffix           VARCHAR2(5));
/
```

The **create type** command in the preceding listing is available as of ORACLE8. You can use your user-defined datatypes to standardize the usage of data within your applications. For example, you can use the NAME_TY datatype anywhere you would use any other datatype. In the following example, the EMPLOYEE table is created again; this time, the NAME_TY datatype is the datatype for the EMPLOYEE.Name column:

```
create table EMPLOYEE
(EmpNo              NUMBER(10)     PRIMARY KEY,
 Name               NAME_TY,
 DeptNo             NUMBER(2)      DEFAULT 10,
 Salary             NUMBER(7,2)    CHECK (salary<1000000),
 Birth_Date         DATE,
 Soc_Sec_Num        CHAR(9)        UNIQUE,
 foreign key (DeptNo) references DEPT(DeptNo))
tablespace USERS;
```

The Name column of the EMPLOYEE table contains four attributes, as shown in the NAME_TY creation statement. If you define methods—programs that act on the attributes of datatypes—on the NAME_TY datatype, then you can apply those methods to the values of the Name column in the EMPLOYEE table. See Chapter 5 for examples of the use and management of abstract datatypes and other object-oriented structures.

Constructor Methods

When you create an abstract datatype, ORACLE automatically creates a constructor method to support **insert**s into the column that uses the datatype. For the NAME_TY datatype, the constructor method is named NAME_TY, and the parameters for the method are the attributes of the datatype. See Chapter 5 for examples of the use of constructor methods.

Object Tables

An object table is a table whose rows are all objects—they all have object ID (OID) values. You can create an object table via the **create table** command. For example, you can use the **create table** command in the following listing to create a NAME table based on the NAME_TY datatype:

```
create table NAME of NAME_TY;
```

You will then be able to create references from other tables to the row objects in the NAME object table. If you create references to the NAME row objects, you will be able to select NAME rows via the references—without directly querying the NAME table. See Chapter 5 for examples of the use of row objects and the simulation of row objects via object views.

Nested Tables and Varying Arrays

A nested table is a column (or columns) within a table that contains multiple values for a single row in the table. For example, if you have multiple addresses for a person, then you may create a row in a table that contains multiple values for an Address column, but only one value for the rest of the columns. Nested tables can contain multiple columns and an unlimited number of rows. A second type of collector, called a varying array, is limited in the number of rows it can contain.

An in-depth discussion of the use of nested tables and varying arrays is beyond the scope of this book; see *ORACLE8: The Complete Reference* (Oracle Press, 1997) for detailed examples of these structures and their related syntax. In general, nested tables give you more flexibility in data management than varying arrays do (particularly in ORACLE8.0, since varying array values can only be selected via PL/SQL). Both nested tables and varying arrays require you to modify the SQL syntax you use to access your data. In general, you can simulate the data relationships of nested tables via related relational tables.

Partitions and Subpartitions

As your tables grow larger, their maintenance grows more difficult. In very large databases, you may greatly simplify your database administration activities by splitting a large table's data across multiple smaller tables. For example, you may split a table into separate smaller tables based on the department or product values in the table.

As of ORACLE8, you can specify ranges for the database to use when splitting a larger table into smaller tables. These smaller tables, called *partitions*, are generally simpler to manage than larger tables. For example, you can **truncate** the data in a single partition without truncating the data in any other partition. ORACLE will treat the partitioned table as a single large table, but you can manage the partitions as separate objects.

Partitions may also improve the performance of an application. Since the optimizer will know the range values used as the basis for the partitions, the optimizer may be able to direct queries to only use specific partitions during table accesses. Because less data may be read during the query processing, the performance of the query should improve.

You can partition indexes as well as tables. The ranges of values for the partitions of a partitioned index may match the ranges used for the indexed table—in which case the index is called a *local index*. If the index partitions do not match the value ranges used for the table partitions, the index is called a *global index*.

As of ORACLE8i, you can partition partitions, creating *subpartitions*. For example, you can partition a table on one set of values and then partition the partitions based on a second partition method. See Chapter 12 for a description of the management issues for partitions, subpartitions, local indexes, and global indexes.

Users

A *user* account is not a physical structure in the database, but it does have important relationships to the objects in the database: users own the database's objects. The user SYS owns the data dictionary tables; these store information about the rest of the structures in the database. The user SYSTEM owns views that access these data dictionary tables, for use by the rest of the users in the database.

When you create objects in the database, the objects are created under user accounts. You can customize each user account to use a specific tablespace as its default tablespace.

You can tie database accounts to operating system accounts, allowing users to access the database from the operating system without having to enter passwords for both the operating system and the database. Users can then access the objects they own or to which they have been granted access.

Schemas

The set of objects owned by a user account is called the user's *schema*. You can create users who do not have the ability to log in to the database. Such user accounts provide a schema that can be used to hold a set of database objects separate from other users' schemas.

Indexes

In a relational database, the physical location of a row is irrelevant—unless, of course, the database needs to find it. In order to make it possible to find data, each row in each table is labeled with a *RowID*. This RowID tells the database exactly where the row is located (by file, block within that file, and row within that block).

NOTE
An index-organized table does not have traditional ORACLE RowIDs. Instead, its primary key acts as a logical RowID.

An index is a database structure used by the server to quickly find a row in a table. There are three types of indexes: cluster indexes, table indexes, and bitmap indexes. Cluster indexes store the cluster key values in clusters; see the next section of this chapter for further details on the use of clusters. A table index stores the values of a table's rows along with the physical location where the row is located (its RowID). A bitmap index is a special type of table index designed to support queries of large tables with columns that have few distinct values.

Each index entry consists of a key value and a RowID. You can index a single column or a set of columns. ORACLE stores index entries using a B*tree mechanism, guaranteeing a short access path to the key value. When a query accesses the index, it finds the index entries that match the query criteria. The entry's matching RowID value provides ORACLE the physical location for the associated row, reducing the I/O burden required to locate the data.

Indexes both improve performance and (optionally) ensure uniqueness of a column. ORACLE automatically creates an index when a UNIQUE or PRIMARY KEY constraint clause is specified in a **create table** command. You can manually create your own indexes via the **create index** command. See Appendix A for the full syntax and options of the **create index** command.

You can create indexes on one or more columns of a table. In the example of the EMPLOYEE table given earlier, ORACLE will automatically create unique indexes on the EmpNo and Soc_Sec_Num columns since they have been specified as PRIMARY KEY and UNIQUE, respectively. Dropping an index will not affect the data within the previously indexed table.

As of ORACLE7.3, you can create *bitmap indexes*. As described in Chapter 12, bitmap indexes are useful when the data is not very selective—there are very few distinct values in the column. Bitmap indexes speed searches in which such nonselective columns are used as limiting conditions in queries. Bitmap indexes are most effective for very static data.

As of ORACLE8, you can create indexes that *reverse* the order of the data prior to storing it. That is, an entry whose data value is 1002 will be indexed as 2001. The reversing of the data order prior to indexing helps keep the data better distributed within the index. Because they reverse the data values, reverse order indexes are only useful if you will be performing equivalence operations in your queries, such as

```
where key_col_value = 1002
```

If you are performing range searches, such as

```
where key_col_value > 1000
```

then reverse order indexes will not effectively meet your needs since consecutive values will not be stored near each other. Because consecutive rows will be stored apart from each other in the index, range queries of reverse key indexes will have to read more blocks than a traditional index would require.

As of ORACLE8, you can create an index-organized table. In an index-organized table (specified via the **organization index** clause of the **create table** command), the entire table is stored within an index structure, with its data sorted by the table's primary key. To create an index-organized table, you must specify a primary key constraint for the table. The index-organized table will not have RowIDs for its rows; ORACLE will use the primary key value as a logical RowID value. As of ORACLE8i, you can create secondary indexes on an index-organized table.

Clusters

Tables that are frequently accessed together may be physically stored together. To store them together, you can create a *cluster* to hold the tables. The data in the tables is then stored together in the cluster to minimize the number of I/Os that must be performed, and thus performance is improved.

The related columns of the tables are called the *cluster key*. The cluster key is indexed using a *cluster index*, and its value is only stored once for the multiple tables in the cluster. You must create a cluster index prior to **insert**ing any rows into the tables in the cluster.

Clusters may be beneficial for tables that are very frequently queried together. Within the cluster, rows from separate tables are stored in the same blocks, so queries joining those tables may perform fewer I/Os than if the tables were stored apart. However, the performance of **insert**s, **update**s, and **delete**s for clustered tables may be significantly worse than the same operations against nonclustered tables. Before clustering tables, evaluate the frequency with which they are queried together. If the tables are always queried together, you should consider merging them into a single table rather than clustering two tables.

Hash Clusters

A second type of cluster, a *hash cluster*, uses *hashing functions* on the row's cluster key to determine the physical location where the row should be stored. Hash clusters will yield the greatest performance benefit for equivalence queries, such as the one shown in the following listing:

```
select Name
   from EMPLOYEE
 where EmpNo = 123;
```

In this example, the EMPLOYEE table is queried for an exact match of the EmpNo column. If EMPLOYEE is part of a hash cluster, and EmpNo is part of the cluster key, then the database can use the hashing function to quickly determine where the data is physically located. The same performance gains would not be expected if the **where** clause had specified a range of values, as in the following listing:

```
select Name
   from EMPLOYEE
 where EmpNo > 123;
```

Finding a row in a standard indexed table may require multiple I/Os—one or more to find the key value in the index and another to read the row from the table. Using a hash algorithm reduces the number of I/Os required to return the row for equivalence queries.

Views

A *view* appears to be a table containing columns and is queried in the same manner that a table is queried. However, a view contains no data. Conceptually, a view can be thought of as a mask overlaying one or more tables, such that the columns in the view are found in one or more underlying tables. Thus, views do not use physical storage to store data. The definition of a view (which includes the query it is based on, its column layout, and privileges granted) is stored in the data dictionary.

When you query a view, the view queries the tables that it is based on and returns the values in the format and order specified by the view definition. Since there is no physical data directly associated with them, views cannot be indexed.

Views are frequently used to enforce row-level and column-level security on data. For example, you could grant a user access to a view that shows only that user's rows from a table, while not granting the user access to all of the rows in the table. Similarly, you could limit the columns the user can see via the view.

As of ORACLE8, you can use *object views* to create an object-oriented layer above your tables. You can use object views to simulate abstract datatypes, object IDs, and references. See Chapter 5 for examples of object views.

Object Views

If you use abstract datatypes, you may encounter consistency issues during their implementation. Accessing the attributes of abstract datatypes requires you to use syntax that is not used for access of regular columns. As a result, you may need to change your enterprise SQL coding standards in order to support abstract datatypes. You will also need to remember which tables use abstract datatypes when performing transactions and queries against the tables.

Object views provide an important bridge on the path to abstract datatypes. You can use object views to give an object-relational presentation to your relational data. The underlying tables are unchanged, but the views support the abstract datatype definitions. From a DBA's perspective, little changes—you manage the tables as you would manage any other tables in the database. From a developer's perspective, object views provide object-relational access to the tables' data. See Chapter 5 for details on the implementation and use of object views.

Sequences

Sequence definitions are stored in the data dictionary. Sequences are used to simplify programming efforts by providing a sequential list of unique numbers.

The first time a sequence is called by a query, it returns a predetermined value. Each subsequent query against the sequence will yield a value that is increased by its specified increment. Sequences can cycle, or may continue increasing until a specified maximum value is reached.

When you use a sequence, there is no guarantee that you will generate an unbroken string of values. For example, if you query the next value from a sequence for use in an **insert**, then yours is the only session that can use that sequence value. If you fail to commit your transaction, then your sequence value is not inserted into the table, and later **insert**s will use succeeding values from the sequence.

Procedures

A *procedure* is a block of PL/SQL statements that is stored in the data dictionary and is called by applications. You can use procedures to store frequently used application logic within the database. When the procedure is executed, its statements are executed as a unit. Procedures do not return any value to the calling program.

You can use stored procedures to help enforce data security. Rather than grant users access directly to the tables within an application, you can grant them the ability to execute a procedure that accesses the tables. When the procedure is executed, it will execute with the privileges of the procedure's owner. The users will be unable to access the tables except via the procedure.

Functions

Functions, like procedures, are blocks of code that are stored in the database. Unlike procedures, though, functions are capable of returning values to the calling program. You can create your own functions and call them within SQL statements just as you execute the functions that ORACLE provides.

For example, ORACLE provides a function called **SUBSTR** that performs "substring" functions on strings. If you create a function called **MY_SUBSTR** that performs custom substring operations, you could call it within a SQL command.

```
select MY_SUBSTR('text') from DUAL;
```

If you do not own the **MY_SUBSTR** function, then you must have been granted EXECUTE permission on the function. You can only use a user-defined function within a SQL statement if the function does not modify any database rows.

Packages

You can use *packages* to arrange procedures and functions into logical groupings. The specifications and bodies are stored in the data dictionary. Packages are very useful in the administrative tasks required for the management of procedures and functions.

Different elements within the package can be defined as being "public" or "private." Public elements are accessible to the user of the package, while private elements are hidden from the user. Private elements may include procedures that are called by other procedures within the package.

The source code for functions, packages, and procedures is stored in the data dictionary tables. If your applications use packages heavily, you may need to greatly increase the size of your SYSTEM tablespace to accommodate the increase in data dictionary size. In ORACLE Financials implementations, for example, you may need a SYSTEM tablespace that is greater than 250MB in size.

The number and complexity of packages in use directly impacts the size of the Shared SQL Pool portion of the SGA. The Shared SQL Pool is described in the "Internal Memory Structures" section later in this chapter.

Triggers

Triggers are procedures that are executed when a specified database event takes place. You may use them to augment referential integrity, enforce additional security, or enhance the available auditing options.

There are two types of triggers:

Statement triggers	Fire once for each triggering statement
Row triggers	Fire once for each row in a table affected by the statements

For example, a statement-level trigger fires once for a **delete** command that deletes 10,000 rows. A row-level trigger would fire 10,000 times for the same transaction.

For each trigger type, you can create a BEFORE trigger and AFTER trigger for each type of triggering event. Triggering events include **insert**s, **update**s, and **delete**s.

Statement triggers are useful if the code in the trigger action does not rely on the data affected. For example, you may create a BEFORE INSERT statement trigger on a table to prevent **insert**s into a table except during specific time periods.

Row triggers are useful if the trigger action relies on the data being affected by the transaction. For example, you may create an AFTER INSERT row trigger to **insert** new rows into an audit table as well as the trigger's base table.

As of ORACLE8, you can create INSTEAD OF triggers. An INSTEAD OF trigger executes instead of the action that caused it to start. That is, if you create an INSTEAD OF INSERT trigger on a table, the trigger's code executes and the **insert** that caused the trigger to be executed never occurs. INSTEAD OF triggers can be applied to views. If your view joins multiple tables in its query, an INSTEAD OF trigger can direct ORACLE's actions if a user attempts to **update** rows via the view.

As of ORACLE8i, you can create triggers on system-level events. You can trigger code to be executed when **create**, **alter**, or **delete** commands are issued. You can also use system events such as logons, logoffs, and database shutdowns and startups as triggering events. See the entry for **create trigger** in Appendix A for the command syntax.

Synonyms

To completely identify a database object (such as a table or view) in a distributed database, you must specify the host machine name, the server (instance) name, the object's owner, and the object's name. Depending on the location of the object, between one and four of these parameters will be needed. To screen this process from the user, developers can create synonyms that point to the proper object; thus, the user only needs to know the synonym name. Public synonyms are shared by all users of a given database. Private synonyms are owned by individual database account owners.

For example, the EMPLOYEE table that was previously described must be owned by an account—let's say that the owner is HR. From a different user account in the same database, that table could be referenced as HR.EMPLOYEE. However, this syntax requires that the second account know that the HR account is the owner of the EMPLOYEE table. To avoid this requirement, you can create a public synonym called EMPLOYEE to point to HR.EMPLOYEE. Anytime the EMPLOYEE synonym is referenced, it will point to the proper table. The following SQL statement creates the EMPLOYEE synonym:

```
create public synonym EMPLOYEE for HR.EMPLOYEE;
```

Synonyms provide pointers for tables, views, procedures, functions, packages, and sequences. They can point to objects within the local database or in remote databases. Pointing to remote databases requires the use of database links, as described later in this chapter.

You cannot create synonyms for abstract datatypes. Furthermore, ORACLE does not check the validity of a synonym when you create it. You should test your synonyms after you create them to ensure they are valid.

Privileges and Roles

In order to access an object owned by another account, the *privilege* to access that object must first have been granted. Typically, nonowners are granted the privilege to **insert**, **select**, **update**, or **delete** rows from a table, snapshot, or view. You can grant users privileges to **select** values from sequences and **execute** procedures, functions, packages, and abstract datatypes. No privileges are granted on indexes or triggers, since they are accessed by the database during table activity. You can grant **read** on directories (for BFILE datatypes) and **execute** on libraries (for external programs called by your application code). You can grant privileges to individual users or to PUBLIC, which gives the privilege to all users in the database.

You can create *roles*—groups of privileges—to simplify the privilege management process. You can grant privileges to a role, and grant the role in turn to multiple users. Adding new users to applications then becomes a much easier process to manage since it is simply a matter of granting or revoking roles for the user.

The relationship between privileges and roles is shown in Figure 1-4. In Figure 1-4a, the privileges required to grant **select** access on two tables to four users are shown as lines. In Figure 1-4b, the role capability is used to simplify the administration of the privileges. The privileges are granted to a single role, and that role is granted to the four users. Roles may be dynamically enabled and disabled within an application.

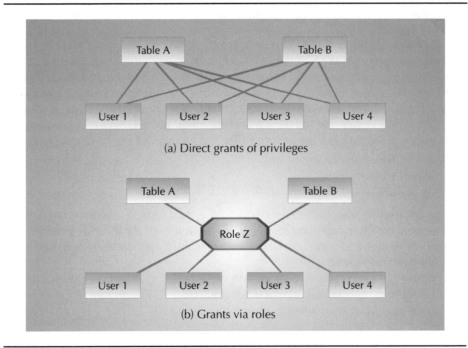

FIGURE 1-4. *Relationship between privileges and roles*

You can also use roles to grant system-level privileges, such as **create table**. System-level roles will be discussed in detail in Chapter 5 and Chapter 9.

Database Links

ORACLE databases can reference data that is stored outside of the local database. When referencing such data, you must specify the fully qualified name of the remote object. In the synonym example given earlier, only two parts of the fully qualified name—the owner and the table name—were specified. What if the table is in a remote database?

To specify an access path to an object in a remote database, you will need to create a *database link*. Database links can either be public (available to all accounts in that database) or private (created by a user for only that account's use). When you create a database link, you specify the name of the account to connect to, the password for the account, and the service name associated with the remote database. If you do not specify an account name to connect to, ORACLE will use your local account name and password for the connection to the remote database. The following example creates a public link named MY_LINK:

```
create public database link MY_LINK
connect to HR identified by PUFFINSTUFF
using 'DB1';
```

In this example, the link specifies that when it is used, it will open up a session in the database identified by the service named DB1. When it opens the session in the DB1 instance, it will log in as the user account HR, with the password puffinstuff. The service names for instances are stored in configuration files used by SQL*Net (the most recent version of SQL*Net is called Net8). The configuration file for service names is called tnsnames.ora, and it specifies the host, port, and instance associated with each service name.

To use this link for a table, the link must be specified in the **from** clause, as in the following example:

```
select * from EMPLOYEE@MY_LINK;
```

The preceding query will access the EMPLOYEE table via the MY_LINK database link. You can create a synonym for this table, as shown in the following SQL command:

```
create synonym EMPLOYEE for EMPLOYEE@MYLINK;
```

Note that the fully qualified designation for the database object has been defined—its host and instance via its service name, its owner (HR) via the database link, and its name (EMPLOYEE).

The location of the EMPLOYEE table is thus completely transparent to the end user. You can move the EMPLOYEE table to a different schema or a different database; changing the database link's definition will redirect the synonym to the new location.

NOTE
If a stored procedure, package, or trigger contains references to a database link, the link must exist for the PL/SQL to compile.

Segments, Extents, and Blocks

Segments are the physical counterparts to logical database objects. Segments store data. Index segments, for example, store the data associated with indexes. The effective management of segments requires that the DBA know the objects that an application will use, how data will be entered into those objects, and the ways in which data will be retrieved.

Because a segment is a physical entity, it must be assigned to a tablespace in the database (and will thus be placed in one of the datafiles of that tablespace). A segment is made up of sections called *extents*—contiguous sets of ORACLE blocks. Once the existing extents in a segment can no longer hold new data, the segment will obtain another extent. The extension process will continue as needed until no more free space is available in the tablespace's datafiles or until an internal maximum number of extents per segment is reached. If a segment has multiple extents, there is no guarantee that those extents will be contiguous.

Each segment has a limit to the maximum number of extents it can acquire. Although the theoretical limit to extents in a segment is in the billions, most database maintenance operations perform best if the number of extents per table is limited to below 10,000. You can specify the maximum number of extents per segment at the segment level, or you can use the default for the segment's tablespace.

When you drop a segment, its used extents become free extents. ORACLE may reuse those free extents for new segments or for extensions of existing segments. Information about the management of specific types of segments is provided in Chapter 4 and Chapter 7.

Rollback Segments

In order to maintain read consistency among multiple users in the database and to be able to roll back transactions, ORACLE must have a mechanism for reconstructing a "before" image of data for uncommitted transactions. ORACLE uses *rollback segments* within the database to provide a before image of data.

Transactions use rollback segments to record the prior image of data that is changed. For example, a large **delete** operation requires a large rollback segment to hold the records to be deleted. If the **delete** transaction is rolled back, ORACLE will use the rollback segment to reconstruct the data.

Queries also use rollback segments. ORACLE performs read-consistent queries, so the database must be able to reconstruct data as it existed when a query started. If a transaction completes after a query starts, ORACLE will continue to use that transaction's rollback segment entries to reconstruct changed rows. In general, you should avoid scheduling long-running queries concurrently with transactions.

Rollback segments will grow to be as large as the transactions they support. The effective management of rollback segments is described in Chapter 7.

Snapshots and Materialized Views

You can use *snapshots* to provide local copies of remote data to your users. A snapshot is based on a query that uses a database link to select data from a remote database. The snapshot's data is replicated from the source database to the target database; users can then query the snapshot. You can implement snapshots to be either read-only or updateable. To improve performance, you can index the local table used by the snapshot.

Depending on the complexity of the snapshot's base query, you may be able to use a *snapshot log* to improve the performance of your replication operations. Replication operations are performed automatically, based on a schedule you specify for each snapshot. See Part III of this book for details on the creation and maintenance of snapshots and snapshot logs.

As of ORACLE8i, you can create *materialized views*. A materialized view is very similar in structure to a snapshot: it stores replicated data based on an underlying query. Whereas a snapshot typically stores data from a remote database, a materialized view stores data that is usually replicated from within the current database. During database operations, the optimizer may dynamically choose to use an available materialized view in place of a query against a larger table, if the materialized view will return the same data. Materialized views thus provide a potential performance gain, at the cost of additional space usage and maintenance. See Chapter 12 for further details on the implementation of materialized views.

Internal Memory Structures

ORACLE uses shared memory areas and background processes to manage its memory and file structures. Background processes will be described in the next section; this section will focus on the global memory areas used by all ORACLE database users.

Depending on the database server option used, the implementation of the memory options available may vary widely. The most common implementations will be described here and in Chapter 2.

The elements described in this section include the following:

- System Global Area (SGA)
- Data block buffer cache

- Dictionary cache

- Redo log buffer

- Shared SQL Pool

- The large pool

- The Java pool

- Multiple buffer pools

- Context areas

- Program Global Area (PGA)

System Global Area (SGA)

If you were to read a chapter of this book, what would be the quickest way of passing that information on to someone else? You could have the other person read that chapter as well, but it would be quickest if you could hold all of the information in memory and then pass that information from your memory to the second person.

The *System Global Area (SGA)* in an ORACLE database serves the same purpose—it facilitates the transfer of information between users. The SGA also holds the most commonly requested structural information about the database.

The composition of the SGA is shown in Figure 1-5. The memory elements shown in Figure 1-5 are described in the following sections.

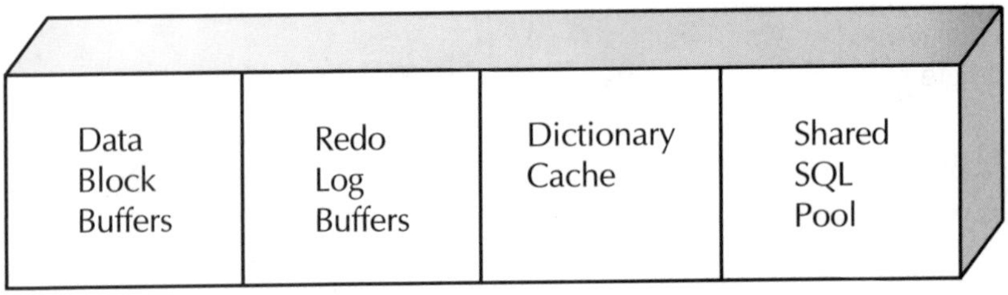

| Data Block Buffers | Redo Log Buffers | Dictionary Cache | Shared SQL Pool |

FIGURE I-5. *SGA structures*

Data Block Buffer Cache

The *data block buffer cache* is a cache in the SGA used to hold the data blocks that are read from the data segments in the database, such as tables, indexes, and clusters. The size of the data block buffer cache is determined by the DB_BLOCK_BUFFERS parameter (expressed in terms of number of database blocks) in the init.ora file for that database server. Managing the size of the data block buffer cache is an important part of managing and tuning the database.

Since the data block buffer cache is fixed in size, and is usually smaller than the space used by database segments, it cannot hold all of the database's segments in memory at once. Typically, the data block buffer cache is about 1 to 2 percent of the size of the database. ORACLE will manage the space available by using a *least recently used (LRU)* algorithm. When free space is needed in the cache, the least recently used blocks will be written out to disk, and new data blocks will take their place in memory. In this manner, the most frequently used data is kept in memory.

However, if the SGA is not large enough to hold the most frequently used data, then different objects will contend for space within the data block buffer cache. This is particularly likely when multiple applications share the same SGA. In that case, the most recently used segments from each application constantly contend for space in the SGA with the most recently used segments from other applications. As a result, requests for data from the data block buffer cache will result in a lower ratio of "hits" to "misses." Data block buffer cache misses result in physical I/Os for data reads, resulting in performance degradation. For information on monitoring the usage of the data block buffer cache, see the "Interpreting the Statistics Reports" section of Chapter 6.

Dictionary Cache

Information about database objects is stored in the data dictionary tables. For example, data dictionary information includes user account data, datafile names, segment names, extent locations, table descriptions, and privileges. When this information is needed by the database (for example, to check a user's authorization to query a table), the data dictionary tables are read and the data that is returned is stored in the SGA in the *dictionary cache.*

The data dictionary cache is managed via an LRU algorithm. The size of the dictionary cache is managed internally by the database; it is part of the Shared SQL Pool, whose size is set via the SHARED_POOL_SIZE parameter in the database's init.ora file.

If the dictionary cache is too small, the database will have to repeatedly query the data dictionary tables for information needed by the database. These queries are called *recursive calls*, and are slower to resolve than are queries that can be handled solely by the dictionary cache in memory. For information on monitoring the usage of the dictionary cache, see the "Interpreting the Statistics Reports" section of Chapter 6.

Redo Log Buffer

Redo log files are described in the section "Redo Logs" later in this chapter. Redo entries describe the changes that are made to the database. Redo entries are written to the online redo log files so that they can be used in roll-forward operations during database recoveries. Before being written to the online redo log files, however, transactions are first recorded in the SGA in an area called the *redo log buffer*. The database then periodically writes batches of redo entries to the online redo log files, thus optimizing this operation.

The size (in bytes) of the redo log buffers is set via the LOG_BUFFER parameter in the init.ora file.

Shared SQL Pool

The *Shared SQL Pool* stores the data dictionary cache and the *library cache*—information about statements that are run against the database. While the data block buffer and dictionary cache enable sharing of structural and data information among users in the database, the library cache allows the sharing of commonly used SQL statements.

The Shared SQL Pool contains the execution plan and parse tree for SQL statements run against the database. The second time that an identical SQL statement is run (by any user), it is able to take advantage of the parse information available in the Shared SQL Pool to expedite its execution. For information on monitoring the usage of the Shared SQL Pool, see the "Interpreting the Statistics Reports" section of Chapter 6.

The Shared SQL Pool is managed via an LRU algorithm. As the Shared SQL Pool fills, less recently used execution paths and parse trees will be removed from the library cache to make room for new entries. If your Shared SQL Pool is too small, statements will be continually reloaded into the library cache, affecting your performance.

The size (in bytes) of the Shared SQL Pool is set via the SHARED_POOL_SIZE init.ora parameter.

The Large Pool

The Large Pool is an optional memory area. If you use the multithreaded server option or frequently perform backup/restore operations, you may manage those operations more efficiently if you create a Large Pool. The Large Pool will be dedicated to supporting large SQL commands. By using a Large Pool, you prevent those large SQL commands from overwriting entries in the Shared SQL Pool, reducing the number of statements reloaded into the library cache.

The size of the Large Pool, in bytes, is set via the LARGE_POOL_SIZE init.ora parameter. In ORACLE8.0, you can use the LARGE_POOL_MIN_ALLOC init.ora parameter to set the minimum allocation within the Large Pool; in ORACLE8i, this parameter is obsolete.

As an alternative to using the Large Pool, you can use the SHARED_POOL_RESERVED_SIZE init.ora parameter to reserve a portion of the Shared SQL Pool for larger SQL statements.

The Java Pool

The Java Pool, as its name suggests, services the parsing requirements for Java commands. The Java Pool's size is set, in bytes, via the JAVA_POOL_SIZE init.ora parameter introduced in ORACLE8i. The JAVA_POOL_SIZE init.ora parameter defaults to 10MB.

Multiple Buffer Pools

You can create multiple buffer pools within your SGA. You can use multiple buffer pools to separate large datasets from the rest of your application, reducing the likelihood they will contend for the same resources within the data block buffer cache. For each buffer pool you create, you need to specify its size and its number of LRU latches. The number of buffers must be at least 50 times greater than the number of LRU latches.

When creating buffer pools, you need to specify the size of the *keep area* and the size of the *recycle area*. Like the reserved area of the Shared SQL Pool, the keep area retains entries, while the recycle area is more frequently recycled. You can specify the size of the keep area via the BUFFER_POOL_KEEP parameter, as shown in the following listing:

```
BUFFER_POOL_KEEP=(buffers:200, lru_latches:3)
BUFFER_POOL_RECYCLE=(buffers:50, lru_latches:1)
```

The sizes of the keep and recycle buffer pools reduce the available space in the data block buffer cache (set via the DB_BLOCK_BUFFERS parameter). For a table to use one of the new buffer pools, specify the name of the buffer pool via the **buffer_pool** parameter within the table's **storage** clause. For example, if you want a table to be quickly removed from memory, assign it to the RECYCLE pool. The default pool is named DEFAULT, so you can use the **alter table** command to redirect a table to the DEFAULT pool at a later date.

Context Areas

Within the shared SQL area, there are both public and private areas. Every SQL statement issued by a user requires a private SQL area, which continues to exist until the cursor corresponding to that statement is closed. As of ORACLE8, a private object cache is also used when object-relational features are used.

Program Global Area (PGA)

The *Program Global Area* (*PGA*) is an area in memory that is used by a single ORACLE user process. The memory in the PGA is not sharable.

If you are using the *multithreaded server* (MTS), part of the PGA may be stored in the SGA. The multithreaded server architecture allows multiple user processes to use the same server process, thus reducing the database's memory requirements. If MTS is used, the user session information is stored in the SGA rather than in the PGA. If you use MTS, you should increase the size of the Shared SQL Pool to accommodate the additional shared memory requirements.

Background Processes

The relationships between the database's physical and memory structures are maintained and enforced by *background processes*. These are the database's own background processes, which may vary in number depending on your database's configuration. These processes are managed by the database and require little administrative work.

Each of the background processes creates a trace file. The trace files are maintained for the duration of the instance's uptime. The naming convention and location for the background process trace files differs across operating systems and database versions. In general, the trace file names will contain either the background process name or the operating system process ID for the background process. You can set the BACKGROUND_DUMP_DEST init.ora parameter to specify a location for the background process trace files, but some versions of ORACLE ignore that setting. The trace files become most important when you are debugging problems with the database. Serious problems that affect the background processes usually are logged in the database's alert log.

The alert log is usually located in the BACKGROUND_DUMP_DEST directory. Typically, that directory is the /admin/*INSTANCE_NAME*/bdump directory under the ORACLE_BASE directory.

SMON

When you start the database, the *SMON* (System Monitor) process performs instance recovery as needed (using the online redo log files). It also cleans up the database, eliminating transactional objects that are no longer needed by the system.

SMON serves an additional purpose: it coalesces contiguous free extents into larger free extents. The free space fragmentation process is conceptually described in Chapter 4. For some tablespaces, DBAs must manually perform the free space coalescence; instructions for performing this task are given in Chapter 8. SMON only coalesces free space in tablespaces whose default **pctincrease** storage value is nonzero.

PMON

The *PMON* background process cleans up failed user processes. PMON frees up the resources that the user was using. Its effects can be seen when a process holding a lock is killed; PMON is responsible for releasing the lock and making it available to other users. Like SMON, PMON wakes up periodically to check if it is needed.

DBWR

The *DBWR* (Database Writer) background process is responsible for managing the contents of the data block buffer cache and the dictionary cache. DBWR performs batch writes of changed blocks from the SGA to the datafiles.

Although there is only one SMON and one PMON process running per database instance, you can have multiple DBWR processes running at the same time, depending on the platform and operating system. Using multiple DBWR processes helps to minimize contention within DBWR during large operations that span datafiles. The number of DBWR processes running is set via the DB_WRITER_PROCESSES parameter in the database's init.ora file. If your system supports asynchronous I/O, you can create a single DBWR process with multiple DBWR I/O slaves; the number of DBWR I/O slaves is set via the DBWR_IO_SLAVES init.ora parameter.

If you create multiple DBWR processes, the processes will not be named DBWR; instead, they will have a numeric component. For example, if you create five DBWR processes, the operating system names of the processes may be DBW0, DBW1, DBW2, DBW3, and DBW4.

LGWR

The *LGWR* (Log Writer) background process manages the writing of the contents of the redo log buffer to the online redo log files. LGWR writes log entries to the online redo log files in batches. The redo log buffer entries always contain the most up-to-date status of the database, since the DBWR process may wait before writing changed blocks from the data block buffers to the datafiles.

LGWR is the only process that writes to the online redo log files and the only one that directly reads the redo log buffers during normal database operation. The online redo log files are written to in sequential fashion, as opposed to the fairly random accesses that DBWR performs against the datafiles. If the online redo log files are mirrored, LGWR writes to the mirrored sets of logs simultaneously. See Chapter 2 for details on this mirroring capability.

As of ORACLE8, you can create multiple LGWR I/O slaves to improve the performance of writes to the online redo log files. In ORACLE8.0, the number of LGWR I/O slaves is set via the LGWR_IO_SLAVES parameter in the database's init.ora file. In ORACLE8i, that parameter is obsolete and the number of LGWR I/O slaves is derived from the DBWR_IO_SLAVES setting.

CKPT

Checkpoints help to reduce the amount of time needed to perform instance recovery. Checkpoints cause DBWR to write all of the blocks that have been modified since the last checkpoint to the datafiles and update the datafile headers and control files to record the checkpoint. Checkpoints occur automatically when an online redo log file fills; the LOG_CHECKPOINT_INTERVAL parameter in the database instance's init.ora file may be used to set a more frequent checkpoint.

The CKPT background process separates the two functions of LGWR in earlier database versions (signaling checkpoints and copying redo entries) between two background processes. The CKPT background process is enabled by setting the CHECKPOINT_PROCESS parameter in the database instance's init.ora file to TRUE.

ARCH

The LGWR background process writes to the online redo log files in a cyclical fashion; after filling the first log file, it begins writing the second, until that one fills, and then begins writing to the third. Once the last online redo log file is filled, LGWR begins to overwrite the contents of the first redo log file.

When ORACLE is run in ARCHIVELOG mode, the database makes a copy of each redo log file before overwriting it. These archived redo log files are usually written to a disk device. They may also be written directly to a tape device, but this tends to be very operator-intensive.

The archiving function is performed by the *ARCH* background process. Databases using this option will encounter contention problems on their redo log disk during heavy data transaction times, since LGWR will be trying to write to one redo log file while ARCH is trying to read another. They may also encounter database lockups if the archive log destination disk fills. At that point, ARCH freezes, which prevents LGWR from writing, which in turn prevents any further transactions from occurring in the database until space is cleared for the archived redo log files.

As of ORACLE8, you can create multiple ARCH I/O slaves to improve the performance of writes to the archived redo log files. In ORACLE8.0, the number of ARCH I/O slaves is set via the ARCH_IO_SLAVES parameter in the database's init.ora file. In ORACLE8i, that parameter is obsolete and the ARCH_IO_SLAVES setting is derived from the DBWR_IO_SLAVES setting.

For details on the management of the archiving and database backup processes, see Chapter 10.

RECO

The *RECO* background process resolves failures in distributed databases. RECO attempts to access databases involved in in-doubt distributed transactions and resolve those transactions. This process is only created if the Distributed Option is supported on the platform and the DISTRIBUTED_TRANSACTIONS parameter in the init.ora file is set to a value greater than zero.

SNP*n*

ORACLE's snapshot refreshes and internal job queue scheduling rely on background processes for their execution. The background processes' names start with the letters SNP and end with a number or letter. The number of SNP processes created for an instance is set via the JOB_QUEUE_PROCESSES parameter in the database's init.ora file (in ORACLE7, the parameter was named SNAPSHOT_REFRESH_PROCESSES).

LCK*n*

Multiple *LCK* processes, named LCK0 through LCK9, are used for interinstance locking when the ORACLE Parallel Server option is used. The number of LCK processes is set via the GC_LCK_PROCS parameter.

D*nnn*

Dispatcher processes are part of the MTS architecture; they help to minimize resource needs by handling multiple connections. At least one dispatcher process must be created for each protocol that is being supported on the database server. Dispatcher processes are created at database startup, based on the SQL*Net (or Net8) configuration, and can be created or removed while the database is open.

Server: S*nnn*

Server processes are created to manage connections to the database that require a dedicated server. Server processes may perform I/O against the datafiles.

Parallel Query Server Processes: P*nnn*

If you enable the Parallel Query Option within your database, a single query's resource requirements may be distributed among multiple processors. The number of parallel query server processes started when the instance starts is determined by the PARALLEL_MIN_SERVERS init.ora parameter. Each of those processes will be present at the operating system level; as more processes are needed to parallelize operations, more parallel query server processes will be started. Each of the parallel query server processes will have a name such as P000, P001, and P002 at the operating system level. The maximum number of parallel query server processes is set via the PARALLEL_MAX_SERVERS init.ora parameter.

Parallel query server processes do not generate trace files. See Chapter 12 for details of the implementation of the Parallel Query Option.

External Structures

The database's datafiles, as described earlier in the "Files" portion of the overview section of this chapter, provide the physical storage for the database's data. Thus, they are both "internal" structures, since they are tied directly to tablespaces, and "external," since they are physical files. The planning process for their distribution across devices is described in Chapter 4.

The following types of files, although related to the database, are separate from the datafiles. These files include the following:

■ Redo logs

■ Control files

■ Trace files and the alert log

Redo Logs

ORACLE maintains logs of all transactions against the database. These transactions are recorded in files called *online redo log files*. Redo log files are used to recover the database's transactions in their proper order in the event of a database crash. The redo log information is stored external to the database's datafiles.

Redo log files also let ORACLE streamline the manner in which it writes data to disk. When a transaction occurs in the database, it is entered in the redo log buffers, while the data blocks affected by the transaction are not immediately written to disk.

Each ORACLE database will have two or more online redo log files. ORACLE writes to online redo log files in a cyclical fashion: after the first log file is filled, it writes to the second log file, until that one is filled. When all of the online redo log files have been filled, it returns to the first log file and begins overwriting its contents with new transaction data. If the database is running in ARCHIVELOG mode, the database will make a copy of the online redo log files before overwriting them. These archived redo log files can then be used to recover any part of the database to any point in time (see Chapter 10).

Redo log files may be mirrored (replicated) by the database. Mirroring the online redo log files allows you to mirror the redo log files without relying on the operating system or hardware capabilities of the operating environment. See Chapter 2 for details on this mirroring capability.

Control Files

A database's overall physical architecture is maintained by its *control files*. Control files record control information about all of the files within the database. Control files maintain internal consistency and guide recovery operations.

Since the control files are critical to the database, multiple copies are stored online. These files are typically stored on separate disks to minimize the potential damage due to disk failures. The database will create and maintain the control files specified at database creation.

The names of the database's control files are specified via the CONTROL_FILES init.ora parameter. Although it is an init.ora parameter, the CONTROL_FILES parameter is usually specified in the config.ora file, since it changes rarely. If you need to add a new control file to a database, you can shut down the instance, copy one of the existing control files to the new location, add the new location to the CONTROL_FILES parameter setting, and restart the instance.

Trace Files and the Alert Log

Each of the background processes running in an instance has a trace file associated with it. The trace file will contain information about significant events encountered by the background process. In addition to the trace files, ORACLE maintains a file called the *alert log*. The alert log records the commands and command results of major events in the life of the database. For example, tablespace creations, redo log switches, recovery operations, and database startups are recorded in the alert log. The alert log is a vital source of information for day-to-day management of a database; trace files are most useful when attempting to discover the cause of a major failure.

You should monitor your alert log daily. The entries in the alert log will inform you of any problems encountered during database operations, including any ORA-0600 internal errors that occur. To make the alert log easier to use, you may wish to automatically rename it each day. For example, if the alert log is named alert_orcl.log, you could rename it so its filename includes the current date. The next time ORACLE tries to write to the alert log, no file with the name alert_orcl.log will be found, so the database will create a new one. You will then have the current alert log (alert_orcl.log) as well as the previous alert log. Separating alert log entries in this fashion may make analyzing the alert log entries a more efficient process.

Basic Database Implementation

In its simplest form, an ORACLE database consists of the following:

- One or more datafiles
- One or more control files
- Two or more online redo logs

Internally, that database contains the following:

- Multiple users/schemas

- One or more rollback segments

- One or more tablespaces

- Data dictionary tables

- User objects (tables, indexes, views, etc.)

The server that accesses that database consists of (at a minimum) the following:

- An SGA (includes the data block buffer cache, redo log buffer cache, and the shared SQL pool)

- The SMON background process

- The PMON background process

- The DBWR background process

- The LGWR background process

- The CKPT background process

- User processes with associated PGAs

This is the base configuration; everything else is optional or dependent on the ORACLE version and options you are using.

The remainder of this section will provide an overview of the recovery and security capabilities of the database, as well as sample logical and physical layouts for ORACLE databases.

Backup/Recovery Capabilities

The ORACLE database features a number of backup and recovery options. Each of these will be described in detail in Chapter 10. The available options are described in the following sections.

Export/Import

The *Export* utility queries the database and stores its output in a binary file. You can select the portions of the database that are exported. You may export the entire database, a user's or a set of users' schema(s), or a specific set of tables. Export also has options that allow it to only export the tables that have changed since the last export (called an *incremental* export) or since the last full system export (called a *cumulative* export).

Full system exports read the full data dictionary tables as well. You can use a full export to completely re-create a database, since the data dictionary tracks users, datafiles, and database objects. Full system exports are commonly used during efforts to eliminate fragmentation in the database (see Chapter 8).

The Export utility performs a logical read of the database. To read information out of the binary dump file created by the export, you must use the *Import* utility. Import can selectively choose objects or users from the dump file to import. The Import utility will then attempt to insert that data into the database (rather than overwriting existing records).

Export and Import are part of most databases' backup and recovery plans. Since Export reads the data at a point in time, you can only use exported data to recover the data as it was at that point in time. Exports are therefore most effective for backups of data that is not very volatile. For example, when you are performing database maintenance activities such as moving tables to different schemas, the data should not be changing. For that sort of activity, Export and Import are effective tools. For transaction-intensive environments, exports are rarely the best primary backup method; online backups are generally preferred.

Offline Backups

In addition to making logical backups of the database, you can make physical backups of its files. To make a physical backup of the database, you can use *online backups* and *offline backups*. Offline backups are performed by first shutting down the database; the files that constitute the database can then be backed up to a storage device (via disk-to-disk copies or tape writes). Once the backup is complete, you may reopen the database.

Even if offline backups are not the main backup and recovery option being implemented, it is still a good idea to make an offline backup of the database periodically (such as when the host it resides on undergoes routine maintenance).

Online Backups

Online backups are available for those databases that are being run in ARCHIVELOG mode (described in the ARCH process section). You can use online backups to make physical database backups while the database is open. During an online backup, you place tablespaces temporarily into a backup state, then restore them to their normal state when their files have been backed up. See Chapter 10 for details on implementing the online and offline backup options.

Recovery Manager (RMAN)

As of ORACLE8, you can use the Recovery Manager (RMAN) utility to perform physical backups of your database. Rather than backing up an entire datafile, RMAN can perform incremental physical backups of your datafiles. During a full (*level 0*) datafile backup, all of the blocks ever used in the datafile are backed up. During a cumulative (*level 1*) datafile backup, all of the blocks used since the last full datafile backup are backed up. An incremental (*level 2*) datafile backup backs up only those blocks that have changed since the most recent cumulative or full backup. You can define the levels used for incremental backups.

The Recovery Manager keeps track of your backups either through a recovery catalog or by placing the required information into the control file for the database being backed up. The number of days' worth of RMAN records stored in a control file is set via the CONTROL_FILE_RECORD_KEEP_TIME init.ora parameter.

The ability to perform incremental and cumulative backups of datafiles may greatly improve the performance of your backups if you have very large databases with isolated areas of transaction activity. See Chapter 10 for details of the implementation of RMAN and other backup methods.

Security Capabilities

The full security-related capabilities within ORACLE will be described in detail in Chapter 9. In this section, you will see an overview of these capabilities within ORACLE.

Account Security

You may protect database accounts via passwords. You can also enable an autologin capability, allowing users who have accessed a host account to access a related database account without entering a database password. Having an account or privileges in one database does not give a user an account or privileges in any other database.

System-Level Privileges

You can create system-level roles from the full set of system-level privileges (such as CREATE TABLE, CREATE INDEX, SELECT ANY TABLE) to extend the basic set of system-level roles. CONNECT, RESOURCE, and DBA are provided as standard roles for application users, developers, and DBAs, respectively.

Object Security

Users who have created objects may grant privileges on those objects to other users via the **grant** command. They can also **grant** a user access to tables **with grant option**, in which case that user (the grantee) can **grant** access to the tables to additional users.

Auditing

You can audit user activities that involve database objects via the **audit** command. **Audit**ed actions may include table accesses, login attempts, and DBA-privileged activities. The results of these **audit**s are stored in an audit table within the database. In addition to the provided **audit**ing capabilities, you can create database triggers to record changes in data values.

Sample Logical Database Layout

The logical layout of an ORACLE database has a great impact on the administrative options the DBA has. The tablespace layout shown in Table 1-2 is based on the design considerations given in Chapter 3. The objective of this layout is to isolate database segments based on their usage and characteristics.

Sample Physical Database Layout

The proper physical layout for the database files is database-specific; however, certain general rules can be applied to correctly separate database files whose I/O requests will conflict with each other. A detailed discussion of this topic is given in Chapter 4. The configuration shown in Figure 1-6 is given as a sample configuration for a 12-disk production system. The procedures given in Chapter 4 should be followed to determine the proper distribution of files that will meet your needs.

Understanding Logical Modeling Conventions

In the previous section on table constraints, several data-modeling terms were shown. In this section, you will see how the relationships implied by those terms are graphically depicted. The information in this section will assist DBAs in interpreting application data models (some of which are used in this book).

A *primary key (PK)* is the column or set of columns that makes each record in a table unique. A *foreign key (FK)* is a set of columns that refers back to an existing primary key.

Tables can be related to each other via three types of relationships: *one to one*, *one to many*, and *many to many*. In a one-to-one (1:1) relationship, the tables share a common primary key. In a one-to-many (1:M) relationship, a single record in one table is related to many records in another table. In a many-to-many (M:M) relationship, many records in one table are related to many records in another table. The following sections provide examples of each type of relationship.

These graphical standards for depicting various types of relationships will be used throughout this book.

Tablespace	Use
SYSTEM	Data dictionary
DATA	Standard-operation tables
DATA_2	Static tables used during standard operations
INDEXES	Indexes for the standard-operation tables
INDEXES_2	Indexes for the static tables
RBS	Standard-operation rollback segments
RBS_2	Specialty rollback segments used for data loads
TEMP	Standard-operation temporary segments
TEMP_*USER*	Temporary segments created by a specific user
TOOLS	RDBMS tools tables
TOOLS_I	Indexes for heavily used RDBMS tools tables
USERS	User objects, in development databases
USERS_I	User indexes, in testing databases
SNAPS	Snapshot tables
SNAPS_I	Indexes on the snapshots
AGG_DATA	Aggregation tables and materialized views
AGG_DATA_I	Indexes on aggregation tables and materialized views
PARTITIONS	Partitions of table or index segments; create multiple tablespaces for them
PARTITIONS_I	Local and global indexes on partitions
TEMP_WORK	Temporary tables used during data load processing

TABLE 1-2. *Logical Distribution of Tablespaces in a Database*

One-to-One Relationships

It is rare to have two tables that share the same primary key unless there are performance or security reasons driving the design. For example, ORACLE recommends that when a LONG datatype is used in a table, it should be stored in a

```
Disk              Contents
1                 Oracle software
2                 SYSTEM tablespace, Control file 1
3                 RBS tablespace, RBS_2 tablespace, Control file 2
4                 DATA tablespace, Control file 3
5                 INDEX tablespace
6                 TEMP tablespace, TEMP_USER tablespace
7                 TOOLS tablespace, INDEX_2 tablespace
8                 Online Redo logs 1, 2, and 3
9                 Application software
10                DATA_2
11                Archived redo log destination disk
12                Export dump file destination disk
```

FIGURE 1-6.   *Sample 12-disk configuration for database files*

separate table for performance reasons, with the two tables related to each other in a 1:1 fashion.

Consider the SALES_REPS table from Figure 1-1 at the beginning of this chapter. What if an additional column, RESUME, with a datatype of LONG, were to be added to the data being stored? Since there is one resume for each sales rep, the RESUME column should be stored in the SALES_REPS table. However, this will force the database to read through the LONG value every time the table is queried, even if only the NAME field is being sought.

To improve performance, you can create a second table, called SALES_REPS_RESUME. This table will have the same primary key (REP_NUMBER), and one additional column (RESUME). The two tables thus have a 1:1 relationship. This is shown graphically in Figure 1-7.

The solid line between the two entities indicates that the relationship is mandatory. Had the relationship been optional, the line would have been partially dashed.

LOB storage in ORACLE8 implicitly uses 1:1 relationships to store LOB data. If the LOB data size exceeds a threshold value, it is stored apart from the base table.

One-to-Many Relationships

One-to-many (1:M) relationships are far more common than 1:1 relationships. In a 1:M relationship, one record in one table is related to many records in another table.

Consider the SALES_REPS table again. For the records given in Figure 1-1, there is only one sales rep per office. However, the data analysis may reveal that multiple

FIGURE 1-7. *Entity relationship diagram for a 1:1 relationship*

sales reps can report to the same office. To support that requirement, a new entity, OFFICE, would be created. The Office column of the SALES_REPS table would then be a foreign key to the Office column of the new OFFICE table.

Since many sales reps (records in the SALES_REPS table) can report to a single office (record in the OFFICE table), there is a 1:M relationship between these tables. The 1:M relationship is shown graphically in Figure 1-8. Note two differences from Figure 1-7 in the connecting line: the addition of a crow's foot on the "many" side of the relationship, and the use of a dashed line on the "one" side. The dashed line signifies that the relation is not mandatory on that side—you can have an office with no sales reps assigned to it.

Many-to-Many Relationships

You may also have a requirement that many rows of a table are related to many rows of another table. Consider the SALES_REPS table (Figure 1-1) again. For this example, assume that the data analysis reveals that sales reps contact multiple companies. Furthermore, a single company can be called upon by multiple sales reps. Thus, there is a many-to-many (M:M) relationship between the SALES_REPS entity and the COMPANIES entity. To understand this relationship, note that a single

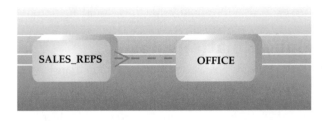

FIGURE 1-8. *Entity relationship diagram for a 1:M relationship*

sales rep (record in the SALES_REPS table) can correspond to multiple companies (records in the COMPANIES table), and that the reverse is also true. This relationship is shown graphically in Figure 1-9.

Many M:M relationships have an *intersection table*. For example, you may wish to record information about each sales representative's interactions with each customer. The primary key for that data should be the combination of the primary keys from the SALES_REPS table and the COMPANIES table. Graphically, the intersection table will be located between the SALES_REPS table and the COMPANIES table.

Creating a Database

When creating databases, you should strive to use a consistent logical and physical distribution of your tablespaces and files. Moreover, you should use a consistent script to create the database so each of your databases will have a similar structure, simplifying later administration efforts.

The simplest way to generate a **create database** script is via the ORACLE Installer utility. When you install ORACLE, the Installer gives you the option to create a database. If you use that option, the Installer will create a small database. The database is not important, and its files can be deleted unless you plan to use it. The important product of the ORACLE Installer is the set of database creation scripts it generates. The **create database** scripts generated by the Installer provide a solid template for your standard **create database** scripts.

Modifying the Template Creation Scripts

The **create database** scripts generated by ORACLE should be modified to match your requirements. Changes to the scripts may include the following:

■   In the **create database** command, setting MAXDATAFILES to its maximum setting for your operating system

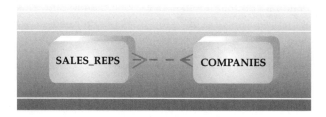

FIGURE 1-9.   *Entity relationship model for a M:M relationship*

- In the config.ora file, setting the DB_BLOCK_SIZE parameter to the highest value supported by your operating system

- In the init.ora file, setting the proper values for the DB_BLOCK_BUFFERS, SHARED_POOL_SIZE, LOG_ARCHIVE_DEST_n, DB_WRITER_PROCESSES, and other init.ora parameters you wish to customize

- In the **create tablespace** portions of the database creation script, implementing the logical and physical database designs you have chosen

With the exception of the DB_BLOCK_SIZE setting, you can make all of these changes after the database has been created. However, it is far simpler to make these changes before the database has been created. Create your own templates for database creations, and modify them to fit each new database you create. See Chapters 3 and 4 for the guidelines for logical and physical tablespace distribution.

Modifying MAXDATAFILES after Database Creation

The MAXDATAFILES setting is specified as part of the **create database** command. MAXDATAFILES sets the upper limit for the number of datafiles you can have in your database; it supersedes any value set for the DB_FILES init.ora parameter. If you need to add a new datafile (for example, to add a new tablespace to a database) and you have reached your MAXDATAFILES limit, your file allocation will fail.

To alter the MAXDATAFILES setting, you will need to re-create the control file. Since re-creating a control file cannot be performed while the database is open, you should limit the number of times this operation is required. To re-create a control file, follow these steps:

1. With the database open, go into Server Manager and execute the following command:

   ```
   alter database backup controlfile to trace;
   ```

   The preceding command will generate a trace file in the user dump file destination directory. The trace file will contain header information that can be deleted, followed by the **create controlfile** command for the database.

2. Shut down the instance, using either **shutdown** or **shutdown immediate**.

3. Edit the **create controlfile** script generated in step 1. Set the MAXDATAFILES setting to a value that you will never reach. The higher the MAXDATAFILES setting, the larger the control file created.

4. Rename the existing control files. Do not delete them at this point, since they will serve as a fallback position.

5. Mount the database via the **startup mount *instance_name* exclusive** command within Server Manager.

6. Run the edited **create controlfile** script generated in step 3. Using the CONTROL_FILES setting in the init.ora or config.ora file, ORACLE will create new control files for the database.

7. Open the database. You may need to use the **resetlogs** option of the **alter database open** command.

8. Once the database has been successfully opened, you can remove the old control files.

Issues with shutdown and startup

In step 2 of the control file re-creation procedure, the database was shut down. When shutting the database down, you can use the **shutdown**, **shutdown immediate**, or **shutdown abort** commands. If you use the **shutdown abort** command to shut down the instance, ORACLE will need to perform recovery prior to reopening the instance during a subsequent **alter database open** command. You should not use the **shutdown abort** command immediately prior to performing an offline backup of the database.

However, you may be required to use **shutdown abort** occasionally. For example, if you frequently have deadlocks in your database application, ORACLE will not be able to shut down the database if you use a **shutdown immediate**. If you need to perform file system backups in such an environment, follow these steps:

1. Perform a **shutdown abort**.

2. Immediately start up the instance.

3. Perform a **shutdown**.

The instance will now be shut down in a consistent fashion and ready to be backed up.

Using OEM

Since ORACLE7.3, the Oracle Enterprise Manager (OEM), a graphical user interface (GUI) tool, has been supplied to enable DBAs to manage their databases from a personal computer. With the release of ORACLE8i, the OEM Toolset, version 2.0.4, provides a much more robust interface for remote database administration. In all 1.x versions of OEM, only one DBA could connect to the OEM repository at a time. Therefore, if you wanted to administer a database while another DBA was using the repository, you either had to wait until that DBA's tasks were completed or create a separate repository from which to work. In that configuration, your database changes could accidentally be overwritten by another DBA. With the release of OEM version 2, all DBAs can use the same central repository to perform their work. In addition to those changes, OEM version 2 includes task scheduling and assignment features to enable around-the-clock database coverage.

With all versions of OEM, you must make several key decisions prior to installing and configuring the tool. You will need to decide where the OEM repository is to be created and how and when you are going perform backups to protect this repository. Since you can use OEM as an interface to the ORACLE Recovery Manager (RMAN), recovery information can be stored in the OEM repository. Although there is nothing to stop you from creating the OEM repository in a production database, if you should lose this database, where will you get the recovery information? You may want to create a small, separate database in which to store the OEM repository. You should ensure that this repository is being backed up frequently so that recovery of the repository is assured.

If you are the only DBA working with the OEM Toolset, you will not have to consider who will handle administration of specific databases in your environment. If, however, there are several DBAs at the site, you will need to determine task definitions, database responsibilities, and schedules. With OEM, you can grant levels of access and privilege to each DBA in the group on a task-by-task basis. You can configure OEM to enable you to send email requests and assignments to other DBAs or take control of a problem to speed resolution.

If you have a previous version of OEM on your system, migrate that repository to the newest version to take advantage of the new features. If you have more than one repository on your system, you will need to take precautions to ensure that you migrate each version of the repository without damaging currently stored information.

Oracle supports SNMP (Simple Network Management Protocol). By supporting SNMP, ORACLE products can be easily integrated into monitoring tools for systems and networks. Its SNMP support enables ORACLE to be monitored by existing tools on enterprise networks. Key benefits of SNMP include the following:

■ Easy integration into enterprise networks managed via SNMP tools

■ Central monitoring of all services required for database access

■ Support for automatic alerts for critical situations

■ Support for automatic reactions to alert conditions

Although you do not have to use OEM to manage your databases, it provides a common interface to your databases. As your enterprise grows in size (and in number of databases and number of DBAs), the consistency of the DBA interface will support consistent implementation of your change control and production control processes.

CHAPTER

2

Hardware Configurations and Considerations

lthough each ORACLE database will be built from the same basic pieces, the options available to you depend on your hardware platform and operating system. For most platforms, you will have a number of options to choose from. In this chapter, you will see the standard architectures available—the ways that the pieces are usually put together. Since ORACLE supports many hardware platforms, it will not be possible to cover all of the options in this chapter. Rather, the focus will be on the most common implementations.

Architecture Overview

An ORACLE database consists of physical files, memory areas, and processes. The distribution of these components varies depending on the database architecture chosen.

The data in the database is stored in physical files (called *datafiles*) on a disk. As it is used, that data is stored in memory. ORACLE uses memory areas to improve performance and to manage the sharing of data between users. The main memory area in a database is called the *System Global Area* (*SGA*). To read and write data between the SGA and the datafiles, ORACLE uses a set of background processes that are shared by all users.

A database *server* (also known as an *instance*) is a set of memory structures and background processes that accesses a set of database files. The relationship between servers and databases is illustrated in Figure 2-1.

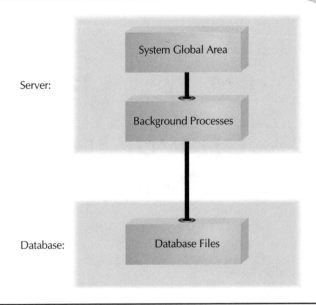

FIGURE 2-1. *Servers and databases in Oracle*

The characteristics of the database server—such as the size of the SGA and the number of background processes—are specified during startup. These parameters are stored in a file called init.ora. The init.ora file for a database usually contains the database name in the filename; a database named ORA1 will typically have an init.ora file named initora1.ora.

The init.ora file may, in turn, call a corresponding config.ora file. If a config.ora file is used, it usually only stores the parameter values for unchanging information, such as database block size and database name. The initialization files are only read during startup; modifications to them will not take effect until the next startup.

Stand-Alone Hosts

The simplest conceptual configuration for a database is a single server accessing a single database on a stand-alone, single-disk host. In this configuration, shown in Figure 2-2, all of the files are stored on the server's sole device, and there are only one SGA and one set of ORACLE background processes on the server.

The architecture shown in Figure 2-2 represents the minimum configuration. All of the other database configurations are modifications to this base structure.

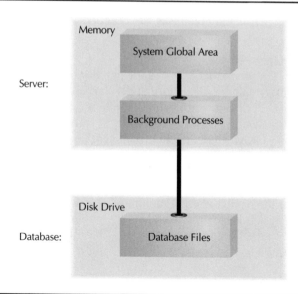

FIGURE 2-2. *Single server on a stand-alone host*

The files stored on the disk include the database datafiles and the host's init.ora file. As shown in Figure 2-2, there are two main interface points in the database:

- Between the database files and the background processes
- Between the background processes and the SGA

Tuning efforts mostly consist of improving the performance of these interface points. If the memory area dedicated to the database is large enough, then fewer repetitive reads will be performed against the database files. Since the files are all stored on the sole available disk device in this configuration, you should try to minimize the number of datafile accesses performed. File tuning topics are covered in detail in Chapter 4 and in Chapter 8.

Stand-Alone Hosts with Disk Arrays

If multiple disks are available, then the database files can be physically separated. Separating files improves database performance by reducing the amount of contention between the database files. During database operation, it is common for information from multiple files to be needed to handle a transaction or query. If the files are not distributed across multiple disks, then the system will need to read from multiple files on the same disk concurrently. The separation of files across multiple disks is shown in Figure 2-3.

The database uses several types of files. These file types, and guidelines for their optimal distribution across multiple disks, are described in Chapter 4.

Control File Mirroring

The init.ora file for the server that accesses the database is stored in the ORACLE software directories, usually in a directory under the ORACLE software base directory. In the default directory configuration, the init.ora file is stored in a directory named /orasw/app/oracle/admin/instance_name/pfile. For example, if the instance name is ORA1, then the init.ora file will be named initora1.ora and it will be stored in /orasw/app/oracle/admin/ORA1/pfile. The init.ora file does not list the names of the datafiles or online redo log files for the database; these are stored within the data dictionary. However, the init.ora file does list the names of the control files for the database. On a multiple-disk host, the control files should be stored on separate disks. The database will keep them in sync. By storing mirrored control files on multiple disks, you greatly reduce the risk of database problems caused by media failures.

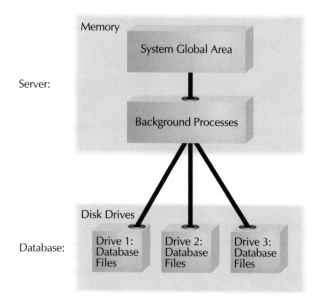

FIGURE 2-3.   *Single server on a stand-alone host with multiple disks*

A second server configuration file, config.ora, is called by init.ora. The config.ora file is used to set values for those parameters that typically do not change within the database; the control files' names are among those parameters. The following listing shows the entry for the CONTROL_FILES parameter in the config.ora file:

```
control_files           = (/db01/oracle/ORA1/ctrl1ora1.ctl,
                           /db02/oracle/ORA1/ctrl2ora1.ctl,
                           /db03/oracle/ORA1/ctrl3ora1.ctl)
```

This entry names the three control files. If it is used during the database creation, then the database will automatically create the three control files listed here. If you want to add additional control files to an existing database, follow this procedure:

1. Shut down the database.

2. Copy one of the current control files to the new location.

3. Edit the config.ora file, adding the new control file's name to the CONTROL_FILES entry.

4. Restart the database.

The new control file will then be activated.

A single init.ora file can call multiple initialization files via the IFILE parameter. The most common IFILE entry is the inclusion of the config.ora parameter file. You can also nest initialization files. For example, init.ora may have an IFILE entry to include a file called tuning.ora. The tuning.ora file, in turn, may have an IFILE entry for a file called disktuning.ora. You can use the support for multiple initialization files to group related parameters; however, you must be careful not to supersede a parameter setting by using it in more than one of the included files.

Redo Log File Mirroring

As noted in the previous section, the database will automatically mirror control files. The database can also mirror online redo log files. To mirror online redo log files, use *redo log groups*. If redo log groups are used, then the operating system does not need to perform the mirroring of the online redo log files; it is done automatically by the database.

When using this functionality, the LGWR (Log Writer) background process simultaneously writes to all of the members of the current online redo log group. Thus, rather than cycling through the redo log files, it instead cycles through *groups* of redo log files. Since the members of a group are usually placed on separate disk drives, there is no disk contention between the files, and LGWR thus experiences little change in performance. See Chapter 4 for further information on the placement of redo log files.

You can create redo log groups via the **create database** command. You can also add redo log groups to the database after it has been created, via the **alter database** command. The following listing shows an example of the addition of a redo log group to an existing database. The group is referred to in this example as GROUP 4. Using group numbers eases their administration; number them sequentially, starting with 1. The **alter database** command in this example is executed from within Server Manager.

```
> svrmgrl
SVRMGR> connect internal as sysdba
SVRMGR> alter database
    2> add logfile group 4
    3> ('/db01/oracle/CC1/log_1c.dbf',
    4>  '/db02/oracle/CC1/log_2c.dbf') size 5M;
```

To add a new redo log file to an existing group, use the **alter database** command shown in the following listing. As in the previous example, this command is executed from within Server Manager. It adds a third member to the GROUP 4 redo log group.

```
> svrmgrl
SVRMGR> connect internal as sysdba
SVRMGR> alter database
    2> add logfile member '/db03/oracle/CC1/log_3c.dbf'
    3> to group 4;
```

Beginning in ORACLE8i, you can log on to SQL*Plus and **connect internal** to perform the same logfile creation or modification activities.

```
> sqlplus internal/<password>
 SQL> alter database
   2  add logfile group 4
   3  ('/db01/oracle/CC1/log_1c.dbf',
   4  '/db02/oracle/CC1/log_2c.dbf') size 5M;
```

To add a new redo log file to an existing group, use the **alter database** command shown in the following listing. As in the previous example, this command is executed from SQL*Plus. The command adds a third member to the GROUP 4 redo log group.

```
> sqlplus internal/<password>
 SQL> alter database
   2  add logfile member '/db03/oracle/CC1/log_3c.dbf'
   3  to group 4;
```

When you use the **add logfile member** option of the **alter database** command, no file sizing information is specified. This is because all members of the group must have the same size. Since the group already exists, the database already knows how large to make the new file.

Archived Redo Log File Mirroring

As of ORACLE8, you can instruct the database to write multiple copies of each archived redo log file as it is written. In init.ora, the LOG_ARCHIVE_DEST parameter sets the primary storage location for the archived redo log files. In ORACLE8.0, you can use the LOG_ARCHIVE_DUPLEX_DEST parameter to specify a second location for your archived redo logs. While writing the archived redo log files, ORACLE will write to both locations. The write to the primary location must always succeed; otherwise, the database will be unavailable until it succeeds.

The write to the second archive log destination area, as specified by LOG_ARCHIVE_DUPLEX_DEST, may be optional. If you set LOG_ARCHIVE_MIN_

SUCCEED_DEST to 1, then the write to only one location (the first one, specified by LOG_ARCHIVE_DEST) must be successful. If the write to the secondary location fails, the database availability will not be interrupted.

The init.ora parameters for archive log destination areas change as of ORACLE8i. In ORACLE8i, the LOG_ARCHIVE_DEST parameter is obsolete, replaced by LOG_ARCHIVE_DEST_*n*. You can specify up to five archive log destination areas, replacing *n* with the number of the destination. For example, you can specify two separate archived redo log destination areas via the LOG_ARCHIVE_DEST_1 and LOG_ARCHIVE_DEST_2 parameters, as shown in the following listing:

```
log_archive_dest_1 = '/db00/arch'
log_archive_dest_2 = '/db01/arch'
```

The ORACLE8.0 LOG_ARCHIVE_MIN_SUCCEED_DEST parameter is obsolete in ORACLE8i. In place of that parameter, you can use the LOG_ARCHIVE_DEST_STATE_*n* parameter to enable or disable archive log destinations. For example, to disable the second archive log destination, set LOG_ARCHIVE_DEST_STATE_2 to DEFER. By default, the state values are set to ENABLE.

If you do not use ORACLE8's internal ability to mirror the archived redo log files, then you must mirror them at the operating system level. You can use RAID techniques (see Chapter 4) as part of the hardware mirroring approach. In general, you should favor the hardware system's mirroring solution over ORACLE's, provided the hardware system can support mirroring without significant performance impact. Mirroring solutions that use ORACLE's methods or the operating system methods are more portable across platforms but may impact your CPU usage.

During a recovery, you cannot skip a missing archived redo log file. See Chapter 10 for further details on backup and recovery.

Stand-Alone Hosts with Disk Shadowing

Many operating systems give you the ability to maintain duplicate, synchronized copies of files via a process known as *disk shadowing* or *volume shadowing.* (This practice is also known as *mirroring.*)

There are two benefits to shadowing your disks. First, the shadow set of disks serves as a backup in the event of a disk failure. In most operating systems, a disk failure will cause the corresponding disk from the shadow set to automatically step into the place of the failed disk. The second benefit is that of improved performance. Most operating systems that support volume shadowing can direct file I/O requests to use the shadow set of files instead of the main set of files. This reduces the I/O load on the main set of disks and results in better performance for file I/Os. The use of disk shadowing is shown in Figure 2-4.

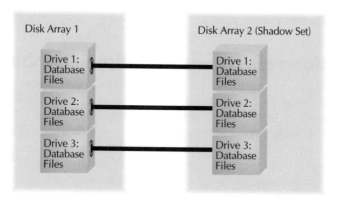

FIGURE 2-4. *Disk shadowing*

NOTE
Operating system–level disk shadowing may impact write performance if the operating system does not support asynchronous writes.

The type of shadowing shown in Figure 2-4 is called RAID-1 (redundant array of independent disks) shadowing. In this type of shadowing, each disk in the main set of disks is paired up, one-to-one, with a disk in the shadow set. Depending on your operating system, other shadowing options may be available. In RAID-3 and RAID-5 shadowing, for example, a set of disks is treated as a single logical unit, and each file is automatically "striped" across each disk. In RAID-3 and RAID-5, a parity-check system provides a means of recovering a damaged or failed member of the set of disks.

The method of shadowing that is used will affect how the files are distributed across devices. For example, datafiles that store tables are usually stored on a different disk than the datafiles that store those tables' indexes. However, if RAID-3 or RAID-5 is used, then the distinction between disks is blurred. Accessing a datafile when using those options will almost always require that all of the disks in the set be accessed. Therefore, contention between the disks is more likely.

Despite this, the contention should not be severe. In RAID-5, for example, the first block of data is stored on the first disk of a set, and the second block is stored on the next disk. Thus, the database only has to read a single block off a disk before moving on to the next disk. In this example, any contention that results from multiple accesses of the same disk should therefore last only as long as it takes to perform a single block read.

Stand-Alone Hosts with Multiple Databases

You can create multiple databases on a single host. Each database will have a separate set of files and will be accessed by a different server. Guidelines for appropriate directory structures are provided in Chapter 4.

Figure 2-5 shows a single host that is supporting two databases. Since each server requires an SGA and background processes, the host must be able to support the memory and process requirements that this configuration will place upon it.

As noted earlier, these configurations are modifications to the base database architecture. In this case, you simply create a second database that mimics the structure of the first. Note that although the two databases are on the same host, they do not (in this case) communicate with each other. The server from the first database cannot access the database files from the second database.

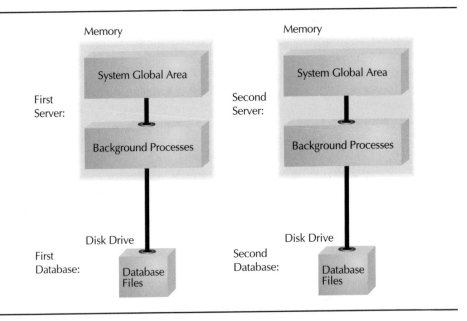

FIGURE 2-5.   *Stand-alone host with multiple databases*

Multiple databases on the same server typically share the same ORACLE source code directories. The init.ora files for the two databases in Figure 2-5 are stored in separate directories, since the instance name is part of the directory structure. For example, if the two server names were ORA1 and ORA2, then the associated init.ora files would be named initora1.ora and initora2.ora, respectively. The first would be stored in /orasw/app/oracle/admin/ORA1/pfile, and the second would be stored in /orasw/app/oracle/admin/ORA2/pfile. Their server parameters, like their datafiles, are completely independent of each other. Their config.ora files should also include the server name in the filename (for example, configora1.ora and configora2.ora) and be stored in the same directories as their respective init.ora files.

Although the databases may share the same source code directories, their datafiles should be stored in separate directories—and, if available, on separate disks. Sample directory structures for datafiles are provided in Chapter 4. If multiple databases have datafiles stored on the same device, then neither database's I/O statistics will accurately reflect the I/O load on that device. Instead, you will need to sum the I/O attributed to each disk by each database.

Simplifying the Upgrade Process

If your operating system can support multiple versions of the ORACLE software, then the process for upgrading your ORACLE database version is greatly simplified. For example, if both ORACLE8i Release 8.1.5 and ORACLE8i Release 8.1.6 are installed on your host, you can upgrade a database from 8.1.5 to 8.1.6 by following these steps:

1. Shut down the database.

2. Edit the environment file (usually /etc/oratab) to point the ORACLE software home directory to the 8.1.6 software directory.

3. Reset your environment variables (such as ORACLE_HOME) to point to the new home software directory for the database.

4. Edit listener.ora (see Part III for an explanation of SQL*Net and Net8) to point to the database's new software home directory. Stop and restart the listener.

5. Go to the /rdbms/doc directory under the new software version. Find the README.doc file and go to the section on upgrades. Depending on the version, one or more "cat" scripts will be necessary to update the data dictionary catalog following the upgrade. Read through the README.doc file to find the cat scripts you will be applying.

6. Go to the /rdbms/admin subdirectory for the new software version.

7. Mount and open the database. For example, for an instance named ORA1:

```
SVRMGRL> connect internal as sysdba
SVRMGRL> startup mount ORA1 exclusive;
SVRMGRL> alter database open;
```

8. Apply the catalog scripts specified in the README.doc file (see Step 5).

9. As an optional step, reapply the full catalog.sql, catexp.sql, and catproc.sql script:

```
SVRMGRL> @catalog
SVRMGRL> @catproc
SVRMGRL> @catexp
```

The database is now fully upgraded to the new version.

NOTE
As always, take a full backup of the database prior to the upgrade.

Networked Hosts

When hosts supporting ORACLE databases are connected via a network, those databases can communicate via ORACLE Net8 (formerly called SQL*Net). As shown in Figure 2-6, the Net8 drivers rely on the local networking protocol to achieve connectivity between two servers. The Net8 portion then supports communications between the application layers on the two servers. Net8 is described in Part III.

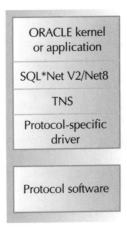

FIGURE 2-6. *ORACLE Net8 architecture*

The database configuration options available in a networked environment depend on the network's configurations and options. The following sections describe the main architectures:

- Networks of databases, used for remote queries

- Distributed databases, used for remote transactions

- Parallel server databases, on which multiple servers access the same database

- Parallel query operations, in which multiple CPUs serve a single operation

- Client/server databases

- Three-tier architectures

- Web-accessible databases

- ORACLE Transparent Gateway access

- Standby databases

- Replicated databases

- External file access

Networks of Databases

Net8 allows ORACLE databases to communicate with other databases that are accessible via a network. Each of the servers involved must be running Net8. This configuration is illustrated in Figure 2-7.

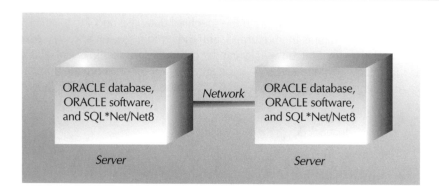

FIGURE 2-7.   *Networked hosts with databases*

In Figure 2-7, two hosts are shown. Each host can operate a database in stand-alone fashion, as was previously shown in Figure 2-2 and Figure 2-3. Each host in this example maintains a copy of the ORACLE software and one or more ORACLE databases.

For the databases to be able to communicate, their respective servers must be able to communicate with each other. As shown in Figure 2-6, the database layers of communication rely on the networking software and hardware to establish the communications link between the servers. Once that communications link is created, the database software can use it to transport data packets between remote databases.

The ORACLE software used to transfer data between databases is called Oracle Net8. In its simplest configuration, it consists of a host process that waits for connections via a specific connection path. When those connections are detected, it follows the instructions passed via the connection and returns the requested data. A full description of Oracle Net8 is found in Part III.

For Net8 to receive and process communications, the host must run a process called the *listener*. The listener process must be running on each host that will be involved in the database communications. Each server must be configured to assign this process to a specific communications port (see Chapter 14 for an example of this).

Examples of the use of database connections are shown in the following sections. They include queries against remote databases and transactions against remote databases.

Remote Queries

Queries against remote ORACLE databases use *database links* to identify the path that the query should take to find the data. A database link specifies, either directly or indirectly, the host, database, and account that should be used to access a specified object. The database link identifies the host and database to access by referring to the *service name* for that database. When a database link is referenced by a SQL statement, ORACLE opens a session in the specified database and executes the SQL statement there. The data is then returned, and the remote session may stay open in case it is needed again. Database links can be created as public links (by DBAs, making the link available to all users in the local database) or as private links.

The following example creates a public database link called HR_LINK:

```
create public database link HR_LINK
connect to HR identified by PUFFINSTUFF
using 'hq';
```

The **create database link** command, as shown in this example, has several parameters:

- The optional keyword **public**, which allows DBAs to create links for all users in a database

- The name of the link (HR_LINK, in this example)

- The account to connect to (if none is specified, then the local username and password will be used in the remote database)

- The service name (hq)

To use this link, simply add it as a suffix to table names in commands. The following example queries a remote table by using the HR_LINK database link:

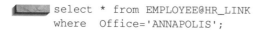
```
select * from EMPLOYEE@HR_LINK
where  Office='ANNAPOLIS';
```

NOTE
Database links cannot be used to return values from fields with LONG datatypes.

Database links allow for queries to access remote databases. They also allow for the information regarding the physical location of the data—its host, database, and schema—to be made transparent to the user. For example, if a user in the local database created a view based on a database link, then any access of the local view would automatically query the remote database. The user performing the query would not have to know where the data resides.

The following listing illustrates this. In this example, a view is created using the HR_LINK database link defined earlier in this section. Access to this view can then be granted to users in the local database, as shown here:

```
create view LOCAL_EMP
as select * from EMPLOYEE@HR_LINK
where Office='ANNAPOLIS';

grant select on LOCAL_EMP to PUBLIC;
```

When a user queries the LOCAL_EMP view, ORACLE will use the HR_LINK database link to open a session using the connection information specified for the HR_LINK database link. The query will be executed and the remote data will be returned to the local user. The local user of LOCAL_EMP will not be informed that the data came from a remote database.

Remote Updates: the Advanced Replication Option

In addition to querying data from remote databases, databases using the Advanced Replication Option can **update** databases that are located on remote hosts. The **update**s against these remote databases can be combined with **update**s against the local database into a single logical unit of work: either they all get **commit**ted or they all get rolled back.

A sample set of transactions is shown in Figure 2-8. One of the transactions goes against a database on a remote host and one against the local host. In this example, a local table named EMPLOYEE is **update**d; a remote table named EMPLOYEE, in a database defined by the HR_LINK database link, is also **update**d as part of the same transaction. If either **update** fails, then both of the transactions will be rolled back. This is accomplished via ORACLE's implementation of Two-Phase Commit, which is described in greater detail in Part III.

The databases involved in this remote update are functionally separate. They each have their own sets of datafiles and memory areas. They each must be running the Advanced Replication Option. The hosts involved must be running Net8 and must be configured to allow host-host communications.

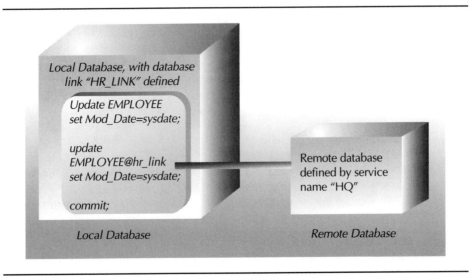

FIGURE 2-8. *Sample distributed transaction*

After Net8 is set up for each host, any files associated with it must be properly configured. These configuration files allow the database to interpret the service names shown in the **create database link** command earlier in this chapter.

Each host that runs Net8 must maintain a file called tnsnames.ora. This file defines the connect descriptors for the service names that are accessible from that host. For example, the following listing shows the tnsnames.ora file entry for the HQ service name used in the HR_LINK example:

```
HQ =(DESCRIPTION=
        (ADDRESS=
            (PROTOCOL=TCP)
            (HOST=HQ)
            (PORT=1521))
        (CONNECT DATA=
            (SID=loc)))
```

This example shows a number of different aspects of the connection process (its parameters are specific to TCP/IP, but the underlying connection needs are the same for all platforms). First, there is the hardware addressing information—the protocol, the host name, and the communications port to use. The second section defines the instance name—in this case, loc. Since the tnsnames.ora file tells the database all it needs to know to connect to remote databases, you should keep the contents of this file consistent across hosts. See Chapter 16 for information on this and other aspects affecting the management of location transparency.

The logical unit of work for distributed transactions is processed via ORACLE's implementation of Two-Phase Commit (2PC). If there is a network or server failure that prevents the unit of work from successfully completing, then it is possible that the data in the databases affected by the transactions will be out of sync. A background process automatically checks for incomplete transactions and resolves them as soon as all of the resources it needs become available.

The maximum number of concurrent distributed transactions for a database is set via the DISTRIBUTED_TRANSACTIONS parameter of its init.ora file. If this parameter is set to 0, then no distributed transactions will be allowed and the recovery background process will not be started when the instance starts.

Two data dictionary views are helpful when diagnosing uncompleted distributed transactions. The DBA_2PC_NEIGHBORS view contains information about incoming and outgoing connections for pending transactions. DBA_2PC_PENDING contains information about distributed transactions awaiting recovery. If your distributed transaction encounters errors, check DBA_2PC_NEIGHBORS and DBA_2PC_PENDING for details.

Clustered Servers: the **ORACLE Parallel Server**

Up to this point, all of the configurations discussed have featured databases that are accessed by a single server. However, depending on your hardware configurations, it may be possible to use multiple servers to access a single database. This configuration, called the *ORACLE Parallel Server* (OPS), is illustrated in Figure 2-9.

As shown in Figure 2-9, two separate servers share the same set of datafiles. Usually, these servers are located on separate hosts of a hardware cluster. A cluster is usually a group of individual hosts that have been connected with a high-bandwidth, low-latency interconnect fabric via which they pass messages to one another, allowing them to operate as a single entity. Using a clustered configuration provides the following benefits:

- More memory resources are available, since two machines are being used.

- If one of the hosts goes down, the other can still access the datafiles, thus providing a means of recovering from disasters.

- Users can be separated by the type of processing they perform, and high-CPU users will be kept on a separate host from regular online processing transactions.

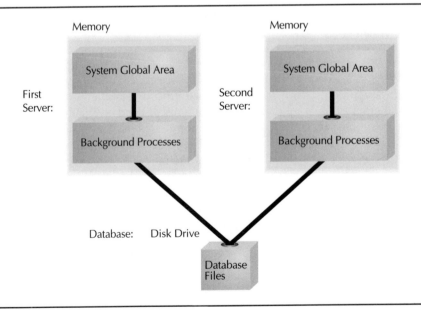

FIGURE 2-9. *ORACLE Parallel Server*

Despite these advantages, there is a significant potential problem with this configuration—what if both servers try to **update** the same records? Following a transaction, ORACLE does not immediately write modified blocks from the SGA back to the datafiles. While those blocks are in the SGA, another instance may request them. To support that request, ORACLE will write the blocks out to disk, and *then* read them into the second SGA. The result is a database request that becomes very I/O-intensive.

The best way around this potential problem is to plan the distribution of users *not* by their CPU usage, but rather by their data usage. That is, users who update the same table should use the same instance to access the database.

When setting up a set of servers to use OPS, a number of database structures and parameters specific to OPS must be specified.

First, the central database must be configured to handle separate servers. Its primary requirement is a set of rollback segments that each server can use. To best manage these, create a separate rollback segment tablespace for each server, using the server name as part of the tablespace name. For example, if the server names were ORA1 and ORA2, then the rollback segment tablespace names should be RBS_ORA1 and RBS_ORA2.

To specify which rollback segments to use, each server must name them in its init.ora file. This method for activating rollback segments is described in Chapter 7. There are several other database initialization parameters that must be set for the parallel servers. Since many of these must be the same for each server, the init.ora IFILE parameter should be used. This specifies an *include file*, which lists values for additional parameters. If both instances refer to the same IFILE, then you will not need to worry about the common values.

In an OPS environment, some of the init.ora parameters (such as INSTANCE_NAME and ROLLBACK_SEGMENTS) must be unique for all instances, while other parameters (such as DB_BLOCK_SIZE) must be the same for all instances.

Further details on all of these parameters are found in the *Oracle Parallel Server Administrator's Guide*. Note that a number of them are tied to the number of servers used. Because of that relationship, the common init.ora parameters must be reevaluated every time a new server is added to the set of servers for a database.

Multiple Processors: the Parallel Query and Parallel Load Options

You can take advantage of multiple processors to perform transactions and queries. The work performed to resolve a single database request can be performed by multiple, coordinated processors. Distributing the workload across multiple processors may improve the performance of transactions and queries.

The Parallel Query Option (PQO) architecture of ORACLE allows almost all database operations to be parallelized. Operations that can take advantage of the

PQO include **create table as select**, **create index**, full table scans, index scans, sorts, **insert**s, **update**s, **delete**s, and most queries.

The extent to which parallelism is employed by the database depends on the **degree** and **instances** parameters of the **parallel** keyword used with these commands (see Appendix A). The **degree** parameter specifies the degree of parallelism—the number of query servers used—for the given operation. The **instances** parameter specifies how the operation is to be split among the instances of an OPS installation. You can specify your instance's parallelism rules—such as the minimum number of query servers—in the instance's init.ora file. The maximum number of concurrently available parallel query server processes is set by the PARALLEL_MAX_SERVERS parameter in init.ora; the minimum number is set by the PARALLEL_MIN_SERVERS parameter. The number of disks on which a table's data is stored and the number of processors available on the server are used to generate the default parallelism for a query.

As of ORACLE7 Release 7.3, you can use the PARALLEL_AUTOMATIC_TUNING init.ora parameter to automatically set many of the available parallel query–related init.ora parameters. One of the automatically set parameters, PARALLEL_ADAPTIVE_ MULTI_USER, will reduce the parallelism of your operations if there are multiple active users in the database. Since there is a limit to the number of parallel query server processes available, reducing parallelism for an operation prevents it from using all of the available resources. You can also use the Database Resource Manager to limit parallelism, as described in Chapter 5.

In addition to parallelizing queries, you can parallelize data loads if you use the SQL*Loader Direct Path loader. See Chapter 8 for details on tuning bulk data inserts.

Client/Server Database Applications

In a host-host configuration, as described earlier in this chapter, an ORACLE database exists on each host, and the databases communicate via Net8. However, a host without a database can access a remote database, typically by having application programs on one host access a database on a second host. In that configuration, the host running the application is called a *client* and the other is called the *server*. This configuration is illustrated in Figure 2-10.

As shown in Figure 2-10, the client must have the ability to communicate across the network to the server. The application programs are run on the client side; therefore, the database is used mainly for I/O. The CPU costs for running the application programs are thus charged to the client PC rather than to the server.

For this configuration to work, the client must be running Net8 or SQL*Net V2. When the client's application program prompts the user for database connection information, the service name should be specified. The application will then open a session in the remote database.

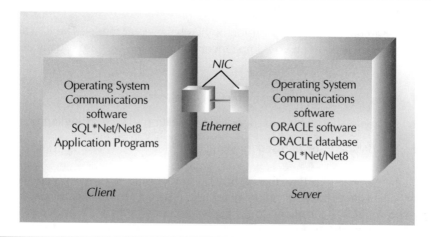

FIGURE 2-10. *Client/server configuration*

Using a client/server configuration helps to reduce the amount of work that is being done by the server. However, shifting an application to a client/server configuration will not automatically improve the system's performance, for two main reasons:

■ CPU resources may not have been a problem before. Usually, CPU resources are used often during the day and infrequently during off-hours. You may wish to alter the schedule of CPU usage by running batch processes or large programs at off-hours.

■ The application may not have been redesigned. Designing for a client/ server environment requires you to take into account the data volumes that are sent across the network for every database access. In server-based applications, this is not a problem. In client/server applications, the network traffic must be considered during planning and tuning.

There are many different ways to implement the client/server configuration, depending on the hardware that is available. The implementation shown in Figure 2-10 is fairly common; it would be used by an ad hoc query tool running on a PC to access an ORACLE database running on a server.

Three-Tier Architectures

A three-tier architecture is an extension of the client/server model. The function of each tier is dependent on your implementation, but the tiers are usually as follows:

- A client, used for presentation of the application

- An application server, used for the application's business logic processing

- The database server, used for storage and retrieval of data

In a three-tier architecture, the application's processing requirements are moved from the client tier to the application server tier. Typically, the application server is more powerful than the client, so the application's performance may benefit. Performance may also be improved by reducing the amount of traffic between the database server and the client. Less data may be sent to the client, since more of the interaction may be performed between the application server and the database server.

The longer-term benefits of a three-tier configuration are derived from the simplified maintenance of the client. Since the application resides on the application server, most of the upgrades will be focused on upgrading the application server. If you do not have extensive configuration control on your client machines, a three-tier architecture may reduce your application maintenance costs.

However, migrating from a client/server architecture to a three-tier architecture is not always simple, straightforward, or beneficial. If you have a well-configured network, controlled client machines, and a well-tuned application, moving to a three-tier architecture may result in no benefits—and potential costs. For example, you will need to redesign your application to reduce network traffic between the clients and the application server; failing to do so may impact the performance of your application. Furthermore, the process for upgrading an application changes—instead of upgrading clients, you will be upgrading an application server used by many clients. Since the application server usage is centralized, you will encounter more difficulty in testing application changes without affecting all application users. However, when changing an application, you will only need to change the application on one server one time.

Figure 2-11 shows a generic three-tier configuration for an ORACLE application. The application server and the database server communicate via SQL*Net. The protocol for communications between the clients and the application server depends on your environment; it may use SQL*Net, or it may use an Internet protocol such as HTTP.

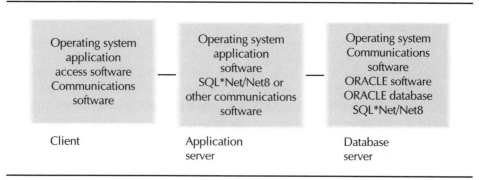

FIGURE 2-11.   *Three-tier configuration*

In any configuration, your application should avoid unnecessary traffic between the client and the database. In a three-tier application, you should be particularly mindful of the traffic between the database and the client, since there are more components between them. The additional components between the client and the database may adversely impact the performance of every database query performed. In many three-tier applications, little data validation is performed at the client side, reducing the number of database lookups required during transaction processing. The lack of data validation queries may be offset via the use of drop-down list boxes of values or multiple-choice check boxes within the application.

Web-Accessible Databases

You can configure your databases to be accessible via the World Wide Web. External clients will communicate with your firewall server (the middle tier), which in turn will pass data requests to the database server. Web-accessible databases, in architecture, are based on the three-tier model shown in Figure 2-11. For example, the client tier may be your personal computer, running a Web browser. Your browser communicates with the middle tier (the firewall server) via HTTP. The middle tier communicates with the database server via SQL*Net/Net8 or via Internet Inter-ORB Protocol (IIOP) if Java is used within the database.

Web configurations, which include the use of Web servers, are described in Chapter 17.

ORACLE Transparent Gateway Access

You can access non-ORACLE databases from within your database. That is, you can create a database link to a service that is not an ORACLE database. You can then query data via the database link, and the data will be queried as if the source data is an ORACLE database.

To access non-ORACLE data, you will need to use the ORACLE Transparent Gateway product. A separate gateway is required for each type of database engine accessed. The gateway is run on the source host for the data being accessed. For example, if the source data is stored in an AS/400 database, then the ORACLE Transparent Gateway software for AS/400 is installed on the AS/400 server. When executed, the gateway software creates a listener on the source server that acts like SQL*Net/Net8 listener. You can then access specific data objects within the AS/400 database, provided you have a username and password for that database.

ORACLE Transparent Gateway is an extension of the server/server configuration shown in Figure 2-7; the difference is that one host's database and database software are non-ORACLE.

Standby Databases

As of ORACLE7, you can configure a second database as a "standby" copy of a primary database. A standby database is a special case of a server/server configuration. Each server has a full copy of the ORACLE software, and the database file structures are usually identical (if they are not, you will need to build a separate control file for the standby database). The two hosts should use the same operating system versions and database software versions.

In the event of a disaster in the production database, you can open the standby database with little data lost—you will usually lose the contents of your online redo log files. As archived redo log files are generated by the production instance in 8i, they must be copied to the standby system. The standby database remains in recovery mode until it is needed. Once the standby database is opened, it becomes the primary database and cannot be easily reconfigured as the standby database.

To automate the transfer of archived redo log files to the standby database, use the LOG_ARCHIVE_DEST_*n* parameters introduced in ORACLE8i. In place of a directory name, use a service name as the destination for the standby database's copy of the archived redo log files.

For example, the production database's init.ora file may contain the following entries:

```
log_archive_dest_1 = '/db00/arch'
log_archive_dest_state_1 = enable
```

The first archive log destination area is the primary destination for new archived redo log files. The second set of init.ora parameters tells the database to write copies of the archived redo log files to the standby database's destination area. For this example, the standby database has a service name of STBY:

```
log_archive_dest_2 = "service=stby.world mandatory reopen=60"
log_archive_dest_state_2 = enable
```

The LOG_ARCHIVE_DEST_2 setting specifies the service name of the standby database. The STBY instance must be accessible via Net8. If there is a connectivity problem, the ARCH process will attempt to reopen the connection 60 seconds later.

See the *ORACLE Server Administrator's Guide* for further directions for setting up and maintaining standby databases.

Replicated Databases

You can use ORACLE's replication features to copy data between databases. You can select the tables, columns, and rows to be replicated from the source database to its replica. In its architecture, a replicated environment is a server/server configuration, as shown in Figure 2-7.

Replicated databases are typically used for the following reasons:

■ To support multiple sites for OLTP access. Large data-entry requirements at remote locations can benefit from replication, since multiple sites around the world can perform data entry concurrently. Transactions can be sent between databases so that the contents of all of the related databases are relatively up-to-date.

■ To create read-only or reporting databases and data warehouses. You can use replication to separate your OLTP database from the database used to support your reporting requirements.

The first option in the preceding list is *multimaster replication*: multiple databases can make changes to the data, and those changes must be propagated to the other databases in the network. Multimaster database systems must account for the resolution of conflicts that may arise during transaction processing.

The second option in the preceding list is *read-only replication*, in which data is only replicated in one direction: from one source to one or more target databases. In general, read-only replication is much simpler to administer and configure than multimaster replication. You can use the read-only copy of the database for reporting, as the basis for a data warehouse, or as a test database. Since it is a separate database, you can create different indexing schemes, tables, and processes in the replica database.

For details on the configuration and administration of a replicated database, see Part III of this book.

External File Access

ORACLE provides numerous methods for interacting with external files. You can use external files as data sources, as script sources, or as output files. The most common external file uses are as follows:

1. As source code for scripts, written in SQL*Plus, SQL, or PL/SQL.

2. As output from a SQL*Plus script, generated via the **spool** command.

3. As input or output from a PL/SQL program, accessed via the UTL_FILE package.

4. As output from a PL/SQL script, generated via use of the DBMS_OUTPUT package.

5. As external data referenced within the database via the BFILE datatype. The BFILE datatype stores a pointer to an external binary file. You must first use the **create directory** command to create a directory pointer within ORACLE to the directory in which the file is stored.

6. As an external program accessed via DBMS_PIPE. The program must be written in a 3GL supported by ORACLE, such as C, Ada, or COBOL.

Any time your application uses external files, you should be concerned about security. The security considerations include the following:

1. Are there passwords hardcoded in any of the files? Scripts that execute repeatedly must have some way of logging into the database.

2. Are the files secure? Can another user read the files?

3. If you use UTL_FILE, is the directory it uses (identified via the UTL_FILE_DIR init.ora parameter) secure? Users will be able to see all of the files in the directory.

4. If you use BFILE datatypes, is the associated directory secure? Are the files protected against modification?

If your application relies on external files, you must be sure those files are backed up using the same schedule as the database backups. Application administrators and database administrators frequently neglect to back up external files along with their database files. If the database is lost due to a disaster, then the database backups may be used during the recovery—but if the associated external files have not been backed up, then the application may not be usable.

Regardless of the configuration you use, you must be able to guarantee its availability, recoverability, and security. As you add components to your environment, you add potential failure points to your environment. Your backup and recovery plans (see Chapter 10), security plans (see Chapter 9), monitoring plans (see Chapter 6), and tuning plans (see Chapter 8) must take all components of your hardware configuration into account.

CHAPTER
3

Logical Database
Layouts

T he logical configuration of a database has a dramatic effect on its performance and its ease of administration. This chapter provides guidelines for choosing the proper tablespace layout for any ORACLE database.

The effective distribution of the database's logical objects was first formalized by Cary Millsap of ORACLE, who named the resulting architecture the *Optimal Flexible Architecture* (OFA). The logical database design described here will define and extend OFA as it relates to logical database design. Planning the layout using this architecture will greatly ease database administration while allowing the DBA greater options when planning and tuning the physical layout. Depending on the installation option you choose, the standard OFA tablespace layout may be automatically created when you install ORACLE. In this chapter, you will see explanations of that layout and useful alternatives to the standard layout.

The End Product

The objective of the database design described here is to configure the database so that its objects are separated by object type and activity type. This configuration will greatly reduce the amount of administrative work that must be done on the database, while decreasing the monitoring needs as well. Problems in one area thus will not affect the rest of the database.

Distributing the database objects in the manner described here will also allow the DBA greater flexibility when planning the database's physical layout. That exercise, described in Chapter 4, is easiest to do when the logical design is as distributive as possible.

In order to distribute the objects effectively within the database, a system of classification must first be established. The logical objects within the database must be classified based on how they are to be used and how their physical structures impact the database. The classification process includes separating tables from their indexes and separating high-activity tables from low-activity tables. Although the volume of activity against objects can only be determined during production usage, a core set of highly used tables can usually be isolated.

The Optimal Flexible Architecture (OFA)

In the following sections you will see the object categories as defined by OFA. Following those descriptions, you will be introduced to suggested OFA extensions.

The Starting Point: The SYSTEM Tablespace

It is possible, though not advisable, to store all of the database's objects in a single tablespace; this is analogous to storing all your files in your root directory. The SYSTEM tablespace, which is the ORACLE equivalent of a root directory, stores the *data dictionary tables* (owned by SYS). The SYSTEM tablespace is also the location of the SYSTEM rollback segment, and during database creation the SYSTEM tablespace is temporarily used to store a second rollback segment (which is then deactivated or dropped).

There is no reason for anything other than the data dictionary tables and the SYSTEM rollback segment to be stored in the SYSTEM tablespace. Storing other segment types in SYSTEM increases the likelihood of space management problems there, which may require the tablespace to be rebuilt. Since the only way to rebuild the SYSTEM tablespace is to re-create the database, anything that can be moved out of SYSTEM should be moved.

The data dictionary tables store all of the information about all of the objects in the database. *Data dictionary segments*, the physical storage for the data dictionary tables, are stored in the SYSTEM tablespace and are fairly static unless large structural changes are made to the applications within the database. Data dictionary segments are created during the database creation process and are generally fairly small. The more procedural objects (such as triggers and procedures) you create and the more abstract datatypes and object-oriented features you use, the larger the data dictionary segments will be. Procedural objects such as triggers store PL/SQL code in the database, and their definitions are stored in the data dictionary tables.

By default, any new user created in your database will have a default tablespace of SYSTEM. To prevent users from creating objects in the SYSTEM tablespace, any quotas on SYSTEM (which gives them the ability to create objects there) must be revoked:

```
alter user USER quota 0 on SYSTEM;
```

When you create a user (via the **create user** command) you can specify a default tablespace:

```
create user USERNAME identified by PASSWORD
default tablespace TABLESPACE_NAME;
```

Once a user has been created, you can use the

```
alter user USERNAME default tablespace TABLESPACE_NAME;
```

command to reassign the default tablespace for a user. Specifying a default tablespace for users and developers will direct objects created without a **tablespace** clause to be stored outside of the SYSTEM tablespace.

NOTE
If a user is granted the UNLIMITED TABLESPACE system privilege or the RESOURCE role, that grant will override any quota set for the user.

The following sections describe each type of database object, its usage, and why it should be stored apart from the rest of the database. The end result will be a standard database configuration with up to 19 standard tablespace types, depending on the manner in which the database is to be used. By developing a consistent logical architecture, you can simplify the development of a consistent physical architecture for your databases. The more consistent your physical database architecture is, the simpler your database administration activities become.

Separating Application Data Segments: DATA

Data segments are the physical areas in which the data associated with tables and clusters is stored. Data segments tend to be very actively accessed by the database, experiencing a high number of data manipulation transactions. Managing the access requests against the data segments is the main goal of a production database.

A typical DATA tablespace contains all of the tables associated with an application. The high I/O volumes against these tables make them ideal candidates for isolation in their own tablespace. If you isolate the application tables to a DATA tablespace, you can separate that tablespace's datafiles from the other datafiles in the database. The separation of datafiles across disk drives may improve performance (through reduced contention for I/O resources) and simplify file management.

Segments in a DATA tablespace are likely to be fragmented. If your data segments are fragmented, they were not properly sized when created. Managing fragmentation, which is described in greater detail in Chapter 4, also drives the need to separate DATA from SYSTEM. Separating data segments from data dictionary segments makes it much easier to isolate and resolve fragmentation problems.

Within DATA, you may have multiple types of tables. Small, static tables have different storage characteristics and management requirements than large, active tables. See the DATA_2 tablespace later in this chapter for details on managing different table types.

Separating Application Index Segments: INDEXES

The indexes associated with tables are subject to the same I/O and growth/fragmentation considerations that encouraged the movement of data segments out of the SYSTEM tablespace. Index segments should not be stored in the same tablespace as their associated tables, since they have a great deal of concurrent I/O during both data manipulation and queries.

Index segments are also subject to fragmentation due to improper sizing or unpredicted table growth. Isolating the application indexes to a separate tablespace greatly reduces the administrative efforts involved in defragmenting either the DATA or the INDEXES tablespace.

Separating existing indexes from their tables may be accomplished by using the **rebuild** option of the **alter index** command. If an index has been created in the same tablespace as the table it indexes, you can move it with a single command. In the following example, the EMPLOYEE$DEPT_NO index is moved to the INDEXES tablespace, and new **storage** values are assigned for it:

```
alter index EMPLOYEE$DEPT_NO rebuild
tablespace INDEXES
storage (initial 2M next 2M pctincrease 0);
```

If you use partitions, then you should separate the partition indexes from the table partitions. For example, you may create a table with ten partitions. If you create local partition indexes, then there will be ten local partition indexes—one for each of the table's partitions. You should store those partition indexes apart from the table partitions they index. If you create a global index on a partitioned table, then the entries in that index may be related to any of the table's partitions. If you use a global index, then you should separate that index from all of the table partitions for the table.

For example, if the SALES table is partitioned, then you can create local indexes on the SALES table's partitions. Each of those local index partitions should be stored apart from their respective table partitions. If you create a global index that spans the entire SALES table, then that index should be stored apart from all of the SALES table's partitions.

When you create a table, the database will dynamically create an index for any PRIMARY KEY or UNIQUE constraint you specify (unless you first create the table without constraints, then create the indexes, then create the constraints). If you do not specify **tablespace** and **storage** parameters for those constraints during table creation, the database will automatically create those indexes in your default tablespace, using the default storage parameters for that tablespace. To avoid this problem, use the **using index** clause of the **create table** command to separate your constraint indexes from the table, as shown in the following listing:

```
create table JOB
(Job_Code      NUMBER,
Description    VARCHAR2(35),
constraint JOB_PK primary key (Job_Code)
using index tablespace INDEXES
storage (initial 2M next 2M pctincrease 0))
tablespace DATA
storage (initial 5M next 5M pctincrease 0);
```

The JOB table will be created in the DATA tablespace, but its primary key index, JOB_PK, will be created in the INDEXES tablespace. Note that the JOB table and its primary key index have separate **storage** and **tablespace** clauses.

Separating Tools Segments: TOOLS

Despite the previous sections' warnings about not storing data segments in the SYSTEM tablespace, many tools do exactly that. They do this not because they specifically call for their objects to be stored in the SYSTEM tablespace, but rather because they store them under the SYSTEM database account, which normally has the SYSTEM tablespace as its default area for storing objects. To avoid this, change the SYSTEM account's default tablespace to the TOOLS tablespace and revoke the SYSTEM account's quota on the SYSTEM tablespace. If SYSTEM has been granted UNLIMITED TABLESPACE, you may also **revoke** that privilege to avoid having nondata dictionary objects stored in the SYSTEM tablespace. However, if you revoke UNLIMITED TABLESPACE from SYSTEM, be sure to grant **quota** on the tablespaces in which SYSTEM may need to create objects such as rollback segments.

Many ORACLE and third-party tools create tables owned by SYSTEM. If the tables have already been created in the database, their objects can be moved by exporting the database, dropping the tool's tables, revoking quota from the SYSTEM tablespace account, granting the SYSTEM user **quota** only on the TOOLS tablespace, and importing the tables.

The following listing shows part of this process. In the first step, the quota is revoked from the SYSTEM user. The second step grants **quota** on the TOOLS tablespace to the SYSTEM user.

```
alter user SYSTEM quota 0 on SYSTEM;
alter user SYSTEM quota 50M on TOOLS;
```

Separating Rollback Segments: RBS

Rollback segments maintain both statement-level and transaction-level read consistency within the database. In order to create non-SYSTEM tablespaces, you must first create a second rollback segment within the SYSTEM tablespace. To isolate rollback segments (which incur I/O for transactions in the database) from the data dictionary, create a rollback segment tablespace that contains nothing but rollback segments. Splitting them out in this fashion also greatly simplifies their management (see Chapter 7).

Once the RBS tablespace has been created, and a rollback segment has been activated within it, the second rollback segment in the SYSTEM tablespace can be dropped. You may find it useful to keep the second rollback segment in SYSTEM inactive but still available in the event of a problem with the RBS tablespace.

Rollback segments dynamically expand to the size of the largest transaction and shrink to a specified optimal size you define (see Chapter 7). I/O against rollback segments is usually concurrent with I/O against the DATA and INDEXES tablespaces. Separating rollback segments from data segments helps avoid I/O contention while making them easier to administer.

Separating Temporary Segments: TEMP

Temporary segments are dynamically created objects within the database that store data during large sorting operations (such as **select distinct**, **union**, and **create index**). Due to their dynamic nature, temporary segments should not be stored with any other types of segments. The proper structure of temporary segments is described in Chapter 4.

As of ORACLE7.3, you can designate a tablespace as a "temporary" tablespace via the **create tablespace** and **alter tablespace** commands. If you designate a tablespace as a temporary tablespace, then you will not be able to create permanent segments such as tables and indexes within that tablespace. Furthermore, the temporary segment in that tablespace will not be dropped when its related command completes, reducing the amount of space management performed for that tablespace.

Unless you designate a tablespace as a temporary tablespace, temporary segments are dropped once the command they support completes. Thus, when a TEMP tablespace is "at rest," there are no segments stored within it. Separating temporary segments from SYSTEM removes a potential problem from the data dictionary area and creates a tablespace that is simple to administer.

You can use the **create user** command to specify a non-SYSTEM temporary tablespace, as shown in the following listing:

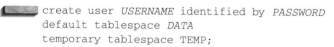

```
create user USERNAME identified by PASSWORD
default tablespace DATA
temporary tablespace TEMP;
```

If the account already exists, you can use the

```
alter user USERNAME temporary tablespace TEMP;
```

command to reassign the temporary tablespace. The **alter user** command will cause all future temporary segments created for that user's account to be created in TEMP.

> **NOTE**
> *It is usually appropriate to alter the SYSTEM and SYS users' temporary tablespace setting to a non-SYSTEM tablespace.*

Separating Users: USERS

Although they typically do not have object creation privileges in production databases, users may have such privileges in development databases. User objects are usually transient in nature, and their sizing efforts are usually not thorough. As a result, user objects should be separated from the rest of the database. Separating user objects from the rest of the database will help to minimize the impact of user experimentation on the functioning of the database.

To separate the users' objects, revoke users' quotas on other tablespaces and change their default tablespace settings to the USERS tablespace. You can use the **create user** command to specify an alternate default tablespace, as shown here:

```
create user USERNAME identified by PASSWORD
default tablespace USERS
temporary tablespace TEMP;
```

After a user's account has been created, you can use the

```
alter user USERNAME default tablespace USERS;
```

command to reassign the default tablespace. Reassigning the default tablespace will direct objects created without a **tablespace** clause to be stored in USERS.

Beyond OFA

The USERS tablespace is the last major section called for by traditional OFA. However, there are several extensions that may be appropriate for your database. These extensions, described in the following sections, help to further isolate objects with differing usage requirements while handling exceptions without impacting the production setup.

Separating Low-Usage Data Segments: DATA_2

When reviewing your list of data tables, you can very likely combine them into two or more groups based on their characteristics: some will contain very dynamic data, others very static data; the latter type of table may contain a list of states, for example. The static data tables tend to experience less I/O than the active data tables; when queried, the access against a static data table is usually concurrent with an access against a dynamic data table.

This concurrent I/O can be split among multiple files (and thus among multiple disks, to reduce I/O contention) by placing all static data tables in a dedicated tablespace. Administrative functions performed against the DATA tablespace, such as defragmentation, now only occur against those tables most likely to require assistance. Meanwhile, the tablespace for static data tables, DATA_2, should remain static and simple to maintain.

Depending on the size of your database and the features you use, you may have multiple types of DATA tablespaces. In addition to having a DATA_2 tablespace for your static tables, you may also have multiple types of DATA tablespaces for the following:

■ **Aggregations**   If you have a data warehouse, you will most likely store aggregations in separate tables. Since these tables are based on derived data and may be frequently dropped and re-created, you should isolate them from your primary transaction tables.

■ **Snapshots**   Like aggregations, snapshots are based on derived data, and may be dropped and re-created on a more frequent basis than your application's transaction tables.

■ **Temporary work tables**   If you frequently load data from other systems into your database, you may load that data into temporary tables before moving it into your transaction tables. Such temporary work tables should be separated from the rest of your database tables.

■ **Partitions**   If you use partitioning extensively, you should separate your partitions across tablespaces (and, therefore, across datafiles). Separating your partitions across tablespaces will enable you to separate current data in the table from archival data in the table.

How can you tell if a table is a static table? If you are not familiar with the application, then you may need to audit the accesses to tables in order to determine which tables are most actively used. Auditing (see Chapter 9) can record every time a table is accessed as well as the type of access performed (insert, select, etc.). Auditing of accesses for many tables may generate a large number of audit records, so perform the audits during a single day and then disable the audits. A single day of standard usage of the application should be sufficient to determine the usage pattern. When analyzing the audit results, you will be looking for the tables that are most frequently accessed as well as the most common types of access against each table. If the table has no **insert**s, **update**s, or **delete**s against it during normal usage, then it should be considered for migration out of the DATA tablespace into a more appropriate tablespace.

Separating Low-Usage Index Segments: INDEXES_2

The indexes for low-usage, static data tables also tend to be low usage and static. To simplify the administrative actions for the INDEXES tablespace, move the static tables' indexes to a separate INDEXES_2 tablespace. This separation also helps to improve performance-tuning options, since concurrent I/O among indexes can now be split across disk drives.

If the low-usage indexes have already been created in the INDEXES tablespace, then they must be dropped and re-created in INDEXES_2. This is usually done concurrent with the moving of low-usage tables to DATA_2. If the index was created via a PRIMARY KEY or UNIQUE constraint definition, then that constraint may need to be modified.

The following listing shows a sample tablespace specification for an automatically created index. This example creates a UNIQUE constraint on the Description column in a static table called EMPLOYEE_TYPE. The UNIQUE index that the database will create for this constraint is directed to be stored in the INDEXES_2 tablespaces.

```
alter table EMPLOYEE_TYPE
   add constraint UNIQ_DESCR  unique(DESCRIPTION)
using index tablespace INDEXES_2;
```

If the index already exists, you can use the **rebuild** clause of the **alter index** command to move the index from its current tablespace to a new tablespace. See the INDEXES section earlier in this chapter.

If you create additional DATA tablespaces for aggregations, snapshots, temporary work tables, and partitions, then you should create additional INDEX tablespaces to support the indexes for those tables.

Separating Tools Indexes: TOOLS_I

If your database shows a lot of activity against the TOOLS tablespace, then the indexes for those TOOLS tables may be moved to a separate tablespace. This is most applicable to those environments in which the TOOLS tablespace is treated as a DATA tablespace; that is, its tables are the subject of much of the I/O in the database.

You can use the **rebuild** clause of the **alter index** command to move an existing index to a different tablespace while rebuilding it. In the following example, the JOB_PK index is moved to the INDEXES tablespace, and new **storage** values are assigned for it:

```
alter index JOB_PK rebuild
tablespace INDEXES
storage (initial 2M next 2M pctincrease 0);
```

Separating Specialty Rollback Segments: RBS_2

The rollback segments in the RBS tablespace should be of the proper size and number to support production usage of the application (see Chapter 7). There will almost always be a transaction (usually a batch transaction) whose size is unsupported by the production rollback segment configuration. When you execute that transaction, it will take over one of the production rollback segments and extend it greatly, using up as much free space as it can before the transaction succeeds or fails.

It doesn't have to be that way. The production rollback segments should be used by production users. Special transactional requirements (such as large data loads, aggregations, or **delete**s) should be handled by a separate rollback segment. To specify this rollback segment, the application code must use the

```
set transaction use rollback segment SEGMENT_NAME
```

command prior to executing the transaction. The need for detailed settings of this sort within application code may call for greater involvement of DBAs within application teams (see Chapter 5). However, the **set transaction** command solves only part of the problem since the chosen rollback segment is still using space in the production RBS tablespace.

Create a separate rollback segment tablespace that will exist solely to support this type of transaction. When the transaction completes, the rollback segment may be either deactivated or dropped (and its tablespace may be dropped as well, thus saving disk space). Once again, separating logical objects based on their functional requirements serves to greatly simplify their administration.

Separating User-Specific Temporary Segments: TEMP_USER

The final major tablespace is, like RBS_2, a specialty tablespace designed to address specific needs of the application users. Certain users, such as GL (the General

Ledger schema) in an ORACLE Applications database, may require much larger temporary segments than the rest of the application's users. In such a case, separate those temporary segments from the standard TEMP tablespace. This separation eases administration, since you can now design for the common usage of the system while handling the exceptions via TEMP_*USER*. In practice, name this tablespace after the name of the user, as in TEMP_GL or TEMP_SCOTT.

You can use the **create user** command to specify a temporary tablespace for a user:

```
create user USERNAME identified by PASSWORD
default tablespace TABLESPACE_NAME
temporary tablespace temp_USER;
```

If the user has already been created, the following command can be used to change the temporary tablespace setting:

```
alter user USERNAME temporary tablespace TEMP_USER;
```

The **alter user** command will cause all future temporary segments created for that user's account to be created in the user's custom TEMP_*USER* tablespace.

If your applications use a single database logon for all users, then your options are more limited. In that environment, a change to the temporary tablespace assignment or sizing affects all users. In that configuration, you have two primary choices:

1. Size the TEMP temporary tablespace to support extremely large transactions in addition to the smaller transactions. Don't create a second temporary tablespace.

2. Create a TEMP_USER tablespace in addition to TEMP. Schedule the large transactions to run at off-hours. Prior to executing the large transactions, change the user's temporary tablespace setting to point to TEMP_USER. When the transaction completes, change the user's temporary tablespace setting back to TEMP.

Additional Application-Specific OFA Extensions

Depending on your application, you may have additional types of objects in your database. Each distinct type of object should be stored in its own tablespace to minimize the impact objects have on each other. The types are listed in the following table.

SNAPS   For snapshots (see Chapter 16). Snapshot tables and indexes are managed differently than most other tables in the database.

SNAPS_I   For the indexes on your snapshots.

AGG_DATA   For materialized views and aggregation tables. Like snapshots, materialized views and aggregations are based on derived data.

AGG_DATA_I   For the indexes on materialized views and aggregation tables.

PARTITIONS   For partitions (see Chapter 12). You can use partitions to distribute the I/O load and improve the ease of management for very large tables. You should identify the most commonly used partitions and manage them as if they were separate tables.

PARTITIONS_I   For the local and global indexes associated with your partitions.

TEMP_WORK   For use during large data loads (see Chapter 12). Temporary work segments are characterized by large batch loads of data followed by deletion of the data or truncation of the table. You may also need a separate tablespace for the indexes for your temporary work tables.

If you do not use replication, materialized views, partitions, or temporary work tables for data loads, then you will not need any of these extra tablespaces. If you use partitions, you can move the partitions to different tablespaces once they exist (see Chapter 12 and the **alter table** command in Appendix A). If you use local partition indexes (see Chapter 12), you should separate the local indexes from their respective table partitions.

Common-Sense Logical Layouts

The resulting logical design of the database should meet the following criteria:

- Segment types that are used in the same way should be stored together.

- The system should be designed for its most common usage (transaction sizes, number of users, number of transactions, etc.).

■ Separate areas should exist for exceptions.

■ Contention among tablespaces should be minimized.

■ The data dictionary should be isolated.

Note that meeting these criteria requires the DBA to know the application being implemented: which tools it will use, which tables will be most active, when data loads will occur, which users will have exceptional resource requirements, and how standard transactions behave. Gaining this knowledge requires a very high level of involvement of the DBA in the application development process (see Chapter 5). Applications provided by a third-party vendor may require additional DBA involvement (see Chapter 11).

Meeting these criteria results in a system whose varied segment types do not interfere with each other's needs. This separation makes it much simpler to manage the database, and to isolate and resolve performance problems. When fragmentation of segments or free space does occur (see Chapter 4 and Chapter 8), it is much simpler to resolve when the database is laid out in this manner.

In this configuration, the only potential non-SYSTEM tablespace in which multiple types of segments may exist is the USERS tablespace. If the development environment is also used as a testing environment, then it may be a good idea to separate users' indexes into a USERS_I tablespace.

The combination of a sensible logical database layout with a well-designed physical database layout (see Chapter 4) results in systems that require very little tuning after the first postproduction check. The up-front planning efforts pay off immediately in both the flexibility and the performance of the database. The cost of implementing this design from the start is minimal; it can be built into all of your database creation scripts automatically, and is now a part of the database creation scripts automatically generated by the ORACLE software installation process. The final overall design of the system should be an appropriate combination of the logical divisions shown in Table 3-1.

Once you establish your standard configuration, apply it whenever you create a new database. Applying a standard configuration will simplify administration, since each database will follow the same set of tablespace usage rules. Those rules, which separate segments by type and characteristics, isolate most problems and simplify their resolution.

Tablespace	Use
SYSTEM	Data dictionary
DATA	Standard-operation tables
DATA_2	Static tables used during standard operations
INDEXES	Indexes for the standard-operation tables
INDEXES_2	Indexes for the static tables
RBS	Standard-operation rollback segments
RBS_2	Specialty rollback segments used for data loads
TEMP	Standard-operation temporary segments
TEMP_*USER*	Temporary segments created by a specific user
TOOLS	RDBMS tools tables
TOOLS_I	Indexes for heavily used RDBMS tools tables
USERS	User objects, in development databases
USERS_I	User indexes, in testing databases
SNAPS	Snapshot tables
SNAPS_I	Indexes on the snapshots
AGG_DATA	Aggregation tables and materialized views
AGG_DATA_I	Indexes on aggregation tables and materialized views
PARTITIONS	Partitions of table or index segments; create multiple tablespaces for them
PARTITIONS_I	Local and global indexes on partitions
TEMP_WORK	Temporary tables used during data load processing

TABLE 3-1. *Logical Distribution of Segments in an Optimal Database*

Solutions

You can use the suggested tablespace types in Table 3-1 to design a configuration that best meets your needs. In Table 3-2, you will see the configurations most commonly found in database applications.

Database Type	Tablespaces
Small development database	SYSTEM DATA INDEXES RBS TEMP USERS TOOLS
Production OLTP database	SYSTEM DATA DATA_2 INDEXES INDEXES_2 RBS RBS_2 TEMP TEMP_USER TOOLS
Production OLTP with historical data	SYSTEM DATA DATA_2 DATA_ARCHIVE INDEXES INDEXES_2 INDEXES_ARCHIVE RBS RBS_2 TEMP TEMP_USER TOOLS

TABLE 3-2. *Common Tablespace Layouts*

Database Type	Tablespaces
Data warehouse	SYSTEM
	DATA
	DATA_2
	INDEXES
	INDEXES_2
	RBS
	RBS_2
	TEMP
	TEMP_USER
	TOOLS
	PARTITIONS
	PARTITIONS_I
	AGG_DATA
	AGG_DATA_I
	SNAPS
	SNAPS_I
	TEMP_WORK
	TEMP_WORK_I

TABLE 3-2.   *Common Tablespace Layouts* (continued)

CHAPTER

4

Physical
Database Layouts

icture a crowded lecture hall, in which every seat is taken. Now, eliminate half of the seats by combining groups of attendees onto seats. For the combinations to work, characteristics of the people must be estimated: their relative weights, their space needs, etc. Now eliminate half of the remaining seats. The cycle of planning the appropriate distribution of attendees must be repeated.

This same repetitive reallocation of resources happens to DBAs every day. In the DBA's case, it occurs when the number of database-related files exceeds the number of disks available. The characteristics of those files must then be considered in order to arrive at the optimal combinations.

In this chapter, you will see the manner in which ORACLE manages physical data storage, along with the optimal physical database layouts for any number of disks. These layouts will be the result of understanding the ways in which various database files operate and interact. You will also see a set of standard solutions for common database configurations.

Too often, the physical layout of the database is not planned; it is only considered when the database is experiencing performance problems. Just as the logical layout of the database should be planned (see Chapter 3), the physical layout of the database's files must be designed and implemented to meet the database's goals. Failure to plan the layouts before creating the database will result in a recurring cycle of layout-related problems and performance tuning efforts.

In this chapter, you will see where to place database-related files relative to each other to ensure optimal recoverability and performance as well as a method for verifying the planned layout. You will also see the suggested directory structure for the system's disks and an overview on database space usage. These four sections, taken together, provide an understanding of the impact of system-level file layout decisions on each level of an ORACLE database.

Database File Layout

By establishing the clear goals of the file distribution design, and by understanding the nature of the database (transaction-oriented versus read-intensive), the proper design can be determined for distributing the files across any number of devices. In this chapter you will see designs for the most common configurations as well as guidelines for applying them to any situations not directly covered.

This process will be accomplished via the following steps:

1. Identifying I/O contention among datafiles

2. Identifying I/O bottlenecks among all database files

3. Identifying concurrent I/O among background processes

4. Defining the security and performance goals for the database

5. Defining the system hardware and mirroring architecture

6. Identifying disks that can be dedicated to the database

In many cases, only the datafile contention, hardware mirroring, and disk acquisition tasks (tasks #1, 5, and 6 above) are performed before creating databases, thus designing contention into the system. When you complete all of the steps listed here, the end product will be a physical database layout that has your needs designed into it.

I/O Contention Among Datafiles

When designing your logical database layout, follow the design procedures given in Chapter 3. Doing so should result in a database that contains some combination of the tablespaces shown in Table 4-1.

Tablespace	Use
SYSTEM	Data dictionary
DATA	Standard-operation tables
DATA_2	Static tables used during standard operation
INDEXES	Indexes for the standard-operation tables
INDEXES_2	Indexes for the static tables
RBS	Standard-operation rollback segments
RBS_2	Specialty rollback segments used for data loads
TEMP	Standard-operation temporary segments
TEMP_*USER*	Temporary segments created by a particular user
TOOLS	RDBMS tools tables
TOOLS_I	Indexes for RDBMS tools tables
USERS	User objects, in development databases
SNAPS	Snapshots (a SNAPS_I can be created for their indexes)
AGG_DATA	Aggregation tables and materialized views
PARTITIONS	Partitions of table or index segments; create multiple tablespaces for them
TEMP_WORK	Temporary tables used during data load processing

TABLE 4-1. *Logical Distribution of Segments in an Optimal Database*

Each of these tablespaces requires a separate datafile. You can monitor database I/O among datafiles *after* the database has been created; this capability is only useful during the planning stages if an analogous database is available for reference. If no such database is available, then the DBA must estimate the I/O load for each datafile.

Start the physical layout planning process by estimating the relative I/O of the datafiles. Assign the most active tablespace an I/O "weight" of 100. Then, estimate the I/O against the other data tablespaces relative to that tablespace. Assign the SYSTEM tablespace files a weight of 35, and the index tablespaces a value equal to one-third of the weighting for their associated data tablespaces.

What about the TOOLS, RBS, and TEMP tablespaces? The I/O against these tablespaces varies widely, depending on the nature of the database. TOOLS will experience very little I/O in a production environment. If the database will be very transaction-oriented, RBS's weight may go as high as 75 (in most cases, it should be between 10 and 40). TEMP, in production, will only be used by large sorts; its weight will therefore vary widely during usage, ranging from 0 to 75. Choose a value that is reflective of the database you are implementing.

The message in this weighting procedure is twofold: first, the file I/O weight has to be estimated before the files are created; and second, this procedure has to be done for each database. Table 4-2 shows the I/O weights for a sample transaction-oriented production database with no RBS_2 or TEMP_*USER* tablespaces.

Tablespace	Weight	Percent of Total
DATA	100	45
RBS	40	18
SYSTEM	35	16
INDEXES	33	15
TEMP	5	2
DATA_2	4	2
INDEXES_2	2	1
TOOLS	1	1
Total	220	

TABLE 4-2. *Estimated I/O Weights for Sample Tablespaces*

In the example shown in Table 4-2, the DATA tablespace has been given a weight of 100. Its associated index tablespace, INDEXES, has a weight of one-third of that—33. The SYSTEM tablespace has been given a weight of 35, and RBS (the rollback segments tablespace) has been given an estimated I/O weight of 40. TEMP and TOOLS have been estimated to have weights of 5 and 1, respectively. The DATA_2 and INDEXES_2 tablespaces have been estimated to be very lightly used, with weights of 4 and 2, respectively.

Note that 94 percent of the I/O is concentrated in the top four tablespaces. In order to properly distribute the datafile I/O, you would therefore need at least five disks: one for each of the top four tablespaces (by I/O weight) and one for the lower I/O tablespaces. The DBA of this database should also avoid putting additional database files on the disks holding the top four tablespaces.

These weightings serve to reinforce several cardinal rules about database file placement on disks: the DATA tablespaces should be stored separate from their INDEXES tablespaces, the RBS tablespaces separate from the DATA tablespaces, and the SYSTEM tablespace separate from the other tablespaces in the database. The weightings and characteristics of the lower I/O tablespaces will be used to determine which of them should be stored on the same devices when that becomes necessary.

You can use the scripts given in the "Verification of I/O Weighting Estimates" section of this chapter to monitor the database (and thus verify the I/O weighting estimates).

Only One DATA Tablespace?

In Table 4-2, only one DATA tablespace is shown. For the sake of keeping this example simple to understand, only one DATA tablespace will be used throughout this chapter. In production databases, you will likely have multiple DATA tablespaces (particularly if you use partitions). When estimating I/O weights, you will then have to estimate the I/O weight of each of your DATA tablespaces.

I/O Bottlenecks Among All Database Files

Once you have estimated the I/O weightings of the datafiles, you can lay out the location of the datafiles relative to each other. However, I/O weighting of datafiles is only part of the picture. Other database file types must be considered as well.

Online Redo Log Files

The most confusing aspect of database file placement concerns *online redo log files*. Online redo log files store the records of each transaction in the database. Each database must have at least two online redo log files available to it. The database will write to one log file in a sequential fashion until it is filled, then it will start writing to the second redo log file. When the last online redo log file is filled, the database will begin overwriting the contents of the first redo log file with new transactions.

Online redo log files are the database's Achilles' heel. Since they maintain information about the current transactions in the database, they cannot be recovered from a backup unless the database was shut down prior to backup (see Chapter 10).

DBAs need to make sure that the online redo log files are mirrored by some means. You can use *redo log groups* to enable the database to dynamically maintain multiple sets of the online redo log files. Redo log groups use the database to mirror the online redo log files, thus minimizing the recovery problems caused by a single disk failure. You can also rely on the operating system to mirror the redo log files.

In general, you should place online redo log files apart from datafiles because of potential performance implications. Understanding the performance implications requires knowing how the two types of files (datafiles and online redo log files) are used.

Every transaction that is not executed with the **nologging** parameter in effect is recorded in the redo log files. Transaction entries are written to the online redo log files by the *LGWR (Log Writer)* background process. The data in the transactions is concurrently written to several tablespaces (such as the RBS rollback segments tablespace and the DATA tablespace). The writes to the tablespaces are done via the *DBWR (Database Writer)* background process. Thus, even though the datafile I/O may be properly distributed, contention between the DBWR and LGWR background processes will occur if a datafile is stored on the same disk as a redo log file.

Redo log files are written sequentially. If there is no concurrent activity on the disk, then the disk hardware will already be properly positioned for the next log write. By contrast, datafiles are read and written to in a comparatively random fashion. Since the log files are written sequentially, they will process I/O the fastest if they do not have to contend with other activity on the same disk.

If you must store a datafile on the same disk as redo log files, then it should not belong to the SYSTEM tablespace, the RBS tablespace, or a very active DATA or INDEX tablespace. All of these will have direct conflicts with the redo log files and will increase the likelihood of the log writes being affected by the database reads.

Control Files

Control files can be internally mirrored by ORACLE. You can specify the number and name of the control files via the CONTROL_FILES parameter in the database's init.ora or config.ora file. If the control filenames are specified via this parameter during database creation, then they will be automatically created during the database creation process. The database will thereafter maintain the control files as identical copies of each other.

Each database should have a minimum of three copies of its control files, located across three drives. Very little I/O occurs in these files relative to that of the other database files.

Archived Redo Log Files

The LGWR background process writes to the online redo log files in a cyclical fashion; after filling the first log file, it begins writing the second until that one fills, and then begins writing to the third. Once the last online redo log file is filled, LGWR begins to overwrite the contents of the first online redo log file.

When ORACLE is run in ARCHIVELOG mode, the database makes a copy of each online redo log file before overwriting it. These archived redo log files are usually written to a disk device. They may also be written directly to a tape device, but this tends to be operator-intensive.

The ARCH background process performs the archiving function. Databases using the ARCHIVELOG option will encounter contention problems on their online redo log disk during heavy data transaction times, since LGWR will be trying to write to one redo log file while ARCH is trying to read another. The only way to avoid this contention is to distribute the online redo log files across multiple disks. Therefore, if you are running in ARCHIVELOG mode on a very transaction-oriented database, avoid LGWR-ARCH contention by splitting up your online redo log files across devices.

You should also be careful with the placement of the archived redo log files. Remember that this device, by its nature, will have the same amount of I/O as the online redo logs device. Therefore, the rules regarding placement of online redo log files apply also to the archived redo log files. They should not be stored on the same device as the SYSTEM, RBS, DATA, or INDEXES tablespaces, and they should not be stored on the same device as any of the online redo log files. Since running out of space on the archived redo log device will freeze the database, archived redo log files should only be stored with small, static files.

ORACLE Software

The specific ORACLE software files that are accessed during normal database operation vary according to the packages that are licensed for the host on which the server resides. The I/O against these files is not recorded within the database. Since the location of the files is also variable (particularly in a distributed or client/server architecture), a system or network monitor should be used to determine the I/O against these files. The actual I/O against these files can then be compared with the I/O measurements for the database files to determine if the files need to be redistributed.

To minimize contention between the database files and the database code, avoid placing database files on the same disk device as the code files. If datafiles must be placed on that disk device, then the least frequently used datafiles should be placed there.

Concurrent I/O Among Background Processes

When evaluating contention among various processes, you should identify the type of I/O being performed and its timing. Files contend with each other if I/O from one file interferes with I/O for the second file, so two random-accessed files that are never accessed at the same time can be placed on the same device.

Based on the discussion in the previous section, two types of I/O contention can be defined: *concurrent I/O* and *interference*. Concurrent I/O contention occurs when multiple accesses are performed against the same device at the same instant. This is the kind of contention that is eliminated by isolating tables from their associated indexes. Interference contention occurs when writes to a sequentially written file are interrupted by reads or writes to other files on the same disk, even if those reads or writes occur at different times than the sequential reads and writes.

There are three database background processes that actively access the database files on disk: the Database Writer (DBWR), the Log Writer (LGWR), and the Archiver (ARCH). DBWR writes to files in a fairly random manner, LGWR writes sequentially, and ARCH reads and writes sequentially. Eliminating the contention possibilities between these three background processes will effectively eliminate all contention at the database level.

Note that LGWR and ARCH are always writing to one file at a time. DBWR, on the other hand, may be attempting to write to multiple files at once. There is thus the potential for DBWR to cause contention with itself! To combat this problem, certain operating systems (including UNIX) can create multiple DBWR processes for each instance. The number of DBWRs is set via the init.ora parameter DBWR_PROCESSES; you can also start multiple I/O slaves for a single DBWR process via the DBWR_IO_SLAVES parameter. ORACLE recommends setting DBWR_IO_SLAVES to a value between n and $2n$, where n is the number of disks. In 8.0, but not in 8.1 or later releases, you can also start multiple LGWR I/O slaves (via the LGWR_IO_SLAVES parameter) and multiple ARCH I/O slaves (via ARCH_IO_SLAVES). As of 8.1, ORACLE uses the DBWR_IO_SLAVES setting to determine how many LGWR and ARCH I/O slaves to start; setting DBWR_IO_SLAVES to a value greater than 0 sets the corresponding LGWR_IO_SLAVES and ARCH_IO_SLAVES settings each to 4. If this option is not available on your system, then you may be able to use asynchronous I/O to reduce internal DBWR contention. With asynchronous I/O, only one DBWR process is started since the I/O processing is performed asynchronously.

The nature of the contention that will occur between the background processes is thus a function of the backup scheme used (ARCH), the transaction load on the system (LGWR), and the host operating system (DBWR). Designing a scheme that will eliminate contention between files and processes requires a clear understanding of the ways in which those files and processes will interact in the production system.

Defining the Recoverability and Performance Goals for the System

Before designing the database's disk layout, the goals for the layout must be clearly defined. Otherwise, you'll end up with contradictory designs.

The database goals that relate directly to disks are (1) *recoverability* and (2) *performance*. The recoverability goals must take into account all processes that impact disks. These should include, at a minimum, the storage area for archived redo log files (if used) and the storage area for Export dump files.

The performance tuning goals must take into account the projected database file I/O distribution and the relative access speeds of the disks available (since heterogeneous systems may feature some disks that are faster than others).

In order to avoid conflicting advice on disk layouts, the goal of the layout must be clearly defined: Are you trying to optimize performance or recoverability? If recoverability is the primary goal of the layout, then all critical database files should be placed on mirrored drives, and the database should be run in ARCHIVELOG mode. In such a scenario, performance is a secondary consideration.

Recoverability of a database should always be a primary concern. But once the database has been secured, the performance goals of the system should be taken into consideration. For example, the server on which the database resides may have fully mirrored disks, in which case performance is the only real issue.

To ensure database recoverability, you must mirror your online redo log files. You can mirror the files via the operating system or via mirrored redo log groups, but it must be done. The architecture put in place for recoverability should complement the performance tuning architecture; the two goals may yield two different file layouts. If the performance tuning design conflicts with the recoverability design, then the recoverability design must prevail. Recoverability issues should only involve a few disks; once the database recovery options have been chosen (see Chapter 10), the performance issues can be addressed.

Defining the System Hardware and Mirroring Architecture

Since the systems management group allocates and manages the server's disk farm, DBAs must work with that team to manage the system's hardware and mirroring architecture. This involves specifying the following:

■ The number of disks required

- The models of disks required (for performance or size)

- The appropriate mirroring strategy

The number of disks required will be driven by the size of the database and the database I/O weights. Wherever possible, those disks should be dedicated to ORACLE files to avoid concurrent I/O and interference contention with non-ORACLE files. If the disk farm is heterogeneous, then the size and speed of the drives available should be taken into consideration when determining which are to be dedicated to ORACLE files.

Disk mirroring provides fault tolerance with regard to media failures. Mirroring is performed either by maintaining a duplicate of each disk online (known as *RAID-1* or *volume shadowing*) or by using a *parity-check* system among a group of disks (usually *RAID-3* or *RAID-5*). The parity-check systems implicitly perform file striping across disks. In RAID-5, for example, each file is striped on a block-by-block basis across the disks in the mirroring group. A parity check is then written on another disk in the set so that if one disk is removed, its contents can be regenerated based on knowing the parity check and the contents of the rest of the mirrored set.

The system mirroring architecture thus impacts the distribution of database files across those disks. Disks that are mirrored on a one-to-one basis (RAID-1) can be treated as stand-alone disks. Disks that are part of a parity-check system (such as RAID-3 or RAID-5) must be considered as a set, and can take advantage of the implicit striping.

NOTE
Often, DBAs are told by systems administrators that disks have been configured in a RAID environment, so that file placement is not a concern. However, if that configuration consists of a small number of disks, then there may be sources for I/O contention at the disk level. Striping across a small number of large disks does not normally resolve disk contention issues in an ORACLE database. Work closely with systems administrators to configure the stripe sets appropriately.

Identifying Disks That Can Be Dedicated to the Database

Whatever mirroring architecture is used, the disks chosen must be dedicated to the database. Otherwise, the nondatabase load on those disks will impact the database, and that impact is usually impossible to forecast correctly. User directory areas, for example, may experience sudden increases in size—and wipe out the space that was intended for the archived redo log files, bringing the database to a halt. Other files may have severe I/O requirements that were not factored into the database I/O weights estimated earlier.

Choosing the Right Layout

The goals for the disk layout are as follows:

- The database must be recoverable.

- The online redo log files must be mirrored via the system or the database.

- The database file I/O weights must be estimated.

- Contention between DBWR, LGWR, and ARCH must be minimized.

- Contention between disks for DBWR must be minimized.

- The performance goals of the system must be defined.

- The disk hardware options must be known.

- The disk mirroring architecture must be known.

- Disks must be dedicated to the database.

The Dream Database Physical Layout: the 22-Disk Solution

The layouts presented in this section assume that the disks involved are dedicated to the database and that the online redo log files are being mirrored via the operating system. It is also assumed that the disks have identical size and performance characteristics.

The configuration shown in Figure 4-1 is not likely to be available, but it's important to start with goals that aim high. This configuration eliminates contention between datafiles completely by giving each a separate disk to occupy. It also eliminates

Disk	Contents
1	Oracle software
2	SYSTEM tablespace
3	RBS tablespace
4	DATA tablespace
5	INDEXES tablespace
6	TEMP tablespace
7	TOOLS tablespace
8	Online Redo log 1
9	Online Redo log 2
10	Online Redo log 3
11	Control file 1
12	Control file 2
13	Control file 3
14	Application software
15	RBS_2
16	DATA_2
17	INDEXES_2
18	TEMP_*USER*
19	TOOLS_I
20	USERS
21	Archived redo log destination disk
22	Export dump file destination disk

FIGURE 4-1. *The 22-disk solution*

LGWR-ARCH contention by giving each redo log a separate disk. It also assigns a disk (number 14) to the software for the application that will access the database.

This configuration is unlikely because of the capital resources that are required; on the control file disks, an entire disk (usually up to 8GB) is used to maintain a single, low-access file that seldom exceeds 200K. To reach a more realistic configuration, the disk layout will be iteratively revised until the available number of disks is reached.

The First Iteration: the 17-Disk Solution

Each successive iteration of the disk layout will involve placing the contents of multiple disks on a single disk. The first iteration (in Figure 4-2) moves the three control files onto the three redo log disks. Control files will cause interference contention with the online redo logs, but only at log switch points and during database recovery. During normal operation of the database, very little interference will occur.

Disk	Contents
1	Oracle software
2	SYSTEM tablespace
3	RBS tablespace
4	DATA tablespace
5	INDEXES tablespace
6	TEMP tablespace
7	TOOLS tablespace
8	Online Redo log 1, *Control file 1*
9	Online Redo log 2, *Control file 2*
10	Online Redo log 3, *Control file 3*
11	Application software
12	RBS_2
13	DATA_2
14	INDEXES_2
15	TEMP_*USER*
16	Archived redo log destination disk
17	Export dump file destination disk

FIGURE 4-2.   *The 17-disk solution*

Assuming that this will be a production database, the TOOLS_I tablespace's contents will be merged with the TOOLS tablespace (they are usually only separated in intense development environments). For production environments, users will not have resource privileges, so the USERS tablespace will not be considered in these configurations.

The Second Iteration: the 15-Disk Solution
The second iteration of file combinations (in Figure 4-3) begins the process of placing multiple tablespaces on the same disk. In this case, the RBS and RBS_2 tablespaces are placed together because they are seldom used concurrently; as previously defined, RBS_2 contains specialty rollback segments that are used during large data loads. Since data loads should not be occurring during production usage (which RBS is used for), there should be no contention between RBS and RBS_2, so they can be placed together.

The TEMP and TEMP_*USER* tablespaces can also be placed on the same disk. The TEMP_*USER* tablespace is dedicated to a specific user (such as GL in ORACLE Financials) who has temporary segment needs that are far greater than the rest of the system's users. The TEMP tablespace's weighting, as previously noted, can vary widely; however, it should be possible to store it on the same device as TEMP_*USER* without overly impacting its I/O.

```
Disk      Contents
1         Oracle software
2         SYSTEM tablespace
3         RBS tablespace, RBS_2 tablespace
4         DATA tablespace
5         INDEXES tablespace
6         TEMP tablespace, TEMP_USER tablespace
7         TOOLS tablespace
8         Online Redo log 1, Control file 1
9         Online Redo log 2, Control file 2
10        Online Redo log 3, Control file 3
11        Application software
12        DATA_2
13        INDEXES_2
14        Archived redo log destination disk
15        Export dump file destination disk
```

FIGURE 4-3. *The 15-disk solution*

The Third Iteration: the 12-Disk Solution

Before putting any more combinations of tablespaces on multiple disks, the online redo logs should be placed together on the same disk (see Figure 4-4). In databases that use ARCHIVELOG backups, this will cause concurrent I/O and interference contention between LGWR and ARCH on that disk. Thus, this combination is not appropriate for very high-transaction systems running in ARCHIVELOG mode.

```
Disk      Contents
1         Oracle software
2         SYSTEM tablespace, Control file 1
3         RBS tablespace, RBS_2 tablespace, Control file 2
4         DATA tablespace, Control file 3
5         INDEXES tablespace
6         TEMP tablespace, TEMP_USER tablespace
7         TOOLS tablespace, INDEXES_2 tablespace
8         Online Redo logs 1, 2, and 3
9         Application software
10        DATA_2
11        Archived redo log destination disk
12        Export dump file destination disk
```

FIGURE 4-4. *The 12-disk solution*

Because the online redo log file disks have been combined into one, the control files must be moved. In this example, they coexist with the three most critical tablespaces (SYSTEM, RBS, and DATA). As previously stated, the control files are not I/O intensive and should cause little contention. The only other change for this configuration is the colocation of the TOOLS tablespace with the INDEX_2 tablespace.

The Fourth Iteration: the 9-Disk Solution

As you may have noted, most of the changes have consisted of moving items from the highest-numbered disks onto the lower-numbered disks. This is because the first disks were assigned to those files that were judged to be most critical to the database. The later disks were assigned to files that would be helpful to have on separate devices, but whose isolation was not a necessity.

This iteration (shown in Figure 4-5) combines the three highest-numbered disks (disks 10, 11, and 12) with good matches for their characteristics. First, the DATA_2 tablespace (weighted as 2 percent of the total datafile I/O) is combined with the TEMP tablespaces, creating a disk that now handles 4 percent of the datafile I/O. This should be a good match because the static tables are less likely to have large group operations performed on them than are the tables in the DATA tablespace. Second, the Export dump files have been moved to the online redo log file disk. This may seem an odd combination at first, but they are well suited to each other since the online redo log files never increase in size (and usually take less than 100MB), while the process of exporting a database causes very little transaction activity (and therefore little contention between the redo log file and the Export dump file). The third combination in this iteration is that of the application software with the archived redo log file destination area. The application software is assumed to be both static and small, using less than 10 percent of the available disk space. This leaves the ARCH background process ample space to write log files to while avoiding conflicts with DBWR.

The Fifth Iteration: the 7-Disk Compromise

From this point onward, the tablespace combinations should be driven by the weights assigned during the I/O estimation process. For the weightings given earlier in this chapter, the distribution of I/O among the disks after the fourth iteration is shown in Table 4-3.

The weighting for disk 1 is not shown because it is installation-specific, since applications may be of widely varying size, and different ORACLE software is licensed for different sites.

The weightings for disks 8 and 9 are based on the weighting for the rollback segments tablespaces, since transactions written to RBS will also be written to the online redo log files. If the database is running in ARCHIVELOG mode, then disk 9's

```
Disk      Contents
1         Oracle software
2         SYSTEM tablespace, Control file 1
3         RBS tablespace, RBS_2 tablespace, Control file 2
4         DATA tablespace, Control file 3
5         INDEXES tablespace
6         TEMP tablespace, TEMP_USER tablespace, DATA_2
           tablespace
7         TOOLS tablespace, INDEXES_2 tablespace
8         Online Redo logs 1, 2, and 3, Export dump file
           destination disk
9         Application software, Archived redo log destination
           disk
```

FIGURE 4-5. *The 9-disk solution*

Disk	Weight	Contents
1		ORACLE software
2	35	SYSTEM tablespace, control file 1
3	40	RBS tablespace, RBS_2 tablespace, control file 2
4	100	DATA tablespace, control file 3
5	33	INDEXES tablespace
6	9	TEMP tablespace, TEMP_USER tablespace, DATA_2 tablespace
7	3	TOOLS tablespace, INDEXES_2 tablespace
8	40+	Online redo logs 1, 2, and 3, Export dump file destination disk
9	40+	Application software, archived redo log destination disk

TABLE 4-3. *Estimated I/O Weightings of the 9-Disk Solution*

archived redo log files will have the same I/O as disk 8's online redo log files. Because other files are on these disks (the Export dump files and the application software), their weight is indicated as being some value greater than the RBS disk's I/O weight.

From the weightings shown in Table 4-3, there are no good solutions going forward. In order to compress the disk farm further, you must either store data on the same disk as its associated index (by combining disks 6 and 7, which feature DATA_2 and INDEXES_2, respectively), or you must store extra tablespaces on one of the top four weighted disks (disks 2, 3, 4, and 5). The last two disks, which are being used to support the online redo log files, exports, application software, and archived redo log files, which are key to the database's recoverability, should not be further burdened.

The I/O weighting for the fifth iteration results in the compromise distribution of files shown in Figure 4-6.

For this iteration, the TOOLS and INDEXES_2 tablespaces are moved from old disk 7 to the disk that contains the SYSTEM tablespace. The TEMP, TEMP_*USER*, and DATA_2 tablespaces are moved from old disk 6 to the disk that features the INDEXES tablespace (since temporary segments dynamically extend, they should be kept separate from the SYSTEM tablespace).

The database's tablespace files are shown in bold in Figure 4-6. They are now spread over just four disks (disks 2, 3, 4, and 5). Each of these four disks features one of the top four I/O weighted files for the database; their relative weightings will be the same for most databases. If systems have a very high transaction volume, then this design will not change since the rollback segments tablespaces (RBS and RBS_2) are already isolated.

```
Disk   Weight   Contents
1               Oracle software
2      38       SYSTEM, TOOLS, INDEXES_2 tablespaces, Control
                  file 1
3      40       RBS, RBS_2 tablespaces, Control file 2
4      100      DATA tablespace, Control file 3
5      42       INDEXES, TEMP, TEMP_USER, DATA_2 tablespaces
6      40+      Online Redo logs 1, 2, and 3, Export dump
                  file destination disk
7      40+      Application software, Archived redo log
                  destination disk
```

FIGURE 4-6. *The 7-disk solution*

Going beyond this level of file combinations forces the DBA to compromise even further. Since the database's recoverability should not be compromised, disks 6 and 7 should remain as they are. Additional combinations of tablespace files will compromise performance. Therefore, any further combinations of datafiles must be based on actual measurements of database I/O against these datafiles.

Verification of I/O Weighting Estimates

"I often say that when you can measure what you are talking about and express it in numbers, you know something about it; but when you cannot measure it, when you cannot express it in numbers, your knowledge is of a meagre and unsatisfactory kind."

—Lord Kelvin

The statistics tables within the data dictionary record the amount of I/O for each datafile. You can query the internal statistics tables to verify the weightings assigned in the estimation process. The following listings provide queries for generating the actual I/O weights.

Note that this script is not run for a specific time interval, but instead records all I/O against the database since it started up; the I/O against the SYSTEM tablespace will therefore be slightly higher than its value during everyday usage. Also note that the weightings are relative to the largest single file's I/O, not to the total I/O in the database.

The query uses a SQL feature available as of ORACLE7.2: the ability to have a subquery as part of the **from** clause. In this case, the subquery selects the maximum file I/O from the V$FILESTAT view. The file with this I/O value will be assigned an I/O weight of 100. The script queries V$FILESTAT for the file I/O of each file and compares the file I/O with the maximum total I/O to determine the file's I/O weighting. The output from the query is written to a file called io_weights.lst via the **spool** command.

NOTE
The script assumes that the devices are consistently named and that the device name is five characters long (see the SUBSTR of the DF.Name column). If your device names are longer than that, you will need to alter the script to meet your specifications.

```
set pagesize 60 linesize 80 newpage 0 feedback off
ttitle skip center "Database File IO Weights" skip center -
"ordered by Drive" skip 2
column Total_IO format 999999999
column Weight format 999.99
column File_Name format A40
break on Drive skip 2
compute sum of Weight on Drive

select
substr(DF.Name, 1,5) Drive,
DF.Name File_Name,
FS.Phyblkrd+FS.Phyblkwrt Total_IO,
100*(FS.Phyblkrd+FS.Phyblkwrt)/MaxIO Weight
from V$FILESTAT FS, V$DATAFILE DF,
   (select MAX(Phyblkrd+Phyblkwrt) MaxIO
     from V$FILESTAT)
where DF.File# = FS.File#
order by Drive, Weight desc

spool io_weights
/
spool off
```

The following listing shows sample output from this query:

```
                    Database File I/O Weights
                       Ordered by Drive


DRIVE    FILE_NAME                          TOTAL_IO      WEIGHT
-----    --------------------------         --------      -------
/db01    /db01/oracle/DEMO/sys01.dbf          31279        40.65
         /db01/oracle/DEMO/tools.dbf           2112         2.74
*****                                                       -------
sum                                                          43.39


/db02    /db02/oracle/DEMO/rbs01.dbf           3799         5.94
         /db02/oracle/DEMO/rbs02.dbf           2465         3.20
         /db02/oracle/DEMO/rbs03.dbf           1960         2.55
         /db02/oracle/DEMO/rbs04.dbf           1675         2.18
*****                                                       -------
sum                                                          13.87


/db03    /db03/oracle/DEMO/ddata.dbf          76950       100.00
*****                                                       -------
sum                                                         100.00
```

```
/db04      /db04/oracle/DEMO/demondx.dbf      36310      47.19
           /db04/oracle/DEMO/temp.dbf          4012       5.21
*****                                                    -------
sum                                                       52.40
```

In this example, the main data tablespace (DDATA, using the ddata.dbf datafile on /db03) is rated at a weight of 100. The index tablespace associated with that data (DEMONDX, using the demondx.dbf datafile on /db04) is rated at 47.19, and the SYSTEM tablespace (using the sys01.dbf datafile on /db01) has a weight of 40.65. The biggest difference between these actual values and the estimates made earlier is in the rollback segments' RBS tablespace, which has a weight of only 13.87, rather than its estimated weight of 40. This information should be used to reorganize the database file layout to take advantage of the lighter-than-forecast transaction load in the database.

The Sixth Iteration: Back to the Planning Stage

Given these actual I/O weights for this database, the disk layout should be reevaluated. The disk layout for this example, with the estimated and actual I/O weights, is shown in Figure 4-7. Note that this example, for a small demo database, did not use the RBS_2, DATA_2, INDEXES_2, USER, or TEMP_*USER* tablespaces.

The INDEXES tablespace is being much more actively used than had been forecast (by about 25 percent). Also, the rollback segment usage is much lower than the estimates (13.87 instead of 40). As a result, two moves can be made for this system to better distribute the I/O weight; first, move TEMP from the INDEXES disk to the RBS disk, then move TOOLS from the SYSTEM to the RBS disk as well. This will result in a more leveled distribution of the I/O weight, as shown in Figure 4-8.

It is worth noting that the final example configuration process consisted of five iterations during the planning stage and only one iteration during the tuning stage.

```
Disk  Est Weight  Actual Weight  Contents
1                                Oracle software
2     38          43.39          SYSTEM, TOOLS tablespaces,
                                     Control file 1
3     40          13.87          RBS tablespace, Control file 2
4     100         100            DATA tablespace, Control file 3
5     42          53.40          INDEXES, TEMP tablespaces
6     40+         13.87+         Online Redo logs 1, 2, and 3,
                                     Export dump files
7     40+         13.87+         Application software,
                                     Archived redo logs
```

FIGURE 4-7. *Estimated and actual I/O weights for the 7-disk compromise*

Disk	Actual Weight	Contents
1		Oracle software
2	40.65	SYSTEM tablespace, Control file 1
3	21.82	RBS, TEMP, and TOOLS tablespaces, Control file 2
4	100	DATA tablespace, Control file 3
5	47.19	INDEX tablespace
6	13.87+	Online Redo logs 1, 2, and 3, Export dump files
7	13.87+	Application software, Archived redo logs

FIGURE 4-8. *The 7-disk compromise, revised for the example's actual weights*

The single tuning iteration's cost, in terms of database downtime, CPU usage, and time for completion, was greater than that of all of the planning stage's costs combined. Planning must not be an afterthought.

What If You Have Very Few Disks?

If you don't have enough disks to properly separate your database files, you will be making performance trade-offs as you try to minimize contention. Here are the design rules to follow when designing a layout for a small database system (such as a system that has only three disks available):

1. *The system is usually an OLTP system.* A small system can't hold a data warehouse, so you should approach the system from an OLTP design standpoint (see Table 4-2). For that database, assume that transactions tend to be small in size, large in number and variety, and fairly randomly scattered among the available tables. To support such a system, design the application to be as index-intensive as possible, with a minimum number of full table scans performed.

2. *Try to isolate the SYSTEM tablespace.* The SYSTEM tablespace stores the data dictionary, and every query of the database performs many queries of the data dictionary. For example, consider a query like:

```
select Code from CODES_TABLE where Description = 'Widget';
```

For an OLTP system, that's a common style of query—the application may have many different simple queries. Each time the user executes that query, the database needs to check:

- The column names of the CODES_TABLE table
- The user's ability to access the CODES_TABLE table

- The user's ability to access the Code column of the CODES_TABLE table

- The user's role definitions

- The indexes defined on the CODES_TABLE table

- The columns of the indexes defined on the CODES_TABLE table

among other data dictionary checks. Because DDL can happen at any time, the database keeps rechecking this information. Those repeated queries of the data dictionary lead to an artificially elevated data block buffer cache hit ratio, but it also adds to the number of queries performed against the data dictionary. In an OLTP system, isolate your SYSTEM tablespace as much as possible—it will account for around 40 percent of your I/O.

3. *Isolate your INDEXES tablespace.* In an OLTP system, your INDEXES tablespace accesses should account for at least 35 percent of the I/O in the system. To properly support those I/O requests, isolate the INDEXES tablespace as much as possible. If you have a low data block buffer cache hit ratio, or you can't predict the user's access paths, then prioritize the isolation of the DATA tablespace over that of the INDEXES tablespace.

4. *If necessary, separate the rollback segments and DATA tablespaces.* At this point, you're making design trade-offs, because that makes four tablespaces (SYSTEM, INDEXES, DATA, and RBS) and only three disks. Monitor the system to determine where to put the RBS tablespace. If you have a high volume of transactions, keep RBS apart from DATA. If the volume of transactions is low, then you can store the rollback segments on the same disk as the DATA tablespace with little contention.

Following those guidelines, the tablespace layout for a three-disk system would begin with one of these two layouts:

Disk 1: SYSTEM tablespace, control file, redo log
Disk 2: INDEXES tablespace, control file, redo log, RBS tablespace
Disk 3: DATA tablespace, control file, redo log

or

Disk 1: SYSTEM tablespace, control file, redo log
Disk 2: INDEXES tablespace, control file, redo log
Disk 3: DATA tablespace, control file, redo log, RBS tablespace

If neither of those layouts is a good fit, you can split the RBS tablespace so it has multiple datafiles, and distribute those datafiles evenly across disk 2 and disk 3.

In systems of this size, you can usually put TEMP on the same disk as INDEXES with little contention, and the TOOLS tablespaces can go on disk 1. As always, you must monitor your I/O balancing after you've implemented the database to make sure your configuration properly addresses the data usage in the database.

NOTE
If you are using only a small number of drives on a RAID unit, you may be able to move some of the "low weight" files to the internal drives to reduce I/O interference contention.

Solutions

You can use the guidelines in this chapter to design a physical configuration for the logical configuration you designed in Chapter 3. The "Solutions" section of Chapter 3 presented four common logical configurations: small development database, production OLTP database, production OLTP database with historical data, and a data warehouse. In this section, you will see common physical layouts for those four database types. None of the solutions in this section considers the space requirements for the application software, ORACLE software, or backups.

Small Development Database Layout

For a small database, you will typically have the following tablespaces (see Table 3-2): SYSTEM, DATA, INDEXES, RBS, TEMP, USERS, and TOOLS. To store them all on separate devices, you only need seven disks. If you have fewer than seven disks, follow the guidelines in the "What If You Have Very Few Disks?" section earlier in this chapter. For a four-disk system, distribute the tablespaces as follows:

Disk 1: SYSTEM and TEMP tablespaces, control file, redo log
Disk 2: INDEXES, RBS, and USERS tablespaces, control file, redo log, Export dump files
Disk 3: DATA and TOOLS tablespaces, control file, redo log
Disk 4: ORACLE software, application software, archived redo logs

If you have more than four disks available, move the RBS tablespace off of the INDEXES tablespace disk. Since this is a development database, you are more likely to be performing data loads and full table scans than you would in production. Therefore, RBS is kept apart from the DATA tablespace in the development database.

Production OLTP Database Layout

A production OLTP database supports many small transactions. An OLTP database typically contains the following tablespaces: SYSTEM, DATA, DATA_2, INDEXES, INDEXES_2, RBS, RBS_2, TEMP, TEMP_*USER*, and TOOLS (see Table 3-2). Since that set of tablespaces was the basis for the iterative planning process illustrated earlier in this chapter, the configuration from Figure 4-8 can serve as the basis for a recommended solution. For a seven-disk system, the configuration should be as follows:

Disk 1: ORACLE software
Disk 2: SYSTEM tablespace, control file
Disk 3: RBS, RBS_2, TEMP, TEMP_*USER*, and TOOLS tablespaces, control file
Disk 4: DATA and INDEXES_2 tablespaces, control file
Disk 5: INDEXES and DATA_2 tablespaces
Disk 6: online redo log files, Export dump files
Disk 7: application software, archived redo log files

In an OLTP system, the configuration is designed to optimize the performance of small transactions and small queries. In an OLTP configuration, the TEMP, TEMP_*USER*, and RBS_2 tablespaces should only be used during batch operations. Therefore, the configuration puts TEMP, TEMP_*USER*, and RBS_2 together and focuses on optimizing the performance I/O distribution of the remaining tablespaces.

If you have fewer than seven disks available for your production OLTP database, then you will need to make further design trade-offs. For example, a six-disk solution may start by combining the online redo log files with the DATA_2 and INDEXES_2 tablespaces (which contain static data and thus participate in few transactions) as shown in the following listing:

Disk 1: ORACLE software
Disk 2: SYSTEM tablespace, control file
Disk 3: RBS, RBS_2, TEMP, TEMP_*USER*, and TOOLS tablespaces, control file
Disk 4: DATA tablespace, control file
Disk 5: INDEXES tablespace
Disk 6: DATA_2 and INDEXES_2 tablespaces, online redo log files, Export dump files
Disk 7: application software, archived redo log files

To reduce the number of disks to six, you will need to colocate the contents of disk 6 with the INDEXES tablespace on disk 5:

Disk 1: ORACLE software
Disk 2: SYSTEM tablespace, control file
Disk 3: RBS, RBS_2, TEMP, TEMP_*USER*, and TOOLS tablespaces, control file
Disk 4: DATA tablespace, control file
Disk 5: INDEXES, DATA_2 and INDEXES_2 tablespaces, online redo log files, Exports
Disk 6: application software, archived redo log files

Colocating other tablespaces with the INDEXES tablespace is not ideal; no ideal production OLTP database has just four disks available for its datafiles.

Production OLTP Database with Historical Data Layout

In addition to your current production data, you may be required to maintain historical data. Since the historical data will have different growth patterns than the current transactional data, you should store the historical data apart from the current DATA tablespace. As shown in Table 3-2, a production OLTP database with historical data will have the same tablespaces as a production OLTP database, plus two new tablespaces: DATA_ARCHIVE and INDEXES_ARCHIVE.

The storage guidelines for a production OLTP database with historical data mirror those for standard production OLTP databases. As described in the previous section, a seven-disk configuration for an OLTP database without historical data could be as follows:

Disk 1: ORACLE software
Disk 2: SYSTEM tablespace, control file
Disk 3: RBS, RBS_2, TEMP, TEMP_*USER*, and TOOLS tablespaces, control file
Disk 4: DATA tablespace, control file
Disk 5: INDEXES tablespace
Disk 6: DATA_2 and INDEXES_2 tablespaces, online redo log files, Export dump files
Disk 7: application software, archived redo log files

When you add historical data to the configuration, you have to know how the historical data will be used. If it is to be constantly referenced, then you will need to separate it from the current DATA and INDEXES tablespaces. If both the current and historical DATA tablespaces are actively used, then you will encounter I/O contention if you store them on the same physical device. The following configuration supports an OLTP database with active historical data:

Disk 1: ORACLE software
Disk 2: SYSTEM tablespace, control file

Disk 3: RBS, RBS_2, TEMP, TEMP_*USER*, and TOOLS tablespaces, control file
Disk 4: DATA tablespace, control file
Disk 5: INDEXES tablespace
Disk 6: DATA_2 and INDEXES_2 tablespaces, online redo log files, Export dump files
Disk 7: DATA_ARCHIVE tablespace
Disk 8: INDEXES_ARCHIVE tablespace
Disk 9: application software, archived redo log files

In this configuration, the current data and the historical data are separated, and each type of DATA tablespace is separated from its corresponding INDEX tablespace.

If the historical data is not actively used, then you can store the historical data on the same devices as the current data without causing I/O contention. For example, if the historical data is only used by rarely executed reports, there will be little I/O against the historical data and little I/O contention between the current and historical DATA tablespaces. As shown in the following listing, seldom-used historical data can be stored on the same devices as the current data:

Disk 1: ORACLE software
Disk 2: SYSTEM tablespace, control file
Disk 3: RBS, RBS_2, TEMP, TEMP_*USER*, and TOOLS tablespaces, control file
Disk 4: DATA and DATA_ARCHIVE tablespaces, control file
Disk 5: INDEXES and INDEXES_ARCHIVE tablespaces
Disk 6: DATA_2 and INDEXES_2 tablespaces, online redo log files, Export dump files
Disk 7: application software, archived redo log files

Data Warehouse Layout

The volume of data in a data warehouse will likely be significantly greater than that of any of your OLTP databases. As shown in Table 3-2, a data warehouse will likely contain each type of segment used by ORACLE: data dictionary tables (SYSTEM tablespace), tables (DATA and DATA_2), indexes (INDEXES and INDEXES_2), small and large rollback segments (RBS and RBS_2), temporary segments (TEMP and TEMP_*USER*), and tools tables (TOOLS). In addition to those segments, a data warehouse will usually also include partitions (PARTITIONS and PARTITIONS_I tablespaces), aggregate data and materialized views (AGG_DATA and AGG_DATA_I), snapshots (SNAPS and SNAPS_I) and "work" tables used only during batch processing (TEMP_WORK and TEMP_WORK_I). When designing a physical layout for all those tablespaces, you need to consider the two entirely separate ways in which the data warehouse will be used: data loading and data retrieval.

In an OLTP database, the data loading process is performed by many users executing small **insert** and **update** transactions. In a data warehouse, the data loading process is a set of large batch operations that may take days or weeks to complete during each data load cycle. You therefore need to tune your database to optimize the batch data loading process. At the same time, you need to consider how users are retrieving the data once it has been loaded.

The data retrieval process in a data warehouse differs little from the OLTP data retrieval process. As in an OLTP database, data warehouse users perform many small queries against a large number of tables. Although the base tables of a data warehouse are large, the end users should not be directly querying them; instead, they should be querying the heavily indexed aggregation tables. The data in the data warehouse should be denormalized so that it best supports the access paths most commonly followed by the end users.

When designing the data warehouse's physical layout, consider the batch loading and data retrieval uses separately. For the batch loading process, the primary tablespaces involved will be as follows:

SYSTEM	Data dictionary tables
TEMP_WORK	Temporary tables used during the data load process
TEMP_WORK_I	Indexes for the temporary work tables
TEMP_*USER*	Large temporary segments to support batch sorts
RBS_2	Large rollback segments to support the batch transactions
DATA	Tables
INDEXES	Indexes for the tables in the DATA tablespace
PARTITIONS	Table partitions
PARTITIONS_I	Indexes for the table partitions
SNAPS	Snapshots
SNAPS_I	Indexes for the snapshots
AGG_DATA	Aggregate tables and materialized views
AGG_DATA_I	Indexes for the aggregate tables and materialized views

Following the guidelines presented earlier in this chapter, you should separate the SYSTEM and RBS tablespaces from all of the other tablespaces. You can optimize the remainder of the configuration by planning out your batch loading process. For example, many data warehouse systems load data from outside sources. If your data comes into the database via flat files, then the normal data loading steps are as follows.

1. Load data from flat files into the TEMP_WORK tables for data cleaning operations.

2. Index the TEMP_WORK tables to improve the performance of data cleaning and movement operations; write indexes to TEMP_WORK_I; use the TEMP_*USER* tablespace for the associated temporary segments during the index creation.

3. Perform database transactions to move data from TEMP_WORK tables to DATA and PARTITIONS tables, using the RBS_2 tablespace for rollback segments.

4. Index the tables in DATA and PARTITIONS, writing the indexes to INDEXES and PARTITIONS_I; use the TEMP_*USER* tablespace for the associated temporary segments during the index creation.

5. If your data warehouse uses data from other databases, create local snapshots of the remote data in the SNAPS database using the RBS_2 tablespace for rollback segments. Index the snapshots in SNAPS_I and use the TEMP_*USER* tablespace for the associated temporary segments during the index creation.

6. Create aggregate tables in AGG_DATA, and index those tables in AGG_DATA_I using the RBS_2 tablespace for rollback segments; use the TEMP_*USER* tablespace for the associated temporary segments during the index creation.

Before colocating tablespaces on the same physical device, you need to consider the end-user data access requirements. Rather than just querying DATA and INDEXES during queries, users may also be accessing AGG_DATA, AGG_DATA_I, PARTITIONS, PARTITIONS_I, SNAPS, and SNAPS_I. You therefore need to separate all of those tablespaces in order to minimize I/O contention during queries.

To design the physical layout, start with an eight-disk configuration, as shown in the following listing. This eight-disk layout is similar to the standard OLTP layout, with the TEMP tablespaces moved apart from the RBS tablespaces.

```
Disk 1: ORACLE software
Disk 2: SYSTEM tablespace, control file
Disk 3: RBS, RBS_2, and TOOLS tablespaces, control file
Disk 4: DATA tablespace, control file
Disk 5: INDEXES tablespace
Disk 6: DATA_2 and INDEXES_2 tablespaces, online redo log files, Export dump files
Disk 7: TEMP and TEMP_USER tablespaces
Disk 8: application software, archived redo log files
```

NOTE
If you are using a purchased application, the vendor may have a preferred disk configuration for that application software. If the vendor has a preferred configuration, follow it. The vendor may rely on the configuration for its application to work, or may rely on that configuration during subsequent application upgrades.

Next, add disks for the PARTITIONS, PARTITIONS_I, SNAPS, SNAPS_I, AGG_DATA, AGG_DATA_I, TEMP_WORK, and TEMP_WORK_I tablespaces:

Disk 1: ORACLE software
Disk 2: SYSTEM tablespace, control file
Disk 3: RBS, RBS_2, and TOOLS tablespaces, control file
Disk 4: DATA tablespace, control file
Disk 5: INDEXES tablespace
Disk 6: DATA_2 and INDEXES_2 tablespaces, online redo log files, Export dump files
Disk 7: TEMP and TEMP_*USER* tablespaces
Disk 8: PARTITIONS tablespace
Disk 9: PARTITIONS_I tablespace
Disk 10: SNAPS tablespace
Disk 11: SNAPS_I tablespace
Disk 12: AGG_DATA tablespace
Disk 13: AGG_DATA_I tablespace
Disk 14: TEMP_WORK tablespace
Disk 15: TEMP_WORK_I tablespace
Disk 16: application software, archived redo log files

As you can see from the preceding listing, supporting a data warehouse requires you to support many types of tablespaces. However, as described earlier, these tablespaces are not all used concurrently. The TEMP_WORK and TEMP_WORK_I tablespaces, for example, are only used during the data loading process. Therefore, you may be able to colocate them with other tablespaces (such as the SNAPS and SNAPS_I tablespaces) to reduce the number of disks used. Furthermore, you may choose to partition all of your nonstatic tables, effectively eliminating the need for the DATA and INDEXES tablespaces, as shown in the following listing:

Disk 1: ORACLE software
Disk 2: SYSTEM tablespace, control file
Disk 3: RBS, RBS_2, and TOOLS tablespaces, control file

Disk 4: PARTITIONS tablespace, control file
Disk 5: PARTITIONS_I tablespace
Disk 6: DATA_2 and INDEXES_2 tablespaces, online redo log files, Export dump files
Disk 7: TEMP and TEMP_*USER* tablespaces
Disk 8: SNAPS and TEMP_WORK tablespaces
Disk 9: SNAPS_I and TEMP_WORK_I tablespaces
Disk 10: AGG_DATA tablespace
Disk 11: AGG_DATA_I tablespace
Disk 12: application software, archived redo log files

The preceding 12-disk layout for a data warehouse is a starting point; your actual layout should reflect the file usage characteristics of your application. In an ideal data warehouse, the most commonly used tablespaces are AGG_DATA_I and PARTITIONS_I, with very little access to the associated tables. If you are able to index your data warehouse tables so effectively that the tables are rarely accessed, you may be able to colocate the AGG_DATA and PARTITIONS tablespaces without causing I/O contention.

The ORACLE Call Interface (OCI) has a feature for Direct Path Loading, introduced with ORACLE8i. When this feature is used, the following limitations apply. These limitations mirror those of the SQL*Loader Direct Path option.

- Triggers are not supported.

- Check constraints are not supported.

- Referential integrity constraints are not supported.

- Clustered tables are not supported.

- Loading of remote objects is not supported.

- User-defined types are not supported.

- LOBS must be specified after all scalar columns.

- LONGS must be specified last.

Some of these limitations may cause problems with existing database policies in your database (such as the lack of support for referential integrity).

File Location

In order to simplify database management, the files associated with a database should be stored in directories created specifically for that database. Database files from different databases should not be stored together.

Furthermore, the database's datafiles should be separated from the software used to access the database (despite the fact that this is the default for some of the installation programs). The disk layouts shown in the previous sections all featured "ORACLE software" as their disk #1. This disk (Figure 4-9) includes all active versions of all ORACLE software, and should not be allowed to cause contention with the datafiles.

The file layout shown in Figure 4-9 uses the most recent version of OFA (optimal flexible architecture) for the software directories. In previous versions of ORACLE, the configuration files such as init.ora were stored in the /dbs subdirectory under the software version directory (such as 8.1.5). The problem with that configuration is that each time the database software version is upgraded, the configuration files must be moved. The modified version shown in Figure 4-9 resolves this problem and stores dump files in directories that are specific to the instance name ("CC1") instead of the database version.

Storing the datafiles at the same level in a directory hierarchy will simplify the management procedures. It also allows you to avoid putting the instance identifier in the filename, using it instead as part of the directory path, as in the sample directory structure listing shown in Figure 4-10.

The layout shown in Figure 4-10 allows the same filenames to be used across instances. In this configuration, the files are logically separated from each other in a consistent fashion. This separation allows wildcards or search lists to be used when referencing them (if the disks are named in a consistent fashion). For example, in

```
Disk 1       (/orasw)
/orasw
   /app
      /oracle
         /product
                 /8.1.5
                       /bin
                       /rdbms (and other directories)
         /admin
                 /CC1
                       /pfile
                            initCC1.ora
                            configCC1.ora
                       /bdump
                       /udump
```

FIGURE 4-9.   *Disk layout for ORACLE software*

```
        Disk 2      (/db01)
/db01
   /oracle
       /CASE
               control1.dbf
               sys01.dbf
               tools.dbf
       /CC1
               control1.dbf
               sys01.dbf
               tools.dbf
       /DEMO
               control1.dbf
               sys01.dbf
```

FIGURE 4-10. *Disk hierarchy for a sample data disk*

UNIX environments, all of the files belonging to a specific instance could be copied to a tape device with a single command, as in the following:

```
> tar /dev/rmt/1hc /db0[1-8]/oracle/CASE
```

In this example, the system will write out to the tape device (/dev/rmt/1hc) the contents of the /oracle/CASE subdirectory on the devices named /db01 through /db08.

Database Space Usage Overview

In order to understand how space should be allocated within the database, you first have to know how the space is used within the database. In this section, you will see an overview of the ORACLE database space usage functions.

When a database is created, it is divided into multiple logical sections called *tablespaces*. The SYSTEM tablespace is the first tablespace created. Additional tablespaces are then created to hold different types of data, as described in Chapter 3.

When a tablespace is created, *datafiles* are created to hold its data. These files immediately allocate the space specified during their creation. There is thus a one-to-many relationship between databases and tablespaces, and a one-to-many relationship between tablespaces and datafiles.

A database can have multiple users, each of whom has a *schema*. Each user's schema is a collection of logical database objects such as tables and indexes. These objects refer to physical data structures that are stored in tablespaces. Objects from a user's schema may be stored in multiple tablespaces, and a single tablespace can contain objects from multiple schemas.

When a database object (such as a table or index) is created, it is assigned to a tablespace via user defaults or specific instructions. A *segment* is created in that tablespace to hold the data associated with that object. The space that is allocated to the segment is never released until the segment is dropped, manually shrunk, or **truncate**d. See the "How to Deallocate Space from Segments" section later in this chapter for details on manually shrinking the space allocated to tables, indexes, and clusters.

A segment is made up of sections called *extents*—contiguous sets of ORACLE blocks. Once the existing extents can no longer hold new data, the segment will obtain another extent. The extension process will continue until no more free space is available in the tablespace's datafiles or until an internal maximum number of extents per segment is reached. If a segment is composed of multiple extents, there is no guarantee that those extents will be contiguous.

The logical interrelationships between these database objects are shown in Figure 4-11.

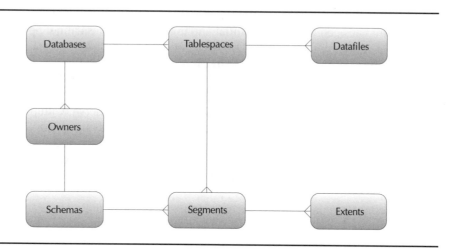

FIGURE 4-11. *Logical relationships between database structures*

As shown in Figure 4-11, a tablespace may contain multiple segments. The segment types available in ORACLE include the following:

TABLE
INDEX
ROLLBACK
TEMPORARY
PARTITION
CLUSTER

Managing the space used by each is one of the basic functions of the DBA. Chapters 6, 7, 8, and 12 contain detailed information on the monitoring and tuning of these segments. The intent of this overview is to aid in the planning of their physical storage.

Implications of the storage Clause

The amount of space used by a segment is determined by its storage parameters. These parameters are determined by the database at segment creation time; if no specific **storage** parameters are given in the **create table**, **create index**, **create cluster**, or **create rollback segment** command, then the database will use the default storage parameters for the tablespace in which it is to be stored. The storage parameters specify the **initial** extent size, the **next** extent size, the **pctincrease** (a factor by which each successive extent will geometrically grow), the **maxextents** (maximum number of extents), and **minextents** (minimum number of extents). After the segment has been created, the **initial** and **minextents** values cannot be altered. The default values for the storage parameters for each tablespace are contained in the DBA_TABLESPACES and USER_TABLESPACES views.

When a segment is created, it will acquire at least one extent (other values can be set via **minextents**). This extent will be used to store data until it no longer has any free space available (the **pctfree** clause can be used to reserve, within each block in each extent, a percentage of space that will remain available for updates of existing rows). When additional data is added to the segment, the segment will extend by obtaining a second extent of the size specified by the **next** parameter. There is no guarantee that the second extent will be physically contiguous to the first extent.

The **pctincrease** parameter is designed to minimize the number of extents in growing tables. A nonzero value for this parameter can be dangerous—it causes the size of each successive extent to increase geometrically by the **pctincrease** factor specified. For example, consider the case of a data segment with an **initial** extent size of 20 ORACLE blocks, a **next** extent size of 20 blocks, and a **pctincrease** of 50. Table 4-4 shows the sizes of the first ten extents in this segment.

Extent Number	Size (in ORACLE Blocks)	Total	Comments on Extent Size
1	20	20	INITIAL
2	20	40	NEXT
3	30	70	NEXT*1.5
4	45	115	NEXT*1.5*1.5
5	70	185	NEXT*1.5*1.5*1.5
6	105	290	etc.
7	155	445	
8	230	675	
9	345	1020	
10	520	1,540	

TABLE 4-4. *The Effect of Using a Nonzero pctincrease*

In just ten extents, the segment's size has increased by 7,700 percent! Besides being an indicator of inappropriate space planning, this is also an administrative problem for the DBA. The table is badly fragmented, the extents are most likely not contiguous, and the next time this table extends (for even one row of data), it will need over 750 ORACLE blocks (for a 2K block size, that's 1.5MB). A preferable situation would be to have a single extent of the right size, with a small value for **next**, and set the table's **pctincrease** of 0. Those settings would avoid the need for segment defragmentation efforts (as described in Chapter 8).

NOTE
*Setting **pctincrease** to 0 at the tablespace level affects ORACLE's ability to automatically coalesce free space in the tablespace. Set the default **pctincrease** for the tablespace to a very low value, such as 1.*

Never change **pctincrease** without also changing **next**. The size of each successive extent is calculated by going back to the storage parameters for the table; the size of the last extent added is not considered. If, for example, you were to now change the **pctincrease** value to 0 for the segment in Table 4-4, then extent number 11 would have a size of 20 ORACLE blocks (**next***1.0*1.0 etc.), *not* 520 blocks. See Chapter 5 for guidance on selecting extent sizes and estimating storage requirements.

Table Segments

Table segments, also called *data segments*, store the rows of data associated with tables or clusters. Each data segment contains a header block that serves as a space directory for the segment.

Unless it is very large, a properly sized table will have one extent. The more extents a data segment has, the more work is involved in managing it. In some cases, you cannot have single-extent data segments; since extents cannot span datafiles, a segment that is larger than the largest datafile available will have multiple extents. You can use multiple extents to stripe a segment across disks; striping data, though, is better handled outside of the database (for example, by using RAID-3 or RAID-5 disk mirroring, as described earlier in this chapter).

Once a data segment acquires an extent, it keeps that extent until the segment is either dropped or **truncate**d. Deleting rows from a table has no impact on the amount of space that has been allocated to that table. The number of extents will increase until either (1) the **maxextents** value is reached, (2) the user's quota in the tablespace is reached, or (3) the tablespace runs out of space. You can also force a datafile to extend automatically; see the "Automating Datafile Extensions" section later in this chapter.

To minimize the amount of wasted space in a data segment, tune the **pctfree** parameter. The **pctfree** parameter specifies the amount of space that will be kept free within each data block. The free space can then be used when **NULL**-valued columns are updated to have values, or when updates to other values in the row force the row to lengthen. The proper setting of **pctfree** is application-specific since it is dependent on the nature of the updates that are being performed. For information on setting this and other storage parameters for tables and indexes, see Chapter 5.

Index Segments

Like table segments, *index segments* hold the space that has been allocated to them until they are dropped; however, they can also be indirectly dropped if the table or cluster they index is dropped. To minimize contention, indexes should be stored in a tablespace that is separated from their associated tables.

Indexes are subject to the same space problems that tables experience. Their segments have **storage** clauses that specify their **initial**, **next**, **minextents**, **maxextents**, and **pctincrease** values, and they are as likely to be fragmented as their tables are. They must be sized properly before they are created; otherwise, their fragmentation will drag down the database performance—exactly the opposite of their purpose.

You can use the **rebuild** option of the **alter index** command to alter the **storage** and **tablespace** settings for an index. For example, if you create an index with an overly large **initial** extent, you can reclaim the space from that extent by rebuilding the index and specifying a new value for **initial**, as shown in the following example. In the following listing, the JOB_PK index is rebuilt with an **initial** extent of 10MB.

```
alter index JOB_PK rebuild
tablespace INDEXES
storage (initial 10M next 10M pctincrease 0);
```

During the index **rebuild** process, both the old and the new indexes will exist in the database. Therefore, you must have enough space available to store both indexes prior to executing the **alter index rebuild** command.

Rollback Segments

Rollback segment functionality will be discussed in detail in Chapter 7. The principles of sound design for tables apply also to rollback segments. However, while ideal tables have one extent that is suited to their size requirements, ideal rollback segments will have multiple evenly sized extents that add up to their optimal total size (they will have a minimum of two extents when created). Each extent should be large enough to handle all of the data from a single transaction. If it is not, or if too many users request the same rollback segment, then the rollback segment may extend.

Rollback segments can dynamically shrink to a specified size, or they can be manually shrunk to a size of your choosing. The **optimal** clause, which allows rollback segments to shrink to an **optimal** size after extending, helps to provide interim support to systems that have not been properly implemented for the way they are being used. Frequent shrinks (see the "Interpreting the Statistics Reports" section of Chapter 6, and Chapter 7) indicate the need for the rollback segments to be redesigned.

How many rollback segments should you have? The answer to that is database-dependent; it's like asking how large your DATA tablespace should be. For guidance in choosing the right number and size of rollback segments, see the "Choosing the Number and Size" section of Chapter 7.

Temporary Segments

Temporary segments store temporary data during sorting operations (such as large queries, index creations, and unions). Each user has a temporary tablespace specified when the account is created via **create user** or altered via **alter user**. The user's temporary tablespace should be pointed to some place other than SYSTEM (the default).

When a temporary segment is created, it uses the default storage parameters for that tablespace. While it is in existence, its storage parameters cannot be altered by changing the default storage parameters for the tablespace. The temporary segment extends itself as necessary, and drops itself when the operation completes or encounters an error. Since the temporary segment itself can lead to errors (by exceeding the maximum number of extents or running out of space in the tablespace), the size of large sorting queries and operations should be taken into consideration when sizing the temporary tablespace.

The temporary tablespace, usually named TEMP, is fragmented by its nature. Temporary segments are constantly created, extended, and then dropped. You must therefore maximize the reusability of dropped extents. For your temporary tablespace, choose an **initial** and **next** extent size of 1/20th to 1/50th of the size of the tablespace. The default settings for **initial** and **next** should be equal for this tablespace. Choose a **pctincrease** of 0; the result will be segments made up of identically sized extents. When these segments are dropped, the next temporary segment to be formed will be able to reuse the dropped extents.

You can specify a tablespace as a "temporary" tablespace. A "temporary" tablespace cannot be used to hold any permanent segments, only temporary segments created during operations. The first sort to use the temporary tablespace allocates a temporary segment within the temporary tablespace; when the query completes, the space used by the temporary segment is not dropped. Instead, the space used by the temporary segment is available for use by other queries; this allows the sorting operation to avoid the costs of allocating and releasing space for temporary segments. If your application frequently uses temporary segments for sorting operations, the sorting process should perform better if a dedicated temporary tablespace is used.

To dedicate a tablespace for temporary segments, specify the **temporary** clause of the **create tablespace** or **alter tablespace** command, as shown in the following listing:

```
alter tablespace TEMP temporary;
```

NOTE
If there are any permanent segments (tables or indexes, for example) stored in TEMP, the command shown in the preceding listing will fail.

To enable the TEMP tablespace to store permanent (i.e., nontemporary) objects, use the **permanent** clause of the **create tablespace** or **alter tablespace** command, as shown in the following listing:

```
alter tablespace TEMP permanent;
```

The Content column in the DBA_TABLESPACES data dictionary view displays the status of the tablespace as either 'TEMPORARY' or 'PERMANENT'.

Free Space

A *free extent* in a tablespace is a collection of contiguous free blocks in the tablespace. A tablespace may contain multiple data extents and one or more free extents (see Figure 4-12a). When a segment is dropped, its extents are deallocated and marked as free. However, these free extents are not always recombined with neighboring free extents; the barriers between these free extents may be maintained (see Figure 4-12b). The SMON background process periodically coalesces neighboring free extents (see Figure 4-12c)—provided the default **pctincrease** for the tablespace is nonzero.

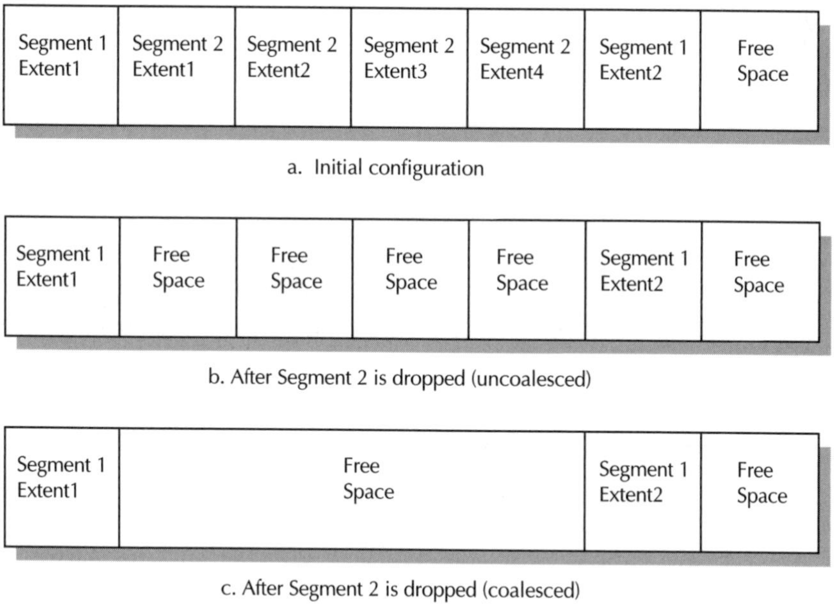

Segment 1 Extent1	Segment 2 Extent1	Segment 2 Extent2	Segment 2 Extent3	Segment 2 Extent4	Segment 1 Extent2	Free Space

a. Initial configuration

Segment 1 Extent1	Free Space	Free Space	Free Space	Free Space	Segment 1 Extent2	Free Space

b. After Segment 2 is dropped (uncoalesced)

Segment 1 Extent1	Free Space	Segment 1 Extent2	Free Space

c. After Segment 2 is dropped (coalesced)

FIGURE 4-12. *Free extent management in ORACLE*

When servicing a space request, the database will not merge contiguous free extents unless there is no alternative; thus, the large free extent at the rear of the tablespace tends to be used while the smaller free extents toward the front of the tablespace are relatively unused, becoming "speed bumps" in the tablespace because they are not, by themselves, of adequate size to be of use. As this usage pattern progresses, the database thus drifts further and further from its ideal space allocation.

If your tablespace has a default **pctincrease** value of 0, then the space coalesce will not happen automatically. However, you can force the database to recombine the contiguous free extents, thus emulating the SMON functionality. Contiguous free space will increase the likelihood of the free extents near the front of the file being reused, thus preserving the free space near the rear of the tablespace file. As a result, new requests for extents are more likely to meet with success.

To force the tablespace to coalesce its free space, use the **coalesce** clause of the **alter tablespace** clause, as shown in the following listing:

```
alter tablespace DATA coalesce;
```

The preceding command will force the neighboring free extents in the DATA tablespace to be coalesced into larger free extents.

> **NOTE**
> The **alter tablespace** command will not coalesce free extents that are separated by data extents.

In an ideal database, all objects are created at their appropriate size (in one extent if possible), and all free space is always stored together, a resource pool waiting to be used. In reality, the image shown in the bottom half of Figure 4-12 is often encountered: fragmented tables and free space that is separated from other free space by data extents. Resolutions to these fragmentation issues are described in Chapter 8. Monitoring scripts to determine the severity of these conditions are given in Chapter 6.

Resizing Datafiles

Existing datafiles can be resized via the **alter database** and **alter tablespace** commands. You can specify values for storage extension parameters for each datafile in a database; ORACLE will use those values when automatically extending the datafile. Datafiles can also be extended manually, and can be resized down (to a smaller size) manually as well.

To manually extend a datafile, use the **alter database** command, as shown in the following example:

```
alter database
datafile '/db05/oracle/CC1/data01.dbf' resize 200M;
```

After the **alter database** command shown in the preceding example is executed, the specified file will be resized to 200MB in size. If the file was already more than 200MB in size, it will decrease in size to 200MB if possible. When the database shrinks the file, it shrinks it from the end. Therefore, if there is any segment stored at the physical end of the file, the database will not be able to shrink the file. If there are any extents stored past the point you specify (in this example, 200MB), then the **alter database** command in the preceding listing will fail. See the "Defragmentation of Free Extents" section of Chapter 8 for a script that maps out your data storage locations within files.

Automating Datafile Extensions

When creating datafiles, you can specify parameters that will allow ORACLE to automatically extend your datafiles. The datafiles could then be automatically extended whenever their current allocated length is exceeded. You can specify three sizing parameters for each datafile:

autoextend	A flag, set to ON or OFF to indicate if the file should be allowed to automatically extend. If set to OFF, the other sizing parameters will be set to zero.
next *size*	The size, in bytes, of the area of disk space to allocate to the datafile when more space is required. You can qualify the *size* value with 'K' and 'M' for kilobytes and megabytes, respectively.
maxsize *size*	The maximum size, in bytes, to which the datafile is allowed to extend. You can qualify the *size* value with 'K' and 'M' for kilobytes and megabytes, respectively.

If no **maxsize** value is specified, then the maximum size of the datafile will be limited by the available space on the file's disk and the maximum file size supported by the operating system. The file size may also be limited by a file size quota set at the operating system level against the "oracle" userid.

The **autoextend**, **next**, and **maxsize** parameters can be specified for a datafile via the **create database**, **create tablespace**, and **alter tablespace** commands. In the following example, the **create tablespace** command creates a datafile that will automatically extend as needed:

```
create tablespace DATA
datafile '/db05/oracle/CC1/data01.dbf' size 200M
autoextend ON
next 10M
maxsize 250M;
```

NOTE
*If disk space is available, you can manually extend the datafile via the **alter database** command, as shown in the prior section.*

The tablespace created in this example will have a single datafile with an initial size of 200MB. When that datafile fills, and the objects within it require additional space, the datafile will extend itself by 10MB. The extension process will continue as needed until the file has reached 250MB in size, at which point the file will have reached its maximum size.

You can add a new datafile, via the **alter tablespace** command, to enable **autoextend** capabilities for a tablespace. The command in the following listing adds a new datafile to the DATA tablespace, specifying **autoextend on** and **maxsize** 300MB:

```
alter tablespace DATA
add datafile '/db05/oracle/CC1/data02.dbf'
size 50M
autoextend ON
maxsize 300M;
```

To change the attributes of an existing datafile, you can use the **alter database** command, as shown here:

```
alter database
datafile '/db05/oracle/CC1/data01.dbf'
autoextend ON
maxsize 300M;
```

NOTE
*Although you can set **maxsize unlimited**, you should always specify a value for the file's maximum size. Otherwise, a transaction that uses all of the space available on the disk device will cause your database to fail.*

How to Move Database Files

Once a file has been created in a database, you may need to move it to better manage its size or I/O requirements. In the following sections you'll see the procedures for moving datafiles, online redo log files, and control files. In all of the procedures, operating system commands are used to move the files; the ORACLE commands serve primarily to reset the pointers to those files.

Moving Datafiles

There are two methods for moving datafiles: via the **alter database** command and via the **alter tablespace** command. The **alter tablespace** method only applies to datafiles whose tablespaces do not include SYSTEM, rollback segments, or temporary segments. The **alter database** method will work for all datafiles.

The alter database Method

When using the **alter database** method to move datafiles, the datafile is moved after the instance has been shut down. The steps involved, detailed in the following sections, are as follows.

1. Shut down the instance, using OEM or Server Manager.

2. Use operating system commands to move the datafile.

3. Mount the database and use **alter database** to rename the file within the database.

4. Start the instance.

Step 1. Shut down the instance, using OEM or Server Manager.

```
> svrmgrl
SVRMGR> connect internal as sysdba;
SVRMGR> shutdown;
SVRMGR> exit;
```

Step 2. Use operating system commands to move the datafile.

Use an operating system command to move the datafile. In UNIX, the **mv** command moves files to new locations. The following example shows the data01.dbf file being moved from the device named /db01 to one named /db02:

```
> mv /db01/oracle/CC1/data01.dbf /db02/oracle/CC1
```

The filename must fully specify a filename using the conventions of your operating system.

Step 3. Mount the database and use alter database to rename the file within the database.

In the following example, the CC1 instance is started and the data01.dbf datafile moved in step 2 is renamed within the database. The database will then be able to find that file during instance startup. The **alter database** command shown here does not rename the file; the file must have already been renamed or moved.

```
> svrmgrl
SVRMGR> connect internal as sysdba;
SVRMGR> startup mount CC1;
SVRMGR> alter database rename file
    2> '/db01/oracle/CC1/data01.dbf' to
    3> '/db02/oracle/CC1/data01.dbf';
```

Do not disconnect after this step is complete; stay logged in to the database and proceed to step 4.

When the **alter database** command is executed, ORACLE will check to see if the name you are naming the file to exists. If this step fails, check the accuracy of the destination filename.

Step 4. Start the instance.

Now that the database knows how to find the moved file, the instance can start.

```
SVRMGR> alter database open;
```

The instance will now be opened, using the new location for the datafile that was moved.

The alter tablespace Method

When using the **alter tablespace** method to move datafiles, the datafile is moved while the instance is still running. The steps involved, detailed in the following sections, are as follows.

1. Take the tablespace offline.

2. Use operating system commands to move the file.

3. Use the **alter tablespace** command to rename the file within the database.

4. Bring the tablespace back online.

NOTE
This method can only be used for non-SYSTEM tablespaces. It cannot be used for tablespaces that contain active rollback segments or temporary segments.

Step 1. Take the tablespace offline.

Use the **alter tablespace** command within Server Manager or OEM to put the tablespace into **offline** state, as shown in the following example. This command is executed while the instance is running. This method cannot be used for the SYSTEM tablespace or for tablespaces containing active rollback segments or temporary segments.

```
> svrmgrl
SVRMGR> connect internal as sysdba;
SVRMGR> alter tablespace DATA offline;
SVRMGR> exit;
```

Step 2. Use operating system commands to move the file.

Use an operating system command to move the datafile. In UNIX, the **mv** command moves files to new locations. The following example shows the data01.dbf file being moved from the device named /db01 to one named /db02:

```
> mv /db01/oracle/CC1/data01.dbf /db02/oracle/CC1
```

The filename must fully specify a filename using the conventions of your operating system.

Step 3. Use the alter tablespace command to rename the file within the database.

In the following example, the data01.dbf datafile moved in step 2 is renamed within the database. The database will then be able to access that file. The **alter tablespace** command shown here does not rename the file; the file must have already been renamed or moved.

```
> svrmgrl
SVRMGR> connect internal as sysdba;
SVRMGR> alter tablespace DATA rename datafile
    2> '/db01/oracle/CC1/data01.dbf' to
    3> '/db02/oracle/CC1/data01.dbf';
```

Do not disconnect after this step is complete; stay logged in to the database and proceed to step 4.

When the **alter tablespace** command is executed, ORACLE will check to see if the name you are naming the file to exists. If this step fails, check the accuracy of the destination filename.

Step 4. Bring the tablespace back online.

Use the **alter tablespace** command to bring the tablespace back online from within Server Manager or OEM.

```
SVRMGR> alter tablespace DATA online;
```

The DATA tablespace will then be brought back online, using the new location for the datafile.

Moving a Datafile with **ORACLE** Enterprise Manager

Although there are two methods that can be used to move a datafile interactively from the system level, there is only one way to perform the same task from the ORACLE Enterprise Manager (OEM). In the following section, you will see the steps to follow within OEM to move a datafile from one directory location to another. In the figures in this section, the datafile for the DATA2 tablespace will be moved from the D:\ora8i\orcl directory to the D:\ora8i\orcl_alt directory.

Steps Required to Move a Datafile Using OEM

To move a datafile from one directory to another using OEM, follow the same steps as described in the prior "The **alter tablespace** Method" section. In the following example, the OEM toolset is used in place of Server Manager and the actions can be accomplished from a remote console.

The alter tablespace Method from OEM

When using the **alter tablespace** method to move datafiles, the datafile is moved while the instance is still running. The steps involved, detailed in the following sections, are as follows.

1. Take the tablespace offline.

2. From the Microsoft Explorer tool on Windows NT, move the datafile from the old folder to the new folder.

3. Use the datafile detail screen to modify the datafile name.

4. Bring the tablespace back online.

NOTE
This method can only be used for non-SYSTEM tablespaces. It cannot be used for tablespaces that contain active rollback segments or temporary segments.

Step 1. Take the tablespace offline.

From the ORACLE Storage Manager screen of the OEM, select the tablespace whose datafile is going to be moved. Figure 4-13 shows the original screen with the details for the DATA2 tablespace.

After selecting the tablespace, use the pull-down menu or the right-click mouse button and select the option Take Offline – Normal to put the tablespace into **offline** state, as shown in Figure 4-14 for the pull-down menu and Figure 4-15 for the right-click mouse button.

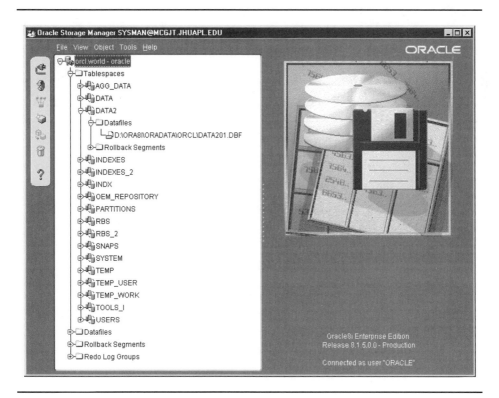

FIGURE 4-13. *Oracle Storage Manager initial screen*

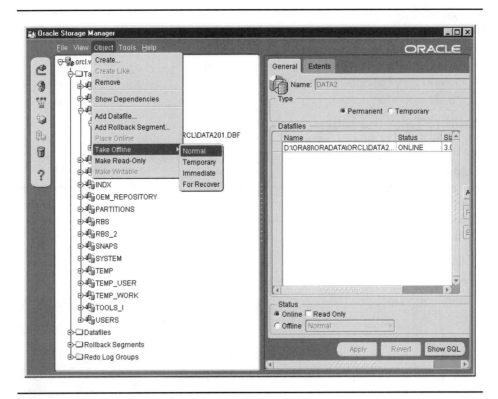

FIGURE 4-14. *Pull-down menu option to take object offline*

The tablespace is changed to **offline** state while the instance is running. After selecting the option to take the tablespace offline, a confirmation screen will be displayed with the question, "Are you sure you want to take this Tablespace Offline?" The options for reply are Yes and No. Figure 4-16 shows the Confirmation screen.

Step 2. Use Microsoft Explorer to move the file.
On Windows NT, use the Microsoft Explorer tool to move the datafile. In UNIX, the **mv** command moves files to new locations. Figures 4-17 and 4-18 show the

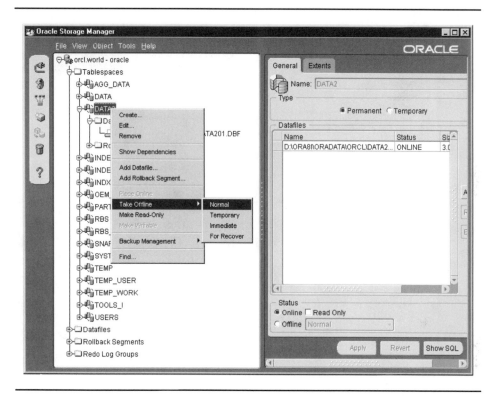

FIGURE 4-15. *Right-click mouse button option to take object offline*

Data201.dbf file being moved from the folder D:\ora8i\ORADATA\orcl to
D:\ora8i\ORADATA\orcl_alt.

In Figure 4-17, the datafile is shown in the D:\ora8i\ORADATA\orcl directory.
The cursor is used to click on the datafile and, with the left mouse button depressed,
the file is dragged from the current directory to the new directory—D:\ora8i\
ORADATA\orcl_alt.

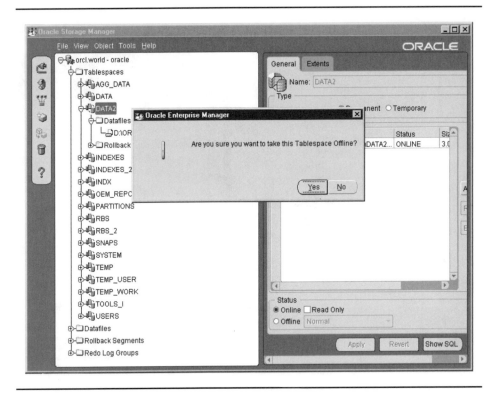

FIGURE 4-16. *Tablespace offline confirmation screen*

In Figure 4-18, the datafile is now shown located in the D:\ora8i\ORADATA\ orcl_alt directory.

Step 3. Use the datafile detail screen to modify the datafile name.

In the following example, the Data201.dbf datafile moved in step 2 is renamed within the database; the database will then be able to access that file. Renaming the directory name of the datafile as shown here does not rename the file; the file must have already been renamed or moved. Figures 4-19, 4-20, 4-21, 4-22, and 4-23 show the progression of steps that are taken to modify the datafile location and see the modification from the OEM console.

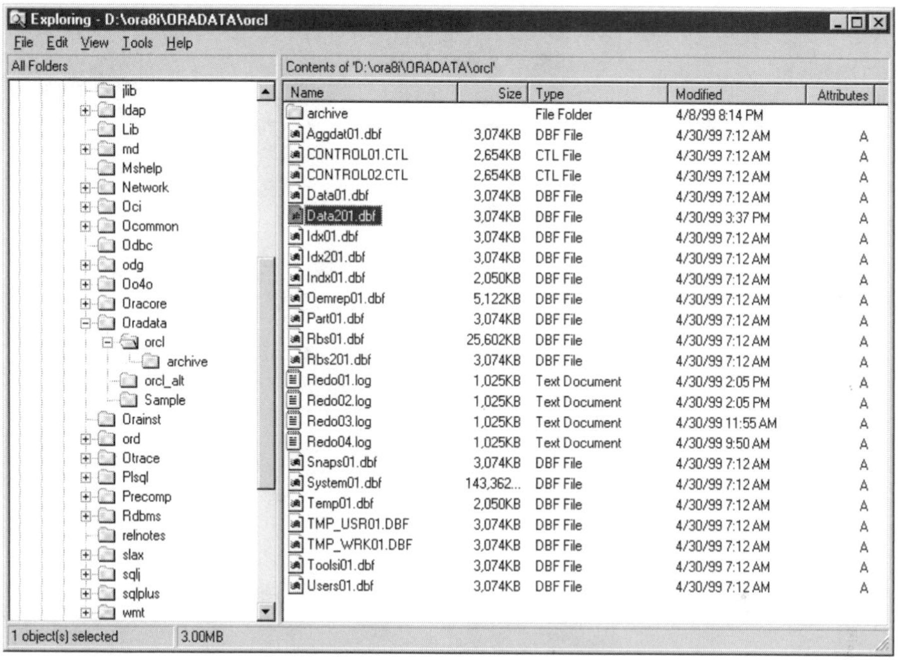

FIGURE 4-17.   *DATA201.DBF original directory location*

Figure 4-19 shows the original appearance of the screen prior to the datafile directory location being changed.

Figure 4-20 shows the datafile detail with the directory change from D:\ora8i\ORADATA\orcl to D:\ora8i\ORADATA\orcl_alt. Notice that the Apply button at the bottom of the datafile detail screen is active. To make the change take effect, click on the Apply button. When you click on the Apply button, ORACLE will check to see if the name you are naming the file to exists. If this step fails, check the accuracy of the destination filename.

To update the left screen of OEM and display the change, use the Refresh option (under the View option on the OEM menu).

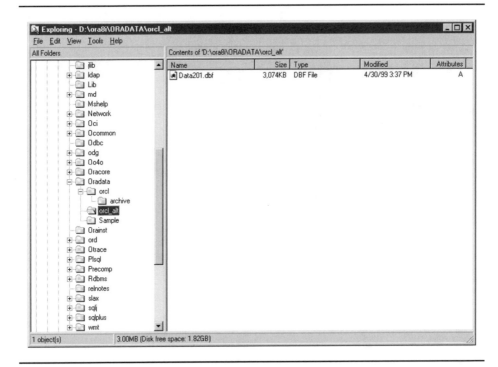

FIGURE 4-18. *DATA201.DBF new directory location*

In Figure 4-21, the screen has been refreshed and both the left screen and datafile detail screen now display the correct information. If the ORACLE Storage Manager OEM tool had been exited and reentered, the change would have also been visible.

Do not disconnect from OEM after this step is complete; stay in this tool and proceed to step 4.

Step 4. Bring the tablespace back online.

Use either the pull-down menu option or the right-click mouse button option to bring the tablespace back online from within ORACLE Storage Manager of OEM. Select the option Place Online to place the tablespace into the **online** state, as

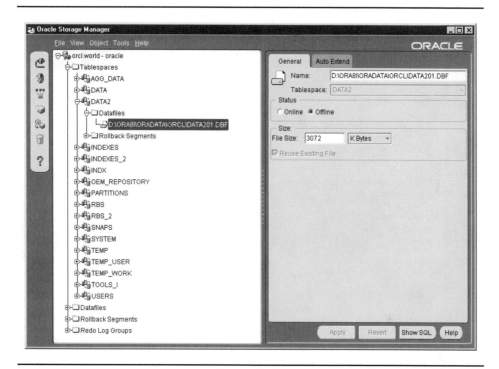

FIGURE 4-19. *DATA201.DBF in original location*

shown in Figure 4-22 for the pull-down menu and Figure 4-23 for the right-click mouse button.

After selecting the option to bring the tablespace online, a Confirmation screen will be displayed with the question, "Are you sure you want to bring this Tablespace Online?" Confirm your selection by clicking on the Yes option, or cancel the operation by selecting No. When you click on Yes, the DATA2 tablespace will be brought back online, using the new location for the datafile.

Moving Online Redo Log Files

Online redo log files can be moved while the database is shut down, and renamed within the database via the **alter database** command. The procedures for moving

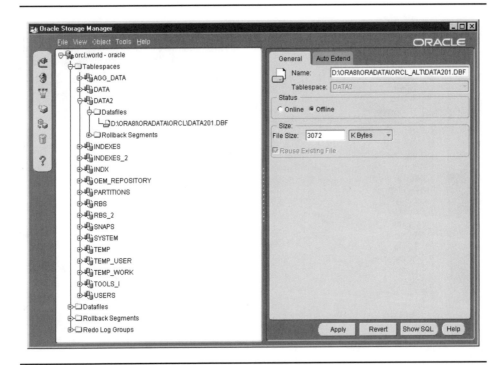

FIGURE 4-20. *General tab with DATA201.DBF location change*

online redo log files are very similar to those used to move datafiles via the **alter database** command.

First, the database is shut down and the online redo log file is moved. The database is then mounted and the **alter database** command is used to tell the database the new location of the online redo log file. The instance can then be opened, using the online redo log file in its new location.

Step 1. Shut down the instance.

```
> svrmgrl
SVRMGR> connect internal as sysdba;
SVRMGR> shutdown;
SVRMGR> exit;
```

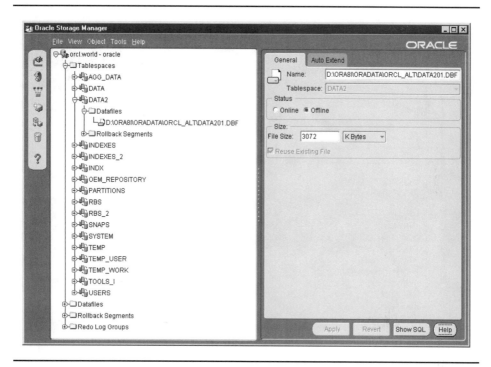

FIGURE 4-21.   *DATA201.DBF relocation complete*

Step 2. Move the online redo log file.

Use an operating system command to move the file. In UNIX, the **mv** command moves files to new locations. The following example shows the redo01CC1.dbf file being moved from the device named /db05 to one named /db02:

```
> mv /db05/oracle/CC1/redo01CC1.dbf /db02/oracle/CC1
```

The filename must fully specify a filename using the conventions of your operating system.

Step 3. Mount the database and use the alter database to rename the file within the database.

In the following example, the CC1 instance is started and the redo01CC1.dbf file moved in step 2 is renamed within the database. The database will then be able to

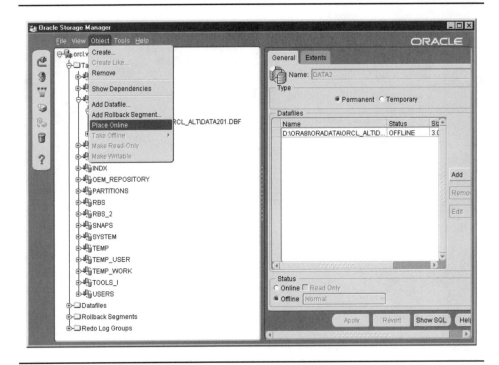

FIGURE 4-22. *Pull-down menu option to put object online*

find that file during instance startup. The **alter database** command shown here does not rename the file; the file must have already been renamed or moved.

```
> svrmgrl
SVRMGR> connect internal as sysdba;
SVRMGR> startup mount CC1;
SVRMGR> alter database rename file
    2> '/db05/oracle/CC1/redo01CC1.dbf' to
    3> '/db02/oracle/CC1/redo01CC1.dbf';
```

Do not disconnect after this step is complete; stay logged in to the database and proceed to step 4.

When the **alter database** command is executed, ORACLE will check to see if the name you are naming the file to exists. If this step fails, check the accuracy of the destination filename.

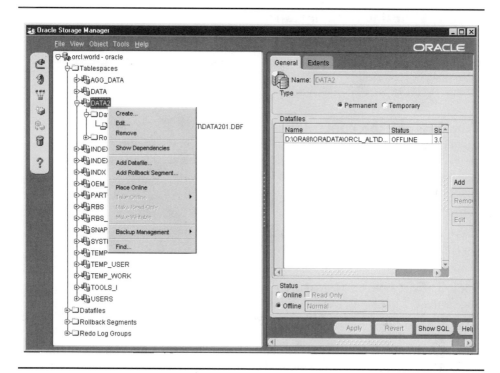

FIGURE 4-23. *Right-click mouse button option to put object online*

Step 4. Start the instance.
Now that the database knows how to find the moved file, the instance can start.

```
SVRMGR> alter database open;
```

The instance will now be opened, using the new location for the online redo log file that was moved.

Moving Control Files

The location of control files is specified in the init.ora or config.ora file for the instance; the config.ora file usually maintains this information. To move a control file, you must shut down the instance, move the file, edit the config.ora file, and then restart the instance.

Step 1. Shut down the instance.

```
> svrmgrl
SVRMGR> connect internal as sysdba;
SVRMGR> shutdown;
SVRMGR> exit;
```

Step 2. Move the control file.

Use an operating system command to move the file. In UNIX, the **mv** command moves files to new locations. The following example shows the ctrl1CC1.ctl file being moved from the device named /db05 to one named /db02:

```
> mv /db05/oracle/CC1/ctrl1CC1.ctl /db02/oracle/CC1
```

The filename must fully specify a filename using the conventions of your operating system.

Step 3. Edit the config.ora or init.ora file.

The config.ora file for an instance is usually located in same directory as the init.ora file. The name of the configuration file typically includes the name of the instance—for the CC1 instance, the config.ora file may be named configCC1.ora. The exact name and location of the config.ora file is specified in the init.ora file for the instance (usually located in the same directory as the config.ora file, with the same naming convention applied).

Within either the config.ora or init.ora file, there will be an entry for the CONTROL_FILES parameter; an example is shown in the following listing:

```
control_files     =  (/db01/oracle/CC1/ctrl1CC1.ctl,
                       /db03/oracle/CC1/ctrl1CC1.ctl,
                       /db05/oracle/CC1/ctrl1CC1.ctl)
```

Edit this entry to reflect the change to the file you moved in step 2:

```
control_files     =  (/db01/oracle/CC1/ctrl1CC1.ctl,
                       /db03/oracle/CC1/ctrl1CC1.ctl,
                       /db02/oracle/CC1/ctrl1CC1.ctl)
```

Step 4. Start the instance.

```
> svrmgrl
SVRMGR> connect internal as sysdba;
SVRMGR> startup;
SVRMGR> exit;
```

The instance will then be started, using the control file in its new location.

How to Deallocate Space from Segments

As of ORACLE7.2, you can reclaim unused space from existing datafiles. As of ORACLE7.3, you can reclaim space from tables, indexes, and clusters. In the following sections, you'll see examples of datafiles, tables, and indexes that are "shrunk" to reclaim previously allocated space.

Shrinking Datafiles

You can use the **alter database** command to reclaim unused space from datafiles. You cannot resize a datafile if the space you are trying to reclaim is currently allocated to a database object.

For example, if the datafile is 100MB in size, and 70MB of the datafile is currently in use, then you will need to leave at least 70MB in the datafile. You can use the **resize** clause of the **alter database** command to reclaim the space, as shown in the following example:

```
alter database datafile '/db05/oracle/CC1/data01.dbf'
resize 80M;
```

As shown in the listing, you specify the name of the file to be shrunk and its new size. If there are no database objects beyond the first 80MB of the specified datafile, the datafile will be shrunk to 80MB.

If space is used within the datafile beyond the first 80MB, then an error will be returned. As shown in the following listing, the error will show the amount of space that is used within the datafile beyond the specified **resize** value:

```
alter database datafile '/db05/oracle/CC1/data01.dbf'
resize 80M;
*
ERROR at line 1:
ORA-03297: file contains 507 blocks of data beyond
requested RESIZE value
```

If the database block size is 4K, then 507 database blocks is equivalent to 1.98MB. If you increase the **resize** value specified to 82MB, then the datafile can be resized.

To minimize the chances of encountering an error during free space reclamation from datafiles, you can "map" the free space within a datafile. See the "Measuring Fragmentation" section of Chapter 8 for a script that maps the free and used space within a tablespace and datafile. If your free space is fragmented, ORACLE may not be able to reclaim it all during a datafile resize operation.

Shrinking Tables, Clusters, and Indexes

When ORACLE writes data to a segment, it updates the *high-water mark* for the segment. The high-water mark is the highest block number in which data has been stored in the segment. If you **insert** thousands of rows in the table, the high-water mark will be incremented; if you **delete** the records, the high-water mark will *not* decrease. Aside from dropping and re-creating the table, the high-water mark for a segment is only reset when you issue a **truncate** command or the segment is dropped and re-created.

As of ORACLE7.3, unused space above the high-water mark in a segment can be reclaimed. If you have overestimated the storage requirements for an object, or have used a nonzero **pctincrease** setting (see Table 4-4), then you may wish to reclaim space that was allocated unnecessarily. You can reclaim the space from the segment without dropping and recreating it—with the limitation that you can only reclaim the space above the high-water mark for the table.

Before you can reclaim space from a table, you should therefore determine the high-water mark for the table. ORACLE provides a package named DBMS_SPACE that you can use to determine how much, if any, space can be reclaimed from a segment. In the following listing, the UNUSED_SPACE procedure within the DBMS_SPACE package is used to determine the space usage of the table named SPACES owned by the user OPS$CC1:

```
declare
        VAR1 number;
        VAR2 number;
        VAR3 number;
        VAR4 number;
        VAR5 number;
        VAR6 number;
        VAR7 number;
begin
    dbms_space.unused_space('OPS$CC1','SPACES','TABLE',
                        VAR1,VAR2,VAR3,VAR4,VAR5,VAR6,VAR7);
    dbms_output.put_line('OBJECT_NAME          = SPACES');
    dbms_output.put_line('--------------------------');
    dbms_output.put_line('TOTAL_BLOCKS         = '||VAR1);
    dbms_output.put_line('TOTAL_BYTES          = '||VAR2);
    dbms_output.put_line('UNUSED_BLOCKS        = '||VAR3);
    dbms_output.put_line('UNUSED_BYTES         = '||VAR4);
    dbms_output.put_line('LAST_USED_EXTENT_FILE_ID  = '||VAR5);
    dbms_output.put_line('LAST_USED_EXTENT_BLOCK_ID = '||VAR6);
    dbms_output.put_line('LAST_USED_BLOCK      = '||VAR7);
end;
/
```

Sample output of the preceding script for a 2MB SPACES table is shown in the following listing:

```
OBJECT_NAME      = SPACES
--------------------------
TOTAL_BLOCKS    = 500
TOTAL_BYTES     = 2048000
UNUSED_BLOCKS   = 200
UNUSED_BYTES    = 819200
```

The high-water mark of the table (in bytes) is the difference between the TOTAL_BYTES value and the UNUSED_BYTES value returned by this procedure call. The UNUSED_BLOCKS value represents the number of blocks above the high-water mark; the TOTAL_BLOCKS value reflects the total number of blocks allocated to the table.

If you want to reclaim space from the table, and its UNUSED_BLOCKS value is nonzero, then you can use the **alter table** command to reclaim the space above the high-water mark. In the preceding example, the TOTAL_BLOCKS value is 500 and the UNUSED_BLOCKS value is 200, with a database block size of 4K. You can reclaim the 200 unused blocks (800 KB).

If you want to leave 20 blocks within the table as unused space above the high-water mark, you can alter the table, specifying that the database keep 20 blocks—80K.

To reclaim space from a table, use the **alter table** command, as shown in the following listing. The **keep** parameter specifies the amount of free space to keep.

```
alter table SPACES deallocate unused keep 80K;
```

If you had not specified the **keep** clause, the **minextents** and **initial** storage values for the table would have been preserved. If **keep** is used, you can eliminate free space from any extent—even from the **initial** extent if there is no data in any other extent!

You can deallocate space from clusters via the **deallocate unused** clause of the **alter cluster** command. After deallocating space from a segment, you should execute the DBMS_SPACE procedure again to see the new values for the total and unused blocks allocated to the segment.

You can deallocate space from indexes via the **deallocate unused** clause of the **alter index** command. However, there is another option for indexes that allows you even greater flexibility when manipulating index space usage—**alter index rebuild**, as described in the next section.

How to Rebuild Indexes

Prior to ORACLE7.3, the only way to rebuild an index was to drop the index and re-create it completely. As of ORACLE7.3, you can use the **alter index rebuild** command to rapidly change the **storage** and **tablespace** parameters for an existing index—without having to drop the original index.

When you use the **alter index rebuild** command, the existing index is used as the data source for the new index (instead of using the table as the data source), improving performance of index creation. During the index re-creation, you can change the index's **storage** and **tablespace** parameters.

In the following example, the IU_SPACES$DB_TS_CD index is rebuilt via the **alter index rebuild** command. Its **storage** parameters are changed to use an **initial** extent size of 10MB and a **next** extent size of 5MB in the INDX_1 tablespace.

```
alter index IU_SPACES$DB_TS_CD rebuild
storage (initial 10M next 5M pctincrease 0)
tablespace INDX_1;
```

While the new IU_SPACES$DB_TS_CD index is being built, it will exist simultaneously with the old index in the database. Therefore, there must be enough space available to store both the old index and the new index in the database in order to use **alter index rebuild**. After the command has completed and the new index is available, the old index will be dropped automatically and the space will be reclaimed—but the space has to be available during the command execution or the new index creation will fail.

You can use the **alter index rebuild** command to quickly move indexes to different tablespaces. Index rebuilds allow you to set up a simple maintenance schedule for the most used indexes in your database. If the records in a table are frequently **delete**d and **insert**ed, the space used by the indexes on the table will continue to grow, even if the overall number of records remains unchanged. As records are **delete**d from the index, the space used by the records' index entries is not available for reuse. Therefore, if the table is volatile, then your indexes may grow even if there is no growth in the number of records—simply due to the increase in unavailable space within the index.

To reclaim the unusable space in an index, you can use the **alter index rebuild** command. Schedule a batch job to run periodically to rebuild the indexes on your most active tables. Run the batch job at off-hours to avoid scheduling conflicts with users. If you adhere to a maintenance schedule for your indexes, you will be able to reclaim the unusable space quickly. During each **alter index rebuild** command, specify both the **tablespace** and **storage** parameters for your index.

For information on rebuilding index partitions, see Chapter 12.

Physically Fit

In your databases, the file allocation must be planned (using I/O weightings) and the weightings must be verified once the system goes into production. The file layout can be modified postproduction to better balance the I/O requirements of the files. The result will be a database that achieves its performance goals without sacrificing recoverability, and its recoverability goals without sacrificing performance.

Each facet of the database—tables, indexes, rollback segments, and temporary segments—must be sized correctly as well. Correct sizing requires knowing the way in which the data is to be entered, how it is to be stored, and the processes that will be performed on it once it gets there. The costs of planning the storage parameters are minimal when compared to the costs of manipulating the system once it has been released to production. Postproduction tuning should be a final, minor step in the database physical design planning process.

PART

II

Database
Management

CHAPTER
5

Managing the
Development Process

anaging application development is a difficult process. From a DBA's perspective, the best way to manage the development process is to become an integral part of teams involved in the process. In this chapter, you will see the activities involved in migrating applications into databases and the technical details needed for implementation. These details will include system role specifications and sizing formulas for database objects.

This chapter focuses on controlling the activities that create objects in the database at various stages. These activities should follow the database planning activities that were described in Chapter 3 and Chapter 4. Chapter 6 and Chapter 8 address the monitoring and tuning activities that follow the database creation.

Implementing an application in a database by merely running a series of **create table** commands fails to integrate the creation process with the other major areas (planning, monitoring, and tuning). The DBA must be involved in the application development process in order to correctly design the database that will support the end product. The methods described in this chapter will also provide important information for structuring the database monitoring and tuning efforts.

The Three Critical Elements of Success

The life cycle of a database is defined by the four actions referred to previously: planning, creating, monitoring, and tuning. The elements of a successful implementation of this cycle can be identified as belonging to three key categories: *cultural processes*, *management processes*, and *technology*.

Managing the implementation efforts of database developers requires action on all three points:

1. **Cultural:** The corporate culture and the development team must support the DBA's involvement in this level of activity.

2. **Management:** The developers' adherence to a life cycle methodology must be enforceable.

3. **Technology:** The developers and DBAs must define mechanisms for making sure the appropriate level of involvement and attention to detail is taking place.

NOTE
Attempting to implement a development life cycle methodology without corporate buy-in or without technology that allows for the tracking of deliverables will yield no long-term benefit.

Cultural Processes

In order to break down the traditional barrier between DBAs and developers, the relationship between them must be formalized. The revised nature of the relationship must be accepted by all of the parties involved. This can only be accomplished if the groups being brought together feel that the new team's structure adds value to the development process. There must be a corporate commitment to the team structure to overcome the initial turf wars that may otherwise disrupt the process from the start.

A joint DBA/developer team adds value by

- Building applications that are easier to maintain

- Building applications that are properly sized and organized, and thus require no downtime for reorganizations

- Creating appropriate indexes to maximize performance

- Identifying the tables and indexes that will be most frequently used by the application

- Identifying and correcting poorly constructed SQL to avoid performance impacts

- Identifying static query-only tables within the application

- Building into each application an understanding of the interface needs of outside applications

- Identifying technical problems earlier in the development process

- Identifying resource scheduling conflicts between online users and long-running batch processes

- Allowing the DBA, who will eventually provide much of the application's support, to accept partial ownership of the application during its development

The value the DBA adds to each of these efforts is greatly enhanced when the DBA understands the application and the business needs it serves. If you understand the business needs, you can better understand the developers' goals in their application development process. As another benefit, understanding the application and the business will greatly improve your ability to communicate effectively with the application developers and users. As a final benefit, working with the application development team from the beginning will improve your ability to properly size and tune the database used by the application.

Difficult to maintain, fragmented, slow, and isolated database applications cost the organization in terms of downtime, tuning time, and user frustration. These costs can be avoided by entering into true team relationships between developers and DBAs. The methodology must clearly define the roles and responsibilities within these relationships and must be accepted by all levels within the personnel groups responsible for applications development. This will greatly ease the need for third-party enforcement of the methodology.

Management Processes

In order to properly manage development efforts, the methodology must not only spell out the relationships between the different functional areas, but must also clearly define the deliverables required in each phase of application development. For example, when does an application move out of development and into test, or from test to production? Who decides?

The answer is, the methodology decides. If the deliverables for the development section are completed, reviewed, and approved, then the application can be moved into the test environment, under whose constraints the developers must then work.

Defining the Environment

Most application environments are divided into two to five areas. They are *development, system test, stress test, acceptance test,* and *production.* For the purposes of this discussion, the three test areas will be combined. The exact number of areas maintained is methodology-specific.

NOTE
Although it is not discussed in depth here, stress testing should be an integral part of the development process. In practice, stress testing is most effective when it is performed before acceptance testing; problems related to the usage load should be resolved prior to any acceptance testing.

Consider each of the areas. The methodology needs to specify what the finished product will be from each area, and what completing that section will provide to subsequent areas. Once this has been defined, the database needs for the different areas can be deduced.

In development, for instance, users may have free reign to make table changes, test new ideas, and create new objects. An integrated CASE (computer-aided systems engineering) tool such as Oracle Designer should be used to maintain a constantly synchronized logical model. The CASE repository should be used to generate the first set of database objects in each environment; the developers should be responsible for maintaining the CASE dictionary thereafter.

Once the system enters the test phase, its final configuration should be within sight. At this point, the table volumes, user accounts, and performance needs should be identified. These will allow the DBA to create a proper database for the application on the first try, and to monitor for performance problems that are outside of the defined acceptable bounds.

In production, developers are locked out. From the database's perspective, they are just another set of users. All changes to database objects in the production database should have first passed through the test environment via a defined change control process. Any modifications to the system's needs should have been clearly defined in the test phase.

In order to maintain the proper level of user system-level privileges, developer accounts must be configured differently for each area. The next section will describe the proper system role definitions for developers given the development/test/production areas previously described.

Role Definitions

Of the system-level roles provided by ORACLE, three roles (CONNECT, RESOURCE, and DBA) apply to the development environment (the others are related to the administration of the database, and are described in Chapter 9). You can create your own system-level roles to define system privileges beyond CONNECT, RESOURCE, and DBA, but these may be more difficult to use and maintain than the system-provided roles. You can grant roles to the users and developers depending on the system privileges they need in their environment.

CONNECT

The CONNECT role gives users privileges beyond just creating sessions in the database. In addition to the CREATE SESSION system privilege, the CONNECT role gives users the following system privileges: ALTER SESSION, CREATE CLUSTER, CREATE DATABASE LINK, CREATE SEQUENCE, CREATE SYNONYM, CREATE TABLE, and CREATE VIEW. That's far more than just connecting to the database. However, the users do not have the ability to create tables or clusters (objects that use space in the database) unless you grant them a quota on a tablespace, or unless they have been granted the RESOURCE role (discussed next). See Chapter 9 for details on the granting of space quotas.

In general, the CONNECT role will be sufficient for your end users in all environments. Depending on the needs of your developers, the CONNECT role may be sufficient for them as well. For example, if your developers do not need to create objects such as procedures, packages, triggers, and abstract datatypes, then the CONNECT role serves their needs.

If you wish to limit the system privileges of your application users, you can create your own role—APPLICATION_USER—which has just the CREATE SESSION privilege:

```
create role APPLICATION_USER;
grant CREATE SESSION to APPLICATION_USER;
grant APPLICATION_USER to username;
```

RESOURCE

The RESOURCE role has the following system privileges: CREATE CLUSTER, CREATE INDEXTYPE, CREATE OPERATOR, CREATE PROCEDURE, CREATE SEQUENCE, CREATE TABLE, CREATE TRIGGER, CREATE TYPE. Users who have the RESOURCE role are also granted the UNLIMITED TABLESPACE privilege, so they can override the quotas defined for them. You should grant the RESOURCE role to developers who will be creating PL/SQL objects such as procedures and triggers. If your developers use the Objects Option, the RESOURCE role gives them the CREATE TYPE privilege, which enables them to create and execute types and methods.

If you wish to restrict developers' privileges, then you can create your own role and grant system-level privileges to it. For example, you may want to restrict developers' ability to create tables and clusters, while permitting them to create indexes and procedural objects. If that is the case, then you could create a system-level role and grant it all of the system privileges that constitute RESOURCE except for the privileges you wish to exclude. In general, you should only grant developers the RESOURCE role in development; in test and production, the CONNECT role should be sufficient. If you give developers RESOURCE access to your production database, you will be giving away control of your database and severely impacting your ability to enforce a change control process.

DBA

The DBA role has all system privileges **with admin option**, which means that the DBA can grant the system privileges to any other user. You should not grant the DBA role to application developers or users in any development, test, or production database. If you grant developers the DBA role in development, they may code their application with the assumption that they will have the same system privileges when the application is released into the production environment. If you cannot restrict access to DBA-privileged accounts, then you cannot guarantee the security of the data in your database—and that is one of the key job functions of the DBA.

In Test and Production

The appropriate role designations for the test environment depend on how that environment is to be used. If it is to be used as a true acceptance test region, mirroring the eventual production database, then its roles should be assigned to mirror the production roles. If, however, developers will be allowed to make modifications to the test database, then they will require access to an account that has the same privileges that they have in the development environment.

The tables and other database objects used by the application are typically owned by a single account in test and production. If the change must be performed within the account that owns the application schema (for example, the creation of a database link), then the DBA can temporarily log in to that account and perform the change. In general, developers should not have the RESOURCE role in a test environment. If a change is to be made to the system, the change should be made first in development and then migrated to test via a documented change control process.

Deliverables

How do you know if the methodology is being followed? Doing so requires establishing a list of items called *deliverables* that must be completed during the application development. The methodology must clearly define, both in format and in level of detail, the required deliverables for each stage of the life cycle. These should include specifications for each of the following items:

- Entity relationship diagram

- Physical database diagram

- Space requirements

- Tuning goals

- Data requirements

- Execution plans

- Acceptance test procedures

In the following sections, you will see descriptions of each of these items.

Entity Relationship Diagram

The *entity relationship (E-R) diagram* illustrates the relationships that have been identified among the entities that make up the application. E-R diagrams are critical for providing an understanding of the goals of the system. They also help to identify interface points with other applications, and to ensure consistency in definitions across the enterprise. Modeling conventions for E-R diagrams are described in Chapter 1.

Physical Database Diagram

A *physical database diagram* shows the physical tables generated from the entities and the columns generated from the defined attributes in the logical model. A physical database diagramming tool is usually capable of generating the DDL necessary to create the application's objects. Modeling conventions for physical database diagrams are described in Chapter 1.

You can use the physical database diagram to identify tables that are most likely to be involved in transactions. You should also be able to identify which tables are commonly used together during a data entry or query operation. You can use this information to effectively plan the distribution of these tables (and their indexes) across the available physical devices to reduce the amount of I/O contention encountered (see Chapters 3 and 4).

Space Requirements

The space requirements deliverable should show the initial space requirements for each database table and index. The recommendations for the proper size for tables, clusters, and indexes are shown in the "Sizing Database Objects" section later in this chapter.

Tuning Goals

Changes to the application design may have significant impact on the application's performance. Application design choices may also directly affect your ability to tune the application. Because application design has such a great effect on the DBA's ability to tune its performance, the DBA must be involved in the design process.

You must identify the performance goals of a system *before* it goes into production. The role of expectation in perception cannot be overemphasized. If the users have an expectation that the system will be at least as fast as an existing system, then anything less will be unacceptable. The estimated response time for each of the most-used components of the application must be defined and approved.

It is important during this process to establish two sets of goals: reasonable goals and "stretch" goals. *Stretch goals* represent the results of concentrated efforts to go beyond the hardware and software constraints that limit the system's performance.

Maintaining two sets of performance goals helps to focus efforts on those goals that are truly mission-critical versus those that are beyond the scope of the core system deliverables.

Security Requirements

The development team must specify the account structure that the application will use. This should include the ownership of all objects in the application and the manner in which privileges will be granted. All roles and privileges must be clearly defined. The deliverables from this section will be used to generate the account and privilege structure of the production application (see Chapter 9 for a full review of Oracle's security capabilities).

Depending on the application, you may need to specify the account usage for batch accounts separately from that of online accounts. For example, the batch accounts may use the database's autologin features, while the online users have to manually sign in. Your security plans for the application must support both types of users.

Like the space requirements deliverable, security planning is an area in which the DBA's involvement is critical. The DBA should be able to design an implementation that meets the application's needs while fitting in with the enterprise database security plan.

Data Requirements

The methods for data entry and retrieval must be clearly defined. Data entry methods must be tested and verified while the application is in the test environment. Any special data archiving requirements of the application must also be documented, since they will be application-specific.

You must also describe the backup and recovery requirements for the application. These requirements can then be compared to the site database backup plans (see Chapter 10 for guidelines). Any database recovery requirements that go beyond the site's standard will require modifying the site's backup standard or adding a module to accommodate the application's needs.

Execution Plans

Execution plans are the steps that the database will go through while executing queries. They are generated via the **explain plan** or **set autotrace** commands, as described in Chapter 8. Recording the execution plans for the most important queries against the database will aid in planning the index usage and tuning goals for the application. Generating them prior to production implementation will simplify tuning efforts and identify potential performance problems before the application is released. Generating the explain plans for your most important queries will also facilitate the process of performing code reviews of the application.

Acceptance Test Procedures

The developers and users should very clearly define what functionality and performance goals must be achieved before the application can be migrated to production. These goals will form the foundation of the test procedures that will be executed against the application while it is in the test environment.

The procedures should also describe how to deal with unmet goals. They should very clearly list the functional goals that must be met before the system can move forward. A second list of noncritical functional goals should also be provided. This separation of functional capabilities will aid in both resolving scheduling conflicts and structuring appropriate tests.

Development Environment Features Introduced in Oracle8i

As of ORACLE8i, developers and DBAs can use two new features to manage the development process. You can use *stored outlines* to migrate execution paths between instances. You can use the *Database Resource Manager* to control the allocation of system resources among database users. Stored outlines and resource management are important components in a managed development environment. The Database Resource Manager gives DBAs more control over the allocation of system resources than is possible with operating system controls alone.

Implementing the Database Resource Manager

You can use the Database Resource Manager to allocate percentages of system resources to classes of users and jobs. For example, you could allocate 75 percent of the available CPU resources to your online users, leaving 25 percent to your batch users. To use the Database Resource Manager, you will need to create *resource plans, resource consumer groups,* and *resource plan directives.* By default, the script catrm.sql is called from catproc.sql to create the structure's necessary for the Database Resource Manager.

Prior to using the Database Resource Manager commands, you must create a "pending area" for your work. To create a pending area, use the CREATE_PENDING_AREA procedure of the DBMS_RESOURCE_MANAGER procedure. When you have completed your changes, use the VALIDATE_PENDING_AREA procedure to check the validity of the new set of plans, subplans, and directives. You can then either submit the changes (via SUBMIT_PENDING_AREA) or clear the changes (via CLEAR_PENDING_AREA). The procedures that manage the pending area do not have any input variables, so a sample creation of a pending area uses the following syntax:

```
execute DBMS_RESOURCE_MANAGER.CREATE_PENDING_AREA();
```

If the pending area is not created, you will receive the following messages:

```
ERROR at line 1:
ORA-29371: pending area is not active
ORA-06512: at "SYS.DBMS_RMIN", line 249
ORA-06512: at "SYS.DBMS_RESOURCE_MANAGER", line 26
ORA-06512: at line 1
```

If you receive this set of error messages, execute the CREATE_PENDING_AREA procedure as shown in the prior listing. You will see the commands for the validation and submission of pending areas at the end of this section.

To create a resource plan, use the CREATE_PLAN procedure of the DBMS_RESOURCE_MANAGER package. Since resource management is a new feature in ORACLE8i, the syntax relies on the execution of PL/SQL procedures rather than SQL commands.

The syntax for the CREATE_PLAN procedure is shown in the following listing:

```
CREATE_PLAN
    (plan                       IN VARCHAR2,
     comment                    IN VARCHAR2,
     cpu_mth                    IN VARCHAR2 DEFAULT 'EMPHASIS',
     max_active_sess_target_mth IN VARCHAR2 DEFAULT
            'MAX_ACTIVE_SESS_ABSOLUTE',
     parallel_degree_limit_mth  IN VARCHAR2 DEFAULT
            'PARALLEL_DEGREE_LIMIT_ABSOLUTE')
```

When you create a plan, give the plan a name (in the Plan variable) and a comment. By default, the CPU allocation method will use the "emphasis" method, allocating CPU based on percentage. The following example shows the creation of a plan called DEVELOPERS:

```
execute DBMS_RESOURCE_MANAGER.CREATE_PLAN -
  (Plan => 'DEVELOPERS', -
   Comment => 'Developers, in Development database');
```

NOTE
The hyphen (-) character is a continuation character in SQL*Plus, allowing a single command to span multiple lines.

In order to create and manage resource plans and resource consumer groups, you must have the ADMINISTER_RESOURCE_MANAGER system privilege enabled for your session. DBAs have this privilege with the **with admin option**. To grant this privilege to non-DBAs, you must execute the GRANT_SYSTEM_PRIVILEGE procedure of the DBMS_RESOURCE_MANAGER_PRIVS package. The example in the following listing grants the user MARTHA the ability to manage the Database Resource Manager:

```
execute DBMS_RESOURCE_MANAGER_PRIVS -
  (grantee_name => 'Martha',  -
   admin_option => TRUE);
```

You can revoke MARTHA's privileges via the REVOKE_SYSTEM_PRIVILEGE procedure of the DBMS_RESOURCE_MANAGER package.

With the ADMINISTER_RESOURCE_MANAGER privilege enabled, you can create a resource consumer group using the CREATE_CONSUMER_GROUP procedure within DBMS_RESOURCE_MANAGER. The syntax for the CREATE_CONSUMER_GROUP procedure is shown in the following listing:

```
CREATE_CONSUMER_GROUP
      (consumer_group IN VARCHAR2,
       comment        IN VARCHAR2,
       cpu_mth        IN VARCHAR2 DEFAULT 'ROUND-ROBIN')
```

You will be assigning users to resource consumer groups, so give the groups names that are based on the logical divisions of your users. The following example creates two groups—one for online developers and a second for batch developers:

```
execute DBMS_RESOURCE_MANAGER.CREATE_CONSUMER_GROUP -
  (Consumer_Group => 'Online_developers', -
   Comment => 'Online developers');

execute DBMS_RESOURCE_MANAGER.CREATE_CONSUMER_GROUP -
  (Consumer_Group => 'Batch_developers', -
   Comment => 'Batch developers');
```

Once the plan and resource consumer groups are established, you need to create resource plan directives and assign users to the resource consumer groups. To assign directives to a plan, use the CREATE_PLAN_DIRECTIVE procedure of the DBMS_RESOURCE_MANAGER package. The syntax for the CREATE_PLAN_DIRECTIVE procedure is shown in the following listing:

```
CREATE_PLAN_DIRECTIVE
      (plan                   IN VARCHAR2,
       group_or_subplan       IN VARCHAR2,
       comment                IN VARCHAR2,
       cpu_p1                 IN NUMBER    DEFAULT NULL,
       cpu_p2                 IN NUMBER    DEFAULT NULL,
       cpu_p3                 IN NUMBER    DEFAULT NULL,
       cpu_p4                 IN NUMBER    DEFAULT NULL,
       cpu_p5                 IN NUMBER    DEFAULT NULL,
```

```
cpu_p6                      IN NUMBER   DEFAULT NULL,
cpu_p7                      IN NUMBER   DEFAULT NULL,
cpu_p8                      IN NUMBER   DEFAULT NULL,
max_active_sess_target_p1 IN NUMBER   DEFAULT NULL,
parallel_degree_limit_p1  IN NUMBER   DEFAULT NULL)
```

The multiple CPU variables in the CREATE_PLAN_DIRECTIVE procedure support the creation of multiple levels of CPU allocation. For example, you could allocate 75 percent of all of your CPU resources (level 1) to your online users. Of the remaining CPU resources (level 2), you could allocate 50 percent to a second set of users. You could split the remaining 50 percent of resources available at level 2 to multiple groups at a third level. The CREATE_PLAN_DIRECTIVE procedure supports up to eight levels of CPU allocations.

The following example shows the creation of the plan directives for the Online_developers and Batch_developers resource consumer groups within the DEVELOPERS resource plan:

```
execute DBMS_RESOURCE_MANAGER.CREATE_PLAN_DIRECTIVE -
 (Plan => 'DEVELOPERS', -
  Group_or_subplan => 'Online_developers', -
  Comment => 'online developers', -
  Cpu_p1 => 75, -
  Cpu_p2=> 0, -
  Parallel_degree_limit_p1 => 12);

execute DBMS_RESOURCE_MANAGER.CREATE_PLAN_DIRECTIVE -
 (Plan => 'DEVELOPERS', -
  Group_or_subplan => 'Batch_developers', -
  Comment => 'Batch developers', -
  Cpu_p1 => 25, -
  Cpu_p2 => 0, -
  Parallel_degree_limit_p1 => 6);
```

In addition to allocating CPU resources, the plan directives also restrict the parallelism of operations performed by members of the resource consumer group. In the preceding example, batch developers are limited to a degree of parallelism of 6, reducing their ability to consume system resources. Online developers are limited to a degree of parallelism of 12.

To assign a user to a resource consumer group, use the SET_INITIAL_ CONSUMER_GROUP procedure of the DBMS_RESOURCE_MANAGER package. The syntax for the SET_INITIAL_CONSUMER_GROUP procedure is shown in the following listing:

```
SET_INITIAL_CONSUMER_GROUP
     (user            IN VARCHAR2,
      consumer_group IN VARCHAR2)
```

If a user has never had an initial consumer group set via the SET_INITIAL_ CONSUMER_GROUP procedure, then the user is automatically enrolled in the resource consumer group named DEFAULT_CONSUMER_GROUP.

To enable the Resource Manager within your database, set the RESOURCE_MANAGER_PLAN init.ora parameter to the name of the resource plan for the instance. Resource plans can have subplans, so you can create tiers of resource allocations within the instance. If you do not set a value for the RESOURCE_MANAGER_PLAN parameter, then resource management is not performed in the instance.

You can dynamically alter the instance to use a different resource allocation plan via the **set initial_consumer_group** clause of the **alter system** command. For example, you could create a resource plan for your daytime users (DAYTIME_USERS) and a second for your batch users (BATCH_USERS). You could create a job that each day executes this command at 6:00 A.M.:

```
alter system set initial_consumer_group = 'DAYTIME_USERS';
```

At a set time in the evening, change consumer groups to benefit the batch users:

```
alter system set initial_consumer_group = 'BATCH_USERS';
```

The resource allocation plan for the instance will thus be altered without needing to shut down and restart the instance.

When using multiple resource allocation plans in this fashion, you need to make sure you don't accidentally use the wrong plan at the wrong time. For example, if the database is down during a scheduled plan change, your job that changes the plan allocation may not execute. How will that affect your users? If you use multiple resource allocation plans, you need to consider the impact of using the wrong plan at the wrong time. To avoid such problems, you should try to minimize the number of resource allocation plans in use.

In addition to the examples and commands shown in this section, you can update existing resource plans (via the UPDATE_PLAN procedure), delete resource plans (via DELETE_PLAN), and cascade the deletion of a resource plan plus all of its subplans and related resource consumer groups (DELETE_PLAN_CASCADE). You can update and delete resource consumer groups via the UPDATE_CONSUMER_GROUP and DELETE_CONSUMER_GROUP procedures, respectively. Resource plan directives may be updated via UPDATE_PLAN_DIRECTIVE and deleted via DELETE_PLAN_DIRECTIVE.

When you are modifying resource plans, resource consumer groups, and resource plan directives, you should test the changes prior to implementing them. To test your changes, create a pending area for your work. To create a pending area, use the CREATE_PENDING_AREA procedure of the DBMS_RESOURCE_ MANAGER package. When you have completed your changes, use the

VALIDATE_PENDING_AREA procedure to check the validity of the new set of plans, subplans, and directives. You can then either submit the changes (via SUBMIT_PENDING_AREA) or clear the changes (via CLEAR_PENDING_AREA). The procedures that manage the pending area do not have any input variables, so a sample validation and submission of a pending area uses the following syntax:

```
execute DBMS_RESOURCE_MANAGER.VALIDATE_PENDING_AREA();
execute DBMS_RESOURCE_MANAGER.SUBMIT_PENDING_AREA();
```

Implementing Stored Outlines

As you migrate from one database to another, the execution paths for your queries may change. Your execution paths may change for several reasons:

1. You may be using a different optimizer in different databases (cost-based in one, rule-based in another).

2. You may have enabled different optimizer features in the different databases.

3. The statistics for the queried tables may differ in the databases.

4. The frequency with which statistics are gathered may differ among the databases.

5. The databases may be running different versions of the Oracle kernel.

The effects of these differences on your execution paths can be dramatic, and can have a significant negative impact on your query performance as you migrate or upgrade your application. To minimize the impact of these differences on your query performance, ORACLE introduced a feature called a *stored outline* in ORACLE8i.

A stored outline stores a set of hints for a query. Those hints will be used every time the query is executed. Using the stored hints will increase the likelihood that the query will use the same execution path each time. Hints do not mandate an execution path (they're hints, not commands), but decrease the impact of database moves on your query performance.

To start creating hints for all queries, set the CREATE_STORED_OUTLINES init.ora parameter to TRUE. If you set CREATE_STORED_OUTLINES to TRUE, then all of the outlines will be saved under the DEFAULT category. As an alternative, you can create custom categories of outlines and use the category name as a value in the init.ora file, as shown in the following listing:

```
CREATE_STORED_OUTLINES = development
```

In this example, stored outlines will be stored for queries within the DEVELOPMENT category.

You must have the CREATE ANY OUTLINE system privilege in order to create an outline. Use the **create outline** command to create an outline for a query, as shown in the following listing:

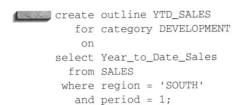

```
create outline YTD_SALES
    for category DEVELOPMENT
      on
select Year_to_Date_Sales
  from SALES
 where region = 'SOUTH'
   and period = 1;
```

NOTE
If you do not specify a name for your outline, the outline will be given a system-generated name.

If you have set CREATE_STORED_OUTLINES to TRUE in your init.ora file, the RDBMS will create stored outlines for your queries; using the **create outline** command gives you more control over the outlines that are created.

NOTE
You can create outlines for DML commands and for **create table as select** *commands.*

Once an outline has been created, you can alter it. For example, you may need to alter the outline to reflect significant changes in data volumes and distribution. You can use the **rebuild** clause of the **alter outline** command to regenerate the hints used during query execution, as shown below:

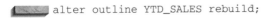
```
alter outline YTD_SALES rebuild;
```

You can also rename an outline via the **rename** clause of the **alter outline** command, as shown here:

```
alter outline YTD_SALES rename to YTD_SALES_REGION;
```

You can change the category of an outline via the **change category** clause, as shown in the following example:

```
alter outline YTD_SALES_REGION change category to DEFAULT;
```

For the stored outlines to be used by the optimizer, set the USE_STORED_OUTLINES init.ora parameter to TRUE or to a category name (such as DEVELOPMENT in the earlier examples). If stored outline use is enabled, any query with a stored outline will use the hints generated when the outline was created. You can also enable USE_STORED_OUTLINES at the session level via the **alter session** command.

To manage stored outlines, use the OUTLN_PKG package. The OUTLN_PKG package gives you three capabilities:

- Drop outlines that have never been used

- Drop outlines within a specific category

- Move outlines from one category to another

Each of these three capabilities has a corresponding procedure within OUTLN_PKG. To drop outlines that have never been used, execute the DROP_UNUSED procedure, as shown in the following listing:

```
execute OUTLN_PKG.DROP_UNUSED;
```

To drop all of the outlines within a category, execute the DROP_BY_CAT procedure. The DROP_BY_CAT procedure has the name of the category as its only input parameter. The following example drops all of the outlines within the DEVELOPMENT category:

```
execute OUTLN_PKG.DROP_BY_CAT -
   (category_name => 'DEVELOPMENT');
```

To reassign outlines from an old category to a new category, use the UPDATE_BY_CAT procedure, as shown in the following example:

```
execute OUTLN_PKG.UPDATE_BY_CAT -
  (old_category_name => 'DEVELOPMENT', -
   new_category_name => 'TEST');
```

To drop a specific outline, use the **drop outline** command.

Sizing Database Objects

Choosing the proper space allocation for database objects is critical. Developers should begin estimating space requirements before the first database objects are created. Afterwards, the space requirements can be refined based on the actual usage statistics. In the following sections, you will see the space estimation methods for tables, indexes, and clusters. You'll also see methods for determining the proper setting for **pctfree** and **pctused**.

Why Size Objects?

You should size your database objects for four reasons:

1. To preallocate space in the database, thereby minimizing the amount of future work required to manage objects' space requirements

2. To reduce the amount of space wasted due to overallocation of space

3. To eliminate potential causes of I/O-related performance problems

4. To improve the likelihood of a dropped free extent being reused by another segment

You can accomplish all of these goals by following the sizing methodology shown in the following sections. This methodology is based on ORACLE's internal methods for allocating space to database objects. Rather than rely on detailed calculations, the methodology relies on approximations that will dramatically simplify the sizing process while simplifying the long-term maintainability of the database.

Why ORACLE Ignores Most Space Calculations

Unless you have calculated your space requests with ORACLE's internal space allocation methods in mind, ORACLE will most likely ignore your detailed space request. ORACLE follows a set of internal rules when allocating space:

1. ORACLE only allocates whole blocks, not parts of blocks.

2. ORACLE allocates sets of blocks, usually in multiples of five blocks.

3. ORACLE may allocate larger or smaller sets of blocks depending on the available free space in the tablespace.

You can apply these internal rules to your space allocations. For this example, assume that the database block size is 4KB. The following tables will be created:

Table Name	Initial	Next	PctIncrease
SmallTab	7K	7K	0
MediumTab	103K	103K	20

Before these tables were created, the DBA diligently estimated the space requirements using the detailed space calculations available in the ORACLE documentation. What happened when the tables were created?

For SmallTab, the DBA specified an initial extent size of 7KB. However, the database block size is 4KB. In order to avoid splitting a block, ORACLE will round the initial extent size up to 8KB. However, 8KB represents only two blocks. In most environments, ORACLE will round the initial extent size up to five blocks—20KB. When the time comes to allocate the next extent, ORACLE will use the specified **next** value—7KB—and perform a similar calculation.

For MediumTab, the **initial** value is 103KB. That value needs to be rounded up to a whole block increment, so ORACLE will round the value up to 104KB, or 26 blocks. At this point, ORACLE will analyze the available space in the tablespace. Ideally, ORACLE will round up the block allocation to the next multiple of five blocks—30 blocks. If there is a free extent in the tablespace that is between 26 and 30 blocks in size, then ORACLE may use that free extent for MediumTab's first extent.

When MediumTab allocates its second extent, ORACLE performs the same space allocation analysis and allocates a second extent of 30 blocks (120KB).

When MediumTab allocates its third extent, ORACLE goes back to the specified value for **next**, not the allocated value. MediumTab has a **pctincrease** value of 20, so the third extent should be 20 percent larger than the second extent. If ORACLE relied on the allocated space in its calculations, then it would start the allocation process for the third extent by trying to allocate 36 blocks (30 blocks × 1.2) and searching for a 40-block free extent. However, ORACLE relies on the specified **next** value when performing its calculations. Thus, it takes the **next** value (103KB), increased by the **pctincrease** value (20 percent), giving it a value of 123.6KB. For a 4KB block size, 123.6KB is 30.9 blocks, rounded up to 31 blocks, which when rounded to the next highest multiple of five yields 35 blocks.

The specified and actual space allocations for SmallTab and MediumTab are as follows:

Table	Initial	Next	PctIncrease	FirstExtent	SecondExt	ThirdExt
SmallTab	7K	7K	0	20K	20K	20K
MediumTab	103K	103K	20	120K	120K	140K

These results may be disheartening to the DBA who performed the space calculations. The SmallTab table only needed 14KB for its first two extents; instead, it allocated 40KB. The MediumTab table should have needed 206KB for its first two extents; instead, it allocated 240KB. Moreover, the **pctincrease** setting for MediumTab called for the third extent to be 20 percent larger than the second extent; instead, it's only 16.6 percent larger.

As shown through this exercise, there is no point in going through a sizing calculation exercise unless you first consider how ORACLE allocates space. If you factor ORACLE's space allocation methods into your space calculation methodology, then you will be able to allocate space effectively, with a minimum of changes made by ORACLE. Before choosing your extent sizes, however, you should first consider how the size of extents impacts performance.

The Impact of Extent Size on Performance

There is no direct performance benefit gained by reducing the number of extents in a table. In some situations (such as in parallel query environments), having multiple extents in a table can significantly reduce I/O contention and enhance your performance. Regardless of the number of extents in your tables, the extents need to be properly sized.

ORACLE reads data from tables in two ways: by RowID (usually immediately following an index access) and via full table scans. If the data is read via RowID, then the number of extents in the table is not a factor in the read performance. ORACLE will read each row from its physical location (as specified in the RowID) and retrieve the data.

If the data is read via a full table scan, then the size of your extents can impact performance. When reading data via a full table scan, ORACLE will read multiple blocks at a time. The number of blocks read at a time is set via the DB_FILE_ MULTIBLOCK_READ_COUNT init.ora parameter, and is limited by the operating system's I/O buffer size. For example, if your database block size is 4KB and your operating system's I/O buffer size is 64KB, then you can read up to 16 blocks per read during a full table scan. In that case, setting DB_FILE_MULTIBLOCK_ READ_COUNT to a value higher than 16 will not change the performance of the full table scans.

Your extent sizes should take advantage of ORACLE's ability to perform multiblock reads during full table scans. Thus, if your operating system's I/O buffer is 64KB, then your extent sizes should be a multiple of 64KB.

Consider a table that has ten extents, each of which is 64KB in size. For this example, the operating system's I/O buffer size is 64KB. To perform a full table scan, ORACLE must perform ten reads (since 64KB is the operating system I/O buffer size). If the data is compressed into a single 640KB extent, ORACLE still must perform ten reads to scan the table. Compressing the extents results in no gain in performance.

If the table's extent size is not a multiple of the I/O buffer size, then the number of reads required may increase. For the same 640KB table, you could create eight extents that are 80KB each. To read the first extent, ORACLE will perform two reads: one for the first 64KB of the extent, and a second read for the last 16KB of the extent (reads cannot span extents). To read the whole table, ORACLE must therefore perform two reads per extent, or 16 reads. Reducing the number of extents from ten to eight increased the number of reads by 60 percent!

To avoid paying a performance penalty for your extent sizes, you must therefore choose between one of the following two strategies:

1. Create extents that are significantly larger than your I/O size. If the extents are very large, then very few additional reads will be necessary even if the extent size is not a multiple of the I/O buffer size.

2. Create extents that are a multiple of the I/O buffer size for your operating system.

If the I/O buffer size for your operating system is 64KB, then your pool of extent sizes to choose is 64KB, 128KB, 192KB, 256KB, etc. In the next section, you will see how to further reduce the pool of extent sizes from which to choose.

Maximizing the Reuse of Dropped Extents

When a segment is dropped, its extents are added back to the pool of available free extents. Other segments can then allocate the dropped extents as needed. If you use a consistent set of extent sizes, ORACLE will be more likely to reuse a dropped extent, resulting in more efficient use of the space in the tablespace.

If you use custom sizes for all of your extents, then you will spend more time managing your free space (such as defragmenting tablespaces). For example, if you create a table with an initial extent size of 100KB, then ORACLE will allocate a 100KB extent for the table. When you drop the table, the 100KB extent is marked as a free extent. As noted in Chapter 4, ORACLE will automatically coalesce neighboring free extents if the default **pctincrease** setting for the tablespace is nonzero. For this example, assume that there is no neighboring free extent—the 100KB free extent is surrounded on each side by data extents. When ORACLE tries to allocate space for another segment, it will consider using the 100KB free extent. For example, suppose a new segment requests two extents that are 60KB each. ORACLE may choose to consume the first 60KB of the 100KB free extent for the new segment, leaving a 40KB free extent in its place. As a result, 40 percent of the free space is wasted.

To avoid wasting free space, you should use a set of extent sizes that meets the following criteria: *Every extent size will hold an integral multiple of every smaller extent size.*

Consider the first six values in the set of extent sizes generated earlier:

64KB, 128KB, 192KB, 256KB, 320KB, 384KB

Evaluating these:

■ 64KB is the base value.

■ 128KB holds an even multiple of 64KB extents, so that value is acceptable.

■ 192KB does not hold an even multiple of 128KB extents, so that value is not acceptable.

■ If 192KB is discarded, then 256KB is acceptable.

■ 320KB and 384KB do not hold an even multiple of 256KB extents, so they are not acceptable.

The pattern emerges quickly. Each extent size must be twice the size of the previous extent size. Thus, the acceptable values for extents are as follows:

64KB, 128KB, 256KB, 512KB, 1MB, 2MB, 4MB, 8MB, 16MB, 32MB, etc.

Using those values for extent sizes will eliminate any potential I/O problems and will enhance the likelihood that dropped extents will be reused.

One Last Obstacle

As noted earlier, ORACLE will round the number of blocks allocated to an extent, usually to a multiple of five. For a 4KB block size, the list of acceptable extent sizes (in blocks) is as follows:

16, 32, 64, 128, 256, 512, 1024, 2048, 4096, 8192

None of those values is evenly divisible by five, so ORACLE may round them to:

20, 35, 65, 130, 260, 515, 1025, 2050, 4100, 8195

But that negates the impact of using the proper extent sizes! However, ORACLE may not round those values after all. During its space allocation process, ORACLE searches the tablespace for available free extents to use. If you request a 32-block extent, and ORACLE finds an available 32-block free extent, you may allocate a 32-block extent rather than a 35-block extent. Furthermore, the larger the extent size, the smaller the impact the rounding has on your multiblock read performance.

Estimating Space Requirements for Nonclustered Tables

To estimate the space required by a table, you only need to know four values:

- The database block size

- The **pctfree** value for the table

- The average length of a row

- The expected number of rows in the table

To calculate the exact space requirements for a table, you will need additional information (such as the number of columns). To perform a quick estimate, these four pieces of information are all you need.

The database block size is set via the DB_BLOCK_SIZE parameter in the database's init.ora file. You cannot change the block size of a database once it is created. To increase a database's block size, you would need to completely re-create it (via the **create database** command) and import any data exported from the old database.

Each database block has an area used for overhead within the block. Estimate the block overhead for tables to account for 90 bytes. Therefore, the available space in a block is as follows:

Database Block Size (in bytes)	Available Space (in bytes)
2,048	1,958
4,096	4,006
8,192	8,102

A portion of that available space will be kept free, available for updates of rows previously inserted into the block. The **pctfree** setting for the table sets the size of the free space that is unused during **insert**s. Multiply the available space by the **pctfree** value to determine how much space is unused. Subtract that value from the available space in the block to determine how much space is available to rows.

For example, for a 4KB block size and a table with a **pctfree** setting of 10, the available space is

```
4006 bytes - (0.1*4006 bytes) = 3605.4 bytes, rounded down to 3605 bytes.
```

In every database block in this example, there are 3,605 bytes available for new records.

Next, estimate your average row length. Estimate the length of a DATE value to be 8 bytes, and estimate the length of a NUMBER value to be 4 bytes. For VARCHAR2 columns, estimate the actual length of the values stored in the columns.

NOTE
These estimates incorporate additional column overhead. In reality, a DATE value stores 7 bytes, while a NUMBER value is typically 3 bytes.

For example, you may have a table with 10 columns and an estimated average row length of 60 bytes. Since there are 3,605 bytes available per block (from the previous estimate), the number of rows per block is

```
3605 bytes per block / 60 bytes per row = 6 rows per block.
```

Now, you need to estimate the number of rows you expect in the table. If the sample table will have 25,000 rows, then the number of blocks you need is

```
25,000 rows / 6 rows per block = 4,166 blocks
```

Your table will require approximately 4,166 blocks. However, that does not match any of the extent sizes specified in the previous sections. You have several choices:

1. Create an **initial** extent of 16MB (4,096 blocks) and a **next** extent of 512KB (128 blocks).

2. If space is available and you anticipate further growth in the table, create an **initial** extent of 32MB.

If you use the first option, your space allocation (4,224 blocks) will exceed your estimate (4,166 blocks) by just over 1 percent. By allocating that additional 1 percent, you will be creating a table whose extents are properly sized both for performance and for optimal reuse of free extents.

In the next section, you will see how to estimate space for indexes, followed by detailed space calculations for tables, indexes, and clusters. In general, detailed calculations are unnecessary; using effective estimates and a predetermined set of allowed extent sizes will greatly simplify your space management process.

Estimating Space Requirements for Indexes

The estimation process for indexes parallels the estimation process for tables. The estimation process described in this section does not generate exact space allocation requirements; rather, it enables you to quickly estimate the space requirements and match them to a set of standard extent sizes. To estimate the space required by an index, you only need to know four values:

- The database block size

- The **pctfree** value for the index

- The average length of an index entry

- The expected number of entries in the index

The database block size is set via the DB_BLOCK_SIZE parameter in the database's init.ora file. Each database block has an area used for overhead within the block. Estimate the block overhead for an index to be 161 bytes. Therefore, the available space in a block is as follows:

Database Block Size (in bytes)	Available Space (in bytes)
2,048	1,887
4,096	3,935
8,192	8,031

A portion of that available space will be kept free, based on the **pctfree** setting for the index. However, index values should not be frequently updated. For indexes, **pctfree** is commonly set to a value below 5. Multiply the available space by the **pctfree** value to determine how much space is unused in each block. Subtract that value from the available space in the block to determine how much space is available to index entries.

For example, for a 4KB block size and an index with a **pctfree** setting of 2, the available space is

```
3935 bytes - (0.02*3935 bytes) = 3856.3 bytes, rounded down to 3856 bytes.
```

In every database block in this example, there are 3,856 bytes available for new index entries.

Next, estimate the average row length of an index entry. If the index is a concatenated index, estimate the length of each column's values and add them together to arrive at the total entry length. Estimate the length of a DATE value to be 8 bytes, and estimate the length of a NUMBER value to be 4 bytes. For VARCHAR2 columns, estimate the actual length of the values stored in the columns.

NOTE
These estimates incorporate additional column
overhead. In reality, a DATE value stores 7 bytes,
while a NUMBER value is typically 3 bytes.

For example, you may have an index with three columns and an estimated average row length of 17 bytes. Since there are 3,856 bytes available per block (from the previous estimate), the number of entries per block is

```
3856 bytes per block / 17 bytes per entry = 226 entries per block.
```

Now, you need to estimate the number of entries you expect in the index. If the sample index will have 25,000 entries, then the number of blocks you need is

```
25,000 rows / 226 entries per block = 111 blocks
```

Your index will require approximately 111 blocks. However, that size (444KB) does not match any of the extent sizes specified in the previous sections. You have several choices:

1. Create an **initial** extent of 256KB and a **next** extent of 64KB, specifying **minextents** 4 and **pctincrease** 0 (112 blocks).

2. If space is available and you anticipate further growth in the table, create an **initial** extent of 512KB (128 blocks).

If you use the first option, your space allocation (112 blocks) will exceed your estimate (111 blocks) by just one block. If you use the second option, you will allocate 13 percent more space than your estimate. By following either of these options, you will be creating an index whose extents are properly sized both for performance and for optimal reuse of free extents.

In the following sections, you will see detailed calculations for the space requirements for tables, indexes, and clusters. You can use these more detailed calculations to validate any of your estimates; before using the detailed methods, go through the estimation process. Regardless of the space estimate you use, be sure your extent sizes conform to the standard extent sizes you establish for your database.

A Note About Approximations

In the formulas provided by ORACLE, there are a number of extremely detailed calculations you must perform in order to size your tables and indexes. The level of detail required in those calculations is unnecessary, since the calculations conclude with the advice to add 10 to 20 percent to the calculated space requirements.

Why make a detailed calculation if you know ahead of time that it will be wrong by at least 10 percent?

The error in the space estimation is caused by the way ORACLE manages space after the objects have been created. As you **insert**, **update**, and **delete** rows, ORACLE manages the space inside the database blocks. Because of the manner in which ORACLE manages the space, your space usage will frequently be less than optimal. As a result, your space needs will increase—in some cases they may double.

Given the dynamic nature of the space management in ORACLE, the precise space calculations provided are only valid if you are loading static data into static tables. Since that represents a small percentage of the tables whose space usage is of a great concern, the calculations in this chapter approximate the space usage rather than carry out extremely detailed calculations. In all cases, the difference between the exact calculation and the approximation should be less than 5 percent—well within the bounds set by ORACLE.

Calculating Size Requirements for Nonclustered Tables

In addition to showing the initial space requirements for a table, the space requirements deliverable should show the estimated yearly percentage increase in number of records for each table. If applicable, you should also define the maximum number of records per table.

Once you know the table's column definitions and data volumes, its storage requirements can be calculated. This is a process of educated guessing, since the true data volumes and row lengths will not be known until after the table is created. It is important that sample data be available during the size calculation process in order to make the results of these calculations as accurate as possible.

First, estimate the amount of space used by the block header; this is space that ORACLE will use to manage the data within the block. The size of the block header is approximately 90 bytes. If you use a 2KB database block size, this leaves 1,958 bytes free; for a 4KB block size, this leaves 4,006 bytes free.

```
4096 - 90 = 4006 bytes available.
```

Next, factor in the table's **pctfree** setting, and multiply that by the free space to determine how much space will be kept free for row updates.

If you use a **pctfree** value of 10, then multiply the available free space by 0.10, as shown in the following listing:

```
4006*(pctfree/100) = 4006*0.1 = 401 (rounded up)
```

Of the available free space, 401 bytes will be kept for row extensions. The available free space is the block free space minus the space kept by **pctfree**.

```
4006 - 401 = 3605 bytes available.
```

Of the 4,096 bytes in the block, 3,605 bytes are available to store rows (see Figure 5-1).

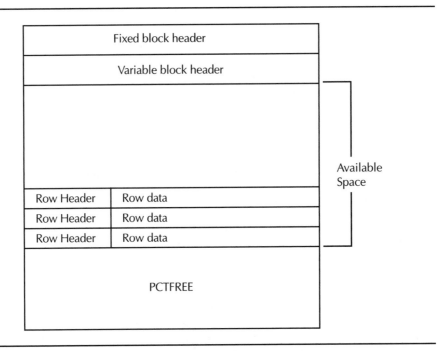

FIGURE 5-1. *Space allocation within blocks*

The next step is to calculate the space used per row. To estimate the space used per row, you need to estimate the *average row length*. The average row length is the total of the average length of each value in a row. If no data is available, then estimate the actual length of the values in a column. Do not use the full length of a column as its actual length unless the data will always completely fill the column.

For example, consider a table containing three columns, all of which are VARCHAR2(10). The average row length cannot exceed 30; its actual length depends on the data that will be stored there.

If the sample data is available, then you can use the **VSIZE** function to determine the actual space used by the data. Again, assume a table has three columns. To determine its average row length, perform the following query:

```
select AVG(NVL(VSIZE(Column1),0))+
       AVG(NVL(VSIZE(Column2),0))+
       AVG(NVL(VSIZE(Column3),0))    Avg_Row_Length
from TABLENAME;
```

In this example, the average length of each column is determined, and the averages are totaled to determine the average row length.

If the table is large, the preceding query may take a long time to execute. As an alternative, you can analyze the table as follows:

```
analyze table TABLENAME compute statistics;
```

For large tables, you can use the **estimate statistics** clause, as shown here:

```
analyze table TABLENAME estimate statistics;
```

Once the table is analyzed, you can select the statistics from the data dictionary, as shown below:

```
select Avg_Row_Len
  from USER_TABLES
 where Table_Name = 'TABLENAME';
```

The Avg_Row_Len value contains the additional bytes used for row overhead such as column headers.

For the sample three-column table, assume that the average row length is 24 bytes. To that total, add 1 byte for each column in the table, for a total of 27 bytes per row. If the table has columns that contain data that is more than 250 characters long, add an extra byte for each such column. Finally, add 3 bytes for the row header.

```
Space used per row = Avg_Row_Length
                   + 3
                   + Number of columns
                   + Number of long columns
```

For the example table, the space per row is

```
Space used per row = 24
                   +3
                   +3
                   +0
                   = 30 bytes per row.
```

Given 3,605 bytes available and 30 bytes per row, you can fit 120 rows in a block.

```
rows per block = TRUNC(3605 free bytes/30 bytes per row)
               = 120 rows per block
```

Since you can fit 120 rows per block, you can estimate the number of blocks needed as soon as you can estimate the number of rows you expect. As noted in the previous section, this is an approximation of the storage requirements of the table. As records in the table are manipulated, their space requirements will increase. The greater the number of **delete**s and **update**s that occur, the greater the amount of space required.

Calculating the Proper pctfree

The proper **pctfree** value must be determined for each table. This value represents the percentage of *each data block* that is reserved as free space. This space is used when a row that has already been stored in that data block grows in length, either by updates of previously **NULL** fields or by updates of existing values to longer values.

There is no single value for **pctfree** that will be adequate for all tables in all databases. But since **pctfree** is tied to the way in which updates occur in an application, determining the adequacy of its setting is a straightforward process. The **pctfree** setting controls the number of records that are stored in a block in a table. To see if **pctfree** has been set correctly, first determine the number of rows in a block. As shown in the preceding section, you can use the **analyze** command to measure row allocation in an existing table. In the following listing, the **compute statistics** clause of the **analyze** command is used to generate statistics for the table; you can then select those statistics from the data dictionary views.

```
analyze table TABLENAME compute statistics;
```

NOTE
*If you are using the rule-based optimizer, delete the statistics after you have calculated the **pctfree** value.*

Once the table has been analyzed, query its record in the USER_TABLES view and record its Num_Rows and Blocks values. Dividing Num_Rows by Blocks yields the number of rows stored per block, as shown in the following query:

```
select Num_Rows,              /*number of rows*/
       Blocks,                /*number of blocks used*/
       Num_Rows/Blocks        /*number of rows per block*/
  from USER_TABLES
 where Table_Name='TABLENAME';
```

Once the number of rows per block is known, **update** records in the table in a manner that mimics its production usage. Once the **update**s are complete, check the number of rows per block by analyzing the table and rerunning these queries. If

pctfree was not set high enough, then some of the rows may have been moved to new data blocks to accommodate their new lengths. If the number of blocks has not changed, then the **pctfree** value is adequate.

NOTE
*When rows are moved due to inadequate space in the **pctfree** area, the move is called a row migration. Row migration will impact the performance of your transactions.*

This **pctfree** value, though, may be too high, resulting in wasted space. The **analyze** command shown earlier also generates values for the Avg_Space column of the USER_TABLES view. This column shows the average number of bytes that are free in each data block. If this value is high after the **update** test, then the **pctfree** value can be decreased.

Determining the Proper pctused

The **pctused** value determines when a used block is re-added to the list of blocks into which rows can be inserted. For example, consider a table that has a **pctfree** value of 20 and a **pctused** value of 50. When rows are inserted into the table, ORACLE will keep 20 percent of each block free (for use by later **update**s of the **insert**ed records). If you now begin to **delete** records from the block, ORACLE will not automatically reuse the freed space inside the blocks. New rows will not be **insert**ed into the block until the block's used space falls below its **pctused** percentage—50 percent.

The **pctused** value, by default, is set to 40. If your application features frequent deletions, and you use the default value for **pctused**, then you may have many blocks in your table that are only 40 percent used.

For best results, set **pctused** so that **pctused** plus **pctfree** equals 85. If your **pctfree** setting is 20 percent, then set your **pctused** value to 65 percent. That way, at least 65 percent of each block will be used, saving 20 percent of the block for **update**s and row extensions.

Calculating Index Sizes

The process of sizing indexes is very similar to the table sizing process described previously. There are several differences in the object sizing, since tables and indexes have differing structures. As with the table space estimates, the sizing calculations provided here are approximations.

Once you know an index's column definitions and data volumes, its space requirements can be calculated. This is a process of educated guessing, since the true data volumes and row lengths will not be known until after the table is created. It is important that sample data be available at this point in order to make the results of these calculations as accurate as possible.

First, estimate the amount of space used by the block header; this is space that ORACLE will use to manage the data within the block. The size of the block header is approximately 161 bytes. If you use a 4KB database block size, this leaves 3,935 bytes free.

```
4096 - 161 = 3935 bytes available.
```

Next, factor in the table's **pctfree** setting, and multiply that by the free space to determine how much space will be kept free for row **update**s.

If you use a **pctfree** value of 5, then multiply the available free space by 0.05, as shown in the following listing:

```
3935*(pctfree/100) = 3935*0.05 = 197 (rounded up)
```

Of the available free space, 197 bytes will be kept for entry extensions. The available free space is the block free space minus the space kept by **pctfree**.

```
3935 - 197 = 3738 bytes available.
```

Of the 4,096 bytes in the block, 3,738 bytes are available to store index entries.

The next step is to calculate the space used per entry. To estimate the space used per entry, you need to estimate the *average row length of the columns in the index*. For tables, you calculate the average row length of all columns; for indexes, you only need to be concerned about the indexed columns. The average row length is the total of the average length of each value in the indexed columns. If no data is available, then estimate the actual length of the values. Do not use the full length of a column as its actual length unless the data will always completely fill the column.

For example, consider an index containing two columns, both of which are VARCHAR2(10). The average indexed row length cannot exceed 20; its actual length depends on the data that will be stored there.

If the sample data is available, then you can use the **VSIZE** function to determine the actual space used by the data. Again, assume an index has two columns. To determine its average row length, perform the following query:

```
select AVG(NVL(VSIZE(Column1),0))+
       AVG(NVL(VSIZE(Column2),0))   Avg_Row_Length
from TABLENAME;
```

In this example, the average length of each column is determined and the averages are totaled to determine the average row length.

For example, in the sample two-column index, assume that the average row length for the indexed columns is 16 bytes. To that total, add 1 byte for each column in the index, for a total of 18 bytes per row. If the index has columns that contain data that is more than 127 characters long, add an extra byte for each such column. Finally, add 8 bytes for the index entry header.

```
Space used per row = Avg_Row_Length
                    + Number of columns
                    + Number of long columns
                    + 8 header bytes
```

For the example index, the space per row is

```
Space used per row = 16
                    +2
                    +0
                    +8
                    = 26 bytes per index entry.
```

If the index is a unique index, add 1 to this total.

```
26 + 1 = 27 bytes per row
```

Given 3,738 bytes available and 27 bytes per row, you can fit 138 index entries in a block.

```
entries per block = TRUNC(3738 free bytes/
                        27 bytes per entry)
                    = 138 entries per block
```

Since you can fit 138 index entries per block, you can estimate the number of blocks needed as soon as you can estimate the number of rows you expect. As noted previously, this is an approximation of the storage requirements of the table. As records in the table are manipulated, their space requirements will increase. The greater the number of **delete**s and **update**s that occur, the greater the amount of space required.

Deleted space within indexes is seldom reused, so indexes may grow even if the table does not. For example, if you **delete** 100 rows from the table and then **insert** 100 new rows, the table may use the freed space from the **delete**d records for the **insert**ed records, and its space usage will remain constant. The table's index, however, will most likely not be able to reuse the space freed by the **delete**d records, so its space usage will increase.

Calculating Sizes for Clustered Tables

Clusters are used to store data from different tables in the same physical data blocks. They are appropriate to use if the records from those tables are frequently queried together. By storing them in the same data blocks, the number of database block reads needed to fulfill such queries decreases, thereby improving performance. They may have a negative performance impact on data manipulation transactions and on queries that only reference one of the tables in the cluster.

Because of their unique structure, clustered tables have different storage requirements than nonclustered tables. Each cluster stores the tables' data, as well as maintaining a *cluster index* that it uses to sort the data.

The columns within the cluster index are called the *cluster key*—the set of columns that the tables in the cluster have in common. Since the cluster key columns determine the physical placement of rows within the cluster, they should not be subject to frequent **update**s. The cluster key is usually the foreign key of one table that references the primary key of another table in the cluster.

After the cluster has been created, the cluster index is created on the cluster key columns. After the cluster key index has been created, data can then be entered into the tables stored in the cluster. As rows are **insert**ed, the database will store a cluster key and its associated rows in each of the cluster's blocks.

> **NOTE**
> *Because of their complex structure, the sizing of clusters is more complex than that of either indexes or tables, even when using this simplified method.*

Sizing a cluster thus involves elements of table sizing and index sizing. For this example, consider the table used in the previous sections: a three-column table, each column of which has a datatype and length of VARCHAR2(10). If this table is very frequently joined to another table, then it may be appropriate to cluster the two tables together. For the purposes of this example, assume that the second table has two columns: a VARCHAR2(10) column and a VARCHAR2(5) column, the former of which is used to join the tables together.

Since the two tables are joined using the VARCHAR2(10) column that they have in common, that column will be the cluster key.

First, estimate the amount of space used by the block header; this is space that ORACLE will use to manage the data within the block. The size of the cluster block header is approximately 110 bytes. If you use a 2KB database block size, this leaves 1,938 bytes free; for a 4KB block size, this leaves 3,986 bytes free.

 `2048 - 110 = 1938 bytes available.`

Next, factor in the cluster's **pctfree** setting and multiply that by the free space to determine how much space will be kept free for row **update**s.

If you use a **pctfree** value of 10, then multiply the available free space by 0.10, as shown in the following listing:

`1938*(pctfree/100) = 1938*0.1 = 194 (rounded up)`

Of the available free space, 194 bytes will be kept for row extensions. The available free space is the block free space minus the space kept by **pctfree**.

```
1938 - 194 = 1744 bytes available.
```

Next, subtract the header space needed for table header entries. The buffer space is four times the number of tables, plus 4 bytes. For a two-table cluster, the available free space will now be

```
bytes available = 1744 bytes available
                  - 4 bytes
                  - 4*number of tables

                = 1744
                  - 4
                  - 8

                = 1732 bytes available
```

Of the 2,048 bytes in the block, 1,732 bytes are available to store cluster entries. Next, calculate the space required for a single row in each of the tables, excluding the length due to the column(s) in the cluster key.

If the sample data is available, then the **VSIZE** function can be used to determine the actual space used by the data. Again, assume a table has three columns and a second table has two columns. To determine the average row length, perform the following query:

```
select AVG(NVL(VSIZE(Column1),0))+
       AVG(NVL(VSIZE(Column2),0))    Avg_Row_Length_1
from TABLE1;

select AVG(NVL(VSIZE(Column1),0))    Avg_Row_Length_2
from TABLE2;
```

In this example, the average length of each column that is not in the cluster key is determined, and the averages are totaled to determine the average row length. This example assumes that the cluster key is Column3 in TABLE1 and Column2 in TABLE2.

For this example, assume the average row length for TABLE1's nonclustered columns will be 20, and the average row length for TABLE2's nonclustered column is 3.

```
Average row length = 23 bytes
```

Each row in the cluster has *row header* information stored with it. The total row space requirements, including the header space requirements, are calculated via the following formula. In the formula, a "long" column is one in which the data value is more than 250 characters long. This distinction is necessary because of the number of length bytes that the database must store for the values.

```
Row header space = 4 bytes
                   + number of columns
                   + number of long columns
```

Combining the average row length with the row header space yields

```
Space used per row = average row length + row header space
         = 23 + 4 + number of columns + number of long columns
         = 23 + 4 + 3 + 0
         = 30 bytes
```

Thus, each cluster entry will require 30 bytes. This space does not take into account the space requirements of the cluster index.

The next step in the cluster sizing process is to determine the value of the **size** parameter, which is unique to clusters. The **size** parameter is the estimated number of bytes required by a cluster key and its associated rows.

The **size** parameter is dependent on the distribution of the data. That is, how many rows are there in a table for each distinct value in the cluster key? To determine these values, query the clustered tables and divide the number of records in the table by the number of distinct cluster key values.

```
select
    COUNT(DISTINCT(column name))/    /* Num of records in table*/
    COUNT(*)  rows_per_key           /* Num of cluster key values*/
from tablename;
```

For this example, assume that in TABLE1 there are 30 rows per cluster key value. In TABLE2, there is one row per cluster key value for this example.

The **size** parameter also needs to know the average length of the cluster key value. Query the clustered tables using the **VSIZE** query shown previously. Since it should be the same in both tables (via referential integrity), only one table has to be queried.

```
select
    AVG(NVL(VSIZE(cluster key column),0)) Avg_Key_Length
 from TABLE1;
```

For this example, assume that the average key column value is 5 bytes.

The value for **size** can now be calculated.

```
SIZE=
   (Rows per cluster key in Table1*Average row size for Table1)+
   (Rows per cluster key in Table2*Average row size for Table2)+
   cluster key header+
   column length of the cluster key+
   average length of cluster key+
   2*(Rows per cluster key in Table1+Rows per cluster key in
   Table2+ Rows per cluster key for any other tables in the cluster)
```

The "cluster key header" is 19 bytes in length. Thus, for the example data,

```
SIZE      = (30 rows per key in Table1*20 bytes per row)+
      (1 row per key in Table2*3 bytes per row)+
      19  bytes for the cluster key header+
      10  bytes for the column length of the cluster key+
      5   bytes for the average length of the cluster key+
      2*(30 rows+1 row)
   = (30*20)+(1*3)+19+10+5+(2*31)
   = 600+3+19+10+5+62
   = 699 bytes
```

Thus, each cluster key will require 699 bytes, rounded up to 700 bytes. This will be placed in the available space in the block. The available space was earlier calculated to be 1,732 bytes. The number of cluster keys per block is

```
cluster keys per block = free space /(SIZE + 42)
                       = 1732/(700+42)
                       = 1732/742
                       = 2 (rounded down)
```

Each database block can store the values for two cluster keys.

Since each block can store values for two cluster keys, the number of blocks required for the cluster is one-half the number of cluster key values. That is, if there are 40 distinct values of the cluster key, then you will need to allocate 20 blocks for the cluster.

Sizing Functional Indexes

As of Oracle8i, you can create *functional indexes*. For example, you can create an index on **UPPER**(Name) instead of just Name. Functional indexes significantly enhance your query tuning capabilities. When sizing a functional index, follow the same method used to size a standard index, as shown in the prior sections of this chapter.

Reverse Key Indexes

In ORACLE8, you can create an index and specify the parameter **reverse** to have the bytes in the index block stored in the reverse order. As of ORACLE8i, you can create *reverse key indexes*. In a reverse key index, the values are stored backwards—for example, a value of 2201 is stored as 1022. If you use a standard index, then consecutive values are stored near each other. In a reverse key index, consecutive values are not stored near each other. If your queries do not commonly perform range scans, and you are concerned about I/O contention in your indexes, reverse key indexes may be a tuning solution to consider. When sizing a reverse key index, follow the same method used to size a standard index, as shown in the prior sections of this chapter.

Sizing Bitmap Indexes

If you create a bitmap index, then ORACLE will dynamically compress the bitmaps generated. The compression of the bitmap may result in substantial storage savings. To estimate the size of a bitmap index, estimate the size of a standard (B*-tree) index on the same columns using the formulas provided in the preceding sections of this chapter. After calculating the space requirements for the B*-tree index, divide that size by 10 to determine the size of a bitmap index for those columns. In general, bitmap indexes will be between 5 and 10 percent of the size of a comparable B*-tree index.

Sizing Index-Organized Tables

An index-organized table is stored sorted by its primary key. The space requirements of an index-organized table closely mirror those of an index on all of the table's columns. The difference in space estimation comes in calculating the space used per row, since an index-organized table does not have RowIDs.

For an index-organized table, the space used per row calculation reflects the reduction of the header bytes from 8 bytes to 2.

```
Space used per row = Avg_Row_Length
                   + Number of columns
                   + Number of long columns
                   + 2 header bytes
```

Sizing Tables That Contain Large Objects (LOBs)

LOB data (in BLOB or CLOB datatypes) is usually stored apart from the main table. You can use the **lob** clause of the **create table** command to specify the storage for the LOB data. In the main table, ORACLE stores a **lob** locator value that points to the LOB data. Estimate a length of 24 bytes for the **lob** locator value.

ORACLE does not always store the LOB data apart from the main table. In general, the LOB data is not stored apart from the main table until the LOB data exceeds 4KB in length. Therefore, if you will be storing short LOB values, you need to consider its impact on the storage of your main table. If your LOB values are less than 4,000 characters, you may be able to use VARCHAR2 datatypes instead of LOB datatypes for the data storage.

Sizing Partitions

As of ORACLE8, you can create multiple *partitions* of a table. In a partitioned table, multiple separate physical partitions constitute the table. For example, a SALES table may have four partitions: SALES_NORTH, SALES_SOUTH, SALES_EAST, and SALES_WEST. You should size each of those partitions using the table sizing methods described earlier in this chapter. You should size the partition indexes using the index sizing methods shown earlier in this chapter. See Chapter 12 for further details on partition management.

Sizing Tables Based on Abstract Datatypes

ORACLE introduced object-relational structures into the database in ORACLE8. Of these new structures, the two most critical features are *abstract datatypes* and *constructor methods*. Abstract datatypes define the structure of data—for example, an ADDRESS_TY datatype may contain attributes for address data, along with methods for manipulating that data. When you create the ADDRESS_TY datatype, ORACLE will automatically create a constructor method called ADDRESS_TY. The ADDRESS_TY constructor method contains parameters that match the datatype's attributes, facilitating **insert**s of new values into the datatype's format. In the following sections, you will see how to create tables that use abstract datatypes, along with information on the sizing and security issues associated with that implementation.

As of ORACLE8, you can create tables that use abstract datatypes for their column definitions. For example, you could create an abstract datatype for addresses, as shown here:

```
create type ADDRESS_TY as object
(Street   VARCHAR2(50),
City      VARCHAR2(25),
State     CHAR(2),
Zip       NUMBER);
/
```

Once the ADDRESS_TY datatype has been created, you can use it as a datatype when creating your tables, as shown in the following listing:

```
create table CUSTOMER
(Name      VARCHAR2(25),
Address    ADDRESS_TY);
```

When you create an abstract datatype, ORACLE creates a *constructor method* for use during **insert**s. The constructor method has the same name as the datatype, and its parameters are the attributes of the datatype. When you **insert** records into the CUSTOMER table, you need to use the ADDRESS_TY datatype's constructor method to **insert** Address values.

```
insert into CUSTOMER values
('Joe',ADDRESS_TY('My Street', 'Some City', 'ST', 10001));
```

In this example, the **insert** command calls the ADDRESS_TY constructor method in order to insert values into the attributes of the ADDRESS_TY datatype.

The use of abstract datatypes increases the space requirements of your tables by 8 bytes for each datatype used. If a datatype contains another datatype, then you should add 8 bytes for each of the datatypes.

Using Object Views

The use of abstract datatypes may increase the complexity of your development environment. When you query the attributes of an abstract datatype, you must use a syntax that is not used against tables that do not contain abstract datatypes. If you do not implement abstract datatypes in all of your tables, you will need to use one syntax for some of your tables and a separate syntax for other tables—and you will need to know ahead of time which queries use abstract datatypes.

For example, the CUSTOMER table uses the ADDRESS_TY datatype described in the previous section.

```
create table CUSTOMER
(Name      VARCHAR2(25),
Address    ADDRESS_TY);
```

The ADDRESS_TY datatype, in turn, has four attributes: Street, City, State, and Zip. If you want to select the Street attribute value from the Address column of the CUSTOMER table, you may write the following query:

```
select Address.Street from CUSTOMER;
```

However, that query *will not work*. When you query the attributes of abstract datatypes, you must use correlation variables for the table names. Otherwise, there may be an ambiguity regarding the object being selected. To query the Street attribute, use a correlation variable (in this case, "C") for the CUSTOMER table, as shown in the following listing:

```
select C.Address.Street from CUSTOMER  C;
```

As shown in this example, you need to use correlation variables for queries of abstract datatype attributes *even if the query only accesses one table*. There are therefore two nonstandard features of queries against abstract datatype attributes:

the notation used to access the attributes and the correlation variables requirement. In order to implement abstract datatypes consistently, you may need to alter your SQL standards to support 100 percent usage of correlation variables. Even if you use correlation variables consistently, the notation required to access attribute values may cause problems as well, since you cannot use a similar notation on tables that do not use abstract datatypes.

Object views provide an effective compromise solution to this inconsistency. The CUSTOMER table created in the previous examples assumed that an ADDRESS_TY datatype already existed. But what if your tables already exist? What if you had previously created a relational database application and are trying to implement object-relational concepts in your application without rebuilding and re-creating the entire application? What you would need is the ability to overlay object-oriented (OO) structures such as abstract datatypes on existing relational tables. ORACLE provides *object views* as a means for defining objects used by existing relational tables.

If the CUSTOMER table already existed, you could create the ADDRESS_TY datatype and use object views to relate it to the CUSTOMER table. In the following listing, the CUSTOMER table is created as a relational table, using only the normally provided datatypes:

```
create table CUSTOMER
(Name          VARCHAR2(25) primary key,
 Street        VARCHAR2(50),
 City          VARCHAR2(25),
 State         CHAR(2),
 Zip           NUMBER);
```

If you want to create another table or application that stores information about people and addresses, you may choose to create the ADDRESS_TY datatype. However, for consistency, that datatype should be applied to the CUSTOMER table as well. The following examples will use the ADDRESS_TY datatype created in the previous section.

You can create an object view based on the CUSTOMER table, using any datatype you have defined. To create an object view, use the **create view** command. Within the **create view** command, specify the query that will form the basis of the view. The code for creating the CUSTOMER_OV object view is shown in the following listing:

```
create view CUSTOMER_OV (Name, Address) as
select Name,
       ADDRESS_TY(Street, City, State, Zip)
  from CUSTOMER;
```

The CUSTOMER_OV view will have two columns: the Name and the Address columns (the latter is defined by the ADDRESS_TY datatype). Note that you cannot specify **object** as an option within the **create view** command.

There are several important syntax issues presented in this example. When a table is built upon existing abstract datatypes, you select column values from the table by referring to the names of the columns (such as Name) instead of their constructor methods. When creating the object view, however, you refer to the names of the *constructor* methods (such as ADDRESS_TY) instead. Also, you can use **where** clauses in the query that forms the basis of the object view. You can therefore limit the rows that are accessible via the object view.

If you use object views, then you as the DBA will administer relational tables the same way as you did before. You will still need to manage the privileges for the datatypes (see the next section of this chapter for information on security management of abstract datatypes), but the table and index structures will be the same as they were before the creation of the abstract datatypes. Using the old structures will simplify your administration tasks while allowing developers to access objects via the object views of the tables.

You can also use object views to simulate the references used by row objects. Row objects are rows within an object table. To create an object view that supports row objects, you need to first create a datatype that has the same structure as the table.

```
create or replace type CUSTOMER_TY as object
(Name        VARCHAR2(25),
 Street      VARCHAR2(50),
 City        VARCHAR2(25),
 State       CHAR(2),
 Zip         NUMBER);
/
```

Next, create an object view based on the CUSTOMER_TY type, while assigning OID (object identifier) values to the records in CUSTOMER.

```
create view CUSTOMER_OV of CUSTOMER_TY
   with object OID (Name) as
select Name, Street, City, State, Zip
  from CUSTOMER;
```

The first part of this **create view** command gives the view its name (CUSTOMER_OV) and tells ORACLE that the view's structure is based on the CUSTOMER_TY datatype. An OID is an object identifier (for a row object). In this object view, the Name column will be used as the OID.

If you have a second table that references CUSTOMER via a foreign key/primary key relationship, then you can set up an object view that contains references to

CUSTOMER_OV. For example, the CUSTOMER_CALL table contains a foreign key to the CUSTOMER table, as shown here:

```
create table CUSTOMER_CALL
(Name            VARCHAR2(25),
 Call_Number    NUMBER,
 Call_Date      DATE,
 constraint CUSTOMER_CALL_PK
     primary key (Name, Call_Number),
 constraint CUSTOMER_CALL_FK foreign key (Name)
    references CUSTOMER(Name));
```

The Name column of CUSTOMER_CALL references the same column in the CUSTOMER table. Since you have simulated OIDs (called pkOIDs) based on the primary key of CUSTOMER, you need to create references to those OIDs. ORACLE provides an operator called **MAKE_REF** that creates the references (called pkREFs). In the following listing, the **MAKE_REF** operator is used to create references from the object view of CUSTOMER_CALL to the object view of CUSTOMER:

```
create view CUSTOMER_CALL_OV as
select MAKE_REF(CUSTOMER_OV, Name) Name,
       Call_Number,
       Call_Date
  from CUSTOMER_CALL;
```

Within the CUSTOMER_CALL_OV view, you tell ORACLE the name of the view to reference and the columns that constitute the pkREF. You could now query CUSTOMER_OV data from within CUSTOMER_CALL_OV by using the DEREF operator on the Customer_ID column.

```
select DEREF(CCOV.Name)
   from CUSTOMER_CALL_OV CCOV
 where Call_Date = TRUNC(SysDate);
```

You can thus return CUSTOMER data from your query without directly querying the CUSTOMER table. In this example, the Call_Date column is used as a limiting condition for the rows returned by the query.

Whether you use row objects or column objects, you can use object views to shield your tables from the object relationships. The tables are not modified; you administer them the way you always did. The difference is that the users can now access the rows of CUSTOMER as if they are row objects.

Sizing Object Tables and REFs

When you create an object table, ORACLE generates an OID value for each of the rows in the table. An OID (Object ID) value adds 16 bytes to the average row length. When you create a table that has a reference to an object table, that table will contain a column with a REF datatype. When estimating the space requirements for a table, estimate the length of the REF datatype column to be 16 bytes.

Security for Abstract Datatypes

The examples in the previous sections assumed that the same user owned the ADDRESS_TY datatype and the CUSTOMER table. What if the owner of the datatype is not the table owner? What if another user wants to create a datatype based on a datatype you have created? In the development environment, you should establish guidelines for the ownership and use of abstract datatypes.

For example, what if the account named DORA owns the ADDRESS_TY datatype, and the user of the account named GEORGE tries to create a PERSON_TY datatype? GEORGE executes the following command:

```
create type PERSON_TY as object
(Name     VARCHAR2(25),
 Address  ADDRESS_TY);
/
```

If GEORGE does not own the ADDRESS_TY abstract datatype, then ORACLE will respond to this **create type** command with the following message:

```
Warning: Type created with compilation errors.
```

The compilation errors are caused by problems creating the constructor method when the datatype is created. ORACLE cannot resolve the reference to the ADDRESS_TY datatype since GEORGE does not own a datatype with that name. He could issue the **create type** command again (using the **or replace** clause) to specifically reference DORA's ADDRESS_TY datatype.

```
create or replace type PERSON_TY as object
(Name     VARCHAR2(25),
 Address  Dora.ADDRESS_TY);
/

Warning: Type created with compilation errors.
```

To see the errors associated with the datatype creation, use the **show errors** command, as shown below:

```
show errors
Errors for TYPE PERSON_TY:
```

```
LINE/COL ERROR
-------- ------------------------------------------------------------
0/0      PL/SQL: Compilation unit analysis terminated
3/11     PLS-00201: identifier 'DORA.ADDRESS_TY' must be declared
```

GEORGE will not be able to create the PERSON_TY datatype (which includes the ADDRESS_TY datatype) unless DORA first **grant**s him EXECUTE privilege on her type. The following listing shows this **grant**:

```
grant EXECUTE on ADDRESS_TY to George;
```

Now that the proper **grant**s are in place, GEORGE can create a datatype that is based on DORA's ADDRESS_TY datatype.

```
create or replace type PERSON_TY as object
(Name      VARCHAR2(25),
 Address   Dora.ADDRESS_TY);
/
```

GEORGE's PERSON_TY datatype will now be successfully created. However, using datatypes based on another user's datatypes is not trivial. For example, during **insert** operations, you must fully specify the name of the owner of each type. GEORGE can create a table based on his PERSON_TY datatype (which includes DORA's ADDRESS_TY datatype), as shown in the following listing:

```
create table GEORGE_CUSTOMERS
(Customer_ID  NUMBER,
 Person       PERSON_TY);
```

If GEORGE owned PERSON_TY and ADDRESS_TY datatypes, then an **insert** into CUSTOMER would use the format:

```
insert into GEORGE_CUSTOMERS values
(1,PERSON_TY('SomeName',
   ADDRESS_TY('StreetValue','CityValue','ST',11111)));
```

Since GEORGE does not own the ADDRESS_TY datatype, this command will fail. During the **insert**, the ADDRESS_TY constructor method is used, and DORA owns it. Therefore, the **insert** command must be modified to specify DORA as the owner of ADDRESS_TY. The following example shows the corrected **insert** statement, with the reference to DORA shown in bold:

```
insert into GEORGE_CUSTOMERS values
(1,PERSON_TY('SomeName',
   Dora.ADDRESS_TY('StreetValue','CityValue','ST',11111)));
```

Can GEORGE use a synonym for DORA's datatype? No. GEORGE *can* create a synonym named ADDRESS_TY:

```
create synonym ADDRESS_TY for Dora.ADDRESS_TY;
```

but this synonym *cannot* be used:

```
create type PERSON2_TY as object
(Name      VARCHAR2(25),
 Address   ADDRESS_TY);
/

create type PERSON2_TY as object
*
ERROR at line 1:
ORA-22863: synonym for datatype DORA.ADDRESS_TY not allowed
```

As shown by the error message, you cannot use a synonym for another user's datatype. Therefore, you will need to refer to the datatype's owner during each **insert** command.

NOTE
When you create a synonym, ORACLE does not check the validity of the object for which you are creating a synonym. If you **create synonym x for y,** *ORACLE does not check to make sure that "y" is a valid object name or valid object type. The validation of that object's accessibility via synonyms is only checked when the object is accessed via the synonym.*

In a relational-only implementation of ORACLE, you grant the EXECUTE privilege on procedural objects, such as procedures and packages. Within the object-relational implementation of ORACLE, the EXECUTE privilege is extended to cover abstract datatypes as well. The EXECUTE privilege is used because abstract datatypes can include *methods*—PL/SQL functions and procedures that operate on the datatype. If you grant someone the privilege to use your datatype, you are granting the user the privilege to execute the methods you have defined on the datatype. Therefore, the proper privilege to grant is EXECUTE. Although DORA did not yet define any methods on the ADDRESS_TY datatype, ORACLE automatically creates special procedures called constructor methods that are used to access the data. Any object (such as PERSON_TY) that uses the ADDRESS_TY datatype uses the constructor method associated with ADDRESS_TY. So, even if you haven't created any methods for your abstract datatype, there are still procedures associated with it.

You cannot create public types, and you cannot create public synonyms for your types. Therefore, you will need to either reference the owner of the type or create the type under each account that can create tables in your database. Neither of these is a simple solution to the problem of datatype management.

Indexing Abstract Datatype Attributes

In the preceding example, the GEORGE_CUSTOMERS table was created based on a PERSON_TY datatype and an ADDRESS_TY datatype. As shown in the following listing, the GEORGE_CUSTOMERS table contains a normal column—Customer_ID—and a Person column that is defined by the PERSON_TY abstract datatype:

```
create table GEORGE_CUSTOMERS
(Customer_ID    NUMBER,
 Person         PERSON_TY);
```

From the datatype definitions shown in the previous section of this chapter, you can see that PERSON_TY has one column—Name—followed by an Address column defined by the ADDRESS_TY datatype.

When referencing columns within the abstract datatypes during queries, **update**s, and **delete**s, specify the full path to the datatype attributes. For example, the following query returns the Customer_ID column along with the Name column. The Name column is an attribute of the datatype that defines the Person column, so you refer to the attribute as Person.Name.

```
select C.Customer_ID, C.Person.Name
   from GEORGE_CUSTOMERS C;
```

You can refer to attributes within the ADDRESS_TY datatype by specifying the full path through the related columns. For example, the Street column is referred to as Person.Address.Street, which fully describes its location within the structure of the table. In the following example, the City column is referenced twice—once in the list of columns to select and once within the **where** clause.

```
select C.Person.Name,
       C.Person.Address.City
  from GEORGE_CUSTOMERS C
 where C.Person.Address.City like 'C%';
```

Because the City column is used with a range search in the **where** clause, the ORACLE optimizer may be able to use an index when resolving the query. If an index is available on the City column, then ORACLE can quickly find all of the rows that have City values starting with the letter 'F' as requested by the query.

To create an index on a column that is part of an abstract datatype, you need to specify the full path to the column as part of the **create index** command. To create an index on the City column (which is part of the Address column), you can execute the following command:

```
create index I_GEORGE_CUSTOMERS$CITY
on GEORGE_CUSTOMERS(Person.Address.City);
```

This command will create an index named I_GEORGE_CUSTOMER$CITY on the Person.Address.City column. Whenever the City column is accessed, the ORACLE optimizer will evaluate the SQL used to access the data and determine if the new index can be useful to improve the performance of the access.

When creating tables based on abstract datatypes, you should consider how the columns within the abstract datatypes will be accessed. If, like the City column in the previous example, certain columns will commonly be used as part of limiting conditions in queries, then they should be indexed. In this regard, the representation of multiple columns in a single abstract datatype may hinder your application performance, since it may obscure the need to index specific columns within the datatype.

When you use abstract datatypes, you become accustomed to treating a group of columns as a single entity, such as the Address columns or the Person columns. It is important to remember that the optimizer, when evaluating query access paths, will consider the columns individually. You therefore need to address the indexing requirements for the columns even when you are using abstract datatypes. In addition, remember that indexing the City column in one table that uses the ADDRESS_TY datatype does not affect the City column in a second table that uses the ADDRESS_TY datatype. For example, if there is a second table named BRANCH that uses the ADDRESS_TY datatype, then *its* City column will not be indexed unless you create an index for it. The fact that there is an index on the City column in the CUSTOMER table will not impact the City column in the BRANCH table.

Iterative Development

Iterative development methodologies typically consist of a series of rapidly developed prototypes. These prototypes are used to define the system requirements as the system is being developed. These methodologies are attractive because of their ability to show the customers something tangible as development is taking place. However, there are a few common pitfalls that occur during iterative development that undermine its effectiveness.

First, effective *versioning* is not always used. Creating multiple versions of an application allows certain features to be "frozen" while others are changed. It also allows different sections of the application to be in development while others are in test. Too often, one version of the application is used for every iteration of every feature, resulting in an end product that is not adequately flexible to handle changing needs (which was the alleged purpose of the iterative development).

Second, the prototypes are not thrown away. Prototypes are developed to give the customer an idea of what the final product will look like; they should not be intended as the foundation of a finished product. Using them as a foundation will not yield the most stable and flexible system possible. When performing iterative development, treat the prototypes as temporary legacy systems. You wouldn't want to base a brand new system on a legacy system; think of the prototypes in the same light.

Third, the development/test/production divisions are clouded. The methodology for iterative development must very clearly define the conditions that have to be met before an application version can be moved to the next stage. It may be best to keep the prototype development completely separate from the development of the full application.

Lastly, unrealistic time lines are often set. The same deliverables that applied to the structured methodology apply to the iterative methodology. The fact that the application is being developed at an accelerated pace does not imply that the deliverables will be any quicker to generate.

Iterative Column Definitions

During the development process, your column definitions may change frequently. As of ORACLE8i, you can drop columns from existing tables; this functionality was not previously available. You can drop a column immediately or you can mark it as "unused," to be dropped at a later time. If the column is dropped immediately, the action may impact performance. If the column is marked as unused, there will be no impact on performance. The column can actually be dropped at a later time when the database is less heavily used.

To drop a column, use either the **set unused** clause or the **drop** clause of the **alter table** command. You cannot drop a pseudocolumn, a column of a nested table, or a partition key column. See Appendix A for the full syntax and restrictions for the **alter table** command.

In the following example, column Col2 is dropped from a table named TABLE1:

```
alter table TABLE1 drop column Col2;
```

You can mark a column as unused.

```
alter table TABLE1 set unused column Col3;
```

Marking a column as "unused" does not release the space previously used by the column. You can drop the unused columns.

```
alter table TABLE1 drop unused columns;
```

You can query USER_UNUSED_COL_TABS, DBA_UNUSED_COL, and ALL_UNUSED_COL_TABS to see all tables with columns marked as unused.

> **NOTE**
> *Once you have marked a column as "unused," you cannot access that column.*

You can drop multiple columns in a single command, as shown in the following listing:

```
alter table TABLE1 drop (Col4, Col5);
```

> **NOTE**
> *When dropping multiple columns, the **column** keyword of the **alter table** command should not be used; it causes a syntax error. The multiple column names must be enclosed in parentheses, as shown in the preceding listing.*

If the dropped columns are part of primary keys or unique constraints, then you will need to also use the **cascade constraints** clause as part of your **alter table** command. If you drop a column that belongs to a primary key, ORACLE will drop both the column and the primary key index.

Technology

The in-process deliverables must be made available while development is underway. Since most development teams include multiple developers (and now, at least one DBA), a means of communication must be established. The communication channels will help maintain consistency in planning and execution.

Four technological solutions are needed in order to make the methodology work. At present, this will require four separate technologies, since no integrated product development package is available. They are CASE tools, shared directories, project management databases, and discussion databases.

CASE Tools

You can use a CASE tool to generate the entity relationship diagram and the physical database diagram. Oracle Designer is a multiuser CASE tool that can create the entity relationship diagram and has an integrated data dictionary. Oracle Designer allows for entities to be shared across applications and can store information about table volumes and row sizes. This functionality will help to resolve several of the deliverables that have been defined in this chapter. Oracle Designer's multiuser capability helps to ensure consistency between developers, allowing different versions of a data model to be maintained or frozen.

The SQL commands that create the database objects for the application should be generated directly from the CASE tool. You may also use the CASE tool to create generic versions of applications based on the defined database objects.

Shared Directories

Several of the deliverables, such as the backup requirements, have no specific tool in which they must be created. These deliverables should be created in whatever tools are most appropriate and available at your site. The resulting files should be stored in shared project directories so that all involved team members can access them. The formats and naming conventions for these files must be specified early in the development process.

Project Management Databases

In order to communicate the status of the application and its deliverables to people outside the development team, a project management database should be maintained. The project management database should provide an outsider with a view of the project and its current milestones. This will allow those people who are not directly involved in the project (such as systems management personnel) to anticipate future requirements. The project management database also allows for the impact of scheduling changes or delays on the critical-path milestones to be analyzed. This analysis may result in modifications to the resource levels assigned to the tasks in the project.

Discussion Databases

Most of the information in these three shared areas—the CASE tools, the shared deliverables directories, and the project management databases—represents a consensus of opinion. For example, several team members may have opinions about the backup strategy, and the system management and DBA staffs must have input as well. To facilitate this communication, a set of discussion databases (usually using a groupware product on a local area network) can be created. Drafts can be posted to these areas before the final resolution is placed in the shared deliverables directory.

Managing Package Development

Imagine a development environment with the following characteristics:

- None of your standards are enforced
- Objects are created under the SYS or SYSTEM accounts
- Proper distribution and sizing of tables and indexes is only lightly considered
- Every application is designed as if it were the only application you intend to run in your database

Welcome to the management of packages.

Properly managing the implementation of packages involves many of the same issues that were described for the application development processes in the previous sections. This section will provide an overview of how packages should be treated so they will best fit with your development environment. See Chapter 11 for a detailed discussion of the management of packaged applications.

Generating Diagrams

Most CASE tools have the ability to *reverse engineer* packages into a physical database diagram. This consists of analyzing the table structures and generating a physical database diagram that is consistent with those structures, usually by analyzing column names and indexes to identify key columns. However, normally there is no one-to-one correlation between the physical database diagram and the entity relationship diagram. Entity relationship diagrams for packages can usually be obtained from the package vendor; they are helpful in planning interfaces to the package database.

Space Requirements

Most Oracle-based packages provide fairly accurate estimates of their database resource usage during production usage. However, they usually fail to take into account their usage requirements during data loads and software upgrades. For this reason, it is wise to create a special rollback segment tablespace (RBS_2) to be used to handle large data loads. A spare data tablespace may be needed as well if the package creates copies of all of its tables during upgrade operations. See Chapter 11 for additional package management guidelines.

Tuning Goals

Just as custom applications have tuning goals, packages must be held to tuning goals as well. Establishing and tracking these control values will help to identify areas of the package in need of tuning (see Chapter 8).

Security Requirements

Unfortunately, most packages that use ORACLE databases fall into one of two categories: either they were migrated to ORACLE from another database system, or they assume they will have full DBA privileges for their object owner accounts.

   If the packages were first created on a different database system, then their ORACLE port very likely does not take full advantage of ORACLE's functional capabilities. These capabilities include row-level locking and the use of sequences, triggers, and methods. Tuning such a package to meet your needs may require modifying the source code.

   If the package assumes that it has full DBA authority, then it must not be stored in the same database as any other critical database application. Most packages that require DBA authority do so in order to add new users to the database. You should determine exactly which system-level privileges the package administrator account actually requires (usually just CREATE SESSION and CREATE USER). You can create a specialized system-level role to provide this limited set of system privileges to the package administrator.

   Packages that were first developed on non-ORACLE databases may require the use of the same account as another ORACLE-ported package. For example, ownership of a database account called SYSADM may be required by multiple applications. The only way to resolve this conflict with any confidence is to create the two packages in separate databases.

Data Requirements

Any processing requirements that the packages have, particularly on the data entry side, must be clearly defined. These are usually well documented in package documentation.

Version Requirements

Applications you support may have dependencies on specific versions and features of ORACLE. For example, a packaged application may be certified on version 8.0.5.1 and 8.1.6 but not on version 8.1.5. If you use packaged applications, you will need to base your kernel version upgrade plans on the vendor's support for the different ORACLE versions. Furthermore, the vendor may switch the optimizer it supports—for example, rule-based in 8.0.5.1 but cost-based in 8.1.6. Your database environment will need to be as flexible as possible in order to support these changes.

Because of these restrictions outside of your control, you should attempt to isolate the application to its own instance. If you frequently query data across applications, the isolation of the application to its own instance will increase your reliance on database links. You need to evaluate the maintenance costs of supporting multiple instances against the maintenance costs of supporting multiple applications in a single instance.

Execution Plans

Generating execution plans requires accessing the SQL statements that are run against the database. The shared SQL area in the SGA (see Chapter 1 and Chapter 6) maintains the SQL statements that are executed against the database. Matching the SQL statements against specific parts of the application is a time-consuming process. It is best to identify specific areas whose functionality and performance are critical to the application's success, and work with the package's support team to resolve performance issues.

Acceptance Test Procedures

The acceptance test procedures for a package are typically created after the application has been installed. However, packages should be held to the same functional requirements that custom applications must meet. The acceptance test procedures should therefore be developed before the package has been selected; they can be generated from the package selection criteria. By testing in this manner, you will be testing for the functionality that you need, rather than what the package developers thought you wanted.

Be sure to specify what your options are in the event the package fails its acceptance test for functional or performance reasons. Critical success factors for the application should not be overlooked just because it is a purchased application.

The Testing Environment

When establishing a test environment, follow these guidelines:

1. It must be larger than your production environment. You need to be able to forecast future performance.

2. It must contain known data sets, explain plans, performance results, and data result sets.

3. It must be used for each release of the database and tools, as well as for new features.

4. It must support the generation of multiple test conditions to enable the evaluation of the features' business costs. You do not want to have to rely on point analysis of results; ideally, you can determine the cost/benefit curves of a feature as the database grows in size.

5. It must be flexible enough to allow you to evaluate different licensing cost options.

6. It must be actively used as a part of your technology implementation methodology.

When implementing and executing tests in your test environment, it simply is not practical to track the execution path and performance of each query in the database. You can use two traditional statistical techniques—grouping and sampling—to perform your tests.

To effectively test the performance results, you should group sets of queries or operations, and test the set as a whole. If the performance of the set fails to meet expectations, you can then investigate the individual components of the set. For example, you may group all operations involved in data warehouse data loads into a single group. If the performance of that group of operations meets your test criteria, then you do not need to evaluate the performance of each operation within that group. If the performance of the group does not meet your expectations, then you should break the group into smaller groups and further isolate the problem. By grouping the operations, you are simplifying the process of identifying problem areas and their causes.

You can use sampling to determine the impact of changes on operations that cannot easily be grouped. For example, you can pick random representative queries from your database (either manually or via the SQL_Text column of the V$SQLAREA view) and run them to determine their expected results and explain plan. You can then execute those queries in your test environment and compare the results of those queries against the expected results. When surveying large populations (such as the population of a country), traditional sample sizes constitute about 1/300,000. For an active database that has thousands of queries, you should be able to represent the most common queries with fewer than 100 SQL statements in your sample set.

Your sample set should not truly be random. Your samples should represent each of the following groups:

- Queries that perform joins, including at least two each representing merge joins, nested loops, outer joins, and hash joins

- Queries that use database links

- DML that uses database links

- At least two of each type of DML statement (**insert**s, **update**s, and **delete**s)

- At least one of each major type of DDL statement, including table creations, index rebuilds, analyze operations, and grants

- At least one query that uses Parallel Query Option, if that option is in use in your environment

The sample set should not be fabricated—it should represent your operations. Thus, generating the sample set should involve reviewing your major groups of operations as well as the OLTP operations executed by your users. The result will not reflect every action within the database, but will allow you to be aware of the implications of upgrades and thus allow you to mitigate your risk and make better decisions about implementing new options.

The Managed Environment

The result of implementing the three critical elements—cultural processes, management processes, and technology—will be a development environment that has quality control built into it. This will allow for improvements to be made in the development process. The production applications will benefit from this in the form of improved performance, better integration with other enterprise applications, and simpler maintenance.

CHAPTER

6

Monitoring Multiple Databases

t the risk of tipping off future interview candidates, here are two questions that I always ask when interviewing to fill DBA positions:

1. "What are the critical success factors for your database?"

2. "How do you monitor them?"

These seem like fairly straightforward questions, but many candidates suddenly realize that they don't know their database's critical success factors—"Something with space, right?" And without knowing those factors, their monitoring systems are either insufficient or overkill. The database must be monitored in a fashion that takes its specific structure and usage into account. Monitoring should focus on revealing problems with the system implementation, rather than tracking the problems' symptoms.

Putting out a fire in a hotel results in an extinguished fire, but it does not make the hotel any less likely to catch fire in the future. Reacting to problems requires understanding the underlying system faults that led to them; otherwise, only the symptom is being treated while the cause remains.

To avoid falling into permanent DBA fire-fighting mode, four things are necessary:

1. A well-defined understanding of how the database will be used by its applications

2. A well-structured database

3. A set of metrics that gauge the database's health

4. A systematic method for making those measurements and determining trends

The first two points, on database design, have been covered in Chapters 3–5. This chapter addresses the third and fourth points, providing measurement guides and a method for monitoring them. The first part of this chapter will concentrate on measuring physical elements of the database via a "Command Center" database; the second section will focus on monitoring memory objects via the ORACLE statistics scripts.

Common Problem Areas

There are several potential problem areas in all ORACLE databases. These include the following:

- Running out of free space in a tablespace
- Insufficient space for temporary segments

- Rollback segments that have reached their maximum extension
- Fragmentation of data segments and free space
- Improperly sized SGA areas

An effective database monitoring system, such as the one whose details are provided in this chapter, should be able to detect unacceptable values for each of these areas. In the following sections you will see a brief synopsis of the problem areas to be tracked, followed by details for creating a system tailored for their monitoring.

Running Out of Free Space in a Tablespace

Each tablespace in the database has datafiles assigned to it. If you are not using autoextending datafiles, then the total space in all of the datafiles in a tablespace serves as the upper limit of the space that can be allocated in the tablespace.

When a segment is created in a tablespace, space is allocated for the initial extent of the segment from the available free space in the tablespace. When the initial extent fills with data, the segment acquires another extent. This process of extension continues either until the segment reaches a maximum number of extents or until the free space in the tablespace is less than the space needed by the next extent.

The free space in a tablespace therefore provides a cushion of unallocated space that can be used either by new segments or by the extensions of existing segments. If the available free space falls to a value that does not allow new segments or extents to be created, additional space will have to be added to the tablespace (by adding new datafiles or resizing existing datafiles).

Therefore, you should monitor not only the current available free space in tablespaces, but also the trend in the available free space—is there more or less available today than there was a week ago? You must be able to determine the effectiveness of the current space allocation and predict what it will look like in the near future.

Insufficient Space for Temporary Segments

Temporary segments store temporary data during sorting operations (such as large queries, index creations, and **union**s). Each user has a temporary tablespace specified when the account is created via the **create user** or **alter user** command. The temporary tablespace should be pointed to someplace other than the SYSTEM tablespace (the default).

When a temporary segment is created, it uses the default storage parameters for that tablespace. While the temporary segment is in existence, its storage parameters cannot be altered by changing the default storage parameters for the tablespace. The temporary segment extends itself as necessary, and drops itself when the operation completes or encounters an error. Since the temporary segment itself can lead to errors (by exceeding the maximum number of extents or running out of space in the tablespace), the size of large sorting queries and operations should be taken into consideration when sizing the temporary tablespace.

If the temporary tablespace runs out of free space during the execution of a sorting operation, the operation will fail. Since it is difficult to accurately size such segments, it is important to monitor whether the temporary tablespace created to hold them is large enough. As with data tablespaces, both the current value and the trend will be monitored via the scripts provided in this chapter.

Rollback Segments That Have Reached Their Maximum Extension

Rollback segments are involved in every transaction that occurs within the database. They allow the database to maintain read consistency between multiple transactions. The number and size of rollback segments available is specified by the DBA during database creation but can be modified later.

Since rollback segments are created within the database, they must be created within a tablespace. The first rollback segment, called *SYSTEM*, is stored in the SYSTEM tablespace. Further rollback segments are usually created in at least one other separate tablespace. Because they are created in tablespaces, their maximum size is limited to the amount of space in the tablespaces' datafiles.

Since they allocate new space in the same manner as data segments, rollback segments are subject to two potential problems: running out of available free space in the tablespace and reaching the maximum allowable number of extents. When either situation is encountered, the transaction that is forcing the rollback segment to extend will fail. A single transaction cannot span multiple rollback segments.

Thus, in addition to tracking the free space (current and trends) for tablespaces that contain rollback segments, the number of extents in each segment must also be monitored.

The **optimal** storage parameter is available only for rollback segments. This parameter sets the optimal size of a rollback segment; when it extends beyond this size, it will later dynamically eliminate unused extents to shrink itself. This capability makes it difficult to determine just by looking at the segment's space usage whether the rollback segments are extending. Instead, the dynamic performance tables, which track the number of times each rollback segment extends and shrinks, must be used. The monitoring system provided here monitors both rollback segment space usage and the number of times they extend and shrink.

Fragmentation of Data Segments

As noted earlier in this chapter, ORACLE manages space in segments by allowing a segment to acquire multiple extents. While this allows for flexibility when sizing tables, it can also cause performance degradation. Ideally, a segment's data will be stored in a manageable number of extents. The data does not have to all be stored in a single extent, but the number of extents should not be so great that it adversely affects your ability to manage the segment.

If a segment has multiple extents, there is no guarantee that those extents are stored near each other. A query against a single table in the database may thus require data that is stored in several different physical locations; this may have a negative impact on performance.

Each segment in the database has a maximum allowable number of extents. As of ORACLE7.3, you can specify that a segment's maximum number of extents is **unlimited**. If a segment's maximum number of extents is not set to **unlimited**, the maximum number of extents may be determined by the database block size. For a 2,048-byte block size, segments are limited to 121 extents; for a 4,096-byte block size, the maximum number of extents is 249.

Any transaction that causes a segment to attempt to exceed its maximum number of extents will fail. Any segment that continually extends has been improperly sized and may contribute to poor performance. Compressing segments into single extents is described in Chapter 8. The monitoring utility provided in this chapter will track the current extension and extension trends for segments in the database.

Fragmented Free Space

Just as data segments can become fragmented, the available free space in a tablespace can become fragmented. This problem is most prevalent in tablespaces whose default **pctincrease** storage value is set to 0. To minimize the impact of **pctincrease 0**, you can run a script to coalesce the tablespace's free space on a nightly basis.

When a segment is dropped, its extents are deallocated and are marked as being "free." However, these free extents are not always recombined with neighboring free extents. The barriers between these free extents may be maintained, affecting the free space available to a new data extent.

If the default **pctincrease** for a tablespace is nonzero, ORACLE automatically combines neighboring free extents into single, large extents. However, it is possible that free extents may be physically separated from each other by data extents, blocking their combination with other free extents.

To detect these potential problems, the utility provided in this chapter tracks the number and size of the available free extents in each tablespace.

Improperly Sized SGA Areas

The size of the System Global Area (SGA) used to store shared memory objects for a database is usually set once, and rarely monitored or tuned after that. However, the proper sizing of the SGA is critical to the performance of the database. Thus, the scripts in the second half of this chapter focus on ways in which the usage of the SGA can be tracked.

Target Selection

Based on the common problem areas described, the following statistics are important:

- Free space in all tablespaces

- Rate of changes in free space for all tablespaces

- Total space usage by temporary segments at any one time

- Sizes and number of extents for rollback segments

- Number of extents for all segments

This target list is a minimum acceptable starting point that should be customized for each database in a system. The target list should be expanded to include those statistics that, combined, determine the success or failure of the system. For each statistic, you should define upper and lower control limits. Once the acceptable ranges have been defined, you can implement the monitoring system. Note that the ranges may be related to either the physical measurements (such as free space in a tablespace) or to the rate at which they change.

The following sections focus on the creation of a system that monitors the database for the targeted statistics. Additional statistics reports are provided following the standard memory and space monitoring scripts.

The End Product

Before describing the configuration and implementation of the monitoring system, decide what the output should provide. In this section, you will see sample listings from the system that will be described in this chapter. If further detail or different information is needed, you can easily modify the system.

The first report, shown in Figure 6-1, is a trend report of free space by tablespace for all databases. This report shows the current percentage of unallocated (free) space in each tablespace (the TS column) of each database (the DB_NM column). The current free space percentage is shown in the Today column of the sample report. The other columns show the free space percentage for each tablespace for the last four weeks. The change between today's free space percentage and its value as of four weeks ago is shown in the Change column. The tablespaces experiencing the greatest negative changes in free space percentage are listed first.

```
                Percent Free Trends for Tablespaces

                      4Wks  3Wks  2Wks  1Wk
DB_NM        TS       Ago   Ago   Ago   Ago   Today  Change
----------   ----------   ----  ----  ----  ----  -----  ------
CASE         CASE         56    56    55    40    40     -16
             USERS        86    64    75    77    76     -10
             SYSTEM       22    22    22    21    21     -1
             TOOLS        25    25    25    25    25
             RBS          32    32    32    32    32
             TEMP         100   100   100   100   100

CC1          CC           94    94    93    92    92     -2
             TESTS        71    70    70    70    70     -1
             SYSTEM       24    24    24    24    24
             RBS          32    32    32    32    32
             CCINDX       51    51    51    51    51
             TEMP         100   100   100   100   100
```

FIGURE 6-1.   *Free space trends of Tablespaces trend report*

The report shown in Figure 6-1 shows the current values, the previous values, and the trend for the percentage of free space in each tablespace. This report is part of the output from the monitoring scripts you will see in this chapter.

The SQL scripts used to generate this report include a variable that can be set to restrict the output to only those tablespaces whose free space percentages have changed more than a given threshold value. It may also be restricted to only show specific databases or tablespaces. Note that these threshold limits, which are used to define whether the system is "in control" or "out of control," can also be hardcoded into the reports. Thus, you could use the report as an exception report for your databases.

You can view extent allocation among segments in the report shown in Figure 6-2. This report, also generated from the monitoring scripts shown in this chapter, shows the trends in extent allocation for all segments that presently have more than ten extents. It shows all rollback segments regardless of their extent procurement.

The report shown in Figure 6-2 shows the current number of extents (the Today column) for each of the segments listed. The segment's database (DB_NM), tablespace (TS), owner (Owner), name (Name), and type (Type) are listed to fully identify it. The segment's current size in ORACLE blocks (the Blocks column) is also

```
              Extent Trends for Segments with 10 or more Extents

                                                  4Wks 3Wks 2Wks  1Wk
  DB_NM TS     Owner    Name     Type     Blocks   Ago  Ago  Ago  Ago Today Change
  ----- ----   -------- -------- -------- ------   ---- ---- ---- ---- ----- ------
  CASE  CASE   CASEMGR  TEMP_TBL TABLE      100                     20    20    20
                        TEMP_IDX INDEX       80                     16    16    16

        RBS    SYSTEM   ROLL1    ROLLBACK  3800    19   19   19   19    19
                        ROLL2    ROLLBACK  3800    19   19   19   19    19

        USERS  AL1      TEST1    TABLE      120         12   12   12    12    12
                        TEST2    TABLE      140         14   14   14    14    14

  CC1   RBS    SYSTEM   ROLL1    ROLLBACK  3800    19   19   19   19    19
                        ROLL2    ROLLBACK  3800    19   19   19   19    19
```

FIGURE 6-2. *Extent trends for Segments sample report*

shown. The current and previous number of extents are shown, as well as the change in the number of extents during the past four weeks (the Change column).

The report shown in Figure 6-2 shows the current values, the previous values, and the trend for the number of extents for fragmented segments. The report also shows these statistics for all rollback segments. This report is part of the output from the monitoring application provided in this chapter.

This report can also be customized to show only those values that have changed. However, it is more informative when all of the alert (>9 extents) records are shown. The report output can then be compared with the free space trends report to reach conclusions about the database. Given these two example reports, one could conclude that:

- All rollback segments appear to be appropriately sized. None of them have increased in size despite the creation of new tables in the databases. (Note: This assumes that the **optimal** sizes of the rollback segment have not yet been reached.)

- The AL1 user in the CASE database has created several tables in the USERS tablespace. Although they have contributed to the decline in the free space in that tablespace, they cannot by themselves account for the dip down to 64 percent three weeks ago. That dip appears to have been caused by transient tables (since the space has since been reclaimed).

■   The CASE_MGR account has impacted a production tablespace by creating a temporary table and index in the CASE tablespace. These segments should be moved unless they are part of the production application.

These two reports, which are generated from the application described in the rest of this chapter, are sufficient to measure all of the variables listed as targets earlier in this section—free space, rollback segments status, extent allocation, and trends for these. More importantly, they provide information about the appropriateness of the database design, given the application's behavior. The sample reports show that the rollback segments were sized correctly, but that the CASE_MGR account has created developmental tables in a production database. This reveals a lack of control in the production system that may eventually cause a production failure.

Since it may be helpful to see a summary of each database, the final sample report summarizes the CC1 database. It lists all files and tablespaces, and the space details for each. The CC1 database is the Command Center database, which will be defined in the next section of this chapter.

The sample output shown in Figure 6-3 is divided into two sections. In the first section, each of the datafiles in the databases is listed (the File nm column), along with the tablespace it is assigned to (the Tablespace column). The number of ORACLE blocks (Orablocks) and disk blocks (DiskBlocks) in each datafile are also displayed in this section.

In the second half of the report, the free space statistics for the tablespaces are displayed. For each tablespace, the number of free extents is displayed (NumFrExts). This column shows how many fragments the available free space in a tablespace is broken into. The largest single free extent, in ORACLE blocks, is shown in the MaxFrExt column, as well as the sum of all free space in the tablespace (SumFrBl). The percentage of the tablespace that is unallocated is shown in the PercentFr column.

The MaxFrPct column displays the ratio of the largest single free extent to the total free space available. A high value for this column indicates that most of the free space available is located in a single extent. The last two columns display the free space available, in disk blocks (DiskFrBl), out of the total available disk blocks (DiskBlocks) for each tablespace. The sample data in Figure 6-3 is for a database that uses a 2KB database block size, with a 512-byte operating system block size.

The report shown in Figure 6-3 provides an overview of the space usage in the database. The first section shows where the free space is coming from—the datafiles assigned to the tablespaces—and the second section shows how that free space is currently being used. This report is part of the output of the monitoring application provided in this chapter.

```
                    Oracle Tablespaces in CC1
                    Check Date = 27-MAY-99


Tablespace     File nm                     Orablocks    DiskBlocks
-------------  --------------------------  ---------    ------------

CC             /db03/oracle/CC1/cc.dbf        30,720      122,880
CCINDX         /db04/oracle/CC1/ccindx.dbf    20,480       81,920
RBS            /db02/oracle/CC1/rbs01.dbf      5,120       20,480
               /db02/oracle/CC1/rbs02.dbf      5,120       20,480
               /db02/oracle/CC1/rbs03.dbf      5,120       20,480
SYSTEM         /db01/oracle/CC1/sys01.dbf     10,240       40,960
TEMP           /db01/oracle/CC1/temp01.dbf    15,360       61,440
TESTS          /db04/oracle/CC1/tests01.dbf   30,720      122,880


                  Oracle Free Space Statistics for CC1
                    (Extent Sizes in Oracle blocks)
                       Check Date = 27-MAY-99


Tablespace    NumFrExts MaxFrExt  SumFrBl PERCENTFR MaxFrPct DiskFrBl DiskBlocks
------------  --------- --------  ------- --------- -------- -------- ----------

CC                1      21504     21504    70.00     100     86016    122880
CCINDX            1      15360     15360    75.00     100     61440     81920
RBS               3       2019      2057    13.39      98      8228     61440
SYSTEM            1       6758      6758    66.00     100     27032     40960
TEMP              6      12800     15360   100.00      83     15360     15360
TESTS             1      21504     21504    70.00     100     86016    122880
```

FIGURE 6-3. *Sample space summary report*

The combination of the reports shown in Figures 6-1, 6-2, and 6-3 is sufficient to measure all of the targets listed earlier. They were all generated based on queries against a single Command Center database. The database design is given in the next section, followed by instructions for data acquisition and a set of standard queries to provide a baseline for your reporting needs.

Creating the Command Center Database

Establishing a separate database that is used solely for monitoring other systems resolves three problems with traditional ORACLE database monitoring capabilities:

- Monitoring activities can be coordinated across multiple databases.

- The monitoring activities will not affect the space usage in the system they are monitoring.

- Trends can be detected for the parameters being monitored.

This section will describe the creation, structure, and implementation of a stand-alone monitoring database.

The system described here is a *reactive monitor*. It is not designed to perform proactive, real-time monitoring of systems, since well-designed, well-implemented, and well-monitored systems should be fundamentally sound. The monitoring system should ideally be called from a system or network monitor, since focusing solely on the database will fail to address the factors that affect the performance of client/server or distributed databases (and this entire function can then be given to the systems management team).

The monitoring database in this example is given the instance name CC1 to designate it as the first Command Center database in the system. Based on your system architecture, you may wish to have multiple databases to perform this function. The database architecture is shown in the following table.

SYSTEM tablespace	20MB
RBS tablespace	30MB
	Two 10MB rollback segments, 10MB free
CC tablespace	30MB
CCINDX tablespace	20MB
TESTS tablespace	30MB
TEMP tablespace	15MB
Redo Logs	Three 2MB redo logs

The design of the application that will store the monitoring results is fairly simple. For each instance, the system will store descriptive information about its location and usage. Information about each file in each database will also be stored (this is very useful information to have during recoveries when the database being recovered is not open). Each tablespace's free space statistics will also be stored, and every segment will be checked for excessive extents. Figure 6-4 shows the physical database diagram for the monitoring tables.

A view of the FILES table, called FILES_TS_VIEW, is created by grouping the FILES table by instance ID, tablespace (TS), and check date (Check_Date). This view is needed when comparing data in the FILES table (allocated space) with data in the

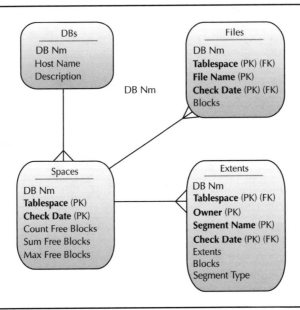

FIGURE 6-4. *Physical database diagram for the Command Center database*

SPACES table (used and free space). The DDL for creating these objects is given in the following listings. The objects are described in Table 6-1.

Object	Description
DBS	Table for storing descriptive information about instances
FILES	Table for storing information about files
FILES_TS_VIEW	View of the FILES table, grouped by tablespace
SPACES	Table for storing information about free space
EXTENTS	Table for storing information about used extents

TABLE 6-1. *Tables and Views in the Command Center Database*

```
drop table dbs;

rem * This table will store information about instances*/

create table DBS
(Db_Nm        VARCHAR2(8),      /*instance name*/
 Host_Nm      VARCHAR2(8),      /*host (server) name*/
 Description  VARCHAR2(80))     /*instance description*/
tablespace CC
storage (initial 64K next 64K pctincrease 0);

drop table FILES;

rem /*This table will store information about datafiles*/

create table FILES
(Db_Nm        VARCHAR2(8),      /*instance name*/
TS            VARCHAR2(30),     /*tablespace name*/
Check_Date    DATE,            /*date entry was made */
File_Nm       VARCHAR2(80),     /*file name*/
Blocks        NUMBER,          /*size of the file*/
primary key(Db_Nm, TS, Check_Date,File_Nm))
tablespace CC
storage (initial 128K next 128K pctincrease 0);

drop view FILES_TS_VIEW;

rem /*This view groups the file sizes by tablespace*/

create view FILES_TS_VIEW as
select
   Db_Nm,                        /*instance name*/
   TS,                           /*tablespace name*/
   Check_Date,                   /*date entry was made */
   SUM(Blocks) Sum_File_Blocks   /*blocks allocated for ts*/
from FILES
group by
   Db_Nm,
   TS,
   Check_Date;

drop table SPACES;

rem /*This table will store information about free space*/

create table SPACES
(Db_Nm        VARCHAR2(8),     /*instance name*/
TS            VARCHAR2(30),    /*tablespace name*/
```

```
Check_Date    DATE,           /*date entry was made */
Count_Free_Blocks NUMBER,     /*number of free extents*/
Sum_Free_Blocks   NUMBER,     /*free space, in Ora blocks*/
Max_Free_Blocks   NUMBER,     /*largest free extent */
primary key (Db_Nm, Ts, Check_Date))
tablespace CC
storage (initial 128K next 128K pctincrease 0);

drop table EXTENTS;

rem /*This table will store information about extents */

create table EXTENTS
(Db_Nm   VARCHAR2(8),        /*instance name*/
TS       VARCHAR2(30),       /*tablespace name*/
Seg_Owner    VARCHAR2(30),   /*segment owner*/
Seg_Name VARCHAR2(32),       /*segment name*/
Seg_Type VARCHAR2(17),       /*segment type*/
Extents  NUMBER,             /*number of extents allocated*/
Blocks   NUMBER,             /*number of blocks allocated*/
Check_Date    DATE,          /*date entry was made */
primary key (Db_Nm, TS, Seg_Owner, Seg_Name, Check_Date))
tablespace CC
storage (initial 128K next 128K pctincrease 0);
```

These database structures will allow the DBA to track all of the targets listed previously, across all databases. Note that there is no table for rollback segments. Rollback segments will be tracked via the EXTENTS table if their extent count exceeds the specified limit.

NOTE
Alter the storage parameters to match your standards, as established in Chapter 5.

Getting the Data

The first object listed in Table 6-1, DBS, is provided as a reference for sites where there are multiple DBAs. You can use the DBS table to enter descriptive information about instances; DBS is the only table of this application that requires manual data entry. All other data will be automatically loaded into the tables. All of the standard data reports will also be automated, with ad hoc capabilities available as well.

The data that is needed to populate these tables is accessible via the SYSTEM account of each database. (A secondary DBA account may also be used for this purpose; this account requires access to DBA-privileged tables, so a specialized system role or the SELECT_CATALOG_ROLE may be used for this purpose.)

Within the CC1 database, you can create an account that will own the monitoring application. This account does not require the DBA role. Within that account, create private database links to a DBA-privileged account in each remote database. The database link's name should be the same as the name of the instance that it links to. For example:

```
create database link CASE
connect to system identified by manager
using 'case';
```

This link accesses the SYSTEM account in the database identified by the service name 'case'. When used, it will log into that database as the user system, with a password of manager.

Note that the **connect to** line is not necessary if the username and password will be the same on the remote system as they are on the local system. See Chapter 9 for details on the **connect to current user** clause for database links.

NOTE
Anyone who is able to gain unauthorized access to your monitoring database may be able to access your production databases via the database links you establish. Be sure to carefully secure the monitoring database.

The outline of the data acquisition process is shown in Figure 6-5.

In the data acquisition process, a batch scheduler will be used to call a command script that will start the process. The job should be scheduled to run daily, at off-peak hours.

As shown in Figure 6-5, the monitoring application will perform the following steps:

1. The command script (called ins_cc1) calls a SQL*Plus script (named inserts.sql) that lists all of the databases to monitor.

2. Each of those databases is checked via a SQL*Plus script (named ins_all.sql).

3. The results of those queries are stored in tables in the Command Center database by ins_all.sql.

4. The command script then generates alert reports based on the latest values in the Command Center database.

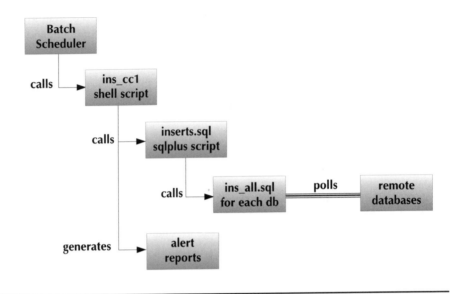

FIGURE 6-5. *Process flow for database monitoring*

To start the system, construct a command file that is run using the operating system's batch scheduler. A sample shell file for UNIX, to be called via **cron**, is shown below. For NT, you can use the **at** command. The following script first sets up its environment variables to point to the CC1 database. It then opens the CC1 database via Server Manager. Once the database is open, a command is executed to start the inserts.sql script. After the data processing completes, the CC1 database is again shut down.

```
# file:  ins_cc1
#
# This script is run once daily to insert records into the
# CC1 database recording the space usage of the databases
# listed in inserts.sql file called by this file.  New
# databases need to have new links created in CC1 and have
# to have entries in the # inserts.sql script.
#
ORACLE_SID=cc1; export ORACLE_SID
ORAENV_ASK=NO; export ORAENV_ASK
. oraenv
cd /orasw/dba/CC1
svrmgrl <<EOF
```

```
connect internal
startup;
!sqlplus / @inserts
shutdown
EOF
```

Note that this file assumes that the database is closed when this monitoring is not taking place. This allows the memory normally used by CC1's SGA and background processes to be freed during regular working hours. Monitoring is assumed to be taking place once a day, at a fixed time when the system is lightly loaded.

The shell script shown in the previous listing calls a file named inserts.sql, located in the /orasw/dba/CC1 directory. A sample inserts.sql file is shown below. This script calls the ins_all.sql script for each database that is to be monitored. Once that is complete, two alert reports, named space_watcher.sql and extent_watcher.sql, are executed.

```
rem
rem   file:  inserts.sql
rem   location:  /orasw/dba/CC1
rem   Called from ins_cc1 shell script.
rem   New entries must be made here every time a new database
rem   is added to the system.
rem
set verify off
@ins_all CASE
@ins_all CC1
analyze table FILES compute statistics;
analyze table SPACES compute statistics;
analyze table EXTENTS compute statistics;
@space_watcher
@extent_watcher
```

The inserts.sql file lists all of the databases for which monitoring statistics will be gathered. When new databases are added to the system, an additional line should be added for each. The inserts.sql file thus provides a layer of process management that allows easy changes without altering the submitted batch program or the SQL statements that access the remote databases.

After executing the ins_all.sql script for two databases (CASE and CC1), the inserts.sql script analyzes the tables that store the monitoring data. The analysis of the tables is necessary to guarantee the performance of the reports against the monitoring tables. Since the data in the monitoring tables changes frequently, these tables should be frequently analyzed.

The last two lines in this script call a pair of SQL scripts named space_watcher.sql and extent_watcher.sql. These scripts will generate versions of the "Percent Free by

Tablespace" and "Segments with over 10 Extents" reports shown earlier in Figures 6-1 and 6-2, respectively. Because they will be used for alerting purposes, only rows with changes exceeding defined limits will be shown in the next listing.

So far, we've seen the first two layers of the data acquisition system. Continuing down the process path depicted in Figure 6-5, the next step is to run a script (ins_all.sql) that inserts records into all applicable monitoring tables based on queries against remote databases. These queries use the database links created earlier to search each instance in turn and record the statistics returned. A sample ins_all.sql SQL*Plus script for **insert**s into the FILES, SPACES, and EXTENTS tables is shown in the next listing.

The first part of the ins_all.sql script **insert**s records into the FILES table. It queries each database for information about all of its datafiles, the tablespaces to which they are assigned, and their sizes.

The second part of the script queries the free space statistics of each database. It stores the output in the SPACES table, recording the number of free extents in each tablespace, the total free space available, and the size of the largest single free extent.

The third part of the script checks the space usage by segments and stores its results in the EXTENTS table. It records the information needed to identify the segment (such as its owner and name), as well as its current size and number of extents. To limit the number of records returned by this query, only rollback segments and segments with greater than nine extents are selected.

```
rem
rem  file:  ins_all.sql
rem  location:  /orasw/dba/CC1
rem  Used to perform all inserts into CC1 monitoring
rem  tables.  This script is called from inserts.sql for
rem  each instance.
rem  For best results, name the database links after the
rem  instances they access.
rem
insert into FILES
    (Db_Nm,
    TS,
    Check_Date,
    File_Nm,
    Blocks)
select
    UPPER('&&1'),        /*insert database link,instance name*/
    Tablespace_Name,     /*tablespace name*/
    TRUNC(SysDate),      /*date query is being performed*/
    File_Name,           /*full name of database file*/
    Blocks               /*number of database blocks in file*/
from sys.DBA_DATA_FILES@&&1
```

```
/
commit;
rem
insert into SPACES
   (Db_Nm,
   Check_Date,
   TS,
   Count_Free_Blocks,
   Sum_Free_Blocks,
   Max_Free_Blocks)
select
   UPPER('&&1'),      /*insert database link,instance name*/
   TRUNC(SysDate),    /*date query is being performed*/
   Tablespace_Name,   /*tablespace name*/
   COUNT(Blocks),     /*num. of free space entries */
   SUM(Blocks),       /*total free space in the tablespace*/
   MAX(Blocks)        /*largest free extent in the ts*/
from sys.DBA_FREE_SPACE@&&1
group by Tablespace_Name
/
commit;
rem
insert into EXTENTS
   (Db_Nm,
   TS,
   Seg_Owner,
   Seg_Name,
   Seg_Type,
   Extents,
   Blocks,
   Check_Date)
select
   UPPER('&&1'),      /*insert database link,instance name*/
   Tablespace_Name,   /*tablespace name*/
   Owner,             /*owner of the segment*/
   Segment_Name,      /*name of the segment*/
   Segment_Type,      /*type of segment (ex. TABLE, INDEX)*/
   Extents,           /*number of extents in the segment*/
   Blocks,            /*number of database blocks in segment*/
   TRUNC(SysDate)     /*date the query is being performed*/
from sys.DBA_SEGMENTS@&&1
where Extents>9          /*only record extended segments*/
or Segment_Type = 'ROLLBACK'   /*or rollback segments*/
/
commit;
rem
undefine 1
```

Note that the inserts into the EXTENTS table only take place for rollback segments and those segments that have exceeded nine extents. This is therefore an incomplete listing of the segments in the database. Since these two **where** clauses establish the threshold for the extent alert report, change the extent limit to best suit your needs.

This series of scripts will perform all of the data acquisition functions necessary to generate the reports shown earlier. It is assumed throughout that they will be run on a daily basis. If more frequent monitoring is needed, the primary keys of the tables will need to be modified to include both Check_Date and Check_Hour (for hourly reporting).

Now that the data has been inserted into the CC1 monitoring tables, ORACLE can automatically generate alert reports. This will be accomplished via the space_watcher.sql and extent_watcher.sql files that are called from the inserts.sql file shown earlier.

Generating Alert Reports

The composition of the alert scripts, described in the previous section, depends entirely on the nature of the databases being monitored. They are simply modifications to the generic free space and extent trends reports shown in Figures 6-1 and 6-2. They feature **where** and **group by** clauses to eliminate those entries that have not exceeded some threshold value. The setting of these values should be customized for each site—they are based on the control limits defined during the target variable selection process.

Since these reports are called automatically following the insertion of records into the Command Center database, the DBA may wish to have them automatically mailed or printed so they are seen each morning before the production users begin to access the databases.

The following script generates the space trend report for tablespaces whose percentage of free space has changed by at least 5 percent in the last four weeks:

```
rem
rem   file:  space_watcher.sql
rem   location:  /orasw/dba/CC1
rem   Called from inserts.sql
rem
rem   ...like some watcher of the skies
rem   when a new planet swims into his ken (Keats)
rem
column Db_Nm format A8
column TS format A20
column Week4 format 999 heading "1Wk|Ago"
column Week3 format 999 heading "2Wks|Ago"
column Week2 format 999 heading "3Wks|Ago"
```

```
column Week1 format 999 heading "4Wks|Ago"
column Today format 999
column Change format 999

set pagesize 60
break on Db_Nm skip 2
ttitle center 'Tablespaces whose PercentFree values have -
decreased 5 pct this month' skip 2

select
   SPACES.Db_Nm,
   SPACES.TS,
   MAX(DECODE(SPACES.Check_Date, TRUNC(SysDate-28),
      ROUND(100*Sum_Free_Blocks/Sum_File_Blocks),0)) Week1,
   MAX(DECODE(SPACES.Check_Date, TRUNC(SysDate-21),
      ROUND(100*Sum_Free_Blocks/Sum_File_Blocks),0)) Week2,
   MAX(DECODE(SPACES.Check_Date, TRUNC(SysDate-14),
      ROUND(100*Sum_Free_Blocks/Sum_File_Blocks),0)) Week3,
   MAX(DECODE(SPACES.Check_Date, TRUNC(SysDate-7),
      ROUND(100*Sum_Free_Blocks/Sum_File_Blocks),0)) Week4,
   MAX(DECODE(SPACES.Check_Date, TRUNC(SysDate),
      ROUND(100*Sum_Free_Blocks/Sum_File_Blocks),0)) Today,
   MAX(DECODE(SPACES.Check_Date, TRUNC(SysDate),
      ROUND(100*Sum_Free_Blocks/Sum_File_Blocks),0)) -
   MAX(DECODE(SPACES.Check_Date, TRUNC(SysDate-28),
      ROUND(100*Sum_Free_Blocks/Sum_File_Blocks),0)) Change
from SPACES, FILES_TS_VIEW FTV
where SPACES.Db_Nm = FTV.Db_Nm          /*same DB name*/
and SPACES.TS = FTV.TS                  /*same TS name*/
and SPACES.Check_Date = ftv.Check_Date  /*same check date*/
and exists                              /*does ts exist?*/
   (select 'x' from spaces x
   where x.db_nm = SPACES.db_nm
   and x.ts = SPACES.ts
   and x.Check_Date = TRUNC(SysDate))
group by
   SPACES.Db_Nm,
   SPACES.Ts
having                  /*has percentfree dropped 5 pct?*/
(  MAX(DECODE(SPACES.Check_Date, TRUNC(SysDate),
        ROUND(100*Sum_Free_Blocks/Sum_File_Blocks),0)) -
   MAX(DECODE(SPACES.Check_Date, TRUNC(SysDate-28),
        ROUND(100*Sum_Free_Blocks/Sum_File_Blocks),0))
>5    )
or                      /*is percentfree less than 10?*/
( MAX(DECODE(SPACES.Check_Date, TRUNC(SysDate),
     ROUND(100*Sum_Free_Blocks/Sum_File_Blocks),0)) <10)
order by SPACES.Db_Nm,
```

```
DECODE(MAX(DECODE(SPACES.Check_Date,TRUNC(SysDate),
   ROUND(100*Sum_Free_Blocks/Sum_File_Blocks),0)) -
MAX(DECODE(SPACES.Check_Date, TRUNC(SysDate-28),
   ROUND(100*Sum_Free_Blocks/Sum_File_Blocks),0)),0,9999,
MAX(DECODE(SPACES.Check_Date,TRUNC(SysDate),
   ROUND(100*Sum_Free_Blocks/Sum_File_Blocks),0)) -
MAX(DECODE(SPACES.Check_Date, TRUNC(SysDate-28),
   ROUND(100*Sum_Free_Blocks/Sum_File_Blocks),0))),
MAX(DECODE(SPACES.Check_Date,TRUNC(SysDate),
   ROUND(100*Sum_Free_Blocks/Sum_File_Blocks),0))

spool space_watcher.lst
/
spool off
```

If the **exists** section is left out of the above query, then all tablespaces will be shown, even after they have been dropped from the database. The two limiting conditions within the **having** clauses define the threshold for the alert report. In this example, only those tablespaces whose percent free values have decreased by more than 5 percent in the past 28 days will pass the first **having** condition. The second **having** condition identifies those tablespaces whose current percent free value is less than 10 percent, regardless of its trends.

If incremental changes in specific databases are critical to their success, then you may wish to add a **having** clause to this report that lists those specific databases regardless of their trends.

Sample output (based on the percent free trend report in Figure 6-1) is shown in Figure 6-6.

```
          Tablespaces whose Percent Free values have
                 decreased 5 pct this month

                       4Wks   3Wks   2Wks   1Wk
DB_NM        TS        Ago    Ago    Ago    Ago   Today   Change
-----------  ---------- ----   ----   ----   ----   -----   ------
CASE         CASE        56     56     55     40      40      -16
             USERS       86     64     75     77      76      -10
```

FIGURE 6-6. *Sample alert report for tablespace percent free trends*

Note that this alert report does not show fluctuations that have since been resolved (for example, a four-week percent free trend of 70-70-20-70-70 would not be shown). This alert report should be run and viewed on a daily basis. If a tablespace's space problems have been resolved, it is no longer shown on the alert reports.

The second report is the extent watcher (extent_watcher.sql). Like the space watcher report, this SQL*Plus query uses the **group by** clause to transpose multiple rows into multiple columns for a single row. This report provides a subset of the data listed in the generic extent trends report that was shown in Figure 6-2.

```
rem
rem   file:  ext_watcher.sql
rem   location:  /orasw/dba/CC1
rem   Called from inserts.sql
rem
rem   ...like some watcher of the skies
rem   when a new planet swims into his ken (Keats)
rem
column Db_Nm format A8
column TS format A18
column Seg_Owner format a14
column Seg_Name format a32
column Seg_Type format a8
column Blocks format 99999999
column Week4 format 999 heading "1Wk|Ago"
column Week3 format 999 heading "2Wks|Ago"
column Week2 format 999 heading "3Wks|Ago"
column Week1 format 999 heading "4Wks|Ago"
column Today format 999
column Change format 999

set pagesize 60 linesize 132
break on Db_Nm skip 2 on TS skip 1 on Seg_Owner
ttitle center 'Segments whose extent count is over 10' -
skip 2

select
   EXTENTS.Db_Nm,
   EXTENTS.TS,
   EXTENTS.Seg_Owner,
   EXTENTS.Seg_Name,
   EXTENTS.Seg_Type,
   MAX(DECODE(EXTENTS.Check_Date, TRUNC(SysDate),
        Blocks,0)) Blocks,
```

```
      MAX(DECODE(EXTENTS.Check_Date, TRUNC(SysDate-28),
           Extents,0)) Week1,
      MAX(DECODE(EXTENTS.Check_Date, TRUNC(SysDate-21),
           Extents,0)) Week2,
      MAX(DECODE(EXTENTS.Check_Date, TRUNC(SysDate-14),
           Extents,0)) Week3,
      MAX(DECODE(EXTENTS.Check_Date, TRUNC(SysDate-7),
           Extents,0)) Week4,
      MAX(DECODE(EXTENTS.Check_Date, TRUNC(SysDate),
           Extents,0)) Today,
      MAX(DECODE(EXTENTS.Check_Date, TRUNC(SysDate),
           Extents,0)) -
      MAX(DECODE(EXTENTS.Check_Date, TRUNC(SysDate-28),
           Extents,0)) Change
from EXTENTS
where exists  /*did this segment show up today?*/
   (select 'x' from EXTENTS x
   where x.Db_Nm = EXTENTS.Db_Nm
   and x.TS = EXTENTS.TS
   and x.Seg_Owner = EXTENTS.Seg_Owner
   and x.Seg_Name = EXTENTS.Seg_Name
   and x.Seg_Type = EXTENTS.Seg_Type
   and x.Check_Date = TRUNC(SysDate))
group by
   EXTENTS.Db_Nm,
   EXTENTS.TS,
   EXTENTS.Seg_Owner,
   EXTENTS.Seg_Name,
   EXTENTS.Seg_Type
order by EXTENTS.Db_Nm, EXTENTS.TS,
   DECODE(MAX(DECODE(EXTENTS.Check_Date,TRUNC(SysDate),
        Extents,0)) -
   MAX(DECODE(EXTENTS.Check_Date, TRUNC(SysDate-28),
        Extents,0)),0,-9999,
   MAX(DECODE(EXTENTS.Check_Date,TRUNC(SysDate),
        Extents,0)) -
   MAX(DECODE(EXTENTS.Check_Date, TRUNC(SysDate-28),
        Extents,0))) desc,
   MAX(DECODE(EXTENTS.Check_Date,TRUNC(SysDate),
        Extents,0)) desc

spool extent_watcher.lst
/
spool off
```

The only portion of this query that limits the records to be shown is the **exists** clause that queries to see if the segment was returned from the current day's query.

The report assumes that the threshold values for the "number of extents" variable was enforced during the **insert** into the EXTENTS table (see ins_all.sql, shown in the "Getting the Data" section of this chapter). The EXTENTS table is the only table that has the threshold enforced during **insert**s rather than during querying, since there may be thousands of segments in a database.

If incremental changes in specific segments are critical to their success, you may wish to add a **where** clause to the portion of the ins_all.sql script that inserts the rows for those segments into the EXTENTS table. The report will then list those specific segments regardless of their trends.

Sample output from the extent_watcher.sql report is shown in Figure 6-7, which is identical to Figure 6-2. This is because the queries used for the **insert**s into the EXTENTS table only selected those segments that were already fragmented. No additional restrictions were needed to produce an alert report.

The Space Summary Report

Since every day's statistics are being stored in the CC1 Command Center database, a summary report can be generated for any database, for any specified date. This report should be generated on a weekly basis via the batch scheduler. It does not have to be printed out at that time. It should, however, be available online to the

```
            Extent Trends for Segments with 10 or more Extents


                                            4Wks 3Wks 2Wks 1Wk
  DB_NM TS     Owner   Name     Type    Blocks Ago  Ago  Ago  Ago Today Change
  ----- ------ ------- -------- -------- ------ ---- ---- ---- ---- ----- ------
  CASE  CASE   CASEMGR TEMP_TBL TABLE      100                  20   20     20
                       TEMP_IDX INDEX       80                  16   16     16


        RBS    SYSTEM  ROLL1    ROLLBACK  3800   19   19   19   19   19
                       ROLL2    ROLLBACK  3800   19   19   19   19   19


        USERS  AL1     TEST1    TABLE      120        12   12   12   12     12
                       TEST2    TABLE      140        14   14   14   14     14


  CC1   RBS    SYSTEM  ROLL1    ROLLBACK  3800   19   19   19   19   19
                       ROLL2    ROLLBACK  3800   19   19   19   19   19
```

FIGURE 6-7. *Sample alert report for extent usage trends*

DBA. Having the report available online will shorten the time delay in getting the report, since the CC1 database is usually kept closed after its daily batch run is completed (as specified in the ins_cc1 shell script).

This SQL*Plus report should be run once for each database. The report generates an output file whose name includes the name of the database link that was used in the query. The script takes three parameters:

1. The database link name (since this will be stored in the output file name, it should have the same name as the instance it accesses).

2. The check date (since this report can be run for any date).

3. The ratio of the ORACLE block size (such as 2KB) to the host operating block size (such as 512 bytes). For these block sizes, the ratio is 2,048/512 = 4.

The report is divided into two sections. The first part queries the FILES table to determine the current filenames and sizes for the database. The second part of the report compares the values in the SPACES table (free space sizes) to those in the FILES table (via the FILES_TS_VIEW view). Because these tables contain information about the space allocated to a tablespace, and the amount of it that has yet to be allocated, the percentage of free space remaining in each tablespace can be measured.

```
rem
rem space_summary.sql
rem   parameter 1: database link name
rem   parameter 2: check date
rem   parameter 3: ratio of Oracle to OS block size
rem
rem   to call this report from within sqlplus:
rem   @space_summary link_name Check_Date block_ratio
rem
rem   Example:
rem   @space_summary CASE 27-MAY-99 4
rem
rem   Should be called weekly for each database.
rem
set pagesize 60 linesize 132 verify off feedback off
set newpage 0
column TS heading 'Tablespace' format A18
column File_Nm heading 'File nm' format A40
column Blocks heading 'Orablocks'
column Percentfree format 999.99
column Diskblocks format 99999999
```

```
column Cfb format 9999999 heading 'NumFrExts'
column Mfb format 9999999 heading 'MaxFrExt'
column Sfb format 9999999 heading 'SumFrBl'
column Dfrb format 9999999 heading 'DiskFrBl'
column Sum_File_Blocks heading 'DiskBlocks'
column Maxfrpct heading 'MaxFrPct' format 9999999

break on TS
ttitle center 'Oracle Tablespaces in ' &&1 skip center -
'Check Date = ' &&2 skip 2 center
spool &&1._space_summary.lst
select
   Ts,                     /*tablespace name*/
   File_Nm,                /*file name*/
   Blocks,                 /*Oracle blocks in the file*/
   Blocks*&&3 Diskblocks   /*OS blocks in the file*/
  from FILES
 where Check_Date = '&&2'
   and Db_Nm = UPPER('&&1')
 order by TS, File_Nm
/
ttitle center 'Oracle Free Space Statistics for ' &&1 -
skip center '(Extent Sizes in Oracle blocks)' skip center -
 'Check Date = ' &&2 skip 2
select
   SPACES.TS,                      /*tablespace name*/
   SPACES.Count_Free_Blocks Cfb,   /*number of free extents*/
   SPACES.Max_Free_Blocks Mfb,     /*lgst free extent*/
   SPACES.Sum_Free_Blocks Sfb,     /*sum of free space*/
   ROUND(100*Sum_Free_Blocks/Sum_File_Blocks,2)
       Percentfree,                /*percent free in TS*/
   ROUND(100*Max_Free_Blocks/Sum_Free_Blocks,2)
    Maxfrpct,                      /*ratio of largest extent to sum*/
   SPACES.Sum_Free_Blocks*&&3 Dfrb, /*disk blocks free*/
   Sum_File_Blocks*&&3 Sum_File_Blocks /*disk blocks allocated*/
   SPACES.Sum_Free_Blocks*&&3 Dfrb, /*disk blocks free*/
   Sum_File_Blocks*&&3 Sum_File_Blocks /*disk blocks allocated*/
 from SPACES, FILES_TS_VIEW FTV
where SPACES.Db_Nm = FTV.Db_Nm
  and SPACES.TS = FTV.TS
  and SPACES.Check_Date = FTV.Check_Date
  and SPACES.Db_Nm = UPPER('&&1')
  and SPACES.Check_Date = '&&2'
/
spool off
undefine 1
undefine 2
undefine 3
```

```
                      Oracle Tablespaces in CC1
                      Check Date = 27-MAY-99


Tablespace    File nm                        Orablocks     DiskBlocks
------------  ---------------------------    ---------     ------------

CC            /db03/oracle/CC1/cc.dbf           30,720        122,880
CCINDX        /db04/oracle/CC1/ccindx.dbf       20,480         81,920
RBS           /db02/oracle/CC1/rbs01.dbf         5,120         20,480
              /db02/oracle/CC1/rbs02.dbf         5,120         20,480
              /db02/oracle/CC1/rbs03.dbf         5,120         20,480
SYSTEM        /db01/oracle/CC1/sys01.dbf        10,240         40,960
TEMP          /db01/oracle/CC1/temp01.dbf       15,360         61,440
TESTS         /db04/oracle/CC1/tests01.dbf      30,720        122,880


                 Oracle Free Space Statistics for CC1
                   (Extent Sizes in Oracle blocks)
                      Check Date = 27-MAY-99


Tablespace   NumFrExts MaxFrExt  SumFrBl PERCENTFR MaxFrPct DiskFrBl DiskBlocks
-----------  --------- --------  ------- --------- -------- -------- ----------

CC               1      21504     21504    70.00      100    86016     122880
CCINDX           1      15360     15360    75.00      100    61440      81920
RBS              3       2019      2057    13.39       98     8228      61440
SYSTEM           1       6758      6758    66.00      100    27032      40960
TEMP             6      12800     61440   100.00       83    15360      15360
TESTS            1      21504     21504    70.00      100    86016     122880
```

FIGURE 6-8. *Sample space summary report*

A sample output report is shown in Figure 6-8. Based on the **spool** command listed in the query, the output file will be called CC1_space_summary.lst. This is based on using the period (**.**) as the concatenation character in SQL*Plus.

Figure 6-8 is identical to Figure 6-3 earlier in this chapter. The sample output shown in Figure 6-8 is divided into two sections. In the first section, each of the datafiles in the databases is listed (the File nm column), along with the tablespace it is assigned to (the Tablespace column). The number of ORACLE blocks (Orablocks) and disk blocks (DiskBlocks) in each datafile is also displayed in this section.

In the second half of the report, the free space statistics for the tablespaces are displayed. For each tablespace, the number of free extents is displayed (NumFrExts).

This column shows how many fragments the available free space in a tablespace is broken into. The largest single free extent, in Oracle blocks, is shown in the MaxFrExt column, as well as the sum of all free space in the tablespace (SumFrBl). The percentage of the tablespace that is unallocated is shown in the PercentFr column.

The MaxFrPct column displays the ratio of the largest single free extent to the total free space available. A high value for this column indicates that most of the free space available is located in a single extent. The last two columns display the free space available, in disk blocks (DiskFrBl), out of the total available disk blocks (DiskBlocks) for each tablespace. The sample data shown in Figure 6-8 is for a database that uses a 2KB database block size, with a 512-byte operating system block.

Purging Data

Left unchecked, the tables described in the previous sections will grow until they use all of the free space in the available tablespaces. To prevent data volume-related problems, you should periodically **delete** records from the EXTENTS, SPACES, and FILES tables.

The amount of data to retain depends on your needs. If you never will need data more than 60 days old from these tables, then you can automate the data purges as part of the data **insert** process. For example, at the end of the ins_all.sql script that performs the **insert**s, you could add the following commands:

```
delete from FILES
  where Check_Date < SysDate-60;

commit;

delete from SPACES
  where Check_Date < SysDate-60;

commit;

delete from EXTENTS
  where Check_Date < SysDate-60;

commit;
```

If you execute this command each day, then the size of the **delete** transactions should be small enough to be supported by the rollback segments.

If the tables become large, you can improve the performance of the **delete**s by creating indexes on the Check_Date columns of the FILES, SPACES, and EXTENTS tables.

Periodic purges of this nature can cause your space usage within indexes to become inefficient. Following a purge, rebuild the primary key indexes on the tables as well as any other indexes you create on the Command Center tables.

Monitoring Memory Objects

ORACLE's memory objects, such as the System Global Area (SGA) and the background processes, can also be monitored. Since most of the monitoring of the background processes is done at the operating system level (and is operating system specific), this section will focus on tuning the SGA.

ORACLE continuously updates a set of internal statistics. These statistics should only be stored in tracking tables (such as the tables used in the space monitoring section of this chapter) when you can be sure that the database will not be shut down between monitoring checks. The internal statistics are reset each time the database is shut down and restarted.

In order to facilitate monitoring of statistics regarding SGA usage, ORACLE provides two scripts that should be modified, called UTLBSTAT.SQL and UTLESTAT.SQL. They are located in the /rdbms/admin subdirectory under the ORACLE software home directory. The first file, UTLBSTAT (Begin Statistics) creates a set of tables and populates them with the statistics in the database at that time. The second file, UTLESTAT, runs at a later time, creates a set of tables based on the statistics in the database at that time, and then generates a report (called REPORT.TXT) that lists the changes in the statistics during the interval between the run times for the beginning and ending scripts.

Necessary Modifications to UTLBSTAT and UTLESTAT

Before running the statistics scripts provided by ORACLE, change them. First, modify the scripts to include database links as part of the **from** clause—this will allow them to be run from a Command Center database. Second, add a **tablespace** clause to allow the segments to be stored in a data or scratch area tablespace.

Why make these modifications? Failing to do so causes two problems: First, since these scripts **insert** records into tables, storing the tables in a database that is being monitored automatically skews the file I/O statistics for the database (since the monitoring activity is being factored into the I/O activity). Second, the scripts are written to be run from within Server Manager, connected internal. If no alternate tablespace is named, then the SYSTEM tablespace will be fragmented by the **create table** and **drop table** operations within these scripts. See Chapter 4 for an explanation of fragmentation and its solutions.

NOTE
*You can now **connect internal** within SQL*Plus;
within Server Manager the Server Manager
formatting commands will be ignored.*

Both the beginning and ending statistics tables are created by utlbstat.sql.
utlestat.sql then creates a series of tables to store the differences between the
beginning and ending statistics before generating report.txt. The scripts must be run
under a DBA account due to a reference to the SYS.FILE$ table. All other tables
referenced by these scripts are accessible to users who have been granted access to
the monitoring views (the V$ views).

To reference a remote database from within the statistics scripts, add a database
link that points to the target database. In order to access all of the tables needed by
these scripts, you will need to either create a link to the target SYS account or grant
the remote SYSTEM account privileges on the SYS tables used by the scripts. To
minimize your risk, create a link to SYS specifying a temporary password.

```
create database link CASE_STAT
connect to SYS identified by only_for_a_minute
using 'case';
```

Once the link is established, log in to the CASE database, change the SYS
password to only_for_a_minute (or whatever you choose), go back to CC1, and run
the statistics script. When it completes, reset the SYS password.

To tell the query to use this link, append the database link name to the table
name being queried. The following listing shows the table creation portion of
utlbstat.sql after it has been modified to use this link. If you are managing multiple
databases, use a variable in place of the database link name.

For this example, the tables will be stored in the CC data tablespace of the CC1
Command Center database. Each **create table** command will have the **tablespace
CC** clause appended to it, and each query of a remote table will have the
@case_stat clause added to it so the database link named CASE_STAT will be used.

After this script has been run, all of the statistics from the remote database's
dynamic performance tables will be stored in the CC tablespace of the local database.

```
rem
rem  Modified version of $ORACLE_HOME/rdbms/admin/utlbstat.sql
rem  Note the addition of tablespace clauses and database links
rem
rem  ************************************************************
rem                 First create all the tables
rem  ************************************************************
```

```
drop table stats$begin_stats;
create table stats$begin_stats
TABLESPACE CC
as select * from v$sysstat@CASE_STAT where 0 = 1;
drop table stats$end_stats;
create table stats$end_stats
TABLESPACE CC
as select * from stats$begin_stats;

drop table stats$begin_latch;
create table stats$begin_latch
TABLESPACE CC
as select * from v$latch@CASE_STAT where 0 = 1;

drop table stats$end_latch;
create table stats$end_latch
TABLESPACE CC
as select * from stats$begin_latch;

drop table stats$begin_roll;
create table stats$begin_roll
TABLESPACE CC
as select * from v$rollstat@CASE_STAT where 0 = 1;

drop table stats$end_roll;
create table stats$end_roll
TABLESPACE CC
as select * from stats$begin_roll;

drop table stats$begin_lib;
create table stats$begin_lib
TABLESPACE CC
as select * from v$librarycache@CASE_STAT where 0 = 1;

drop table stats$end_lib;
create table stats$end_lib
TABLESPACE CC
as select * from stats$begin_lib;

drop table stats$begin_dc;
create table stats$begin_dc
TABLESPACE CC
as select * from v$rowcache@CASE_STAT where 0 = 1;

drop table stats$end_dc;
create table stats$end_dc
```

```
TABLESPACE CC
as select * from stats$begin_dc;

drop table stats$begin_event;
create table stats$begin_event
TABLESPACE CC
as select * from v$system_event@CASE_STAT where 0 = 1;

drop table stats$end_event;
create table stats$end_event
TABLESPACE CC
as select * from stats$begin_event;

drop table stats$begin_bck_event;
create table stats$begin_bck_event
  (event varchar2(200),
   total_waits number,
   time_waited number)
TABLESPACE CC;
drop table stats$end_bck_event;
create table stats$end_bck_event
as select * from stats$begin_bck_event;

drop table stats$dates;
create table stats$dates (stats_gather_times varchar2(100))
TABLESPACE CC;

drop view stats$file_view;
create view stats$file_view
as                /*NOTE:  Have to change the FROM clause here*/
  select ts.name   ts,
         i.name    name,
         x.phyrds pyr,
         x.phywrts pyw,
         x.readtim prt,
         x.writetim pwt,
         x.phyblkrd pbr,
         x.phyblkwrt pbw,
         ROUND(i.bytes/1000000) megabytes_size
  from    v$filestat@CASE_STAT x,
          ts$@CASE_STAT ts,
          v$datafile@CASE_STAT i,
          file$@CASE_STAT f
 where i.file#=f.file#
```

```
    and ts.ts#=f.ts#
    and x.file#=f.file#;

drop table stats$begin_file;
create table stats$begin_file   /*No link needed here*/
TABLESPACE CC
as select * from stats$file_view where 0 = 1;

drop table stats$end_file;
create table stats$end_file
TABLESPACE CC
as select * from stats$begin_file;

drop table stats$begin_waitstat;
create table stats$begin_waitstat
TABLESPACE CC
as select * from v$waitstat@CASE_STAT where 1=0;
drop table stats$end_waitstat;
create table stats$end_waitstat
TABLESPACE CC
as select * from stats$begin_waitstat;
```

A modification that was added for the ORACLE8 version of utlbstat introduced a math error. In the STATS$FILE_VIEW view creation script, the following column was added for ORACLE8:

```
ROUND(i.bytes/1000000) megabytes_size
```

However, there are not 1,000,000 bytes in a megabyte. There are 1,048,576 bytes in a megabyte (1,024*1,024). You should correct this entry to read:

```
ROUND(i.bytes/1048576) megabytes_size
```

The utlestat.sql script also needs to be changed, since it creates tables and inserts data based on queries of remote tables. In the following listing, the statistics gathering portion of utlestat.sql is shown with the appropriate database links:

```
insert into stats$end_latch select * from v$latch@CASE_STAT;
insert into stats$end_stats select * from v$sysstat@CASE_STAT;
insert into stats$end_lib select * from v$librarycache@CASE_STAT;
update stats$dates set end_time = sysdate;
insert into stats$end_event select * from v$system_event@CASE_STAT;
insert into stats$end_bck_event
   select event, sum(total_waits), sum(time_waited)
     from v$session@CASE_STAT s, v$session_event@CASE_STAT e
     where type = 'BACKGROUND' and s.sid = e.sid
     group by event;
insert into stats$end_waitstat select * from v$waitstat@CASE_STAT;
```

```
insert into stats$end_roll select * from v$rollstat@CASE_STAT;
insert into stats$end_file select * from stats$file_view; /*no link*/
insert into stats$end_dc select * from v$rowcache@CASE_STAT;
```

The following listing shows the table creation portion of utlestat.sql, assuming that the original tables have been created in the CC tablespace of the CC1 Command Center database.

For this example, the tables will once again be stored in the CC data tablespace of the CC1 Command Center database. Each **create table** command will have the **tablespace CC** clause appended to it, and each query of a remote table will have the **@case_stat** clause added to it so the database link named CASE_STAT will be used.

```
create table stats$stats
TABLESPACE CC
as select  e.value-b.value change , n.name
    from v$statname n ,  stats$begin_stats b , stats$end_stats e
    where n.statistic# = b.statistic# and n.statistic# = e.statistic#;

create table stats$latches
TABLESPACE CC
as select e.gets-b.gets gets,
    e.misses-b.misses misses,
    e.sleeps-b.sleeps sleeps,
    e.immediate_gets-b.immediate_gets immed_gets,
    e.immediate_misses-b.immediate_misses immed_miss,
    n.name
    from v$latchname n ,  stats$begin_latch b , stats$end_latch e
    where n.latch# = b.latch# and n.latch# = e.latch#;

create table stats$event
TABLESPACE CC
as select  e.total_waits-b.total_waits event_count,
        e.time_waited-b.time_waited time_waited,
        e.event
    from  stats$begin_event b , stats$end_event e
    where b.event = e.event
  union all
  select  e.total_waits event_count,
        e.time_waited time_waited,
        e.event
    from  stats$end_event e
    where e.event not in (select b.event from stats$begin_event b);

create table stats$bck_event tablespace CC_ as
  select  e.total_waits-b.total_waits event_count,
        e.time_waited-b.time_waited time_waited,
        e.event
```

```
     from  stats$begin_bck_event b , stats$end_bck_event e
    where b.event = e.event
  union all
  select  e.total_waits event_count,
          e.time_waited time_waited,
          e.event
    from  stats$end_bck_event e
    where e.event not in (select b.event from stats$begin_bck_event b);

update stats$event e
  set (event_count, time_waited) =
    (select e.event_count - b.event_count,
            e.time_waited - b.time_waited
      from stats$bck_event b
        where e.event = b.event)
    where e.event in (select b.event from stats$bck_event b);

create table stats$waitstat as
select  e.class,
        e.count - b.count count,
        e.time - b.time time
  from stats$begin_waitstat b, stats$end_waitstat e
    where e.class = b.class;

create table stats$roll
TABLESPACE CC
as select  e.usn undo_segment,
        e.gets-b.gets trans_tbl_gets,
    e.waits-b.waits trans_tbl_waits,
    e.writes-b.writes undo_bytes_written,
    e.rssize segment_size_bytes,
        e.xacts-b.xacts xacts,
    e.shrinks-b.shrinks shrinks,
        e.wraps-b.wraps wraps
    from stats$begin_roll b, stats$end_roll e
        where e.usn = b.usn;

create table stats$files
TABLESPACE CC
as select b.ts table_space,
      b.name file_name,
      e.pyr-b.pyr phys_reads,
      e.pbr-b.pbr phys_blks_rd,
      e.prt-b.prt phys_rd_time,
      e.pyw-b.pyw phys_writes,
      e.pbw-b.pbw phys_blks_wr,
```

```
        e.pwt-b.pwt phys_wrt_tim,
        e.megabytes_size
  from stats$begin_file b, stats$end_file e
        where b.name=e.name;

create table stats$dc
TABLESPACE CC
as select b.parameter name,
        e.gets-b.gets get_reqs,
        e.getmisses-b.getmisses get_miss,
        e.scans-b.scans scan_reqs,
        e.scanmisses-b.scanmisses scan_miss,
        e.modifications-b.modifications mod_reqs,
        e.count count,
        e.usage cur_usage
  from stats$begin_dc b, stats$end_dc e
        where b.cache#=e.cache#
        and  nvl(b.subordinate#,-1) = nvl(e.subordinate#,-1);

create table stats$lib
TABLESPACE CC
as select e.namespace,
        e.gets-b.gets gets,
        e.gethits-b.gethits gethits,
        e.pins-b.pins pins,
        e.pinhits-b.pinhits pinhits,
        e.reloads - b.reloads reloads,
        e.invalidations - b.invalidations invalidations
  from stats$begin_lib b, stats$end_lib e
        where b.namespace = e.namespace;
```

The before and after "snapshots" of these statistics tables will provide information about all of the relevant memory objects that can be monitored in ORACLE. These include the dictionary cache, the hit ratio ((db block gets + consistent gets)/physical reads) and the I/O statistics on a file-by-file basis. Information about rollback segment usage and latch usage is also reported.

Interpreting the Statistics Reports

The utlbstat/utlestat scripts create a report called report.txt that lists information about all sections of the database. The ORACLE8 report.txt contains the 13 sections listed in Table 6-2.

The following discussion describes the sections of the report, in the order in which they appear in the report.

Report Sections

Library Cache statistics

Overall statistics

Average length of dirty buffer write queue

System-wide wait events

System-wide wait events for background processes

Latch statistics

No-wait gets of latches

Buffer busy wait statistics

Rollback segments

init.ora values

Dictionary cache

File I/O, summed by tablespace

File I/O

TABLE 6-2.   *report.txt Sections*

Library Cache Statistics

The Library Cache (LC) contains shared SQL and PL/SQL areas. The statistics in this section of the report help determine if shared SQL statements are being reparsed due to insufficient memory being allocated to the LC. The listing shown in Figure 6-9 shows sample data that will be used for this discussion.

The Pins column shows the number of times that an item was executed, while Reloads shows the number of misses. The ratio of reloads to pins indicates the percentage of executions that resulted in reparsing. For this sample data, that ratio is 6/378, or 1.6 percent. That means that 1.6 percent of the time a statement had to be reparsed prior to execution. An ideal value for this ratio is 0; ORACLE recommends adding memory to the Shared SQL Pool if the value is greater than 1 percent (as in this example). Memory is added to this pool via the init.ora SHARED_POOL_SIZE parameter.

If your application consists mostly of dynamic SQL, your SQL commands are reparsed each time they are executed. The commands are reparsed even if identical

LIBRARY	GETS	GETHITRATI	PINS	PINHITRATI	RELOADS	INVALIDATI
BODY	0	1	0	1	0	0
SQL AREA	89	.843	282	.879	5	0
TABLE/PROCED	106	.83	96	.802	1	0
TRIGGER	0	1	0	1	0	0

Note: Sum of Pins column = 378. Sum of Reloads column = 6.

FIGURE 6-9. *Sample Library Cache statistics*

SQL commands have previously been executed. In such an application, increasing the SHARED_POOL_SIZE value will have little effect on the Library Cache statistics. Due to the continual reparsing of statements, the Library Cache will have a high number of reloads compared to the number of pins.

Overall Statistics

The Overall Statistics section of the report shows the total changes for many system statistics, as well as giving *per transaction* and *per logon* values (but since running utlestat requires logging in to the database, the per logon numbers will always reflect one more logon than actually took place). Only nonzero changes are shown. This section of the report is useful for determining the overall hit ratio and for detecting indications of possible problems in the database setup.

To determine the hit ratio, use the formula (logical reads-physical reads)/logical reads. logical reads is the sum of the "consistent gets" and "db block gets" statistics; physical reads is shown on the report as "physical reads." For the statistics shown in Figure 6-10, the hit ratio is 93.4 percent ((1,358 + 214) - 103) / (1,358 + 214).

Statistic	Total	Per Transact	Per Logon
consistent gets	1358	1358	226.33
db block gets	214	214	35.67
physical reads	103	103	17.17

FIGURE 6-10. *Sample hit ratio statistics*

When analyzing the other statistics, note that many of them should be zero or very low for best results. These include recursive calls (which should also show up in the Dictionary Cache section of the report), Table scans (long tables), and enqueue timeouts. High values for these statistics indicate that the database and the applications that use it should be altered in order to improve performance.

Average Length of Dirty Buffer Write Queue

The query for this portion of the report revisits the statistics tables used by the Overall Statistics section. It compares two of the entries there, calculating the ratio of the change in the "summed dirty queue length" record to the change in the "write requests" record. If the average length (the value returned by the query) is greater than 0.25 times the value of the db_block_buffers init.ora parameter (see "init.ora values" section), then either (1) the database I/O is unevenly distributed among the datafiles, or (2) the db_file_simultaneous_writes parameter is set low. In either case, the database write operations are performing poorly.

System-Wide Wait Events

This part of the report lists the count, total time, and average time for a number of system events. There is no documentation in the report to establish ranges for the values shown. Since the query for this part of report.txt calculates the time spent per event, the initiation parameter—TIMED_STATISTICS—should be set to TRUE in init.ora to get nonzero values.

System-Wide Wait Events for Background Processes

This part of the report lists the event, total number of waits, and total time waited for the background processes. Since the query for this part of report.txt calculates the time spent per event, the initiation parameter—TIMED_STATISTICS—should be set to TRUE in init.ora to get nonzero values. Background processes that experience a high number of waits may use options available as of ORACLE8. The DBWR process can have multiple I/O slave processes; their number is determined by the setting of the DBWR_IO_SLAVES parameter in the init.ora file. The LGWR and ARCH processes can also have I/O slaves. You can initiate multiple DBWR processes via the DBWR_PROCESSES init.ora parameter.

Latch Statistics

You can use this section of the report to determine the proper number of redo log allocation latches and redo log copy latches that are appropriate for your database.

Redo log copy latches are used on multiple-CPU servers to distribute the processing that is normally done via the redo log allocation latch. In such a setup, the copy latches are used to copy a process's redo information into the redo log buffer area in the SGA. If copy latches are not used, the allocation latch must both manage the latch allocation and perform the copy, thus slowing down the transaction logging process.

If the Misses value for redo allocation is greater than 10 percent of the Gets column, and if you have multiple processors on your server, consider adding redo log copy latches. To do this, decrease the init.ora parameter LOG_SMALL_ENTRY _SIZE and increase the LOG_SIMULTANEOUS_COPIES and LOG_ENTRY_PREBUILD_THRESHOLD values. These will determine the number of latches and the maximum size of a redo entry that should be copied using the allocation latch (all others will be passed on to the copy latches). After changing these values, regenerate the statistics reports to see if further latch changes are necessary.

No-Wait Gets of Latches

This section of the report calculates the percentage of no-wait latch requests that were satisfied immediately. For the sample data shown in Figure 6-11, all of the no-wait hit ratios are calculated to be 100 percent.

Buffer Busy Waits

This section of the report identifies the type of block for which contention is occurring. If you have too few rollback segments, you will see a high value (> 2,000) for 'undo segment headers'. A high value for 'data block' waits (> 10,000) indicates that you should add DBWR I/O slaves to additional DBWR processess.

LATCH_NAME	NOWAIT_GETS	NOWAIT_MISSES	NOWAIT_HIT_RATIO
cache buffers chai	60643	0	1
cache buffers lru	1021	0	1
library cache	96	0	1
library cache pin	14	0	1
row cache objects	11	0	1

FIGURE 6-11.   *Sample no-wait latch gets statistics*

Rollback Segments

This section of the report shows statistics regarding the usage of rollback segments. You should consider making several changes to this section of the report to improve its usefulness:

- Remove the XACTS column, which is the number of active transactions. Since this statistic is not a cumulative statistic, it is not really helpful to determine the difference between the starting and ending values.

- Add the Extends column, which is cumulative and can be added to the rollback segment queries of the utlbstat queries. The Extends column lists the number of times the rollback segment was extended.

The actions that these columns track are described in Chapter 7.

The Undo_Segment column's value can be used to determine the rollback segment name by querying the V$ROLLNAME table.

```
select Name from V$ROLLNAME
where USN = &UNDO_SEGMENT;
```

Waits for the rollback segment, as indicated in the Trans_Tbl_Waits column of the report, indicate that more rollback segments may be needed in the database. Nonzero values for Shrinks and Wraps indicate that the rollback segments are dynamically expanding and shrinking (back to their **optimal** settings). This activity shows that the rollback segments need to be redesigned in order to reflect the kinds of transactions being performed against the database.

init.ora Values

This section shows the nondefault init.ora parameter settings. You may wish to remove the **where** clause in this query so that all of the parameters and their values will be listed.

Dictionary Cache

The Dictionary Cache (DC) portion of report.txt reflects the setting (Count) and current usage (Usage) of the dictionary cache in the shared SQL area. The report only shows those parameters that have nonzero values for the time interval being reported. The ratio of misses to gets should be low (generally less than 10 percent). Figure 6-12 shows the DC portion of report.txt.

NAME	GET_REQS	GET_MISS	SCAN_REQ	SCAN_MIS	MOD_REQS	COUNT	CUR_USAG
dc_free_extents	246	0	0	0	0	97	82
dc_segments	2	1	0	0	0	128	126
dc_rollback_seg	36	0	0	0	0	17	7
dc_users	46	0	0	0	0	14	13
dc_user_grants	32	0	0	0	0	43	10
dc_objects	60	10	0	0	0	221	218
dc_tables	116	5	0	0	0	195	190
dc_columns	446	27	53	5	0	1880	1871
dc_table_grants	54	24	0	0	0	1626	764
dc_indexes	17	1	37	2	0	261	140
dc_constraint_d	1	0	9	0	0	396	13
dc_synonyms	3	0	0	0	0	18	17
dc_usernames	15	0	0	0	0	20	15
dc_sequences	5	0	0	0	0	7	1

FIGURE 6-12. *Sample dictionary cache statistics*

File I/O, Summed by Tablespace

This section of the report provides the same information as the File I/O section, except that it is summed at the tablespace level instead of the file level. For a description of the most relevant columns in this report, see the "Extensions to the Statistics Reports" section of this chapter.

File I/O

This section records the physical and logical I/O against the datafiles in the database. A description of the most relevant columns is provided in the "Extensions to the Statistics Reports" section of this chapter.

Extensions to the Statistics Reports

By using the queries that generated the report.txt file, you can generate very useful reports that can be run in an ad hoc manner. These queries will be run against the current values of the statistics in the database, rather than against the tables created by the utlbstat and utlestat scripts. The statistics generated from these queries will thus reflect all of the activities in the database since it was last started.

File I/O

The following SQL*Plus scripts generate a listing of all database files, by disk, and total the I/O activities against each disk. The scripts' output helps to illustrate how well the file I/O is currently being distributed across the available devices.

NOTE
*Both queries assume that the drive names are five characters long (such as /db01). If your drive names are other than five characters long, you will need to modify the **SUBSTR** functions in the queries and the formatting commands for the Drive column.*

```
clear columns
clear breaks
column Drive format A5
column File_Name format A30
column Blocks_Read format 99999999
column Blocks_Written format 99999999
column Total_IOs format 99999999
set linesize 80 pagesize 60 newpage 0 feedback off
ttitle skip center "Database File I/O Information" skip 2
break on report
compute sum of Blocks_Read on report
compute sum of Blocks_Written on report
compute sum of Total_IOs on report

select substr(DF.Name,1,5) Drive,
       SUM(FS.Phyblkrd+FS.Phyblkwrt) Total_IOs,
       SUM(FS.Phyblkrd) Blocks_Read,
       SUM(FS.Phyblkwrt) Blocks_Written
  from V$FILESTAT FS, V$DATAFILE DF
 where DF.File#=FS.File#
 group by substr(DF.Name,1,5)
 order by Total_IOs desc;
```

Sample output is shown in the following listing:

```
DRIVE TOTAL_IOS BLOCKS_READ BLOCKS_WRITTEN
----- --------- ----------- --------------
/db03    57217       56820            397
/db01    39940       27712           6228
/db04    15759       14728           1031
/db02     1898          10           1888
         ---------   -----------   --------------
sum     108814       99270           9544
```

The second file I/O query shows the I/O attributed to each datafile, by disk:

```
clear breaks
clear computes
break on Drive skip 1 on report
compute sum of Blocks_Read on Drive
compute sum of Blocks_Written on Drive
compute sum of Total_IOs on Drive
compute sum of Blocks_Read on Report
compute sum of Blocks_Written on Report
compute sum of Total_IOs on Report
ttitle skip center "Database File I/O by Drive" skip 2

select substr(DF.Name,1,5) Drive,
       DF.Name File_Name,
       FS.Phyblkrd+FS.Phyblkwrt Total_IOs,
       FS.Phyblkrd Blocks_Read,
       FS.Phyblkwrt Blocks_Written
  from V$FILESTAT FS, V$DATAFILE DF
 where DF.File#=FS.File#
 order by Drive, File_Name desc;
```

Sample output for this query is shown in the following listing:

```
DRIVE FILE_NAME                         TOTAL_IOS BLOCKS_READ BLOCKS_WRITTEN
----- ------------------------------   --------- ----------- --------------
/db01 /db01/oracle/CC1/sys.dbf            29551      27708           1843
      /db01/oracle/CC1/temp.dbf            4389          4           4385
      *****                             --------- ----------- --------------
sum                                       33940      27712           6228

/db02 /db02/oracle/CC1/rbs01.dbf           1134          3           1131
      /db02/oracle/CC1/rbs02.dbf            349                       349
      /db02/oracle/CC1/rbs03.dbf            415          7            408
      *****                             --------- ----------- --------------
sum                                        1898         10           1888

/db03 /db03/oracle/CC1/cc.dbf             57217      56820            397
      *****                             --------- ----------- --------------
sum                                       57217      56820            397

/db04 /db04/oracle/CC1/ccindx.dbf         15759      14728           1031
      /db04/oracle/CC1/tests01.dbf
      *****                             --------- ----------- --------------
sum                                       15759      14728           1031

      *****                             --------- ----------- --------------
sum                                      108814      99270           9544
```

The data in the preceding listing shows the format of the queries' output. The first part of the report shows a drive-by-drive comparison of the database I/O against datafiles. It shows that the device called /db03 is the most heavily used device during database usage. The second report shows that the I/O on device /db03 is due to one file, since no other database files exist on that drive for the CC1 database.

It also shows that accesses against the file on /db03 are read-intensive by an overwhelming margin.

The second most active device is /db01, which has two database files on it. Most of the activity on that disk is against the SYSTEM tablespace file, with the TEMP tablespace demanding much less I/O. The SYSTEM tablespace's readings will be high during these queries because you are not looking at I/O for a specific interval, but for the entire time that the database has been opened. Since this is the case, all of the I/O involved in database startup and initial SGA population show up here.

This report is excellent for detecting possible conflicts among file I/O loads. Given this report and the I/O capacity of your devices, you can correctly distribute your database files to minimize I/O contention and maximize throughput. See Chapter 4 for further information on minimizing I/O contention.

Segments at Maximum Extension

The alert reports in this chapter use control limit criteria that are established at the system level (for example, ten extents per segment). However, you should compare the current extent usage of segments against the limits defined specifically for that segment, via the **maxextents** storage parameter.

The following SQL*Plus report queries remote databases to detect any segment that is within a specified factor of its maximum extension. It is written to access those databases via a database link, and the link name is used as part of the output file name. The multiplier value should always be greater than 1—it is the value by which the actual extent count will be multiplied when it is compared with the maximum extent count. To determine which segments are within 20 percent of their maximum extension, set the multiplier value to 1.2.

This query checks four different types of segments: clusters, tables, indexes, and rollback segments. For each one, it determines whether the current number of extents is approaching the maximum number of extents that segment can have (as set via the **maxextents** storage parameter). The "multiplier" variable is used to determine how close to its maximum extension a segment must be before it is returned via this query. If the segment is approaching its maximum extension, then its owner, name, and current space usage information will be returned.

NOTE
*As of ORACLE7.3, you can specify a **maxextents** value of **unlimited**. When you specify a **maxextents** value of **unlimited** for a segment, ORACLE assigns the segment a **maxextents** value of 2,147,483,645. Therefore, a segment with a **maxextents** value of **unlimited** could theoretically reach its maximum extension, although that is highly unlikely.*

```
rem
rem   file:  over_extended.sql
rem   parameters:  database link name (instance name), multiplier
rem
rem   The "multiplier" value should always be greater than 1.
rem   Example:  To see segments that are within 20 percent of
rem   their maximum extension, set the multiplier to 1.2.
rem
rem   Example call:
rem   @over_extended CASE 1.2
rem

select
   Owner,                  /*owner of segment*/
   Segment_Name,           /*name of segment*/
   Segment_Type,           /*type of segment*/
   Extents,                /*number of extents already acquired*/
   Blocks                  /*number of blocks already acquired*/
from DBA_SEGMENTS@&&1 s
where                      /*for cluster segments*/
(S.Segment_Type = 'CLUSTER' and exists
(select 'x' from DBA_CLUSTERS@&&1 c
where C.Owner = S.Owner
and C.Cluster_Name = S.Segment_Name
and C.Max_Extents <= S.Extents*&&2))
or                        /*for table segments*/
(s.segment_type = 'TABLE' and exists
(select 'x' from DBA_TABLES@&&1 t
where T.Owner = S.Owner
and T.Table_Name = S.Segment_Name
and T.Max_Extents <= S.Extents*&&2))
or                        /*for index segments*/
(S.Segment_Type = 'INDEX' and exists
(select 'x' from DBA_INDEXES@&&1 i
where I.Owner = S.Owner
and I.Index_Name = S.Segment_Name
and I.Max_Extents <= S.Extents*&&2))
or                        /*for rollback segments*/
(S.Segment_Type = 'ROLLBACK' and exists
(select 'x' from DBA_ROLLBACK_SEGS@&&1 r
where R.Owner = S.Owner
and R.Segment_Name = S.Segment_Name
and R.Max_Extents <= S.Extents*&&2))
order by 1,2

spool &&1._over_extended.lst
/
spool off
undefine 1
undefine 2
```

The output file for this report will contain the database link name in its title. The output filename uses the period (.) as the concatenation character in SQL*Plus.

Segments That Cannot Extend into the Available Free Space

In addition to monitoring the segments that are near their extent limits, you should regularly query the database to determine if any of the segments cannot extend into the available free space in the tablespace. This query does not have to be part of the Command Center database; it is an alert report, and the records returned by the query should be addressed immediately.

There are two separate queries for this report. The first query, shown in the following listing, determines if there is enough space in the tablespace for a segment's next extent:

```
select Owner, Segment_Name, Segment_Type
   from DBA_SEGMENTS
 where Next_Extent >
(select SUM(Bytes) from DBA_FREE_SPACE
   where Tablespace_Name = DBA_SEGMENTS.Tablespace_Name);
```

The preceding query may report segments that are not problems. For example, the tablespace's datafiles may be set to **autoextend**, in which case the tablespace's available free space is limited by the maximum datafile size.

If a table name is returned by the preceding query, there is not enough free space in the tablespace to store the next extent of the table, even if all the space in the tablespace were coalesced. This is an alert condition; you can create a separate query that may identify the table as a problem before it reaches the alert stage. The following query returns the name of any segment whose next extent will not fit in the single largest free extent in the tablespace:

```
select Owner, Segment_Name, Segment_Type
   from DBA_SEGMENTS
 where Next_Extent>
(select MAX(Bytes) from DBA_FREE_SPACE
   where Tablespace_Name = DBA_SEGMENTS.Tablespace_Name);
```

Coalescing free space may resolve some of the space issues. However, if the tablespace's free space is divided among datafiles or separated by data segments, you may not be able to increase the maximum available free extent size.

If you cannot support another extent for an actively used segment, you may need to either add space to the tablespace or change the storage parameters for your segments.

Rate of Space Allocation Within an Object

As described in Chapters 4 and 5, you can simplify your database space administration activities by properly sizing your database objects. However, a properly sized object may not be reported by the Command Center database and similar alert reports, even if it has the potential to cause problems.

For example, you may create a SALES table that is estimated to need 1GB per year. If you allocate a 1GB extent for the table, it should not acquire a new extent for many months, and thus it will not show up in the Command Center reports. If the table does not acquire any new extents, the free space in the tablespace may be unchanged, so the space watcher report will not list that tablespace. However, the space usage within the table may present a problem.

If the space in the table is being used at a greater rate than expected, the table will need to extend sooner than anticipated. For a large transaction table, an unexpected extension may have a significant impact on the space available. Using the scripts provided in the preceding section, you should be able to anticipate segment extensions that will encounter space problems. You can use the query provided in this section to determine which segments are likely to extend.

The following query uses the statistics columns of the data dictionary views, so it is only valid for objects that have been analyzed. Furthermore, the value of the query's output is directly related to the frequency with which the objects are analyzed and the type of analysis performed. For best results, use a full **compute statistics** analysis shortly before executing the query. The query will report any object whose block usage is within 10 percent of its current allocated usage.

The first part of the **union** query, shown in the following listing, selects the data for the database's tables. The **column** commands format the data so it will fit in an 80-column screen width.

```
column Owner format A12
column Table_Name format A20
column Empty format 99999
column Pctusd format 999.99

select T.Owner,
       T.Table_Name,
       S.Segment_Type,
       T.Blocks Used,
       T.Empty_Blocks Empty,
       S.Blocks Allocated,
       T.Blocks/S.Blocks Pctusd
  from DBA_TABLES T, DBA_SEGMENTS S
 where T.Owner = S.Owner
   and T.Table_Name = S.Segment_Name
   and S.Segment_Type = 'TABLE'
   and T.Blocks/S.Blocks > 0.95
 order by 7  desc
```

Sample data for the preceding query is shown in the following listing:

```
OWNER          TABLE_NAME              SEGMENT       USED   EMPTY   ALLOCATED   PCTUSD
-------------  ----------------------  -------  ----------  ------  ----------  -------
APPOWN         REGION                  TABLE            46       0          47      .98
APPOWN         MANUFACTURER            TABLE           210       4         215      .98
APPOWN         VOUCHER_HEADER          TABLE           251       5         257      .98
APPOWN         PO_HEADER               TABLE           459      10         470      .98
APPOWN         VOUCHER_LINE            TABLE           869       5         890      .98
APPOWN         PO_LINE                 TABLE           491       0         505      .97
```

As shown in the output, several of the tables in the database have used over 95 percent of the blocks they have allocated. The tables with the highest percentage of space usage, if they are active transaction tables, are likely to extend. You should evaluate the tables to determine if the tables are likely to extend. For example, the first table in the output listing, REGION, may be unlikely to extend unless you are frequently adding new regions. The VOUCHER_HEADER and VOUCHER_LINE tables, however, are transaction tables and are likely to extend.

The full query, shown in the following listing, reports the tables and indexes approaching their current space allocation:

```
column Owner format A12
column Table_Name format A20
column Empty format 99999
column Pctusd format 999.99

select T.Owner,
       T.Table_Name,
       S.Segment_Type,
       T.Blocks Used,
       T.Empty_Blocks Empty,
       S.Blocks Allocated,
       T.Blocks/S.Blocks Pctusd
  from DBA_TABLES T, DBA_SEGMENTS S
 where T.Owner = S.Owner
   and T.Table_Name = S.Segment_Name
   and S.Segment_Type = 'TABLE'
   and T.Blocks/S.Blocks > 0.95
union all
select I.Owner,
       I.Index_Name,
       S.Segment_Type,
       I.Leaf_Blocks Used,
       S.Blocks-1-I.Leaf_Blocks Empty,
       S.Blocks Allocated,
       I.Leaf_Blocks/S.Blocks Pctusd
  from DBA_INDEXES I, DBA_SEGMENTS S
 where I.Owner = S.Owner
   and I.Index_Name = S.Segment_Name
   and S.Segment_Type = 'INDEX'
   and I.Leaf_Blocks/S.Blocks > 0.95
order by 7 desc, 2, 1
```

The preceding query will display the data for tables and indexes in the same report. The data will be ordered by the percentage of allocated space used, with the highest percentages listed first.

You can extend this report by building a history table and storing the allocated percentage used over time. However, such a history may not be very valuable. For example, the allocated percentage will be reduced when a segment acquires a new extent, so the allocated percentage used will fluctuate over time even for active tables. This report is most useful either as an alert for all of your segments or for tracking the space usage of specific segments.

The Well-Managed Database

The effective management of any system requires strategic planning, quality control, and action to resolve out-of-control parts of the system. The database management systems described in this chapter provide a broad foundation for the monitoring of all of your databases. Individual databases may require additional monitoring to be performed, or may have specific thresholds. These can be easily added to the samples shown here.

Establishing a Command Center database allows the other databases in the system to be monitored without impacting the measures being checked. It also allows for easy addition of new databases to the monitoring system and trend analysis of all statistics. The Command Center database should be tied in to your existing operating system monitoring programs in order to coordinate the distribution and resolution of alert messages.

Like any system, the Command Center database must be planned. The examples in this chapter were designed to handle the most commonly monitored objects in the database, and threshold values were established for each. Do not create the CC1 database until you have fully defined what you are going to monitor and what the threshold values are. Once that has been done, create the database—and in a great example of recursion, use the monitoring database to monitor itself.

CHAPTER
7

Managing Rollback
Segments

ollback segments are ORACLE's version of time machines. They capture the "before" image of data as it existed prior to the start of a transaction. Queries by other users against the data that is being changed will return the data as it existed *before* the change began. No matter how well behaved the rest of the database is, rollback segments will almost always require special attention. And since rollback segments control the database's ability to handle transactions, they play a key role in the database's success.

This chapter will cover the key managerial tasks that DBAs need to perform for rollback segments. You will see

- The basic functional aspects of rollback segments

- The unique way in which they use available space

- How to monitor their usage

- How to select the correct number and size of rollback segments for your database

Rollback Segments Overview

The SQL command **rollback** allows users to undo transactions that have been made against a database. This functionality is available for any **update**, **insert**, or **delete** transaction; it is not available for changes to database objects (such as **alter table** commands). When you select data that another user is changing, ORACLE uses the rollback segments to show you the data as it existed before the changes began.

How the Database Uses Rollback Segments

Rollback segments are involved in every transaction that occurs within the database. They allow the database to maintain read consistency between multiple transactions. The number and size of rollback segments available are specified by the DBA during database creation.

Since rollback segments are created within the database, they must be created within a tablespace. The first rollback segment, called *SYSTEM*, is stored in the SYSTEM tablespace. Further rollback segments are usually created in at least one other tablespace. Because rollback segments are created in tablespaces, their maximum size is limited to the amount of space in the tablespaces' datafiles. Appropriate sizing of rollback segments is therefore a critical task. Figure 7-1 depicts the storage of rollback segments in tablespaces.

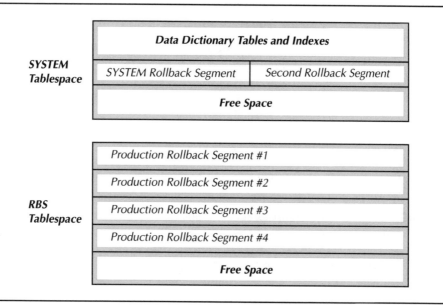

FIGURE 7-1.   *Storage of rollback segments in tablespaces*

A *rollback segment entry* is the set of "before" image data blocks that contain rows modified by a transaction. Each rollback segment entry must be completely contained within one rollback segment. A single rollback segment can support multiple rollback segment entries. This makes the number of rollback segments available a critical factor for the database's performance. Figure 7-2 illustrates the relationship between rollback segments and rollback segment entries.

The database assigns transactions to rollback segments in a round-robin fashion. This assignment method results in a fairly even distribution of the number of transactions in each rollback segment. Although it is possible to specify which rollback segment a transaction should use (see "Specifying a Rollback Segment for a Transaction," later in this chapter), most transactions use the default. Because of the round-robin assignment method used, it is usually not advantageous to have rollback segments of varied sizes.

You can create rollback segments that are designated as *private* or *public*. These designations refer to whether the rollback segment is available to a single instance or to multiple instances that access that database. Private rollback segments are explicitly acquired when an instance opens a database (as shown in the "Activating Rollback Segments" section of this chapter). If a second instance accesses the same database, then it may not use the same private rollback segment that the first

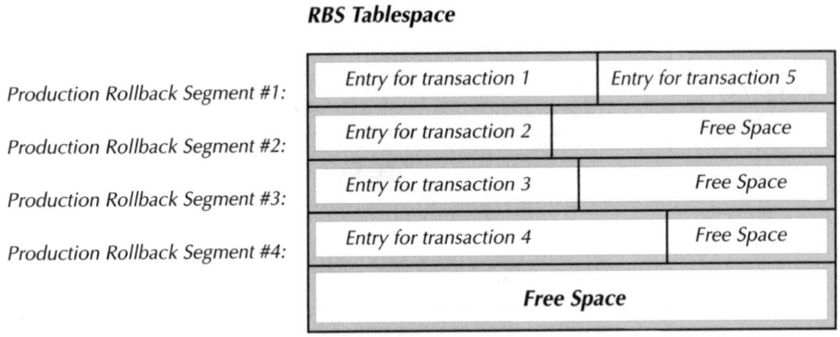

RBS Tablespace

Entry for transaction 1	Entry for transaction 5
Entry for transaction 2	Free Space
Entry for transaction 3	Free Space
Entry for transaction 4	Free Space
Free Space	

Production Rollback Segment #1:
Production Rollback Segment #2:
Production Rollback Segment #3:
Production Rollback Segment #4:

FIGURE 7-2. *Storage of rollback segment entries in rollback segments*

instance has already acquired. Instead, it can either use its own private rollback segments or it can draw from a pool of public rollback segments.

The SYSTEM Rollback Segment

The SYSTEM rollback segment is created automatically during database creation. Its name and storage parameters are not specified in the **create database** command. Rather, the SYSTEM rollback segment is automatically created in the SYSTEM tablespace.

The usage of the SYSTEM rollback segment varies depending on your configuration. If your database has multiple tablespaces (as almost all databases do), then you will have to create a second rollback segment to support them. If other rollback segments are available, then the SYSTEM rollback segment is used only to manage database-level transactions (such as modifications to the data dictionary tables that record user privileges).

The Second Rollback Segment

If your database will have multiple tablespaces, then you will have to create a second rollback segment. You cannot write to any objects in a non-SYSTEM tablespace unless there are at least two rollback segments available. During database creation, the second rollback segment must be created in the SYSTEM tablespace. Postcreation, however, the second rollback segment should not be made available for production transactions; doing so would put the SYSTEM tablespace's free space in jeopardy during large transactions.

Therefore, the second rollback segment should be used only during database creation. As soon as a tablespace for rollback segments has been created, create rollback segments in it and deactivate or drop the second rollback segment in the SYSTEM tablespace.

With regard to rollback segments, your database creation procedures should do the following:

1. Create a database, which automatically creates a SYSTEM rollback segment in the SYSTEM tablespace.

2. Create a second rollback segment, named r0, in the SYSTEM tablespace.

3. Make the new rollback segment available. You can then create other tablespaces.

4. Create a tablespace called RBS for further rollback segments.

5. Create additional rollback segments in the RBS tablespace.

6. Deactivate the second rollback segment (r0) in the SYSTEM tablespace and activate the new rollback segments in RBS.

Although it is no longer needed after database creation, you may want to keep the second rollback segment available but inactive. To do this, deactivate the rollback segment (see "Activating Rollback Segments" later in this chapter), but do not drop it. This rollback segment can then be quickly reactivated during emergency situations that affect the RBS tablespace.

The Production Rollback Segments

Non-SYSTEM *production rollback segments* support the rollback segment entries generated by production usage of the database. They support the use of the **rollback** command to restore the previous image of the modified records. They also roll back transactions that are aborted prior to completion, either because of a problem with the rollback segment or because of user cancellation of the transaction. During queries, rollback segments are used to construct a consistent "before" image of the data that was changed—but not committed—prior to the execution of the query.

The database assigns rollback segment entries to the production rollback segments in a round-robin fashion. This method is designed to distribute the transaction load being carried by the rollback segments (as seen in Figure 7-2). Since a single rollback segment can support multiple transactions, you can create a single, large rollback segment to handle all transactions in a database. However, such a design would result in performance problems due to contention for the rollback segment.

Conversely, you may choose to create many small rollback segments, so that each transaction will be guaranteed its own rollback segment. This implementation will also run into performance problems if the rollback segments are created so small that they must dynamically extend in order to service their transactions. Planning a database's rollback segment design involves finding the proper balance between the two extremes. The "Choosing the Number and Size" section of this chapter addresses this critical design issue.

Activating Rollback Segments

Activating a rollback segment makes it available to the database users. A rollback segment may be deactivated without being dropped. It will maintain the space already allocated to it, and can be reactivated at a later date. The following examples provide the full set of rollback segment activation commands.

An active rollback segment can be deactivated via the **alter rollback segment** command.

```
alter rollback segment SEGMENT_NAME offline;
```

To drop a rollback segment, use the **drop rollback segment** command.

```
drop rollback segment SEGMENT_NAME;
```

To create a rollback segment, use the **create rollback segment** command, as shown in the following listing:

```
create rollback segment SEGMENT_NAME
tablespace RBS;
```

Note that the example **create rollback segment** command creates a private rollback segment (since the **public** keyword was not used) and that it creates it in a non-SYSTEM tablespace called RBS. Since no storage parameters are specified, the rollback segment will use the default storage parameters for that tablespace (you will see the space management details for rollback segments in later sections of this chapter).

Although the rollback segment has been created, it is not yet in use by the database. To activate the new rollback segment, bring it online using the following command:

```
alter rollback segment SEGMENT_NAME online;
```

Once a rollback segment has been created, you should list it in the database's init.ora file. This file is only read during database startups. A sample init.ora entry for rollback segments is shown in the following listing:

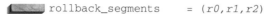

```
rollback_segments    = (r0,r1,r2)
```

NOTE
The SYSTEM rollback segment should never be listed in the init.ora file. The SYSTEM rollback segment can never be dropped; it is always acquired along with any other rollback segments the instance may acquire.

For this database, the rollback segments named r0, r1, and r2 are online. If you take a rollback segment offline, remove its entry from the init.ora file. When you take a rollback segment offline, it will remain online until its current active transactions complete. You can view the PENDING OFFLINE status of a rollback segment via the V$ROLLSTAT view, as described later in this chapter.

Specifying a Rollback Segment for a Transaction

You can use the **set transaction** command to specify which rollback segment a transaction should use. You should execute the **set transaction** command before large transactions to ensure that they use rollback segments that are created specifically for them.

The settings that are specified via the **set transaction** command will be used only for the current transaction. The following example shows a series of transactions. The first transaction is directed to use the ROLL_BATCH rollback segment. The second transaction (following the second **commit**) will be randomly assigned to a production rollback segment.

```
commit;

set transaction use rollback segment ROLL_BATCH;
insert into TABLE_NAME
select * from DATA_LOAD_TABLE;

commit;

REM*  The commit command clears the rollback segment assignment.
REM*  Implicit commits, like those caused by DDL commands, will
REM*  also clear the rollback segment designation.

insert into TABLE_NAME select * from SOME_OTHER_TABLE;
```

Space Usage Within Rollback Segments

When a transaction begins, ORACLE starts writing a rollback segment entry in a rollback segment. The entry cannot expand into any other rollback segments, nor can it dynamically switch to use a different rollback segment. The entry begins writing sequentially to an extent within the rollback segment. Each block within that extent must contain information for only one transaction. Blocks from different transactions can be stored in the same extent (see Figure 7-3).

Figure 7-3 shows the first five blocks of an extent of a rollback segment. Two separate transactions are storing active rollback information in that rollback extent.

In an ideal database, each transaction will fit within a single extent. However, this is rarely the case. When a transaction can no longer acquire space within an extent, the rollback segment looks for another extent to which it can continue writing the rollback segment entry.

The database will first try to extend the entry into the next extent within the rollback segment. If the current extent is the last extent within the rollback segment, then the database will attempt to extend the entry into its first extent.

However, that extent may already be in use. If it is, then the rollback segment will be forced to acquire a new extent. The entry will then be continued in this new extent. This process of selective extension is illustrated in Figure 7-4.

As shown in Figure 7-4a, a transaction (referred to here as "transaction A") presently has its entry data stored in four extents of rollback segment r1. Since it started in extent #3 of this rollback segment, the first two extents must have been unavailable when the transaction started. At this point, it has acquired four extents and is in search of a fifth.

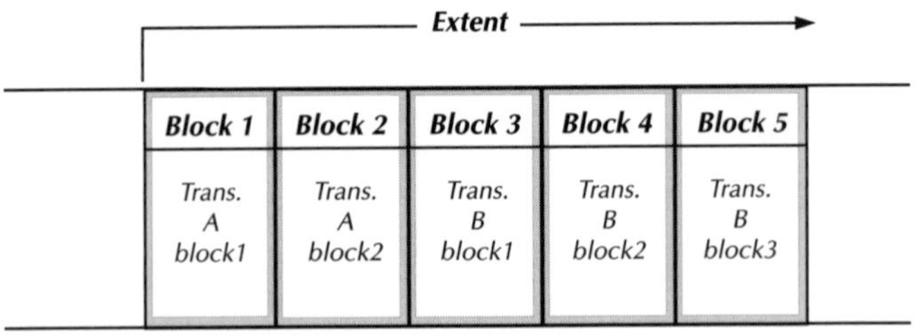

FIGURE 7-3.   *Two transactions in a single rollback segment extent*

Since it already occupies the last extent (extent #6) of the rollback segment, the database checks to see if the first extent of that rollback segment contains any active transaction data. If it does not, then that extent is used as the fifth extent of transaction A's entry (see Figure 7-4b). If, however, that extent is actively being used by a transaction, then the rollback segment will dynamically extend itself and extent #7 will then be used as the fifth extent of transaction A (see Figure 7-4c).

Once a transaction is complete, its data is not deleted from the rollback segment. The old rollback data remains in the rollback segment to service the queries and transactions that began executing before the transaction was committed. This may cause a problem with long queries; namely, they may get the following error message:

```
ORA-1555:  snapshot too old (rollback segment too small)
```

This error arises from the definition of "active" data. Consider the large transaction referred to as "transaction A" in Figure 7-4. If a long-running query accesses the same table as transaction A, then it will need to use the data blocks

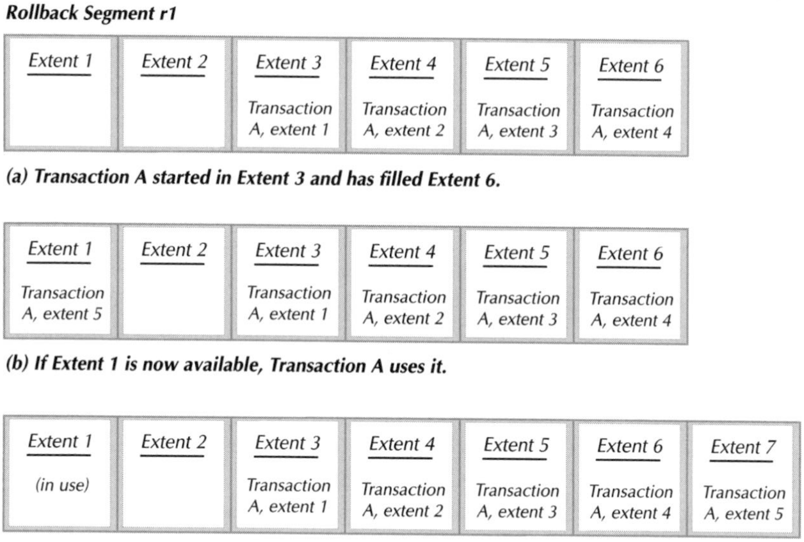

Rollback Segment r1

(a) Transaction A started in Extent 3 and has filled Extent 6.

(b) If Extent 1 is now available, Transaction A uses it.

(c) If Extent 1 is in use, the rollback segment will extend.

FIGURE 7-4. *Selective extension of rollback segments*

stored by transaction A's rollback segment entry. However, once transaction A has completed, those blocks are marked as being *inactive*. Those blocks may then be overwritten by other transactions, even though the separate long-running query against those blocks has not completed. The query, upon attempting to read the blocks that have been overwritten, will fail. This situation is depicted in Figure 7-5.

As shown in Figure 7-5, a transaction can span multiple extents. In Figure 7-5a, transaction A uses five extents of a rollback segment and then completes. Other users may be using that data even after the transaction completes. For example, if other users were querying the data before transaction A completed, they would need the rollback segment entry in order to reconstruct the table's data for their queries. The rollback entry data for transaction A is inactive, but it is in use. When transaction B begins (Figure 7-5b), it starts in the first available extent of the rollback segment. When it extends beyond the second extent, the rollback segment entry data from transaction A is overwritten (since it is inactive) and any process using that rollback segment entry data will fail (since it is in use).

Extent 1	Extent 2	Extent 3	Extent 4	Extent 5	Extent 6	Extent 7
		Transaction A, extent 1	Transaction A, extent 2	Transaction A, extent 3	Transaction A, extent 4	Transaction A, extent 5

(a) Transaction A is in progress; its data is used by a large query.

Extent 1	Extent 2	Extent 3	Extent 4	Extent 5	Extent 6	Extent 7
Transaction B, extent 1		OLD Trans. A, extent 1	OLD Trans. A, extent 2	OLD Trans. A, extent 3	OLD Trans. A, extent 4	OLD Trans. A, extent 5

(b) Transaction A completes. Its entry data stays and is used by the long-running query. Transaction B starts.

Extent 1	Extent 2	Extent 3	Extent 4	Extent 5	Extent 6	Extent 7
Transaction B, extent 1	**Transaction B, extent 2**	**Transaction B, extent 3**	OLD Trans. A, extent 2	OLD Trans. A, extent 3	OLD Trans. A, extent 4	OLD Trans. A, extent 5

(c) Transaction B overwrites blocks used by the large query. Query fails.

FIGURE 7-5.   *Query failure due to "snapshot too old" error*

There are two problems that are the true cause of the query's failure. First, a long-running query is being executed at the same time as data manipulation transactions. In other words, batch processing and online transaction processing are being performed simultaneously in the database. From the earlier discussions of rollback segment functionality, the problems with this strategy should be clear: the long-running query must not only access all of the tables and indexes it needs to complete, but must also access data stored in the rollback segments to return a consistent version of the data.

Since it must continue to access the rollback segments until it completes, the long-running query requires that the rollback segment entries it is using not be overwritten. But once those entries have completed, there is no guarantee that this will be the case. The advice given in the error message ("rollback segment too small") solves the problem by resolving the second, related problem: to avoid overwriting existing entries in the rollback segment, add more space to it so it will take longer to wrap around back to the first extent.

Adding more space to the rollback segment is not a true solution. It is only a delaying tactic, since the rollback segment may eventually overwrite all of its data blocks. The proper solution is to schedule long-running queries at times when online transaction processing is at a minimum.

The optimal storage Clause

As shown previously in Figure 7-4, rollback segments dynamically extend to handle large transaction entry loads. Once the transaction that forced the extension completes, the rollback segment *keeps* the space that it acquired during the extension. This can be a major cause of rollback segment space management problems. A single large transaction may use all of the available free space in the rollback segment tablespace, preventing the other rollback segments in that tablespace from extending.

This problem is solved via two changes in the **storage** clause used for rollback segments. First, the **pctincrease** parameter is not supported for rollback segments. This is important because it forces rollback segments to grow at an even pace, rather than at a geometrically increasing rate (see Chapter 4, the "Implications of the Storage Clause" section, for an illustration of this problem).

The second change in the **storage** clause for rollback segments is the addition of a parameter called **optimal**. The **optimal** parameter allows DBAs to specify an optimal length of the rollback segment (in bytes). When the rollback segment extends beyond this length, it later dynamically *shrinks* itself by eliminating its oldest extent.

At first glance, this seems like a terrific option—it prevents a single rollback segment from using all of the free space in a tablespace. However, note that the database is

1. Dynamically extending the rollback segment, causing a performance hit

2. Dynamically choosing and eliminating old extents, causing a performance hit

3. Eliminating inactive data earlier than it would have under the old method

The last point causes databases with **optimal** sizes set too low to experience a greater incidence of the "snapshot too old" scenario depicted in Figure 7-5. The increased incidence of this scenario is due to the fact that old transaction data may now be eliminated in two ways: by being overwritten and by being discarded during shrinks.

The process of extending and shrinking a rollback segment via the **optimal** parameter is shown in Figure 7-6. Note that this parameter is very useful for handling situations in which the transaction size is completely unknown and the available free space in the rollback segment tablespace is limited. However, it is not a substitute for the correct sizing of the rollback segments. This topic will be covered in the "Choosing the Number and Size" section later in this chapter.

As shown in Figure 7-6, when a transaction completes, the rollback segment checks its **optimal** size value. If it is beyond its **optimal** size, it will eliminate its oldest extent (extent #1). This keeps the rollback segment to the **optimal** size while servicing queries. Shrinking the rollback segment has the side effect of reducing the amount of inactive rollback data available to current transactions.

What would have happened if there had been no inactive extents in the rollback segment when it exceeded its **optimal** size? The rollback segment would have continued to extend to support the transaction. If the rollback segment is forced (for instance, by a single, large transaction) to extend beyond its **optimal** size, then the space it acquires will remain part of that rollback segment temporarily. The next transaction that goes beyond the **optimal** setting will, when it completes, force the database to reclaim any space that forced it to exceed its **optimal** setting.

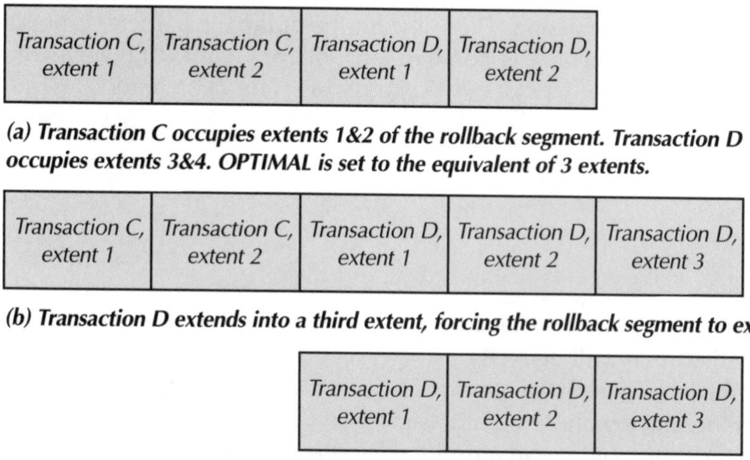

Transaction C, extent 1	Transaction C, extent 2	Transaction D, extent 1	Transaction D, extent 2

(a) Transaction C occupies extents 1&2 of the rollback segment. Transaction D occupies extents 3&4. OPTIMAL is set to the equivalent of 3 extents.

Transaction C, extent 1	Transaction C, extent 2	Transaction D, extent 1	Transaction D, extent 2	Transaction D, extent 3

(b) Transaction D extends into a third extent, forcing the rollback segment to extend.

Transaction D, extent 1	Transaction D, extent 2	Transaction D, extent 3

(c) Transaction C completes, then Transaction D completes. The oldest extents are dropped from the rollback segment and it shrinks to its defined optimal size.

FIGURE 7-6. *Dynamic shrinking of rollback segments to an optimal size*

Monitoring Rollback Segment Usage

The monitoring requirements for rollback segments are similar to those for data segments. See Chapter 6 for methods of monitoring the space and memory usage of segments. Since rollback segments are dynamic objects that are accessed during transactions, they have additional features that should be monitored.

Monitoring Current Space Allocation

To see the current space allocation for a database's rollback segments, query the DBA_SEGMENTS dictionary view, where the Segment_Type column equals 'ROLLBACK':

```
select * from DBA_SEGMENTS
 where Segment_Type = 'ROLLBACK';
```

Table 7-1 lists the columns of interest that will be returned from this query.

There's one column missing. The value for the **optimal** parameter is not stored in DBA_SEGMENTS. Rather, it is stored in the OptSize column of the dynamic performance table named V$ROLLSTAT. To retrieve this value, query V$ROLLSTAT, joining it to V$ROLLNAME to get the rollback segment's name.

```
select N.Name,         /* rollback segment name */
       S.OptSize       /* rollback segment OPTIMAL size */
from V$ROLLNAME N, V$ROLLSTAT S
where N.USN=S.USN;
```

If no **optimal** size was specified for the rollback segment, then the OptSize value returned by this query will be **NULL**.

Since rollback segments are physical segments in the database, they are included in the space monitoring scripts given in Chapter 6. The tablespace space monitoring programs will report any change in the free space available in the RBS or SYSTEM tablespaces. The extent monitoring scripts store records for all of the rollback segments regardless of their number of extents. By doing this, all changes in the rollback segment space allocations can be detected immediately.

Column Name	Description
Segment_Name	Name of the rollback segment
Tablespace_Name	Tablespace in which the rollback segment is stored
Header_File	File in which the first extent of the rollback segment is stored
Bytes	Actual allocated size of the rollback segment, in bytes
Blocks	Actual allocated size of the rollback segment, in ORACLE blocks
Extents	Number of extents in the rollback segment
Initial_Extent	Size, in ORACLE blocks, of the initial extent
Next_Extent	Size, in ORACLE blocks, of the next extent
Min_Extents	Minimum number of extents for the rollback segment
Max_Extents	Maximum number of extents for the rollback segment

TABLE 7-I. *Rollback Segment-Related Columns in DBA_SEGMENTS*

The queries for the Command Center space monitoring scripts in Chapter 6 query the DBA_SEGMENTS view, the main columns of which are listed in Table 7-1.

Shrinking Rollback Segments

You can force rollback segments to shrink. You can use the **shrink** clause of the **alter rollback segment** command to shrink rollback segments to any size you want. If you do not specify a size the rollback segment should **shrink** to, then it will **shrink** to its **optimal** size. You cannot **shrink** a rollback segment to fewer than two extents.

In the following listing, the r1 rollback segment is altered twice. The first command **shrink**s r1 to 15MB. The second command **shrink**s the R1 rollback segment to its **optimal** size.

```
alter rollback segment R1 shrink to 15M;

alter rollback segment R1 shrink;
```

Monitoring Current Status

You can query the DBA_ROLLBACK_SEGS view for information about the rollback segments' status. This view contains the storage parameters (including Tablespace_Name, Initial_Extent, Next_Extent, Min_Extents, Max_Extents, and Relative_FNo) provided in DBA_SEGMENTS. It includes two additional columns, which are listed in Table 7-2.

The status of a rollback segment will be one of the values listed in Table 7-3. You can only bring a rollback segment online if its current status is either OFFLINE or PARTLY AVAILABLE. A rollback segment will have a status value of PARTLY AVAILABLE if it contains data used by an in-doubt or recovered transaction that spans databases (see Part III for information on distributed transactions).

Column Name	Description
Status	Status of the rollback segment.
Instance_Num	Instance the rollback segment belongs to. For a single-instance system, this value is **NULL**.

TABLE 7-2.   *Additional Columns in DBA_ROLLBACK_SEGS*

Status	Description
IN USE	The rollback segment is online.
AVAILABLE	The rollback segment has been created, but has not been brought online.
OFFLINE	The rollback segment is offline.
PENDING OFFLINE	The rollback segment is in the process of going offline.
INVALID	The rollback segment has been dropped. Dropped rollback segments remain listed in the data dictionary with this status.
NEEDS RECOVERY	The rollback segment contains data that cannot be rolled back, or is corrupted.
PARTLY AVAILABLE	The rollback segment contains data from an unresolved transaction involving a distributed database.

TABLE 7-3. *Rollback Segment Status Values in DBA_ROLLBACK_SEGS*

Monitoring Dynamic Extensions

Rollback segments can extend and shrink. In addition, rollback segment entries *wrap* from one extent to another within a rollback segment each time they grow beyond their present extent. All three of these actions require the database to perform additional work to handle transactions. This extra work affects performance.

Consider the case of a large transaction that extends beyond its **optimal** value when an entry wraps and causes the rollback segment to expand into another extent. The sequence of events to handle this looks like this:

1. The transaction begins.

2. An entry is made in the rollback segment header for the new transaction entry.

3. The transaction entry acquires blocks in an extent of the rollback segment.

4. The entry attempts to wrap into a second extent. None is available, so the rollback segment must extend.

5. The rollback segment extends.

6. The data dictionary tables for space management are updated.

7. The transaction completes.

8. The rollback segment checks to see if it is past its **optimal** value. It is.

9. The rollback segment chooses its oldest inactive extent.

10. The oldest inactive extent is eliminated.

If the rollback segment had been sized so that the entry fit in one extent, the sequence of events would instead look like this:

1. The transaction begins.

2. An entry is made in the rollback segment header for the new transaction entry.

3. The transaction entry acquires blocks in an extent of the rollback segment.

4. The transaction completes.

The savings in the amount of overhead needed for space management are clear.

You can use the V$ROLLSTAT dynamic performance table to monitor the incidence of shrinks, wraps, and extensions. You may retrieve the records from this view for a specified time interval or via ad hoc queries, as described in the next two sections.

Dynamic Extensions During a Time Interval

To determine the changes in the values of the V$ROLLSTAT columns during a specific time interval, the system statistics scripts can be used. These scripts, located in the /rdbms/admin subdirectory under the ORACLE software home directory, are UTLBSTAT.SQL and UTLESTAT.SQL. Running these scripts is described in Chapter 6.

The UTLBSTAT script creates a table that stores the current values in the V$ROLLSTAT table. When UTLESTAT is run at a later date, V$ROLLSTAT's values at that time will be compared to those that were stored. The difference will be reported. It is important that the database not be shut down between the running of the UTLBSTAT script and the UTLESTAT script. Because the database resets the statistics in the V$ROLLSTAT table during system startup, the baseline values generated by UTLBSTAT would be of no use following a database restart.

In the UTLBSTAT script, the following commands are used to create the tables at the beginning of the time interval. The first two **create table** commands create tables called STATS$BEGIN_ROLL and STATS$END_ROLL, both with no records in them. The **insert** command then stores the current values from the V$ROLLSTAT table into STATS$BEGIN_ROLL.

```
DROP TABLE stats$begin_roll;
CREATE TABLE stats$begin_roll
AS SELECT * FROM v$rollstat WHERE 0 = 1;

DROP TABLE stats$end_roll;
CREATE TABLE stats$end_roll
AS SELECT * FROM stats$begin_roll;

INSERT INTO stats$begin_roll SELECT * FROM v$rollstat;
```

When UTLESTAT is run, it populates the STATS$END_ROLL table by querying the V$ROLLSTAT table for the then-current values. A table called STATS$ROLL is then created. The sole purpose of the STATS$ROLL table is to hold the results of a query that determines the difference between the records in STATS$BEGIN_ROLL and STATS$END_ROLL.

```
INSERT INTO stats$end_roll SELECT * FROM v$rollstat;

CREATE TABLE stats$roll
AS SELECT  e.usn undo_segment,
        e.gets-b.gets trans_tbl_gets,
    e.waits-b.waits trans_tbl_waits,
    e.writes-b.writes undo_bytes_written,
    e.rssize segment_size_bytes,
        e.xacts-b.xacts xacts,
    e.shrinks-b.shrinks shrinks,
        e.wraps-b.wraps wraps
    FROM stats$begin_roll b, stats$end_roll e
        WHERE e.usn = b.usn;
```

The data in the STATS$ROLL table lists each rollback segment and the statistics that accumulated during the time between the running of UTLBSTAT and UTLESTAT.

Querying the STATS$ROLL table will return the columns listed in Table 7-4 for the interval.

You should make two modifications to the rollback segment portion of UTLESTAT.SQL. First, the Xacts reference in the UTLESTAT query should be changed. The Xacts column reflects the *current* number of active transactions, not

Column Name	Description
Trans_Tbl_Gets	The number of rollback segment header requests.
Trans_Tbl_Waits	The number of rollback segment header requests that resulted in waits.
Undo_Bytes_Written	The number of bytes written to the rollback segment.
Segment_Size_Bytes	The size of the rollback segment, in bytes. Note that this column only considers the ending value.
Xacts	The number of active transactions.
Shrinks	The number of **shrink**s that the rollback segment had to perform in order to stay at the **optimal** size.
Wraps	The number of times a rollback segment entry wrapped from one extent into another.

TABLE 7-4.   *Columns Available in STATS$ROLL*

the *cumulative* number of transactions. As such, the difference between the beginning and ending values for Xacts has no significance. Change that line from

```
e.xacts-b.xacts xacts,
```

to

```
e.xacts        xacts,
```

if you care about this value. Otherwise, remove it entirely.

Second, you may wish to include the Extends column (which *is* cumulative) in the report. The Extends column shows the number of times the rollback segment was extended. Monitoring the Extends column value is most appropriate for those rollback segments whose **optimal** size has not yet been reached.

The monitoring of dynamic extension, wrapping, and shrinking of the rollback segments is thus fairly simple. You can use the rollback segment portions of the UTLBSTAT/UTLESTAT reports to determine the nature of all dynamic extension within the rollback segments.

If the value of (Trans_Tbl_Waits/Trans_Table_Gets) is greater than 0.01 (that is, over 1 percent of gets result in waits) then there is contention for rollback segments in the database.

A final note of caution: these scripts **insert** records into tables. In other words, they perform transactions, which in turn generate rollback segment entries, skewing the results. The number of bytes generated via these queries is less than 100. This skew can be avoided by performing the queries from a remote database (see Chapter 6 for information on this topic).

Ad Hoc Querying

You can query the V$ROLLSTAT table in an ad hoc fashion. The columns available in V$ROLLSTAT are shown in Table 7-5. When querying V$ROLLSTAT, you will also want to query V$ROLLNAME. The V$ROLLNAME table maps the rollback segment number to its name (for example, 'SYSTEM','R0').

Column Name	Description
Usn	Rollback segment number.
Extents	Number of extents in the rollback segment.
RsSize	The size of the rollback segment, in bytes.
Writes	The number of bytes of entries written to the rollback segment.
Xacts	The number of active transactions.
Gets	The number of rollback segment header requests.
Waits	The number of rollback segment header requests that resulted in waits.
Optsize	The value of the **optimal** parameter for the rollback segment.
Hwmsize	The highest value (high-water mark), in bytes, of RsSize reached during usage.
Shrinks	The number of shrinks that the rollback segment has had to perform in order to stay at the **optimal** size.
Wraps	The number of times a rollback segment entry has wrapped from one extent into another.

TABLE 7-5. *Columns Available in V$ROLLSTAT*

Column Name	Description
Extends	The number of times that the rollback segment had to acquire a new extent.
Aveshrink	The average number of bytes freed during a shrink.
Aveactive	The average size of active extents.
Status	Status of the rollback segment; similar to the status values listed earlier. Values are ONLINE (same as 'IN USE') and PENDING OFFLINE (same as 'PARTLY AVAILABLE').
Curext	Current extent.
Curblk	Current block.

TABLE 7-5. *Columns Available in V$ROLLSTAT* (continued)

There is a one-to-one relationship between V$ROLLNAME and V$ROLLSTAT. They both have a primary key called USN (Undo Segment Number). When querying the tables in an ad hoc fashion, join them on this key as shown in the following example:

```
select
    N.Name,                        /* rollback segment name */
    S.RsSize                       /* rollback segment size */
from V$ROLLNAME N, V$ROLLSTAT S
where N.USN=S.USN;
```

Transactions per Rollback Segment

Determining the users who own active entries in each rollback segment effectively answers two questions: how are the rollback segments currently distributed, and who is where?

Understanding this query requires knowing that transactions acquire locks within the rollback segment header. The V$LOCK table can thus be joined to V$ROLLNAME. Since locks are owned by processes, you can join the V$LOCK to V$PROCESS to see a mapping of user processes in V$PROCESS to rollback segment names in V$ROLLNAME.

```
REM  Users in rollback segments
REM
column rr heading 'RB Segment' format a18
```

```
column us heading 'Username' format a15
column os heading 'OS User' format a10
column te heading 'Terminal' format a10
select R.Name rr,
       nvl(S.Username,'no transaction') us,
       S.Osuser os,
       S.Terminal te
  from V$LOCK L, V$SESSION S, V$ROLLNAME R
 where L.Sid = S.Sid(+)
   and trunc(L.Id1/65536) = R.USN
   and L.Type = 'TX'
   and L.Lmode = 6
order by R.Name
/
```

Sample output for the preceding query is shown in the following listing:

```
RB Segment           Username          OS User    Terminal
-----------------    ---------------   ---------- ----------
R01                  APPL1_BAT         georgehj   ttypc
R02                  APPL1_BAT         detmerst   ttypb
```

The output shows that only two users are actively writing to the rollback segments (two different sessions of the APPL1_BAT ORACLE user, by two different operating system users). Each user is writing to a rollback segment that no one else is using. Rollback segments r01 and r02 are the only rollback segments presently used by active transactions. If there were more than one user using a rollback segment, there would be multiple records for that rollback segment.

Data Volumes in Rollback Segments

You can query V$ROLLSTAT to determine the number of bytes written to a rollback segment. V$ROLLSTAT contains a column called Writes that records the number of bytes that have been written to each rollback segment since the database was last started.

To determine the amount of activity in a rollback segment for a specific time interval, select the Writes value at the start of the test period. When the testing completes, query that value for the then-current value. The difference will be the number of bytes written to the rollback segment during that time interval. Since shutting down the database resets the statistics in the V$ROLLSTAT table, it is important that the database remain open during the testing interval.

Select the Writes value from the V$ROLLSTAT table using the following query:

```
select
    N.Name,                        /* rollback segment name */
    S.Writes                       /* bytes written to date */
from V$ROLLNAME N, V$ROLLSTAT S
where N.USN=S.USN;
```

Detecting the size of the rollback segment entry created by a single transaction requires combining these queries with a command given earlier in this chapter. First, isolate the transaction by executing it in a database in which it is the only process. Direct the transaction to a specific rollback segment via the

```
set transaction use rollback segment SEGMENT_NAME
```

command. Then, query the Writes column of the V$ROLLSTAT table for that rollback segment. When the transaction completes, requery V$ROLLSTAT. The exact size of the transaction's rollback segment entry will be the difference between the two Writes values.

Using Oracle Enterprise Manager to Manage Rollback Segments

You can use Oracle Enterprise Manager (OEM) to perform many rollback segment management functions. You can use OEM to create rollback segments, make them available by placing them online and offline, shrink them, or remove them. You can also create a new rollback segment with the same characteristics as an existing one; this option is called **create like**. In this section, you will see the steps required to manage your rollback segments via OEM.

Creating a Rollback Segment from OEM

To create a rollback segment from within OEM, follow these steps:

1. Select the "Rollback Segment" option from the left side of the OEM screen, but do not select an individual rollback segment.

2. From the menu or using the right-click mouse button, select the Create option.

3. Fill in the appropriate information in the Create Rollback Segment screen. OEM will confirm the creation of the new rollback segment.

The next illustration shows the use of the pull-down menu to select the option to create a rollback segment,

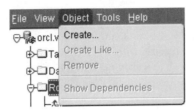

and this illustration shows the use of the right-click mouse button to select the option to create a rollback segment:

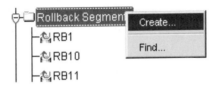

Once you have made your selection, OEM will display the "Create Rollback Segment" window. In this window, enter the following information about the new rollback segment:

- The new rollback segment's name
- Whether it is to be placed online or offline
- Whether it is to be public or private
- The tablespace in which it should be created

The following illustration shows the "Create Rollback Segment" window with the appropriate information filled in. The default tablespace that is selected for the new rollback segment is the first tablespace in the tablespace list. The other default values are public and offline. You must be careful to select the correct tablespace for the rollback segment.

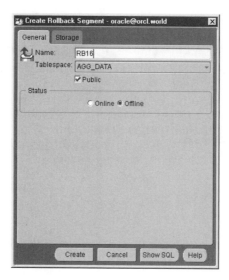

Once the new rollback segment has been created, an informational screen will be displayed to show you that the rollback segment has been created. Click "Okay" to confirm the creation of the new rollback segment.

Creating a Rollback Segment like an Existing Rollback Segment

OEM gives you the ability to create a rollback segment whose structure is an exact duplicate of a current rollback segment. To create a new rollback segment based on the structure of an existing rollback segment, follow these steps:

1. Select the rollback segment to be duplicated.

2. From the menu or using the right-click mouse button, select the Create Like option.

3. Fill in the appropriate information in the "Create Rollback Segment" window. OEM will confirm the creation of the new rollback segment.

Figure 7-7 shows the OEM ORACLE Storage Manager screen with rollback segment RB15 selected for duplication and the pull-down menu with the Create Like option highlighted.

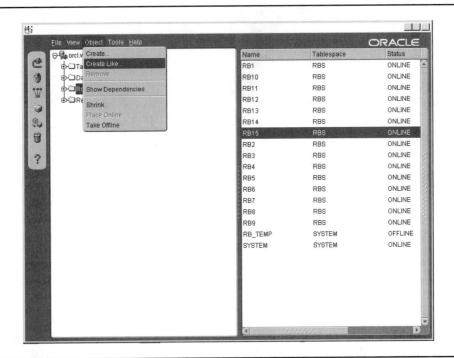

FIGURE 7-7. *Selecting a rollback segment for duplication*

The following illustration shows the use of the right-click mouse button to select the option to create the rollback segment like the one selected.

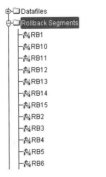

Once you have selected the rollback segment to duplicate, OEM will display the "Create Rollback Segment" window. At this point, enter the following information about the new rollback segment:

- The new rollback segment's name

- Whether it is to be placed online or offline

- Whether it is to be public or private

- The tablespace in which it should be created

The following illustration shows the "Create Rollback Segment" window. The default values for the rollback segment are the current values of the rollback segment that was chosen for duplication.

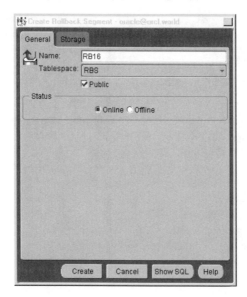

Once the new rollback segment has been created, an informational screen will be displayed to show you that the rollback segment has been created. Confirm the creation of the new rollback segment by clicking on the "Okay" prompt and the new rollback segment will be available.

Placing a Rollback Segment Online

To place a rollback segment online and make it available, follow these steps:

1. Select the rollback segment that is currently offline.

2. From the pull-down menu or using the right-click mouse button, select the Place Online option.

3. Confirm the selection.

Figure 7-8 shows the OEM Oracle Storage Manager screen with rollback segment RB15 selected. As shown in the figure, the status of RB15 is currently "offline".

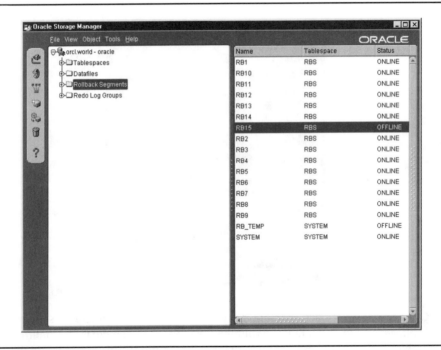

FIGURE 7-8. *Selecting an offline rollback segment*

The following illustration shows the use of the pull-down menu to select the option to place RB15 online,

and the following illustration shows the use of the right-click mouse button to select the option to place RB15 online.

Step 3. Confirm the selection.

Once the selection has been made, the action confirmation window will be displayed to confirm that the action selected is the correct one. OEM will prompt you with the question "Are you sure you want to bring the Rollback Segment Online?" Choose "Yes" to bring the rollback segment online; Figure 7-9 shows the online rollback segment.

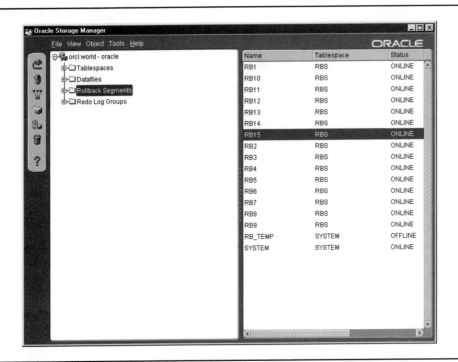

FIGURE 7-9. *Rollback segment with online status*

Placing a Rollback Segment Offline

The steps that are used to place a rollback segment offline and make it unavailable are as follows:

1. Select the rollback segment that is currently online.

2. From the pull-down menu or using the right-click mouse button, select the Place Offline option.

3. Confirm the selection.

Figure 7-9 shows the OEM Oracle Storage Manager screen with rollback segment RB15 selected. Note that the status of RB15 is currently "online". You can choose the "Take Offline" option for RB15 by either using the pull-down menu, shown here,

or by right-clicking the mouse button:

Once the selection has been made, the action confirmation window will be displayed to confirm that the action selected is the correct one. The following illustration shows the action confirmation window with the prompt "Are you sure you want to take the Rollback Segment Offline?" The response options are "Yes" and "No".

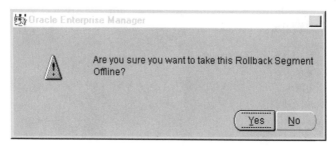

Figure 7-10 shows the results of the action with RB15 now offline.

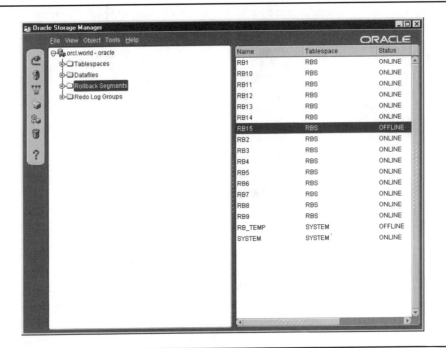

FIGURE 7-10. *Offline rollback segment*

Removing a Rollback Segment

To remove a rollback segment, follow these steps:

1. Select the rollback segment to be removed.

2. From the pull-down menu or using the right-click mouse button, select the Remove option.

3. Confirm the selection.

Figure 7-11 shows the OEM Oracle Storage Manager screen with rollback segment RB15 selected.

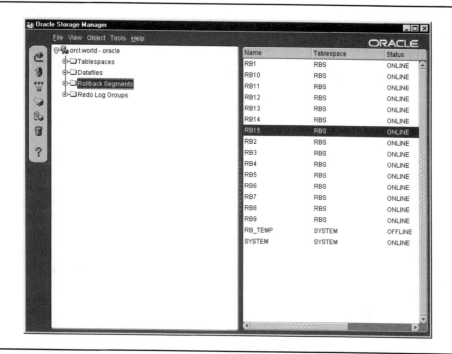

FIGURE 7-11. *Rollback segment selected for removal*

The following illustration shows the use of the pull-down menu to select the option to remove RB15,

and this illustration shows the use of the right-click mouse button to select the option to remove RB15:

Once the selection has been made, the action confirmation window will be displayed to confirm that the action selected is the correct one. When OEM displays the prompt "Are you sure you want to remove rollback segment RB15?", choose "Yes" to confirm the removal of the rollback segment, or "No" to cancel the operation.

Figure 7-12 shows the results of the action with RB15 removed.

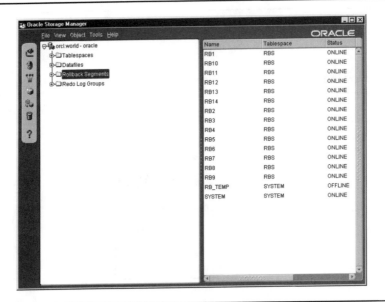

FIGURE 7-12.   *Rollback segment list following removal*

Choosing the Number and Size

You can use the descriptions of rollback segment entries given in this chapter to properly design the appropriate rollback segment layout for your database. Note that the final design will be different for each database—unless your databases are functionally identical with respect to their transactions.

The design process involves determining the transaction volume and estimating the number and type of transactions. In the following sections you will see this process illustrated for a sample application. You can derive the proper number, size, and structure of the rollback segments from this transaction data.

Transaction Entry Volume

The first step in the design process is to determine the total amount of rollback segment entry data that will be active or in use at any instant. Note that there are two distinct types of entries being considered here:

- *Active* entries, which have not yet been committed or rolled back

- *Inactive, in-use* (IIU) entries, which have been committed or rolled back, but whose data is in use by separate processes (such as long-running queries)

Rollback segment entries that are inactive, and are not in use by separate processes, are unimportant in these calculations.

The key to managing rollback segments effectively is to minimize the amount of "inactive, in-use" (IIU) entry data. As a DBA, you have no way of detecting the amount of rollback segment space being used by inactive, in-use entries. Their existence only becomes evident when users begin reporting the ORA-1555 "snapshot too old" error described previously in this chapter (see Figure 7-5).

Minimizing the amount of IIU data in rollback segments involves knowing when long-running queries are being executed. If they are occurring concurrently with multiple transactions, there will be a steady accumulation of IIU rollback segment entries. No matter how large the rollback segments are, poor transaction distribution will ultimately cause queries to fail.

To solve this problem, isolate all large queries so that they run at times when very little transaction activity is occurring. This isolation minimizes the amount of IIU rollback segment entry data while also helping to prevent potential concurrent I/O contention between the queries and the transactions.

To determine the amount of rollback segment entry data being written to the rollback segments, use the queries given in the "Data Volumes in Rollback Segments" section shown previously. Each large transaction should be sized via the methods described there (in a test environment). Sizing of transactions should be a standard part of the database sizing process during application development.

Care should also be taken to minimize the amount of inactive, in-use rollback data that is shared between transactions. Large amounts of IIU data would result from concurrent transactions in which one transaction referenced a table that the other was manipulating. If this is minimized, the result will be a system whose rollback segment data needs are distributed and measurable.

There is overhead associated with each transaction. However, this header information is counted in the statistics queries given in the previous sections of this chapter. Thus, those queries give a very accurate report of the amount of rollback segment space that is needed.

Number of Transactions

Once the total amount of rollback segment entry data is known, the number of transactions must be considered. Segregate the transactions into types by their relative volume. For each group, determine the maximum and average transaction size. For this part of the rollback segment sizing process, only consider the transactions that occur during normal production usage of the system, excluding all data loads.

Create a spreadsheet of the structure shown in Table 7-6. Sample data is shown for reference. The "Transaction Types" for this table are for a data entry application at a zoo safari exhibit. The "Number" column refers to the number of *concurrent* transactions of each type. The "Total Entry Size" column refers to the total entry size, in bytes, of all the *concurrent* entries of this type.

Note that the "Number" column refers to the number of separate transactions. If multiple records are being updated in a single transaction, then that still counts as only one transaction.

Transaction Type	Number	Total Entry Size	Average Entry Size	Largest Entry
FEEDING_LOG	3	210K	70K	70K
NEW_BIRTH	1	500K	500K	500K
VISITOR_LOG	20	800K	40K	40K
VISITOR_EATEN	1	700K	700K	700K
TIME_SHEETS	10	500K	50K	50K
Total	35	2,710K		

TABLE 7-6. *Sample Transaction Distribution*

The transactions listed in Table 7-6 reflect that, for this application, users **commit** after every 10 to 100 records. For example, the average VISITOR_LOG transaction is 40KB in size—which may be ten 4KB records or 100 400-byte records, depending on the record length and the frequency of **commit**s.

According to the data in Table 7-6, there are, on average, 35 concurrent transactions in the database. They take, on average, 2,710KB of data at any one time.

The largest single transaction in the database is 700KB long. Use this as the starting point for the rollback segment sizing. That transaction must fit in a single rollback segment. That rollback segment will contain rollback segment header space as well, and may also contain inactive data. To calculate the minimum possible size for a rollback segment that can support this single transaction, use the following formula. This formula makes the following assumptions:

■ Twenty percent of the rollback segment will remain as free space.

■ Fifteen percent of the rollback segment will be used for inactive, in-use data.

■ Five percent of the rollback segment will be used by the rollback segment header area.

```
Minimum Possible Size (MPS) = Largest Transaction Size *100 /
                             (100 - (Free Pct + In Use Pct + Header Pct))
                           = Largest Transaction Size *100 /
                             (100-(20+15+5))
                           = Largest Transaction Size *100/60
                           = Largest Transaction Size * 1.67
                           = 700 KB * 1.67
                           = 1170 KB
```

Since the database chooses a rollback segment to use in a round-robin fashion, each rollback segment that may have to handle this transaction must be at least this size.

The total rollback segment space needed at any one time can also be calculated. The same space assumptions will be used.

```
Minimum Total Size (MTS)   = Sum(Total Entry Size) *100 /
                             (100 - (Free Pct + In Use Pct + Header Pct))
                           = Sum(Total Entry Size) *100 /
                             (100 - (20 + 15 + 5))
                           = Sum(Total Entry Size) * 100/60
                           = Sum(Total Entry Size) * 1.67
                           = 2710 KB * 1.67
                           = 4525 KB
```

So, the minimum total rollback space available in all of the rollback segments combined at any one time must be at least 4,525KB for this example.

How many rollback segments should this space be divided among? Since the rollback segments should all be of the same size, the minimum value is easy to estimate. You have already seen that the minimum size of each rollback segment is 1,170KB. The total minimum size of all rollback segments is 4,525KB. The following equation compares these two values to determine the minimum number of rollback segments needed:

```
Minimum Num of Rollback Segs (MNRS) = Minimum Total Size /
                                      Minimum Possible Size
                                    = 4525 KB / 1170 KB
                                    = 3.87 (round up to 4)
```

This will be our starting point for the number of rollback segments needed. Note that it only considers the space requirements at this point.

To refine this calculation, consider the number of concurrent transactions. The fewer transactions there are in a rollback segment, the less work the database will have to do to manage its space needs. The maximum number of rollback segments is the number of concurrent transactions (assuming one transaction per rollback segment). For the example data shown in Table 7-6, this number is 35.

```
Maximum Number of Rollback Segs = Number of Concurrent Transactions
                                = 35
```

The production database requires somewhere between 4 and 35 rollback segments. To restrict this range further, you must determine the number of transactions per rollback segment. Each transaction will now be fit into its own extent, rather than into its own rollback segment. To do this, you must evaluate the distribution of transaction sizes.

As shown in Table 7-7, there are two distinct groupings of the safari transactions. The first group features entries whose average entry sizes are between 40KB and 70KB. The second grouping contains entries whose average sizes are between 500KB and 700KB. Since there is an order of magnitude of difference between average entry size for these two groups, it will not be possible to resolve their space needs without wasting space or forcing wraps to occur.

The transactions in the large entry size group are very few in number. Of the 35 concurrent transactions, they constitute just two. Therefore, you can design to handle the small entry group, while leaving space to handle the exceptions in the large entry group. The sizing for the small entry group size will thus form the lower bound for the design requirements.

For the small entry size group, the sum of the total entry sizes is 1,510KB. So, the minimum total size of the rollback segments needed just for that group is

```
MTS = 1510K * 1.67  = 2522 KB
```

Transaction Type	Number	Total Entry Size	Average Entry Size	Largest Entry
VISITOR_LOG	20	800K	40K	40K
TIME_SHEETS	10	500K	50K	50K
FEEDING_LOG	3	210K	70K	70K
Subtotal	**33**	**1,510K**		
NEW_BIRTH	1	500K	500K	500K
VISITOR_EATEN	1	700K	700K	700K
Subtotal	**2**	**1,200K**		
Total	**35**	**2,710K**		

TABLE 7-7. *Sample Transaction Distribution, Grouped by Average Entry Size*

The minimum extent size for that group is the size of the largest transaction in that group.

```
Minimum Extent Size (MES) = 70 KB bytes
```

A 70KB extent size will handle each of the small entry transactions. For the large entry transactions, it will require a minimum of seven wraps (eight 70KB extents for the 500KB entry). To minimize the number of wraps for the large entry transactions, consider a larger extent size. An extent size of 125KB would require fewer wraps, at the cost of increased storage space. An extent size of 250KB would require even fewer wraps for all transactions. However, it would require a great deal of additional physical space, as shown in Table 7-8.

In Table 7-8, three different extent sizes are compared. The first, 70KB, was based on the calculated minimum average extent size. The second, 125KB, was proposed to reduce the number of wraps needed to support the larger transactions.

The third, 250KB, was proposed to reduce even further the number of wraps needed to support the larger transactions.

The "Space Req" column in Table 7-8 shows that with a 70KB extent, and one transaction per extent, 3,570KB of rollback segment space would be needed while incurring 16 wraps. Increasing the extent size to 125KB increases the space requirements by a third, to 5,350KB, while decreasing the number of wraps to 7.

Extent Size	Transaction Entry Type	Number	Space Req	Number of Wraps
70K	small (< 70K)	33	2,310K	0
	large (500K)	1	560K	7
	large (700K)	1	700K	9
		Totals	3,570K	16
125K	small (< 70K)	33	4,125K	0
	large (500K)	1	500K	3
	large (700K)	1	750K	5
		Totals	5,350K	8
250K	small (< 70K)	33	8,250K	0
	large (500K)	1	500K	1
	large (700K)	1	750K	2
		Totals	9,500K	3

TABLE 7-8.   *Extent Sizing Trade-Offs*

Doubling that extent size, to 250KB, increases the space requirement to 9,500KB while only reducing the number of wraps to 3. The space calculations all assume one transaction per extent; that assumption may result in overestimating the space requirements, but it is usually an accurate starting point.

Based on Table 7-8, you can cut this example application's number of wraps in half by increasing the extent size by only two-thirds. Extending the extent size much beyond 125KB will not reduce the number of wraps appreciably. Note that these calculations still assume one transaction per extent, even for the larger extent sizes.

You have to be able to estimate your transaction volume in order to reach this point. Since this calculation assumes that only 15 percent of the rollback segment is being used to support IIU entries, such entries must be minimized via scheduling. You have to be able to estimate the type, quantity, and nature of the system's transactions in order to be able to reach this decision point.

Given the trade-off between the options in Table 7-8, a small extent size will almost always be the proper choice since it is usually the most common type of transaction. The deciding factor will be the distribution of the number of transactions. Since 33 of 35 concurrent transactions are small in this example, the largest extent size can be discarded. The choice is then between the two smaller extent sizes (70KB and 125KB). Since the number of wraps falls so rapidly with the small increase in extent size, choose the 125KB size. Note that the choice of an extent size, falling between the minimum extent size (MES) and the minimum extent size necessary to eliminate all wraps, should always be the best compromise. This compromise assumes that (1) the additional disk space needed is available and (2) the performance penalties due to the wraps are acceptable.

The minimum total size of all rollback segments for the database was previously calculated as 4,525KB. The minimum possible size for a rollback segment was calculated as 1,170KB, yielding a minimum of four rollback segments.

In that configuration, each of the four rollback segments would support nine transactions at a time (35 transactions divided by 4 rollback segments, rounded). ORACLE recommends a number closer to four transactions per rollback segments. For this implementation, split the difference and start with six transactions per rollback segment, yielding six rollback segments (35/6, rounded). The actual space requirements for them can now be determined.

Each of the six rollback segments will contain an extent that is used for the rollback segment header. Its extent distribution is listed in Table 7-9.

The resulting rollback segment consists of a total of 2,250KB, in 18 evenly sized extents. It can handle the high transaction load of the small entry transactions. It can support the large transactions. And it contains free space in the event that the transaction volume or the transaction load is greater than has been predicted.

For details on monitoring the adequacy of this design, see Chapter 6. The next section describes the calculations used to reach this final layout.

Extent Number	Description
1	Rollback segment header
2	Transaction #1
3	Transaction #2
4	Transaction #3
5	Transaction #4
6	Transaction #5
7	Transaction #6
8	Inactive, in-use data
9	Inactive, in-use data
10	Expansion space for large transactions
11	Expansion space for large transactions
12	Expansion space for large transactions
13	Expansion space for large transactions
14	Expansion space for large transactions
15	Expansion space for large transactions
16	Free space
17	Free space
18	Free space

TABLE 7-9.   *Extent Distribution Within the Sample Rollback Segments*

Determining the optimal *Size*

The **optimal** size of a rollback segment must accommodate the transaction volume and the overhead needed to manage the transactions. The design should allow most of the transactions to be handled within a single extent.

The amount of transaction data in a rollback segment should therefore be measured in extents. The number of extents required for each rollback segment is

```
Min Num of Extents/Segment = Number of Single-Extent Transactions
   +((Number of Wraps in Long Transactions +1)*
                     Average Number of Long Transactions)
```

Applying this to our sample data,

```
Min Num of Extents/Segment      = (33 small-entry transactions
                                   /6 rollback segments) +
                                   (5 wraps +1 )*1
                                 = 5.6 + 6
                                 = 11.6, rounded up to 12
```

The longest transaction is 700KB, which will require six 125KB extents. This requires five wraps. Since only one such transaction is active at a time, a rollback segment needs to have an extent for each transaction, plus an additional extent for each wrap.

Using this many extents will allow the rollback segment to handle its share of the small entry transaction load while also having room to support an average large transaction load. This distribution of extents was shown graphically in Table 7-9. In that table, extents 2 through 7 support the first extents of six different transactions. Extents 10 through 15 handle the expansion needs of the large transactions.

The transaction data thus requires 12 extents. The overhead needs of the rollback segment must now be estimated. They consist of three parts.

```
Rollback Segment Overhead = Rollback segment header space +
                            Inactive, In-Use space +
                            Free Space
```

The rollback segment header should always be estimated to take an extent (shown as extent #1 in Table 7-9).

The IIU space is determined by the transaction scheduling for the application. If long-running queries are executing concurrently with online transactions that use the same data, then this value will have to be set high. It is possible that the amount of IIU data may exceed the currently used transaction volume.

If the transactions have been distributed correctly, then no long-running queries will be run concurrently with data manipulation transactions. Even so, there may be some overlap between the transactions. This overlap results in IIU space, and usually requires at least 10 percent of the rollback segment's transaction volume.

For the safari example, the overlap between transactions is estimated to be 15 percent.

```
IIU Space           = (Per cent Inactive, In-Use) *
                         Number of Data Extents
                    = .15*12
                    = 1.80, rounded up to 2 extents.
```

These two extents are shown as extents #8 and #9 in Table 7-9.

The final overhead factor is the free space. The free space must accommodate the worst-case scenario of transaction allocations. In this case, that would be for both of the large entry transactions to be assigned to the same rollback segment.

The space needed for a single large transaction has already been factored into the minimum number of extents per segment calculation. Therefore, you only need to add the number of wraps that would occur for a second large transaction. Since that is listed as 500KB (Table 7-7), and the extent size is 125KB (Table 7-8), such a transaction would require four extents (three wraps).

```
Free Space Extents  = Maximum Number of Additional Extents Needed
                    = 3
```

These extents are shown as extents #16, #17, and #18 of Table 7-9.

The **optimal** size of the rollback segment, and the value for the **optimal** storage parameter, is thus

```
OPTIMAL  = (Minimum Number of Data Extents per Segment
               + Rollback Segment Header extents
               + Inactive, In Use extents
               + Free Space extents)
            * Extent Size

         = (12+1+2+3) * 125K/extent
         = 18 * 125K/extent
         = 2250K bytes
```

To minimize the dynamic extension of the rollback segment in reaching this size, set **minextents** to 18. The **optimal** size of the rollback segment will then be preallocated.

Creating the Rollback Segments

You can now create the rollback segments. They should all be created with identical storage parameters. The storage parameters for the safari application are listed in Table 7-10.

All of the production rollback segments will be created in the RBS tablespace. Therefore, you can use the default storage settings for that tablespace to enforce the desired storage values for the rollback segments. Use the following command to set these parameters:

```
alter tablespace RBS
default storage
(initial 125K next 125K minextents 18 maxextents 249)
```

Parameter	Value
INITIAL	125K
NEXT	125K
MINEXTENTS	18
MAXEXTENTS	249
OPTIMAL	2,250K

TABLE 7-10. *Storage Parameters for the Sample Rollback Segments*

When creating rollback segments in that tablespace, you now only have to specify the tablespace and the **optimal** value, as shown in the following set of commands:

```
create rollback segment R4 tablespace RBS
    storage (optimal 2250K);
alter rollback segment R4 online;
```

The RBS tablespace will have to contain at least enough space to hold six 2,250KB rollback segments (13,500KB). When planning its space requirements, think of the tablespace graphically. Figure 7-13, which should call to mind Figures 7-1 and 7-2, shows a potential layout for the RBS tablespace.

In the layout shown in the figure, six equally sized rollback segments are shown. An additional area of free space of the same size is added at the bottom. That free space will be available for adding a seventh segment (if rollback segment header contention is a problem) or for temporary extensions of the six rollback segments.

Figure 7-13 also shows that these rollback segments may be separated into their own files. In such files, a small amount of space will be reserved for overhead. The figure shows seven 2,300KB files; you could also have stored all of the rollback segments in a single datafile. Using multiple files may improve your options during database tuning efforts, since these files could be placed on different disks to distribute the transaction I/O load.

Production Versus Data Load Rollback Segments

All of the calculations performed here assumed that the application had no way of assigning transactions to specific rollback segments. The rollback segments thus had

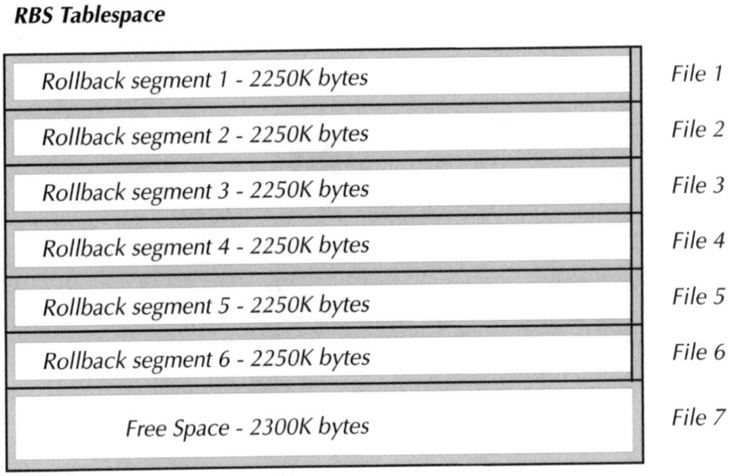

RBS Tablespace

Rollback segment 1 - 2250K bytes	File 1
Rollback segment 2 - 2250K bytes	File 2
Rollback segment 3 - 2250K bytes	File 3
Rollback segment 4 - 2250K bytes	File 4
Rollback segment 5 - 2250K bytes	File 5
Rollback segment 6 - 2250K bytes	File 6
Free Space - 2300K bytes	File 7

FIGURE 7-13. *Potential layout for the sample RBS tablespace*

to support both large and small entry sizes. This is acceptable for most production usage, but it is not acceptable for handling data load transactions.

Data load transactions are used to manipulate large volumes of data in an application. These transactions may include initial data loads or the creation of large summary tables from detail tables. Either way, they involve transaction volumes that are orders of magnitude greater than those designed for here.

Data loads not only deal with large volumes of data, but the transactions within those loads are larger. For example, when using the ORACLE Import utility, its default functionality is to perform one **commit** for each table's data. To support that, a rollback segment the size of the table would be needed. See Chapter 10 for alternatives to Import's default transaction size.

Data load transactions must be assigned to specific rollback segments. You can use the

```
set transaction use rollback segment SEGMENT_NAME
```

command, or you can deactivate all but one production rollback segment (during off-peak hours). The size of the data load transactions should be measured using the V$ROLLSTAT queries shown previously in this chapter.

Once the data load transactions have been isolated to specific rollback segments, those rollback segments should be isolated in the RBS_2 tablespace. This tablespace, as described in Chapter 3, is used solely for rollback segments that have extraordinary space requirements. Placing them in RBS_2 allows their extensions into the RBS_2 free space to be performed without impacting the free space available to the production rollback segments (in the RBS tablespace). See Chapter 12 for a discussion of the support of large batch transactions.

The result will be production rollback segments that are properly sized and preallocated. Their extents are designed to be large enough to handle an entire transaction. Space is allocated to handle those transactions that are not properly distributed. The worst-case scenario is covered, and the best-case scenario is achieved: the time machine works.

Solutions

In the preceding sections, you saw the process for configuring the rollback segment layout for a sample application. In this section, you will see common rollback segment configurations for two types of applications: OLTP applications and data warehouses.

OLTP applications

An OLTP (online transaction processing) application supports many users executing small transactions. To support many small transactions, you should have many rollback segments, each of which has many extents. To begin configuring your rollback segments for an OLTP database, you must first determine the number of concurrent users in your database. If you have an active database, you can query the Sessions_Highwater column of the V$LICENSE view to see the highest number of concurrent users reached since the database was last started.

```
select Sessions_Highwater from V$LICENSE;
```

The Sessions_Highwater value is the maximum number of rollback segments required for the database. If the number of rollback segments equals the Sessions_Highwater value, then each transaction will have its own rollback segment. Since your database is not always at its maximum usage (and users in OLTP applications are not constantly entering new transactions), divide the Sessions_Highwater value by 4 to determine your starting value for the number of rollback segments. If your Sessions_Highwater value is 100, then you should create 25 rollback segments to support your users.

Each of those rollback segments will be supporting up to four users, so you should create at least four extents for those transactions. In addition, you will need to allocate space for large transactions and IIU space. Start by allocating 20 extents for each rollback segment; the size of the extents should be based on the average transaction size in your application. If the average transaction size is 50KB, then you could create each rollback segment with 20 extents of 50KB each. You will need to monitor your rollback segments post-production to determine if there are wraps, extends, and shrinks occurring.

Data Warehouses/Batch Applications

Data warehouses support two distinct types of transactions: small transactions executed by users and very large transactions executed during the loading of data into the database. To support the small transactions, determine the maximum number of concurrent users by querying V$LICENSE.

```
select Sessions_Highwater from V$LICENSE;
```

Since data warehouse users typically perform a small number of transactions, divide the Sessions_Highwater value by 10 to establish a starting value for the number of rollback segments. If you have 100 concurrent users, create ten rollback segments to support them. Create those ten rollback segments with 20 extents each, and size the extents to support the transaction sizes your users are executing.

For your batch processing, you will need to create a separate set of rollback segments. The rollback segments that support batch processing are typically stored in their own tablespace (such as RBS_2; see Chapters 3 and 4). You should not use the end users' rollback segments to support the batch data loading process.

In many data warehouses, the data loading process is serialized—only one table load or aggregation is occurring at a time. If your data warehouse data loading process is serialized, then you only need to have one rollback segment to support the data load. If you have multiple large transactions concurrently active in the data loading process, then you will need to have multiple large rollback segments available. The data loading rollback segments should have a small number of large extents.

Although you can set the datafiles for a rollback segment tablespace to **autoextend**, doing so prevents you from having control over the space usage in your database. If you set a limit to the maximum number of extents in the rollback segment, and the tablespace's datafiles cannot extend, then the maximum size of any batch transaction is limited. Any transaction that attempts to acquire more rollback segment space than the defined maximum will fail, and will force you to reevaluate your space estimates. If you use the **autoextend** option for your datafiles and do not limit the maximum size of your rollback segments, then a single large transaction can use all of the available space on your disks. If possible, limit the size of your transactions during your batch data loads.

In a data warehouse, your batch loading processes typically do not occur at times when online warehouse users are accessing the database. Therefore, you should be able to place all but the batch load rollback segments in OFFLINE state. If the small rollback segments for the users are online, then your batch loading transactions may accidentally use them, causing problems with your ability to manage the rollback segment space allocation in the rest of the database. If you effectively isolate your batch data loading rollback segments from your users' rollback segments, you will be able to effectively manage the space requirements of those very different types of transactions.

CHAPTER

8

Database Tuning

uning is a part of the life of every database application. As noted in previous chapters, most performance problems are not isolated symptoms, but rather are the result of the system design. Tuning efforts should therefore focus on identifying and fixing the underlying flaws that yield the unacceptable performance.

Tuning is the final step in a four-step process: planning (Chapters 3 and 4), doing (Chapter 5), and monitoring (Chapter 6) must precede it. If you tune only for the sake of tuning, then you are failing to address the full cycle of activity, and will likely never resolve the underlying flaws that caused the performance problem.

Most of the database objects that can be tuned are discussed elsewhere in this book—for example, rollback segments are covered thoroughly in Chapter 7. This chapter will only discuss the tuning-related activities for such objects, while their own chapters cover planning and monitoring activities.

In the following sections, you will see tuning activities for the following areas:

- Application design

- SQL

- Memory usage

- Data storage

- Data manipulation

- Physical storage

- Logical storage

- Network traffic

Tuning Application Design

Why should a DBA tuning guide include a section on application design? And why should this section come first? Because *nothing* you can do as a DBA will have as great an impact on the system performance as the design of the application. The requirements for making the DBA's involvement in application development a reality are described in Chapter 5. In designing an application, you can take several steps to make effective and proper use of the available technology, as described in the following sections.

Effective Table Design

"No major application will run in Third Normal Form."

George Koch—*ORACLE8: The Complete Reference*

No matter how well designed your database is, poor table design will lead to poor performance. Not only that, but overly rigid adherence to relational table designs will lead to poor performance. That is due to the fact that while fully relational table designs (said to be in the *third normal form*) are logically desirable, they are physically undesirable.

The problem with such designs is that although they accurately reflect the ways in which an application's data is related to other data, they do not reflect the normal access paths that users will employ to access that data. Once the user's access requirements are evaluated, the fully relational table design will become unworkable for many large queries. Typically, the first problems will occur with queries that return a large number of columns. These columns are usually scattered among several tables, forcing the tables to be joined together during the query. If one of the joined tables is large, then the performance of the whole query may suffer.

In designing the tables for an application, developers should therefore consider denormalizing data—for example, creating small summary tables from large, static tables. Can that data be dynamically derived from the large, static tables on demand? Of course. But if the users frequently request it, and the data is largely unchanging, then it makes sense to periodically store that data *in the format in which the users will ask for it.*

User-centered table design, rather than theory-centered table design, will yield a system that better meets the users' requirements. Design options include separating a single table into multiple tables, and the reverse—combining multiple tables into one. The emphasis should be on providing the users the most direct path possible to the data they want in the format they want.

Distribution of CPU Requirements

When effectively designed, and given adequate hardware, an ORACLE database application will be *CPU-bound.* That is, the limiting factor to its performance will be the availability of CPU resources. Short of purchasing additional CPU power for the available servers, you have several options for managing the CPU resources.

First, the CPU load should be scheduled. This topic was mentioned in Chapter 7 with regard to reducing rollback segment overhead. However, it applies in general as well: schedule long-running batch query or update programs to run at off-peak hours. Rather than run them at lower operating system priority while online users are performing transactions, run them at normal operating system priority *at an appropriate time*. This will minimize potential locking, rollback, and CPU conflicts.

Second, as distributed computing becomes more widespread, take advantage of the opportunity to physically shift CPU requirements from one server to another. Wherever possible, isolate the database server from the application's CPU requirements. The data distribution techniques described in Part III of this book will result in data being stored in its most appropriate place, and the CPU requirements of the application may be separated from the I/O requirements against the database.

Third, you can use database resource management features introduced in ORACLE8i. You can use the Database Resource Manager to establish resource allocation plans and resource consumer groups. You can use ORACLE's capabilities to change the resource allocations available to the consumer groups. See Chapter 5 for details on creating and implementing resource consumer groups and resource plans via the Database Resource Manager.

Fourth, you can use the Parallel Query Option (PQO) to distribute the processing requirements of SQL statements among multiple CPUs. Parallelism can be used by almost every SQL command, including the **select**, **create table as select**, **create index**, **recover**, and SQL*Loader Direct Path loading options.

The degree to which a transaction is parallelized depends on the defined degree of parallelism for the transaction. Each table has a defined degree of parallelism (see the **create table** and **alter table** commands in Appendix A), and a query can override the default degree of parallelism by using the PARALLEL hint. As of ORACLE7.3, the database evaluates the number of CPUs available on the server and the number of disks on which the table's data is stored in order to determine the default degree of parallelism.

The maximum available parallelism is set at the instance level. The PARALLEL_MAX_SERVERS init.ora parameter sets the maximum number of parallel query server processes that can be used at any one time by all the processes in the database. For example, if you set PARALLEL_MAX_SERVERS to 32 for your instance, and you run a query that uses 30 parallel query server processes for its query and sorting operations, then only two parallel query server processes are available for all of the rest of the users in the database. Therefore, you need to carefully manage the parallelism you allow for your queries and batch operations. As of ORACLE7.3, you can use the PARALLEL_ADAPTIVE_MULTI_USER init.ora parameter to limit the parallelism of operations in a multiuser environment. The PARALLEL_ADAPTIVE_MULTI_USER feature is automatically turned on if you set the PARALLEL_AUTOMATIC_TUNING init.ora value to TRUE. As of ORACLE8i, you can limit the parallelism available to the resource consumer groups defined within your database. See Chapter 5 for details on implementing the Database Resource Manager and resource plans.

For each table, you can set a default degree of parallelism via the **parallel** clause of the **create table** and **alter table** commands. The *degree of parallelism* tells

ORACLE how many parallel query server processes to attempt to use for each part of the operation. For example, if a query that performed both table scanning and data sorting operations had a degree of parallelism of 5, then there could be ten parallel query server processes used—five for scanning, five for sorting. You can also specify a degree of parallelism for an index when it is created, via the **parallel** clause of the **create index** command.

The minimum number of parallel query server processes started is set via the PARALLEL_MIN_SERVERS init.ora parameter. In general, you should set this parameter to a very low number (less than 5). Setting this parameter to a low value will force ORACLE to repeatedly start new query server processes, but it will greatly decrease the amount of memory held by idle parallel query server processes. If you set a high value for PARALLEL_MIN_SERVERS, then you may frequently have idle parallel query server processes on your server, holding onto the memory they had previously acquired but not performing any functions. You can set an idle time parameter that tells ORACLE how many minutes a parallel query server process can be idle before it is terminated by the database.

Parallelizing operations distributes their processing requirements across multiple CPUs; however, you should use these features carefully. If you use a degree of parallelism of 5 for a large query, then you will have five separate processes accessing the data. If you have that many processes accessing the data, then you may create contention for the disks on which the data is stored, hurting performance! When using the PQO, you should selectively apply it to those tables whose data is well distributed over many physical devices. Also, you should avoid using it for all tables; as noted earlier, a single query may use all of the available parallel query server processes, eliminating the parallelism for all of the rest of the transactions in your database.

Effective Application Design

In addition to the application design topics described later in this chapter, there are several general guidelines for ORACLE applications.

First, they should minimize the number of times they request data from the database. Options for doing this include the use of sequences and PL/SQL blocks. The denormalization of tables discussed earlier in this chapter also applies here. You can use distributed database objects such as snapshots and (as of ORACLE8i) materialized views to help reduce the number of times a database is queried.

Second, different users of the same application should query the database in a very similar fashion. This will increase the likelihood that their requests may be resolved by information that is already available in the SGA. This sharing of data includes not only the tables and rows retrieved, but also the actual queries that are used. If the queries are identical, then the parsed version of a query may already exist in the Shared SQL Pool, reducing the amount of time needed to process the query.

Third, you should restrict the use of dynamic SQL. Dynamic SQL, which uses the DBMS_SQL package, is always reparsed even if an identical query exists in the Shared SQL Pool. Dynamic SQL is a useful feature, but it should not be used for the majority of an application's database accesses.

Stored procedures are available for use in application development. When they are used, it is very likely that the same code will be executed multiple times, thus taking advantage of the Shared SQL Pool. You can also manually compile procedures, functions, and packages to avoid run-time compilation. For example, to create a procedure, use a **create procedure** command, as shown in the following listing:

```
create procedure MY_RAISE (My_Emp_No IN NUMBER, Raise IN NUMBER)
as begin
      update EMPLOYEE
         set Salary = Salary+Raise
         where Empno = My_Emp_No;
end;
/
```

When you create a procedure, ORACLE automatically compiles it. If the procedure later becomes invalid, the database must recompile it before executing it. To avoid incurring this compilation cost at run time, use the **alter procedure** command shown in the following listing:

```
alter procedure MY_RAISE compile;
```

You can view the SQL text for all procedures in a database via the Text column in the DBA_SOURCE view. The USER_SOURCE view will display the procedures owned by the user performing the query. Text for packages, functions, and package bodies is also accessible via these views. These views reference a table named SYS.SOURCE$. Since this table is part of the data dictionary, the procedural code is stored in the SYSTEM tablespace. Therefore, if you use these objects, you must be sure to allocate more space to the SYSTEM tablespace—usually doubling its size.

The two design guidelines discussed—limiting the number of user accesses and coordinating their requests—require that the application developer know as much as possible about how the data is to be used and the access paths involved. For this reason, it is critical that users be as involved in the application design as they are in the table design. If the users spend long hours drawing pictures of tables with the data modelers, and little time with the application developers discussing the access paths, then the application will most likely not meet the users' needs.

Tuning SQL

As with application design, the tuning of SQL statements seems far removed from a DBA's duties. However, DBAs should be involved in reviewing the SQL that is written as part of the application. A well-designed application may still experience performance problems if the SQL it uses is poorly constructed. Application design and SQL problems cause most of the performance problems in properly designed databases.

In a relational database, the physical location of data is not as important as its logical place within the application design. However, the database has to find the data in order to return it to a user performing a query. The key to tuning SQL is to minimize the search path that the database uses to find the data.

In most ORACLE tables, each row has a RowID associated with it. The RowID contains information about the physical location of the row—its file, the block within that file, and the row within the database block. The RowID format changed significantly between ORACLE7 and ORACLE8.

When a query with no **where** clause is executed, the database will usually perform a *full table scan*, reading every block from the table. To do this, the database locates the first block of the table and then reads sequentially through all other blocks in the table. For large tables, this can be a very time-consuming process.

When specific rows are queried, the database may use an index to help speed the retrieval of the desired rows. An index maps logical values in a table to their RowIDs—which in turn map them to a specific physical location. Indexes may either be unique—in which case there is no more than one occurrence for each value—or nonunique. Indexes only store RowIDs for **NOT NULL** values in the indexed columns.

You may index several columns together. This is called a *concatenated* index, and it will be used if its leading column is used in the query's **where** clause. Simply throwing an index at a query will not necessarily make it run faster—the index must be tailored to the access path needed.

Consider the case of a three-column, concatenated index. As shown in the following listing, it is created on the City, State, and Zip columns of the EMPLOYEE table:

```
create index CITY_ST_ZIP_NDX
on EMPLOYEE(City, State, Zip)
tablespace INDEXES;
```

If a query of the form

```
select * from EMPLOYEE
  where State='NJ';
```

is executed, then the index will *not* be used, because its *leading* column (City) is not used in the **where** clause. If users will frequently run this type of query, then the index's columns should be reordered with State first in order to reflect the actual usage pattern.

It is also important that the table's data be as ordered as possible. Again, this is unimportant in relational theory, but plays a critical role in retrieving data for queries. If users are frequently executing *range* queries—selecting those values that are within a specified range—then having the data ordered may require fewer data blocks to be read while resolving the query, thus improving performance. The ordered entries in the index will point to a set of neighboring blocks in the table rather than blocks that are scattered throughout the datafile(s).

For example, a range query of the type shown in this listing:

```
select *
  from EMPLOYEE
 where Empno between 1 and 100;
```

will require fewer data blocks to be read if the physical records in the EMPLOYEE table are ordered by the Empno column. This should improve the performance of the query. To guarantee that the rows are properly ordered in the table, extract the records to a flat file, sort the records in the file, and then **delete** the old records and reload them from the sorted file.

As an alternative to extracting data to a flat file, you can use ORACLE's internal sorting procedures to sort your data. Ideally, you could reorder rows for a table by creating a second table, via the **create table as select** command. However, the **create table as select** and **insert as select** commands do not allow you to specify an **order by** clause.

To circumvent this limitation, create a view on the base table. The view should group by *all* of the columns of the table plus the RowNum pseudocolumn. The view shown in the following listing selects and groups by all of the columns in the EMPLOYEE table:

```
create or replace view EMPLOYEE_VIEW as
select Empno,
       Name,
       Address,
       City,
       State,
       Zip,
```

```
        RowNum
  from COMPANY
group by Empno,
         Name,
         Address,
         City,
         State,
         Zip,
         RowNum;
```

The **group by** clause will force the use of a sorting operation within ORACLE during queries—and the rows selected from EMPLOYEE_VIEW will be sorted in order of Empno. This allows you to then create a table selecting from EMPLOYEE_VIEW; the effect will be that a duplicate copy of EMPLOYEE will be created, with the rows properly sorted.

```
create table EMPLOYEE_ORDERED
    as select * from EMPLOYEE_VIEW;
```

In the preceding example, the data was ordered by the Empno value. Often, you may need to order the data by an attribute column instead, such as the Name column. If the data is ordered to support the most-used range queries, and is densely stored within each block, then you can minimize the number of blocks read during each query and thereby improve the performance of your queries. You need to add RowNum to the **group by** clause so duplicate rows in EMPLOYEE will be copied from EMPLOYEE to EMPLOYEE_ORDERED. Note that EMPLOYEE_ORDERED contains the data from EMPLOYEE, but does not contain its constraints, indexes, triggers, or privileges. You will need to re-create the privileges and other objects prior to using the EMPLOYEE_ORDERED data.

If the data is not very selective, then you may consider using *bitmap indexes*. As described in Chapter 12, bitmap indexes are most effective for queries against large, static data sets with few distinct values. You can create both bitmap indexes and normal (B*-tree) indexes on the same table, and ORACLE will perform any necessary index conversions dynamically during query processing. See Chapter 12 for details on using bitmap indexes.

If two tables are frequently queried together, then *clusters* may be effective in improving performance. Clusters store rows from multiple tables in the same physical data blocks, based on their logical values (the cluster key). See Chapter 5 for more information on clusters.

Queries in which a column's value is compared to an exact value (rather than a range of values) are called *equivalence* queries. A *hash cluster* stores a row in a specific location based on its value in the cluster key column. Every time a row is inserted, its cluster key value is used to determine which block it should be stored in; this same logic can be used during queries to quickly find data blocks that are needed for retrieval. Hash clusters are designed to improve the performance of equivalence queries; they will not be as helpful in improving the performance of the range queries discussed earlier.

Reverse indexes provide another tuning solution for equivalence queries. In a reverse index, the bytes of the index are stored in reverse order. In a traditional index, two consecutive values are stored next to each other. In a reverse index, consecutive values are not stored next to each other. For example, values 2004 and 2005 are stored as 4002 and 5002, respectively, in a reverse index. While not appropriate for range scans, reverse indexes may reduce contention for index blocks if many equivalence queries are performed.

NOTE
You cannot reverse a bitmap index.

As of ORACLE8i, you can create *functional indexes*. Prior to ORACLE8i, any query that performed a function on a column could not use that column's index. Thus, this query could not use an index on the Name column:

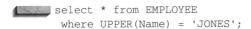

```
select * from EMPLOYEE
  where UPPER(Name) = 'JONES';
```

but this query could:

```
select * from EMPLOYEE
  where Name = 'JONES';
```

since the second query does not perform the **UPPER** function on the Name column. As of ORACLE8i, you can create indexes that allow function-based accesses to be supported by index accesses. Instead of creating an index on the column Name, you can create an index on the column expression UPPER(Name), as shown in the following listing.

```
create index EMP_UPPER_NAME on
EMPLOYEE(UPPER(Name));
```

Although functional indexes can be useful, be sure to consider the following points when creating them:

■ Can you restrict the functions that will be used on the column? If so, can you restrict all functions from being performed on the column?

■ Do you have adequate storage space for the additional indexes?

- When you drop the table, you will be dropping more indexes (and therefore more extents) than before. How will that impact the time required to drop the table?

Functional indexes are useful, but you should implement them sparingly. The more indexes you create on a table, the longer all **insert**s, **update**s, and **delete**s will take.

Generating Explain Plans

How can you determine which access path the database will use to perform a query? This information can be viewed via the **explain plan** command. This command will evaluate the execution path for a query and will place its output into a table (named PLAN_TABLE) in the database. A sample **explain plan** command is shown in the following listing:

```
explain plan
set Statement_Id = 'TEST'
for
select * from EMPLOYEE
where City > 'Y%';
```

The first line of this command tells the database that it is to explain its execution plan for the query without actually executing the query. The second line labels this query's records in the PLAN_TABLE with a Statement_Id equal to TEST. Following the keyword **for**, the query to be analyzed is listed.

The account that is running this command must have a PLAN_TABLE in its schema. ORACLE provides the **create table** commands needed for this table. The file, named utlxplan.sql, is usually located in the /rdbms/admin subdirectory under the ORACLE software home directory. Users may run this script to create the table in their schemas.

Query the plan table using the query in the following listing. Records in that table are related to each other, so the **connect by** clause of the **select** statement can be used to evaluate the hierarchy.

```
select
  LPAD(' ',2*Level)||Operation||' '||Options||' '||Object_Name
  Q_Plan
  from PLAN_TABLE
 where Statement_Id = 'TEST'
connect by prior ID = Parent_ID and Statement_ID = 'TEST'
 start with ID=0 and Statement_ID = 'TEST';
```

This query will report on the types of operations the database must perform to resolve the query. Sample output is shown in the following listing:

```
Q_PLAN
-----------------------------------------------------------
SELECT STATEMENT
  TABLE ACCESS BY ROWID EMPLOYEE
    INDEX RANGE SCAN CITY_ST_ZIP_NDX
```

To read the explain plan, read the order of operations from inside out of the hierarchy until you come to a set of operations at the same level of indentation; then read from top to bottom. In this example, there are no operations at the same level of indentation; therefore, you read the order of operations from inside out. The first operation is the index range scan, followed by the table access; the SELECT STATEMENT operation displays the output to the user.

This plan shows that the data that is returned to the user comes via a Table Access by ROWID. The RowIDs are supplied by an index range scan, using the CITY_ST_ZIP_NDX index described earlier in this section.

As of ORACLE7.3, you can use the **set autotrace on** command in SQL*Plus to automatically generate the **explain plan** output and trace information for every query you run. The autotrace-generated output will not be displayed until after the query has completed (while the **explain plan** output is generated without running the command). To enable autotrace-generated output, a PLAN_TABLE must either be created in the schema in which the autotrace utility will be used or created in the SYSTEM schema and access granted to the schema that will use the autotrace utility. The script plustrce.sql, located in the $ORACLE_HOME/sqlplus/admin directory, must also be run as SYS before you can **set autotrace on**. Users must have the PLUSTRACE role enabled prior to executing **set autotrace on**.

When evaluating the output of the **explain plan** command, you should make sure that the most selective indexes (that is, the most nearly unique indexes) are used by the query. If a nonselective index is used, you may be forcing the database to perform unnecessary reads to resolve the query. A full discussion of SQL tuning is beyond the scope of this book, but you should focus your tuning efforts on making sure that the most resource-intensive SQL statements are using the most selective indexes possible.

When using the **explain plan** command, you need to make sure you are using the latest version of PLAN_TABLE. Each time you upgrade your database to a new kernel version, drop and re-create your PLAN_TABLE table (using the current version of UTLXPLAN.SQL to create the table). In ORACLE8.0 and again in ORACLE8i, new columns were added to the PLAN_TABLE table. If you do not drop and re-create your PLAN_TABLE, you will never see the new columns or the data they contain.

The **set autotrace on** command described earlier will automatically display all of the new PLAN_TABLE columns as part of its output.

You can use the **set autotrace on** command to measure the "cost" of each step within an **explain plan**. In general, transaction-oriented applications (such as multiuser systems used for data entry) evaluate performance based on the time it takes to return the first row of a query. For transaction-oriented applications, you should focus your tuning efforts on using indexes to reduce the database's response time to the query.

If the application is batch-oriented (with large transactions and reports), you should focus on improving the time it takes to complete the overall transaction instead of the time it takes to return the first row from the transaction. Improving the overall throughput of the transaction may require using full table scans in place of index accesses—and may improve the overall performance of the application. Since full table scans can take advantage of the Parallel Query Option, you may be able to involve more computing resources in the execution of the scan, thereby improving its performance. See Chapter 12 for details on the implementation of the Parallel Query Option.

As of ORACLE8i, you can use *stored outlines* to save the execution path for a query. See Chapter 5 for details on the implementation of stored outlines.

If the application is distributed across multiple instances, focus on reducing the number of times database links are used in queries. If a remote database is frequently accessed during a query, then the cost of accessing that remote database is paid each time the remote data is accessed. Even if the cost of accessing the remote data is low, accessing it thousands of times will eventually place a performance burden on your application. See the "Reducing Network Traffic" section later in this chapter for additional tuning suggestions for distributed databases.

See *ORACLE8 Advanced Tuning and Administration* (Osborne/McGraw-Hill/ Oracle Press) for further details on tuning SQL.

Tuning Memory Usage

Monitoring the usage of ORACLE's memory areas is discussed in Chapter 6. Specifically, that chapter describes the proper use of the ORACLE statistics scripts and the interpretation of their output. These scripts, called UTLBSTAT.SQL and UTLESTAT.SQL, summarize the changes in system statistics for a given period. They help point out areas to which not enough resources have been given.

The data block buffer cache and the Shared SQL Pool are managed via a *least recently used (LRU)* algorithm. A preset area is set aside to hold values; when it fills, the least recently used data is eliminated from memory and written back to disk. An adequately sized memory area keeps the most frequently accessed data in memory; accessing less frequently used data requires physical reads.

Sizing of both the dictionary cache and the Shared SQL Pool is described in Chapter 6. The hit ratio calculation in that chapter also helps to alert you to an improperly sized data buffer cache.

The hit ratio is a measure of how well the data buffer cache is handling requests for data. It is calculated as

```
Hit Ratio = (Logical Reads - Physical Reads)/Logical Reads
```

Thus, a perfect hit ratio would have a value of 1.00. In that instance, all requests for database blocks (logical reads) would be fulfilled without requesting any data from datafiles (physical reads); all requests would be handled by the data that is already in memory.

In general, the online transaction portion of applications should have hit ratios in excess of 0.97. In a batch-oriented system, the hit ratio should not fall below 0.89. The overall hit ratio for an application will be lowered by its batch activity. The method for measuring the hit ratio is described in Chapter 6. Note that the hit ratio in a database is cumulative, reflecting all of the processing performed since the last time the database was started. A single poorly written query or long-running batch job will adversely affect your hit ratio long after it completes. To avoid this impact, you can use the methods described in Chapter 6 to measure the hit ratio during specific time intervals.

You can manipulate the actions of the LRU algorithm in the data block buffer cache via the **cache** option. The option automatically loads an entire table into the SGA the first time that table is accessed, and will mark it as *most* recently used. That table's data will still be subject to the LRU algorithms that manage the SGA caches, but it will stay in the SGA longer than if it had been treated normally. The **cache** option can be specified at a table level via the **create table** and **alter table** commands, and can also be specified via query hints. The **cache** option is most useful for frequently accessed tables that change infrequently. You can then run queries that will reload the most-used tables into the SGA caches each time the database is restarted.

With all of the areas of the SGA—the data block buffers, the dictionary cache, and the Shared SQL Pool—the emphasis should be on sharing data among users. Each of these areas should be large enough to hold the most commonly requested data from the database. In the case of the Shared SQL Pool, it should be large enough to hold the parsed versions of the most commonly used queries. When they are adequately sized, the memory areas in the SGA can dramatically improve the performance of individual queries and of the database as a whole.

As of ORACLE8, you can create a *large pool* within the SGA. The large pool will be used when ORACLE requests large contiguous areas of memory within the shared pool (such as during use of the multithreaded server). To create the large pool, set a value (in bytes) for the LARGE_POOL_SIZE init.ora parameter. By default, the large pool is not created. In ORACLE8.0, you can specify the minimum allocation size for an object in the large pool via the LARGE_POOL_MIN_ALLOC init.ora parameter. The LARGE_POOL_MIN_ALLOC parameter defaults to 16KB in ORACLE8.0, and is obsolete as of ORACLE8i.

Rather than using the large pool, you can reserve an area within the shared pool for large objects via the SHARED_POOL_RESERVED_SIZE init.ora parameter. The "reserved size" is set aside for the shared pool entries of large objects (such as large packages). The minimum size for an entry in the reserved area is set via the SHARED_POOL_RESERVED_MIN_ALLOC init.ora parameter. You can use the reserved area of the shared pool in ORACLE7, ORACLE8.0, and ORACLE8i, although the SHARED_POOL_RESERVED_MIN_ALLOC parameter is obsolete as of ORACLE8i.

Rather than reserving space in the shared pool, you may wish to selectively "pin" packages in memory. Pinning packages in memory immediately after starting the database will increase the likelihood that a large enough section of contiguous free space is available in memory. The KEEP procedure of the DBMS_SHARED_POOL package designates the packages to pin in the shared pool. As shown in the following listing, you must first reference the object to be pinned:

```
alter procedure APPOWNER.ADD_CLIENT compile;
execute DBMS_SHARED_POOL.KEEP('APPOWNER.ADD_CLIENT','P');
```

Pinning of packages is more related to application management than application tuning, but it can have a performance impact. If you can avoid dynamic management of fragmented memory areas, you minimize the work ORACLE has to do when managing the shared pool.

As noted in Chapter 5, ORACLE reads multiple blocks at a time during a full table scan. The number of blocks read during each physical read is determined by the setting of the DB_FILE_MULTIBLOCK_READ_COUNT init.ora parameter. The number of blocks read at a time is limited by the I/O buffer size of your operating system. If your operating system buffer size is 128KB, and your database block size is 4KB, then you should set DB_FILE_MULTIBLOCK_READ_COUNT to a value of 32 (128KB divided by the 4KB block size). If you set it to a lower value, the performance of your full table scans will be adversely affected.

Using the Cost-Based Optimizer

With each release of its software, ORACLE has added new features to its optimizer, and has improved its existing features. As a result, performance when using the cost-based optimizer (CBO) should be consistently improving. Although the RULE hint and rule-based optimization is available in ORACLE8, the role of rule-based optimization will probably diminish over time, and you should begin converting to cost-based optimization if you have not already done so.

Effective use of the cost-based optimizer requires that the tables and indexes in your application be analyzed regularly. The frequency with which you analyze the objects depends on the rate of change within the objects. For batch transaction applications, you should reanalyze the objects after each large set of batch transactions. For OLTP applications, you should reanalyze the objects on a time-based schedule (such as via a weekly or nightly process).

Statistics on objects are gathered via the **analyze** command. If you **analyze** a table, then its associated indexes are automatically analyzed as well. You can specify that only the table be reanalyzed, but this should only be done if the only changes to the table were in nonindexed columns. You can **analyze** only the indexed columns, speeding the analysis process. In general, you should **analyze** a table's indexes each time you **analyze** the table. In the following listing, the COMPANY table and all of its indexes are completely scanned and their statistics are gathered by the first **analyze** command. The second command analyzes just the table and its indexed columns.

```
analyze table COMPANY compute statistics;

analyze table COMPANY compute statistics for table
     for all indexed columns;
```

You can view the statistics on the COMPANY table and its indexes via DBA_TABLES, DBA_TAB_COL_STATISTICS, and DBA_INDEXES. Some column-level statistics are still provided in DBA_TAB_COLUMNS, but they are provided there strictly for backward compatibility. The statistics for the columns of partitioned tables are found in DBA_PART_COL_STATISTICS.

As of ORACLE7.3, you can use the **analyze** command to generate histograms. A histogram reflects the distribution of data values within a table. For example, there may be many distinct values for a column, in which case the column may seem ideal as a limiting value for a query. However, 90 percent of those values may all be clustered together, with the remaining 10 percent of the values outside the cluster. If your query performs a range scan with a limiting value inside the cluster, the index may not help the performance of your query. The use of an index for values outside the cluster would have a greater performance impact.

How does the optimizer know where data value clusters are? When you run the **analyze** command, you can tell ORACLE to generate a histogram for the cluster. By default, ORACLE will create a histogram that divides the data values into 75 *buckets*. Each bucket has the same number of records as every other bucket. The more buckets you create, the better the distribution of database values will be reflected via the histogram. You can specify the number of buckets to use via the **size** parameter of the **analyze** command. The maximum number of buckets per table is 254.

To **analyze** all objects in a schema, you can use the ANALYZE_SCHEMA procedure within the DBMS_UTILITY package. As shown in the following listing, it has two parameters: the name of the schema and the **analyze** option used (COMPUTE or ESTIMATE):

```
execute DBMS_UTILITY.ANALYZE_SCHEMA('APPOWNER','COMPUTE');
```

When the command in the preceding listing is executed, all of the objects belonging to the APPOWNER schema will be analyzed, using the **compute statistics** option of the **analyze** command. If you are using rule-based optimization, then the statistics, although not used during the optimization process, will provide useful information to the developers during the query tuning process. See the **analyze** command entry in Appendix A for the full syntax of the command.

Implications of compute statistics

In the examples in the preceding section, the **compute statistics** option of the **analyze** command was used to gather statistics about objects. ORACLE also provides an **estimate statistics** option which, by default, scans only the first 1,064 rows of a table during its analysis. The **estimate statistics** option, therefore, may not be appropriate if your tables will be growing—since new records added to the table might not be considered during subsequent analyses of the table. If you choose to use **estimate statistics**, **analyze** as much of the table as possible (you can specify a percentage of the rows to **analyze**)—**analyze** at least 20 percent of the table. If you do not **analyze** enough of the table, then your statistics will not accurately reflect the data in the table.

To generate the most accurate statistics, you should use the **compute statistics** option wherever possible. There are, however, management issues associated with the **compute statistics** option of the **analyze** command. Specifically, **compute statistics** can require large amounts of temporary segment space (up to four times the size of the table). You need to make sure that the user performing the analysis has the proper temporary tablespace settings and that the temporary tablespace can handle the space requirements. As the table grows over time, the temporary segment space requirements of **compute statistics** will grow. Although **compute statistics** places an additional management burden on the system, the benefits gained from the use of accurate statistics should outweigh the management burdens.

If the table is very large, then even the **estimate statistics** option may take too long to complete, or consume too much temporary segment space. In that case, you may need to partition the table in order to reduce the administrative costs of the analysis. You can analyze individual partitions of a table. For example, if the table TAB1 has a partition PART1, you can **analyze** the partition via the following command:

```
analyze table TAB1 partition (PART1) compute statistics;
```

Tuning Data Storage

How the database actually *stores* data also has an effect on the performance of queries. If the data is fragmented into multiple extents, then resolving a query may cause the database to look in several physical locations for related rows.

Free space fragmentation may slow performance when storing new records. If the free space in a tablespace is fragmented, then the database may have to dynamically combine neighboring free extents to create a single extent that is large enough to handle the new space requirements. Tuning data storage thus involves tuning both used space and free space, as described in the next sections.

Defragmentation of Segments

Space: The **initial** Frontier.

As described in Chapter 4, when a database object (such as a table or index) is created, it is assigned to a tablespace via user defaults or specific instructions. A *segment* is created in that tablespace to hold the data associated with that object. The space that is allocated to the segment is never released until the segment is dropped, shrunk, or truncated.

A segment is made up of sections called *extents*. The extents themselves are contiguous sets of ORACLE blocks. Once the existing extents can no longer hold new data, the segment will obtain another extent. This extension process will continue until no more free space is available in the tablespace's datafiles, or until an internal maximum number of extents per segment is reached. If a segment consists of multiple extents, there is no guarantee that those extents will be contiguous.

To simplify the management of segments, it is beneficial to have each data segment have only one extent. A segment's **initial** storage parameter, which specifies the size of its initial extent, should be set large enough to handle all of the segment's data. The monitoring system provided in Chapter 6 checks for fragmented data segments via its EXTENTS table.

Having a large number of extents does not impact query performance if the extents are properly sized. As described in Chapter 5, your extent sizes should be a multiple of the operating system's I/O buffer size. If your extents are properly sized, then neither full table scans nor RowID-based lookups will be impacted by the number of extents in the table. DDL operations, however, may be impacted.

When an object allocates an extent, ORACLE **update**s the entries in the used extents table, SYS.UET$. At the same time, it **update**s the entries in the free extents table, SYS.FET$. The SYS.UET$ table has one record for every extent in the database, and SYS.FET$ has one row for every free extent in the database. If you have a large number of extents in a table or index, then DDL commands that **update** SYS.UET$ and SYS.FET$ may impact the performance of your commands.

For example, consider a table that has 10,000 extents (either by itself or as a collection of partitions that together have 10,000 extents). When you drop that table, ORACLE will need to perform 10,000 **update**s of SYS.UET$ (since the data in SYS.UET$ must always be consistent for everyone in the database). At the same time, ORACLE must **update** SYS.FET$ and the other data dictionary tables used for object maintenance (for privileges, columns, etc.). Unfortunately, SYS.UET$ is not tuned to support the drops of tables with thousands of extents. In a test environment, a **drop table** of a 5,000 extent table took two minutes to complete. In the same environment, a **drop table** of a 10,000 extent table took ten minutes to complete. As more extents were added, the time required to drop the table grew exponentially worse. When the table reached 60,000 extents, the **drop table** command took almost a day to complete.

When considering the impact of the number of extents on your DDL commands' performance, you should consider not only your tables but also the indexes, partitions, and index partitions that will be dropped along with the table. If you have a table with 100 partitions, and each of the partitions has 300 extents, and each of the partitions has a local index that in turn has 300 extents, then dropping the table will require dropping 60,000 extents—and that may cause performance problems. To resolve this problem, ORACLE8i introduced *locally managed tablespaces*, in which the extent usage information is stored in a bitmap in the datafile header rather than in the data dictionary. See Chapter 12 for further details on locally managed tablespaces.

The monitoring system provided in Chapter 6 checks the DBA_SEGMENTS data dictionary view to determine which segments have ten or more extents. A general query of the DBA_SEGMENTS view is shown in the following listing. This query will retrieve the tablespace name, owner, segment name, and segment type for each segment in the database. The number of extents and blocks used by the segment will be displayed.

```
select
        Tablespace_Name,    /*Tablespace name*/
        Owner,              /*Owner of the segment*/
        Segment_Name,       /*Name of the segment*/
        Segment_Type,       /*Type of segment (ex. TABLE, INDEX)*/
        Extents,            /*Number of extents in the segment*/
        Blocks,             /*Number of db blocks in the segment*/
        Bytes               /*Number of bytes in the segment*/
from DBA_SEGMENTS
/
```

Segment types include TABLE, INDEX, CLUSTER, ROLLBACK, TEMPORARY, DEFERRED ROLLBACK, and CACHE. The DBA_SEGMENTS view does not list the size of the individual extents in a segment. To see that, query the DBA_EXTENTS view, as shown in the following listing:

```
select
        Tablespace_Name,    /*Tablespace name*/
        Owner,              /*Owner of the segment*/
        Segment_Name,       /*Name of the segment*/
        Segment_Type,       /*Type of segment (ex. TABLE, INDEX)*/
```

```
        Extent_ID,          /*Extent number in the segment*/
        Block_ID,           /*Starting block number for the extent*/
        Bytes,              /*Size of the extent, in bytes*/
        Blocks              /*Size of the extent, in Oracle blocks*/
  from DBA_EXTENTS
where Segment_Name = 'segment_name'
order by Extent_ID;
```

This query selects the extent information for a single segment (identified via the **where** clause). It returns the storage information associated with the segment's extents, including the size and location of each data extent. A similar query shown later in this chapter is used when mapping the distribution of free extents and used extents in a tablespace.

If a segment is fragmented, the easiest way to compress its data into a single extent is to rebuild it with the proper storage parameters. Since the **initial** storage parameter cannot be changed after a table has been created, a new table must be created with the correct storage parameters. The old data can then be **insert**ed into the new table, and the old table can be dropped.

This process can be automated via the Export/Import utilities. As noted in Chapter 10, the Export command has a COMPRESS flag. This flag will cause Export, when reading a table, to determine the total amount of space allocated to that table. It will then write to the export dump file a new **initial** storage parameter—equivalent to the total of the allocated space—for the table. If the table is then dropped, and Import is used to re-create it, then its data should all fit in the new, larger initial extent.

Note that it is the *allocated,* not the *used,* space that is compressed. An empty table with 300MB allocated to it in three 100MB extents will be compressed into a single, empty 300MB extent. No space will be reclaimed. Also, the database will not check to see if the new **initial** extent size is greater than the size of the largest datafile for the tablespace. Since extents cannot span datafiles, this would result in an error during import.

The data segment compression procedure is shown in the following example. First, export the tables.

```
exp system/manager file=exp.dmp compress=Y grants=Y indexes=Y
    tables=(HR.T1,HR.T2)
```

Next, if the Export succeeded, then go into SQL*Plus and drop the exported tables. Then, import the tables from the export dump file.

```
imp system/manager file=exp.dmp commit=Y buffer=64000 full=Y
```

In this example, the DBA exported two tables, named T1 and T2, owned by the user HR. The tables were exported with the COMPRESS=Y flag, which modified their storage parameters during the Export. The tables were then dropped. When they were then imported, the Import utility created the tables with the new, compressed storage parameters. Because the Export used the INDEXES=Y clause, the tables indexes were also Exported and re-created during Import.

This method may also be used on the entire database. Export the database with the COMPRESS=Y flag, re-create the database, and then perform a full Import. With some restrictions, it may also be applied to the defragmentation of tablespaces. See Chapter 10 for further details on the use of Export and Import for tablespace rebuilds.

Defragmentation of Free Extents

As noted in Chapter 4, a *free extent* in a tablespace is a collection of contiguous free blocks in the tablespace. When a segment is dropped, its extents are deallocated and marked as free. However, these free extents are not always recombined with neighboring free extents; the barriers between these free extents may be maintained. The SMON background process periodically coalesces neighboring free extents if the default **pctincrease** setting for the tablespace is nonzero. If the default **pctincrease** setting for a tablespace is zero, then the free space in the tablespace will not be coalesced automatically by the database. You can use the **coalesce** option of the **alter tablespace** command to force neighboring free extents to be coalesced, regardless of the default **pctincrease** setting for the tablespace.

NOTE
*The SMON background process only coalesces tablespaces whose default **pctincrease** value is nonzero. A **pctincrease** of 1 will force SMON to coalesce the adjacent free space in a tablespace while having little impact on the next extent value.*

Not forcing the coalescing of free extents affects the allocation of space within the tablespace during the next space request (such as by the creation or expansion of a table). In its quest for a large enough free extent, the database will not merge contiguous free extents unless there is no other alternative; thus, the large free extent at the rear of the tablespace tends to be used while the smaller free extents toward the front of the tablespace are relatively unused, becoming "speed bumps" in the tablespace because they are not, by themselves, of adequate size to be of use. As this usage pattern progresses, the database thus drifts further and further from its ideal space allocation. Free space fragmentation is particularly prevalent in environments in which database tables and indexes are frequently dropped and re-created, especially if their storage parameters are changed in the process.

However, you can force the database to recombine the contiguous free extents, thus emulating the SMON functionality. Coalescing the free extents will increase the likelihood of the free extents near the front of the file being reused, thus preserving the free space near the rear of the tablespace file. As a result, new requests for extents are more likely to meet with success.

In the ideal ORACLE tablespace, each database object is stored in a single extent and all of the available free space is in one large contiguous extent. This will minimize recursive calls during retrievals while maximizing the likelihood of acquiring a large enough free extent when an object needs additional storage space. The commands presented here will provide a means of accomplishing the second goal, that of automated free space defragmentation, as well as mapping database space allocations and providing a means of evaluating the severity of the free space fragmentation problems you may experience.

Measuring Free Space Fragmentation

To judge whether a tablespace could benefit from a free space rebuild, you must first establish a baseline on an arbitrary scoring system. Since free space fragmentation is made up of several components (number of extents, size of largest extent), create a scoring index that considers both. The weightings presented here are arbitrary, and were chosen to reflect the potential for the database to acquire a large extent. Thus, the number of extents is given little importance. The critical factor is the size of the largest extent as a percentage of the total free space (that is, how close is the tablespace to the ideal?). The score for each tablespace is referred to as the *free space fragmentation index* (FSFI). You may wish to tailor your index to give greater importance to other criteria. Note that it does not consider how much free space is available, only its structure.

$$FSFI = 100 * sqrt\left(\frac{largest\ extent}{sum\ all\ extents}\right) * \frac{1}{(number\ of\ extents)^{1/4}}$$

The largest possible FSFI (for an ideal single-file tablespace) is 100. As the number of extents increases, the FSFI rating drops slowly. As the size of the largest extent drops, however, the FSFI rating drops rapidly. The following script calculates the FSFI values for all tablespaces in a database:

```
rem
rem   file: fsfi.sql
rem
rem   This script measures the fragmentation of free space
rem   in all of the tablespaces in a database and scores them
rem   according to an arbitrary index for comparison.
rem
set newpage 0 pagesize 60
column fsfi format 999.99

select
```

```
       Tablespace_Name,
       SQRT(MAX(Blocks)/SUM(Blocks))*
       (100/SQRT(SQRT(COUNT(Blocks)))) Fsfi
from DBA_FREE_SPACE
group by
       Tablespace_Name
order by 1

spool fsfi.lis
/
spool off
```

Output from this query, showing the FSFI values for a sample database, is shown in Figure 8-1.

Given your database's FSFI ratings, you must then establish a baseline. You should rarely encounter free space availability problems in tablespaces that have adequate free space available and FSFI ratings over 30. If a tablespace appears to be approaching that borderline, you may wish to generate a mapping of space usage in the tablespace. The following script will show all space marked as free or used by database objects. This is useful (1) to show the distribution and size of the free extents and (2) to determine which database objects are barriers between free extents.

```
rem
rem    file: mapper.sql
rem    Parameters: the tablespace name being mapped
rem
rem    Sample invocation:
rem    @mapper DEMODATA
rem
rem    This script generates a mapping of the space usage
rem    (free space vs used) in a tablespace. It graphically
rem    shows segment and free space fragmentation.
rem
set pagesize 60 linesize 132 verify off
column file_id heading "File|Id"

select
       'free space' Owner,       /*"owner" of free space*/
       '    ' Object,             /*blank object name*/
       File_ID,                   /*file ID for the extent header*/
       Block_ID,                  /*block ID for the extent header*/
       Blocks                     /*length of the extent, in blocks*/
  from DBA_FREE_SPACE
where Tablespace_Name = UPPER('&&1')
union
select
       SUBSTR(Owner,1,20),               /*owner name (first 20 chars)*/
```

```
       SUBSTR(Segment_Name,1,32),  /*segment name*/
       File_ID,                    /*file ID for extent header*/
       Block_ID,                   /*block ID for block header*/
       Blocks              /*length of the extent in blocks*/
  from DBA_EXTENTS
where Tablespace_Name = UPPER('&&1')
order by 3,4

spool &&1._map.lst
/
spool off
undefine 1
```

Sample output from this mapping query is shown in Figure 8-2. The query output displays the owner and segment name for each extent in the tablespace. If the extent is a free extent, then the owner is listed as "free space," and the segment name (the OBJECT column) is left blank.

The output in Figure 8-2 shows 12 rows. Five of them are of free space extents, and seven are from data segments. Note that the first three free space extents are contiguous. Following two more data extents, there is another free space extent. Because it is separated from the other free extents in the tablespace, the fourth free extent cannot be combined with any of the other free extents unless the tablespace is defragmented.

Combining the Free Extents

If a tablespace would benefit from having its free extents coalesced (as shown in its FSFI value and free extent map), then you should either manually coalesce the extents or enable the SMON process to coalesce the extents.

Tablespace_Name	FSFI
DEMODATA	87.91
DEMONDX	30.39
RBS	68.24
SYSTEM	73.78
TEMP	100.00
TOOLS	100.00

FIGURE 8-1. *Sample free space fragmentation index values*

Owner	OBJECT	File Id	BLOCK_ID	Blocks
OPS$CC1	FILES	6	2	20
OPS$CC1	SPACES	6	22	20
OPS$CC1	EXTENTS	6	42	20
OPS$CC1	FILES	6	62	20
free space		6	82	5
free space		6	87	5
free space		6	92	5
OPS$CC1	SPACES	6	97	20
OPS$CC1	EXTENTS	6	117	20
free space		6	137	10
OPS$CC1	FILES	6	147	20
free space		6	167	14,833

FIGURE 8-2. *Sample extent map of used and free space*

To enable the SMON process to coalesce the extents, you should set the default **pctincrease** value for the tablespace to a nonzero value. In the following listing, the default storage for the DEMONDX tablespace is altered to use a **pctincrease** of 1:

```
alter tablespace DEMONDX
default storage (pctincrease 1);
```

If an object is created in the DEMONDX without a specified **pctincrease** value, then the object will use the default **pctincrease** value for the tablespace. In general, low **pctincrease** values accurately reflect the normal linear growth in the number of rows in the database. Therefore, the lowest allowable nonzero value (1) was used for the **pctincrease** value. You can override the default via the **storage** clause of the object you create.

To manually coalesce the free extents of the tablespace, use the **coalesce** option of the **alter tablespace** command.

```
alter tablespace DEMONDX coalesce;
```

The neighboring free extents will then be coalesced. You can reexecute the mapper.sql script shown earlier in this chapter to see the new structure of used and free extents in the tablespace. If there are many free extents located between data extents, then you will need to re-create the tablespace (for example, by exporting and importing its data) in order to be able to coalesce the free extents.

Identifying Chained Rows

When a data segment is created, a **pctfree** value is specified. This parameter tells the database how much space should be kept free *in each data block*. This space is then used when rows that are already stored in the data block extend in length via **update**s.

If an **update** to a row causes that row to no longer completely fit in a single data block, then that row may be moved to another data block, or the row may be *chained* to another block. If you are storing rows whose length is greater than the ORACLE block size, then you will automatically have chaining.

Chaining affects performance because it requires ORACLE to look in multiple physical locations for data from the same logical row. By eliminating unnecessary chaining, you reduce the number of physical reads needed to return data from a datafile.

You can avoid chaining by setting the proper value for **pctfree** during creation of data segments. For instructions for setting this value, see the "Determining the Proper **pctfree**" section of Chapter 5.

You can use the **analyze** command to collect statistics about database objects. The cost-based optimizer can use these statistics to determine the best execution path to use. The **analyze** command has an option that detects and records chained rows in tables. Its syntax is

```
analyze table TABLE_NAME list chained rows into CHAINED_ROWS;
```

This command will put the output from this operation into a table called CHAINED_ROWS in your local schema. The SQL to create the CHAINED_ROWS table is in a file named utlchain.sql, in the /rdbms/admin subdirectory under your ORACLE software directory. The following query will select the most significant columns from the CHAINED_ROWS table:

```
select
        Owner_Name,       /*Owner of the data segment*/
        Table_Name,       /*Name of the table with the chained rows*/
        Cluster_Name,     /*Name of the cluster, if it is clustered*/
        Head_RowID        /*Rowid of the first part of the row*/
from CHAINED_ROWS;
```

The output will show the RowIDs for all chained rows. This will allow you to quickly see how many of the rows in the table are chained. If chaining is prevalent in a table, then that table should be rebuilt with a higher value for **pctfree**.

You can see the impact of row chaining by querying V$SYSSTAT. The V$SYSSTAT entry for the 'table fetch continued row' statistic will be incremented each time ORACLE selects data from a chained row. This statistic will also be incremented when ORACLE selects data from a *spanned row*—a row that is chained because it is greater than a block in length. Tables with LONG, BLOB, CLOB, and NCLOB datatypes are most likely to have spanned rows.

In addition to chaining rows, ORACLE will occasionally move rows. If a row exceeds the space available to its block, the rows may be **insert**ed into a different block. The process of moving a row from one block to another is called *row migration*, and the moved row is called a *migrated row*. During row migration, ORACLE has to dynamically manage space in multiple blocks and access the free list (the list of blocks available for **insert**s). A migrated row does not appear as a chained row, but it does impact the performance of your transactions.

Increasing the **ORACLE** Block Size

The effect of increasing the database block size is stunning. In most environments, at least two block sizes are supported—for example, 2KB and 4KB. Most of the installation routines are set to use the lower of the two. However, using the next higher value for the block size may improve the performance of query-intensive operations by up to 50 percent.

This gain comes relatively free of charge. To increase the database block size, the entire database must be rebuilt, and all of the old database files have to be **delete**d. The new files can be created in the same location as the old files, with the same size, but will be managed more efficiently by the database. The performance savings comes from the way that ORACLE manages the block header information. More space is used by data, improving the ability of multiple users to access the same block of data in memory. Doubling the size of the ORACLE blocks has little effect on the block header; thus, a smaller percentage of space is used to store block header information. For a Windows NT environment, a 4KB block size aligns nicely with the NTFS file system and is recommended.

To change the block size, modify the parameter called DB_BLOCK_SIZE. The DB_BLOCK_SIZE parameter may be specified in the database init.ora parameter file or the config.ora file that your database's init.ora file calls.

Be careful when doing this, since several of the database's init.ora parameters are set in terms of the number of ORACLE blocks. Most importantly, the DB_BLOCK_BUFFERS parameter, which sets the size of the data buffer cache, is set in this manner. If you double the block size, you should cut the DB_BLOCK_BUFFERS parameter in half. Failing to modify the DB_BLOCK_BUFFERS parameter when doubling the database block size will double the size of the data buffer cache, possibly causing problems with the memory management on your server.

Using Index-Organized Tables

As of ORACLE8.0, you can use index-organized tables (IOTs) to store your data. In ORACLE8i, the most important constraints on IOT usage have been eliminated, and significant new capabilities have been added. As a result, you should consider IOTs as a tuning solution both for storage tuning and for performance tuning.

Conceptually, an IOT is an index in which an entire row is stored, rather than just the key values for the row. Rather than storing a RowID for the row, the primary key for the row is treated as the logical identifier for the row. Rows in IOTs do not have RowIDs.

Within the IOT, the rows are stored sorted by their primary key values. Thus, any range query that is based on the primary key may benefit, since the rows are stored near each other (see the "Tuning SQL" section earlier in this chapter for the steps involved in ordering the data within normal tables). Additionally, any equivalence query based on the primary key may benefit, since the table's data is all stored in the index. In the traditional table/index combination, an index-based access requires an index access followed by a table access. In an IOT, only the IOT is accessed; there is no companion index.

However, the performance gains from a single index access in place of a normal index/table combination access may be minimal—any index-based access should be fast. To help improve performance further, index-organized tables offer additional features:

- *An overflow area*   By setting the **pctthreshold** parameter when the IOT is created, you can store the primary key data apart from the row data. If the row's data exceeds the threshold of available space in the block, then it will dynamically be moved to an overflow area. You can designate the overflow area to be in a separate tablespace, improving your ability to distribute the I/O associated with the table.

- *Secondary indexes*   In ORACLE8.0, you cannot create additional indexes on an IOT; the primary key is the only index, limiting the IOT's usefulness. As of ORACLE8i, you can create secondary indexes on the IOT. ORACLE will use the primary key values as the logical RowID for each row.

- *Key compression*   If the same data is repeated in the same columns of multiple rows, then you can configure the IOT to only store the repeated data once. Via key compression, ORACLE creates a one-to-many relationship between the unique column values and those that are repeated.

- *Reduced storage requirements*   In a traditional table/index combination, the same key values are stored in two places. In an IOT, they are stored once, reducing the storage requirements.

To create an IOT, use the **organization index** clause of the **create table** command. You must specify a primary key when creating an IOT. Within an IOT, you can drop columns or mark them as inactive via the **set unused** clause of the **alter table** command. See Chapter 5 for details concerning column management.

Tuning Issues for Index-Organized Tables

Like indexes, IOTs may become internally fragmented over time, as values are **insert**ed, **update**d, and **delete**d. To rebuild an IOT, use the **move** clause of the **alter table** command. In the following example, the EMPLOYEE_IOT table is rebuilt, along with its overflow area:

```
alter table EMPLOYEE_IOT
 move tablespace DATA
overflow tablespace DATA_OVERFLOW;
```

You should avoid storing long rows of data in IOTs. In general, you should avoid using an IOT if the data is longer than 75 percent of the database block size. If the database block size is 4KB, and your rows will exceed 3KB in length, you should investigate the use of normal tables and indexes instead of IOTs. The longer the rows are, and the more transactions are performed against the IOT, the more frequently it will need to be rebuilt.

NOTE
You cannot partition an IOT, and you cannot reference an IOT via distributed transactions or replication.

Tuning Data Manipulation

There are several data manipulation tasks that may involve the DBA. These tasks tend to involve manipulation of large quantities of data. You have several options when loading and deleting large volumes of data, as described in the following sections.

You can improve the performance of database reads and writes by creating multiple DBWR (Database Writer) I/O slaves. Creating multiple DBWR slaves will prevent access requests against multiple disks from causing performance bottlenecks. ORACLE recommends creating at least as many DBWR slaves as you have disks. The number of DBWR slaves that should be created for an instance is set via the DBWR_IO_SLAVES parameter in the database's init.ora file. As an alternative to creating DBWR I/O slaves, you can create multiple DBWR processes. In ORACLE7, the DB_WRITERS init.ora parameter sets the number of DBWR processes to create; in ORACLE8.0 and ORACLE8i, the parameter name is DB_WRITER_PROCESSES.

In addition to creating I/O slaves for DBWR, you can create I/O slaves for the LGWR and ARCH processes. In ORACLE8.0, you can create multiple LGWR I/O slaves by setting a value for the LGWR_IO_SLAVES init.ora parameter, and multiple ARCH I/O slaves by setting a value for ARCH_IO_SLAVES. The number of ARCH I/O slaves is set via the ARCH_IO_SLAVES init.ora parameter. As of ORACLE8i, the LGWR_IO_SLAVES and ARCH_IO_SLAVES parameters are no longer supported; their values are derived from the DBWR_IO_SLAVES setting. Also, as of ORACLE8i you can use the LOG_ARCHIVE_MAX_PROCESSES init.ora parameter to set the number of ARCH processes initiated. Thus, you can choose between having multiple processes or a single process with multiple I/O slaves.

Bulk Inserts: Using the SQL*Loader Direct Path Option

When used in the Conventional Path mode, SQL*Loader reads a set of records from a file, generates **insert** commands, and passes them to the ORACLE kernel. ORACLE then finds places for those records in free blocks in the table and **update**s any associated indexes.

In Direct Path mode, SQL*Loader creates formatted data blocks and writes directly to the datafiles. This requires occasional checks with the database to get new locations for data blocks, but no other I/O with the database kernel is required. The result is a data load process that is dramatically faster than Conventional Path mode.

If the table is indexed, then the indexes will be placed in DIRECT PATH state during the load. After the load is complete, the new keys (index column values) will be sorted and merged with the existing keys in the index. To maintain this temporary set of keys, the load will create a temporary index segment that is at least as large as the largest index on the table. The space requirements for this can be minimized by presorting the index and using the SORTED INDEXES clause in the SQL*Loader control file.

To use the Direct Path option, a series of views must be created in the database. These views are created during database creation via the script catldr.sql, located in $ORACLE_HOME/rdbms/admin.

To get the best performance from the load, the data segment that you are loading into should already be created, with all of the space it will need already allocated. This will minimize the amount of dynamic space allocation necessary. You should also presort the data on the columns of the largest index in the table. Sorting the data and leaving the indexes on the table during a Direct Path load will usually yield better performance than if you were to drop the indexes before the load and then re-create them after it completed.

To take advantage of this option, the table cannot be clustered, and there can be no other active transactions against it. During the load, only NOT NULL, UNIQUE, and PRIMARY KEY constraints will be enforced; after the load has completed, the CHECK and FOREIGN KEY constraints can be automatically reenabled. To force this to occur, use the

```
REENABLE DISABLED_CONSTRAINTS
```

clause in the SQL*Loader control file.

The only exception to this reenabling process is that table insert triggers, when reenabled, are not executed for each of the new rows in the table. A separate process must manually perform whatever commands were to have been performed by this type of trigger.

The SQL*Loader Direct Path loading option provides significant performance improvements over the SQL*Loader Conventional Path loader in loading data into ORACLE tables by bypassing SQL processing, buffer cache management, and unnecessary reads for the data blocks. The Parallel Data Loading option of SQL*Loader allows multiple loading processes to work on loading the same table, utilizing spare resources on the system and thereby reducing the overall elapsed times for loading. Given enough CPU and I/O resources, this can significantly reduce the overall loading times.

To use Parallel Data Loading, start multiple SQL*Loader sessions using the **parallel** keyword (otherwise, SQL*Loader puts an exclusive lock on the table). Each session is an independent session requiring its own control file. The following listing shows three separate Direct Path loads, all using the PARALLEL=TRUE parameter on the command line:

```
sqlload USERID=ME/PASS CONTROL=PART1.CTL DIRECT=TRUE PARALLEL=TRUE
sqlload USERID=ME/PASS CONTROL=PART2.CTL DIRECT=TRUE PARALLEL=TRUE
sqlload USERID=ME/PASS CONTROL=PART3.CTL DIRECT=TRUE PARALLEL=TRUE
```

Each session creates its own log, bad, and discard files (part1.log, part2.log, part3.log, part1.bad, part2.bad, etc.) by default. Since you have multiple sessions loading data into the same table, only the APPEND option is allowed for Parallel Data Loading. The SQL*Loader REPLACE, TRUNCATE, and INSERT options are not allowed for Parallel Data Loading. If you need to **delete** the table's data before starting the load, you must manually **delete** the data (via **delete** or **truncate** commands). You cannot use SQL*Loader to **delete** the records automatically if you are using Parallel Data Loading.

NOTE
If you use Parallel Data Loading, indexes are not maintained by the SQL*Loader session. Before starting the loading process, you must drop all indexes on the table and disable all of its PRIMARY KEY and UNIQUE constraints. After the loads complete, you can re-create the table's indexes.

In serial Direct Path loading (PARALLEL=FALSE), SQL*Loader loads data into extents in the table. If the load process fails before the load completes, some data could be **commit**ted to the table prior to the process failure. In Parallel Data Loading, each load process creates temporary segments for loading the data. The temporary segments are later merged with the table. If a Parallel Data Load process fails before the load completes, the temporary segments will not have been merged with the table. If the temporary segments have not been merged with the table being loaded, then no data from the load will have been **commit**ted to the table.

You can use the SQL*Loader FILE parameter to direct each data loading session to a different datafile. By directing each loading session to its own datafile, you can balance the I/O load of the loading processes. Data loading is very I/O-intensive and must be distributed across multiple disks for parallel loading to achieve significant performance improvements over serial loading.

After a Parallel Data Load, each session may attempt to reenable the table's constraints. As long as at least one load session is still underway, attempting to reenable the constraints will fail. The final loading session to complete should attempt to reenable the constraints, and should succeed. You should check the status of your constraints after the load completes. If the table being loaded has PRIMARY KEY and UNIQUE constraints, you can create the associated indexes in parallel prior to enabling the constraints.

Bulk Inserts: Common Traps and Successful Tricks

If your data is not being inserted from a flat file, SQL*Loader will not be a useful solution. For example, if you need to move a large set of data from one table to another, you will likely want to avoid having to write the data to a flat file and then read it back into the database. The fastest way to move data in your database is to move it from one table to another without going out to the operating system.

When moving data from one table to another, there are four common methods for improving the performance of the data migration:

    1. Tuning the structures – removing indexes and triggers

    2. Disabling constraints during the data migration

3. Using hints and options to improve the transaction performance

4. Isolating the rollback segments for the large transaction

The first of the four tips, tuning the structures, involves disabling any triggers or indexes that are on the table into which data is being loaded. For example, if you have a row-level trigger on the target table, that trigger will be executed for every row **insert**ed into the table. If possible, disable the triggers prior to the data load. If the trigger should be executed for every **insert**ed row, then you may be able to do a bulk operation once the rows have been **insert**ed, rather than a repeated operation during each **insert**. If properly tuned, the bulk operation will complete faster than the repeated trigger executions. You will need to be sure that the bulk operations execute for all rows that have not already been processed by the triggers.

In addition to disabling triggers, you should disable the indexes on the target table prior to starting the data load. If the indexes are left on the table, then ORACLE will dynamically manage the indexes as each row is **insert**ed. Rather than continuously manage the index, drop it prior to the start of the load and re-create it when the load has completed.

NOTE
Disabling indexes and triggers resolves most of the performance problems associated with large table-to-table data migration efforts.

In addition to disabling indexes, you should consider disabling constraints on the table. If the source data is already in a table in the database, you can check that data for its adherence to your constraints (such as foreign keys or CHECK constraints) prior to loading it into your target table. Once the data has been loaded, reenable the constraints.

If none of those options gives you adequate performance, you should investigate the options ORACLE has introduced for data migration tuning in ORACLE8. Those options include the following:

- *The APPEND hint for **insert** commands*   Like the Direct Path loader, the APPEND hint loads blocks of data into a table, starting at the high-water mark for the table (see Chapter 4). Thus, use of the APPEND hint may impact your space usage.

- *The NOLOGGING option*   If you are performing a **create table as select** command, use the **nologging** option to avoid writing to the redo logs during the operation.

■ *The parallel options* As described in Chapter 12, the Parallel Query Options use multiple processes to accomplish a single task. For a **create table as select**, you can parallelize both the **create table** portion and the query. If you use the parallel options, you should also use the **nologging** option; otherwise the parallel operations will have to wait due to serialized writes to the online redo log files.

Before using any of these three advanced options, you should first investigate the target table's structures to make sure you've avoided the common traps cited earlier in this section.

The fourth tip, isolating the rollback segment activity for the transaction, may require the creation of a new tablespace. For example, you can create a new tablespace for rollback segments and create one or more large rollback segments within it. The datafiles associated with that tablespace should be placed on disks that are isolated from the rest of the database. Create one rollback segment for each of the concurrent data migration transactions. You can then use the **set transaction use rollback segment** command to force the transaction to use the new rollback segment. If you cannot use this command, you may need to take the rest of the rollback segments offline before starting the large data migration transactions. To minimize the size of the rollback segments required, perform **commit**s frequently during the transaction.

You can also use programming logic to force **insert**s to be processed in arrays rather than as an entire set. For example, COBOL and C support array **insert**s, reducing the size of the transactions required to process a large set of data.

Bulk Deletes: the truncate Command

Occasionally, users attempt to **delete** all of the records from a table at once. When they encounter errors during this process, they complain that the rollback segments are too small, when in fact their transaction is too large.

A second problem occurs once the records have all been **delete**d. Even though the segment no longer has any records in it, it still maintains all of the space that was allocated to it. Thus, deleting all those records saved you not a single byte of allocated space.

The **truncate** command resolves both of these problems. It is a DDL command, not a DML command, *so it cannot be rolled back.* Once you have used the **truncate** command on a table, its records are gone, and none of its **delete** triggers are executed in the process. However, the table retains all of its dependent objects—such as grants, indexes, and constraints.

The **truncate** command is the fastest way to **delete** large volumes of data. Since it will **delete** all of the records in a table, this may force you to alter your application design so that no protected records are stored in the same table as the records to be

deleted. If you use partitions, you can **truncate** one partition of a table without affecting the rest of the table's partitions (see Chapter 12).

A sample **truncate** command for a table is shown in the following listing:

```
truncate table EMPLOYEE drop storage;
```

This example, in which the EMPLOYEE table's records are **delete**d, shows a powerful feature of **truncate**. The **drop storage** clause is used to deallocate the non**initial** space from the table (this is the default option). Thus, you can **delete** all of a table's rows, and reclaim all but its initial extent's allocated space, without dropping the table.

This command also works for clusters. In this example, the **reuse storage** option is used to leave all allocated space empty within the segment that acquired it:

```
truncate cluster EMP_DEPT reuse storage;
```

When this example command is executed, all of the records in the EMP_DEPT cluster will be instantly **delete**d.

To **truncate** partitions, you need to know the name of the partition. In the following example, the partition named PART3 of the EMPLOYEE table is **truncate**d via the **alter table** command:

```
alter table EMPLOYEE
truncate partition PART3
drop storage;
```

The rest of the partitions of the EMPLOYEE table will be unaffected by the truncation of the PART3 partition. See Chapter 12 for details on creating and managing partitions.

As an alternative, you can create a PL/SQL program that uses dynamic SQL to divide a large **delete** operation into multiple smaller transactions. See Chapter 12 for an example of a program that forces **commit**s during a large **delete**.

Partitions

You can use partitions to isolate data physically. For example, you can store the data from one department in a separate partition of the EMPLOYEE table. If you perform a bulk data load or deletion on the table, you can customize the partitions to tune the data manipulation operation. For example:

- You can **truncate** a partition and its indexes without affecting the rest of the table.

- You can drop a partition, via the **drop partition** clause of the **alter table** command.

- You can drop a partition's local index.

- You can set a partition to **nologging**, reducing the impact of large transactions.

From a performance perspective, the chief advantage of partitions lies in their ability to be managed apart from the rest of the table. For example, being able to **truncate** a partition enables you to **delete** a large amount of data from a table (but not all of the table's data) without generating any redo information. In the short term, the beneficiary of this performance improvement is the DBA; in the longer term, the entire enterprise benefits from the improved availability of the data. See Chapter 12 for details on implementing partitions and subpartitions.

Tuning Physical Storage

Although the database should be CPU-bound, this can only happen if its physical I/O is evenly distributed and handled correctly. Chapter 4 describes a process for planning file distribution across disks. Planning file distribution involves understanding the interactions of the DBWR, LGWR, and ARCH background processes. A means of verifying the adequacy of the final layouts is also provided there.

In addition to that level of physical storage tuning, several other factors should be considered. The following sections address factors that are external to the database but may have a profound impact on its ability to access data quickly.

Tuning File Fragmentation

Back in ORACLE version 5, there was a command called CCF—Create Contiguous File. This command created datafiles that were contiguous on the physical disk. In the current version of ORACLE, however, there is no way to guarantee that any of the database's files are created in contiguous areas on their disks.

Why is this significant? Consider the case of a perfectly sized and compressed table. All of its data is in a single extent. However, that extent is located in a datafile—and that datafile may not be contiguous on the disk. Thus, the disk hardware has to keep moving to find the data, even though the database considers the table to be contiguous.

The method for determining whether a file is contiguous or not is operating system–dependent. In most cases, you will have to dump the header of the file and analyze the output to determine how many fragments the file is physically broken into. This process should be done in coordination with the systems management personnel.

Their participation is important because they hold the key to resolving the situation. To have the best chance at creating a contiguous file, create a new file on an unused disk and then check its fragmentation. To minimize file fragmentation, keep nondatabase files off of database disks, and avoid dropping and re-creating files. This problem highlights the need for disks that are dedicated to your database files.

Using Raw Devices

Raw devices are available with some UNIX operating systems. When they are used, the DBWR process bypasses the UNIX buffer cache and eliminates the file system overhead. For I/O-intensive applications, they may result in a performance improvement of around 20 percent.

Raw devices cannot be managed with the same commands as file systems. For example, the **tar** command cannot be used to back up individual files; instead, the **dd** command must be used. This is a much less flexible command to use and limits your recovery capabilities.

NOTE
ORACLE files should not reside on the same physical devices as non-ORACLE files, particularly if you use raw devices. Mixing an active UNIX file system with an active ORACLE raw device will cause I/O performance problems.

Using RAID and Mirroring

See Chapter 4 for details concerning the use of RAID and mirroring technologies for performance enhancement. In general, RAID 0+1 will yield the best performance, while RAID-5 is the cheapest to implement. The performance benefit derived from a RAID implementation is directly related to the manner in which the system is implemented.

Tuning Logical Storage

From a logical standpoint, like objects should be stored together. As discussed in Chapter 3, objects should be grouped based on their space usage and user interaction characteristics. Based on these groupings, tablespaces should be created that cater to specific types of objects.

A suggested tablespace layout is presented in Table 8-1, along with details about the characteristics of the types of objects stored in each tablespace.

Tablespace	Use
SYSTEM	Data dictionary
DATA	Standard-operation tables
DATA_2	Static tables used during standard operations
INDEXES	Indexes for the standard-operation tables
INDEXES_2	Indexes for the static tables
RBS	Standard-operation rollback segments
RBS_2	Specialty rollback segments used for data loads
TEMP	Standard-operation temporary segments
TEMP_*USER*	Temporary segments created by a specific user
TOOLS	RDBMS tools tables
TOOLS_I	Indexes for heavily used RDBMS tools tables
USERS	User objects, in development databases
USERS_I	User indexes, in testing databases
SNAPS	Snapshot tables
SNAPS_I	Indexes on the snapshots
AGG_DATA	Aggregation tables and materialized views
AGG_DATA_I	Indexes on aggregation tables and materialized views
PARTITIONS	Partitions of table or index segments; create multiple tablespaces for them
PARTITIONS_I	Local and global indexes on partitions
TEMP_WORK	Temporary tables used during data load processing

TABLE 8-1. *Logical Distribution of Segments in an Optimal Database*

For further information on this distribution of segment types and extensions to the Optimal Flexible Architecture (OFA), see Chapter 3. For information on detecting and managing contention for rollback segments, see Chapter 7.

As listed in Table 8-1, materialized views can be used to aggregate data and improve query performance. A materialized view is very similar in structure to a snapshot—it is a physical table that holds data that would usually be read via a view. When you create a materialized view, you specify the view's base query as well as a schedule for the refreshes of its data. You can then index the materialized view to enhance the performance of queries against it. As a result, you can provide data to your users in the format they need, indexed appropriately. For details on the implementation of materialized views, see Chapter 16.

Reducing Network Traffic

As databases and the applications that use them become more distributed, the network that supports the servers may become a bottleneck in the process of delivering data to the user. Since DBAs typically have little control over the network management, it is important to use the database's capabilities to reduce the number of network packets that are required for the data to be delivered. Reducing network traffic will reduce your reliance on the network, and thus eliminate a potential cause of performance problems.

Replication of Data

As described in Chapter 1 and Part III of this book, you can manipulate and query data from remote databases. However, it is not desirable to have large volumes of data constantly sent from one database to another. To reduce the amount of data being sent across the network, different data replication options should be considered.

In a purely distributed environment, each data element exists in one place, as shown in Figure 8-3. When data is required, it is accessed from remote databases via database links. In the example shown in Figure 8-3, the EMPLOYEE data is queried from the MASTER1 database, and the DEPT data is queried from the REMOTE1 database. Both databases are accessible via database links created within the REMOTE2 database.

This purist approach (having data stored in only one place) is similar to implementing an application in third normal form—and as stated earlier in this chapter, that approach will not support any major production application. Modifying the application's tables to improve data retrieval performance involves denormalizing data. The denormalization process deliberately stores redundant data in order to shorten users' access paths to the data.

In a distributed environment, replicating data accomplishes this goal. Rather than force queries to cross the network to resolve user requests, selected data from remote servers is replicated to the local server. This can be accomplished via a number of means, as described in the following sections.

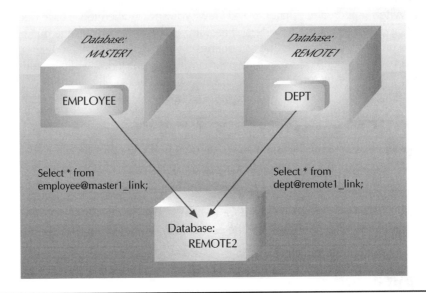

FIGURE 8-3. *Sample distributed environment*

Using the copy Command to Replicate Data

In the first option, the data can be periodically copied to the local server. This is best accomplished via the SQL*Plus **copy** command, as described in Part III. The **copy** command allows selected columns and rows to be replicated to each server. This option is illustrated in Figure 8-4.

For example, the remote server may have a table called EMPLOYEE. The local server would be able to replicate the data that it needs by using the **copy** command to select records from the remote EMPLOYEE table. You can use the **copy** command to store those selected records in a table in the local database. The **copy** command includes a query clause; thus, it is possible to return only those rows that meet the specified criteria.

In this example, a portion of the EMPLOYEE table is copied down from the headquarters database to a local database. A **where** clause is used to restrict which records are selected.

```
set copycommit 1
set arraysize 1000
copy from HR/PUFFINSTUFF@loc -
create EMPLOYEE -
using -
select * from EMPLOYEE -
where State = 'NM'
```

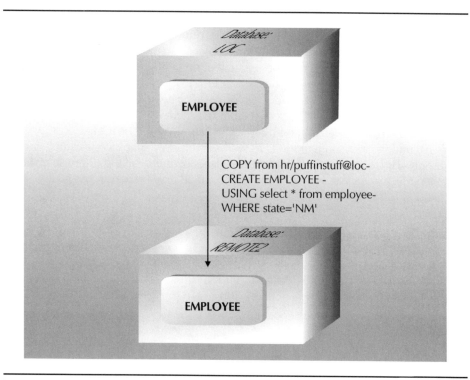

FIGURE 8-4. *Data replication using the **copy** command*

The **copy from** clause in this example specifies the name of the remote database. In this case, the query is told to use the database identified by the service name LOC. During the connection, a session should be started by using the hr account, with the password puffinstuff.

The **set copycommit** and **set arraysize** commands specify the size of array of data. Setting the array size allows the DBA to force the database to **commit** during the data copy, thus reducing the size of the transactions to be supported. For more details on this capability and other **copy** options, see Part III.

As soon as the data is stored locally, it is accessible to the local users. They can thus query the data without traversing the network; a network access is performed during the **copy** instead of separate network accesses for each query.

The downside to replicating data in this manner is that the replicated data is out of date as soon as it is created. Replicating data for performance purposes is thus most effective when the source data is very infrequently changed. The **copy** command must be performed frequently enough so that the local tables contain useful, sufficiently accurate data. The **replace** option of the **copy** command can be used to replace the contents of the local tables during subsequent **copy**s. See Part III of this book for further usage notes for the **copy** command.

Although the local table may be updatable, none of the changes made to it will be reflected in the source table. Thus, this scenario is only effective for improving the performance of query operations. If you need to be able to **update** the local data and have those changes sent back to the master database, then you will need to use some of the advanced replication options available within ORACLE. ORACLE supports multimaster configurations as well as read-only snapshots and updatable snapshots. The following section provides a brief overview of the use of snapshots from a performance standpoint; for a more detailed explanation of snapshots, see Part III of this book.

Using Snapshots to Replicate Data

The ORACLE Distributed Option offers a means of managing the data replication within a database. This option uses *snapshots* to replicate data from a master source to multiple targets. It also provides tools for refreshing the data, updating the targets at specified time intervals. This option is illustrated in Figure 8-5.

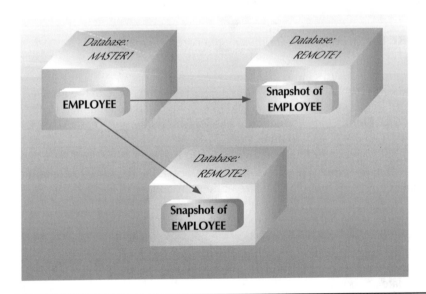

FIGURE 8-5. *Data replication using snapshots*

Snapshots may be read-only or updatable. The management issues for snapshots are covered in Chapter 16; in this section, you will see the performance-tuning aspects of snapshots.

Before creating a snapshot, a database link to the source database should first be created. The following example creates a private database link called HR_LINK, using the LOC service name:

```
create database link HR_LINK
connect to HR identified by PUFFINSTUFF
using 'loc';
```

The **create database link** command, as shown in this example, has several parameters:

- The name of the link (HR_LINK, in this example).

- The account to connect to.

- The service name of the remote database (as found in the tnsnames.ora file for the server). In this case, the service name is LOC.

For more information on this command, see the entry for the **create database link** command in Appendix A.

There are two styles of snapshots available: *simple snapshots* and *complex snapshots*. The proper type to use for your environment depends on the amount of replicated data and the manner in which it is queried. The type of snapshot used affects which data-refresh options are available.

The type of snapshot is determined by the query that defines it. A simple snapshot is based on a query that does not contain **group by** clauses, **connect by** clauses, joins, or set operations. A complex snapshot contains at least one of these options. For example, a snapshot based on the query

```
select * from EMPLOYEE@HR_LINK;
```

would be a simple snapshot, while a snapshot based on the query

```
select DEPT, MAX(Salary)
  from EMPLOYEE@HR_LINK
 group by DEPT;
```

would be a complex snapshot because it uses grouping functions.

The syntax used to create the snapshot on the local server is shown in the following listing. In this example, the snapshot is given a name (LOCAL_EMP), and its storage parameters are specified. Its base query is given, as well as its refresh interval. In this case, the snapshot is told to immediately retrieve the master data, then to perform the snapshot operation again in seven days (SysDate+7).

```
create snapshot LOCAL_EMP
pctfree 5
tablespace data_2
storage (initial 100K next 100K pctincrease 0)
refresh fast
      start with SysDate
      next SysDate+7
as select * from EMPLOYEE@HR_LINK;
```

The **refresh fast** clause tells the database to use a snapshot log to refresh the local snapshot. The ability to use snapshot logs during refreshes is only available with simple snapshots. When a snapshot log is used, only the changes to the master table are sent to the targets. If you use a complex snapshot, then the **refresh complete** clause must be used in place of the **refresh fast** clause. In a complete refresh, the refresh completely replaces the existing data in the snapshot table.

Snapshot logs must be created in the master database, via the **create snapshot log** command. An example of the **create snapshot log** command is shown in the following listing:

```
create snapshot log on EMPLOYEE
tablespace DATA
storage (initial 10K next 10K pctincrease 0 );
```

The snapshot log is always created in the same schema as the master table.

You can use simple snapshots with snapshot logs to reduce the amount of network traffic involved in maintaining the replicated data. Since only the changes to the data will be sent via a snapshot log, the maintenance of simple snapshots should use fewer network resources than complex snapshots require. This is particularly true if the master tables for the snapshots are large, fairly static tables. If the master tables are not static, then the volume of transactions sent via the snapshot log may not be any less than would be sent to perform a complete refresh.

Replication plays a part in your application design as well. If your data access paths require joining information from multiple remote tables, then you have two choices, as shown in Figure 8-6. The first option—see Figure 8-6a—is to create multiple simple snapshots and then perform the join query on the local server. The second option—see Figure 8-6b—is to create a single complex snapshot on the local server based on multiple remote tables.

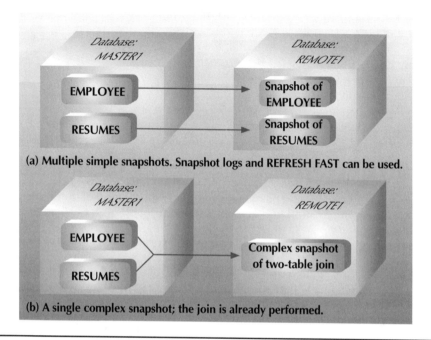

(a) Multiple simple snapshots. Snapshot logs and REFRESH FAST can be used.

(b) A single complex snapshot; the join is already performed.

FIGURE 8-6.   *Data replication options for joins*

Which option will retrieve data faster? The answer to that depends on several factors:

- The size of the master tables. How long does a complete refresh take?

- The volume of transactions against the master tables. How large are the snapshot logs?

- The frequency of the refreshes. How often will the data be replicated?

If the data is rarely refreshed, and there are few transactions against the master tables, then it should be quicker to use a complex snapshot—see Figure 8-6b. If the data is frequently updated and refreshed, then the time savings from using fast refreshes should outweigh the cost of performing the join when the query is executed (rather than ahead of time via the snapshot). In that case, using a set of simple snapshots would result in a faster response time.

NOTE
In general, a fast refresh will outperform a complete refresh if fewer than 25 percent of the rows have changed. If more than 25 percent of the rows have changed, then you should consider using a complete refresh instead. Although a complete refresh may complete faster in that case, it will generate a greater volume of network traffic than a fast refresh will.

The tuning goal of data replication is to minimize the time it takes to satisfy the user's request for remote data. The decision on the proper type of snapshot configuration to use can only be made if you know most common joins ahead of time. For further information on the management of snapshots, see Chapter 16.

Using Remote Procedure Calls

When using procedures in a distributed database environment, there are two options: to create a local procedure that references remote tables or to create a remote procedure that is called by a local application. These two options are illustrated in Figure 8-7.

The proper location for the procedure depends on the distribution of the data and the way the data is to be used. The emphasis should be on minimizing the amount of data that must be sent through the network in order to resolve the data request. The procedure should reside within the database that contains most of the data that is used during the procedure's operations.

For example, consider this procedure:

```
create procedure MY_RAISE (My_Emp_No IN NUMBER, Raise IN NUMBER)
as begin
     update EMPLOYEE@HR_LINK
     set Salary = Salary+Raise
     where Empno = My_Emp_No;
end;
/
```

In this case, the procedure only accesses a single table (EMPLOYEE) on a remote node (as indicated by the database link HR_LINK). To reduce the amount of data sent across the network, move this procedure to the remote database identified by the database link HR_LINK and remove the reference to that database link from the

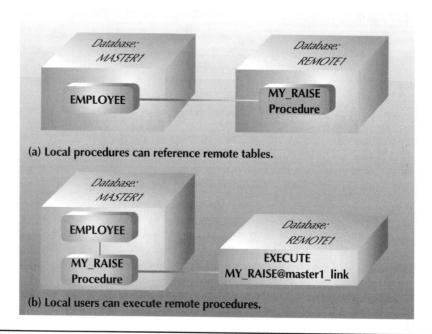

FIGURE 8-7. *Options for procedure location*

from clause in the procedure. Then, call the procedure from the local database by using the database link, as shown in the following listing:

```
execute MY_RAISE@HR_LINK(1234,2000);
```

In this case, two parameters are passed to the procedure—My_Emp_No is set to 1234 and Raise is set to 2000. The procedure is invoked using a database link to tell the database where to find the procedure.

The tuning benefit of performing a remote procedure call is that all of the procedure's processing is performed in the database where the data resides. The remote procedure call minimizes the amount of network traffic necessary to complete the procedure's processing.

To maintain location transparency, you may create a local synonym that points to the remote procedure. The database link name will be specified in the synonym so that user requests will automatically use the remote database.

```
create synonym MY_RAISE for MY_RAISE@HR_LINK;
```

A user could then enter the command:

```
execute MY_RAISE(1234,2000);
```

and it would execute the remote procedure defined by the synonym MY_RAISE.

Using OEM and the Performance Tuning Packs

For an additional cost, Oracle supplies three packs that can be used in conjunction with the Oracle Enterprise Manager to perform tuning and change management control, and to generate system and database diagnostics.

The Tuning Pack option offers three choices: Oracle Expert, SQL Analyze, and Tablespace Management. In this section, you will see the use of the Oracle Expert option. You can configure the Oracle Expert option to collect various forms of information, make suggestions about tuning steps, and create the SQL scripts to implement the tuning suggestions.

Within the Diagnostics pack, a Performance Management option is offered, as described in the "The Performance Manager Option" section later in this chapter.

The Oracle Expert Pack

When you install the Tuning pack and access the Oracle Expert option for the first time, two choices are offered: either to create a new tuning session or load a sample tuning session. Figure 8-8 shows the initial Tuning Session Wizard screen with a new session selected.

After at least one session has been created, a third option—to connect to an existing session—is also offered.

The options associated with configuring a new session are Scope, Collect, View/Edit, Recommendations, and Scripts. The first step in configuring a new session is setting the scope for the areas in which you want to perform tuning. Figure 8-9 shows the initial Oracle Expert screen with a new tuning session configured to check for:

- Instance optimization

- SQL reuse opportunities

- Appropriate space management

- Optimal data access

Once you have established the scope of the tuning session, you will be prompted to choose the collection criteria. Figure 8-10 shows the collection criteria screen with four options selected: Database, Instance, Environment, and Workload.

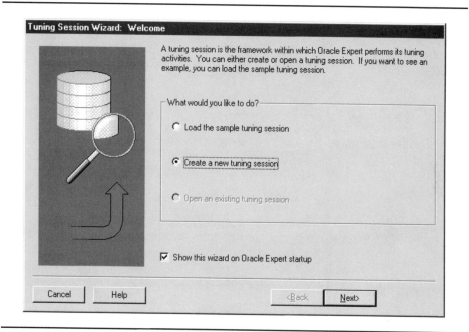

FIGURE 8-8. *Tuning Session Wizard welcome screen*

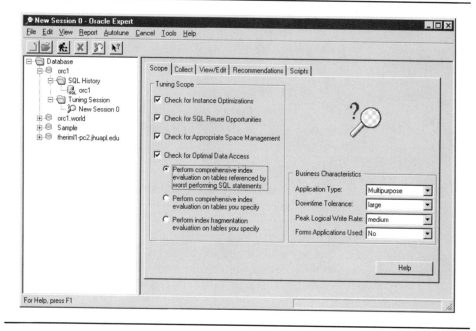

FIGURE 8-9. *Initial Oracle Expert screen*

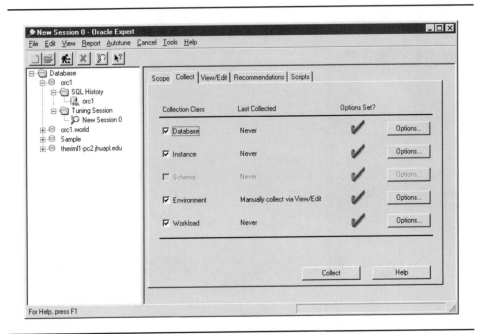

FIGURE 8-10. *Oracle Expert Collection screen*

After you select the collection criteria, click on the Collect button and the tool will perform the requested data collection. In order to view suggestions and take further action, the data collection must either complete or be manually stopped. If you do not specify a collection time range, the tool will continue to collect data at the specified intervals until you stop the process.

You can use the View/Edit option to change various dynamic parameters within the database. Figure 8-11 shows the View/Edit screen with some of the available areas in which parameters can be modified.

Once the data has been collected, you can select the Recommendations option shown in Figure 8-12 to view conclusions and suggestions for tuning the database. Finally, you can use the Scripts option to generate the scripts to implement the recommended database tuning suggestions. Figure 8-13 shows the Scripts screen. If you click on the Generate button of the Scripts screen, the tool will generate the scripts.

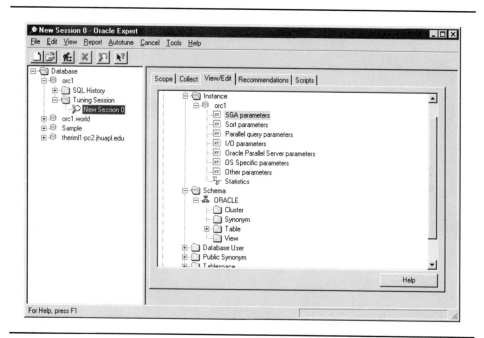

FIGURE 8-11. *Oracle Expert View/Edit screen*

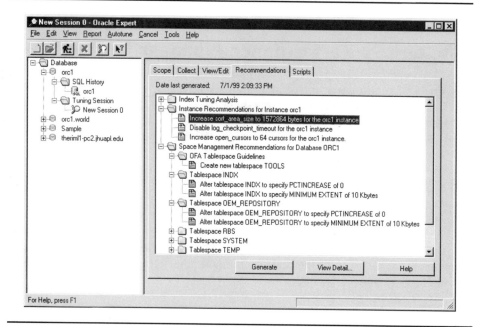

FIGURE 8-12. *Oracle Expert Conclusions screen*

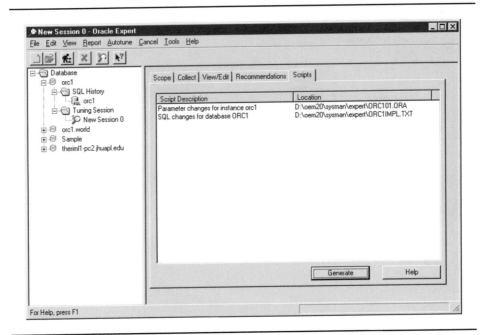

FIGURE 8-13. *Oracle Expert Scripts screen*

The Oracle Performance Manager Option

The Oracle Performance Manager option is available through the Diagnostics pack and enables the display of one or more performance charts to provide immediate feedback on the current state of the database.

Figure 8-14 shows the initial Performance Manager screen with the I/O option selected. Within this option, the instance-wide I/O statistics chart, shown in Figure 8-15, is selected.

You can view the charts in several different chart forms, including pie, bar, strip, table, hierarchical, horizontal orientation, and vertical orientation; not all of the chart types will be available for all of the chart options. When a chart type is unavailable for the selected option, the icon for that chart type will be grayed out and depressed so that it cannot be chosen.

The interval at which statistics are updated can be designated by either using the Stopwatch icon or by using the pull-down menu (see Figure 8-15). The statistics can be recorded for viewing at a later time.

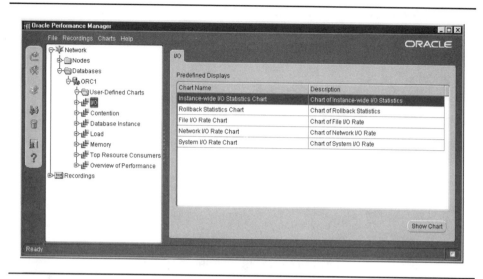

FIGURE 8-14. *Performance Manager initial screen*

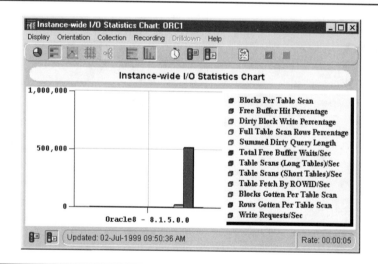

FIGURE 8-15. *Performance Manager instance-wide I/O statistics chart*

This tool is designed to give you a quick look at the state of various database areas. One of the most useful areas is the Overview of Performance option, which enables you to get a quick summary view of several charts at once. Figure 8-16 shows the overview of cache utilization while Figure 8-17 shows the overview of throughput.

Tuning Solutions

There is an underlying approach to the techniques and tools presented throughout this chapter. Before spending your time and resources on the implementation of a new feature, you should first stabilize your environment and architecture—the server, the database, and the application. If the environment is stable, then you should be able to quickly accomplish two goals:

1. Successfully re-create the performance problem

2. Successfully isolate the cause of the problem

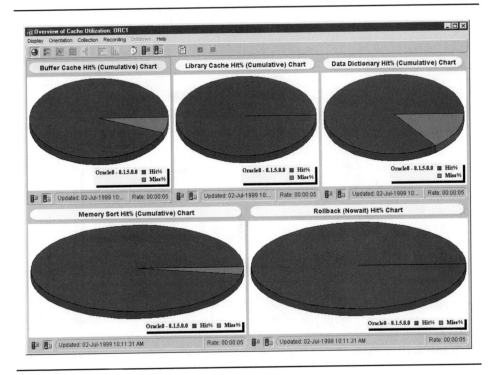

FIGURE 8-16. *Overview of the Cache Utilization screen*

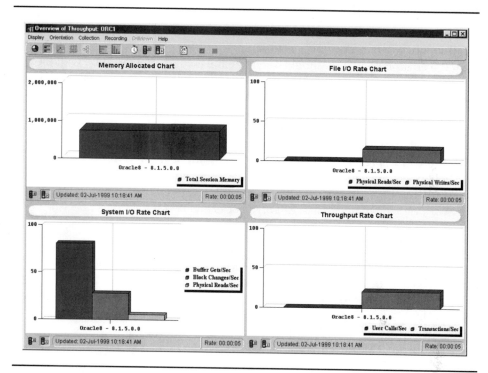

FIGURE 8-17. *Overview of the Throughput screen*

To achieve these goals, you may need to have a test environment available for your performance tests. See Chapter 5 for guidance on the creation of a test environment. Once the problem has been successfully isolated, you can apply the steps outlined in this chapter to the problem. In general, your tuning approach should mirror the order of the sections of this chapter:

1. Evaluate application design

2. Tune SQL

3. Tune memory usage

4. Tune data storage

5. Tune data manipulation

6. Tune physical and logical storage

7. Tune network traffic

Depending on the nature of your application, you may choose a different order for the steps, or you may combine steps. For example, in a Web-based three-tier application, you may encounter performance problems during online data entry. In those environments, you should minimize the amount of interaction with the database. Often, the data validity checks (such as code table lookups) that perform well for server-based applications cause performance problems for three-tier applications. Data validity checks require data to be sent back and forth across the application's data components. In general, you should avoid querying data from the database that the application doesn't directly use.

How can you resolve this issue and still perform data validity checks? There are several options available:

- *Combine multiple data validity checks and perform a single query of the database rather than multiple queries.* Be sure to tune the combined query.

- *Use local variables or drop-down lists of choices at the application level to avoid querying the database.* For example, create a list of states or countries at the application level rather than querying the database for a list.

- *Trust the users.* Rather than perform data validity at the instant the data is entered, perform the validity checks during the **commit** process. If you use constraints, the data will be checked during the **commit** anyway; the additional checks at the application level are usually in place to provide quicker feedback to the users. However, experienced users of an application don't make many data-related mistakes, so the cost of checking their work at the application level may not add any value to their work. If you remove the data checks from the application level, you may remove many of the performance bottlenecks from the data-entry portion of the application.

If the application design cannot be altered, and the SQL cannot be altered, then you can tune the memory and disk areas used by the application. As you alter the memory and disk area settings, you must be sure to revisit the application design and SQL implementation to be sure that your changes do not adversely impact the application. The need to revisit the application design process is particularly important if you choose to use a data replication method such as snapshots or materialized views, since the timeliness of the replicated data may cause problems within the application.

CHAPTER

9

Database Security and Auditing

reating and enforcing security procedures helps to protect what is rapidly becoming the most important corporate asset: data. And while storing that data in a database makes it more useful and available company-wide, it also makes it susceptible to unauthorized access. Such access attempts must be detected and prevented.

The ORACLE database has several layers of security, and the ability to audit each level. In this chapter, you will see descriptions for each layer in the auditing process. You will also see methods for setting impossible passwords and forcing passwords to expire.

Security Capabilities

ORACLE makes several levels of security available to the DBA:

- Account security for validation of users

- Access security for database objects

- System-level security for managing global privileges

Each of these capabilities is described in the following sections; the "Implementing Security" section of this chapter provides details for effectively using the available options.

Account Security

In order to access data in an ORACLE database, you must have access to an account in that database. This access can be direct—via user connections into a database—or indirect. Indirect connections include access via preset authorizations within database links. Each account must have a password associated with it. A database account can also be tied to an operating system account.

Passwords are set for a user when the user's account is created, and may be altered after the account is created. A user's ability to alter the account password will be limited by the tools to which he or she is granted access. The database stores an encrypted version of the password in a data dictionary table. If the account is directly related to an operating system account, it is possible to bypass the password check.

As of ORACLE8, passwords can expire, and the DBA can establish the conditions under which a password can be reused (via a database password history setting). Also, you can use profiles to enforce standards for the passwords (such as minimum length), and you can automatically lock accounts if there are multiple consecutive failures to connect to the account.

Object Privileges

Access to objects within a database is enabled via *privileges*. These allow specific database commands to be used against specific database objects via the **grant** command. For example, if the user THUMPER owns a table called EMPLOYEE, and executes the command

```
grant select on EMPLOYEE to PUBLIC;
```

then all users (PUBLIC) will be able to select records from THUMPER's EMPLOYEE table. You can create *roles*—named groups of privileges—to simplify the administration of privileges. For applications with large numbers of users, roles greatly reduce the number of **grant** commands needed. Since roles can be password-protected and can be dynamically enabled or disabled, they add an additional layer of security to the database.

System-Level Roles and Privileges

You can use roles to manage the system-level commands available to users. These commands include **create table** and **alter index**. Actions against each type of database object are authorized via separate privileges. For example, a user may be granted the CREATE TABLE privilege, but not the CREATE TYPE privilege. You can create customized system-level roles that grant users the exact privileges they need without granting them excessive authority within the database. As noted in Chapter 5, the CONNECT and RESOURCE roles are useful for the basic system privileges required by end users and developers, respectively.

Users who have the RESOURCE role are also granted the UNLIMITED TABLESPACE system privilege, enabling them to create objects anywhere in the database. Because of this additional privilege, you should restrict the use of the RESOURCE role to development and test environments.

Implementing Security

The security capabilities in ORACLE include roles, profiles, and direct grants of privileges. The Oracle Enterprise Manager tool set provides a Security Manager tool to enable the management of user accounts, roles, privileges, and profiles. In the following sections you will see the usage of all of these features, including several undocumented capabilities.

The Starting Point: Operating System Security

You cannot access a database unless you can first access, either directly or indirectly, the server on which the database is running. The first step in securing your database is to secure the platform and network on which it resides. Once that has been accomplished, the operating system security must be considered.

ORACLE uses a number of files that its users do not require direct access to. For example, the datafiles and the online redo log files are written and read only via ORACLE's background processes. Thus, only DBAs who will be creating and dropping these files require direct access to them at the operating system level. Export dump files and other backup files must also be secured.

Your data may be copied to other databases—either as part of a replication scheme or to populate a development database. To secure your data, you will need to secure each of the databases in which your data resides, along with the backups of each of those databases. If someone can walk off with the backup tapes from a database that contains a copy of your data, then all of the security you've implemented in your database is worthless. You must prevent unauthorized access to all copies of your data.

Creating Users

When creating a user, your goal is to establish a secure, useful account that has adequate privileges and proper default settings. You can use the **create user** command to create a new database account. When the account is created, it will not have any capabilities—and users will not even be able to log in until that privilege is granted.

All of the necessary settings for a user account can be specified within a single **create user** command. These settings include values for all of the parameters listed in Table 9-1.

The following listing shows a sample **create user** command. In this example, the user THUMPER is created, with a password of RABBIT, a default tablespace of USERS, a temporary tablespace of TEMP, no quotas, and the default profile.

```
create user THUMPER
identified by RABBIT
default tablespace USERS
temporary tablespace TEMP;
```

Since no profile was specified, the default profile for the database will be used. This is an actual profile named DEFAULT; its initial settings are for all resource consumption limits to be set to UNLIMITED. See the "User Profiles" section of this chapter for further details on profiles.

Since no quotas were specified, the user cannot create objects in the database.

To grant resource quotas, use the **quota** parameter of the **create user** or **alter user** command, as shown in the following listing. In this example, THUMPER is granted a quota of 100MB in the USERS tablespace.

Parameter	Usage
Username	Name of the schema.
Password	Password for the account; may also be tied directly to the operating system host account name or authenticated via a network authentication service. For host-based authentication, use **identified externally**. For network-based authentication, use **identified globally as**.
Default tablespace	The default tablespace in which objects created in this schema will be stored. This setting does not give the user rights to create objects; it only sets a default value.
Temporary tablespace	The tablespace in which temporary segments used during sorting transactions will be stored.
Quota [on tablespace]	Allows the user to store objects in the specified tablespace, up to the total size specified as the quota.
Profile	Assigns a profile to the user. If none is specified, then the default profile is used. Profiles are used to restrict the usage of system resources and to enforce password management rules.
Default Role[s]	Sets the default roles to be enabled for the user.

TABLE 9-1. *Parameters for the **create user** Command*

```
alter user THUMPER
quota 100M on USERS;
```

The THUMPER user can now create up to 100MB worth of segments in the USERS tablespace.

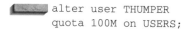

NOTE
Users do not need space quotas on the TEMP tablespace in order for their queries to create temporary segments there.

Except for the username, all of the parameters in the **create user** command may be altered via the **alter user** command.

From the OEM Security Manager screen, you can create a new user or create a user "like" another user. This feature enables you to create a new user with the same attributes as an existing user. Figure 9-1 shows the initial Security Manager

screen with the user THUMPER selected. With the OEM tool, roles, system
privileges, object privileges, and quotas can be assigned as the user is created.
On the first user screen, in Figure 9-1, the password authentication enables the
designation of a specific password, the designation that the account is to be a
global—used for remote database administration—or the account is to be identified
externally. The option to preexpire the password is available and the account can
be created locked or unlocked (see the "Password Management" section later in this
chapter for details on password expirations and account locking).

You can create a new user by selecting the General tab and clicking the right
mouse button or by selecting the "Create" option from the Object menu while the
Users area of the screen is selected. When you select the "Create" or "Create Like"
option, a User Creation Wizard is activated and you can fill in the roles, privileges,
etc., that you want for the user you are creating. By default, the CONNECT role is
assigned to the new user and the SYSTEM tablespace is entered for both the default
and temporary tablespace for the user. Figure 9-2 shows the "Create User" window
with the options available for creating a new user like the user THUMPER. Since

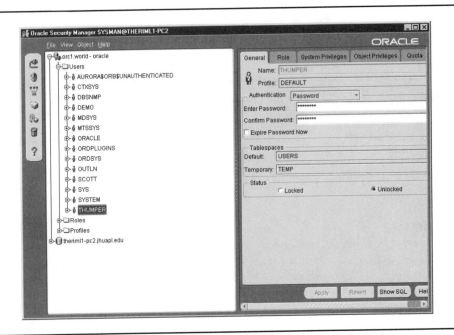

FIGURE 9-1. *Password authentication*

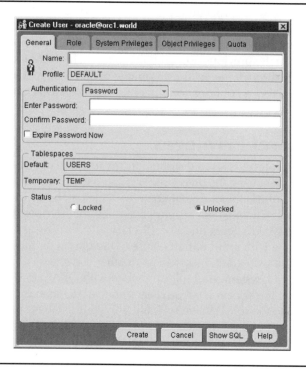

FIGURE 9-2.   *Create User window, General tab*

THUMPER's default tablespace was selected as USERS and his temporary tablespace was designated as TEMP, the new user, by default, has the tablespace assignments as well as all of the other grants and privileges that THUMPER has. The only information that needs to be filled out to create the new user is the user's name, password, and anything different from THUMPER's information that is required.

Dropping Users

You can drop a user from the database via the **drop user** command. The **drop user** command has one parameter, **cascade**, which drops all objects in the user's schema before dropping the user. If the user owns objects, you must specify **cascade** in order to drop the user. A sample **drop user** command is shown in the following listing:

```
drop user THUMPER cascade;
```

Any views, synonyms, procedures, functions, or packages that referenced objects in the schema of the dropped user will be marked as INVALID. If another user with the same name is created at a later date, there will be nothing for the new user to inherit from the previous user with that name. The OEM tool provides a **remove** capability through the Security Manager option that enables a user to be dropped. Within OEM, a confirmation screen is displayed to verify that the user should really be dropped.

System-Level Privileges

You can use system-level roles to distribute the availability of system-level commands used to manage the database. You can either create customized system-level roles or use the ones that come with the database. The available privileges that can be granted via system-level roles are listed in Appendix A under the "GRANT (System Privileges and Roles)" entry.

You can use the **with grant option** clause of the **grant** command to pass along to the grantee the ability to grant the privilege to other users.

Table 9-2 lists 11 system-level roles provided with ORACLE. Using these roles allows you to limit the system-level privileges granted to database management roles. In addition to the roles shown in Table 9-2, your database may include roles generated in support of the Advanced Queuing Option (AQ_USER_ROLE and AQ_ADMINISTRATOR_ROLE) and for use by the OEM Intelligent Agents (the SNMPAGENT role).

Role Name	Privileges Granted To Role
CONNECT	ALTER SESSION, CREATE CLUSTER, CREATE DATABASE LINK, CREATE SEQUENCE, CREATE SESSION, CREATE SYNONYM, CREATE TABLE, CREATE VIEW
RESOURCE	CREATE CLUSTER, CREATE PROCEDURE, CREATE SEQUENCE, CREATE TABLE, CREATE TRIGGER
DBA	All system privileges WITH ADMIN OPTION
EXP_FULL_DATABASE	SELECT ANY TABLE, BACKUP ANY TABLE, INSERT, DELETE, AND UPDATE ON THE TABLES SYS.INCVID, SYS.INCFIL, AND SYS.INCEXP

TABLE 9-2. *System-Level Roles Provided in ORACLE8i*

Role Name	Privileges Granted To Role
IMP_FULL_DATABASE	BECOME USER
DELETE_CATALOG_ROLE	DELETE privileges on all dictionary packages
EXECUTE_CATALOG_ROLE	EXECUTE privilege on all dictionary packages.
SELECT_CATALOG_ROLE	SELECT privilege on all catalog tables and views
CREATE TYPE	CREATE TYPE, EXECUTE, EXECUTE ANY TYPE, ADMIN OPTION, GRANT OPTION
RECOVERY_CATALOG_OWNER	DROP ROLE RECOVERY_CATALOG_OWNER, CREATE ROLE RECOVERY_CATALOG_OWNER, CREATE TRIGGER, CREATE PROCEDURE TO RECOVERY_CATALOG_OWNER
HS_ADMIN_ROLE	HS_EXTERNAL_OBJECT, HS_EXTERNAL_USER

TABLE 9-2. *System-Level Roles Provided in ORACLE8i* (continued)

NOTE
In addition to the privileges listed in Table 9-2, users of the DBA and RESOURCE roles also receive the UNLIMITED TABLESPACE system privilege.

The CONNECT role is typically granted to end users. Although it does have some object creation abilities (including the CREATE TABLE privilege), it does not give the user any quota on any tablespace. Since the users will not have tablespace quotas unless you grant them to them, the users will not be able to create tables.

The RESOURCE role is granted to developers. As described in Chapter 5, the RESOURCE role gives developers the most-used application development privileges.

The DBA role includes all of the system-level privileges, with the option to grant those privileges to other users.

The IMP_FULL_DATABASE and EXP_FULL_DATABASE roles are used during Import and Export, respectively, when you perform a full database Import or Export (see Chapter 10). These roles are part of the DBA role; you can use these roles to grant users limited database management privileges.

The SELECT_CATALOG_ROLE, EXECUTE_CATALOG_ROLE, and DELETE_CATALOG_ROLE roles are new roles as of ORACLE8.

The simplest of these three roles is DELETE_CATALOG_ROLE. If you grant a user DELETE_CATALOG_ROLE, then the user can delete records from the table SYS.AUD$. The SYS.AUD$ table is the table into which audit records are written. By granting this role to a user, you are giving the user the ability to delete records from the audit trail table without giving the user any other DBA-level commands. The use of this role may simplify your audit trail management process.

The SELECT_CATALOG_ROLE and EXECUTE_CATALOG_ROLE roles grant users privileges to select or execute exportable data dictionary objects. That is, not every database object is exported during a full system export (see Chapter 10). For example, the dynamic performance views (see Chapter 6) are not exported. Thus, SELECT_CATALOG_ROLE does not give the user the ability to select from the dynamic performance tables; it does, however, give the user the ability to query from most of the data dictionary. Similarly, EXECUTE_CATALOG_ROLE grants users the ability to execute procedures and functions that are part of the data dictionary.

The CREATE TYPE role is enabled if you use the Objects Option in ORACLE8. Users who have the CREATE TYPE role enabled can create new abstract datatypes.

Given the system-level privileges and roles available, you may wish to reexamine your account creation process. Like the database backup process, DBA-level privileges are required to perform account creation. However, you can select out a subset of privileges that are needed to create new users.

For example, you can create a new system-level role called ACCOUNT_CREATOR. It will only be able to create users; it will not be able to perform any other DBA-level commands. The commands that create this role are shown in the following listing:

```
create role ACCOUNT_CREATOR;
grant CREATE SESSION, CREATE USER, ALTER USER
   to ACCOUNT_CREATOR;
```

The first command in this listing creates a role called ACCOUNT_CREATOR. The second command grants that role the ability to log in (CREATE SESSION) and create and alter accounts (CREATE USER and ALTER USER). The ACCOUNT_CREATOR role can then be granted to a centralized help desk, which will then be able to coordinate the creation of all new accounts. You can create this role using the OEM tool by selecting the Create Role option and filling in the appropriate information. Figure 9-3 shows the ACCOUNT_CREATOR role being created using the OEM Security Manager tool while Figure 9-4 shows the assignment of the privileges to the role.

Centralizing account creation helps to ensure that proper authorization procedures are followed when accounts are requested. The flexibility of system-level privileges and roles allows this capability to be given to a user—in this case, a help desk—without also giving that user the ability to query data from the database.

The ability to create an ACCOUNT_CREATOR role is particularly useful when you are implementing packaged software. Many third-party packaged applications

FIGURE 9-3. *Creating the Account Creator role*

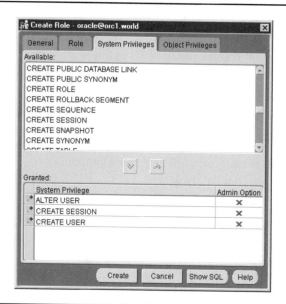

FIGURE 9-4. *Assigning system privileges to the Account Creator role*

assume they will have full DBA authority in your database, when in fact they only need the ability to execute **create user** and **alter user** commands. By creating an ACCOUNT_CREATOR role, you can limit the package schema owner's privileges in the rest of your database.

By default, your roles are enabled each time you log in. You can alter the default role for a user via the **default role** clause of the **alter user** command. For example, you can alter a user to have no roles enabled by default.

```
alter user THUMPER default role NONE;
```

You can specify the roles to enable.

```
alter user THUMPER default role CONNECT;
```

And you can specify the roles that should not be enabled when the session starts.

```
alter user THUMPER default role all except ACCOUNT_CREATOR;
```

If the specified roles have not been granted to the user, then the **alter user** commands will fail. If the user has not been granted a specified system-level role such as CONNECT, then attempting to set that role as a default role for a user will result in the following error:

```
ORA-01919: role 'CONNECT' does not exist
```

If the specified role is a database-specific role that has not been granted to the user, the **alter user** command will fail with the following error:

```
ORA-01955: DEFAULT ROLE 'ACCOUNT_CREATOR' not granted to user
```

You must grant the roles to the users before establishing the users' default roles.

If you use the **default role all** clause, then all of a user's roles will be enabled when the user's session begins. If you plan to dynamically enable and disable roles at different parts of an application (via **set role** commands), then you should control which of the roles are enabled by default.

NOTE
The MAX_ENABLED_ROLES init.ora parameter limits the number of roles any user can have enabled simultaneously. The default value is 20.

NOTE
When you create a role, it is enabled for you by default. If you create many roles, then you may exceed the MAX_ENABLED_ROLES setting even if you are not the user of those roles.

User Profiles

You can use profiles to place limits on the amount of system and database resources available to a user and to manage password restrictions. If no profiles are created in a database, then the default profile, which specifies unlimited resources for all users, will be used.

The resources that can be limited via profiles are listed in Table 9-3.

Resource	Description
SESSIONS_PER_USER	The number of concurrent sessions a user can have in an instance.
CPU_PER_SESSION	The CPU time, in hundredths of seconds, that a session can use.
CPU_PER_CALL	The CPU time, in hundredths of seconds, that a parse, execute, or fetch can use.
CONNECT_TIME	The number of minutes a session can be connected to a database.
IDLE_TIME	The number of minutes a session can be connected to the database without being actively used.
LOGICAL_READS_PER_SESSION	The number of database blocks that can be read in a session.
LOGICAL_READS_PER_CALL	The number of database blocks that can be read during a parse, execute, or fetch.
PRIVATE_SGA	The amount of private space a session can allocate in the SGA's Shared SQL Pool (for MTS).

TABLE 9-3. *Resources Limited by Profiles*

Resource	Description
COMPOSITE_LIMIT	A compound limit, based on the preceding limits.
FAILED_LOGIN_ATTEMPTS	The number of consecutive failed login attempts that will cause an account to be locked.
PASSWORD_LIFE_TIME	The number of days a password can be used before it expires.
PASSWORD_REUSE_TIME	The number of days that must pass before a password can be reused.
PASSWORD_REUSE_MAX	The number of times a password must be changed before a password can be reused.
PASSWORD_LOCK_TIME	The number of days an account will be locked if the FAILED_LOGIN_ATTEMPTS setting is exceeded.
PASSWORD_GRACE_TIME	The length, in days, of the "grace period" during which a password can still be changed when it has reached its PASSWORD_LIFE_TIME setting.
PASSWORD_VERIFY_FUNCTION	The name of a function used to evaluate the complexity of a password; ORACLE provides one you can edit.

TABLE 9-3. *Resources Limited by Profiles* (continued)

NOTE
PASSWORD_REUSE_MAX and PASSWORD_REUSE_TIME are mutually exclusive. If one of these resources is set to a value, the other must be set to UNLIMITED.

As shown in Table 9-3, a number of resources may be limited. However, all of these restrictions are *reactive*; no action takes place until the user has exceeded the resource limit. Thus, profiles will not be of much assistance in preventing runaway queries from using large amounts of system resources before they reach their defined limit. Once the limit is reached, the SQL statement will be stopped.

Profiles are created via the **create profile** command. The **alter profile** command, shown in the following example, is used to modify existing profiles. In this example, the DEFAULT profile for the database is altered to allow a maximum idle time of one hour:

```
alter profile DEFAULT
limit idle_time 60;
```

The OEM Security Manager tool provides a GUI approach to creating and managing profiles. Figure 9-5 shows the default profile screen with the resources allocated to the profile.

You can use profiles to manage password complexity and lifetime, as described in the next section.

Password Management

As of ORACLE8, you can use profiles to manage the expiration, reuse, and complexity of passwords. For example, you can limit the lifetime of a password, and lock an account whose password is too old. You can also force a password to be at least moderately complex, and lock any account that has repeated failed login attempts.

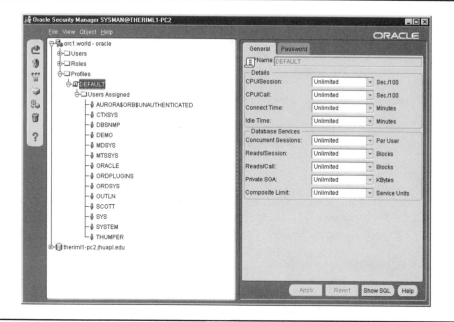

FIGURE 9-5.   *DEFAULT profile settings*

For example, if you set the FAILED_LOGIN_ATTEMPTS resource of the user's profile to 5, then five consecutive failed login attempts will be allowed for the account; the sixth will cause the account to be locked.

NOTE
If the correct password is supplied on the fifth attempt, then the 'failed login attempt count' is reset to 0, allowing for five more consecutive unsuccessful login attempts before the account is locked.

In the following listing, the LIMITED_PROFILE profile is created, for use by the JANE user:

```
create profile LIMITED_PROFILE limit
FAILED_LOGIN_ATTEMPTS 5;

create user JANE identified by EYRE
profile LIMITED_PROFILE;

grant CREATE SESSION to JANE;
```

If there are five consecutive failed connects to the JANE account, the account will be automatically locked by ORACLE. When you then use the correct password for the JANE account, you will receive an error.

```
connect jane/eyre
ERROR: ORA-28000: the account is locked
```

To unlock the account, use the **account unlock** clause of the **alter user** command (from a DBA account), as shown in the following listing:

```
alter user JANE account unlock;
```

Following the unlocking of the account, connections to the JANE account will once again be allowed. You can manually lock an account via the **account lock** clause of the **alter user** command.

```
alter user JANE account lock;
```

If an account becomes locked due to repeated connection failures, it will automatically become unlocked when its profile's PASSWORD_LOCK_TIME value is exceeded. For example, if PASSWORD_LOCK_TIME is set to 1, then the JANE account in the previous example would be locked for one day, at which point the account would be unlocked.

You can establish a maximum lifetime for a password via the PASSWORD_LIFE_TIME resource within profiles. For example, you could force users of the LIMITED_PROFILE profile to change their passwords every 30 days.

```
alter profile LIMITED_PROFILE limit
PASSWORD_LIFE_TIME 30;
```

In this example, the **alter profile** command is used to modify the LIMITED_PROFILE profile. The PASSWORD_LIFE_TIME value is set to 30, so each account that uses that profile will have its password expire after 30 days. If your password has expired, you must change it the next time you log in unless the profile has a specified grace period for expired passwords. The grace period parameter is called PASSWORD_GRACE_TIME. If the password is not changed within the grace period, the account expires.

NOTE
If you are going to use the PASSWORD_LIFE_TIME parameter, then you need to give the users a way to change their passwords easily.

An "expired" account is different from a "locked" account. A locked account, as shown earlier in this section, may be automatically unlocked by the passage of time. An expired account, however, requires manual intervention by the DBA to be reenabled.

NOTE
If you use the password expiration features, make sure the accounts that own your applications have different profile settings; otherwise, they may become locked and the application may become unusable.

To reenable an expired account, you will need to execute the **alter user** command, as shown in the following example. In this example, the user JANE first has her password expired manually by the DBA:

```
alter user jane password expire;

User altered.
```

Next, JANE attempts to connect to her account. When she provides her password, she is immediately prompted for a new password for the account.

```
connect jane/eyre
ERROR: ORA-28001: the account has expired

Changing password for jane
Old password:
New password:
Retype new password:
Password changed
Connected.
SQL>
```

You can also force users to change their passwords when they first access their accounts, via the **password expire** clause of the **create user** command. The **create user** command does not, however, allow you to set an expiration date for the new password set by the user; to do that, you must use the PASSWORD_LIFE_TIME profile parameters shown in the previous examples.

To see the password expiration date of any account, query the Expiry_Date column of the DBA_USERS data dictionary view. Users who wish to see the password expiration date for their accounts can query the Expiry_Date column of the USER_USERS data dictionary view (via either SQL*Plus or a client-based query tool).

Preventing Password Reuse

To prevent a password from being reused, you can use one of two profile parameters: PASSWORD_REUSE_MAX or PASSWORD_REUSE_TIME. These two parameters are mutually exclusive; if you set a value for one of them, the other must be set to UNLIMITED.

The PASSWORD_REUSE_TIME parameter specifies the number of days that must pass before a password can be reused. For example, if you set PASSWORD_REUSE_TIME to 60, then you cannot reuse the same password within 60 days.

The PASSWORD_REUSE_MAX parameter specifies the number of password changes that must occur before a password can be reused. If you attempt to reuse the password before the limit is reached, ORACLE will reject your password change.

For example, you can set PASSWORD_REUSE_MAX for the LIMITED_PROFILE profile created earlier in this chapter.

```
alter profile LIMITED_PROFILE limit
PASSWORD_REUSE_MAX 3
PASSWORD_REUSE_TIME UNLIMITED;
```

If the user JANE now attempts to reuse a recent password, the password change attempt will fail. For example, suppose she changes her password, as below:

```
alter user JANE identified by austen;
```

and then changes it again:

```
alter user JANE identified by eyre;
```

During her next password change, she attempts to reuse a recent password, and the attempt fails.

```
alter user jane identified by austen;
alter user jane identified by austen
*
ERROR at line 1:
ORA-28007: the password cannot be reused
```

She cannot reuse any of her recent passwords; she will need to come up with a new password.

Password histories are stored in the table named USER_HISTORY$ under the SYS schema. In this table, ORACLE stores the userid, encrypted password value, and the date/timestamp for the creation of the password. When the PASSWORD_REUSE_TIME value is exceeded or the number of changes exceeds PASSWORD_REUSE_MAX, the old password records are deleted from the SYS.USER_HISTORY$ table. If a new encryption matches an existing encryption, the new password is rejected.

Because the old passwords are stored in a table owned by SYS, the data is stored in the SYSTEM tablespace. Therefore, if you will maintain a very large password history for a very large number of users who are forced to change passwords frequently, the space requirements of the password history table (SYS.USER_HISTORY$) may impact the space requirements of your SYSTEM tablespace.

Setting Password Complexity

You can force users' passwords to meet standards for complexity. For example, you can require that they be of at least a minimum length, that they not be simple words, and that they contain at least one number or punctuation mark. The PASSWORD_VERIFY_FUNCTION parameter of the **create profile** and **alter profile** commands specifies the name of the function that will evaluate the passwords. If a user's proposed password does not meet the criteria, it is not accepted. For example, you could have rejected 'austen' and 'eyre' as passwords since they do not contain any numeric values.

To simplify the process of enforcing password complexity, ORACLE provides a function called VERIFY_FUNCTION. By default, this function is *not* created. The VERIFY_FUNCTION function is only created if you run the utlpwdmg.sql script located in the /rdbms/admin subdirectory under the ORACLE software home directory. In the following listing, an abridged version of this file is shown. The sections shown in bold will be referenced in the description following the listing.

```
Rem utlpwdmg.sql
Rem
Rem  Copyright (c) Oracle Corporation 1996. All Rights Reserved.
Rem
Rem    NAME
Rem      utlpwdmg.sql - script for Default Password Resource Limits
Rem
Rem    DESCRIPTION
Rem      This is a script for enabling the password management features
Rem      by setting the default password resource limits.
Rem
Rem    NOTES
Rem      This file contains a function for minimum checking of password
Rem      complexity. This is more of a sample function that the customer
Rem      can use to develop the function for actual complexity checks
Rem      that the customer wants to make on the new password.
Rem
Rem    asurpur     12/12/96 - Changing the name of
Rem    password_verify_function
-- This script sets the default password resource parameters
-- This script needs to be run to enable the password features.
-- However the default resource parameters can be changed based
-- on the need.
-- A default password complexity function is also provided.
-- This function makes the minimum complexity checks like
-- the minimum length of the password, password not same as the
-- username, etc. The user may enhance this function according to
-- the need.
-- This function must be created in SYS schema.
-- connect sys/<password> as sysdba before running the script

CREATE OR REPLACE FUNCTION verify_function
(username varchar2,
  password varchar2,
  old_password varchar2)
  RETURN boolean IS
   n boolean;
   m integer;
   differ integer;
   isdigit boolean;
   ischar  boolean;
   ispunct boolean;
   digitarray varchar2(20);
   punctarray varchar2(25);
   chararray varchar2(52);

BEGIN
    digitarray:= '0123456789';
    chararray:= 'abcdefghijklmnopqrstuvwxyzABCDEFGHIJKLMNOPQRSTUVWXYZ';
    punctarray:='!"#$%&()''*+,-/:;<=>?_';

    — Check if the password is same as the username
IF password = username THEN
```

```
raise_application_error(-20001, 'Password same as user');
END IF;

   - Check for the minimum length of the password
IF length(password) < 4 THEN
raise_application_error(-20002, 'Password length less than 4');
   END IF;

   - Check if the password is too simple. A dictionary of words may be
   - maintained and a check may be made so as not to allow the words
   - that are too simple for the password.
   IF password IN ('welcome', 'password', 'oracle', 'computer', 'abcd') THEN
      raise_application_error(-20002, 'Password too simple');
   END IF;

   - Check if the password contains at least one letter, one digit and one
   - punctuation mark.
   - 1. Check for the digit
   isdigit:=FALSE;
   m := length(password);
   FOR i IN 1..10 LOOP
       FOR j IN 1..m LOOP
          IF substr(password,j,1) = substr(digitarray,i,1) THEN
             isdigit:=TRUE;
              GOTO findchar;
          END IF;
       END LOOP;
   END LOOP;
   IF isdigit = FALSE THEN
      raise_application_error(-20003, 'Password should contain at
least one digit, one character and one punctuation');
   END IF;
   -- 2. Check for the character
<<findchar>>
   ischar:=FALSE;
   FOR i IN 1..length(chararray) LOOP
      FOR j IN 1..m LOOP
         IF substr(password,j,1) = substr(chararray,i,1) THEN
            ischar:=TRUE;

             GOTO findpunct;
         END IF;
      END LOOP;
   END LOOP;
   IF ischar = FALSE THEN
      raise_application_error(-20003, 'Password should contain at least one \
             digit, one character and one punctuation');
   END IF;
   -- 3. Check for the punctuation
<<findpunct>>
   ispunct:=FALSE;
   FOR i IN 1..length(punctarray) LOOP
      FOR j IN 1..m LOOP
         IF substr(password,j,1) = substr(punctarray,i,1) THEN
            ispunct:=TRUE;
             GOTO endsearch;
         END IF;
      END LOOP;
   END LOOP;
```

```
   END LOOP;
   IF ispunct = FALSE THEN
      raise_application_error(-20003, 'Password should contain at least one \
             digit, one character and one punctuation');
   END IF;

   <<endsearch>>
   -- Check if the password differs from the previous password by at least
   -- 3 letters
IF old_password = '' THEN
      raise_application_error(-20004, 'Old password is null');
   END IF;
   — Everything is fine; return TRUE ;
   RETURN(TRUE);
   differ := length(old_password) - length(password);

   IF abs(differ) < 3 THEN
      IF length(password) < length(old_password) THEN
        m := length(password);
      ELSE
        m := length(old_password);
      END IF;
      differ := abs(differ);
      FOR i IN 1..m LOOP
         IF substr(password,i,1) != substr(old_password,i,1) THEN
            differ := differ + 1;
         END IF;

      END LOOP;
      IF differ < 3 THEN
         raise_application_error(-20004, 'Password should differ by at \
            least 3 characters');
      END IF;
   END IF;
   — Everything is fine; return TRUE ;
   RETURN(TRUE);
END;
/

— This script alters the default parameters for Password Management

— This means that all the users on the system have Password Management

— enabled and set to the following values unless another profile is

— created with parameter values set to different value or UNLIMITED

— is created and assigned to the user.

ALTER PROFILE DEFAULT LIMIT
PASSWORD_LIFE_TIME 60
PASSWORD_GRACE_TIME 10
PASSWORD_REUSE_TIME 1800
PASSWORD_REUSE_MAX UNLIMITED
FAILED_LOGIN_ATTEMPTS 3
PASSWORD_LOCK_TIME 1/1440
PASSWORD_VERIFY_FUNCTION verify_function;
```

NOTE
*This function should be created under the
SYS schema.*

The first three **if** clauses in the function check if the password is the same as the username, if the password is fewer than four characters, and if the password is in a set of specific words. You can modify any of these checks or add your own. For example, your corporate security guideline may call for passwords to have a minimum of six characters; simply update that portion of the utlpwdmg.sql file prior to running it.

The next major section of the function is a three-part check of the contents of the password string. In order to pass these checks, the password must contain at least one character, number, and punctuation mark. As with the earlier checks, these can be edited. For example, you may not require your users to use punctuation marks in their passwords; simply bypass that part of the password check.

The next section of the function compares the old password to the new password on a character-by-character basis. If there are not at least three differences, the new password is rejected.

The last command in the script is not part of the function; it is an **alter profile** command that changes the DEFAULT profile. If you change the DEFAULT profile, then every user in your database who uses the DEFAULT profile will be affected. The command shown in the listing creates the following limits: password lifetimes of 60 days, with a ten-day grace period; no password reuse for 1,800 days; and account locks after three failed attempts with automatic unlocking of the account after one minute (1/1,440 of a day). These parameters may not reflect the settings you want. The most important setting is the last one—it specifies that the PASSWORD_VERIFY_FUNCTION to use is the VERIFY_FUNCTION function created by the utlpwdmg.sql script.

NOTE
*This function will only apply to the users of the
specified profile.*

Notice that the VERIFY_FUNCTION function does not make any database accesses and does not update any database values. If you modify the function, you should make sure that your modifications do not require database accesses or modifications.

You can alter the default profile to use the VERIFY_FUNCTION without altering the password expiration parameters.

```
alter profile DEFAULT limit
PASSWORD_VERIFY_FUNCTION VERIFY_FUNCTION;
```

If you alter the DEFAULT profile, you need to make sure that all users of the profile can successfully use it. For example, the SYS and SYSTEM users use DEFAULT; can you manage their passwords according to the settings specified here? You may wish to create a new profile and assign the new profile to non-DBA users and nonapplication owners to simplify profile management. The problem with that approach is that you will need to remember to assign the new profile to all new users. The more you standardize your user administration activities, the better your chances of implementing this process.

The name of the password verification function does not have to be VERIFY_FUNCTION. As shown in the last listing, you pass the name of the function as a parameter in the **alter profile** command. Since the name VERIFY_FUNCTION could apply to almost any function, you should change it to a name that makes sense for your database. For example, you could change it to VERIFY_ORACLE_PASSWORD. You should give it a name that is descriptive and easy to remember; doing so will improve the likelihood of other DBAs understanding what functions the program performs.

The OEM Security Manager tool enables the creation of profiles. You can use this tool to easily define the limits both for the general profile-controlled resources and the password resources. Figure 9-6 shows the general profile values while Figure 9-7 shows the password values screen.

Additional management options for passwords are described in the "Password Encryption and Trickery" section later in this chapter.

Tying Database Accounts to Host Accounts

Users are allowed to access a database once they have entered a valid username and password for that database. However, it is possible to take advantage of the operating system to provide an additional level of user authentication.

A database account may be paired with an operating system account on the same server. The two account names will differ only in the prefix of the database account name. The prefix defaults to OPS$, but can be set to another value via the OS_AUTHENT_PREFIX parameter of the database's init.ora file. This prefix can even be set to a null string, so that no prefix will be used.

NOTE
If you change the OS_AUTHENT_PREFIX to anything other than OPS$, then the database accounts can either be used as autologin accounts or accessed via username/password—but not both ways. If you use OPS$ as the authentication prefix, then you can access the account both as an autologin account and via a username/password combination. Most installations use OPS$.

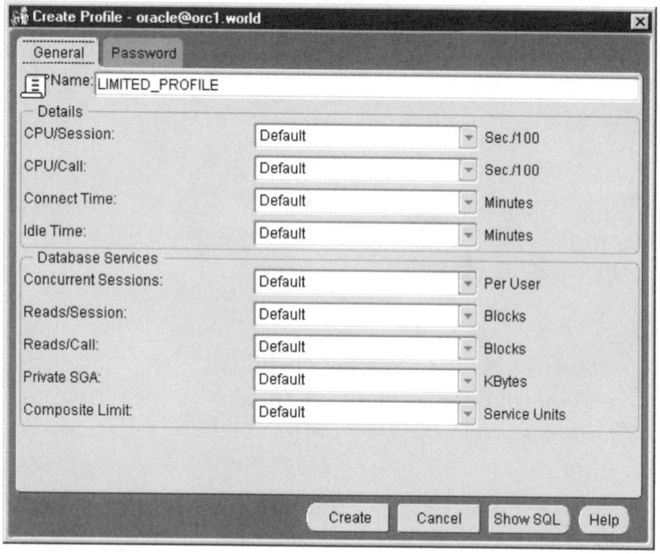

FIGURE 9-6. *LIMITED_PROFILE general settings*

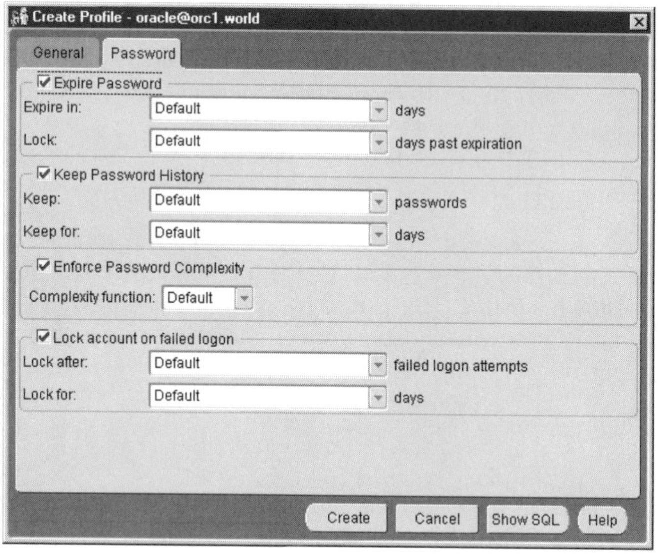

FIGURE 9-7. *LIMITED_PROFILE password settings*

For example, consider an operating system account named FARMER. The matching database account name for this user is OPS$FARMER. When the FARMER user is logged in to his or her operating system account, he or she can access the OPS$FARMER account without specifying a password, as shown in the following listing:

```
> sqlplus /
```

The **/** takes the place of the username/password combination that would normally be required for access.

NOTE
*The autologin feature is not supported on all platforms. Entering **sqlplus /** from an NT DOS prompt will return an ORA-01004 error message.*

Accounts may be created with passwords. Considering the OPS$FARMER account again. Its creation command may be in the following format:

```
create user OPS$FARMER
identified by SOME_PASSWORD
default tablespace USERS
temporary tablespace TEMP;
```

Even though the password will not be used, it still may be specified. Because the account has a password, it is possible to access the OPS$FARMER database account from a different operating system account if you know the password for the database account. The following listing shows a sample connection to the OPS$FARMER account from a different operating system account:

```
> sqlplus ops$farmer/some_password
```

There are two ways around this potential problem. First, you can create the account without a specific password, using the **identified externally** clause, as shown in the following listing. This clause bypasses the need for an explicit password for the account while keeping the connection between the host account name and the database account name.

```
create user OPS$FARMER
identified externally
default tablespace USERS
temporary tablespace TEMP;
```

When you use the **identified externally** clause, you force the database to validate the operating system account being used to access the database. The operating system account name and the database account name must be identical (except for the database account name prefix).

The second option is to create the account with an impossible password. This method, described in the "Setting Impossible Passwords" section of this chapter, prevents the user from logging in to any database account other than through the operating system account associated with it.

There is one situation in which you may want to allow users to have an OPS$ account with a usable password. If the user will both log on directly from the operating system level and from a remote account via SQL*Net, the use of an account that has a password for remote access may be advantageous. If a developer is connecting to the database at the operating system level, she will not want to display her password in order to test a script, and the OPS$ autologin feature supports that need. If she is connecting via remote access (and REMOTE_OS_AUTHENT is not set to TRUE in init.ora), she will need a password to be able to access the database.

How to Use a Password File for Authentication

In most situations, your DBA users can be authenticated by your operating system. For example, on UNIX systems, a member of the DBA group in the /etc/group file can **connect internal**. If your DBA users cannot be authenticated by the operating system, you will need to create and maintain a password file.

To create a password file, follow these steps:

1. Create the password file using the ORAPWD utility.

```
> ORAPWD FILE=filename PASSWORD=password ENTRIES=max_users
```

ORAPWD is an ORACLE utility that generates the password file. When you execute ORAPWD, you specify the name of the password file to be created, along with the password for SYS and INTERNAL access. The ENTRIES parameter tells ORACLE how many entries you will be creating in the password file. You cannot expand the file at a later date, so set the ENTRIES value high. If the password file entries limit is exceeded, you will receive an ORA-1996 error. When you re-create the password file, you will need to regrant the SYSDBA and SYSOPER privileges.

2. Set the REMOTE_LOGIN_PASSWORDFILE initialization parameter to EXCLUSIVE in your init.ora file. Shut down and restart the database so the changed parameter takes effect.

3. Grant the SYSOPER and SYSDBA privileges to each user who needs to perform database administration, as shown in the following examples. SYSDBA gives the user DBA authority; SYSOPER lets the user perform database operations support activities. In order to grant a user SYSOPER or SYSDBA privilege, you must be connected as internal. Privileged users should now be able to connect to the database by using a command similar to the one shown below:

```
connect george/mch11@PROD.world AS SYSDBA
```

You can use the **revoke** command to revoke the SYSDBA or SYSOPER system privilege from a user, as shown in the following example:

```
revoke SYSDBA from George;
```

To see users who have the SYSDBA and SYSOPER system privileges, query V$PWFILE_USERS. V$PWFILE_USERS will have a value of TRUE in its SysDBA column if the user has SYSDBA privilege, and a value of TRUE in its SysOper column if the user has SYSOPER privilege.

Password Protection

Both accounts and roles can be protected via passwords. Passwords for both are set when they are created, and may be modified via the **alter user** and **alter role** commands.

The initial password for an account is set via the **create user** command, as shown in the following listing. In this example, the THUMPER account is created with an initial password of RABBIT:

```
create user THUMPER
identified by RABBIT;
```

Passwords for accounts should be changed via the **alter user** command. A sample **alter user** command is shown in the following listing:

```
alter user THUMPER identified by NEWPASSWORD;
```

As of ORACLE8, you can use the SQL*Plus **password** command to change a user's password. The **password** command will prompt you for the old password, a new password, and a verification of the new password. The password values entered are not echoed to the screen.

To change your own password within SQL*Plus, type the **password** command, as shown in the following listing:

```
password
```

To change another user's password, use the **password** command followed by the username.

```
password JANE
```

You will be prompted for JANE's new password and a verification. The **password** command is very useful for your end users, since it greatly simplifies the commands they need to use when changing passwords. If they do not use the **password** command, then they will need to use the following command:

```
alter user USERNAME identified by NEWPASSWORD;
```

NOTE
*The **alter user** command does not fully enforce the password verification function shown earlier in this chapter. Oracle recommends using the **password** command when changing passwords.*

The **password** command simplifies the password-changing process, which is important in ORACLE8 since you can force the users to change their passwords.

Passwords for roles are set at the time the role is created, via the **create role** command. You do not need to set a password for a role; if one is specified, the password must be entered when the role is enabled by the user.

```
create role ACCOUNT_CREATOR identified by HELPDESK_ONLY;
```

You can use the **alter role** command to change the password associated with roles. Like user passwords, roles can also be **identified externally**, thereby enforcing a link between the host account name and the role name. Unlike user accounts, it is possible to have roles with no passwords (the default). You can remove a password from a role via the **not identified** clause, as shown in the following example:

```
alter role ACCOUNT_CREATOR not identified;
```

After this command has been executed, the ACCOUNT_CREATOR role will not be password-protected.

Roles can be tied to operating system privileges. If this capability is available on your operating system, then you invoke it by using the **identified externally** clause of the **alter role** command. When the role is enabled, ORACLE will check the operating system to verify your access. Altering a role to use this security feature is shown in the following example:

```
alter role MANAGER identified externally;
```

In VMS, the verification process uses operating system rights identifiers. In most UNIX systems, the verification process uses the /etc/group file. In order to use this for any operating system, the OS_ROLES database startup parameter in the **init.ora** file must be set to TRUE.

The following example of this verification process is for a database instance called Local on a UNIX system. The server's /etc/group file may contain the following entry:

```
ora_local_manager_d:NONE:1:dora
```

This entry grants the MANAGER role to the account named Dora. The _d suffix indicates that this role is to be granted by default when Dora logs in. An _a suffix would indicate that this role is to be enabled **with admin option**. If this role were also the user's default role, then the suffix would be _ad. If more than one user were granted this role, then the additional usernames would be appended to the /etc/group entry, as shown in the following listing:

```
ora_local_manager_d:NONE:1:dora,judy
```

If you use this option, then all roles in the database will be enabled via the operating system.

Object-Level Privileges

Object-level privileges give users access to data that they do not own. You can use roles to ease the administration of privileges. Explicit privileges are also available, and are in fact necessary in some circumstances.

Privileges are created via the **grant** command, and are recorded in the data dictionary. Access to tables, views, sequences—as well as synonyms for these—plus the ability to execute procedures, functions, packages, and types can be granted to users. The privileges that may be granted on objects are listed in Table 9-4.

You can use the **with grant option** clause to pass along to the grantee the ability to make further grants on the base object. The following listing from SQL*Plus shows an example of this. In this example, the user named THUMPER grants the user named MCGREGOR both SELECT and partial UPDATE access on a table called EMPLOYEE, **with grant option**. This user then grants one of these privileges to another user (named JFISHER).

```
grant select, update (Employee_Name, Address)
on EMPLOYEE to MCGREGOR
with grant option;

connect MCGREGOR/FARMER
grant select on THUMPER.EMPLOYEE to JFISHER;
```

Privilege	Capabilities Granted
SELECT	Can query the object.
INSERT	Can insert rows into the object. This privilege may be granted for specific columns of the object.
UPDATE	Can update rows in the object. This privilege may be granted for specific columns of the object.
DELETE	Can delete rows from the object.
ALTER	Can alter the object.
INDEX	Can create indexes on the table.
REFERENCES	Can create foreign keys that reference the table.
EXECUTE	Can execute the function, package, procedure, library, or type.
READ	Can access the directory.

TABLE 9-4. *Available Object Privileges*

NOTE
Granting the privileges to PUBLIC makes them available to all users in the database.

If EMPLOYEE is a partitioned table, you cannot grant SELECT access to just one partition of it. However, you can create a view that selects data just from one partition, and then grant SELECT access on that view to your users. The view will be an additional object to manage, but you can use it to enforce partition-level data security.

The management of privileges can quickly become a time-consuming task. Each user must be granted the appropriate privileges for each object in a database application. Consider a small application that has 20 tables and 30 users; 600 privileges (20 tables times 30 users) must be managed.

With the advent of roles, the management of such privileges became much easier. Roles are groups of privileges; the roles are then granted to users, greatly simplifying the privilege management process.

The following listing shows an example of the usage of roles. In this example, two roles are created. The first, APPLICATION_USER, is given the system-level privilege CREATE SESSION; a user who has been granted this role will be able to log in to the database. The second role, DATA_ENTRY_CLERK, is granted privileges on tables.

```
create role APPLICATION_USER;
grant CREATE SESSION to APPLICATION_USER;

create role DATA_ENTRY_CLERK;
grant select, insert on THUMPER.EMPLOYEE to DATA_ENTRY_CLERK;
grant select, insert on THUMPER.TIME_CARDS to DATA_ENTRY_CLERK;
grant select, insert on THUMPER.DEPARTMENT to DATA_ENTRY_CLERK;
```

Roles can be granted to other roles. For example, you can grant the APPLICATION_USER role to the DATA_ENTRY_CLERK role, as shown in this example:

```
grant APPLICATION_USER to DATA_ENTRY_CLERK;
```

The role can then be granted to a user. This role can be dynamically enabled and disabled during the user's session via the **set role** command.

```
grant DATA_ENTRY_CLERK to MCGREGOR;
```

From the OEM Security Manager tool, select the specific user or role to whom object grants are to be given and use the Object Privileges window to select the schema and grants. Figure 9-8 shows the user THUMPER being granted SELECT, INSERT, and UPDATE privileges on the LOCATION table.

Roles and system privileges (such as CREATE TABLE) may be granted to users with the privilege to pass them on to other users. For roles, the **with admin option** clause is used. In the following listing, the DATA_ENTRY_CLERK role created earlier is granted to a user (BPOTTER), along with the privilege to administer the role:

```
grant DATA_ENTRY_CLERK to BPOTTER with admin option;
```

Given this privilege, the user BPOTTER can now **grant** and **revoke** the role to and from other users, and can drop the role as well.

NOTE
Users who have table privileges via roles cannot create views or procedures based on those tables. This restriction is needed because the grants made via a role are only valid while the user is logged in and the role is enabled. The creation of views by nonowners requires explicit privileges on the tables.

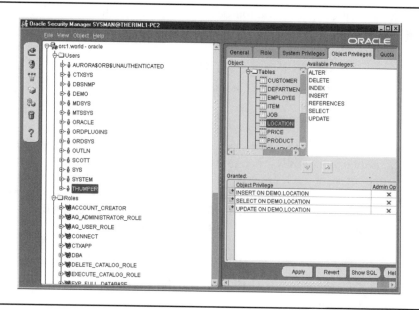

FIGURE 9-8. *Granting object privileges to a user*

The dynamic nature of roles is very useful for restricting users' privileges. If a role is enabled when a user starts an application (via the **set role** command), and then disabled upon leaving the application, the user cannot take advantage of the role's privileges except when using the application.

For example, when MCGREGOR logs into an application, the command

```
set role DATA_ENTRY_CLERK;
```

may be executed. When this user leaves the application, the command

```
set role NONE;
```

will disable any privileges that had been granted via roles.

You can use the **revoke** command to revoke privileges and roles from users. You may either revoke some of a user's privileges (by explicitly listing them) or all of the user's privileges (via the **all** keyword). In the following example, a specific privilege is revoked for the EMPLOYEE table from one user, while another user's privileges are completely revoked:

```
revoke delete on EMPLOYEE from PETER;
revoke all on EMPLOYEE from MCGREGOR;
```

In the following example, the role ACCOUNT_CREATOR is revoked from the user account named HELPDESK:

```
revoke ACCOUNT_CREATOR from HELPDESK;
```

Because user accounts can be completely deleted via the

```
drop user USERNAME cascade;
```

command, privilege cleanup of deleted accounts is not required. The **revoke** command is thus used mostly when users change status, or when applications move from one environment (such as acceptance test) to another (such as production).

There is an important distinction between **revoke**s of privileges granted **with grant option** and those granted **with admin option**. Suppose THUMPER grants MCGREGOR access to the EMPLOYEE table **with grant option**:

```
grant SELECT on EMPLOYEE to MCGREGOR with grant option;
```

MCGREGOR can now pass on that grant to the BPOTTER user, along with the **with grant option** privilege:

```
grant SELECT on THUMPER.EMPLOYEE to BPOTTER with grant option;
```

If THUMPER now **revoke**s the earlier grant to MCGREGOR:

```
revoke SELECT on EMPLOYEE from MCGREGOR;
```

Then what privilege does BPOTTER have, since BPOTTER received access to the EMPLOYEE table via MCGREGOR? BPOTTER can no longer access THUMPER's EMPLOYEE table since MCGREGOR can no longer access that table.

Revokes of privileges granted **with admin option** function differently. If you grant MCGREGOR a system privilege **with admin option**, then MCGREGOR can grant that system privilege to BPOTTER. If you then **revoke** MCGREGOR's privilege, then BPOTTER *retains* the new system privilege.

Listing Privileges

Information about privileges that have been granted is stored in the data dictionary. This data is accessible via the data dictionary views.

You can use the data dictionary views listed in Table 9-5 to list the privileges that have been granted within the database. User-level views are also available.

Data Dictionary View	Contents
DBA_ROLES	Names of roles and their password status
DBA_ROLE_PRIVS	Users who have been granted roles
DBA_SYS_PRIVS	Users who have been granted system privileges
DBA_TAB_PRIVS	Users who have been granted privileges on tables
DBA_COL_PRIVS	Users who have been granted privileges on columns
ROLE_ROLE_PRIVS	Roles that have been granted to other roles
ROLE_SYS_PRIVS	System privileges that have been granted to roles
ROLE_TAB_PRIVS	Table privileges that have been granted to roles

TABLE 9-5. *Privilege-Related Data Dictionary Views*

For example, you may wish to display which system privileges have been granted to which roles. In that case, the following query would display that information:

```
select
    Role,          /*Name of the role*/
    Privilege,     /*System privilege*/
    Admin_Option   /*Was admin option granted?*/
 from ROLE_SYS_PRIVS;
```

To retrieve table grants for users, you now have to look for two types of grants: explicit grants of privileges to users and those that are granted via roles. To view the grants made via explicit grants, query the DBA_TAB_PRIVS view, as shown in the following listing:

```
select
    Grantee,      /*Recipient of the grant*/
    Owner,        /*Owner of the object*/
    Table_Name,   /*Name of the object*/
    Grantor,      /*User who made the grant*/
    Privilege,    /*Privilege granted*/
    Grantable     /*Was admin option granted?*/
 from DBA_TAB_PRIVS;
```

To view the table privileges granted via a role, find the user's records in DBA_ROLE_PRIVS and compare those to the role's table privileges (which are listed in ROLE_TAB_PRIVS).

```
select
      DBA_ROLE_PRIVS.Grantee,        /*Recipient of the grant*/
      ROLE_TAB_PRIVS.Owner,          /*Owner of the object*/
      ROLE_TAB_PRIVS.Table_Name,     /*Name of the object*/
      ROLE_TAB_PRIVS.Privilege,      /*Privilege granted*/
      ROLE_TAB_PRIVS.Grantable       /*Was admin option granted?*/
  from DBA_ROLE_PRIVS, ROLE_TAB_PRIVS
 where DBA_ROLE_PRIVS.Granted_Role = ROLE_TAB_PRIVS.Role
   and DBA_ROLE_PRIVS.Grantee = 'some username';
```

This query will retrieve the role-granted table privileges for a particular user.

To view the profile limits that are in place for your current session, you can query USER_RESOURCE_LIMITS. Its columns are

Resource_Name	The name of the resource (e.g., SESSIONS_PER_USER)
Limit	The limit placed upon this resource

USER_PASSWORD_LIMITS describes the password profile parameters for the user. It has the same columns as USER_RESOURCE_LIMITS.

There is no "DBA" version of the USER_PASSWORD_LIMITS view; it is strictly limited to the user's current session. To see the cost associated with each available resource, you can query the RESOURCE_COST view. DBAs can access the DBA_PROFILES view to see the resource limits for all profiles. The Resource_Type column of DBA_PROFILES indicates whether the resource profile is a PASSWORD or KERNEL profile.

In addition to these views, there are two views, each with a single column, that list the privileges and roles currently enabled for the current session. They are

SESSION_PRIVS	The Privilege column lists all system privileges available to the session, whether granted directly or via roles.
SESSION_ROLES	The Role column lists all roles that are currently enabled for the session.

SESSION_PRIVS and SESSION_ROLES are available to all users.

Limiting Available Commands: Product User Profiles

Within SQL*Plus, an additional level of security is provided—individual commands may be disabled for specific users. That way, users with the UPDATE privilege on a table can be prevented from using the SQL*Plus command-line interface to update the table in an uncontrolled fashion.

This capability allows DBAs to prevent users from accessing the operating system from within SQL*Plus (via the **host** command). This prevention is useful when an application includes an option to access SQL*Plus and you do not want the users to have access to the operating system.

In addition to revoking users' ability to use the **host** command from within SQL*Plus, you may also revoke their use of the **connect** command. Eliminating the access to those commands will force users to stay within their own accounts. The following listing shows the results of these commands when this level of security is in place:

```
SQL> host
invalid command: host
SQL> connect system/manager
invalid command: connect
```

In each case, the "invalid command" message is returned. The user must remain in his or her own account.

To create this level of security, the Product User Profile tables must be created. The script for creating them is called pupbld.sql, and it is found in the /sqlplus/admin subdirectory under the ORACLE software home directory. This script creates several tables and views, and should be run from within the SYSTEM account.

For SQL*Plus, the most important table is accessed via a synonym named PRODUCT_USER_PROFILE. The key columns for security purposes are listed in Table 9-6. Insert records into this table to create the desired level of security.

You can also use the Product User Profiles tables to disable roles. To disable a role, set the Attribute column to ROLES, and place the role name in the Char_Value column. Disabling of roles is usually done in coordination with the disabling of the **set** command (see Table 9-6).

Column Name	Description
PRODUCT	Set to SQL*Plus. The name must be in mixed case, as shown here.
USERID	Username, in uppercase, for users whose commands are being disabled. The % wildcard may be used to specify multiple users. An entry for % used by itself will apply to all users.
ATTRIBUTE	The name, in uppercase, of the command being disabled. Disabling the SET command in SQL*Plus also disables **set role** and **set transaction**.
CHAR_VALUE	Set to DISABLED, in uppercase.

TABLE 9-6. *Columns in PRODUCT_USER_PROFILE*

Password Security During Logins

When you connect to a database server from a client machine, or from one database to another via a database link, ORACLE transmits the password you enter in an unencrypted format unless you specify otherwise. As of ORACLE8, you can set parameters that force ORACLE to encrypt the password values prior to transmitting them. To enable password encryption, set the following parameters:

- For your client machines, set the ORA_ENCRYPT_LOGIN parameter in your sqlnet.ora file to TRUE.

- For your server machines, set the DBLINK_ENCRYPT_LOGIN parameter in your init.ora file to TRUE.

Once these parameters are set (and the database is shut down and restarted), your passwords will be sent from client to server and server to server in an encrypted form.

Password Encryption and Trickery

Knowing how the database encrypts and sets passwords enables DBAs to perform a number of otherwise impossible tasks. These tasks include the setting of impossible passwords and the ability to become other users, as described in the following sections.

How Passwords Are Stored

When a password is specified for a user account or a role, the database stores the *encrypted* version of that password in the data dictionary. Setting the same password for two different accounts will result in different encryptions. For all passwords, the encrypted value is 16 characters long and contains numbers and capital letters.

How are passwords validated? When a password is entered during a user validation, that password is encrypted, and the encryption that is generated is compared to the one in the data dictionary for that account. If they match, then the password is correct and the authorization succeeds.

Setting Impossible Passwords

Knowing how the database stores passwords is important because it adds new options to account security. What would happen if you could specify the *encryption* of a password, rather than the password itself? And what if the encryption you generated did not follow the format rules for encrypted passwords? The result would be an account that could never be logged in to, since no password could generate the invalid encryption.

Consider the accounts and encrypted passwords selected by the following query. The query selects the Username and Password fields from the DBA_USERS view.

```
select
      Username,            /*Username*/
      Password             /*Encrypted password*/
from DBA_USERS
where Username in ('MCGREGOR','THUMPER','OPS$FARMER');

USERNAME           PASSWORD
---------------    ----------------
MCGREGOR           1A2DD3CCEE354DFA
THUMPER            F3DE41CBB3AB4452
OPS$FARMER         4FF2FF1CBDE11332
```

Note that each of the encrypted passwords in the output is 16 characters in length.

Since the password is not stored in the data dictionary—but its encryption is—how does Import know what the passwords are? After all, when a Full import is done from an export dump file, the passwords are imported as well.

Import executes SQL commands. During a Full import, Import executes an undocumented version of the **create user** command. Importing the MCGREGOR user from the database shown in the last listing would generate the following **create user** command:

```
create user MCGREGOR identified by VALUES '1A2DD3CCEE354DFA';
```

In other words, Import uses the undocumented **values** clause within the **identified by** clause to specify the *encrypted* password for the user it is creating.

Import shouldn't get to have all the fun. You can use this same command to set an encryption for any account. As long as the encryption you set violates the encryption rules (16 characters, all capitals), it will be impossible to match during user authentication. The result will be an account that is only accessible from the correct operating system account on the server. In the following listing, the encryption is set to the phrase 'no way'. The DBA_USERS view is then queried.

```
alter user OPS$FARMER identified by VALUES 'no way';

select
      Username,            /*Username*/
      Password             /*Encrypted password*/
from DBA_USERS
where Username in ('MCGREGOR','THUMPER','OPS$FARMER');

USERNAME             PASSWORD
---------------- ----------------
MCGREGOR             1A2DD3CCEE354DFA
THUMPER              F3DE41CBB3AB4452
OPS$FARMER           no way
```

It is now impossible to access the OPS$FARMER account except via the FARMER account on the server, and even then it is only accessible via the **/** autologin. Impossible passwords are useful for locking non-OPS$ accounts that should never be logged into directly, such as SYS.

Becoming Another User

Since the encrypted passwords can be set, you can temporarily take over any account and then set it back to its original password without ever knowing the account's password. This capability allows you to become another user (which is very useful when testing applications or troubleshooting problems in production).

Temporarily becoming another user requires going through the following steps:

1. Query DBA_USERS to determine the current encrypted password for the account.

2. Generate the **alter user** command that will be needed to reset the encrypted password to its current value after you are done.

3. Spool the **alter user** command to a file.

4. Change the user's password.

5. Access the user's account and perform your testing.

6. When the testing is complete, run the file containing the **alter user** command to reset the user's encrypted password to its original value.

This process is automated via the following SQL*Plus script. This script automatically generates the command necessary to reset the user's account once your testing is complete.

```
REM*  become_another_user.sql
REM*
REM*  This script generates the commands necessary to allow
REM*  you to temporarily become another user.
REM*
REM*  It MUST be run from a DBA account.
REM*
REM*  Input variable: The username of the account to be taken
REM*  over.
REM*
REM*  Steps 1, 2, and 3: Query DBA_USERS. Generate the ALTER USER
REM*  command that will be necessary to reset the password to its
REM*  present value.
REM*
set pagesize 0 feedback off verify off echo off termout off
REM*
REM*  Create a file called reset.sql to hold the commands
REM*  generated
REM*
spool reset.sql
REM*
REM*  Select the encrypted password from DBA_USERS.
REM*
SELECT 'alter user &&1 identified by values '||''''||
password||''''||' profile '||profile||';'
FROM dba_users WHERE username = upper('&&1');
```

```
prompt 'host rm -f reset.sql'
prompt 'exit'
spool off
exit
```

NOTE
*In the **select** statement, there are two sets of four single quotes.*

This script generates as its output a script called reset.sql. This file will have three lines in it. The first line will contain the **alter user** command, with the **values** clause followed by the encrypted password. The second line will contain a **host** command that deletes the reset.sql file (since it will not be needed after it is used in step 6). The third line contains an **exit** command to leave SQL*Plus. A sample reset.sql file is shown in the following listing:

```
alter user MCGREGOR identified by values '1A2DD3CCEE354DFA' profile DEFAULT;
host rm -f reset.sql
exit
```

The **rm -f** command in the second line should be replaced by the appropriate file deletion command for your operating system.

You may now proceed with steps 4 and 5, which involve changing the user's password (via the **alter user** command) and accessing the account. These actions are shown in the following listing:

```
alter user MCGREGOR identified by MY_TURN;
connect MCGREGOR/MY_TURN
```

You will now be logged in to the MCGREGOR account. When you have completed your testing, log in to SQL*Plus and run the reset.sql script shown above. The execution of the reset.sql script is shown in the following listing:

```
sqlplus system/manager @reset
```

If you are testing multiple accounts simultaneously, you may wish to embed the username in the reset.sql filename; otherwise, the first reset.sql file may be overwritten by later versions. If you are doing this for OPS$ accounts, be careful, since **$** is a special character in some operating systems (such as UNIX).

The account will now be reset to its original encrypted password—and thus its original password. The testing of the account took place without your needing to know what its password was and without its password being destroyed.

Overriding Password Restrictions During "Become Another User" Operations

As of ORACLE8, you can prevent users from reusing old passwords (see the "Preventing Password Reuse" section earlier in this chapter). Preventing the reuse of old passwords may impact your ability to become other users. As shown previously, the standard set of steps for becoming another user is as follows:

1. Query DBA_USERS to determine the current encrypted password for the account.

2. Generate the **alter user** command that will be needed to reset the encrypted password to its current value after you are done.

3. Spool the **alter user** command to a file.

4. Change the user's password.

5. Access the user's account and perform your testing.

6. When the testing is complete, run the file containing the **alter user** command to reset the user's encrypted password to its original value.

What if the user is not allowed to reuse the old password? Step 6 will fail, and you will be unable to set the user's password back to its original value. You will need to set a new password for the user—significantly reducing the effectiveness of the "become another user" procedure.

To avoid this situation, create a profile that does not enforce a password history constraint. Prior to becoming the user, assign the new profile to the user. When you have completed your session as the user, assign the original profile to the user. In the script provided in the preceding section, the user's **profile** setting is captured and is integrated into the **alter user** command that resets the user's password. The steps are as follows:

1. Check the profile settings for the user.

2. Assign the user to a profile that does not have a password history limit, does not have a password verification function, and has unlimited password reuse times. For example, the profile creation command could be:

```
create profile temp_profile limit
password_verify_function   null
password_reuse_time        unlimited
password_reuse_max         unlimited;
```

3. Query DBA_USERS to determine the current encrypted password and profile for the account.

4. Generate the **alter user** command that will be needed to reset the encrypted password and profile to their current values after you are done.

5. Spool the **alter user** command to a file.

6. Change the user's password.

7. Access the user's account and perform your testing.

8. When the testing is complete, run the file containing the **alter user** command to reset the user's encrypted password and profile to their original value.

Auditing

The database has the ability to audit all actions that take place within it. Audit records may be written to either the SYS.AUD$ table or the operating system's audit trail. The ability to use the operating system's audit trail is operating system–dependent.

Three different types of actions may be audited: login attempts, object accesses, and database actions. Each of these action types will be described in the following sections. When performing audits, the database's default functionality is to record both successful and unsuccessful commands; this may be modified when each audit type is set up.

To enable auditing in a database, the init.ora file for the database must contain an entry for the AUDIT_TRAIL parameter. The AUDIT_TRAIL values are as follows:

NONE	Disables auditing
DB	Enables auditing, writing to the SYS.AUD$ table
OS	Enables auditing, writing to the operating system's audit trail (operating system–dependent)

The **audit** commands described in the following sections can be issued regardless of the setting of the AUDIT_TRAIL parameter. They will not be activated unless the database is started using an init.ora AUDIT_TRAIL value that enables auditing.

If you elect to store the audit records in the SYS.AUD$ table, then that table's records should be periodically archived, and the table should then be **truncate**d. Since it is in the data dictionary, this table is in the SYSTEM tablespace and may cause space problems if its records are not periodically cleaned out. You can grant

DELETE_CATALOG_ROLE to a user to give the user the ability to delete from the SYS.AUD$ table.

Login Audits

Every attempt to connect to the database can be audited. The command to begin auditing of login attempts is

```
audit session;
```

To audit only those connection attempts that result in successes or failures, use one of the commands shown in the following listing:

```
audit session whenever successful;
audit session whenever not successful;
```

If the audit records are stored in the SYS.AUD$ table, then they may be viewed via the DBA_AUDIT_SESSION data dictionary view of that table.

The query shown in the following listing retrieves login audit records from the DBA_AUDIT_SESSION view. It lists the operating system account that was used (OS_Username), the ORACLE account name (Username), and the terminal ID that was used (Terminal). The Returncode column is evaluated: if it is 0, the connection attempt succeeded; otherwise, two common error numbers are checked to determine the cause of the failure. The login and logoff times are also displayed.

```
select
    OS_Username,              /*Operating system username used.*/
    Username,                 /*Oracle username of the account used.*/
    Terminal,                 /*Terminal ID used.*/
    DECODE(Returncode,'0','Connected',
                '1005','FailedNull',
                '1017','Failed',Returncode),       /*Failure check*/
    TO_CHAR(Timestamp,'DD-MON-YY HH24:MI:SS'),     /*Login time*/
    TO_CHAR(Logoff_Time,'DD-MON-YY HH24:MI:SS')    /*Logoff time*/
from DBA_AUDIT_SESSION;
```

The error numbers that are checked are ORA-1005 and ORA-1017. These two error codes cover most of the login errors that occur. ORA-1005 is returned when a user enters a username but no password. ORA-1017 is returned when a user enters an invalid password.

To disable session auditing, use the **noaudit** command, as shown in this example:

```
noaudit session;
```

Action Audits

Any action affecting a database object—such as a table, database link, tablespace, synonym, rollback segment, user, or index—can be audited. The possible actions—such as **create**, **alter**, and **drop**—that can affect those objects can be grouped together during auditing. This grouping of commands reduces the amount of administrative effort necessary to establish and maintain the audit settings.

All of the system-level commands can be audited, and groups of commands are provided. For example, to audit all commands that affect roles, enter the command

```
audit role;
```

To disable this setting, enter the command

```
noaudit role;
```

The SQL command groupings for auditing are listed in Appendix A, under the entry for "AUDIT (SQL Statements)". Each group can be used to audit all of the SQL commands that affect it (see Table 9-2 for a detailed listing of the related privileges). For example, the **audit role** command shown earlier will audit **create role**, **alter role**, **drop role**, and **set role** commands.

In addition to the core audit options shown in Appendix A, you may audit each individual command covered (such as **create table**). ORACLE also provides the following groups of statement options:

CONNECT	Audits ORACLE logons and logoffs
DBA	Audits commands that require DBA authority, such as **grant, revoke, audit, noaudit, create**, or **alter tablespace**; and **create** or **drop public synonym**
RESOURCE	Audits **create** and **drop** for tables, clusters, views, indexes, tablespaces, types, and synonyms
ALL	Audits all of these commands
ALL PRIVILEGES	All of the preceding commands plus **delete**s, **insert**s, **update**s, and several other commands; see Appendix A

Each action that can be audited is assigned a numeric code within the database. These codes are accessible via the AUDIT_ACTIONS view. The following query will display the available action codes for your database:

```
select
      Action,        /*Action code.*/
      Name           /*Name of the action, such as ALTER USER.*/
from AUDIT_ACTIONS;
```

Once the action code is known, you can use the DBA_AUDIT_OBJECT view to determine how an object was affected by the action. The query shown in the following listing retrieves login audit records from the DBA_AUDIT_OBJECT view. It lists the operating system account that was used (OS_Username), the ORACLE account name (Username), and the terminal ID that was used (Terminal). The object owner (Owner) and name (Obj_Name) are selected, along with the action code (Action_Name) for the action performed. The Returncode column is evaluated: if it is 0, then the connection attempt succeeded; otherwise, the error number is reported. The login and logoff times are also displayed.

```
select
    OS_Username,            /*Operating system username used.*/
    Username,               /*Oracle username of the account used.*/
    Terminal,               /*Terminal ID used.*/
    Owner,                  /*Owner of the affected object.*/
    Obj_Name,               /*Name of the affected object.*/
    Action_Name,            /*Numeric code for the action.*/
    DECODE(Returncode,'0','Success',Returncode),   /*Failure check*/
    TO_CHAR(Timestamp,'DD-MON-YYYY HH24:MI:SS')       /*Timestamp*/
from DBA_AUDIT_OBJECT;
```

You can also specify particular users to audit, using the **by *username*** clause of the **audit** command, as shown in the following listing. In this example, all **update** actions by the user MCGREGOR will be audited:

```
audit update table by MCGREGOR;
```

Object Audits

In addition to system-level actions on objects, data manipulation actions to objects can be audited. These may include auditing **select**, **insert**, **update**, and **delete** operations against tables. Actions of this type are audited in a manner that is very similar to the action audits described in the previous section. The only difference is the addition of a new clause in the **audit** command.

The additional clause for object audits is the **by session** or **by access** clause. This clause specifies whether an audit record should be written once for each session (**by session**) or once for each time an object is accessed (**by access**). For example, if a user executed four different **update** statements against the same table, then auditing **by access** would result in four audit records being written—one for each table access. On the other hand, auditing the same situation **by session** would result in only one audit record being written.

Auditing **by access** can therefore dramatically increase the rate at which audit records are written. It is generally used on a limited basis to gauge the number of separate actions taking place during a specific time interval; when that testing is done, the auditing should be reverted to **by session** status.

Examples of these options are shown in the following listing. In the first command, all **insert** commands against the EMPLOYEE table are audited. In the second command, every command that affects the TIME_CARDS table is audited. In the third command, all **delete** operations against the DEPARTMENT table are audited, on a per-session basis.

```
audit insert on THUMPER.EMPLOYEE;
audit all on THUMPER.TIME_CARDS;
audit delete on THUMPER.DEPARTMENT by session;
```

The resulting audit records can be viewed via the query against the DBA_AUDIT_OBJECT view shown in the previous section.

Protecting the Audit Trail

Since the database audit trail table, SYS.AUD$, is stored within the database, any audit records that are written there must be protected. Otherwise, a user may attempt to delete his or her audit trail records after attempting unauthorized actions within the database.

The ability to write audit records to the operating system audit trail helps to get around this problem by storing the records external to the database. However, this option is not available for all operating systems.

If you must store the audit trail information in SYS.AUD$, then you *must* protect that table. First, audit actions against the table via the following command:

```
audit all on SYS.AUD$ by access;
```

If any actions are made against the SYS.AUD$ table (**insert**s generated via audits of other tables don't count), then those actions will be recorded in the audit trail. Not only that, but actions against SYS.AUD$ can only be deleted by users who have the ability to CONNECT INTERNAL (i.e., are in the DBA group). Any actions made while connected as INTERNAL are automatically written to the audit trail.

Wherever possible, coordinate your database auditing and your operating system auditing. This will make it easier to track problems and coordinate security policies across the two environments. Since the system managers will most likely not want to see reams of audit trail entries, it also forces the DBA to analyze exactly which actions are the most critical to audit. Your aim should be to have an audit trail in which every record is significant. If it is not, then use the commands given in this chapter to modify the auditing options to reflect the true actions of interest.

Security in a Distributed Environment

Opening up a database to access from other servers also opens it up to potential security threats from those servers. Since such access comes via Net8 (and SQL*Net), modifications to Net8 parameters can provide most of the protection against unauthorized remote access. For details on the security aspects of Net8, see Part III of this book. As a guiding principle, all access to data should be on a "need-to-know" basis. Extending this principle, all access to your server and operating system and network should be on a "need-to-know" basis. You should periodically review the current access privilege within the database and at the operating system level, and work with the systems management team to evaluate current network access privileges.

Solutions

Effective security management in an ORACLE database requires resolving all known security issues and auditing attempted breaches of security. Your security plan should include, at a minimum, the following:

1. Change the passwords of the SYS and SYSTEM accounts from their default values.

2. Change the password for all DBA-privileged accounts on a regular basis.

3. Drop any of the demo accounts that were created (such as SCOTT/TIGER).

4. Change the password on the DBSNMP account, and put the new password in the snmp.ora file.

5. Set the proper protection levels for all database files.

6. If your development database contains data from your production database, make sure the security rules enforced for production are also enforced for development.

7. Audit all access to SYS.AUD$.

8. Audit all failed connection attempts.

9. Audit all DBA actions.

10. Regularly generate audit listing reports and clean out old records from SYS.AUD$.

11. Secure your database backups.

12. Secure the physical facility in which your database server and backups are stored.

If you follow these 12 steps, you will be able to secure your database. As noted earlier in this chapter, you will still need to work with the system administration and network administration teams to eliminate any unauthorized access to the server's operating system.

CHAPTER
10

Optimal Backup and Recovery Procedures

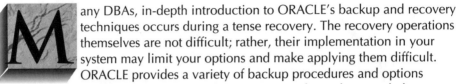 any DBAs, in-depth introduction to ORACLE's backup and recovery techniques occurs during a tense recovery. The recovery operations themselves are not difficult; rather, their implementation in your system may limit your options and make applying them difficult. ORACLE provides a variety of backup procedures and options that help protect an ORACLE database. If they are properly implemented, these options will allow you to effectively back up your database—and recover them easily and efficiently.

ORACLE's backup capabilities include both logical and physical backups, both of which have a number of options available. This chapter will not detail every possible option and recovery scenario; ORACLE's documentation has already accomplished that. Rather, the focus in this chapter is on using the best options in the most effective manner possible. You will see how to best integrate the available backup procedures with each other and with the operating system backups. Backup capabilities introduced as of ORACLE8 will also be highlighted.

Capabilities

There are three standard methods of backing up an ORACLE database: *Exports*, *offline backups*, and *online (ARCHIVELOG) backups*. An export is a *logical* backup of the database; the other two backup methods are *physical* file backups. In the following sections, you will see each of these options fully described.

Logical Backups

A *logical backup* of the database involves reading a set of database records and writing them to a file. These records are read independently of their physical location. In ORACLE, the *Export* utility performs this type of database backup. To recover using the file generated from an export, ORACLE's *Import* utility is used.

Export

ORACLE's Export utility reads the database, including the data dictionary, and writes the output to a binary file called an *export dump file*. You can export the full database, specific users, or specific tables. During exports, you may choose whether or not to export the data dictionary information associated with tables, such as the grants, indexes, and constraints associated with them. The file written by Export will contain the commands necessary to completely re-create all of the chosen objects.

You can perform full database exports for all tables (called *Complete* exports) or for only those tables that have changed since the last export. There are two different types of incremental exports: *Incremental* and *Cumulative*. *Incremental* exports will export all tables that have changed since the last export, while *Cumulative* exports will export all tables that have changed since the last Full export.

You can use the Export utility to compress the extents of fragmented data segments (see Chapter 8).

Import

Once data has been exported, it may be imported via ORACLE's Import utility. The Import utility reads the binary export dump file created by Export and executes the commands found there. For example, these commands may include a **create table** command, followed by an **insert** command to load data into the table.

The data that has been exported does not have to be imported into the same database, or the same schema, as was used to generate the export dump file. You may use the export dump file to create a duplicate set of the exported objects under a different schema or in a separate database.

You can import either all or part of the exported data. If you import the entire export dump file from a Full export, then all of the database objects—including tablespaces, datafiles, and users—will be created during the import. However, it is often useful to precreate tablespaces and users in order to specify the physical distribution of objects in the database.

If you are only going to import part of the data from the export dump file, then the tablespaces, datafiles, and users that will own and store that data must be set up prior to the import.

The data may also be imported into an ORACLE database created under a higher version of the ORACLE kernel. You can use this data migration strategy between consecutive major releases of ORACLE (such as from ORACLE7 to ORACLE8.0 or ORACLE8.0 to ORACLE8i). The reverse capability—importing from an export file created by a more recent major release—is supported, but an extra action will be required. When migrating data from ORACLE8 back to ORACLE7, the script catexp7.sql must be run once in the ORACLE8 database to enable the ORACLE7 Export and Import utilities to perform properly.

When migrating data between nonconsecutive major releases (for example, from ORACLE6 to ORACLE8), you should first import the data into the intermediate release (in this example, ORACLE7), then from that database into the later major release (ORACLE8).

Physical Backups

Physical backups involve copying the files that constitute the database without regard to their logical content. These backups are also referred to as *file system backups* since they involve using operating system file backup commands.

ORACLE supports two different types of physical file backups: the *offline* backup and the *online* backup (also known as the "hot" or "ARCHIVELOG" backup).

Offline Backups

Offline backups occur when the database has been shut down normally (that is, not due to instance failure). While the database is "offline," the following files are backed up:

- All datafiles
- All control files
- All online redo logs
- The init.ora file (optional)

It is easiest to back up the datafiles if the database file architecture uses a consistent directory structure. A sample of such an architecture is shown in the "Database File Layout" section of Chapter 4.

Having all of these files backed up *while the database is closed* provides a complete image of the database as it existed at the time it was closed. The full set of these files could be retrieved from the backups at a later date and the database would be able to function. It is *not* valid to perform a file system backup of the database while it is open unless an online backup is being performed.

Online (ARCHIVELOG) Backups

You can use online backups for any database that is running in ARCHIVELOG mode. In this mode, the online redo logs are archived, creating a full log of all transactions within the database.

ORACLE writes to the online redo log files in a cyclical fashion; after filling the first log file, it begins writing to the second until that one fills, and then begins writing to the third. Once the last online redo log file is filled, the LGWR (Log Writer) background process begins to overwrite the contents of the first redo log file.

When ORACLE is run in ARCHIVELOG mode, the ARCH (Archiver) background process makes a copy of each redo log file before overwriting it. These archived redo log files are usually written to a disk device. The archived redo log files may also be written directly to a tape device, but this tends to be very operator-intensive.

You can perform file system backups of a database while that database is open, provided the database is running in ARCHIVELOG mode. An online backup involves setting each tablespace into a backup state, then backing up its datafiles, then restoring the tablespace to its normal state.

NOTE
When using the ORACLE-supplied Recovery Manager (RMAN) utility, you do not have to place each tablespace into a backup state. The utility will put the tablespace into and take it out of the backup state automatically.

The database can be fully recovered from an online backup, and can, via the archived redo logs, be rolled forward to any point in time. When the database is then opened, any committed transactions that were in the database at that time will have been restored and any uncommitted transactions will have been rolled back.

While the database is open, the following files are backed up:

- All datafiles

- All archived redo log files

- One control file, via the **alter database** command

Online backup procedures are very powerful for two reasons. First, they provide full point-in-time recovery. Second, they allow the database to remain open during the file system backup. Thus, even databases that cannot be shut down due to user requirements can still have file-system backups. Keeping the database open also keeps the System Global Area (SGA) of the database instance from being reset, as occurs during database startups. Keeping the memory from being reset will improve the database's performance since it will reduce the number of physical I/Os required by the database.

Implementations

In this section, you will find the commands and procedures necessary to use each of the backup methods available in ORACLE, as well as sample command files and step-by-step examples using the Oracle Enterprise Manager (OEM) and the Recovery Manager (RMAN) for performing them.

Export

The Export utility has three levels of functionality: *Full* mode, *User* mode, and *Table* mode. You can Export partitions via a modified version of Table mode exports.

In Full mode, the full database is exported. The entire data dictionary is read, and the DDL needed to re-create the full database is written to the export dump file.

This file includes definitions for all tablespaces, all users, and all of the objects, data, and privileges in their schemas.

In User mode, a user's objects are exported, as well as the data within them. All grants and indexes created by the user on the user's objects are also exported. Grants and indexes created by users other than the owner are not exported via this mode.

In Table mode, a specified table is exported. The table's structure, indexes, and grants are exported along with or without its data. Table mode can also export the full set of tables owned by a user (by specifying the schema owner but no table names). You can also specify partitions of a table to Export.

Export can be run interactively, through OEM or RMAN, or via command files. The run-time options that can be specified for Export are listed in Table 10-1.

Keyword	Description
userid	Username/password of the account running the export. If this is the first parameter after the **exp** command, then the **userid** keyword does not have to be specified.
buffer	Size of the buffer used to fetch data rows. The default is system dependent; this value is usually set to a high value (> 64,000).
file	Name of the export dump file.
filesize	The maximum size for an export dump file. If multiple files are listed in the **file** entry, the export will be directed to those files based on the **filesize** setting.
compress	A Y/N flag to indicate whether export should compress fragmented segments into single extents. This affects the **storage** clauses that will be stored in the export file for those objects.
grants	A Y/N flag to indicate whether **grant**s on database objects will be exported.
indexes	A Y/N flag to indicate whether indexes on tables will be exported.
rows	A Y/N flag to indicate whether rows should be exported. If this is set to N, then only the DDL for the database objects will be created in the export file.

TABLE 10-1. *Export Option*

Keyword	Description
constraints	A Y/N flag to indicate whether constraints on tables are exported.
full	If set to Y, then a Full database export is performed.
owner	A list of database accounts to be exported; User exports of those accounts may then be performed.
tables	A list of tables to be exported; Table exports of those tables may then be performed.
recordlength	The length, in bytes, of the export dump file record. Usually left at the default value unless you are going to transfer the export file between different operating systems.
inctype	The type of export being performed (valid values are COMPLETE (default), CUMULATIVE, and INCREMENTAL). The export types are described in the following sections.
direct	A Y/N flag to indicate if a Direct export should be performed. A Direct export bypasses the buffer cache during the export, generating significant performance gains for the export process.
record	For Incremental exports, this Y/N flag indicates whether a record will be stored in data dictionary tables recording the export.
parfile	The name of a parameter file to be passed to Export. This file may contain entries for all of the parameters listed here.
statistics	A parameter to indicate whether **analyze** commands for the exported objects should be written to the export dump file. Valid values are COMPUTE, ESTIMATE (the default), and N. In earlier versions of ORACLE, this parameter was called ANALYZE.
consistent	A Y/N flag to indicate whether a read-consistent version of all exported objects should be maintained. This is needed when tables that are related to each other are being modified by users during the Export process.
log	The name of a file to which the log of the export will be written.
feedback	The number of rows after which to display progress during table exports. The default value is 0, so no feedback is displayed until a table is completely exported.

TABLE 10-1. *Export Option* (continued)

Keyword	Description
point_in_time _recover	A Y/N flag used to signal ORACLE if you are exporting metadata for use in a tablespace point-in-time recovery. This is an advanced recovery technique; see the "Recovery Scenarios" section of this chapter.
recovery_ tablespaces	The tablespaces whose metadata should be exported during a tablespace point-in-time recovery; see the "Recovery Scenarios" section of this chapter.
query	A **where** clause that will be applied to each table during the export.
transport_tab lespace	Set to Y if you are using the pluggable tablespace option available as of ORACLE8i. Use in conjunction with the **tablespaces** keyword.
tablespaces	The tablespaces whose metadata should be exported during a tablespace move.

TABLE 10-1. *Export Option* (continued)

A number of the parameters conflict with each other or may result in inconsistent instructions for Export. For example, setting FULL=Y and OWNER=HR would fail, since the FULL parameter calls for a Full export, while the OWNER parameter specifies a User export.

The default values for these keywords for ORACLE8i are shown in Table 10-2. The last two parameters, TRANSPORT_TABLESPACE and TABLESPACES, only apply to transportable tablespaces, while POINT_IN_TIME_RECOVER and RECOVERY_TABLESPACES only apply to tablespace point-in-time recovery.

You can display these parameters online via the following command:

```
exp help=Y
```

The COMPRESS=Y option alters the **initial** parameter of the **storage** clause for segments that have multiple extents. The total allocated space for that segment is thus compressed into a single extent. There are two important points to note concerning this functionality:

- First, it is the *allocated,* not the *used,* space that is compressed. An empty table with 300MB allocated to it in three 100MB extents will be compressed into a single empty 300MB extent. No space will be reclaimed.

Keyword	Oracle8 Default Value
userid	Undefined
buffer	System dependent
file	EXPDAT.DMP
compress	Y
grants	Y
indexes	Y
rows	Y
constraints	Y
full	N
owner	Current user
tables	Undefined
recordlength	System dependent
inctype	COMPLETE
record	Y
parfile	Undefined
statistics	ESTIMATE
triggers	Y
consistent	Y
log	Undefined
direct	N
feedback	0
filesize	Undefined
query	Undefined
transport_tablespace	Undefined
tablespaces	Undefined

TABLE 10-2. *Default Values for Export Parameters*

■ Second, if the tablespace has multiple datafiles, a segment may allocate space that is greater than the size of the largest datafile. In that case, using COMPRESS=Y would change the **storage** clause to have an **initial** extent size that is greater than any datafile size. Since a single extent cannot span more than one datafile, the object creation will fail during Import.

In the following example, the COMPRESS=Y option is used, as the HR and THUMPER owners are exported:

```
exp system/manager file=expdat.dmp compress=Y owner=(HR,THUMPER)
```

The step-by-step procedure for performing an export from the Oracle Enterprise Manager tool will be shown in the "Tablespace Export Using OEM" section later in this chapter.

Complete Versus Incremental/Cumulative Exports

The INCTYPE Export parameter, when used with the FULL parameter, allows the DBA to export only those tables that have changed since the last Export. If *any* row in a table has changed, then *every* row of that table will be exported via an Incremental or Cumulative export. The available INCTYPE options are described in Table 10-3.

Complete exports form the basis for an export backup strategy. Incremental and Cumulative exports may be useful if very few of the database's tables change, and if those tables are very small. For example, in a decision support database that featured large, static tables, Incremental exports would be helpful since only the smaller, changed tables would be Exported. For databases using Incremental exports, Cumulative exports should be run periodically. The Incremental exports run

Option	Description
COMPLETE	The default value. All tables specified will be exported.
CUMULATIVE	If FULL=Y, then this can be specified. Only those tables that contain rows that have changed since the last Full export of any type will be exported.
INCREMENTAL	If FULL=Y, then this can be specified. This option exports all tables whose rows have changed since the last Cumulative, Complete, or Incremental export.

TABLE 10-3. *INCTYPE Options for Export*

prior to the last Cumulative export can then be discarded. During a recovery in such a database, you will need

- The last Complete export
- The last Cumulative export
- Every Incremental export since the last Cumulative or Complete export, whichever was run later

You should investigate using Complete exports in place of Incremental exports. For example, in the decision support database example, you could create a parameter file (specified via the PARFILE parameter) that lists the tables to be exported. If you can use Complete exports, then you can reduce the number of files required during a recovery and thereby simplify the recovery process.

Consistent Exports

During the process of writing the database's data to the export dump file, Export reads one table at a time. Thus, although the Export started at a specific point in time, each table is read at a different time. The data as it exists in each table at the moment Export starts to read *that table* is what will be exported. Since most tables are related to other tables, this may result in inconsistent data being exported if users are modifying data during the Export.
    Consider the following scenario:

1. The Export begins.
2. Sometime during the Export, table A is exported.
3. After table A is exported, table B, which has a foreign key to table A, is exported.

What if transactions are occurring at the same time? Consider a transaction that involves both table A and table B, but does not **commit** until after table A has been exported.

1. The Export begins.
2. A transaction against table A and table B begins.
3. Later, table A is exported.
4. The transaction is **commit**ted.
5. Later, table B is exported.

The transaction's data will be exported with table B, but not with table A (since the **commit** had not yet occurred). The export dump file thus contains inconsistent data—in this case, foreign key records from table B without matching primary key records from table A.

To avoid this problem, there are two options. First, you should schedule Exports to occur when no one is making modifications to tables. Second, you can use the CONSISTENT parameter. This parameter is only available for Complete exports; Incremental and Cumulative exports cannot use it.

When CONSISTENT=Y, the database will maintain a rollback segment to track any modifications made since the Export began. The rollback segment entries can then be used to re-create the data as it existed when the Export began. The result is a consistent set of exported data, with two major costs: the need for a very large rollback segment and the reduced performance of the Export as it searches the rollback segment for changes.

Whenever possible, guarantee the consistency of exported data by running Exports while the database is not being used or is mounted in **restricted session** mode. If you are unable to do this, then perform a CONSISTENT=Y export of the tables being modified, and a CONSISTENT=N export of the full database. This will minimize the performance penalties you incur while ensuring the consistency of the most frequently used tables.

Tablespace Exports

In order to defragment a tablespace, or to create a copy of its objects elsewhere, you will need to do a tablespace-level export. As you may have noted, there is a TABLESPACE parameter for Export. This parameter, along with the TRANSPORT_TABLESPACE option, is used to move an entire tablespace from one database to another and not to defragment a tablespace in the current database.

There really is no way to export a specific tablespace. However, if your users are properly distributed among tablespaces, you can use a series of User exports that, taken together, produce the desired result. As noted in Chapter 4, you should separate your objects among tablespaces based on the object types and their uses. For example, application tables should be stored apart from their indexes, and static tables should be stored apart from volatile tables. If multiple users own tables, then you may further divide your tablespace assignments so that each user has its own tablespace for volatile tables. Separating the tables in this manner will greatly enhance your ability to manage them via Export/Import while following the tablespace layout guidelines provided in Chapter 3 and Chapter 4.

User exports record those database objects that are created by a user. However, there are certain types of user objects that are not recorded by User exports. Specifically, indexes and grants on tables owned by other accounts are not recorded via User exports.

Consider the case of two accounts, THUMPER and FLOWER. If THUMPER creates an index on one of FLOWER's tables, then a User export of THUMPER will not record the index (since THUMPER does not own the underlying table). A User export of FLOWER will also not record the index (since the index is owned by THUMPER). The same thing happens with **grant**s: when a second account is capable of creating **grant**s on objects, the usefulness of User exports rapidly diminishes.

Assuming that such *third-party objects* do not exist, or can be easily re-created via scripts, the next issue involves determining which users own objects in which tablespaces. This information is available via the data dictionary views. The following query maps users to tablespaces to determine their distribution of their objects. It does this by looking at the DBA_TABLES and DBA_INDEXES data dictionary views, and spools the output to a file called user_locs.lst.

```
rem
rem    user_tablespace_maps.sql
rem
rem  This script maps user objects to tablespaces.
rem
set pagesize 60
break on Owner on Tablespace_Name
column Objects format A20
select
      Owner,
      Tablespace_Name,
      COUNT(*)||' tables' Objects
 from DBA_TABLES
where Owner <> 'SYS'
group by
      Owner,
      Tablespace_Name
union
select
      Owner,
      Tablespace_Name,
      COUNT(*)||' indexes' Objects
 from DBA_INDEXES
where Owner <> 'SYS'
group by
      Owner,
      Tablespace_Name

spool user_locs.lst
/
spool off
```

Sample output from this query is shown in the following listing:

```
OWNER          TABLESPACE_NAME    OBJECTS
-------------  -----------------  ---------------
FLOWER         USERS              3 tables
                                  2 indexes
HR             HR_TABLES          27 tables
               HR_INDEXES         35 indexes
THUMPER        USERS              5 tables
```

The sample output shown in the preceding listing shows that the user account FLOWER owns tables and indexes in the USERS tablespace, and that THUMPER owns several tables in that tablespace as well. The user HR owns objects in both the HR_TABLES and the HR_INDEXES tablespaces.

Before determining the proper combinations of users to export for a tablespace, the inverse mapping—of tablespaces to users—should be done. The following query accomplishes this task. It queries the DBA_TABLES and DBA_INDEXES data dictionary views, and stores the output in a file called ts_locs.lst.

```
rem
rem    user_tablespace_maps.sql
rem
rem  This script maps user objects to tablespaces.
rem
set pagesize 60
break on Tablespace_Name on Owner
column Objects format A20
select
       Tablespace_Name,
       Owner,
       COUNT(*)||' tables' Objects
 from DBA_TABLES
where Owner <> 'SYS'
group by
       Tablespace_Name,
       Owner
union
select
       Tablespace_Name,
       Owner,
       COUNT(*)||' indexes' Objects
 from DBA_INDEXES
where Owner <> 'SYS'
group by
       Tablespace_Name,
       Owner
```

```
spool ts_locs.lst
/
spool off
```

Sample output from this query is shown in the following listing:

```
TABLESPACE_NAME    OWNER       OBJECTS
----------------   ----------- ------------
HR_INDEXES         HR          35 indexes
HR_TABLES          HR          27 tables
USERS              FLOWER      3 tables
                               2 indexes
                   THUMPER     5 tables
```

The sample output shown in the preceding listing shows that the HR_TABLES tablespace contains objects from just one user (the HR account). The HR_INDEXES tablespace is similarly isolated. The USERS tablespace, on the other hand, contains both tables and indexes from several accounts.

The results of the preceding queries illustrate the importance of properly distributing users' objects among tablespaces. Since the HR_TABLES tablespace only contains tables owned by the HR account (from the second query), exporting the HR tables will export all of the objects in the HR_TABLES tablespace. As seen from the first query, HR does not own any tables anywhere else in the database. Because HR's tables are isolated to the HR_TABLES tablespace, and because that tablespace is only used by the HR account, a User export of HR will export all of the tables in HR_TABLES. Since the indexes on those tables are stored in HR_INDEXES, that tablespace can be defragmented at the same time from the same export dump file.

```
exp system/manager file=hr.dmp owner=HR indexes=Y compress=Y
```

The tablespaces can then be dropped and re-created, and the Full export file can be imported. They will contain all of HR's tables and indexes. The following listing shows this process, using Server Manager to manipulate the tablespaces. The full **create tablespace** commands are not shown since those details are not relevant to this example.

```
svrmgrl
SVRMGR> connect internal as sysdba
SVRMGR> drop tablespace HR_INDEXES including contents;
SVRMGR> drop tablespace HR_TABLES including contents;
SVRMGR> create tablespace HR_TABLES...
SVRMGR> create tablespace HR_INDEXES...
SVRMGR> exit

imp system/manager file=hr.dmp full=Y buffer=64000 commit=Y
```

Tablespace Export Using OEM

To perform the tablespace defragmentation task using the Oracle Enterprise Manager (OEM) tool, you must be logged on to the management service for the database of interest. You can use the Storage Manager to drop and create the tablespace and perform the Export and Import. The steps to follow are shown here:

1. Export the schema associated with the tablespaces.

2. Remove the tablespaces.

3. Create the tablespaces.

4. Import the schema associated with the tablespaces.

Step 1. Export the schema.

To perform an export or import using the OEM tools, you must connect to the OEM management server by logging in to the console. From the console, you will alternate between the Schema Management option and the Storage Management option. To export the schema of interest, select the Schema Management option and click on the database of interest. Figure 10-1 shows the database option selected.

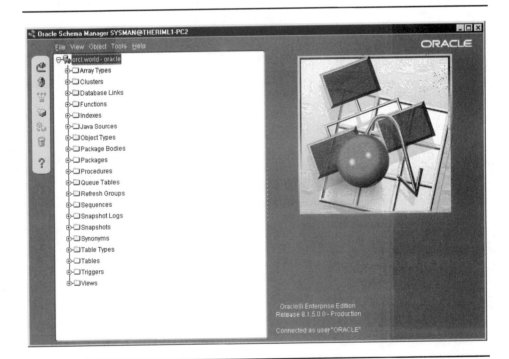

FIGURE 10-1. *The Oracle Schema Manager initial screen*

Using the pull-down menu Tools option, you can only select the Data Management option. Under the Data Management option are Export, Import, and Load. When you select the Export option, the Export Wizard is activated. Figure 10-2 shows the first Export Wizard screen.

Figure 10-3 displays the declaration of the dump file name and location.

In Figure 10-4, the designation of export type—entire database, user, or tables—is shown. In Figure 10-4, the User export option has been chosen.

The next screen, shown in Figure 10-5, is used to select the user or users whose objects are to be exported. The HR user has been selected.

The next decision to make is whether or not grants, indexes, rows of data, and constraints are to be exported. Figure 10-6 shows the selection screen. Note the Advanced option on this screen. The Advanced option, as shown in Figures 10-7 and 10-8, enables modification of the default Export Wizard parameters for statistics, direct path export, and log location declaration as well as tuning options like consistency, extent compression, record length, and buffer size.

The options for scheduling the Export are displayed as shown in Figure 10-9. You can choose to perform the Export immediately, once, or on a daily, weekly, or monthly basis and establish a schedule for day of the week and time of the day. In Figure 10-9, an immediate Export has been selected.

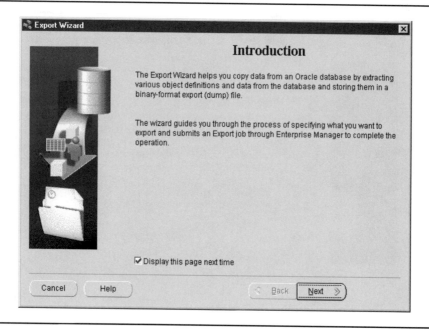

FIGURE 10-2. *The Export Wizard initial screen*

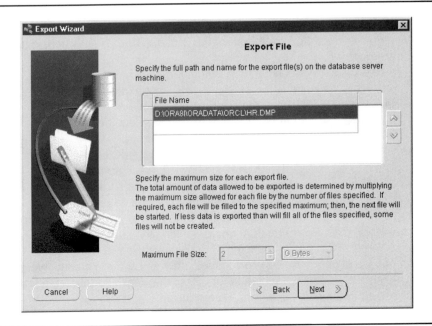

FIGURE 10-3. *The Export File screen*

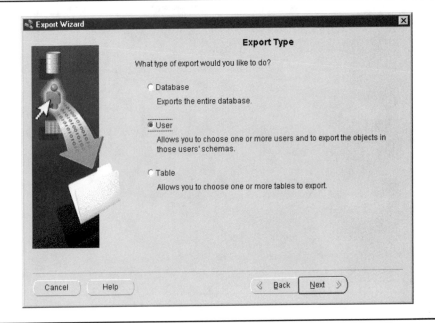

FIGURE 10-4. *The Export Type screen*

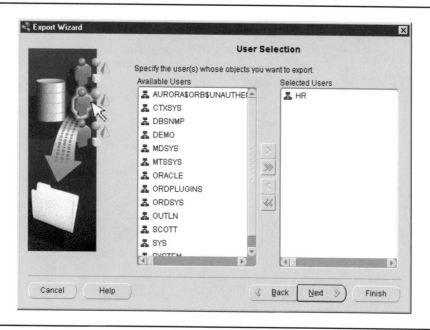

FIGURE 10-5. *The Export User Selection screen*

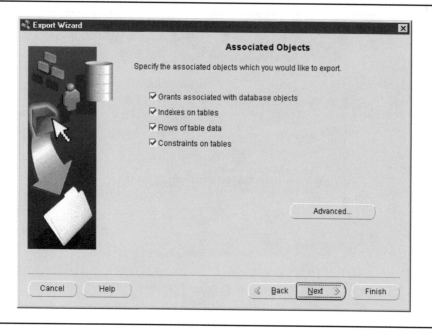

FIGURE 10-6. *The Export Initial Parameter selection screen*

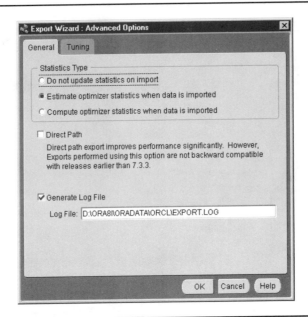

FIGURE 10-7. *The Export Advanced Parameter selection screen 1*

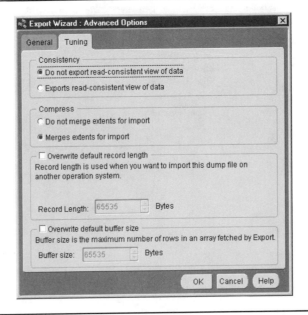

FIGURE 10-8. *The Export Advanced Parameter selection screen 2*

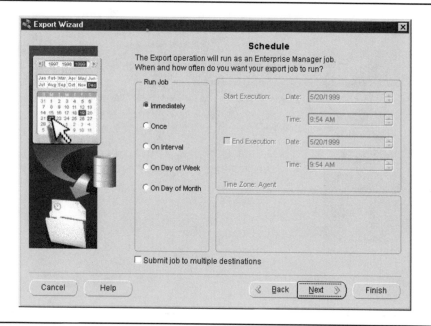

FIGURE 10-9. *The Export Schedule screen*

The actual job information is displayed next. In Figure 10-10, you can see that a job number is assigned to the job and the description for the job action has been filled in. The last decision to make is whether the job is to be run immediately, not run but saved to the job library, or run and saved to the job library. Figure 10-10 shows that the job is to be run immediately.

When you select the Finish option, a summary of the Export job is displayed. Figure 10-11 shows the summary of the Export job actions, including the parameters to be used.

The final option available is to select either OK to execute the job or Cancel to exit the wizard without performing the task.

Step 2. Remove the tablespaces.

To remove (drop) the tablespaces associated with the HR user, you will use the Storage Management option. You can access the Storage Management option either from the Management Server console screen or from the Management Packs option of the DBA Management Pack item on your operating system's Start menu. Once you have selected the Storage Management option, choose the database with which you will work. Figure 10-12 shows the Storage Management screen with the database and tablespace options selected.

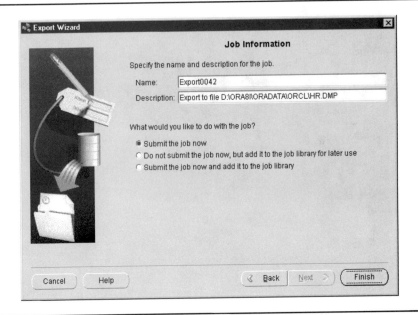

FIGURE 10-10. *The Export Job Information screen*

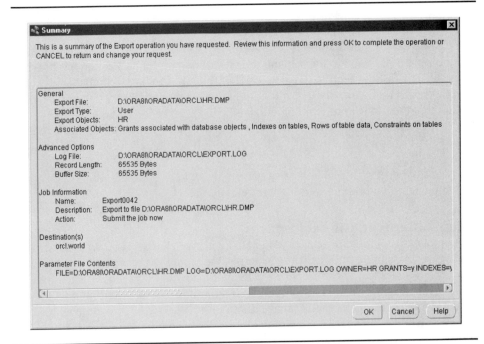

FIGURE 10-11. *The Export Summary screen*

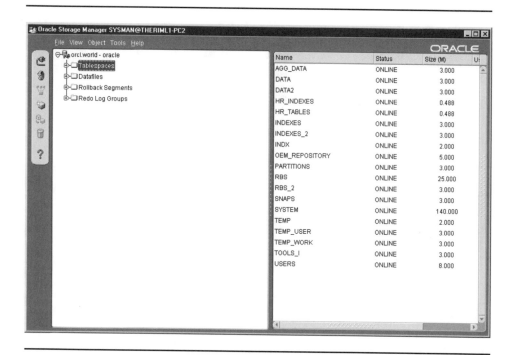

FIGURE 10-12.   *The Oracle Storage Manager screen with options selected*

For this example, the HR_TABLES tablespace will be removed and created. Before removing the tablespace, be sure to record the current tablespace size and datafile information for the tablespace. Figure 10-13 shows the tablespace information screen.

To drop the tablespace, select the Remove option from the Tools menu or click the right mouse button with the tablespace selected and choose Remove. A verification message asking, "Are you sure you want to remove tablespace 'HR_TABLES'? Yes/No" will be displayed. When you select Yes, the tablespace will be logically removed from the data dictionary. To physically remove the datafile from the system, you must delete the file at the operating system level. Figure 10-14 shows that the HR_TABLES tablespace has been removed.

The removal of the HR_INDEXES tablespace will not be shown here since it follows the same procedure.

Step 3. Create the tablespaces.

To create the new HR_TABLES tablespace, from the Tools pull-down menu or from the mouse right-button click, select the Create option. Figure 10-15 shows the Create Tablespace window with the tablespace name already entered.

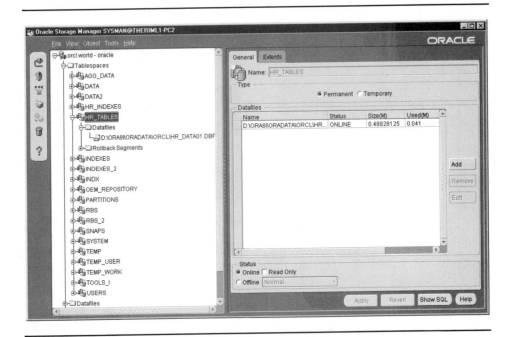

FIGURE 10-13. *The Tablespace Information screen*

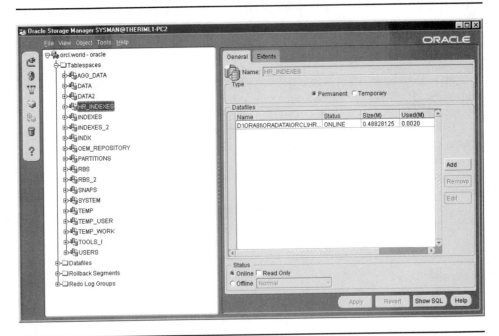

FIGURE 10-14. *The Tablespace Information screen with HR_TABLES removed*

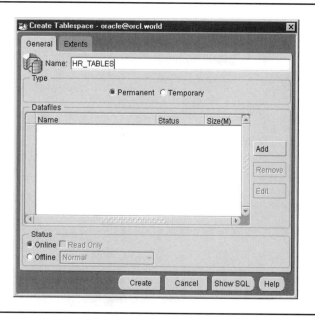

FIGURE 10-15. *The Create Tablespace screen*

To declare the datafile name, select the Add option shown in Figure 10-15. Figure 10-16 shows the information for the new datafile filled in. Note that the datafile name and size have been changed. If the original datafile for the tablespace is to be reused, choose the Reuse Existing File option.

The second tab, shown in Figure 10-16, is used to enable **autoextend**. By default, this option is not enabled. Once the information for the datafile is entered, select OK to return to the Create Tablespace window. If you want to change the parameters for the default storage clause of the tablespace creation statement, use the Extents tab shown in Figure 10-17.

As you can see in Figure 10-17, the default storage parameters are not displayed so there is no guide to default storage parameter sizing.

Once the parameters are established or the default parameters are accepted, click the Create button and the tablespace will be created. An acknowledgement will be displayed stating that the tablespace has been created. Figure 10-18 shows the tablespace with its new size.

Creating the HR_INDEXES tablespace will not be shown here since it follows the same procedure.

FIGURE 10-16. *The Datafile Information screen*

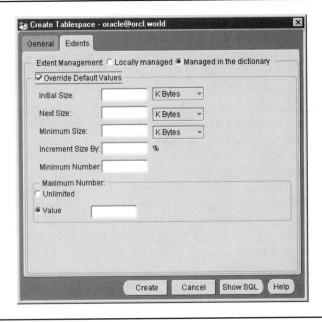

FIGURE 10-17. *The Datafile Extents Tab screen*

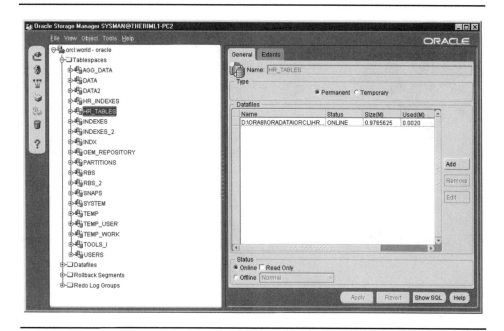

FIGURE 10-18. *The newly created and resized tablespace*

Step 4. Import the schema objects.

To import the HR user, select the Schema Management option from the Server Management console. From the Schema Management option pull-down Tools menu, select the Import option from the Data Management submenu. When you select this option, an Import Wizard will activate. Figure 10-19 shows the Introduction Import Wizard screen.

The next step in the Import procedure is to specify the full path of the file that is to be used for the Import. Figure 10-20 shows the file specification screen.

Once the file has been specified and the Next button pressed, the job immediately begins to run. Figure 10-21 shows the job in progress.

After the Import has completed, a completion notification will be displayed.

Analyzing the Object Distribution

Before performing the Exports in the prior examples, you had to first analyze the distribution of users' objects in the database. If users are isolated to tablespaces, and if tablespaces are dedicated to users, then analyzing user object distribution becomes simple.

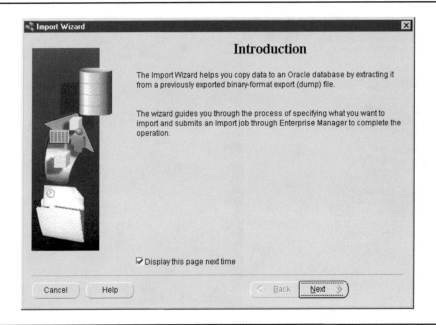

FIGURE 10-19. *The Import Wizard Introduction screen*

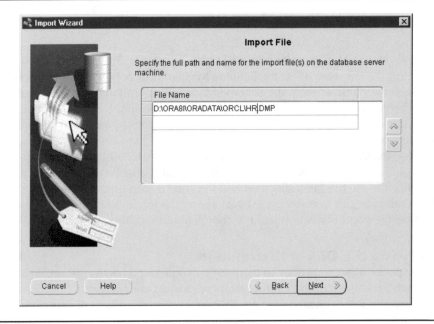

FIGURE 10-20. *The Import Wizard File declaration screen*

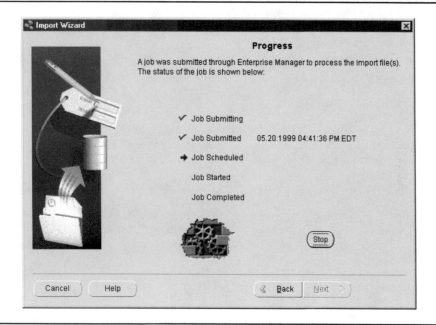

FIGURE 10-21.   *The In-Progress Import Job screen*

What if HR had also owned objects in the USERS tablespace in this example? In that case, there would have been two alternatives. First, you could have queried the data dictionary views to determine the table names involved and then specified the rest of HR's tables in the Export command via the TABLES parameter. Second, you could have exported HR's objects via a User export, dropped the HR_TABLES and HR_INDEXES tablespaces, dropped any HR objects located elsewhere in the database, re-created the HR_TABLES and HR_INDEXES tablespaces, and then performed the Import.

For the sample data given in the earlier listings, re-creating the USERS tablespace requires performing User exports of both the THUMPER and the FLOWER accounts. Neither of these accounts owns objects in tablespaces other than USERS.

NOTE
*This procedure cannot be used for tablespaces that contain temporary segments or rollback segments. The **drop tablespace** command will result in errors in those cases.*

As noted previously, User exports do not export third-party grants and indexes. To determine if third-party grants or indexes exist, query the data dictionary views, as shown in the following queries.

The first set of queries searches for third-party grants.

```
Rem
rem   third_party_grants.sql
rem
rem   This query searches for grants made by users
rem   other than the table owners.  These grants cannot
rem   be exported via User exports.
rem
break on Grantor skip 1 on Owner on Table_Name
select
        Grantor,           /*Account that made the grant*/
        Owner,             /*Account that owns the table*/
        Table_Name,        /*Name of the table*/
        Grantee,           /*Account granted access*/
        Privilege,         /*Privilege granted*/
        Grantable          /*Granted with admin option?*/
from DBA_TAB_PRIVS
where Grantor ! = Owner
order by Grantor, Owner, Table_Name, Grantee, Privilege

spool third_parts_privs.lst
/
spool off
```

As shown in the following listing, the search for third-party indexes queries the DBA_INDEXES data dictionary view to retrieve those records in which the index owner and the table owner columns do not have the same value.

```
rem
rem   third_party_indexes.sql
rem
rem   This query searches for indexes created by
rem   anyone other than the table owner.
rem
select
        Owner,             /*Owner of the index*/
        Index_Name,        /*Name of the index*/
        Table_Owner,       /*Owner of the table*/
        Table_Name         /*Name of the indexed table*/
from DBA_INDEXES
where Owner != Table_Owner

spool third_party_indexes.lst
/
spool off
```

If these queries show that third-party indexes or grants exist, and you plan to rely on User exports, then you must supplement those exports with scripts that generate the third-party grants and indexes. Those supplemental scripts are necessary because those grants and indexes will not be recorded during User exports.

Gathering Information with OEM

There is no simple way to determine complete object ownership through OEM. Although you can alter a user and change a user's default tablespace just as you can through SQL*Plus, the existing objects are not modified when you change a user's default tablespace setting.

There is no easy way to see all of a specific user's tablespaces from the Security Management option—you must go in on a user-by-user basis, which is very cumbersome. You can use the Schema Management option to view the owner and tablespace for objects on an object group–by–object group basis. Figure 10-22 shows the Schema Management screen with a partial printout of the tables and their ownership and tablespaces.

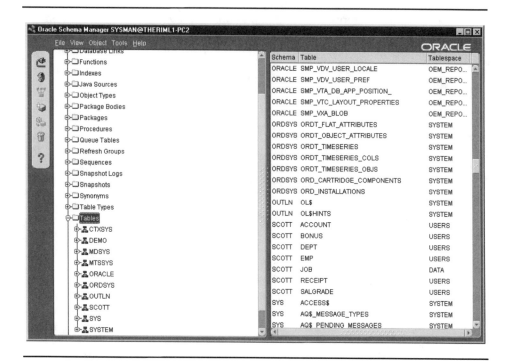

FIGURE 10-22.   *The Oracle Schema Management screen with some tables*

Exporting Partitions

You can reference partitions within tables when you perform Table exports. For example, if the SALES table in the THUMPER schema is partitioned into PART1, PART2, and PART3, then you can export the entire table or its partitions.

To export the entire table, use the TABLES parameter of Export.

```
exp system/manager FILE=expdat.dmp TABLES=(Thumper.SALES)
```

To export a specific partition, list the partition following the table name. The table name and the partition name should be separated by a colon (:). In the following listing, the PART1 partition is exported:

```
exp system/manager FILE=expdat.dmp TABLES=(Thumper.SALES:Part1)
```

As shown in this example, you can list specific partitions to export. This capability is frequently used during reorganizations of partitioned tables (see Chapter 12 for full details on partitioned tables). For example, you can export a full table, drop and re-create the table with different partition ranges, and then import the table, effectively altering the partition ranges for the partitions.

If you use the composite subpartitioning options available as of ORACLE8i, then you can specify subpartition names via the same syntax used for partition names. In the prior example, the "Part1" partition of the SALES table was exported. The syntax of that example would be identical if "Part1" were the name of a subpartition instead of a partition. You can export partitions and subpartitions via the same Export command. If you export a partition, then all of its subpartitions will be exported.

Exporting Table Rows

You can use the OEM Schema Manager tool to export a subset of rows. In Figure 10-23, the EMP table has been selected from the HR schema. However, making this selection will not influence the Export Wizard; it is shown to illustrate that there are times when making selections from the Navigator will not affect the task that you want to perform.

The same export procedure as shown earlier is used, but the Table option is selected instead of the Database or User option, as shown in Figure 10-24.

Figure 10-25 shows the EMP table selected from the HR schema. Inside the wizard, this selection will affect the task.

The next set of screens that you will see match those shown earlier in this chapter in Figures 10–8, so they will not be shown again here. To select a subset of rows to be exported from a table, use the Query tab option shown in Figure 10-26. The query has been entered to select only the rows where the department number equals the value 10.

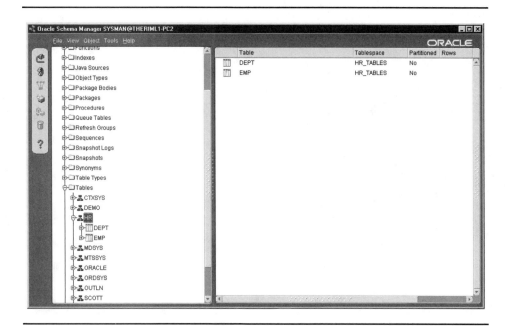

FIGURE 10-23.   *The Schema Manager with EMP table highlighted*

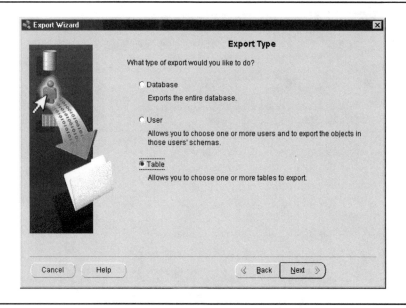

FIGURE 10-24.   *The Export Wizard with Table option selected*

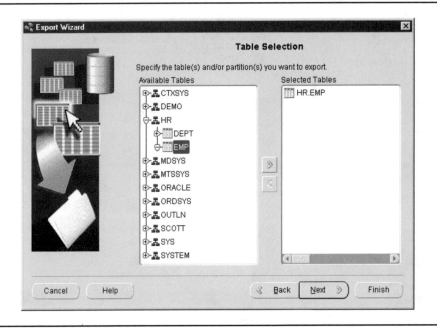

FIGURE 10-25. *The Export Wizard with the EMP table selected*

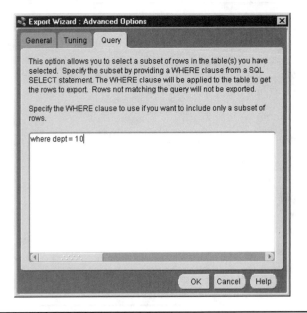

FIGURE 10-26. *Using the Query tab option*

After the job scheduler and summary screens have been displayed and approved, the export is performed.

In the next section, you will see how to use the Import utility to recover data. Since the Import steps used with the OEM have already been discussed, they will not be shown again in the next section.

Import

The Import utility reads the export dump file and runs the commands stored there. Import may be used to selectively bring back objects or users from the export dump file.

When importing data from an Incremental or Cumulative export, you must first import from the most recent Incremental export, followed by the most recent Complete export. After that Import is complete, the most recent Cumulative export must be imported, followed by all Incremental exports since that export.

You can run Import either interactively or via command files. The run-time options that can be specified for Import are listed in Table 10-4.

Keyword	Description
userid	Username/password of the account running the import. If this is the first parameter after the **imp** command, then the **userid** keyword does not have to be specified.
buffer	Size of the buffer used to fetch data rows. The default is system dependent; this value is usually set to a high value (> 100,000).
file	Name of the export dump file to be imported.
show	A Y/N flag to specify whether the file contents should be displayed rather than executed.
ignore	A Y/N flag to indicate whether the Import should ignore errors encountered when issuing **create** commands. This is used if the objects being imported already exist.
grants	A Y/N flag to indicate whether grants on database objects will be imported.
indexes	A Y/N flag to indicate whether indexes on tables will be imported.
constraints	A Y/N flag to indicate whether constraints on tables will be imported.

TABLE 10-4. *Import Keywords*

Keyword	Description
rows	A Y/N flag to indicate whether rows should be imported. If this is set to "N", then only the DDL for the database objects will be executed.
full	A Y/N flag; if set to "Y", then the Full export dump file is imported.
fromuser	A list of database accounts whose objects should be read from the export dump file (when **full**=N).
touser	A list of database accounts into which objects in the export dump file will be imported. **fromuser** and **touser** do not have to be set to the same value.
tables	A list of tables to be imported.
recordlength	The length, in bytes, of the export dump file record. Usually left at the default value unless you are going to transfer the export file between different operating systems.
inctype	The type of import being performed (valid values are COMPLETE [default], CUMULATIVE, and INCREMENTAL).
commit	A Y/N flag to indicate whether Import should **commit** after each array (whose size is set by BUFFER). If this is set to "N", then Import will **commit** after every table is imported. For large tables, **commit**=N requires equally large rollback segments.
parfile	The name of a parameter file to be passed to Import. This file may contain entries for all of the parameters listed here.
indexfile	This very powerful option writes all of the **create table**, **create cluster**, and **create index** commands to a file, rather than running them. All but the **create index** commands will be commented out. This file can then be run (with slight modifications) after importing with **indexes**=N. It is very useful for separating tables and indexes into separate tablespaces.
charset	Character set to use during the Import for v5 and v6 (obsolete but retained)
point_in_time_recover	A Y/N flag to indicate if the Import is part of a tablespace point-in-time recovery. This is an advanced recovery technique; see the "Recovery Scenarios" section of this chapter. (Removed for 8i)

TABLE 10-4. *Import Keywords* (continued)

Keyword	Description
destroy	A Y/N flag to indicate whether the **create tablespace** commands found in dump files from Full exports will be executed (thereby destroying the datafiles in the database being imported into).
log	The name of a file to which the log of the Import will be written.
skip_unusable_ indexes	A Y/N flag that indicates if Import should skip partition indexes marked as "unusable". You may wish to skip the indexes during Import and manually create them later to improve index creation performance.
analyze	A Y/N flag to indicate whether Import should execute the **analyze** commands found in the export dump file.
feedback	The number of rows after which to display progress during table imports. The default value is 0, so no feedback is displayed until a table is completely imported.
tiod_novalidate	Enables Import to skip validation of specified object types. This option is generally used with cartridge installs. One or more object types can be specified.
filesize	The maximum dump size that was specified on Export if the parameter FILESIZE was used on Export.
recalculate_ statistics	A Y/N flag to indicate whether optimizer statistics should be generated.
transport_ tablespace	A Y/N flag to indicate that transportable tablespace metadata is to be imported into the database.
tablespaces	The name or list of names of tablespaces to be transported into the database.
datafiles	The list of datafiles to be transported into the database.
tts_owner	The name or list of names of owners of data in the transportable tablespace.

TABLE 10-4.   *Import Keywords* (continued)

A number of the Import parameters conflict with each other or may result in inconsistent instructions for Import. For example, setting FULL=Y and OWNER=HR would fail, since the FULL parameter calls for a Full import, while the OWNER parameter specifies a User import.

The default values for these options are shown in Table 10-5.

The DESTROY parameter is very useful for DBAs who run multiple databases on a single server. Since Full database Exports record the entire data dictionary, the

Keyword	Oracle8 Default Value
userid	Undefined
buffer	System dependent
file	EXPDAT.DMP
show	N
ignore	N
grants	Y
indexes	Y
constraints	Y
rows	Y
full	N
fromuser	Undefined
touser	Undefined
tables	Undefined
recordlength	System dependent
inctype	Undefined
commit	N
parfile	Undefined
indexfile	Undefined
destroy	N
log	Undefined
charset	NLS_LANG for the instance (obsolete)

TABLE 10-5. *Default Values for Import Parameters*

Keyword	Oracle8 Default Value
point_in_time_ recover	N (replaced by Transport_Tablespaces)
skip_unusable_ indexes	N
analyze	Y
feedback	0
toid_novalidate	None
filesize	O/S dependent—must match Export value
recalculate_statistics	N
transportable_ tablespaces	N
tablespaces	None
datafiles	None
tts_owners	None

TABLE 10-5.   *Default Values for Import Parameters* (continued)

tablespace and datafile definitions are written to the export dump file. The datafile definitions will include the full path name for the files. If this export dump file is used to migrate to a separate database on the same server, a problem may arise.

NOTE
Tablespace names are exported as part of an object's definition. If you are importing data from one instance into a separate instance, be sure to create tablespaces with the target database that have the same names as those in the source instance.

The problem is that when importing into the second database from the Full export of the first database, Import will execute the **create tablespace** commands found in the export dump file. These commands will instruct the database to create files in exactly the same directory, with the same name, as the files from the first database. Without using DESTROY=N (the default option), the first database's datafiles may be overwritten. The only alternative when doing such an Import is to precreate all of the tablespaces, forcing the **create tablespace** commands to return errors (and thus not attempt to create any datafiles during the Import).

Rollback Segment Requirements

By default, the database will issue a **commit** after every table is completely imported. Thus, if you have a table with 300MB of data in it, then your rollback segments must accommodate a rollback segment entry that is at least that large. This is an unnecessary burden for the rollback segments. To shorten the sizes of the rollback segment entries, specify COMMIT=Y along with a value for BUFFER. A **commit** will then be executed after every BUFFER worth of data, as shown in the following example. In the first **import** command shown, a **commit** is executed after every table is loaded. In the second command shown, a **commit** is executed after every 64,000 bytes of data are inserted.

```
imp system/manager file=expdat.dmp
imp system/manager file=expdat.dmp buffer=64000 commit=Y
```

How large should BUFFER be? BUFFER should be large enough to handle the largest single row to be imported. In tables with LONG or LOB datatypes, this may be greater than 64K. If you do not know the longest row length that was exported, start with a reasonable value (e.g., 50,000) and run the Import. If an IMP-00020 error is returned, then the BUFFER size is not large enough. Increase it and try the Import again.

When using COMMIT=Y, remember that a **commit** is being performed for each BUFFER array. This implies that if the Import of a table fails, it is possible that some of the rows in that table may have already been imported and **commit**ted. The partial load may then be either used or **delete**d prior to running the Import again.

Importing into Different Accounts

To move objects from one user to another user via Export/Import, perform a User export of the owner of the objects. During the Import, specify the owner as the FROMUSER and the account that is to own the objects as the TOUSER.

For example, to copy THUMPER's objects into the FLOWER account, execute the following commands. The first command exports the THUMPER owner and the second command imports the THUMPER objects into the FLOWER account.

```
exp system/manager file=thumper.dat owner=thumper grants=N
   indexes=Y compress=Y rows=Y

imp system/manager file=thumper.dat FROMUSER=thumper TOUSER=flower
     rows=Y indexes=Y
```

Importing Structures that Failed to Import

The ROWS parameter is very useful for two reasons. First, it can be used to re-create just the database structure, without the tables' data, even if that data was exported. Second, it is often needed during successive Imports to recover objects that were not created during the first Import attempt. Multiple Imports may be necessary because of the order in which objects are exported and imported.

When you export tables, ORACLE exports users in the order in which they were created in the database. A user's tables are then exported alphabetically. While this order of operations does not cause a problem during Exports, it may cause problems when those same objects are imported. The problems arise from the dependencies that may exist between objects in the database. If Import attempts to create an object (such as a view) before it creates the objects on which it depends, then an error may result. In such cases, the Import can be rerun, with ROWS=N and IGNORE=N, which will only import the structures that did not get imported during the first Import.

The following example shows this usage. The first Import attempts to bring in the entire export dump file. If there are failures during this Import, then a second pass is made to attempt to bring in those structures that failed the first time.

```
imp system/manager file=expdat.dmp full=Y commit=Y buffer=64000
```

During the import, several views fail with an ORA-00942 (table or view does not exist) error. Now run the Import a second time, with IGNORE=N and ROWS=N.

```
imp system/manager file=expdat.dmp ignore=N rows=N commit=Y buffer=64000
```

The IGNORE=N parameter in the second command tells Import to ignore any objects that were created during the first pass. It will only import those objects that failed. These are usually views that reference tables owned by multiple users.

> **NOTE**
> *If a table referenced by a view is dropped, the view definition stays in the data dictionary. This definition can be exported, and the view creation will fail during an Import. In that case, since the view was invalid to begin with, a second Import will fail as well.*

You may need to run multiple Imports with ROWS=N in order to successfully re-create all of your database objects.

Using Import to Separate Tables and Indexes

You can use two Import options—INDEXFILE and INDEXES—to reorganize the tablespace assignments of tables and indexes.

Using the INDEXFILE option during an Import will result in the export dump file being read and, instead of being imported, its table and index creation scripts will be written to an output file. You can edit this file to alter the **tablespace** and **storage** parameters of the tables and indexes listed there. You can then run the altered file via SQL*Plus to either precreate all objects prior to importing their data or to create only specified objects (such as indexes).

When the indexfile is created, the **create index** scripts are the only commands in the file that are not commented out via the **rem** command. This default functionality allows DBAs to separate a user's tables and indexes into separate tablespaces during Import. To do so, create the indexfile and alter the **tablespace** clauses for the indexes. Then import the user, with indexes=N, so that the user's indexes will not be imported. Then run the altered indexfile to create the indexes in their new tablespace.

Note that the indexfile may contain entries for multiple users (if multiple users were exported). In practice, it is useful to separate the indexfile into multiple files, one for each user. This will make it easier to keep the tablespace assignments consistent. The following listing shows the steps involved in this process. In this example, THUMPER's objects are being copied into the FLOWER account, and the indexes are being separated from the tables in the process.

NOTE
The INDEXFILE parameter requires that either FULL=Y or a FROMUSER value is specified.

1. Export the user.

   ```
   exp system/manager file=expdat.dmp owner=thumper
   ```

2. Create the indexfile from this export dump file.

   ```
   imp system/manager file=expdat.dmp indexfile=indexes.sql full=Y
   ```

3. Edit the indexfile to change the **tablespace** settings of the indexes. Be careful performing global edits on the indexfile, since the **tablespace** keyword and the tablespace name may be split over two lines.

4. Import the user, without its indexes.

   ```
   imp system/manager file=expdat.dmp fromuser=thumper touser=flower
       indexes=N commit=Y buffer=64000
   ```

5. Log in to SQL*Plus as the user and run the altered indexfile to create the indexes.

```
sqlplus flower/password
SQL> @indexes
```

If you are separating a small number of indexes from their tables, you should investigate the use of the **rebuild** option of the **alter index** command instead of using Export/Import. See Chapter 3 for details on this alternative method of moving indexes.

Offline Backups

A cold backup is a physical backup of the database files, made after the database has been shut down via either a **shutdown normal** or a **shutdown immediate**. While the database is shut down, each of the files that are actively used by the database is backed up. These files thus capture a complete image of the database as it existed at the moment it was shut down.

NOTE
*You should not rely on an offline backup performed following a **shutdown abort**. If you must perform a **shutdown abort**, you should restart the database and perform a normal **shutdown** or a **shutdown immediate** prior to beginning your offline backup.*

The following files should be backed up during cold backups:

- All datafiles

- All control files

- All online redo logs

- The init.ora file and config.ora file (optional)

It is easiest to back up the datafiles if the database file architecture uses a consistent directory structure. A sample of such an architecture is shown in the "Database File Layout" section of Chapter 4.

In that architecture, all of the datafiles are located in directories at the same level on each device. The following listing shows a sample directory tree for a data disk named /db01:

```
/db01
         /oracle
                 /CASE
                         control1.dbf
                         sys01.dbf
                         tools.dbf
                 /CC1
                         control1.dbf
                         sys01.dbf
                         tools.dbf
                 /DEMO
                         control1.dbf
                         sys01.dbf
```

In the sample directory tree, all database files are stored in an instance-specific subdirectory under an /oracle directory for the device. Directories such as these should contain all of the datafiles, redo log files, and control files for a database. The only file you may optionally add to the cold backup that will not be in this location is the production init.ora file, which should be in the /app/oracle/admin/*INSTANCE_NAME*/pfile subdirectory under the Oracle software base directory.

If you use the directory structure in the prior example, your backup commands are greatly simplified. The following listing shows a sample UNIX **tar** command, which is used here to back up files to a tape drive called /dev/rmt/0hc. Because the directory structure is consistent and the drives are named /db01 through /db09, the following command will back up all of the CC1 database's datafiles, redo log files, and control files:

```
> tar -cvf /dev/rmt/0hc /db0[1-9]/oracle/CC1
```

The **-cvf** flag creates a new **tar** saveset. To append the init.ora file to this saveset, use the **-rvf** flag. This option, which appends files to the tape, is not available on all UNIX systems. If your installation does not support this, then the best alternative is to copy the files directly to a staging area on another disk (see "Database and Operating System Backups Integration" later in this chapter).

```
> tar -rvf /dev/rmt/0hc /orasw/app/oracle/CC1/pfile/initcc1.ora
```

NOTE
If necessary, you can also back up the config.ora file at the same time.

These two commands, taken together, will back up all of the database's files to one tape device. Alternatively, you could combine the two **tar** commands into a single command, as shown in the following listing:

```
> tar -rvf /dev/rmt/0hc /db0[1-9]/oracle/CC1
/orasw/app/oracle/CC1/pfile/initcc1.ora
```

Since offline backups involve changes to the database's availability, they are usually scheduled to occur at night. A command file to automate these backups would resemble the following listing. In this example, the ORACLE_SID and ORACLE_HOME environment variables are set to point to the CC1 database. This database is then shut down and the backup commands are executed. The database is then restarted.

```
ORACLE_SID=cc1; export ORACLE_SID
ORAENV_ASK=NO; export ORAENV_ASK
. oraenv
svrmgrl <<EOF1
connect internal as sysdba
shutdown immediate;
exit
EOF1
insert backup commands like the "tar" commands here
svrmgrl <<EOF2
connect internal as sysdba
startup
EOF2
```

These examples are generic so that non-UNIX operating systems can use them with little modification. In VMS, for example, environment variables are set via instance-specific command files. For example, if the ORACLE software home directory was DB01:[ORASW], then to set the environment variables, you would first go to the instance directory (via the **set def** command). Once there, you would run the instance-specific ORAUSER file there. This is shown in the following example:

```
set def DB01:[ORASW.DB_instance_name]
@ORAUSER_DB_instance_name
```

The Server Manager commands are the same across operating systems. The backup commands are operating system–specific. For VMS systems, the backup commands are of the form shown in the following example.

In this example, the VMS **backup** command is used. The command is told to back up the files even if they have been marked as NOBACKUP, and even if they are interlocked (the interl parameter in this example). The /log clause logs the results of the **backup** command.

```
$Backup/ignore=(nobackup,interl)/log file tape1:oracle_backup.bck/sav
```

The file in this example is backed up to a tape device called tape1. It is written to a saveset (as indicated by the /sav clause) called oracle_backup.bck. As with the UNIX **tar** command, you can back up multiple files at once via this command. The same **backup** command can be used to back up different files to savesets on the same tape. Those savesets will be appended to the tape.

Online (ARCHIVELOG) Backups

Offline backups can only be performed while the database is shut down. However, you can perform physical file backups of a database while the database is open—provided the database is running in ARCHIVELOG mode and the backup is performed correctly. These backups are variously referred to as "hot" backups, "online" backups, or "ARCHIVELOG" backups.

ORACLE writes to the online redo log files in a cyclical fashion; after filling the first log file, it begins writing the second until that one fills, and it then begins writing to the third. Once the last online redo log file is filled, the LGWR (Log Writer) background process begins to overwrite the contents of the first redo log file.

When ORACLE is run in ARCHIVELOG mode, the ARCH background process makes a copy of each redo log file before overwriting it. These archived redo log files are usually written to a disk device. They may also be written directly to a tape device, but this tends to be very operator-intensive.

Getting Started

To make use of the ARCHIVELOG capability, the database must first be placed in ARCHIVELOG mode. The following listing shows the steps needed to place a database in ARCHIVELOG mode:

```
svrmgrl
SVRMGR> connect internal as sysdba
SVRMGR> startup mount cc1;
SVRMGR> alter database archivelog;
SVRMGR> archive log start;
SVRMGR> alter database open;
```

The following command will display the current ARCHIVELOG status of the database from within Server Manager:

```
archive log list
```

To change a database back to NOARCHIVELOG mode, use the following set of commands:

```
svrmgrl
SVRMGR> connect internal as sysdba
```

```
SVRMGR> startup mount cc1;
SVRMGR> alter database noarchivelog;
SVRMGR> alter database open;
```

A database that has been placed in ARCHIVELOG mode will remain in that mode until it is placed in NOARCHIVELOG mode.

The location of the archived redo log files is determined by the settings in the database's init.ora file. The archive log destination parameter may also be set via the config.ora file that is referenced as a parameter file in the init.ora. The two parameters to note are as follows (with sample values):

```
log_archive_dest            = /db01/oracle/arch/CC1/arch
log_archive_start           = TRUE
```

NOTE
See the following section for information on the ORACLE8i parameters that supersede these parameters.

In this example, the archived redo log files are being written to the directory /db01/oracle/arch/CC1. The archived redo log files will all begin with the letters "arch", followed by a sequence number. For example, the archived redo log file directory may contain the following files:

```
arch_170.dbf
arch_171.dbf
arch_172.dbf
```

Each of these files contains the data from a single online redo log. They are numbered sequentially, in the order in which they were created. The size of the archived redo log files varies, but does not exceed their size of the online redo log files.

If the destination directory of the archived redo log files runs out of space, then ARCH will stop processing the online redo log data and the database will stop itself. This situation can be resolved by adding more space to the archived redo log file destination disk or by backing up the archived redo log files and then removing them from this directory.

NOTE
Never delete archived redo log files until you have backed them up. There is no way to skip a missing archived redo log file during a recovery.

In a database that is currently running, you can show the current ARCHIVELOG settings (including the destination directory) via the **archive log list** command within Server Manager, as shown earlier in this section. You can also query the parameter settings from the V$PARAMETER dynamic performance view.

```
select Name,
       Value
  from V$PARAMETER
 where Name like 'log_archive%';
```

Although the LOG_ARCHIVE_START parameter may be set to TRUE, the database will *not* be in ARCHIVELOG mode unless you have executed the **alter database archivelog** command shown earlier in this section. Once the database is in ARCHIVELOG mode, it will remain in that mode through subsequent database shutdowns and startups until you explicitly place it in NOARCHIVELOG mode via the **alter database noarchivelog** command.

Automating Multiplexing of Archived Redo Log Files

As of ORACLE8.0, you can instruct the database to write to two separate archived redo log file destinations areas simultaneously. Writing to two separate destination areas allows you to recover in the event that one of those destination disks fails. The archiving process must be able to write to both locations in order for the database to continue functioning.

NOTE
ORACLE writes to multiple archived redo log file destination areas simultaneously, not consecutively.

In ORACLE8.0, the LOG_ARCHIVE_DUPLEX_DEST init.ora parameter specifies the second destination area for archived redo log files. A second parameter, LOG_ARCHIVE_MIN_SUCCEED_DEST, specifies the minimum number of archived redo log destination areas that must be successfully written to during an ARCH write. Both of these parameters are supported in ORACLE8i, but they are officially obsolete and have been superseded by a new set of options.

As of ORACLE8i, you can use the LOG_ARCHIVE_DEST_n parameter to specify up to five locations for your archived redo log files (LOG_ARCHIVE_DEST_1, LOG_ARCHIVE_DEST_2, etc.). The ARCH process will write files to all of the specified locations simultaneously. Each of the archive destinations has a corresponding "state" set via the LOG_ARCHIVE_DEST_STATE_n parameter. An archive destination's state may be either ENABLED, in which case files are written there, or DEFER, in which case the destination is not presently active. You should create a LOG_ARCHIVE_DEST_STATE_n entry (such as

LOG_ARCHIVE_DEST_STATE_1, LOG_ARCHIVE_DEST_STATE_2, etc.) for each LOG_ARCHIVE_DEST_*n* entry in your init.ora file.

The LOG_ARCHIVE_DEST_*n* parameter replaces the LOG_ARCHIVE_DEST parameter supported in earlier versions of ORACLE.

Using OEM to Get Started

From the Instance Manager screen of the OEM tool, you can see whether or not ARCHIVELOG mode has been enabled. Figure 10-27 shows this screen with the Information tab selected. The database is not in ARCHIVELOG mode in Figure 10-27. In order to use the startup, shutdown, and ARCHIVELOG options within Instance Manager, you must connect through the Management Pack menu using an account with preferred credentials enabled and the SYSDBA role available.

To enable ARCHIVELOG mode, select the pull-down menu Database option and check the Archive Log option. When this box is checked, the database must

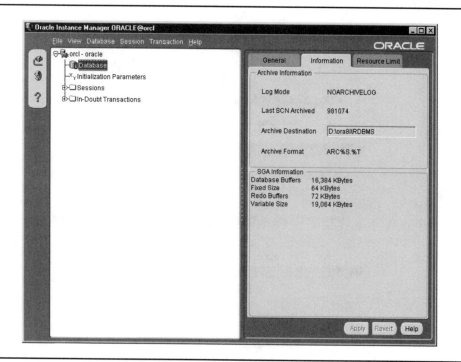

FIGURE 10-27. *The Oracle Instance Manager Database Information screen*

be in startup mount mode but not opened, or a prompt to shut down and start the database will be displayed. The next illustration shows this screen.

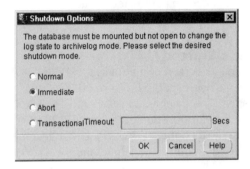

If a shutdown option is selected, a database shutdown and then a database startup screen will display, followed by a prompt screen to verify that ARCHIVELOG mode should be enabled:

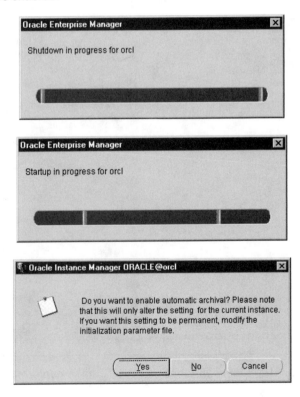

Figure 10-28 shows that ARCHIVELOG mode has been enabled.

NOTE
Although ARCHIVELOG is now enabled for the instance, the init.ora file has not been modified. For the change to be permanent, the init.ora file must be modified and the database stopped and restarted before ARCHIVELOG mode will be completely enabled.

Performing Online Database Backups

Once a database is running in ARCHIVELOG mode, you can back it up while it is open and available to users. This capability allows round-the-clock database availability to be achieved while still guaranteeing the recoverability of the database.

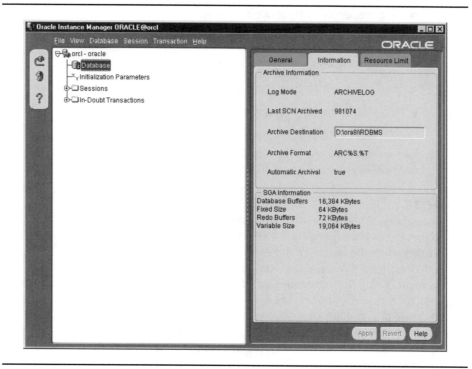

FIGURE 10-28. *The Instance Manager Information screen with Archivelog Mode enabled*

Although hot backups can be performed during normal working hours, they should be scheduled for the times of the least user activity for several reasons. First, the hot backups will use operating system commands to back up the physical files, and these commands will use most of the available I/O resources in the system (impacting the system performance for interactive users). Second, while the tablespaces are being backed up, the manner in which transactions are written to the archived redo log files changes. If the physical block size of the operating system is less than the ORACLE block size, then changing one record in a block will cause the record's entire database block, not just the transaction data, to be written to the archived redo log file. This will use a great deal more space in the archived redo log file destination directory.

The command file for a hot backup has three parts:

1. A tablespace-by-tablespace backup of the datafiles, which in turn consists of

    a. Setting the tablespace into backup state

    b. Backing up the tablespace's datafiles

    c. Restoring the tablespace to its normal state

2. Backing up the archived redo log files, which consists of

    a. Recording which files are in the archived redo log destination directory

    b. Backing up the archived redo log files, then (optionally) deleting or compressing them

3. Backing up the control file via the **alter database backup controlfile** command.

NOTE
During step 2, the archiver may be stopped briefly to prevent new archived redo log files from being written while the names of the existing archived redo log files are recorded. If you don't stop the archiver during this operation, you may delete (in step 2b) files not recorded. There is no way to re-create the contents of a deleted archived redo log file, and no way to skip past it during a recovery if you cannot recover the file. Be careful when deleting archived redo log files.

A command file to perform a hot backup of a database will resemble the following listing. It is structured the same as the description just given. This example is for a UNIX database. In the first section, the environment variables ORACLE_SID and ORACLE_HOME are set for the database. Server Manager is then used to put each tablespace in **begin backup** state. The datafiles associated with each tablespace are then backed up.

When the datafiles are being backed up, there are two choices available: they may be backed up directly to tape or they may be backed up to disk. If you have enough disk space available, choose the latter option since it will greatly reduce the time necessary for the backup procedures to complete. For this example, the datafiles will be written directly to tape.

NOTE

You can simplify this script significantly, as described in the "Automation of Backup Scripts" section later in this chapter.

```
#
# Sample Hot Backup Script for a UNIX File System database
#
# Set up environment variables:
ORACLE_SID=cc1; export ORACLE_SID
ORAENV_ASK=NO; export ORAENV_ASK
. oraenv
#
#   Step 1.  Perform a tablespace-by-tablespace backup
#   of the datafiles.  Set each tablespace, one at a time,
#   into begin backup state.  Then back up its datafiles
#   and return the tablespace to its normal state.
#
# Note for UNIX:  Set up an indicator for Server Manager
# (called EOFarch1 here) so that the command file will
#  stay within Server Manager.
#
svrmgrl <<EOFarch1
connect internal as sysdba
REM
REM    Back up the SYSTEM tablespace
REM
alter tablespace SYSTEM begin backup;
!tar -cvf /dev/rmt/0hc /db01/oracle/CC1/sys01.dbf
alter tablespace SYSTEM end backup;
REM
```

```
REM  The SYSTEM tablespace has now been written to a
REM   tar saveset on the tape device /dev/rmt/0hc.  The
REM   rest of the tars must use the "-rvf" clause to append
REM   to that saveset.
REM
REM   Back up the RBS tablespace
REM
alter tablespace RBS begin backup;
!tar -rvf /dev/rmt/0hc /db02/oracle/CC1/rbs01.dbf
alter tablespace RBS end backup;
REM
REM   Back up the DATA tablespace
REM   For the purposes of this example, this tablespace
REM   will contain two files, data01.dbf and data02.dbf.
REM   The * wildcard will be used in the filename.
REM
alter tablespace DATA begin backup;
!tar -rvf /dev/rmt/0hc /db03/oracle/CC1/data0*.dbf
alter tablespace DATA end backup;
REM
REM   Back up the INDEXES tablespace
REM
alter tablespace INDEXES begin backup;
!tar -rvf /dev/rmt/0hc /db04/oracle/CC1/indexes01.dbf
alter tablespace INDEXES end backup;
REM
REM   Back up the TEMP tablespace

REM
alter tablespace TEMP begin backup;
!tar -rvf /dev/rmt/0hc /db05/oracle/CC1/temp01.dbf
alter tablespace TEMP end backup;
REM
REM   Follow the same pattern to back up the rest
REM   of the tablespaces.
REM
REM
REM        Step 2.  Back up the archived redo log files.
REM
REM   First, stop the archiving process.  This will keep
REM   additional archived redo log files from being written
REM   to the destination directory during this process.
REM   This process takes just a few seconds.
REM
archive log stop
REM
REM   Exit Server Manager, using the indicator set earlier.
exit
```

```
EOFarch1
#
#  Record which files are in the destination directory.
#     Do this by setting an environment variable that is
#  equal to the directory listing for the destination
#  directory.
#  For this example, the log_archive_dest is
#  /db01/oracle/arch/CC1.
#
FILES='ls /db01/oracle/arch/CC1/arch*.dbf'; export FILES
#
#  Now go back into Server Manager and restart the
#  archiving process.  Set an indicator (called EOFarch2
#  in this example).
#
svrmgrl <<EOFarch2
connect internal
archive log start;
exit
EOFarch2
#
#  Now back up the archived redo logs to the tape
#  device via the "tar" command, then delete them
#  from the destination device via the "rm" command.
#  You may choose to compress them instead.
#
tar -rvf /dev/rmt/0hc $FILES
rm -f $FILES
#
#     Step 3.  Back up the control file to a disk file.
#
svrmgrl <<EOFarch3
connect internal
alter database backup controlfile to
   '/db01/oracle/CC1/CC1controlfile.bck';
exit
EOFarch3
#
#  Back up the control file to the tape.
#
tar -rvf /dev/rmt/0hc /db01/oracle/CC1/CC1controlfile.bck
#
#  End of hot backup script.
```

This backup script explicitly lists each datafile within each tablespace.
Therefore, this backup procedure must be altered each time a datafile is added to
the database.

In this version of the backup script, only one tablespace is in **begin backup** state at a time. Having only one tablespace in **begin backup** state at a time minimizes vulnerability to potential damage caused by database crashes. If the database is closed abnormally while a tablespace is in **begin backup** state, then recovery may be necessary. Using the one-at-a-time method shown here greatly reduces the possible impact of such a crash. If your disk environment guards against disk failures (such as a mirrored or RAID environment), then you can simplify your backup scripts by placing all of the tablespaces into **begin backup** state concurrently.

In the "Database and Operating System Backups Integration" section later in this chapter, this script will be modified to take advantage of file system backups performed by systems management personnel.

To back up an ORACLE database in a VMS operating system, make several small changes to the backup script above:

1. Instead of the # signs in the UNIX script, use **$!** to signal a remark in the command file.

2. Remove the references to EOFarch1, EOFarch2, and EOFarch3. These aren't needed in VMS.

3. Replace the UNIX **tar** commands with VMS **backup** commands, as shown earlier in this chapter.

4. Replace the UNIX **rm** command with a VMS **delete** command.

5. Set up the environment variables that point to the instance via the instance-specific command file referred to earlier in this chapter.

6. When backing up the archived redo logs, set the FILES variable equal to the directory listing of the archived redo log destination directory.

Automation of the Backup Scripts

In the preceding section, the backup scripts explicitly list each file to be backed up. Although you should know whenever a file is added or moved in your database, changing the backup scripts may be a process you wish to avoid as the number of databases you support increases. Therefore, you may wish to automate the backup script generation process.

When automating the backup script generation process, you will find it simplest to put all of the tablespaces into **begin backup** state at once. As noted earlier in this chapter, you should only put all of your tablespaces into the **begin backup** state simultaneously if both of these conditions are met:

1. There are very few transactions occurring in the database. Tablespaces in **begin backup** state generate very high volumes of redo log information.

2. The hardware used by the database is mirrored. Since having all of the tablespaces in **begin backup** state greatly increases your vulnerability to media failures, you should make sure that the disk drives and other hardware used by the datafiles are well protected.

If both of these conditions are met, then you can consider placing all of your tablespaces in **begin backup** state. In the revised backup script, the order of events will be

1. A backup of all datafiles, which consists of

   a. Setting all tablespaces into backup state

   b. Backing up all datafiles

   c. Restoring all tablespaces to their normal state

2. Backing up the archived redo log files, which consists of

   a. Recording which files are in the archived redo log destination directory

   b. Backing up the archived redo log files, then (optionally) deleting or compressing them

3. Backing up the control file via the **alter database backup controlfile** command.

The differences between this order of commands and the commands given earlier in this chapter are found in step 1. Instead of placing tablespaces into **begin backup** state one at a time, all of the tablespaces are placed into **begin backup** state at the same time. To automatically generate the commands needed to alter the tablespaces, query DBA_TABLESPACES as shown in the following listing:

```
set pagesize 0 feedback off

select
    'alter tablespace '||Tablespace_Name||' begin backup;'
  from DBA_TABLESPACES
 where Status <> 'INVALID'

spool alter_begin.sql
/
spool off
```

The output of this query will be a command named alter_begin.sql. Its entries will resemble the following:

```
alter tablespace SYSTEM begin backup;
alter tablespace RBS begin backup;
alter tablespace TEMP begin backup;
alter tablespace DATA begin backup;
alter tablespace INDEXES begin backup;
```

When you execute this command file, all of the tablespaces will be placed into **begin backup** state. You can now back up all of the datafiles. Instead of backing up specific datafiles, you can back up all datafiles in the proper directories without regard to their tablespace affiliations. In the following listing, the datafiles from disks /db01 to /db09 are backed up via a single **tar** command:

```
tar -cvf /dev/rmt/0hc /db0[1-9]/oracle/CC1
```

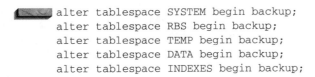

NOTE
You may want to exclude the archived redo log file directory from this backup step since those files will be backed up via step 2 of the backup procedure.

Once the datafiles are backed up, you can change them from **begin backup** state to their normal state. You can automatically generate the script to perform this change, as shown in the following listing:

```
set pagesize 0 feedback off

select
    'alter tablespace '||Tablespace_Name||' end backup;'
  from DBA_TABLESPACES
 where Status <> 'INVALID'

spool alter_end.sql
/
spool off
```

When you execute the alter_end.sql script generated by this query, your tablespaces will be back in their normal state and you can now proceed to steps 2 (archived redo log file backups) and 3 (control file backup) of the backup process.

The automation of backup scripts generates the greatest benefit when you have many databases that are changing frequently. If you rely on automated backup scripts, you should make sure your server hardware is very reliable. As of

ORACLE7.2, you can alter a tablespace to **end backup** state prior to opening the database if the database shut down abnormally while the tablespace was in **begin backup** state. Ideally, you should avoid server activity—and server failures—during your database backup process.

Archived Redo Log File Backups

Since the archived redo log file destination directory may become full before the hot backup procedure is run, you should have a backup procedure that only backs up that directory. The files in that directory can then be deleted, leaving space for new archived redo log files.

This procedure is simply a portion of the full hot backup process. It is a five-step process:

1. Temporarily stop the archiving process.

2. Record which files are in the archived redo log destination directory.

3. Restart the archiving process.

4. Back up the archived redo log files.

5. Delete those files from the destination directory.

The following script performs this function. It is for UNIX databases using file systems. The **tar** command is used to back up the files to tape.

```
#       Step 1: Stop the archiving process. This will keep
#       additional archived redo log files from being written
#       to the destination directory during this process.
#
svrmgrl <<EOFarch1
connect internal as sysdba
archive log stop;
REM
REM    Exit Server Manager using the indicator set earlier.
exit
EOFarch1
#
#       Step 2: Record which files are in the destination
#  directory.
#       Do this by setting an environment variable that is
#  equal to the directory listing for the destination
#  directory.
#  For this example, the log_archive_dest is
#  /db01/oracle/arch/CC1.
#
```

```
FILES='ls /db01/oracle/arch/CC1/arch*.dbf'; export FILES
#
#     Step 3: Go back into Server Manager and restart the
#     archiving process. Set an indicator (called EOFarch2
#     in this example).
#
svrmgrl <<EOFarch2
connect internal as sysdba
archive log start;
exit
EOFarch2
#
#     Step 4. Back up the archived redo logs to the tape
#     device via the "tar" command, then delete them
#     from the destination device via the "rm" command.
#
tar -rvf /dev/rmt/0hc $FILES
#
#     Step 5. Delete those files from the destination directory.
#
rm -f $FILES
#
#     End of archived redo log file backup script.
```

The archived redo logs that are backed up via this procedure should be stored with the last previous hot backup.

Alternatives to Stopping the Archiver

As part of the backup process shown in the preceding sections, the ARCH process is temporarily stopped via the **archive log stop** command. Once a directory of files in the archive log destination area is generated, the ARCH process is reenabled via the **archive log start** command. The ARCH process is temporarily stopped because the backup scripts in the preceding sections all end by deleting the old archived redo log files. You need to be sure that you do not delete a file that has not been backed up. By temporarily disabling archiving, no new files will be created and you can generate a consistent listing of the archive destination directory. This method assumes that if any file is currently being written to the archive destination directory, it will be closed by the time the file is backed up.

There are several alternatives to this method, none of which requires the disabling of the ARCH process. First, you can choose not to delete the old files. If you have enough space available on your disk arrays, keep several days' worth of archived redo log files available on your servers. You can compress the older files to reduce the amount of space required, but you will need to have enough space available to uncompress them during a recovery operation.

As a second option, you can query the V$LOG dynamic dictionary view. The Archived column of the V$LOG will contain a value of YES if the log has been completely archived. You could select the highest archived log from V$LOG (using the Sequence# column) and use that as the basis for your listing of files to be backed up. For example, if V$LOG says that Sequence# 2334 was the last log file to be archived, then you can successfully back up all of the files in your archived redo log destination directory that have sequence numbers of 2334 and below. If you attempt to back up #2335, your backup may succeed at an operating system level, but since the file is not yet fully archived, that backup may be only half-written and therefore may not be useful during a recovery operation.

Ideally, you should maintain enough free space in your archive destination area to store enough compressed archived redo logs to enable you to perform a recovery without needing to recover archived redo log files from tape.

Standby Databases

You can maintain a *standby database* for quick disaster recovery. A standby database maintains a copy of the production database in a permanent state of recovery. In the event of a disaster in the production database, the standby database can be opened with a minimal amount of recovery necessary. You may, however, lose the contents of your online redo log files in your production database during the switch to the standby database. As of ORACLE7.3, the management of standby databases is greatly simplified, and with ORACLE8i the management has become fully automatic.

The standby database must use the same version of the kernel that the production system uses. You can create a standby database from a copy of the current production database (generated via either an offline backup or an online backup). As archived redo log files are generated by the production instance in ORACLE8i, they will be copied to the standby system and applied to the standby database automatically. Maintaining a standby database requires keeping the file structures and software versions of the production and standby databases continuously synchronized. See the *ORACLE Server Administrator's Guide* for detailed directions for setting up and maintaining standby databases.

As of ORACLE8i, you can use the standby database as a read-only database to enable large queries to be run in a nontransaction processing database. However, while the database is in read-only mode, redo log files will not be automatically applied to the database. The database could be placed in read-only mode during the day and then placed into standby mode at night and the redo logs resynchronized. If the standby database—in read-only mode—is needed for recovery during the day, the redo log files must be applied before the standby database can be made available.

Integration of Backup Procedures

Since there are three different methods for backing up the ORACLE database, there is no need to have a single point of failure. Depending on your database's characteristics, one of the three methods should be chosen, and at least one of the two remaining methods should be used to back it up.

In the following sections, you will see how to choose the primary backup method for your database, how to integrate logical and physical backups, and how to integrate database backups with file system backups.

For backup strategies specific to very large databases, see Chapter 12.

Logical and Physical Backups Integration

Which backup method is appropriate for your database? Or rather, which backup method is appropriate to use as the *primary* backup method for your database?

The backup method selection process should take into account the characteristics of each method, as listed in Table 10-6.

As shown in Table 10-6, offline backups are the least flexible method of backing up the database if the database is running in NOARCHIVELOG mode. Offline backups are a point-in-time snapshot of the database; and since they are a physical backup, DBAs cannot selectively recover logical objects (such as tables) from them. Although there are times when they are appropriate, offline backups should normally be used as a fallback position in the event that the primary backup method fails. If you are running the database in ARCHIVELOG mode, you can use the offline backups as the basis for a media recovery, but an online backup would normally be more appropriate for that situation.

Method	Type	Recovery Characteristics
Export	Logical	Can recover any database object to its status as of the moment it was exported.
Offline backups	Physical	Can recover the database to its status as of the moment it was shut down; if the database is run in ARCHIVELOG mode, you can recover the database to its status at any point in time.
Online backups	Physical	Can recover the database to its status at any point in time.

TABLE 10-6.   *Comparison of Characteristics of Backup Methods*

Of the two remaining methods, which one is more appropriate? The answer depends on the nature of your database.

First, consider the recovery requirements. If your database is transaction-intensive, you will most likely want to use online backups. Using online backups will minimize the amount of transaction data lost in the event of a database failure. Using an Export-based strategy would limit you to only being able to go back to the data as it existed the last time the data was exported.

Next, consider the size of the database and what objects you will likely be recovering. Given a standard recovery scenario—such as the loss of a disk—how long will it take for the data to be recovered? If a file is lost, the quickest way to recover it is usually via a physical backup, which again favors online backups over Exports.

There are, however, scenarios in which other methods are preferable. If the database is small and transaction volume is very low, then either offline backups or Export will serve your needs. If you are only concerned about one or two tables, then use Export to selectively back them up. However, if the database is large, then the recovery time needed for Export/Import may be prohibitive. For such large, low-transaction environments, offline backups may be appropriate.

Regardless of your choice for primary backup method, the final implementation should include an Export and a physical backup. This is necessary because these methods validate different aspects of the database: Export validates that the data is logically sound, and physical backups that it is physically sound. Three sample integrations of these methods are shown in Table 10-7.

As shown in Table 10-7, a good database backup strategy integrates logical and physical backups, based on the database's usage characteristics.

Other database activities may call for ad hoc backups. These may include offline backups before performing database upgrades and Exports during application migration between databases.

Database Type	Online Backups	Offline Backups	Exports
All sizes, transaction-intensive	Nightly	Weekly	Weekly
Small, mostly read only	Not done	Weekly	Nightly
Large, mostly read only	Not done	Weekly	Weekly

TABLE 10-7.   *Sample Integration of Database Backup Methods*

Database and Operating System Backups Integration

As described in this chapter, the DBA's backup activities involve a number of tasks normally assigned to a systems management group: monitoring disk usage, maintaining tapes, and so on. Rather than duplicate these efforts, it is best to integrate them. The database backup strategy should be modified so that the systems management personnel's file system backups will take care of all tape handling, allowing you to centralize the production control processes in your environment.

How is this to be done? It is usually accomplished by dedicating disk drives as destination locations for physical file backups. Instead of backing up files to tape drives, the backups will instead be written to other disks on the same server. Those disks should be targeted for backups by the systems management personnel's regular file system backups.

Consider the datafile backups shown earlier in the online backups section of this chapter. The datafiles were written directly to tape via a **tar** command, as shown in this example:

```
REM
REM    Back up the RBS tablespace - directly to tape
REM
alter tablespace RBS begin backup;
!tar -rvf /dev/rmt/0hc /db02/oracle/CC1/rbs01.dbf
alter tablespace RBS end backup;
REM
```

Instead of backing up the files to tape, copy them to the target device for database file backups. For this example, /db10 will be used as the device name. As shown in this listing, the RBS tablespace is put into **begin backup** state. Its files are then copied (here, via the UNIX **cp** command) to a new device, and the tablespace is returned to its normal state.

The commands in the following listing are executed from within Server Manager:

```
REM
REM    Back up the RBS tablespace - to another disk (UNIX)
REM
alter tablespace RBS begin backup;
!cp /db02/oracle/CC1/rbs01.dbf /db10/oracle/CC1/backups
alter tablespace RBS end backup;
REM
```

The VMS version is identical except for the operating system command used. In this case, the **backup** command is used.

The commands in the following listing are executed from within Server Manager:

```
REM
REM    Back up the RBS tablespace - to another disk (VMS)
REM
alter tablespace RBS begin backup;
!backup/ignore=(no backup, interl)DB01:[ORACLE.CC1]RBS01.DBF
DB10:[ORACLE.CC1.BACKUPS]
alter tablespace RBS end backup;
REM
```

To minimize the amount of space required for this task, you may also wish to have the operating system compress the file on the destination device once it has been copied there, if that option is available in your operating system.

Using disk-to-disk backups also changes the way in which archived redo log files are backed up. The new process is shown in the following listing. The UNIX **mv** command is used to move the files to the backup destination device. This does away with the need for the FILES environment variable that was used in the backup-to-tape method. As shown in this listing, the archiving process is temporarily stopped; when the files have all been moved, it is restarted:

```
#
# Procedure for moving archived redo logs to another device
#
svrmgrl <<EOFarch2
connect internal as sysdba
archive log stop;
!mv /db01/oracle/arch/CC1 /db10/oracle/arch/CC1
archive log start;
exit
EOFarch2
#
# end of archived redo log directory move.
```

The control file can also be automatically backed up to the backup destination device. The final distribution of files will resemble that shown in Table 10-8. In this example, the destination device is named /db10.

The /db10 device can then be backed up by the systems management file system backups. The DBA does not have to run a separate tape backup job.

Disk /db01-/db09	**Disk /db10**
Datafiles	Copies of datafiles
Online redo logs	
Archived redo log file directory	Old archived redo log files
Control files	Backed up control file

TABLE 10-8. *File Distribution After Online Backups to a Destination Device*

However, the DBA does need to verify that the systems management team's backup procedures executed correctly and completed successfully.

Recovery Scenarios When Using These Procedures

Unless you test and validate your backup procedures, you cannot be certain that you will be able to recover from *any* type of database failure. Recovery thus begins with testing. Create a sample database and use your chosen procedures. Then test your ability to recover from different types of database failures.

On most servers, the mean time between failure (MTBF) for disks is between three and four years. Failures due to disk errors are the most common hardware failures encountered. The *ORACLE Server Administrator's Guide, ORACLE8 Backup and Recovery Guide,* and the *ORACLE Backup and Recovery Handbook* (by Rama Velpuri, published by Oracle Press) include an exhaustive description of the recovery procedures needed for each type of possible failure.

In the following sections, you will see how to apply the integrated database backups to the three most common scenarios: instance failure, disk failure, and user failure. "User failure" occurs when users execute DDL commands (such as **drop table**) that they need to undo.

Instance Failure

Recovery from instance failure should be automatic. The database will need access to all of its control files, online redo log files, and datafiles—in their proper locations. Any uncommitted transactions that existed in the database will be rolled back. Following an instance failure, such as one brought on by a server failure, be sure to check the alert log for the database for any error messages when the database attempts to restart itself.

When the database is started following an instance failure, ORACLE checks the datafiles and the online redo log files and synchronizes all the files to the same point in time. ORACLE will perform this synchronization even if the database is not running in ARCHIVELOG mode.

Media (Disk) Failure

Disk failure, also called *media failure,* occurs when a disk on which an active database file resides becomes unreadable by the database. Media failure may occur due to a disk crash or to a compilation of read errors on the disk. Either way, the files on the disk must be replaced.

The disks on which *online redo log files* reside should always be mirrored (either by using redo log groups or by mirroring files at the operating system level). Since these files are mirrored, they should never be lost due to a media failure.

This leaves three types of files to consider: control files, archived redo log files, and datafiles.

If the lost file is a *control file,* it is easy to recover regardless of the backup method chosen. Every database should have multiple copies of its control file (which the database will keep in sync), all stored on different devices. The default database creation scripts generated by the ORACLE Installer create three control files for each database and locate them on three different drives. To recover from the loss of a control file, shut the database down and copy one of the remaining control files to the proper location.

If all control files are lost, you can use the **create controlfile** command. This command allows you to create a new control file for the database, specifying all of the datafiles, online redo logs, and database parameters that are in the database. If you are unsure of the parameters to use here and you are running ARCHIVELOG backups, there is a helpful command available. It is

```
alter database backup controlfile to trace;
```

When you execute this command, the proper **create controlfile** command will be written to a trace file. You can then edit the trace file created by ORACLE as necessary. Do not use the **create controlfile** command unless *all* of the control files have been lost.

If the lost file is an *archived redo log file,* you cannot recover it. For this reason, it is important that the archived redo log file destination device be mirrored as well. Archived redo log files should be regarded as being as important as the online redo log files. See the "Automating Multiplexing of Archived Redo Log Files" section earlier in this chapter for methods to automatically maintain multiple copies of your archived redo log files.

If the lost file is a *datafile*, it can be recovered from the previous night's hot backup. Follow these steps:

1. Restore the lost file from the backup to its original location.

   ```
   cp /db10/oracle/CC1/data01.dbf /db03/oracle/CC1/data01.dbf
   ```

   You will now have the current control files, the current online redo log files, and current versions of all datafiles except for the one you just recovered. ORACLE will realize the old datafile is not current and will not open the database. You can now recover the data in the old file (making it current) by applying all of the archived redo log files since the old datafile was backed up.

2. Mount the database.

   ```
   ORACLE_SID=cc1; export ORACLE_SID
   ORAENV_ASK=NO; export ORAENV_ASK
   . oraenv
   svrmgrl
   SVRMGR> connect internal as sysdba
   SVRMGR> startup mount cc1;
   ```

3. Recover the database. You will be prompted for the name of each archived redo log file that is needed for recovery.

   ```
   SVRMGR> recover database;
   ```

   When prompted, enter the filenames for the requested archived redo log files. Alternatively, you can use the AUTO option when prompted by the database recovery operation. The AUTO option uses the defined archive log destination directory and filename format to generate default values for archived redo log filenames. If you have moved archived redo log files, you will not be able to use the AUTO option.

4. Open the database.

   ```
   SVRMGR> alter database open;
   ```

When the datafile is restored from the backup, the database will recognize that it is from an earlier point in time than the rest of the database. To bring it forward in time, it will apply the transactions it finds in the archived redo log files.

The datafiles may be recovered from either the hot or the cold backup (if the database was in ARCHIVELOG mode at the time). If there are complications with the recovery, such as corruption in the files, see the recovery documentation referred to earlier in this chapter for a full list of your options.

Usually, a media recovery is performed using the current control file. If no current control file is available, then you can restore an old control file and use it during the recovery. In that scenario, you would have current online redo log files, at least one old datafile, the rest of the current datafiles, and old control files. When you recover the database while using old control files, you need to let ORACLE know that you are using a backup control file; otherwise, there would be no way to apply changes from the archived redo logs that occurred at a time after the timestamp in the control file. In this case, use the following command to recover the database:

```
SVRMGR> recover database using backup controlfile;
```

Recovering Accidentally Dropped or Altered Objects

Occasionally, users will make errors that they will not be able to roll back or undo. Such errors may consist of DDL commands, such as **alter table** and **drop table**, or DML commands, such as **update** and **delete**.

In such cases, the users' desire is to return to a point in time prior to the database event that they wish to retract. This calls for a point-in-time recovery.

The simplest type of point-in-time recovery uses the most recent export dump file. If the user can go back that far in time, then this may be an acceptable alternative. Use the Import commands shown earlier in this chapter to selectively import the objects and users desired.

However, going back to the last Export may not suffice. The users may need a more up-to-date version of the table—for example, as it existed an hour before the offending command was executed.

To perform a point-in-time recovery, you must be running in ARCHIVELOG mode. Follow these steps:

1. There are two options for the first step for this method of recovery:

   a. Back up the current database (via an offline backup, usually) and replace it with a prior version of itself, then roll that version forward in time to the desired time;

   b. Create a database with the same instance name on a different server, leaving the current database intact, while using the prior version of the primary database as the basis for the second database.

   Regardless of the option chosen, the second step is the same.

2. Roll the temporary database forward in time, using the following command from within Server Manager in place of the **recover database** command used for normal recoveries: The date is in the format

"YYYY-MM-DD:HH24:MI:SS". The sample date below is for August 7 (08-07), 1999, at 2:40 P.M. (14:40).

```
SVRMGR> connect internal as sysdba
SVRMGR> startup mount instance_name;
SVRMGR> recover database until time '1999-08-07:14:40:00';
```

3. While still in Server Manager, open the database using the **resetlogs** option of the **alter database open** command. This command forces the database to reset the redo log sequence number information in the control files and the online redo log files. This in turn makes sure that any redo log entry data that followed the **recover database until time** specification will not be applied to the database.

```
SVRMGR> alter database open resetlogs;
```

The database will now be opened and available, and will look as it did at the time specified during the **recover database until time** command. The dropped or altered objects can now be backed up via Export.

4. Export the logical objects that were affected.

```
> exp system/manager file=saved.dmp tables=(owner.tablename)
```

The altered or dropped objects are now recorded in the export dump file. The temporary database created in step 1 can now be dropped.

5. Restore the production database to its former state. Then use the export dump file created in step 4 to Import the altered/dropped objects back into the production database in their former state.

6. After restoring the production database, prepare it for the Import of the old version of the data. These preparations may involve dropping the objects that were altered by the users. Once this is complete, Import the earlier versions of those objects from the export dump file. The production database is thus returned to its state before step 1, and the damaged objects have been replaced by their earlier incarnations.

```
> imp system/manager file=saved.dmp full=Y commit=Y buffer=64000
```

The purpose of the integration of the available backup methods is to be able to recover easily from the most common types of failures. Since each backup method has different characteristics, the proper combination of backup methods will vary from database to database. Regardless of the backup methods chosen, they should be integrated with the regular file system backups and *tested*. Properly used, they will be able to support the recovery from any type of database crash.

The steps shown in this section allow you to perform a point-in-time recovery of one part of the database. For example, you could create a temporary database, roll it forward to a point in time, and Export just one table from it. You could then Import that data into your primary database, and the Imported data would reflect data from a different point in time than the rest of the database.

Because you are relying on Export and Import, the performance of this recovery option may not meet your timing requirements. As of ORACLE8, ORACLE provides a new mechanism for performing point-in-time recovery for part of the database. ORACLE now supports point-in-time recovery for tablespaces. The method provided by ORACLE may improve the performance of your recoveries since they do not involve using Import to load the data into the primary database, but rather rely on using the temporary database's datafiles during the recovery. The ORACLE tablespace point-in-time recovery option is limited to tablespaces; you cannot recover only one object out of a tablespace. For full details on this advanced recovery option, see the *ORACLE8 Backup and Recovery Guide*, part of the standard ORACLE documentation set.

Parallel Recovery

You can use the Parallel Recovery option to execute multiple recovery processes. A single Server Manager session can read the archived redo log files during a media recovery, and can pass the recovery information to multiple recovery processes, which apply the changes to the datafiles concurrently. The recovery processes are automatically started and managed by ORACLE. If you have a very long recovery process and your datafiles are distributed among many disks, using Parallel Recovery may improve your recovery performance.

To use Parallel Recovery, set a value for the RECOVERY_PARALLELISM parameter in your instance's init.ora file. RECOVERY_PARALLELISM specifies the number of concurrent processes that will participate in Parallel Recovery during instance or media recovery. A value of 0 indicates that recovery is performed serially by a single process.

For media recovery, the RECOVERY_PARALLELISM setting is the default degree of parallelism unless overridden by the **parallel** clause of the **recover** command. The RECOVERY_PARALLELISM setting cannot be greater than the PARALLEL_MAX_SERVERS setting.

If you have an I/O-intensive recovery process (which is typical), and you cannot spread the I/O across many disks, then you may not see any performance benefit from Parallel Recovery. In fact, the increased I/O bottleneck may degrade your performance. You should therefore be sure that your disk environment is highly distributed before implementing Parallel Recovery.

Recovery Manager

As of ORACLE8, the OEM tool set includes a Recovery Manager tool. There are really two forms of interaction you can use—RMAN command line mode or the

Backup Manager from within the Storage Manager tool. To use the Backup Manager, you must enter the tool using the Management Server console.

The Recovery Manager keeps track of your backups either through a Recovery Catalog or by placing the required information into the control file for the database being backed up. The Recovery Manager adds new backup capabilities that are unavailable in the other ORACLE backup utilities. The Recovery Manager product replaces the Enterprise Backup Utility introduced with later versions of ORACLE7.

Recovery Manager does not shield you from the backup steps described in this chapter and it does not simplify your recovery strategy. In fact, since it adds new features, it may complicate your recovery strategy.

The most significant new capability provided via Recovery Manager is the ability to perform incremental physical backups of your datafiles. During a full (called a *level 0*) datafile backup, all of the blocks ever used in the datafile are backed up. During a cumulative (*level 1*) datafile backup, all of the blocks used since the last full datafile backup are backed up. An incremental (*level 2*) datafile backup backs up only those blocks that have changed since the most recent cumulative or full backup. You can define the levels used for incremental backups.

The ability to perform incremental and cumulative backups of datafiles may greatly improve the performance of your backups. The greatest performance improvements will be realized by very large databases in which only a small subset of a large tablespace changes. Using the traditional backup methods, you would need to back up all of the datafiles in the tablespace. Using Recovery Manager, you only back up the blocks that have changed since the last backup.

Using Recovery Manager, however, does not diminish your backup planning issues. For example, what type of datafile backup will you use? What are the implications for your recovery procedures? What tapes and backup media will you need to have available in order to perform a recovery? Will you use a recovery catalog or have the catalog data be placed in your control file? You should only use backup procedures that fit your specific database backup performance and capability requirements.

During database recovery using Recovery Manager, you will need to know which files are current, which are restored, and the backup method you plan to use. In its present form, Recovery Manager does not shield you from the commands needed to recover the database. Also, Recovery Manager stores its catalog of information in an ORACLE database—and you need to back up *that* database or else you may lose your entire backup and recovery catalog of information.

Using the OEM Backup Manager

The first decision to make when using the Backup Manager is whether to store the recovery catalog information in a recovery catalog in a database or in the database control file. By default, if a recovery catalog does not exist when the Backup Manager is activated, the control file will be used. Since the Recovery Manager can obtain its required information directly from the database control file, the Recovery Manager can function without a recovery catalog being created. If the control file is used, no operational setup must be performed. However, using the control file in place of a recovery catalog is only recommended for small databases. If the control file is used and gets damaged or lost, the database cannot be recovered.

To create a recovery catalog, perform the following steps:

1. Create a tablespace named RCVCAT to house the recovery catalog.

2. Create a user to own the recovery catalog using the Security Manager.

3. Use the RMAN line mode commands to create the recovery catalog.

4. Register the recovery catalog.

Step 1. Create a tablespace named RCVCAT to house the recovery catalog.

The steps for creating a tablespace within OEM were shown earlier in this chapter (see Figures 10-15 to 10-18). Use the Storage Manager to create the tablespace and ensure that the tablespace's datafile is large enough to house the recovery catalog. The size will depend on the number of databases whose recovery information will be housed in the catalog.

NOTE
The tablespace's default storage parameters will be used to size all of the objects that are created when the utility to create the recovery catalog is run.

Step 2. Create a user to own the recovery catalog.

Using the Security Manager, create a user to own the recovery catalog. The ORACLE documentation suggests using the name RMAN identified by RMAN. The user's default tablespace is RCVCAT and the temporary tablespace is the name of the temporary tablespace in the database. The user should be granted the RECOVERY_CATALOG_OWNER privilege and unlimited quota on the RCVCAT tablespace.

Step 3. Use the RMAN line-mode commands to create the recovery catalog.

To create the recovery catalog for the user RMAN identified by RMAN, from the operating system command line type the following command:

```
rman rcvcat rman/rman@<database_service_name>
```

Issue the catalog creation commands as follows:
For UNIX, type:

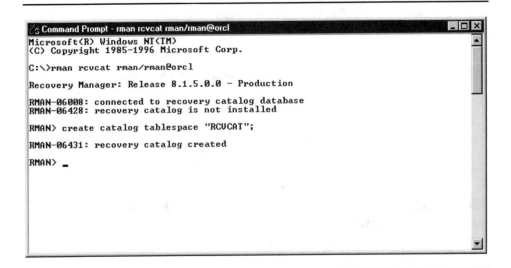

```
RMAN> create catalog tablespace rcvcat;
```

For Windows NT, type:

```
RMAN> create catalog tablespace "RCVCAT";
```

Figure 10-29 shows the output of the procedure for a Windows NT recovery catalog creation. Note the two RMAN messages when connecting to the RMAN utility. They are normal and expected.

Step 4. Register the recovery catalog.

To register the recovery catalog, start the OEM console. Select the database for which you are registering the recovery catalog. Either click the right mouse button and select the Backup Manager option to Create Backup Configuration or use the pull-down Create Backup Configuration option from the Backup Manager option under the Tools menu. Figure 10-30 shows the General tab filled in. Figure 10-31 shows the channel information. When a channel is allocated, a connection is made from the Recovery Manager to the database. The channel starts an ORACLE server session and performs the necessary backup or recovery operation. The type of

```
Command Prompt - rman rcvcat rman/rman@orcl                    _ □ ×
Microsoft(R) Windows NT(TM)
(C) Copyright 1985-1996 Microsoft Corp.

C:\>rman rcvcat rman/rman@orcl

Recovery Manager: Release 8.1.5.0.0 - Production

RMAN-06008: connected to recovery catalog database
RMAN-06428: recovery catalog is not installed

RMAN> create catalog tablespace "RCVCAT";

RMAN-06431: recovery catalog created

RMAN> _
```

FIGURE 10-29. *Creating the RMAN recovery catalog*

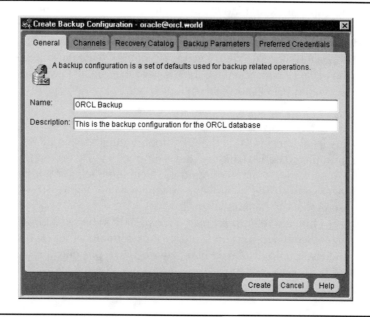

FIGURE 10-30.   *The Create Backup Configuration General screen*

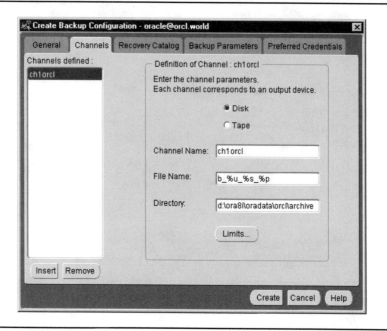

FIGURE 10-31.   *The Create Backup Configuration Channels screen*

channel designated will determine the action to be performed—a read, write, or that a third-party media manager is to be used. Channels can always read and write to and from datafiles regardless of the channel type that has been designated.

Figure 10-32 shows the Recovery Catalog tab of the Create Backup Configuration screen with the initial information filled in. The last tab to be filled out is the Preferred Credentials tab. Figure 10-33 shows this tab filled out.

Performing a Backup with OEM

To perform any level backup using the OEM tool, connect to the OEM console, select the appropriate database and use the right-click mouse button to bring up the database options. From the database options, select the Backup option from the Backup Manager menu. The Backup Wizard will activate. Figure 10-34 shows the Introduction screen of the Backup Wizard.

The Strategy choice screen, presented after you click the Next button, gives the option of using a predefined backup strategy or customizing your own strategy. The predefined strategy will be displayed here. Figure 10-35 presents the backup strategy screen.

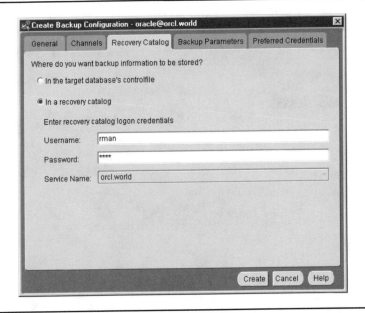

FIGURE 10-32. *The Create Backup Configuration Recovery Catalog screen*

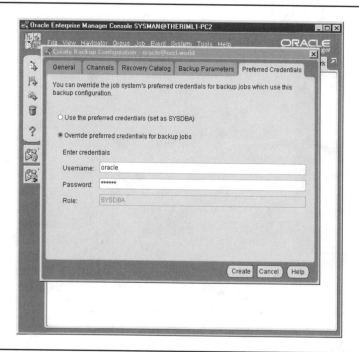

FIGURE 10-33. *The Create Backup Configuration Preferred Credentials screen*

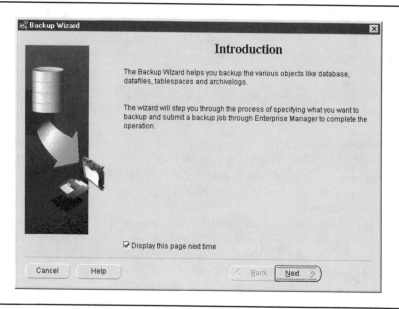

FIGURE 10-34. *The Backup Wizard Introduction screen*

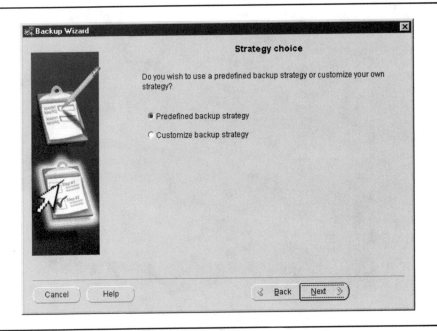

FIGURE 10-35. *The Backup Wizard Strategy Choice screen*

Figure 10-36 displays the Backup Frequency options screen with three choices:

1. A Decision Support System (DSS) with a backup frequency of once a week

2. A moderately updated system (OLTP) that is not very large with a backup frequency of every day

3. A frequently updated, medium to large database with a backup frequency of full backups weekly and incremental backups nightly

The default option is a DSS system backed up once a week on Sunday. For the once-a-week backup, the next screen enables you to select an appropriate time for the backup to be performed. Figure 10-37 shows the Backup Time screen.

The default value is 12:00 A.M. The next screen, Figure 10-38, shows the selected configuration.

Once the configuration is accepted, the tool enables you to declare whether the configuration should be used on multiple destinations. In this example, only one database is available and has been preselected by the tool. Figure 10-39 shows the Multiple Destinations screen.

The only choices from this screen are Back, Finish, Cancel, and Help. When Finish is selected, a summary sheet is presented. Figure 10-40 displays the summary sheet.

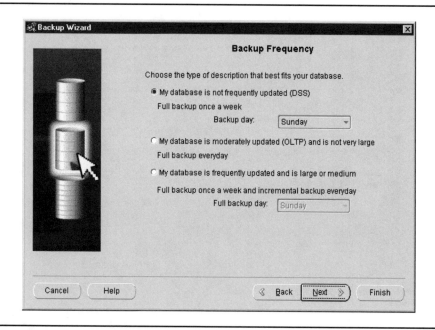

FIGURE 10-37.   *The Backup Wizard Backup Frequency screen*

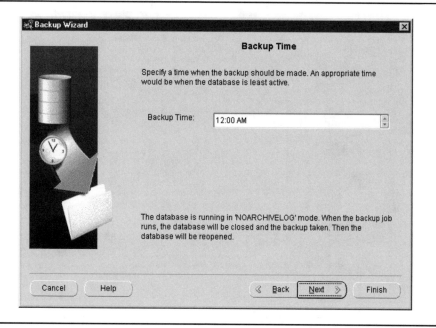

FIGURE 10-36.   *The Backup Wizard Backup Time screen*

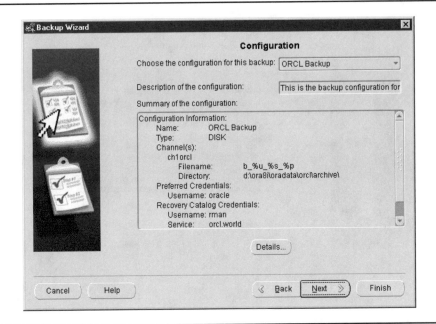

FIGURE 10-38. *The Backup Wizard Configuration Confirmation screen*

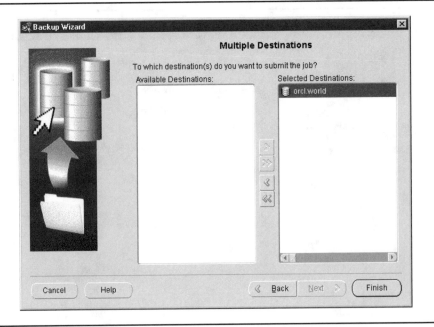

FIGURE 10-39. *The Backup Wizard Multiple Destinations screen*

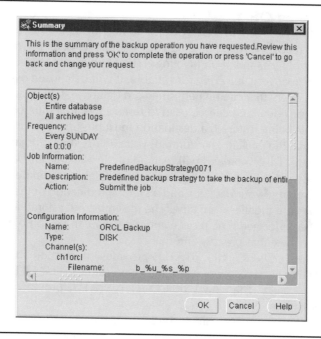

FIGURE 10-40.   *The Backup Wizard Summary screen*

To verify that the backup job has been stored in the Backup Manager, use the right-click mouse button from the Database option in the OEM console to enable selecting the Backup configuration library screen under the Backup Manager option. The next illustration shows this screen with the newly created configuration.

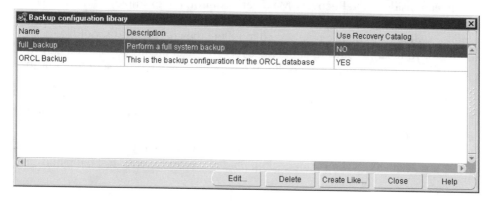

To perform an immediate backup, you can choose the Customize option. The option, although not selected, is shown in Figure 10-35.

Recovery Using OEM

You can use RMAN directly through command line prompts or through the OEM tool to perform recovery. Using RMAN, you can recover datafiles, tablespaces, full databases, control files, and/or archive logs. The Recovery Manager will select the best strategy for recovery. If a copy is available, it will be chosen over a backup set. The types of recovery that can be performed are database, tablespace, and datafile. The **set newname** command can be used to restore files to a different location and, if a control file is being restored, a destination must be supplied.

To ensure that the backup is restorable, you can use the command **restore database validate**. This command will read all of the backups and validate the tape for I/O errors. By periodically running the **restore database validate** command, you will get a validation of your backups and a general indication of the amount of time it will take to restore the files from tape. The files must be restored from tape before recovery can be performed. The restore and recovery can be combined in one routine to make the entire process automatic.

The view V$RECOVERY_FILE_STATUS provides information about the particular files that need recovery while the view V$RECOVER_FILE shows which datafiles need recovery. The view V$RECOVERY_STATUS provides overall recovery information.

You can track the progress of the recovery using the view V$SESSION_LONGOPS while using the following query and look for increasing values:

```
select ROUND(Sofar/Totalwork*100,2)
   from V$SESSION_LONGOPS;
```

Your recovery job should be the only job running at the time, so the query result will show the percentage of the recovery that has completed.

Whether you use RMAN directly or through the OEM facility, you need to ensure that the recovery catalog remains synchronized with any files that have been changed outside of the Recovery Manager's control. For example, if an archived redo log file is moved or a file-level backup is performed manually, the recovery catalog will need to be resynchronized to reflect the change. You should store copies of your scripts outside of the Recovery Manager facility so that you can manually run them if you need to. Be sure to periodically test the scripts to ensure that they will operate properly when needed.

You can use the scripts and methods provided in this chapter to successfully back up your database. As the Recovery Manager product matures, you may wish to migrate your backup procedures to use that tool. No matter what tool you use, you should ensure that your backups accurately reflect your recovery requirements. Once you have established your backup procedures and scripts, test them and document your recovery procedures and the performance you experienced. You will then be able to implement the available procedures in a way that makes the most sense for your installation. The result should be a well-protected database and quick, efficient recoveries. And that, in turn, should lead to fewer calls to ORACLE Support at 3:00 A.M.

CHAPTER
11

Managing Oracle
Financials and Other
Packages and Utilities

hen you install a software package that will be used with your ORACLE database, you will normally customize the front-end portion of the application to reflect your business practices. Just as your business requirements lead to customizations of the front end, the back-end portion of the application will likely need to be modified. To get the most out of the package, you will need to modify the default database structures used by the package. In this chapter, you will see guidelines for managing packages. Specific guidelines are provided for ORACLE Financials, Oracle Designer (ORACLE's CASE tool), and the ORACLE utilities such as ConText and SQL*Loader.

General Guidelines for Managing Packages

To effectively manage packages, you must know the technical details of the packages and the business processes being served by the packages. In most cases, the default installation of packaged software does not seamlessly meet your business process requirements. As a result, there may be a problem with the space management or performance of the package when it is installed. As the package use increases, the number of problems associated with the package increases.

If you start with a database environment that does not properly support the package, then the burden of production usage will quickly cause a problem. Production problems may include transactions that fail to complete, queries that run excessively long, or segments that cannot allocate enough space. All of these production problems will cause either a production service outage or a severe performance problem for the package. On the other hand, if you start with a production environment that is flexible and supportive of the package, then you will improve your ability to respond to production crises. The better you understand how the package will be used, the better you will be able to tune the environment prior to production release of the package.

To effectively manage packaged software, you need to provide a database environment that is as stable as possible. In this section, you will see guidelines for customizing database structures, managing transactions, monitoring, and other system-level considerations. Following this section of this chapter, you will see application-specific guidelines for ORACLE Financials, Oracle Designer, ConText, and other packages.

Customizing Database Structures

If you are installing third-party software that was not written by ORACLE Corporation, you should not assume that the software will take proper advantage of

ORACLE-specific features such as sequences, stored procedures, triggers, and the ORACLE optimizer. You should also question the package's data distribution, space allocation assumptions, and indexing schemes. Many software vendors support multiple database platforms, requiring them to keep their products as generic as possible.

If the package was developed by ORACLE Corporation (such as ORACLE Financials or Oracle Designer), then you should focus your database structure customization efforts on supporting the business processes unique to your business. For example, if your business performs many iterations of its budgeting process, you should size the ORACLE Financials tables that store budgeting information differently than if your business performs few budgeting iterations.

Database structures that should be customized include tablespaces, indexes, and rollback segments, as described in the following sections.

Tablespaces

In general, most packages developed by companies other than ORACLE Corporation will use as few tablespaces as possible. For example, a package may expect the following tablespaces to be created within your database (in addition to SYSTEM, TEMP, and ROLLBACK):

APP_TABLES	For all application tables
APP_INDEXES	For all application indexes

When the package is installed, all of its tables are created within the APP_TABLES tablespace, and all of its indexes are created within the APP_INDEXES tablespace (although some packages do not, by default, store their tables and indexes in different tablespaces). Although this may make it simpler to manage tables and indexes, this design fails to take into account the different kinds of tables involved in an application. For example, some of their tables may be small and static, while others are large and highly volatile.

In Chapter 3, you saw recommendations for extensions beyond the typical Optimal Flexible Architecture (OFA) tablespace architecture. The DATA_2 tablespace was identified for low-usage data segments, and INDEXES_2 for those tables' indexes. Consider a modified set of application tablespaces:

APPS_TABLES	For high-use application tables
APPS_STATIC_TABLES	For static application tables
APPS_INDEXES	For high-use application indexes
APPS_STATIC_INDEXES	For static application indexes

By removing the static tables and indexes from the main application tablespaces, you simplify the management of the space within all tablespaces. Under the revised tablespace organization, the APPS_STATIC_TABLES and APPS_STATIC_INDEXES tablespaces should require very little direct management, allowing you to focus your management and tuning efforts on the main data tablespaces. Isolating the tables across tablespaces in this manner also separates the active and static tables into separate datafiles, simplifying the management of I/O distribution.

You may wish to further divide the highly used application tables. For example, if your package uses many "interim" tables that are used during data interface processing, you may separate those tables from the rest of the high-use application tables. You can also add tablespaces to support the specific temporary segment requirements and transaction sizes for the package.

NOTE
If you modify the tablespace assignments of the package's tables and indexes, you may need to modify scripts provided by the vendor for subsequent upgrades, since the vendor's scripts may assume that the objects are in their original tablespaces. Also, if the owning schema for the application has APPS_TABLES as its default tablespace, then any upgrade script that performs a **create table** *or* **create index** *command will create the objects in the APPS_TABLES tablespace unless the command explicitly names a tablespace. This may cause objects you have moved out of APPS_TABLES to be moved back into APPS_TABLES during the upgrade process.*

Indexes

You cannot conceive all of the questions your users may ask of the database; a developer who does not work for your company likely cannot conceive of your users' demands either. As a result, any package in which users can perform ad hoc queries will likely encounter performance problems for a small set of queries. Although those queries may be few in number, they can consume enough of the available system resources to negatively impact every other user of the database.

The most common cause of such resource-intensive queries is a lack of appropriate indexes. Until you understand how your users, in carrying out their business processes, will use the package, you cannot fully understand the data access paths required. As such, you cannot fully identify all of the indexes the users require. If you understand the business processes well, you may identify many of the key indexes; but since you are using package software, you may not be able to see all of the SQL that the package is executing, and thus may be unable to properly index the tables until the problem SQL is identified—via user complaints.

Indexes may become stale over time. As records are deleted from a table, the matching entries are deleted from the table's indexes. The space released within the table may be reused, but the space released within the index may not be reused. Thus, an indexed table from which rows are frequently deleted should have its indexes periodically rebuilt in order to avoid space fragmentation within the index. The most common occurrence of this problem is found in tables used temporarily during loading processes. For example, if the package **insert**s received records into an interim table, processes the records, and then **delete**s the records from the interim table, then the table's indexes will continue to grow over time, even though there are no rows in the table. To avoid this problem, you should periodically **truncate** the table when it is empty; the **truncate** command cannot be rolled back, and it deletes all rows from the table. The **truncate** command also eliminates the index fragmentation and reduces the table to a single extent (by default; you can use the **reuse storage** option of the **truncate** command to retain the previously allocated extents).

If the tables grow so quickly that the vendor provides a data archiving mechanism, be prepared to frequently rebuild the indexes. The data archiving process usually consists of deleting data older than a set time. As a result of periodic large **delete**s, the index becomes more fragmented and stagnant with each archive. Following each archiving operation, you should rebuild the indexes.

Rollback Segments

Most packages contain an online user component—for data entry or ad hoc reporting—and a batch processing component—for large data processing operations. The online users need enough rollback segments to support the number of concurrent transactions they generate. The batch processes require rollback segments large enough to support the largest batch transaction. In Chapter 7, you saw how to determine the number of rollback segments needed, and their size. If one of the transactions in the package is significantly larger than any other transaction in the package, then you should create a rollback segment that is specifically designed to support this transaction. The special rollback segment should be stored in its own tablespace (see Chapter 3). Before starting the transaction, issue the **set transaction use rollback segment** command to force the transaction to use that rollback segment. You will need to repeat that command after every **commit** within the transaction.

If you cannot alter the transaction code to include the **set transaction use rollback segment** command, then you should schedule the transaction to occur at a specific time when no online users will be active within the database. Immediately prior to the start of the transaction, take the other rollback segments in the database offline, leaving only the SYSTEM rollback segment and the special rollback segment online. Use the **alter rollback segment** *segment_name* **offline** command to take the rollback segments offline (see Chapter 7 for the Oracle Enterprise Manager methods for activating and deactivating rollback segments). When the transaction starts, it will be forced to use the special rollback segment. When the transaction completes, bring the rest of the rollback segments back online.

Temporary Segments

Batch transactions may require large temporary segments for their processing. For example, large data loads using the SQL*Loader Direct Path option require temporary segments to hold the data from the table's indexes during the data load. If you make extensive use of the Parallel Query Option (PQO) during index creations, then you may need to support a large number of temporary segments since each parallel query server process may obtain a temporary segment. If you use many concurrent parallel query server processes during the batch processing, your temporary segment space requirements will most likely exceed the resources normally available for users of the package.

Depending on the nature of the application, you may want to segregate users—or application schema owners—into different sets of temporary tablespaces. You could, for example, create four separate temporary tablespaces and split your online user community into four sets. If the users' temporary tablespace requirements are separated in this manner, users will have less impact on each other during processes that require temporary segments. If a single transaction or query requires a much larger temporary segment than any other transaction or query in the package, then you should give the users of that transaction or query a default temporary tablespace that is specifically designed to support the transaction.

Table and Index Sizes

For small, stagnant tables, the default table and index sizes that come with the package are usually accurate—particularly if the package was developed by ORACLE Corporation. You should, however, still validate the default storage parameters against your space estimates (see Chapter 5). For large or very active tables, you should assume that the default storage parameters for the tables are incorrect. There is no way for the application developers to know exactly how you will use the package, so you will need to customize the table and index sizes to support your anticipated data volumes.

Do not rely on periodic table defragmentation via Export/Import to do all of the resizing work that needs to be done. For example, consider a table that was not properly sized when the package was first made available to users. The table has an **initial** extent size of 100KB, with a **next** extent size of 100KB and a **pctincrease** value of 0. Each extent of the table will be 100KB in size. Within the first month of usage, the table reaches ten extents—and it is clear that as more users are added to the system, the rate of space increases in the table will increase. If you use Export/Import to compress the table's extents to a single extent, then the new storage parameters will be **initial** 1MB, **next** 100KB. Thus, although the Export/Import process may give you a better size for your **initial** extent, it will do nothing to resolve the problems with your **next** extent size. You will need to manually alter the table to reflect a more appropriate **next** extent size.

Many vendors provide sizing spreadsheets you can use to estimate the space usage for the application's objects. DBAs must work with the application team to ensure the sizing exercise is performed prior to application implementation. Depending on the calculations involved, the vendor's sizing calculations may be very time-consuming.

Managing the PCTUSED Setting

Each ORACLE table has a setting for the **pctused** storage parameter; the parameter's value defaults to 40. In most applications, setting **pctused** to 40 does not cause a problem. However, package applications that have been ported to ORACLE may cause space usage problems associated with the **pctused** setting.

The **pctused** parameter sets the minimum percentage of a database block that must be used. If the database block's used space percentage falls below **pctused**, then the block will be added to the list of free blocks in the table and a new record may be written to the block. If the space usage stays above **pctused**, then the block will not be eligible to receive any new records.

Some applications that are ported to ORACLE do not take advantage of ORACLE's locking mechanisms. To avoid encountering a locking problem, those applications may perform **delete**s followed by **insert**s. If an application performs many **delete**s and **insert**s, then the blocks in the tables will not use their space efficiently unless you have altered **pctused**.

Consider this scenario: an application creates many rows in a table whose **pctused** parameter is set to the default value of 40. A large number of rows are then **update**d, which the application performs by deleting old rows and inserting new rows. When the old rows are **delete**d, ORACLE evaluates the used space percentage for the block. If the used space percentage is greater than 40, then the block cannot accept new rows. When the **insert** is performed, the new row is written to a different block, and the space used by the old row is left empty. When this occurs repeatedly, you will find that your tables will have blocks that are only 40 to 50 percent used, doubling your space requirements!

To avoid this problem, set the **pctused** parameter to a high value (70 or greater) for any table that is subject to frequent **delete/insert** transactions. You will need to work with your package application vendor to determine if this will be a problem in your environment.

Managing the Shared SQL Pool

NOTE
*In this section only, the term "package" refers to stored PL/SQL objects created via the **create package** command.*

PL/SQL objects, when used, are stored in the library cache of the shared SQL area within the System Global Area (SGA). If a package has already been loaded into memory by a user, then other users will experience improved performance when executing that package. Keeping a package "pinned" in memory decreases the response time for the user during procedure executions.

To improve the ability to keep large PL/SQL objects pinned in the library cache, you should load them into the SGA as soon as the database is opened. Pinning packages immediately after startup increases the likelihood that a contiguous section of memory will be available to store the package. You can use the DBMS_SHARED_POOL package to pin PL/SQL objects in the SGA. To use DBMS_SHARED_POOL, you first need to reference the objects that you want to pin in memory. To load a package in memory, you can reference a dummy procedure defined in the package or you can recompile the package.

Once the object has been referenced, you can execute the DBMS_SHARED_POOL.KEEP procedure to pin the object. The KEEP procedure of DBMS_SHARED_POOL, as shown in the following listing, takes as its input parameters the name of the object and the type of object ('P' for packages is the default).

```
alter procedure APPOWNER.ADD_CLIENT compile;
execute DBMS_SHARED_POOL.KEEP('APPOWNER.ADD_CLIENT','P');
```

NOTE
The DBMS_SHARED_POOL package is not created by the catalog.sql file. You may need to run the dbmspool.sql script (while logged in as SYS) in order to create this package. The script is located in the /rdbms/admin subdirectory under the ORACLE software home directory.

The example shown in the preceding listing illustrates the two-step process involved in pinning packages in memory: the package is first referenced (via the compilation step) and is then marked for keeping. Pinning your most-used packages in memory immediately after startup will improve your chances of acquiring contiguous space for them within the SGA.

Each database will have two sets of packages to pin: the core set used by each database and the set of packages specific to a particular application. The core set of packages to pin usually includes the SYS-owned packages STANDARD, DBMS_SQL, DBMS_UTILITY, and DIUTIL. To determine which packages should be pinned for your instance, query DBA_OBJECT_SIZE. You should pin the largest packages first. To determine packages to pin and the order in which to pin them, use the script shown in the following listing. The script uses the DBA_OBJECT_SIZE view to list the order in which the objects will be pinned.

```
select Owner,
       Name,
       Type,
  Source_Size+Code_Size+Parsed_Size+Error_Size   Total_Bytes
   from DBA_OBJECT_SIZE
  where Type in ('PACKAGE BODY','PROCEDURE')
  order by 4 desc;
```

In addition to pinning packages, there are two additional options that you can use to improve your management of the shared SQL area. Both are controlled via init.ora parameters: SHARED_POOL_RESERVED_SIZE and LARGE_POOL_SIZE.

SHARED_POOL_RESERVED_SIZE sets the size, in bytes, of the portion of the shared SQL area that will be devoted to requests for large amounts of contiguous memory. By default, SHARED_POOL_RESERVED_SIZE will be set to 5 percent of the shared SQL area. If you use SHARED_POOL_RESERVED_SIZE effectively, you will not need to pin many packages. You can establish a minimum size for entries in the reserved area via the SHARED_POOL_RESERVED_MIN_ALLOC; however, that parameter is being desupported as of ORACLE8i.

Despite its name, the LARGE_POOL_SIZE parameter does not provide an area for pinning large objects; rather, it devotes a portion of the shared SQL area to parallel query operations, multithreaded server memory, and backup operations. In ORACLE8.0, you can set the minimum size for an entry in the large pool via the LARGE_POOL_MIN_ALLOC parameter, but that parameter is being desupported as of ORACLE8i. ORACLE will automatically set a value for LARGE_POOL_SIZE whenever you use the Parallel Query Option, DBWR I/O slaves, or the multithreaded server.

Security and Data Access Control

In addition to the database structures you need to alter, you should examine the way in which the package implements security. The assumptions that the developers of the package made regarding security may not be valid in your environment since the developers did not have access to your database and your company's security policies when developing the package. As a result, you may find that the application requires that all users have DBA privilege, or that users share accounts, or that user passwords can be easily seen during regular use of the package. You should work with the package vendor to determine whether the package can be implemented along the guidelines specified in your corporate security guidelines.

Within the database, you should determine if the application makes extensive use of roles, and which roles must be the default roles for the user. If there are many roles within the package, or if the database supports multiple applications, then you may reach the limit on the number of roles permitted per user (set via the MAX_ENABLED_ROLES init.ora parameter). Try to reduce the number of system privileges (such as ALTER ANY TABLE) granted to the roles used by the package. Often, packages will by default use a higher level of access than required—such as requiring DBA role access when the users just need the ALTER USER privilege so they can change their passwords. See Chapter 9 for details on user configuration commands.

Some applications provide little or no security within the database; if you can connect to the database then you can access most of the data. In order to provide a generic security interface, the vendor may have to create its own table of users and passwords; connections to the application would be validated against this table. Although such a scheme may give the vendor a flexible, generic security solution, it may be a source of security vulnerabilities within your database. To avoid malicious or accidental damage to the database, usernames and passwords should be closely guarded. You should also use the PRODUCT_USER_PROFILE tables to restrict access within SQL*Plus, as described in Chapter 9.

Transaction Management

Transaction management for a package requires understanding the batch and online portions of the application, and separating their processing to the greatest extent possible. Most of the problems with transactions in an application arise from the concurrent scheduling of long-running batch processes and online transactions. See Chapter 7 for information on the implications of different types of transactions on your rollback segments. As noted earlier in this chapter, you will need to have enough rollback segments to support the online users and special rollback segments to handle the extraordinary requirements of large batch transactions.

In addition to properly sizing your rollback segments, you should determine how the package implements locking. If the package has been ported from another RDBMS to ORACLE, then the package may not take full advantage of the granularity of locking available in ORACLE. You need to discover *when* the records are locked—are they locked **for update** when a user first queries them? If so, then another user attempting to query the same set of records **for update** will be forced to wait for the first user to release the locks for their query to complete. You should be aware of how the package resolves data concurrency issues, particularly if it is a client/server application. For example, if two users separately query and **update** the same row, which **update** is accepted? Different packages answer this question differently, and you need to be aware of the implementation in your package. Once you know the locking scheme used, you can help the application team to implement the package in a manner that makes the best use of the available technology and resources.

When you administer a three-tier or network-based application, your locking considerations multiply. How is data accessed? When are records locked by the application? What happens to the user sessions and locks if the middle tier of the architecture shuts down?

In a server-based application, you can easily relate a user on the server to activity within the database. As more and more tiers are added to your application architecture, the process of identifying the source of a problem becomes much more difficult. In a multitier environment, you are reliant on each tier properly administering users' rights and their acquired lock information. As part of an implementation test before migrating the application to production, you should test how the database handles the loss of each part of the technical architecture.

File Locations

In your development and test environment, you should monitor the package to determine which files are the most-used files (see Chapter 4). In the production environment, you should move the most-used files so they do not contend with each other for I/O resources on the server. You should be aware of the disk layout on the server so you can distribute the database across disks and across disk controllers. Postproduction, you should monitor the package's usage to determine if the actual usage mirrors the anticipated usage, and alter your file locations accordingly. See Chapter 4 for details on planning physical I/O distribution.

Monitoring

Monitoring the package involves implementing the basic environment monitoring described in Chapter 6, along with any special monitoring required for the package. For example, the package's batch transactions may vary wildly in size, forcing you to closely monitor their scheduling and resource usage. You should automate the monitoring process as much as possible, reducing the amount of time you need to spend actively watching the database activity. The best method for accomplishing this goal is to isolate the nonstandard activities (such as batch loads or a sudden increase in the number of users). During the period of nonstandard activity, monitor the database closely. The rest of the time, the database activity should fall within the normal control boundaries. If the database exceeds the normal control boundaries—for example, if the overall hit ratio for the day is less than the threshold value—then you should be notified, and you should evaluate the causes of the problem.

Versioning Considerations

How will you develop a new version of the package while supporting the current version of the package? Does a second copy of the package require a second instance, or can two copies of the package coexist in the same instance? You need to be able to answer these questions in order to properly plan the support environment required for the implementation of new versions of the package.

For example, suppose a package assumes that its objects will be accessed via public synonyms. Thus, when a user queries EMPLOYEE, the user is really accessing the object defined by the public synonym EMPLOYEE. In that environment, you can create a second set of application tables within the same instance. For example, the main package object owner—call it APP_SYS—will own the first set of tables. The public synonyms will all point to the APP_SYS objects. The second set of tables can be created under a second user—call it APP_SYS_TWO. Users who should be accessing the second set of tables should have private synonyms pointing to the APP_SYS_TWO tables. The users' private synonyms will override the public synonyms when object names are resolved by the database.

If a package requires its tables to be stored under specific usernames, then you may not be able to create a copy of the package within the same database. Instead, you will need to create a separate instance for the second copy of the package. Thus, if you have a development database, a test database, and a production database, then when you upgrade to a new version of the package, you may need a second development database, a second test database, and a second production database. You may not be able to use your first development database during the upgrade because you will need to have that database available to support the development of modifications for the current production database. Once you know how the package handles such versioning considerations, you can plan for the resources you'll need to support the required instances.

In addition to the application versioning considerations, you will need to be aware of the package's dependencies on different versions of the ORACLE RDBMS and tools; an application may only be certified to run on ORACLE RDBMS versions 7.2.3.2, 7.3.4.3, and 8.0.5.1. That restriction may impact your overall version migration strategy. For example, you may have limited disk space available, impacting the number of ORACLE software versions you can maintain online. If the application is only certified on a small number of ORACLE RDBMS versions, you may be forced to choose one of the supported versions as the base version for all of your databases.

If you have other databases that interact with the application's tables, you will need to evaluate those dependencies during each upgrade of the package's database. As a result, you may need to "bundle" database version upgrades of multiple databases. The coordinated upgrade may reduce the dependency-related problems but will increase the complexity and importance of your preupgrade testing.

When moving an application from one version to the next, always ensure that the vendor provides data migration utilities. You should always test data migration utilities in an isolated test environment prior to executing the migration in the production environment. Migrating application data from one version to the next is data-dependent; there is rarely a generic test that will accurately forecast your success or failure. When possible, test the migration with a full set of the production data. Data migrations that fail in production after succeeding in the test environment are usually attributed to one of two reasons:

- **Very large data volumes**   The migration performs transactions on the entire data set, requiring large rollback segments or temporary segments.

- **Modifications to the production system**   The production system may contain data that is specific to modifications made to the production application. The vendor's migration utilities may not take your modifications into account.

The data migration effort may not provide you with a simple way to re-create the production environment as it was before the migration began. Therefore, you should perform an offline backup of the data before performing the migration; you may also be able to isolate the data by instance in order to further guard against creating an unrecoverable situation.

The DBA's Role

If you are implementing a custom application, the DBA should be involved at each step of the development process (see Chapter 5). The DBA should serve as a technical consultant to the development team, assisting in the planning, testing, and implementation of the application.

If you purchase a package to implement, the DBA's role expands. Instead of just dealing directly with the development team, the DBA must now also deal directly with the technical support staff of the vendor that developed the package. Since the package was not developed by your developers, you may need direct contact with the package vendor in order to understand how the application performs locking, or how you can manage its batch transactions. You will also need to determine which versions of the RDBMS are supported by the package, and how this affects your database software upgrade path for the rest of your applications.

As with all database application implementations, the DBA must work with the application team to develop a plan for creating and monitoring the database. Any special considerations—such as large batch transactions or tables known to be highly used by the package—should be addressed prior to the creation of the database for use by the package. It is simple to change the tablespace designation of a table that has not yet been created; once the table has been created within the database, there are more steps involved in managing it (not the least of which is arranging for a service interruption in your production environment so you can move the table).

The DBA should also be involved in clarifying the processes involved in obtaining support for the package. If you purchase your ORACLE license via the package vendor, you may not be allowed to call ORACLE Support directly. Rather, you may need to contact the package vendor, who in turn will call ORACLE Support as needed. The support procedures must be clearly defined during the package purchase process, and their impact on your ability to receive answers and resolve problems must be clarified for the business users. If you cannot contact ORACLE Support directly, then the time required to get an answer for any ORACLE-specific question will be delayed based on the responsiveness and availability of the vendor's support organization.

In the following sections, you will see specific guidelines for managing ORACLE Financials, Oracle Designer, ConText, and other packages and utilities. The general guidelines outlined in the previous sections apply to all packages.

Specific Guidelines for Managing ORACLE Financials

ORACLE's accounting package, ORACLE Financials, is an application developed and sold by ORACLE to manage corporate accounting. It includes modules for the General Ledger (GL), Accounts Payable (AP), Purchase Orders (PO), Fixed Assets (FA), and other major financial categories. It is created using a wide variety of ORACLE tools. This chapter will focus on issues related to the management of Oracle Financials Release 10 and 11, although its implementation recommendations will be applicable to earlier versions as well.

From the DBA's perspective, ORACLE Financials is a complex application, even in those installations that do not use all of the modules. The following sections describe the key features of the database that you should be aware of, and the specific package management guidelines for ORACLE Financials.

Database Structures

Because ORACLE Financials relies so heavily on stored objects such as packages and triggers, the size of your SYSTEM tablespace will need to be increased to at least 150MB in order to store the code. The space required by the code is independent of the rest of the database sizing; you will need that space even if there are no records in the ORACLE Financials tables. ORACLE Financials databases commonly have SYSTEM tablespaces up to 300MB in size.

Each module of ORACLE Financials corresponds to an ORACLE account. That account, such as "GL" for the General Ledger module, owns all of the tables and indexes for that module. Another account, "FND," owns the tables that the application uses to generate the front-end forms. The FND tables are queried by the applications during production usage of the forms.

Since each module's objects are created under its own account, create two tablespaces for each account: one for its tables (such as GL_TABLES) and one for its indexes (such as GL_INDEXES). You can edit the application creation scripts to separating the tables and indexes into different tablespaces. You may further separate the application tables by moving the most-used tables to separate tablespaces. For example, if you actively use the GL journal entry tables, you may move the GL_JE_LINES table to a separate tablespace to minimize its impact on other GL tables.

Even if you are not using all of the modules of Financials, each module's tables must be installed. Many of the views in ORACLE Financials will query tables from multiple modules—and thus from multiple owners. Failing to install the unused modules will therefore cause the views to be unusable.

These views may present problems during database rebuilds, particularly if developers create their own views. Since the order in which the structures are imported may cause the view to be imported before its underlying tables are, the view may fail to be created via the Import. In order to resolve this problem, you can run the Import multiple times: first with only the structures being imported (using the rows=N flag), then a second run to bring in the data (using the rows=Y and ignore=Y flags). The second Import will create any views that experienced errors during the first Import. The two Import commands are

```
imp system/manager file=export.dmp rows=N
imp system/manager file=export.dmp full=y buffer=64000
    commit=Y ignore=Y
```

The first command imports all of the database structures, but none of the rows (rows=N). The second Import brings in the structures and the data, with a commit point set for every 64,000 bytes of data imported. The ignore=Y flag allows the second Import to succeed even though the objects already exist. The use of Import is described in greater detail in Chapter 10.

Sizing Tables and Indexes

Sizing for the Financials application objects is the responsibility of the Financials systems administrator. The database size required is dependent on a number of factors specific to the implementation of the application. The calculations needed to determine the proper size are in the Oracle Financials Installation Guide.

Managing Rollback Segments

ORACLE Financials contains both online and batch modules. You should monitor the online usage to determine the number of rollback segments required; see Chapter 7 for details. For the batch modules, you should create rollback segments that are designed to support the specific transactions being run. Use the methods described earlier in this chapter to force the package to use the special rollback segments during large batch transactions.

Managing Temporary Segments

The GL user in the ORACLE Financials package has processing space requirements that exceed those of all the rest of the database users combined. It needs to have a large temporary tablespace available for its processing. Since its requirements are unique, isolate its temporary tablespace from the rest of the users by creating a tablespace that is used only for GL's temporary segments. Start with a tablespace that is between 50MB and 100MB in size. Create it so that it has 20 to 50 divisions (as shown in the following listing) so that you can measure the actual usage in the tablespace; then assign the GL user to this tablespace using the commands shown in the following listing:

```
create tablespace TEMP_GL
datafile '/db01/oracle/FIN/temp_gl.dbf' size 100m
default storage
(initial 5m next 5m pctincrease 0);

alter user GL temporary tablespace TEMP_GL;
```

In the preceding listing, the tablespace is created with a size of 100MB. Its default storage parameters will use that space in 5MB extents. Therefore, as a large GL transaction is running, you can determine how large a temporary segment is created by querying DBA_SEGMENTS, as shown in the following listing:

```
select
    Extents,   /*how many extents does the segment have?*/
    Bytes,     /*how large is the temp segment, in bytes? */
    Blocks     /*how large is it, in Oracle blocks? */
from DBA_SEGMENTS
where Segment_Type = 'TEMPORARY'
  and Tablespace_Name = 'TEMP_GL';
```

The query in the preceding listing will provide information about each of the GL user's temporary segments currently in use in the database. The query output will display the number of extents and total size of each such segment.

If the TEMP_GL tablespace will not contain any permanent objects, you can create it as a temporary tablespace. See Chapter 3 for details on temporary tablespaces.

Pinning Packages

To facilitate the pinning of packages in the shared SQL area, ORACLE Financials provides a script that pins the most commonly used packages. The script, named ADXCKPIN.sql, is usually stored in the /sql subdirectory under the directory identified by the $AD_TOP environment variable. You can edit the script to remove packages from the pinning list if you know they will not be commonly used in your implementation. The script should be run immediately following each database startup.

As an alternative to pinning packages, you can use the SHARED_POOL_RESERVED_SIZE init.ora parameter to allocate a portion of your shared SQL area to large objects. Many Financials installations use the SHARED_POOL_RESERVED_SIZE parameter in place of pinning in order to reduce the time required to start the database.

Managing Interim Tables

ORACLE Financials maintains a set of "interim" tables that are used to process data received via interfaces. For example, budget loads use the GL_BUDGET_INTERIM table. Because these tables are only used for transitional data—data that is loaded and then unloaded—the tables and their indexes expand. As noted in the "Indexes" section earlier in this chapter, indexes may not reuse space freed by deleted entries. Therefore, even if the interim tables remain constant in size, their indexes may increase in size.

To eliminate problems with the space consumption by the interim tables, you should be sure to periodically **truncate** the tables after the records have been removed from them. The **truncate** command will delete any remaining records from the table (and this operation *cannot* be rolled back). The **truncate** command will also truncate the table's indexes, freeing unused space within the index. By default, the **truncate** command will also reduce the table to a single extent.

You should schedule periodic **truncate**s for all of your interim tables. As your ORACLE Financials implementation grows in size and complexity, the number of interfaces to the package will increase, so the number of uses of the interim tables will increase. To avoid persistent space usage problems caused by these tables, you must actively manage them.

Database Access

Access to the Financials application is controlled within the application. Users log in to the application as themselves, are validated, and are then logged in to the modules they are using as the module owners. This means that all users of GL get logged in as GL.

The use of common database accounts removes the administration of user accounts from the DBA's tasks. The only accounts in a production Financials database will be those that belong to the module owners. The Financials systems administrator will be responsible for all user authorizations. From an account management perspective, the DBA will only be involved in setting up the module owner accounts (such as GL and PO) and any accounts created for access to the Financials database from outside databases, typically created to allow query-only access to restricted views of Financials data.

The DBA must also grant SELECT access on the V$SESSION and V$PROCESS dynamic performance tables to all Financials users, via the commands shown in the following listing. You should grant direct SELECT access on V$PROCESS and V$SESSION to the APPLSYS user using the **with grant option** clause.

```
svrmgrl
SVRMGR> connect internal as sysdba;
SVRMGR> grant select on V$PROCESS to applsys with grant option;
SVRMGR> grant select on V$SESSION to applsys with grant option;
SVRMGR> grant select on V$PROCESS to public;
SVRMGR> grant select on V$SESSION to public;
```

The APPLSYS user needs explicit grants to the V$PROCESS and V$SESSION views because that user creates views based on those system views. The APPLSYS-owned views are named FND_V$PROCESS and FND_V$SESSION. If you do not grant the privileges shown in the preceding listing, the APPLSYS views cannot be created.

These privileges may cause problems during database re-creations. After you create a new database, create the APPLSYS user prior to importing data from a Financials database. Grant the V$PROCESS and V$SESSION privileges to APPLSYS prior to performing an Import. If you do not, then APPLSYS will not be able to create its views that are based on those system views. The privileges on V$PROCESS and V$SESSION are not maintained during an Export/Import process.

Concurrent Managers

ORACLE Financials features an internal job queue manager called the Concurrent Manager. A single Financials database can run several Concurrent Managers (but usually fewer than five). These are set up by the Financials SysAdmin and run as background processes, waking up at specified intervals to check for jobs waiting to be executed.

Jobs in the Concurrent Manager queue are stored in a table called FND_CONCURRENT_REQUESTS, owned by the FND account. They will have one of the following status values:

Status	Description
Q	The job is waiting in the queue.
R	The job is running.
C	The job has completed.

Once a request has been run and completed, its record remains in the FND_CONCURRENT_REQUESTS table. These old records provide an audit trail of request submissions, but they do so at the expense of database space. Records of completed jobs should be archived to flat files on a regularly scheduled basis and then **delete**d from the table. The Financials systems administrator should be responsible for doing this, since the Concurrent Manager should be shut down during this process. If the FND_CONCURRENT_REQUESTS table begins extending, the DBA should advise the Financials systems administrator to decrease the time between these data archiving operations.

The regular deletion of records can cause fragmentation in indexes, as described earlier in this chapter. Therefore, you should periodically **truncate** the FND_CONCURRENT_REQUESTS table after archiving its records, or rebuild its indexes (see "How to Rebuild Indexes" in Chapter 4).

The Financials systems administrator can customize the Concurrent Managers. Concurrent managers can be restricted to run jobs of a particular type or those run by a specific user. Concurrent managers may also be restricted based on the program run. These restrictions allow long-running reports to be executed at off-peak hours. Separating jobs in this manner will greatly reduce the amount of rollback segment space needed by minimizing the inactive, in-use rollback segment data (see Chapter 7).

Although it is possible to configure the Concurrent Managers so that their processes run at a low operating system priority, this is not an optimal choice. The better solution is to run all jobs at the same priority *at the appropriate times*, resulting in better performance for everyone. The DBA should work with the Financials systems administrator to evaluate system usage cycles and determine how jobs can be more effectively scheduled.

The Demo Database

ORACLE delivers a full copy of a demo database along with Financials. This is actually an export dump file, which can be imported into a single user account. This account should point to its own tablespace. It will own all 1,000+ tables that are part of Financials, as well as the associated views and indexes. Since the demo database may be modified during training or demos, DBAs should be prepared to reimport this data periodically.

Versioning

Financials is a modifiable package, so there must be a development area established. Since the data is critical to corporate finances, a test area is normally used as well. For further information on the development process, see Chapter 5. You may need six instances—one each for development, test, and production, plus a second set of instances for development, testing, and rollout of a new version of Financials.

Since ORACLE Financials uses ORACLE tools for its data entry and reporting capabilities, developers may create new reports and add them to the application. Because of this capability, the development of add-ons to Financials must be managed via a methodology based on the guidelines in Chapter 5.

The tools used to access Financials may actively use the database during execution. All development must take place outside of the production instance. Since a separate development database will be needed, the demo database is unnecessary in the production instance. The demo database should be loaded into the test database for system testing or training purposes.

File Locations

The optimal file locations for the files used by the Financials database depend on your specific implementation of the application. However, there are several generic guidelines you can use to establish a baseline configuration. You can use the solutions and guidelines presented in Chapter 4 to further refine the file placements.

When designing the file layout on the available server hardware, you should follow these guidelines:

- ORACLE software and the application software for Financials should be stored on separate disks to avoid concurrent I/O contention.

- Online redo logs should be fairly large in size—at least 5 to 10MB each. There should be at least six of them for each Financials instance. Since they will typically experience heavy usage, they should be stored on a disk with little other activity.

- The FND account should have two tablespaces: one for its tables and one for its indexes. These tables and indexes will store the data used by the applications. These tablespaces will generally have a high I/O weight (see Chapter 4), and they should be stored on separate devices to minimize concurrent I/O contention.

■ Each module (such as General Ledger) will need a pair of tablespaces: one for its tables and one for its indexes. These tablespaces should be created on different devices to help minimize concurrent I/O contention. The main modules installed at your site (such as GL, FA, and AP) should be separated across disks as well. That is, you should not store the GL tables on the same disk as the AP tables since entries into one module's tables may impact another module's tables, triggering concurrent I/O contention.

■ There should be at least two rollback segment tablespaces. Create one for the production data entry usage, and another (RBS_2) to be used during large data loads and month-end closings. They may be stored on the same device, since they are rarely used at the same time.

■ A small TOOLS tablespace will be needed to support the ORACLE tools that are installed with Financials. It typically experiences very little I/O relative to the rest of the database files.

■ As previously noted, two temporary tablespaces are needed: TEMP for all users but GL and TEMP_GL for the GL account's exclusive use. They may be stored on the same device. Of the two, TEMP_GL will experience far greater I/O. The TEMP_GL tablespace's relative I/O weight within the database is dependent on the way in which the application is being used. If many periods are open at once, then the processing requirements for postings will increase greatly, which will in turn increase the size of the temporary tables created by GL.

■ In the development and test databases, a DEMO tablespace will be needed to hold the objects created for the demo account. This tablespace should be relatively dormant outside of training times.

init.ora Parameters

There are several database initialization parameters you can set (via the init.ora initialization parameter file) to improve the performance of ORACLE Financials. The major parameters to set are listed in the following sections.

SGA Size

The System Global Area (SGA) is the memory area that is available to the instance. Data read from the database is held in the SGA for quick retrieval by other users. Structural information about the database and the data returned by transactions is stored in the SGA. An additional area, called the Shared SQL Pool, stores the parsed version of statements run against the database.

For Financials, make the SGA as large as possible given the memory available on your server. The Oracle Financials Installation Guide gives calculations for the minimum SGA size that should be used. In general, expect the data buffer cache in the Financials production SGA to take at least 80MB in order to function effectively. The Shared SQL Pool should also be at least 80MB in size in order to support the pinning of packages. The size of the shared SQL area is set, in bytes, by the SHARED_POOL_SIZE init.ora parameter. The size of the data block buffer cache is set, in database blocks, by the DB_BLOCK_BUFFERS init.ora parameter.

Open Cursors

The init.ora OPEN_CURSORS parameter limits the number of open cursors (context areas) that can be simultaneously held by each user process. The maximum value for the parameter is operating system dependent. Set this parameter to its maximum value; although this may be documented as 255, you can exceed 255 on most operating systems.

Optimizer Changes

Prior to the release of ORACLE7, the internal ORACLE optimizer was modified to change the manner in which nested subqueries were handled by the optimizer. A side effect of this change was to slow down the performance of Financials reports that had been created with the previous optimizer functionality in mind.

To offset this change, a special init.ora parameter must be used. Its first character is an underscore (_), and its entry is shown in the following listing:

```
_optimizer_undo_changes     = TRUE
```

When this parameter is detected at startup, the changes made to the handling of subqueries will be ignored by the optimizer during query processing.

Block Size

To maximize performance within Financials, increase the ORACLE block size used. Rather than using a 2,048-byte block size, increase it to 4,096 or 8,192. Increasing the database block size will reduce the percentage of each block that is devoted to overhead. As a result, more data will be read with each I/O. Since more data will be read with each I/O, fewer I/Os will be necessary to resolve a query, thus improving performance. The init.ora entry for this parameter is

```
db_block_size    = 4096
```

You cannot change the block size of a database after it has been created. You can only change the database block size by completely re-creating the database and all of its datafiles (along with an Export/Import of the current data).

Most Active Tables and Indexes

The tables and indexes that are most likely to extend depend on the specific modules that have been installed and the manner in which they are being used. In general, several tables and their indexes experience growth spurts that cause them to become fragmented quickly. Since Financials is heavily indexed, expect the indexes to encounter problems first. The tables to monitor are listed in the following. Their indexes will be the ones most likely to extend.

Owner	Table Name
AR	AR_CUSTOMER_PROFILES
AR	AR_PAYMENT_SCHEDULES
AP	AP_INVOICES
AP	AP_PAYMENT_SCHEDULES
GL	GL_BALANCES
GL	GL_BUDGET_INTERIM
GL	GL_JE_HEADERS
GL	GL_JE_LINES
GL	GL_SUMMARY_INTERIM
PO	PO_VENDOR_SITES
PO	PO_VENDORS

The actual tables that will experience extension problems in your Financials database will vary. Creating and running a Command Center monitoring database (see Chapter 6) will greatly simplify the process of identifying problem areas. Note that most of the FND tables, since they define the application's forms interface, are fairly static and large in size. Other tables, such as GL.GL_CODE_COMBINATIONS, may experience great expansion during initial database load and setup, then become very static.

The Optimizer

ORACLE Financials relies on the rule-based optimizer to resolve the query execution paths to be used. You should not analyze the ORACLE Financials tables.

In order to enhance the performance of ORACLE Financials, a custom cost-based optimizer was developed to serve the application. This optimizer populates the GL.GL_SEGMENT_RATIOS table, which is then used to determine which index should be used for each of the Financial Statement Generator (FSG) reports. When an FSG report is run, the optimizer suppresses all but the most selective index for that report.

Since the FSG reports rely on the GL.GL_SEGMENT_RATIOS table, they will only choose the proper index if the GL.GL_SEGMENT_RATIOS table is up to date. The optimizer should be run to repopulate this table when the account structure of the general ledger changes, when the summary template structure changes, and periodically during regular usage (for example, following month-end closings). To run the GL optimizer, the Financials systems administrator chooses the optimizer option from the Financials Navigate | Setup | System menu. Although the DBA is not directly involved in this task, the GL optimizer has a direct effect on performance and appropriate scheduling and should thus be coordinated between the DBA and the Financials systems administrator.

Specific Guidelines for Managing Oracle Designer

Oracle Designer is the successor to its earlier Oracle*CASE product. Oracle Designer is a client/server application, with the data repository stored on the server and the application's presentation on the client (usually a Windows-based PC). The client software usually requires over 300MB for its installation.

On the server, you should set up the database and applications by following the guidelines in Chapter 4. In the following sections, you will see guidelines for setup and administration of the Oracle Designer package. Much of the administration of Oracle Designer database structures can be performed via the Repository Administration Utility provided with Oracle Designer.

Database Structures

The Oracle Designer repository should be stored in an isolated instance, apart from any active application development databases. You should create several instances of the Oracle Designer repository—one for development, one for test, and one for production. When it is time to implement a new version of the tool, you may need a second set of instances if you will be providing development support to the current production version while testing the new version.

Because Oracle Designer makes extensive use of stored procedures and packages, the SYSTEM tablespace will need to be large enough to hold the stored code. You should start with a SYSTEM tablespace that is between 100MB and 150MB in size, and monitor its freespace availability.

Within the application, you can use the Repository Management screen of the Repository Administration Utility to manipulate the database objects (such as indexes, views, triggers, and packages) in an ad hoc fashion. This screen can simplify the process of dropping and re-creating your indexes following a large deletion of data. You can use the "Pre-Check" option on this screen to check the SQL that is generated prior to executing it. Since the SQL commands that are executed (such as **create view** and **create trigger**) require DDL (Data Dictionary Language) locks, these commands should only be executed when no other users are using the database.

Sizing Tables and Indexes

The majority of the records in the Oracle Designer repository are stored in two tables: SDD_ELEMENTS and SDD_STRUCTURE_ELEMENTS. You should carefully size these tables and their indexes; the required size is heavily influenced by your *model versioning* strategy and the amount of *model sharing* implemented. The frequency of extracts, described in the next section, also influences the space requirements of the repository.

Model versioning allows developers to maintain different versions of the same model within the Oracle Designer repository. Since the application design's data is stored in the database, this means that two versions of the same application will double that application's storage requirements in the repository. You must work with the Oracle Designer users to make sure a consistent versioning strategy is in place for all application teams. If creating multiple versions of a model is to be the exception to the rule, then the frequency of such exceptions must still be estimated. Use those estimates to calculate the amount of additional space that the repository is likely to need.

Model sharing involves sharing objects between separate models within the repository. For example, if a model contains a CUSTOMER entity, a second model can share the first model's CUSTOMER entity. The ability to share common objects in your repository facilitates the development of enterprise-wide entities and objects, and thus an enterprise model encompassing all of your applications.

When you share an object belonging to a different model and then create a new version of your model, the repository will make copies of *all* models that own objects that have been shared into your model. If you shared the CUSTOMER entity from another model and then created a new version of your model, then the repository would make a new version of your model *and* of the model containing the CUSTOMER entity. Thus, your strategies for model versioning and model sharing have a great impact on the amount of space required within your repository. If you have five models and they each share objects from each other, then creating a new version of one model would require the creation of five new models (for the one that you're copying plus the four that are shared). Although you have only created a new version of one model, you have doubled the space usage within the repository.

Managing Rollback Segments

The Oracle Designer application has an online component and a batch component. The online component is used by the developers during application design and development. The batch component is used during large data manipulation transactions (such as extracts or model versioning) performed by the repository administrator.

You should design your rollback segments to support the online users. Typically, the amount of online activity in a repository will be less than that in a comparable online application since there is not usually a consistent volume of transactions to be entered into the repository.

To support large transactions such as model versioning and extracts, you will need to have at least one large rollback segment that is dedicated to these activities. Extracts do not, as their name might suggest, write data from the repository into a flat file external to the database. Rather, they create tables that are copies of the repository tables via commands like those shown in the following listing:

```
create table EXTRACT_TABLE
as select * from REP_TABLE;
```

The command shown in the preceding listing combines a **create table** command with a single implicit **insert** command. The **insert** command creates a single transaction that holds all of the data from the REP_TABLE table for inserting into the extract table. Since a transaction cannot span rollback segments, there must be a single rollback segment available that is large enough to handle such a transaction. Therefore, a single large-volume rollback segment is needed for use during the repository administrator's extracts. However, this large rollback segment does not reflect the online requirements of the application. Typically, an Oracle Designer environment features very low transaction volume. To support this transaction volume, rollback segments of 10MB in size are usually sufficient. Create one rollback segment for every four to six active transactions. See Chapter 7 for information on how to monitor the amount of rollback segment data being written and the number of active transactions per rollback segment.

The storage requirements for extract tables mirror the storage requirements for the application design data. Therefore, at least 50 percent of the space in the repository's tablespace must be unused before the extract starts. The space used by the extract tables is only temporary; the application assumes that those tables will be either exported to flat files or read into another repository. Thus, the additional space in the repository tablespace is not used by the online users, and is used for very short periods of time by the repository administrator during extracts. However, the additional space is critical to the success of the extraction procedure.

Pinning Packages

You can use the Repository Management screen within the Repository Administration Utility to pin any package in the Oracle Designer repository. However, you should perform pinning operations in a batch mode, not via an ad hoc administration utility. You should write a script that queries all of the repository's packages and procedures from DBA_OBJECTS (where Object_Type='PACKAGE') and alter your database startup scripts to automatically include the pinning script. If you include pinning as part of your database startup, then your database will always have its packages pinned when the application is in use.

init.ora Parameters

There are several database initialization parameters that can be set (via the init.ora initialization parameter file) to improve the performance of Oracle Designer. The major parameters to set are listed in the following sections.

SGA Size

The System Global Area (SGA) is the memory area that is available to the instance. Data read from the database is held in the SGA for quick retrieval by other users. Structural information about the database and the data returned by transactions is stored in the SGA. An additional area called the Shared SQL Pool stores the parsed version of statements run against the database.

For Oracle Designer, the data buffer cache in the SGA is usually at least 30MB in size in order to function effectively. The shared SQL area should also be at least 30MB in size in order to support the pinning of packages. The size of the shared SQL area is set, in bytes, by the SHARED_POOL_SIZE init.ora parameter. The size of the data block buffer cache is set, in database blocks, by the DB_BLOCK_BUFFERS init.ora parameter.

Open Cursors

The init.ora OPEN_CURSORS parameter limits the number of open cursors (context areas) that can be simultaneously held by each user process. The maximum value for the parameter is operating system dependent. Set this parameter to its maximum value; although this may be documented as 255, you can exceed 255 on most operating systems.

Block Size

To maximize performance within Oracle Designer, increase the ORACLE block size used. Rather than using a 2,048-byte block size, increase it to 4,096 or 8,192. Increasing the database block size will reduce the percentage of each block that is devoted to overhead. As a result, more data will be read with each I/O. Since more data will be read during each I/O, fewer I/Os will be necessary to resolve a query, improving performance. The init.ora entry for this parameter is

```
db_block_size    = 4096
```

You cannot alter the database block size of an existing database.

Most Active Tables and Indexes

As noted previously in this section of this chapter, the SDD_ELEMENTS and SDD_STRUCTURE_ELEMENTS tables are the most frequently accessed tables in the repository. If you **delete** elements from the repository, you are deleting records from these two tables. As records are **delete**d, the indexes on these tables may become fragmented. You should schedule periodic re-creations of the indexes in order to relieve the performance and space management problems caused by the indexes. You should monitor the segment extensions for the tables and indexes in the repository to determine which other tables are being actively used in your Oracle Designer implementation. See Chapter 6 for details on extent allocation trend monitoring.

The Optimizer

Oracle Designer relies on the rule-based optimizer to resolve the query execution paths to be used. You should not analyze the Oracle Designer repository tables.

Managing Other Packages and Utilities

In the following sections, you will see management directions for several common packages: ConText, SQL*Loader, and the programmatic interfaces.

ConText

The ConText Cartridge for ORACLE relies on a series of background servers to process text portions of queries. Thus, you can execute queries combining relational and text criteria for limiting conditions, as shown in the following listing. The example assumes that a Resume column exists in the PROSPECT table; the column can either contain the text data or can point to an external file containing the data.

```
select Name
  from PROSPECT
 where Name like 'B%'
   and contains (Resume, 'digging') > 0;
```

The query shown in the preceding listing has a **contains** clause, so ConText will be invoked to determine which Resume values contain the word "digging." If the score of the **contains** search is greater than 0 and the prospect's Name value starts with B, the row will be returned by the query.

You can also use ConText to perform "fuzzy matches," proximity searches, and wildcard searching. When the preceding query is executed, the text portion is processed via ConText, and the relational portion is processed via the RDBMS. The results are merged and returned to the user.

To process the text portion of the query, ConText uses a series of background processes and queues within the database. The DBA should work with the teams developing ConText-based applications to determine the number and categories (DML, DDL, and Document) of the servers required. The servers must be started each time the database is started.

Use the CTXSRV utility to start the ConText servers. When you start a ConText server, you specify the server's *personality*. The personality of a server defines the categories of commands that the server can process. In the following example, a server is started with a personality that enables it to support three categories of commands: D for DDL, M for DML, and S for Document Services. When executing the following command, you should replace *ctxsys_pass* with the password for the CTXSYS account:

```
ctxsrv -user ctxsys/ctxsys_pass -personality DMS
```

You can view the status of ConText servers via the CTX_SERVERS view, as shown in the following query:

```
column Ser_Name format A32

select Ser_Name,
       Ser_Status,
       Ser_Started_At
from CTX_SERVERS;
```

Sample output from CTX_SERVERS is shown in the following listing:

```
SER_NAME                         SER_STAT SER_START
-------------------------------- -------- ---------
DRSRV_42736                      IDLE     03-MAY-99
```

The sample output shows that a single ConText server has been started in the instance. The system-assigned name of the server is DRSRV_42736. To shut down all of the servers in an instance, you can use the SHUTDOWN procedure within the CTX_ADM package, as shown in the following listing:

```
execute CTX_ADM.SHUTDOWN;
```

To shut down a single ConText server, you specify the ConText server name as a parameter when executing the CTX_ADM.SHUTDOWN procedure, as shown in the following listing. The server name is listed in the Ser_Name column of CTX_SERVERS.

```
execute CTX_ADM.SHUTDOWN('DRSRV_42736');
```

The SHUTDOWN procedure of the CTX_ADM package has a second parameter, SDMode, that defaults to **NULL**. An SDmode value of 0 or **NULL** will force a normal shutdown of the ConText servers. An SDmode value of 1 indicates an immediate shutdown, and a value of 2 forces an abort.

To enable ConText searches (that is, queries using the **contains** clause), you should set the following parameter within your database's init.ora file:

```
text_enable = TRUE
```

Within the database, the ConText data dictionary is owned by the CTXSYS user. The CTXSYS user is the only user who should have the CTXADMIN role. Other ConText-related roles include CTXAPP (application owner) and CTXUSER (application user). You should grant the CTXAPP role to all users who will be developing ConText applications. When a user executes a ConText-related query, records are stored in an interim table. When the query completes, the database **truncate**s the interim table, thus eliminating any space management problems that may occur because of the use of the interim tables.

ORACLE has significantly changed the administration of ConText in ORACLE8i. In prior versions of ConText, you create *policies*, and then create text indexes based on those policies. In ORACLE8i, you create a text index via an extended version of the **create index** command.

Before creating a text index, you first must specify your preferences. You specify preferences via the CREATE_PREFERENCE procedure of the CTX_DDL package.

```
ctx_ddl.create_preference(preference_name  in varchar2,
                          object_name      in varchar2);
```

If you specify no preferences, ORACLE will use the system defaults (see the CTX_PARAMETERS view). Once you have created your preferences, create attributes for those preferences via the SET_ATTRIBUTE procedure of the CTX_DDL package.

```
ctx_ddl.set_attribute(preference_name in varchar2,
                      attribute_name  in varchar2,
                      attribute_value in varchar2);
```

For example, the following command creates a text index called Resume_Index on the Resume column of the PROSPECT table:

```
create index Resume_Index on PROSPECT(Resume)
indextype is context
parameters('stoplist MY_STOP');
```

In the preceding example, the **indextype is context** clause tells ORACLE that this is a text index. Only one parameter (a stoplist) is specified; the other parameters will use the default system preferences.

Prior to ORACLE8i, reorganizing a text index required the use of the CTX_DDL.OPTIMIZE_INDEX procedure. As of ORACLE8i, you can administer a text index with the **alter index** and **drop index** commands. For example, the following command will rebuild the Resume_Index text index:

```
alter index Resume_Index rebuild;
```

To improve the performance of a text index rebuild, use a ConText-specific **optimize fast** parameter. When you use the **optimize fast** parameter, as shown in the following example, deleted values are not removed from the text index during the rebuild.

```
alter index Resume_Index rebuild parameters('optimize fast');
```

You can also use the **alter index** command to rename a text index, to change its storage parameters, or to change the text indexing preferences. To drop a text index, use the **drop index** command, as shown in the following listing:

```
drop index Resume_Index;
```

SQL*Loader

SQL*Loader is a utility for loading data into ORACLE tables from external files. As a DBA, you have to be concerned with two aspects of its usage:

1. Are the tables and indexes properly sized for the data load that is expected?

2. Is the Direct Path option being used?

The table and index size calculations (see Chapter 5) should take into account the data that is coming in via flat files. Typically, this data's length and volume are very well defined, so the sizing estimates should be accurate. If it is a one-time load used for initial population of the data, then do not create the indexes until after the data has been loaded and the table's sizing has been verified.

The Direct Path option is a high-speed method for inserting data into tables. It bypasses the normal processing of **insert** statements and instead writes directly to the table's data blocks. When using Direct Path, the data in the flat file should be presorted by the indexed columns of the tables. For large data loads, the performance gains are considerable.

Of course, such performance gains must have a cost. In this case, the cost is borne by the tablespace used for temporary segments. When a Direct Path load is started, the table's indexes are placed in an invalid state for the duration of the load. As data is loaded into the table, the new index key values are written to a temporary segment. When the load completes, the old index values and the new values are merged, and the index once again becomes valid.

The implication of Direct Path loads for temporary segment storage space can be considerable. SQL*Loader requires that enough space be available in the temporary tablespace to hold, at a minimum, the **initial** extent sizes of all the indexes on the table being loaded. Since the Direct Path option is normally used on large data loads, the space requirements for the temporary tablespace are usually large. For unsorted data loads, the temporary tablespace size requirements may be twice the index size requirements.

To determine the status of an index, query the DBA_INDEXES view, as shown in the following listing. Valid Status values are DIRECT LOAD and VALID.

```
select Owner,        /*Owner of the index*/
       Index_Name,   /*Name of the index*/
       Status        /*Either DIRECT LOAD or VALID*/
  from DBA_INDEXES;
```

If an index is left in DIRECT PATH state following a data load, then the load did not meet the index's criteria. For example, you may have loaded duplicate records into a table with a unique index. When the load completed, the index could not be reapplied to the table, and the index was left in DIRECT PATH state. As a result, you will need to drop the index, correct the data, and then re-create the index.

High-Water Mark Issues with SQL*Loader Direct Path Option

As described in Chapter 4, ORACLE maintains a high-water mark for every table in the database. The high-water mark is the highest block to which data has been written; if the data is then deleted, the high-water mark does not change. To reset the high-watermark, you must **truncate** the table.

The high-water mark is significant for SQL*Loader Direct Path users because Direct Path loads blocks of data rather than individual records. Direct Path loads the data into the table starting at the high-water mark. Thus, if your table has a high-water mark that is not reflective of its actual data usage, then you may be wasting a significant amount of space.

For example, if you have loaded 100MB of data into a table and then **delete** that data, the high-water mark will still be set at the 100MB point. If you then perform a Direct Path load into that table, the newly loaded data will be added *starting* at the 100MB point; the first 100MB of the table's storage will still be empty.

To avoid wasting the space, you will need to use the **truncate** command to reset the high-water mark for the table back to its original value. However, **truncate** is a DDL command that deletes all of the records from a table, with no way to roll back the deletion. Therefore, if you will be using the Direct Path load option, you should consider using ORACLE's table partitioning options. You can **truncate** a partition without affecting any of the other partitions of the table. To truncate a partition, use the **truncate partition** clause of the **alter table** command. If you are using the subpartition options introduced in ORACLE8i, you can specify a specific subpartition to **truncate**. If you do not specify a subpartition, ORACLE will truncate all of the partition's subpartitions.

As of ORACLE8i, the ORACLE Call Interface (OCI) now includes a direct load facility that SQL*Loader uses. Vendors may begin to use this new capability to perform bulk loads via OCI calls. As with SQL*Loader Direct Path loads, these bulk loads will not reuse any free space below the table's high-water mark.

Programmatic Interfaces

The programmatic interfaces to ORACLE allow application developers to write programs in 3GL programming languages (such as C) that can access the database. For a DBA, the most important support note for the programmatic interfaces concerns upgrades to the database or operating system software. Since the users' programs use the ORACLE kernel's software libraries, and since the operating system software libraries are also used, any modification to either library requires that the users' programs be relinked. A relink should take place any time the database software is upgraded (for example, from version 8.0.5 to 8.1.5) or the operating system software is upgraded.

CHAPTER
12

Managing Large
Databases

he definition of a "large" database keeps changing. In 1995, a large database was considered to be one that was greater than 100GB in size. Just a few years later, multiterabyte databases were going into production. The acronym VLDB, meaning very large database, quickly loses its meaning unless it is defined by something other than a numerical threshold for size. The technological changes that support faster backups, larger systems, and I/O distribution constantly increase the largest supportable database size.

Instead of defining "large" by a given size, define it by its recovery time: if you can't completely recover the database from a full offline backup in an 18-hour period, it's a large database. This definition allows the size of a "large" database to increase over time as operating systems and hardware performance is improved.

When you are managing a large database, you need to view the database from a nonstandard perspective. In this chapter, you will see management advice specific to large databases, including the following:

- Setting up the environment, including partitions and materialized views

- Managing transactions, including data loads

- Implementing backup strategies

- Tuning

- Using transportable tablespaces for data movement

Some of the advice in this chapter will not be applicable for smaller systems. If you are managing a database that can be fully recovered in less than 18 hours, you should follow the advice found in the other chapters of this book.

Setting Up the Environment

Within a large database, a small number of tables use the majority of the space allocated to tables. For example, in a large database used for decision support purposes, you may have 100 tables, five of which account for over 90 percent of the records in the database. The remaining 95 tables are used for codes tables or special reporting functions. To improve the performance of queries against the application, you may choose to create tables that contain aggregations of data from the largest table; each of those aggregation tables will be small relative the largest table. Codes tables will be even smaller. If the application and the end users access the aggregation tables instead of the large transaction tables, your tuning efforts will be focused on tuning access to the aggregation tables.

When you create and manage a large database, the bulk of your effort will likely be devoted to managing the few very large tables that account for the majority of the rows. The database configuration tips provided in this section include methods for transparently splitting the large table into smaller (more easily managed) tables and distributing the I/O requirements of the large table across many devices.

Sizing Large Databases

When creating a large database, categorize each table you will be creating according to the following types:

- **Small codes table**   A codes table rarely increases in size.

- **Large business transactions table**   This is the type of table that accounts for the majority of the records in the database. It may increase in size over time.

- **Aggregation table**   This type of table may increase in size over time or may remain at a constant size, depending on your application design. Ideally, it does not increase in size over time. Its data is based on aggregations of data from the large transaction tables.

- **Temporary work table**   A temporary work table is used during data load processing and bulk data manipulation.

In the following sections, you will see sizing and configuration advice for each type of table.

Sizing Codes Tables

A codes table contains a list of codes and descriptions—such as a list of country abbreviations and country names. A codes table should be fairly constant in size.

Since a codes table's data may be very static, you should be able to properly size the codes table and not have to worry about it becoming fragmented over time. If the codes tables are small, you should be able to create them with the proper storage parameters so that each table fits in a single extent. If there are multiple codes tables with the same relative size, you can place them in a tablespace whose default storage parameters are correct for the codes tables. For example, if all of your codes tables require between 500KB and 1MB, you may store them all in the CODES_TABLES tablespace.

```
create tablespace CODES_TABLES
datafile '/u01/oracle/VLDB/codes_tables.dbf'
default storage
  (initial 1M next 1M pctincrease 0 pctfree 2);
```

If you create a table in the CODES_TABLES tablespace, the table will use the default storage parameters for the tablespace unless you specify values of your own. In this example, each table created in CODES_TABLES that uses the default storage values will have an initial extent 1MB in size, and all subsequent extents will be 1MB in size. Having all of the extents the same size maximizes the likelihood that a dropped extent will be reused. If you must use differently sized extents, they should be sized to maximize the reuse of dropped extents. A common strategy for extent sizing is to use extent sizes of 1MB, 2MB, 4MB, 8MB, 16MB, etc.

As part of the **default storage** clause for the CODES_TABLES tablespace, the **pctfree** setting is set very low. The low setting for **pctfree** means that very little space will be held free in each database block for subsequent **update**s. In general, codes table values are rarely **update**d (for example, country names do not change frequently). If one of your codes tables has values that are frequently **update**d, then you will need to set **pctfree** to a higher value to support the space requirements of the **update**s.

Because they have similar storage and usage characteristics, codes tables are frequently stored together. If you have multiple sets of codes tables, you can store them in multiple tablespaces. For example, if some of your codes tables are used more frequently than others, you can move them to their own tablespace so they do not cause contention with the other codes tablespaces.

As another possibility, you may choose to eliminate codes tables from your database and store static codes values as arrays in your programs. If the codes table data is small and static, then hardcoding the values into programs will have little impact on your long-term maintenance costs. For example, you may have a table that tracks units of measure:

Abbreviation	Unit of Measure
V	Volt
KW	Kilowatt
F	Degrees Fahrenheit

Rather than storing this data in an ORACLE table, you could store it in arrays in your programs. In C and C++, you could store the array data in a header file; in COBOL, you could store the values in a copybook. When the data is stored as arrays, no database access is required to reference the units of measure. If the application required a new unit of measure, the header file for the program would need to be amended and the code regenerated. Modifying the programs to accommodate code value changes may not be a significant maintenance cost, since the programs may have to be edited to create new functions, classes, and procedures to handle the new unit of measure. If you hardcode static codes values into your programs, you remove them entirely from the database. You will need to weigh the costs and benefits of this approach for your environment, based on the volatility of your codes table data.

Sizing Business Transaction Tables

The business transaction tables store the majority of the data in the database. They store the raw data on which the aggregation tables are based. When sizing the business transaction tables, you first need to understand how historical data is handled within the application. Does the application always store the same volume of data in its transaction tables, or are past records kept indefinitely?

If the business transaction tables always store the same volume of data, sizing the tables is straightforward. You should be able to estimate the number of rows in the table and the size of each row. In large databases, the business transaction tables are typically loaded via batch programs. Thus, you know two things about the data: the size of the input file and the source of data changes.

By analyzing the input file, you should be able to estimate the size of the rows in the business transaction tables. The source of data changes is equally important. If the table is **truncate**d and reloaded with each subsequent data load, then there is no need for a high **pctfree** setting for the table. If records are **update**d, however, you will need to set **pctfree** high enough so that an **update**d row can still fit in its original block. If a row cannot fit in its original block, then ORACLE may migrate the row to a new block or cause the row to span multiple blocks.

The **pctincrease** value for a table should support the growth pattern of the table. If the table grows at a constant rate, you should use a **pctincrease** of 0. If the table's data volume grows geometrically, you should use a nonzero value for **pctincrease**. For most tables, a **pctincrease** setting of 0 correctly mirrors their growth.

NOTE
In most tables, the number of rows grows at a linear rate—such as 10 rows, then 20, then 30, then 40 for the cumulative number of records. In each case, a constant volume of 10 rows was added. If the number of records increases at a geometric rate, then the number of records added each time could be 10, then 20, then 40, then 80, yielding a cumulative total of 10, then 30, then 70, then 150.

As of ORACLE8, you can partition a large business transaction table into multiple smaller tables. When you split a table into partitions, you need to size each of the partitions. Correctly sizing partitions requires that you know the distribution of data values within the table. Since the data is typically loaded in batch, the data distribution information may already be available to you prior to loading the data. The creation of partitions is described in the "Partitions" section later in this chapter.

Sizing Aggregation Tables

An aggregation table stores summaries of the data in the business transaction table. This redundant data storage is usually designed to improve the performance of frequently accessed screens or reports within an application. Most users of an application rarely need to see the detailed business transaction data. By storing the aggregations of the business transaction tables' data in aggregation tables, you can achieve two goals:

■ Improving the performance of queries against the application. You don't want your database to have to support users who frequently perform aggregation operations (**SUM**, **MIN**, **MAX**, **AVG**, for example) of the largest table in your database. If you store the aggregated data in its own set of tables, then the users query the smaller, customized aggregation tables instead of the huge transaction data.

■ Reducing the number of times the business transaction tables are accessed. The aggregation tables are created via a batch process, so the business transaction tables are only accessed via the batch programs. This reduction in the number of accesses significantly improves your ability to maintain, load, alter, and manage the business transaction tables. For example, if users only directly access aggregation tables, you can **truncate** the main transaction table without affecting the availability of the application.

If the business transaction table grows in size over time, then the aggregation tables may grow in size over time. However, it is more common for the aggregation tables to grow in number, not size, over time. For example, you may create an aggregation table that holds the sales data for a particular time period, such as the first sales period after a product is launched. Where do you store data for the next time period? You can either expand the existing aggregation table or you can create a new table to hold the new data. If the data is placed in a new table (as is often the case), you should be able to accurately predict the data volume of the new table based on the storage requirements of the existing aggregation tables. If the new data is stored in an existing aggregation table, you will need to estimate the number of periods' worth of data to be stored in a single aggregation table. If there is no limit to the data volume in the aggregation tables, those tables will eventually become large and the performance and management of those tables may become problematic.

Sizing Temporary Work Tables

A temporary work table is used during the processing of batch data loads. For example, you may use a loading process that performs no constraint checking of the incoming data. Prior to loading the new data into the business transaction table, you should "clean" the data to make sure it is correct and acceptable. Since batch loads typically use outside data sources, some of the records to be inserted may fail your system's criteria. You can either apply the logic checks during the data load or, if you use temporary work tables, following the data load.

Applying the data-cleaning logic following the data load allows you to tune the data load for very rapid processing of rows. However, it increases the amount of space required within the database since the data must be stored in a separate table prior to being loaded into the production business transaction tables. The temporary work tables should be stored in a tablespace apart from any production tables, and their size should match the space required to hold the records from a data load.

In addition to allocating space for the temporary work tables, you should allocate space for any indexes you will create on those tables during the data loading and validation process.

Sizing Other Database Areas

In addition to the space required by the production tables and their associated indexes, you also need to provide adequate space for other core database objects: the data dictionary, rollback segments, and temporary segments.

The data dictionary is stored in the SYSTEM tablespace. The source code for packages, procedures, functions, triggers, and methods is stored in the data dictionary tables. If your application makes extensive use of these objects, you may need to increase the space available to the SYSTEM tablespace. The use of auditing (see Chapter 9) also increases the potential space usage within the SYSTEM tablespace.

Rollback segments support the transactions within the database. In a large database, there are typically three distinct types of transactions:

- **Large batch loads** These should be supported by large, dedicated rollback segments.

- **Batch aggregations** The data volume and transaction size for aggregations are typically smaller than those of large data loads. You will need several dedicated rollback segments to support aggregations. Although the individual aggregation rollback segments may be smaller than the rollback segment used to support the initial data loads, their total space allocation may exceed the data load rollback segment space allocation.

- **Small transactions executed by users** If your users will frequently be making small transactions in the database, you need to provide a number of rollback segments with multiple extents to support the transactions.

See Chapter 7 for information on determining the required number, size, and structure for your rollback segments.

ORACLE creates temporary segments during the processing of sorting operations. The initial data load may use temporary segments if you use the SQL*Loader Direct Path option and the loaded table is indexed. In general, most of the temporary segment activity in a large database comes from the aggregation activity and the creation of indexes. When estimating the required size of a temporary segment, first estimate the size of the table or index being created. For instance, suppose the aggregation table being created will be 50MB in size. Next, multiply that size by 4. For the aggregation table being created, you should be able to support a temporary segment that is 200MB in size. The temporary segment will be created in the user's temporary tablespace, using the default storage parameters for the tablespace, so you need to make sure that those storage values are large enough to support the aggregations and sorting operations performed.

NOTE
*If you are using the SQL*Loader Direct Path loading option, your temporary segments must be large enough to store the indexes used by the tables being loaded.*

Sizing Support Areas

Outside of the database, there are several types of files that may use considerable disk space; you need to plan for this area prior to implementing your system.

First, you may need space for the raw datafiles to be loaded. Unless you are loading data directly from a tape or CD, you will likely be storing raw datafiles on the disks of your system. Second, you may need space for file processing that occurs before the data is loaded into the database. For example, it is common to sort the data prior to loading it; you therefore need space for both the original file and the sorted version of that file. Third, you may be required to keep the files online for a set period of time. Ensure there is enough space to hold multiple sets of files, and that old files are removed when they are no longer required to be online.

Lastly, depending on your backup strategy, you may need disk space available for archived redo log files or export files. You will see details on backup strategies for large databases in the "Backups" section of this chapter.

The sizes for these three areas vary depending on your implementation of your application and your backup strategies. Prior to finalizing your space estimate for the new system, be sure to finalize the size of the nondatabase areas you will need.

Choosing a Physical Layout

In implementing the physical layout for a large database, you should have two primary objectives:

1. Spread the I/O burden across as many disks as possible.

2. Reduce I/O contention among dissimilar types of objects.

In order to spread the I/O burden across many disks, many large systems use RAID arrays of disks. A RAID array treats a set of disks as a single logical volume; when a file is created within that volume, the operating system spreads the file across the disks. For example, if there are four disks in the RAID array, then the first disk may contain the first block of a file, the second disk may contain the second block, the third disk may contain the third block, and the fourth disk may contain a parity block. If one of the disks is lost due to a media failure, the RAID unit can use the existing disks to reconstruct the missing data.

The more disks there are in the RAID array, the more the I/O burden is distributed. Because they involve writing and maintaining parity information, RAID arrays are usually most effective for write-once, read-many applications. If the data will frequently be updated, you should consider an alternative storage mechanism (such as mirroring, described presently). During an **update** to a data value, for example, a RAID system would need to read the original data block, read the original parity block, and update and write both blocks back to the disk. Many large RAID systems use a disk cache to improve the performance of such operations, but they still may experience performance degradation.

An alternative architecture uses *mirroring*. In a mirrored system, there are multiple copies of each disk maintained by the operating system. For example, there may be Disk1 and a second disk that is a duplicate of Disk1. During reads and writes, the operating system may read or write to either copy of Disk1. The operating system maintains the read consistency of the files on the mirrored disks. Mirroring is effective (for writes as well as for reads), but you will need to double your disk space availability in order to use it.

To reduce I/O contention between dissimilar types of objects, use the strategies described in Chapter 4 to categorize the types of files you will be storing. Then, categorize the tables within your application based on the categories described earlier in this chapter (codes tables, aggregation tables, etc.). You should separate the temporary work tables from their data source (the external data files). You should store the business transaction tables apart from their data source (either the temporary work tables or the external data files). You should store the aggregation tables apart from their data source (the business transaction tables). All of these should be separated from the rollback segments, data dictionary, and temporary segments.

What if you are using RAID devices? In that case, treat each set of RAID disks as a single disk. Store the business transaction tables on a different RAID set than the aggregation tables are stored on. Store the tables' indexes on a different RAID set than the tables are stored on.

NOTE
Determining the optimal RAID configuration may require a great deal of interaction with the system administration team. You need to explain the file access patterns of your database to the system administrators, and you need to understand their approach for distributing the I/O burden.

Partitions

In order to make large tables easier to manage, you can use partitions. Partitions dynamically separate the rows in your table into smaller tables. You can have ORACLE create a view that spans all of the partitions; thus, the data will appear to be together logically although it is separated physically. Splitting a large table into multiple smaller partitions may improve the performance of maintenance operations, backups, recoveries, transactions, and queries.

The criteria used to determine which rows are stored in which partitions are specified as part of the **create table** command. Dividing a table's data across multiple tables in this manner is called *partitioning* the table; the table that is partitioned is called a *partitioned table*, and the parts are called *partitions*.

The ORACLE optimizer will know that the table has been partitioned; as you will see later in this section, you can also specify the partition to use as part of the **from** clause of your queries.

As of ORACLE8i, ORACLE supports three types of partitioning: range partitioning, hash partitioning, and composite partitioning. In ORACLE8.0, only range partitioning is supported. The examples in the following section focus on range partitioning; composite and hash partitioning are shown in the "Using Subpartitions" section later in this chapter.

Creating a Partitioned Table

To create a partitioned table, you must specify the ranges of values to use for the partitions as part of the **create table** command.

Consider the EMPLOYEE table:

```
create table EMPLOYEE (
    EmpNo           NUMBER(10) primary key,
    Name            VARCHAR2(40),
    DeptNo          NUMBER(2),
    Salary          NUMBER(7,2),
    Birth_Date      DATE,
    Soc_Sec_Num     VARCHAR2(9),
    State_Code      CHAR(2),
```

```
constraint FK_DeptNO foreign key (DeptNo)
   references DEPT(DeptNo),
constraint FK_StateCode foreign key (State_Code)
   references State(State_Code)
);
```

If you will be storing a large number of records in the EMPLOYEE table, you may want to separate the EMPLOYEE rows across multiple tables. To partition the table's records by range, use the **partition by range** clause of the **create table** command. The ranges will determine the values stored in each partition.

The column used as the basis for the partition logic is rarely the primary key for the table. More often, the basis for partitioning is one of the foreign key columns in the table. In the EMPLOYEE table, the DeptNo and State_Code columns are foreign keys. If you frequently query by the DeptNo column, and it makes sense to split the data based on that column, then use it as the partition key. In a system that tracks historical data (such as sales history or salary history), it may be more appropriate to partition the data based on one of the time-based columns (such as sales period or effective date of salary change).

```
create table EMPLOYEE (
EmpNo           NUMBER(10) primary key,
Name            VARCHAR2(40),
DeptNo          NUMBER(2),
Salary          NUMBER(7,2),
Birth_Date      DATE,
Soc_Sec_Num     VARCHAR2(9),
 constraint FK_DeptNO foreign key (DeptNo)
   references DEPT(DeptNo)
)
partition by range (DeptNo)
 (partition PART1    values less than (11)
   tablespace PART1_TS,
  partition PART2    values less than (21)
   tablespace PART2_TS,
  partition PART3    values less than (31)
   tablespace PART3_TS,
  partition PART4    values less than (MAXVALUE)
   tablespace PART4_TS)
;
```

The EMPLOYEE table will be partitioned based on the values in the DeptNo column:

```
partition by range (DeptNo)
```

For any DeptNo values less than 11, the record will be stored in the partition named PART1. The PART1 partition will be stored in the PART1_TS tablespace. Any DeptNo in the range between 11 and 20 will be stored in the PART2 partition; values between 21 and 30 will be stored in the PART3 partition. Any value greater than 30 will be stored in the PART4 partition. Note that in the PART4 partition definition, the range clause is

```
partition PART4    values less than (MAXVALUE)
```

You do not need to specify a maximum value for the last partition; the **maxvalue** keyword tells ORACLE to use the partition to store any data that could not be stored in the earlier partitions. For each partition, you only specify the maximum value for the range. The minimum value for the range is implicitly determined by ORACLE.

When partitioning a table, you should store the partitions in separate tablespaces. Separating them by tablespace allows you to control their physical storage location and avoid contention between the partitions.

How many partitions should you have? You should have as many partitions as are required to logically separate your data. The additional maintenance work involved in having many partitions is negligible. Focus on dividing the rows of your table into logical groups. If the partition ranges make sense for your application, then they are the ones you should use. If your largest table is 100GB in size, using 100 evenly sized partitions generates 100 partitions that are each 1GB in size. Although a 1GB table is not always simple to manage, it is certainly simpler to manage than a 100GB table is. Use enough partitions to reduce the size of the tables to a size that is easily manageable in your operating system and hardware configuration.

NOTE
You cannot partition object tables or tables that use LOB datatypes.

QUERYING DIRECTLY FROM PARTITIONS   If you know the partition from which you will be retrieving your data, you can specify the name of the partition as part of the **from** clause of your query. For example, what if you wanted to query the records for the employees in Departments 11 through 20? The optimizer should be able to use the partition definitions to determine that only the PART2 partition could contain data that can resolve this query. If you wish, you can tell ORACLE to use PART2 as part of your query.

```
select *
  from EMPLOYEE partition (PART2)
 where DeptNo between 11 and 20;
```

This example explicitly names the partition in which ORACLE is to search for the matching employee records. If the partition is modified (for example, if its range of values is altered), then PART2 may no longer be the partition that contains the needed records. Thus, you should use great care when using this syntax.

In general, this syntax is not necessary because ORACLE places CHECK constraints on each of the partitions. When you query from the partitioned table, ORACLE uses the CHECK constraints to determine which partitions should be involved in resolving the query. This process may result in a small number of rows being searched for the query, improving query performance. Additionally, the partitions may be stored in different tablespaces (and thus on separate disk devices), helping to reduce the potential for disk I/O contention during the processing of the query.

During an **insert** into the partitioned table, ORACLE uses the partitions' CHECK constraints to determine which partition the record should be inserted into. Thus, you can use a partitioned table as if it were a single table, and rely on ORACLE to manage the internal separation of the data.

Indexing Partitions

When you create a partitioned table, you should create an index on the table. The index may be partitioned according to the same range values that were used to partition the table. In the following listing, the **create index** command for the EMPLOYEE table is shown:

```
create index EMPLOYEE_DEPTNO
   on EMPLOYEE(DeptNo)
    local
    (partition PART1
      tablespace PART1_NDX_TS,
     partition PART2
      tablespace PART2_NDX_TS,
     partition PART3
      tablespace PART3_NDX_TS,
     partition PART4
      tablespace PART4_NDX_TS);
```

Notice the **local** keyword. In this **create index** command, no ranges are specified. Instead, the **local** keyword tells ORACLE to create a separate index for each partition of the EMPLOYEE table. There were four partitions created on EMPLOYEE. This index will create four separate indexes—one for each partition. Since there is one index per partition, the indexes are "local" to the partitions.

Local partitions mimic the way indexes traditionally work in ORACLE; a single index applies to only one table. If you use local partitions, it should be simple to manage the index along with its matching table.

You can also create "global" indexes. A global index may contain values from multiple partitions. That is, the index's values span multiple tables. A global index is typically used when there are many transactions occurring in the partitions and you need to guarantee the uniqueness of the data values across all partitions. Local indexes will also guarantee uniqueness, but global indexes should perform the uniqueness check faster. The index itself may be partitioned, as shown in this example:

```
create index EMPLOYEE_DEPTNO
on EMPLOYEE(DeptNo)
 global partition by range (DeptNo)
 (partition PART1   values less than (11)
   tablespace PART1_NDX_TS,
  partition PART2   values less than (21)
   tablespace PART2_NDX_TS,
  partition PART3   values less than (31)
   tablespace PART3_NDX_TS,
  partition PART4   values less than (MAXVALUE)
   tablespace PART4_NDX_TS)
;
```

The **global** clause in this **create index** command allows you to specify ranges for the index values that are different from the ranges for the table partitions. In this case, the same partition ranges were used. Even though the same partition ranges are used for both the table and the global index, the index partitions are not directly related to the table partitions. Instead, the index partitions are part of a global index whose values span all of the table partitions. There is only a direct relationship between table partitions and index partitions when the index is a local index.

In most cases, you should use local index partitions. If you use local partitions of your indexes, you will be able to easily relate index partitions to table partitions. Local indexes are simpler to manage than global indexes since they represent only a portion of the data in the partitioned table. In the next section, you will see other aspects of partition management.

Managing Partitions

You can use the **alter table** command to **add**, **drop**, **exchange**, **move**, **modify**, **rename**, **split**, and **truncate** partitions. These commands allow you to alter the existing partition structure, as may be required after a partitioned table has been used heavily. For example, the distribution of the DeptNo values within the partitioned table may have changed or the maximum value may have increased.

For the full syntax for the **alter table** command, see Appendix A.

You can use the **alter table** command to manage the storage parameters of the partitions. When the EMPLOYEE table was partitioned earlier in this chapter, no storage parameters were specified for its partitions. For example, the first partition, PART1, was assigned to the PART1_TS tablespace, with no **storage** clause.

```
partition by range (DeptNo)
  (partition PART1   values less than (11)
    tablespace PART1_TS,
```

The PART1 partition will use the default storage for the PART1_TS tablespace. If you wish to use different storage parameters, you must either specify them when the table is created (via a **storage** clause) or alter the partition's storage after it has been created.

For example, the following command changes the storage parameters for the PART1 partition of the EMPLOYEE table:

```
alter table EMPLOYEE
    modify partition PART1
    storage (next 1M pctincrease 0);
```

You can **truncate** partitions, leaving the rest of the table's partitions unaffected, as shown here:

```
alter table EMPLOYEE
   truncate partition PART3
   drop storage;
```

You can also use the **alter table** command to move partitions to new tablespaces, split existing partitions into multiple new partitions, exchange partitions, drop partitions, and add new partitions.

For index partitions, the options are more limited. The partition-related syntax for the **alter index** command is shown in Appendix A. You can use the **alter index** command to modify an index partition's storage or rename, drop, split, or rebuild the partition. You can use the partition-related extensions to the **alter index** command to manage the index partitions the same way you manage normal indexes. For example, you can rebuild an existing index partition via the **rebuild partition** clause of the **alter index** command.

```
alter index EMPLOYEE_DEPTNO
rebuild partition PART4
storage (initial 2M next 2M pctincrease 0);
```

When you use the **rebuild** option for an index or an index partition, you must have enough storage space available to simultaneously hold both the old index and the new index.

Managing Subpartitions

As of ORACLE8i, you can create subpartitions—partitions of partitions. You can use subpartitions to combine two separate types of partitions: range partitions and hash partitions. Range partitions were the only type of partition available in ORACLE8.0.

A hash partition, like a hash cluster, determines the physical placement of data by performing a hash function on the values of the partition key. In range partitioning, consecutive values of the partition key are usually stored in the same partition. In hash partitioning, consecutive values of the partition key are not necessarily stored in the same partition. Hash partitioning distributes a set of records over a greater set of partitions than range partitioning does, potentially decreasing the likelihood for I/O contention.

To create a hash partition, use the **partition by hash** clause in place of the **partition by range** clause, as shown in the following listing:

```
create table EMPLOYEE (
EmpNo           NUMBER(10) primary key,
Name            VARCHAR2(40),
DeptNo          NUMBER(2),
Salary          NUMBER(7,2),
Birth_Date      DATE,
Soc_Sec_Num     VARCHAR2(9),
 constraint FK_DeptNO foreign key (DeptNo)
   references DEPT(DeptNo)
)
partition by hash (DeptNo)
partitions 10;
```

You can name each partition and specify its tablespace, just as you would for range partitioning, as shown here:

```
create table EMPLOYEE (
EmpNo           NUMBER(10) primary key,
Name            VARCHAR2(40),
DeptNo          NUMBER(2),
Salary          NUMBER(7,2),
Birth_Date      DATE,
Soc_Sec_Num     VARCHAR2(9),
 constraint FK_DeptNO foreign key (DeptNo)
   references DEPT(DeptNo)
)
partition by hash (DeptNo)
partitions 2
store in (PART1_TS, PART2_TS);
```

Following the **partition by hash (DeptNo)** line, you have two choices for format:

■   As shown in the preceding listing, you can specify the number of partitions and the tablespaces to use:

```
partitions 2
store in (PART1_TS, PART2_TS);
```

This method will create partitions with system-generated names of the format SYS_P*nnn*. The number of tablespaces specified in the **store in** clause does not have to equal the number of partitions. If more partitions than tablespaces are specified, the partitions will be assigned to the tablespaces in a round-robin fashion.

■   You can specify named partitions:

```
partition by hash (DeptNo)
(partition P1 tablespace P1_TS,
 partition P2 tablespace P2_TS);
```

In this method, each partition is given a name and a tablespace, with the option of using an additional **lob** or **varray** storage clause. This method gives you more control over the location of the partitions, with the added benefit of letting you specify meaningful names for the partitions.

NOTE
You cannot create global indexes for hash partitions.

You can use hash partitions in combination with range partitions, creating hash partitions of the range partitions. For very large tables, this composite partitioning may be an effective way of separating the data into manageable and tunable divisions.

The following example range partitions the EMPLOYEE table by the DeptNo column, and hash partitions the DeptNo partitions by Name values:

```
create table EMPLOYEE (
EmpNo          NUMBER(10) primary key,
Name           VARCHAR2(40),
DeptNo         NUMBER(2),
Salary         NUMBER(7,2),
Birth_Date     DATE,
Soc_Sec_Num    VARCHAR2(9),
 constraint FK_DeptNO foreign key (DeptNo)
   references DEPT(DeptNo)
)
partition by range (DeptNo)
subpartition by hash (Name)
```

```
subpartitions 10
 (partition PART1   values less than (11)
   tablespace PART1_TS,
  partition PART2   values less than (21)
   tablespace PART2_TS,
  partition PART3   values less than (31)
   tablespace PART3_TS,
  partition PART4   values less than (MAXVALUE)
   tablespace PART4_TS);
```

The EMPLOYEE table will be range-partitioned into four partitions, using the ranges specified for the four named partitions. Each of those partitions will be hash-partitioned on the Name column.

Creating Materialized Views

The underlying technology for materialized views should be familiar to anyone who has created and maintained snapshots. A materialized view is a table that stores derived data. During its creation, you specify the SQL used to populate the materialized view.

For a large database, a materialized view may offer several performance advantages. Depending on the complexity of the base SQL, you may be able to populate the materialized view with incremental changes (via a materialized view log) instead of completely re-creating it during data refreshes.

Unlike snapshots, materialized views can be used dynamically by the optimizer to change the execution paths for queries. This feature, called query rewrite, enables the optimizer to use a materialized view in place of the table queried by the materialized view, even if the materialized view is not named in the query. For example, if you have a large SALES table, you may create a materialized view that sums the SALES data by region. If a user queries the SALES table for the sum of the SALES data for a region, ORACLE can redirect that query to use your materialized view in place of the SALES table. As a result, you can reduce the number of accesses against your largest tables, improving the system performance.

To enable a materialized view for query rewrite, all of the master tables for the materialized view must be in the materialized view's schema, and you must have the QUERY REWRITE system privilege. If the view and the tables are in separate schemas, you must have the GLOBAL QUERY REWRITE system privilege. In general, you should create materialized views in the same schema as the tables on which they are based; otherwise, you will need to manage the permissions and grants required to create and maintain the materialized view.

Like a snapshot, a materialized view creates a local table to store the data and a view that accesses that data. Depending on the complexity of the materialized view, ORACLE may also create an index on the materialized view's local table. You can index the materialized view's local table to improve the performance of queries against the materialized view.

To create a materialized view, use the **create materialized view** command (see Appendix A for the full syntax for this command). The example shown in the following listing creates a materialized view against the SALES table:

```
create materialized view SALES_MONTH_MV
tablespace AGG_DATA
refresh complete
start with sysdate
next sysdate+1
enable query rewrite
as
select Sales_Month, SUM(Amount)
  from SALES
 group by Sales_Month;
```

As shown in the preceding listing, the **create materialized view** command specifies the name of the view and its refresh schedule. In this example, a complete refresh of the view is chosen—each time the view is refreshed, its data will be completely deleted and re-created. For views that are not based on aggregations, you can use fast refreshes in combination with materialized view logs to send only incremental changes to the materialized view. The **start with** and **next** clauses tell ORACLE when to schedule refreshes of the data. The data will be automatically refreshed if you have enabled background job processes (via the JOB_QUEUE_PROCESSES init.ora parameter). The **tablespace** clause tells ORACLE where to store the local table for the materialized view. The **enable query rewrite** clause enables the optimizer to redirect queries of SALES to SALES_MONTH_MV if appropriate.

Fast refreshes of materialized views use materialized view logs. A materialized view log is a table stored along with the master table for the materialized view. As rows change in the master table, the changes are written to the materialized view log. During a fast refresh, the changed rows from the master table, as identified via the materialized view log, are sent to the materialized view. If the changes account for less than 25 percent of the rows in the master table, a fast refresh is generally faster than a complete refresh. For the full syntax of the **create materialized view log** command, see Appendix A.

Creating Fully Indexed Tables

You should consider fully indexing tables that have few columns and contain static data. To fully index a table is to create a set of indexes that contain all of the columns of a table, with each column used as the leading column of at least one index. For example, if the STATE table has two columns—State_Code and

Description—then you would need to create two indexes in order to fully index the table: one two-column index with State_Code as the leading column and one two-column index with Description as the leading column. The **create index** commands required are shown in the following listing:

```
create index STATE_CODE_DESCRIPTION
on STATE(State_Code, Description);

create index STATE_DESCRIPTION_CODE
on STATE(Description, State_Code);
```

Whenever you query from the STATE table using a **where** clause, one of these two indexes can be used. Since each index contains all of the data available in the table, there is no need for any subsequent table accesses. The indexes contain all of the data that users could query from the table.

Fully indexing tables is particularly useful for the codes tables, which tend to have few columns and fairly static data. As of ORACLE8, you can create index-organized tables, as described in the next section.

Creating and Managing Index-Organized Tables

An *index-organized table* keeps its data sorted according to the primary key column values for the table. Index-organized tables store their data as if the entire table was stored in an index. A normal index only stores the indexed columns in the index; an index-organized table stores all of the table's columns in the index.

Because the table's data is stored as an index, the rows of the table do not have RowIDs. Therefore, you cannot select the RowID pseudocolumn values from an index-organized table. Prior to ORACLE8i, you cannot create additional indexes on the table; the only valid index is the primary key index. As of ORACLE8i, you can create secondary indexes on an index-organized table.

To create an index-organized table, use the **organization index** clause of the **create table** command, as shown in the following example:

```
create table STATE (
State_Code      CHAR(2) primary key,
Description     VARCHAR2(25)
)
organization index;
```

In order to create STATE as an index-organized table, you must create a PRIMARY KEY constraint on it, as shown in the example. When you create STATE as an index-organized table, its data is stored in sorted order (sorted by the primary key values).

An index-organized table is appropriate if you will always be accessing the STATE data by the State_Code column (in the **where** clauses of your queries). To minimize the amount of active management of the index required, you should use index-organized tables only if the table's data is *very* static. If the table's data changes frequently, or if you need to index additional columns of the table, then you should use a regular table, with indexes as appropriate. In most cases, fully indexing tables gives you greater performance benefits, but at higher costs in terms of space allocation.

An index-organized table will require less space than if the data were stored in a normal table. Within the index, no RowID values are stored (since the table has none), so it also takes less space than an index would if the index contained all of the columns of the table.

Creating and Managing Bitmap Indexes

Normally, indexes are created on columns that are very selective; that is, there are very few rows that have the same value for the column. A column whose values are only ever Y or N is a very poor candidate for an index because the index contains only two unique values, so any access via that column will return an average of half of the table. However, if the values in those columns belong to a fairly static group of values, then you should consider using bitmap indexes for them.

For example, if there are very few distinct State_Code values in a very large EMPLOYEE table, then you would not usually create a B*tree index on State_Code, even if it is commonly used in **where** clauses. However, State_Code may be able to take advantage of a bitmap index.

Internally, a bitmap index maps the distinct values for the columns to each record. For this example, assume there are only two State_Code values (NH and DE) in a very large EMPLOYEE table. Since there are two State_Code values, there are two separate bitmap entries for the State_Code bitmap index. If the first five rows in the table have a State_Code value of DE and the next five have a State_Code value of NH, the State_Code bitmap entries would resemble those shown in the following listing:

```
State_Code bitmaps:
    DE:   < 1 1 1 1 1 0 0 0 0 0 >
    NH:   < 0 0 0 0 0 1 1 1 1 1 >
```

In the preceding listing, each number represents a row in the EMPLOYEE table. Since there are ten rows considered, there are ten bitmap values shown. Reading the bitmap for State_Code, the first five records have a value of DE (the 1 values), and the next five do not (the 0 values). You could have more than two possible values for the column, in which case there would be a separate bitmap entry for each possible value.

The ORACLE optimizer can dynamically convert bitmap index entries to RowIDs during query processing. This conversion capability allows the optimizer to use indexes on columns that have many distinct values (via B*tree indexes) and those that have few distinct values (via bitmap indexes).

To create a bitmap index, use the **bitmap** clause of the **create index** command, as shown in the following listing. You should indicate its status as a bitmap index within the index name so that it will be easy to detect during tuning operations.

```
create bitmap index EMPLOYEE$STATE_CODE$BMAP
    on EMPLOYEE(State_Code);
```

If you choose to use bitmap indexes, you will need to weigh the performance benefit during queries against the performance cost during data manipulation commands. The more bitmap indexes there are on a table, the greater the cost will be during each transaction. You should not use bitmap indexes on a column that frequently has new values added to it. Each addition of a new value to the State_Code column will require that a new bitmap be created for the new State_Code value.

When creating bitmap indexes, ORACLE compresses the bitmaps that are stored. As a result, the space required for a bitmap index may be only 5 to 10 percent of the space required for a normal index. Therefore, you should consider using bitmap indexes for any nonselective column that is frequently used in **where** clauses, provided the set of values for the column is limited. If there are new values frequently added to the column's list of values, then the bitmaps will have to be constantly adjusted.

Within a large database, bitmap indexes will yield the biggest impact when used on columns in the business transaction and aggregation tables. Codes tables are usually better served by fully indexing them; larger tables typically benefit from bitmap indexing strategies. You can create both bitmap indexes and normal (B*tree) indexes on the same table, and ORACLE will perform any necessary index conversions dynamically during query processing.

Bitmap indexes are usually not suitable for tables that are involved in many **insert**, **update**, and **delete** operations. A single bitmap index entry against a column with few unique values will contain references to several RowIDs, and thus several rows will be locked during transactions that **update** the bitmap. The locking of rows for bitmap index **update**s may significantly degrade performance of DML operations. The same performance penalty is not suffered when bitmap indexes are used as part of query-intensive decision support systems.

Managing Transactions

In a large database, batch data loads usually account for the bulk of the transactions. There is a simple logistical reason for this: machines can collect and insert data faster than an individual can process it and type it in. Consider a very effective data processing operator who enters two purchase orders per minute into a database application. At that rate, the operator would insert 120 records per hour into the system, with a total of 960 rows per day; an extra 20 minutes' work rounds the total up to 1,000 rows per day.

Contrast that with the work done by a batch-load process. Using SQL*Loader Direct Path loads, you should be able to insert 1,000 rows in less than a second. Thus, you can match a full day's output of a very skilled and consistent operator with less than a second of work. In a way, this is good news for the operators since they can now turn their attention to things more appropriate for their minds—such as analyzing data trends—rather than endlessly typing in values. The entire data collection and data loading process can occur without requiring any person to enter any command, and it can work much faster than any comparable operator-driven system.

There may be small transactions within your large database, but most of the transactions will be generated by batch operations. Therefore, when managing the transactions within a large database, you should pay special attention to the batch transactions involved in loading and aggregating the data.

The timing of your batch transactions is critical. As discussed previously in Chapter 7, executing large batch operations concurrently with small online transactions is a common cause of rollback segment–related problems in the database. Additionally, a batch process (such as SQL*Loader Direct Path loading or the ORACLE8i OCI direct loading) using a direct load option will put indexes into a load state. While the indexes are in a load state, online **update**s to the table will fail.

Ideally, the batch loads should occur when there is no online processing occurring. The more you can isolate the batch-load transactions, the more likely they will be to succeed.

Configuring the Batch Transaction Environment

In the following sections, you will see management advice for loading and deleting data from the large tables in your database. Prior to performing large batch transactions, you should create an environment that is capable of supporting the transactions.

Create Dedicated Rollback Segments

The rollback segments used by batch transactions have different characteristics than those used by transactions entered by online application users. Instead of having many small transactions, batch systems tend to have few, larger transactions. Therefore, your rollback segments that support the batch transactions will typically be few in number and have larger extent sizes than those that support online users. For example, you may have ten rollback segments with 20 extents each to support your online users, but only a single large rollback segment with ten extents to support the batch transaction.

To force a transaction to use a particular rollback segment, use the

```
set transaction use rollback segment SEGMENT_NAME;
```

command within SQL*Plus. This command should immediately follow a **commit**, even if you have not yet entered any transactions in your session. You will need to provide the name of the rollback segment you will be using for the transaction. If you are working with multiple databases, you should standardize the names of your batch transaction rollback segments to simplify your load processing. For example, you could call the batch data load rollback segment ROLL_BATCH in each database. If you use a consistent naming standard, you won't have to alter your data loading programs as you move from one database to another.

Disable Archiving of Redo Logs

Archiving the contents of your online redo log files allows you to recover in the event of a media failure. However, consider the transactions that are being written to the online redo log files during the batch load: they are the **insert**s that are occurring because of the data load. If you can completely re-create those **insert**s by reexecuting your data load, then you do not need to enable archiving of the transactions.

For example, if you are already running in ARCHIVELOG mode, you could shut the database down prior to the data load (which we'll call time T1). Start the database in NOARCHIVELOG mode (point in time T2). Execute the data load until it completes (time T3). Then, shut down and restart the database in ARCHIVELOG mode. If a media failure occurs prior to time T1, you can use the archived redo log files to recover your data. If it fails between time T2 and time T3, you can recover from that as well: recover to time T1 and reexecute the data load. At time T3, take a new backup of the database.

If you turn off the archiving of online redo log files during your data load, you need to make sure that no other transactions are occurring during your data load. If other transactions are occurring at the same time, their data may be lost during a recovery. As of ORACLE8, you can use the **nologging** parameter to avoid logging transactions against specific tables or parts of tables, as described in the next section.

Disable Logging for the Large Tables

When ORACLE7.2 was released, a new keyword was introduced to the **create table as select** and **create index** commands: **unrecoverable**. The **unrecoverable** keyword eliminated the writing of online redo log file entries during the execution of the command. As of ORACLE8, the keyword **unrecoverable** has been replaced with the more widely applicable **nologging** keyword.

When you create a table using the **nologging** keyword, the transactions that initially populate the table are not written to the online redo log. Additionally, any subsequent SQL*Loader Direct Path loads and any **insert** commands using the APPEND hint will not write redo log entries to the online redo log files. Thus, you can target specific tables (such as your large business transaction tables or the aggregation tables) for no logging. Being able to avoid writing these transactions to the online redo log files allows you to keep the full database in ARCHIVELOG state while the largest tables are essentially in NOARCHIVELOG state. You can also specify **nologging** for the LOB portions of tables that use BLOB or CLOB datatypes.

Rebuild Indexes After Data Loads

Efficient indexes are the key to fast data access in a large database. ORACLE does not perfectly manage the data in its indexes, so you must periodically rebuild your indexes. You should rebuild your indexes after every major data load. You can use the **rebuild** clause of the **alter index** command to build a new index that uses the old index as its data source.

Even if you use the SQL*Loader Direct Path option (while leaving the indexes on during the data load), you should still periodically rebuild your indexes. If you are not using that load option, then you should drop your indexes prior to the data load and then re-create them once the load completes.

The same advice holds true for mass deletions and **update**s: if many index values have been **delete**d or **update**d, you should rebuild the indexes. The better organized an index is, the faster the associated data access will be.

Loading Data

When loading data from files into your business transaction tables, you should try to eliminate factors that can slow down **insert**s. You should disable the constraints on the table and disable any triggers on the table (although batch-loaded tables should typically not have triggers anyway), and you should drop indexes prior to the data load. If you do not drop the indexes and the data is sorted prior to loading, you can use the SQL*Loader Direct Path option. In addition to managing indexes, this option allows you to insert entire blocks at a time rather than performing one **insert** per row. If the partition or table being loaded via the Direct Path load is marked as **nologging**, the loaded blocks are not written to the redo log files.

During a normal **insert** of a row, ORACLE checks the list of free blocks in the table—those new blocks that have more than **pctfree** space left in them. ORACLE finds the first block that can hold the record and **insert**s it. For the next record, ORACLE performs the search for free space again. The search is repeated for each record. SQL*Loader Direct Path avoids the cost of these searches by inserting entire blocks of data at a time.

To know where to load data, SQL*Loader first determines the *high-water mark* of the table. The high-water mark is the highest-numbered block that has ever held data in the table. For example, if you load 1,000 blocks' worth of rows into the table and then **delete** the rows, the high-water mark will point to block number 1,000. During a SQL*Loader Direct Path insert, ORACLE does not search for open space in currently used blocks. Instead, it loads blocks of data at the first block after the high-water mark. If there is space available below the high-water mark, the SQL*Loader Direct Path option will not use it.

There are only two ways to reset the high-water mark for a table: drop and re-create the table or **truncate** the table. Thus, you need to be aware of the methods used to **delete** records from a table. If you load 1,000 blocks' worth of rows into a table and later **delete** them, the high-water mark is left unchanged. A subsequent SQL*Loader Direct Path load of the same data would use 1,000 blocks—starting at block 1,001. Instead of using 1,000 blocks, the table would now use 2,000 blocks.

In addition to allowing you to use the very efficient Direct Path option, SQL*Loader also has options for parallel operations and unlogged operations. See the "Tuning" section later in this chapter for further details on parallel operations. See the "Disable Logging for the Large Tables" section earlier in this chapter for information on the **nologging** parameter.

Inserting Data

If the data being **insert**ed is from another table (such as an **insert as select** used to populate an aggregation table), you can take advantage of a new hint provided as of ORACLE8. The hint, called APPEND, uses the high-water mark as the basis for **insert**s of blocks of data, the same way SQL*Loader Direct Path does (see the previous section of this chapter for a discussion of high-water marks).

The APPEND hint tells ORACLE to find the last block into which the table's data has been **insert**ed. The new records will be **insert**ed starting in the next block following the high-water mark.

For instance, if a table had previously used 20 blocks within the database, an **insert** command that used the APPEND hint would start writing its data in the 21st block. Since the data is being written into new blocks of the table, there is much less space management work for the database to do during the **insert**. Therefore, the **insert** may complete faster when the APPEND hint is used. The table's space requirements may increase because of unused space below the high-water mark.

You specify the APPEND hint within the **insert** command. A hint looks like a comment—it starts with **/*** and ends with ***/**. The only difference in syntax is that the starting set of characters includes a **+** before the name of the hint. The following example shows an **insert** command whose data is appended to the table:

```
insert /*+ APPEND */ into SALES_PERIOD_CUST_AGG
select Period_ID, Customer_ID, SUM(Sales)
  from SALES
 group by Period_ID, Customer_ID;
```

The records from the SALES business transaction table will be **insert**ed into the SALES_PERIOD_CUST_AGG aggregation table. Instead of attempting to reuse previously used space within the SALES_PERIOD_CUST_AGG table, the new records will be placed at the end of the table's physical storage space.

Since the new records will not attempt to reuse available space that the table has already used, the space requirements for the SALES_PERIOD_CUST_AGG table may increase. In general, you should use the APPEND hint only when **insert**ing large volumes of data into tables with little reusable space.

The APPEND hint is ideal for the creation of aggregate tables, since their data source is a table stored elsewhere in the database. Since they store redundant data, aggregate tables are also good candidates for the **nologging** parameter discussed earlier in this chapter. Rows **insert**ed via the APPEND hint do not generate redo log entries if the table being loaded has the **nologging** parameter enabled.

NOTE
*Some purchased applications are designed to be database-independent and may not use SQL*Loader for data loading. If the application provides an executable that performs loads, check with the vendor or the application support team to make sure array processing is performed during **insert**s. Avoid row-by-row **insert**s, even in batch mode.*

Deleting Data

When managing large volumes of data, you should try to set up your tables so you can use the **truncate** command. If the data is all stored in a single large table, you should consider using partitions since you can **truncate** partitions via the **alter table** command shown earlier in this chapter. If you need to **delete** large volumes at once via the **delete** command, however, you will need to either configure your environment to support a large transaction or you will need to use a procedural method to break the transaction into smaller pieces.

Configuring the Environment

The configuration requirements for large **delete**s are identical to those required for large **insert**s; you need to create and maintain a rollback segment that is large enough to support the transaction. To force the rollback segment to be used by the transaction, use the **set transaction use rollback segment** command immediately following a **commit**. You should schedule the bulk **delete** to occur during a time when there are few other transactions occurring in the database to avoid potential read concurrency problems.

Using a Procedural Method

You can use PL/SQL to break a single deletion into multiple transactions. You can create a PL/SQL block that takes as its input the **delete** command and the number of records to **commit** in each batch. For example, if there are one million records to **delete** and you cannot use the **truncate** command, you can force a **commit** after every 1,000 records. To do this, you will need to use dynamic PL/SQL and loops. In the following PL/SQL procedure (developed and distributed by ORACLE Support), the two input parameters are the SQL statement and the number of records to be committed in each batch. For example, suppose the **delete** command is

```
delete from SALES where Customer_ID=12;
```

and you want to **commit** after each 1,000 rows committed. The procedure, named DELETE_COMMIT, will be called with those two parameters, as shown here:

```
execute DELETE_COMMIT('delete from SALES where Customer_ID=12',1000);
```

If the values in the **where** clause are character strings, enclose them in double sets of quotes.

```
execute DELETE_COMMIT('delete from SALES where State_Code = ''NH''',500)
```

The code for the DELETE_COMMIT procedure is shown here:

```
create or replace procedure DELETE_COMMIT
( p_statement in varchar2,
  p_commit_batch_size   in number default 10000)
is
        cid                             integer;
        changed_statement               varchar2(2000);
        finished                        boolean;
        nofrows                         integer;
        lrowid                          rowid;
        rowcnt                          integer;
        errpsn                          integer;
```

```
        sqlfcd                          integer;
        errc                            integer;
        errm                            varchar2(2000);
begin
        /* If the actual statement contains a WHERE clause, then
           append a rownum < n clause after that using AND, else
           use WHERE rownum < n clause */
        if ( upper(p_statement) like '% WHERE %') then
                changed_statement := p_statement||' AND rownum < '
                ||to_char(p_commit_batch_size + 1);
        else
changed_statement := p_statement||' WHERE rownum < '
||to_char(p_commit_batch_size + 1);
        end if;
        begin
  cid := dbms_sql.open_cursor; -- Open a cursor for the task
                dbms_sql.parse(cid,changed_statement, dbms_sql.native);
                        -- parse the cursor.
  rowcnt := dbms_sql.last_row_count;
                        -- store for some future reporting
        exception
           when others then
                    errpsn := dbms_sql.last_error_position;
                        -- gives the error position in the changed sql
                        -- delete statement if anything happens
     sqlfcd := dbms_sql.last_sql_function_code;
                        -- function code can be found in the OCI manual
                    lrowid := dbms_sql.last_row_id;
                        -- store all these values for error reporting.
                        -- However all these are really useful in a
                        -- stand-alone proc execution for dbms_output
                        -- to be successful, not possible when called
                        -- from a form or front-end tool.
                    errc := SQLCODE;
                    errm := SQLERRM;
                    dbms_output.put_line('Error '||to_char(errc)||
                            ' Posn '||to_char(errpsn)||
               ' SQL fCode '||to_char(sqlfcd)||
          ' rowid '||rowidtochar(lrowid));
                        raise_application_error(-20000,errm);
                        -- this will ensure the display of at least
                        -- the error message if something happens,
                        -- even in a front-end tool.
        end;
        finished := FALSE;
      while not (finished)
      loop -- keep on executing the cursor till there is no more
              -- to process.
                  begin
 nofrows := dbms_sql.execute(cid);
```

```
                        rowcnt := dbms_sql.last_row_count;
                exception
                        when others then
                                errpsn := dbms_sql.last_error_position;
                                sqlfcd := dbms_sql.last_sql_function_code;
                                lrowid := dbms_sql.last_row_id;
                                errc := SQLCODE;
                                errm := SQLERRM;
                        dbms_output.put_line('Error '||to_char(errc)||
                                ' Posn '||to_char(errpsn)||
                        ' SQL fCode '||to_char(sqlfcd)||
                ' rowid '||rowidtochar(lrowid));
                                raise_application_error(-20000,errm);
                        end;
                        if nofrows = 0 then
                                finished := TRUE;
                        else
                         finished := FALSE;
                        end if;
                        commit;
                end loop;
                begin
                        dbms_sql.close_cursor(cid);
                                -- close the cursor for a clean finish
                exception
                        when others then
                                errpsn := dbms_sql.last_error_position;
                                sqlfcd := dbms_sql.last_sql_function_code;
                                lrowid := dbms_sql.last_row_id;
        errc := SQLCODE;
                                errm := SQLERRM;
          dbms_output.put_line('Error '||to_char(errc)||
          ' Posn '||to_char(errpsn)||
                                        ' SQL fCode '||to_char(sqlfcd)||
                                        ' rowid '||rowidtochar(lrowid));
                                raise_application_error(-20000,errm);
                        end;
end;
/
```

Much of the code in the DELETE_COMMIT procedure handles any exceptions that may be encountered during statement processing. Conceptually, the executable command section follows this logic: If the **delete** command contains a **where** clause already, append an **and** clause to the statement; otherwise, append a **where** clause. These clauses are used to limit the number of rows **delete**d at a time. Process and

commit the **delete** for the specified number of records. The second time the **delete** is executed, a second set of rows will be **delete**d. Reexecute the **delete** until there are no more records that match the **where** clause criteria.

The exceptions that may be raised are documented within the procedure and are rarely encountered. For best performance, be sure that the **delete** command's **where** clause can use indexes. You can use the **explain plan** command prior to executing the command to determine if a **delete** command will use indexes. See Chapter 8 for information on the **explain plan** command.

Backups

Why bother backing up a large database?

That may seem a bit of a heretical question for a DBA to ask, but it is relevant and appropriate. By definition, you cannot recover the large database in less than 18 hours. Often, you can reload the database and re-create the aggregations in less time than it would take to recover the data using the ORACLE backup and recovery utilities. If you can reload the data faster than you can recover it, do you need to back up the data at all? The answer depends on the way in which your data load processing occurs.

Evaluating Backup Needs and Strategies

As described earlier in this chapter, most large databases have four types of tables:

- Large business transaction tables, which contain the majority of the raw data in the database

- Aggregation tables, which store aggregated data from the business transaction tables

- Codes tables

- Temporary work tables

When evaluating your database's backup needs, you should evaluate the backup needs for each type of table.

The backup requirements for business transaction tables are driven by the data load processing methods used. If the business transaction data is completely replaced with each data load, then you can use the data load process to recover the data; you do not need to rely on ORACLE's tools such as Export. If the business transaction data is not completely replaced with each data load, you may be able to use a combination of backup methods to recover the data.

For example, if each data load consists of only one period's worth of data in the SALES table, you will need to back up the prior periods' data as well as the current period's data. There are two ways to do this:

1. Export the old data and use the data load process to re-create the current period's data.

2. Save the old data files and during a recovery run the data load for each period separately.

Depending on your data load procedures, the second option may allow your recovery to complete faster. You can still use the Export utility as a backup to your data load recovery method.

If the data in your business transaction tables can be updated after loading, you will need to be able to re-create those transactions. You can either Export the data following the transactions or you can run the database in ARCHIVELOG mode. If you are relying on the archived redo log files to re-create the transaction data, you cannot place the business transaction table in **nologging** mode. You can also use RMAN (see Chapter 10) to minimize the amount of data backed up during file system backups.

In an ideal scenario, the business transaction table is completely reloaded during each data load and no **update**s occur following the data load. If you need to recover the business transaction table, you can simply reexecute the data load procedure and the table can be kept in **nologging** state. As an additional backup method, you can Export the data following each data load. If your data can be **update**d following a data load, or if the data load does not account for all of the data in the table, then you need to back up the user transactions or the historical data.

Aggregation tables store redundant data. All of the data in the aggregation tables can be generated by rerunning the commands used to create them. If you lose an aggregation table (for example, if it is accidentally dropped), you can re-create it by executing the **create table as select** command used to populate it. You should not permit modifications to the aggregation tables following their creation. If data needs to be changed, it should be changed in the business transaction tables that are the data source of the aggregation tables, and the aggregation tables should then be re-created.

Given these characteristics of aggregation tables, there is no need to use ARCHIVELOG backups for them. You may wish to export the data following the table creation, but you can usually re-create the table faster via SQL than via Import. This performance difference is greatest if you use the APPEND hint of the **insert** command as described earlier in this chapter.

Codes tables store static data. There should be very few transactions occurring in the codes tables. Therefore, exports are usually sufficient for the codes tables. Since there are so few transactions occurring, there is no need to use archived redo log files to recover them; if you time your export properly, you should be able to use the exports during recovery with no data loss.

Temporary work tables are used during data load processing and are typically not accessed as part of the production application. Therefore, the only recovery needs for the temporary work tables arise as part of the data load process. For example, you may wish to back up the temporary work tables at different points in the data load in order to minimize the amount of recovery activity needed if the data load process fails. Since there are no online transactions occurring within the temporary work tables, exports are usually used to back up these tables.

Developing the Backup Plan

Consider a large database whose business transaction tables are fully reloaded during each load (with no subsequent transactions in them) and whose codes tables are unchanging. What is the appropriate backup strategy? For such a system, there is no need to use ARCHIVELOG mode anywhere; indeed, it may be appropriate to put many of the tables into **nologging** state. The backup strategy could be as follows:

1. Export the business transaction tables following data loads. Rely primarily on the data load process for recovery.

2. Export the aggregation tables following their creation. Rely primarily on table re-creation for recovery.

3. Export the codes tables after major changes. If the tables are small enough, you can also create copies of the codes tables via **create table as select** commands. Rely primarily on the exports for recovery.

4. Export the temporary work tables after critical steps in the data load process. Rely primarily on the data load process for recovery.

Although each of the table types relies on exports, the exports are performed at different times in the data processing. Only one of the table types (codes tables) relies on exports as its primary recovery method.

It is very likely that this kind of backup strategy is inconsistent with the backup strategy used on your other, online transactions systems. However, there are a few key similarities:

1. Each table has a primary backup method and a secondary backup method. If, for example, the **create table as select** for an aggregation table fails, you can rely on the export of that table as a secondary recovery method. Never rely on just one backup method.

2. Each recovery type should be fully tested. If you have not tested a recovery operation, then you cannot rely on it.

If you follow these guidelines, your large database will be recoverable—even if you rely on exports only for the backup of the codes tables. As you tune your data load process, you should be able to reduce the time required to recover the database, giving you greater flexibility in its management.

Tuning

Tuning a large database is a two-part process: first tune the environment, then tune the specific queries and transactions that place the largest performance burden on the database. The tuning of database environments was discussed in Chapter 8, and some transaction tuning tips were provided earlier in this chapter. For example, your data load processes should use the block insert methods found in the SQL*Loader Direct Path loader and the APPEND hint of the **insert** command.

For a large database, the data block buffer portion of the System Global Area (SGA) should be approximately 2 percent of the database size. For a 100GB database, the SGA may be 2GB. An SGA that large implies that the database is being run on a host and operating system that can support the management of large memory areas.

When creating the database, you should set the database block size to the highest value supported by ORACLE on your operating system. The larger the database block is, the more efficiently data is stored. When you are managing a small database, the improvements in storage efficiency and data access that come from using a larger database block size are noticeable. When you are managing a large database, they are substantial. Doubling the database block size typically results in performance gains of about 40 percent on most batch operations.

NOTE
You cannot alter the database block size after a database has been created. The database block size is set based on the value of the DB_BLOCK_SIZE parameter in the init.ora file used when the database is created.

You should consider partitioning the main tables of the large database as described in the "Partitions" section of this chapter. By partitioning the table, you can dramatically improve your ability to effectively manage it. For example, you can use partitioning to distribute the I/O burden due to a table's accesses across multiple smaller tables, based on the table values. You can then **truncate** or modify one partition of the table without affecting the rest of the table. Use local indexes for the greatest flexibility in managing index partitions. You can also use materialized views to automate the aggregation process and enable the query rewrite capability within the optimizer.

Outside of the database, you should take advantage of the available devices and disk storage architectures to properly distribute the system I/O requirements. See the "Choosing a Physical Layout" section earlier in this chapter for information on disk options and architectures such as RAID devices and disk mirroring.

If your host machine has multiple CPUs available, you may be able to take full advantage of ORACLE's Parallel Query Option (PQO). When you use PQO, multiple processes are created to complete a single task—such as a query or an index creation. Because they involve large transactions and sorts, large databases typically benefit from the use of the PQO. See Chapter 8 for information on the usage of the PQO.

Tuning Queries of Large Tables

In addition to creating fully indexed tables, creating bitmap indexes, partitioning tables and indexes, and using the PQO for queries of large tables, you can further tune queries of large tables to minimize their impact on the rest of the database. Whereas multiple users can benefit from sharing data from small tables in the SGA, that benefit disappears when very large tables are accessed. For very large tables, index accesses can have a negative effect on the rest of the database.

When a table and its indexes are small, there can be a high degree of data sharing within the SGA. Multiple users performing table reads or index range scans can use the same blocks over and over. As a result of the reuse of blocks within the SGA, the *hit ratio*—a measure of the reuse of blocks within the SGA—increases.

As a table grows, the table's indexes grow too. If a table and its indexes grow much larger than the available space in the SGA, it becomes less likely that the next row needed by a range scan will be found within the SGA. The reusability of data within the SGA's data block buffer cache will diminish. The hit ratio for the database will decrease. Eventually, each logical read will require a separate physical read.

The SGA is designed to maximize the reuse (among multiple users) of the blocks read from the datafiles. To do this, the SGA maintains a list of the blocks that have been read; if the blocks were read via index accesses or via table access by RowID, those blocks are kept in the SGA the longest. If a block is read into the SGA via a full table scan, that block is the first to be removed from the SGA when more space is needed in the data block buffer cache.

For applications with small tables, the data block buffer cache management in the SGA maximizes the reuse of blocks and increases the hit ratio. What happens, though, if an index range scan is performed on a very large table? The index's blocks will be kept for a long time in the SGA, even though it is likely that no other users will be able to use the values in the index's blocks. Since the index is large, many of its blocks may be read, consuming a substantial portion of the available space in the SGA's data block buffer cache. A greater amount of space will be consumed by the table blocks accessed by RowID, and those blocks will be even less likely to be reused. The hit ratio will begin to drop—ironically, because index scans are being performed. The tuning methods used for very large tables therefore focus on special indexing techniques and on alternatives to indexes.

Manage Data Proximity

If you intend to continue using indexes during accesses of very large tables, you must be concerned about *data proximity*—the physical relationship between logically related records. To maximize data proximity, **insert** records into the table sequentially, ordered by columns commonly used in range scans of the table. For example, the primary key of the large SALES table is the combination of Period_ID, Customer_ID, and Sale_No. Accesses that use Period_ID as a limiting condition will be able to use the unique index on the primary key; but if range scans are commonly performed on the SALES.Customer_ID column, the data should be stored in order of Customer_ID.

If the data is stored in an ordered format, then during range searches, such as

```
where Customer_ID between 123 and 241
```

you will more likely be able to reuse the table and index blocks read into the SGA because all of the Customer_ID values with a value of 123 will be stored together. Fewer index and table blocks will be read into the SGA's data block buffer cache, minimizing the impact of the index range scan on the SGA. Storing data in an ordered fashion helps range scans regardless of the size of the table, but it is particularly critical for large tables due to the negative implications of large range scans.

Avoid Unhelpful Index Scans

If you are going to use index scans against a large table, you cannot assume that the index scan will perform better than a full table scan. Unique scans or range scans of indexes that are not followed by table accesses perform well, but a range scan of an index followed by a table access by RowID may perform poorly. As the table grows to be significantly larger than the data block buffer cache, the break-even point between index scans and full table scans decreases—eventually, if you read more than 1 percent of the rows in a 10,000,000-row table, you are better off performing a full table scan rather than an index range scan and table access by RowID combination.

Full table scans may perform better because of the way ORACLE manages the data block buffer cache of the SGA. If a large index scan is performed in a large table, then many index blocks will be stored in the SGA—and they will be kept in the SGA as long as possible. By contrast, blocks read by the full table scan will be flushed out of the SGA as quickly as possible. Therefore, if any other objects have blocks of data in the SGA, they will be unaffected by the full table scan; the index-based access, however, would flush them from the cache.

There are a few blocks from the full table scan that are retained in the SGA. The blocks held in the SGA because of the full table scan are those blocks read in via the last read; the number of blocks read is determined by the setting of the DB_FILE_MULTIBLOCK_READ_COUNT init.ora parameter. The size of the cache area used by the full table scan blocks is the product of the DB_FILE_MULTIBLOCK_READ_COUNT parameter and the DB_BLOCK_SIZE parameter.

As of ORACLE8i, you can also specify multiple buffer pools and assign objects to those pools. For example, you can create a RECYCLE pool, and assign your largest tables to that pool. Using a RECYCLE pool will minimize the impact of scans of the large table on the memory management within the SGA.

Favoring full table scans is not a typical tuning method. However, if a table is so large that its index-based accesses will override the SGA, you should consider using a full table scan for queries of very large tables in multiuser environments. To improve the performance of the full table scan, consider parallelizing the operation.

Using Transportable Tablespaces

ORACLE has introduced a significant number of features designed to improve the performance of data movement operations. As highlighted in the earlier sections of this chapter, these data movement features include the following:

- The **truncate** command for bulk **delete**s

- The APPEND hint and SQL*Loader Direct Path loads for **insert**s

- Partitions for dividing tables and indexes into smaller sets of data

- **nologging** operations

As of ORACLE8i, you can use another new feature—transportable tablespaces—to improve the performance of data movement operations. Transportable tablespaces should improve the performance of operations that move large amounts of data between databases. You can transport both data and indexes, but you cannot transport bitmap indexes or tables containing collectors (nested tables and varying arrays).

To transport tablespaces, you need to generate a tablespace set, move that tablespace set to the new database, and plug the set into the new database. In the following section, you will see the steps to follow along with implementation tips. The databases should be on the same operating system, with the same version of ORACLE, database block size, and character set.

Generating a Transportable Tablespace Set

A transportable tablespace set contains all of the datafiles for the tablespaces being moved, along with an export of the metadata for those tablespaces. The tablespaces being transported should be self-contained—they should not contain any objects that are dependent on objects outside of the tablespaces. For example, if you want to move a table, you must also transport the tablespace that contains the table's indexes. The better you have organized and distributed your objects among tablespaces (see Chapter 3), the easier it is to generate a self-contained set of tablespaces to transport.

You can optionally choose whether to include referential integrity constraints as part of the transportable tablespace set. If you choose to use referential integrity constraints, the transportable tablespace set will increase to include the tables required to maintain the key relationships. Referential integrity is optional because you may have the same codes tables in multiple databases. For example, you may be planning to move a tablespace from your test database to your production database. If you have a COUNTRY table in the test database, then you may already have an identical COUNTRY table in the production database. Since the codes tables are identical in the two databases, you do not need to transport that portion of the referential integrity constraints. You could transport the tablespace and then reenable the referential integrity in the target database once the tablespace has been moved, simplifying the creation of the transportable tablespace set.

To determine if a tablespace set is self-contained, you can execute the TRANSPORT_SET_CHECK procedure of the DBMS_TTS package. This procedure takes two input parameters: the set of tablespaces and a Boolean flag set to TRUE if you want referential integrity constraints to be considered. In the following example, referential integrity constraints are not considered for the combination of the AGG_DATA and AGG_INDEXES tablespaces:

```
execute DBMS_TTS.TRANSPORT_SET_CHECK('AGG_DATA,AGG_INDEXES','FALSE');
```

If there are any self-containment violations in the specified set, ORACLE will populate the TRANSPORT_SET_VIOLATIONS data dictionary view. If there are no violations, the view will be empty.

Once you have selected a self-contained set of tablespaces, make the tablespaces read only, as shown here:

```
alter tablespace AGG_DATA read only;
alter tablespace AGG_INDEXES read only;
```

Next, export the metadata for the tablespaces, using the TRANSPORT_ TABLESPACE and TABLESPACES Export parameters:

```
exp TRANSPORT_TABLESPACE=Y TABLESPACES=(AGG_DATA,AGG_INDEXES) CONSTRAINTS=N  GRANTS=Y TRIGGERS=N
```

As shown in the example, you can specify whether triggers, constraints, and grants are exported along with the tablespace metadata. You should also note the names of the accounts that own objects in the transportable tablespace set. You can now copy the tablespaces' datafiles to a separate area. If needed, you can put the tablespaces back into read-write mode in their current database. After you have generated the transportable tablespace set, you can move its files (including the export) to an area that the target database can access.

Plugging in the Transportable Tablespace Set

Once the transportable tablespace set has been moved to an area accessible to the target database, you can plug the set into the target database. First, use Import to import the exported metadata:

```
imp TRANSPORT_TABLESPACE=Y DATAFILES=(agg_data.dbf, agg_indexes.dbf)
```

In the import, you specify the datafiles that are part of the transportable tablespace set. You can optionally specify the tablespaces (via the TABLESPACES parameter) and the object owners (via the OWNERS parameter).

After the import completes, all tablespaces in the transportable tablespace set are left in read-only mode. You can issue the **alter tablespace read write** command in the target database to place the new tablespaces in read-write mode.

```
alter tablespace AGG_DATA read write;
alter tablespace AGG_INDEXES read write;
```

Note that you cannot change the ownership of the objects being transported.

Transportable tablespaces support very fast movement of large datasets. In a data warehouse, you could use transportable tablespaces to publish aggregations from core warehouse to data marts, or from the data marts to a global data warehouse. Any read-only data can be quickly distributed to multiple databases—instead of sending SQL scripts, you can send datafiles and exported metadata. This modified data movement process may greatly simplify your procedures for managing remote databases, remote data marts, and large data movement operations.

Locally Managed Tablespaces

In ORACLE8i, there are two different methods that can be used to track free and used space in a tablespace. The first method, which has been available since the advent of tablespaces and is the default behavior, is to handle extent management via the data dictionary (dictionary-managed tablespaces). In a dictionary-managed tablespace, each time an extent is allocated or freed for reuse in a tablespace, the appropriate entry is **update**d in the data dictionary table. Rollback information is also stored about each **update** of the dictionary table. Dictionary tables and rollback segments are part of the database and the rules that apply to other data activity apply to them as well. Therefore, recursive space management operations can occur as extents are acquired and released.

The second method, available as of ORACLE8i, is to handle extent management within the tablespaces themselves (locally managed tablespaces). In locally managed tablespaces, the tablespace manages its own space by maintaining a bitmap in each datafile of the free and used blocks or sets of blocks in the datafile. Each time an extent is allocated or freed for reuse, ORACLE **update**s the bitmap to show the new status.

When you use locally managed tablespaces, the dictionary is not **update**d and rollback activity is not generated. Locally managed tablespaces automatically track adjacent free space, so there is no need to coalesce extents. Within a locally managed tablespace, all extents can have the same size or the system can automatically determine the size of extents.

To use this feature, you must specify the **local** option for the **extent management** clause in the **create tablespace** command. An example of the **create tablespace** command declaring a locally managed tablespace is shown here:

```
create tablespace CODES_TABLES
datafile '/u01/oracle/VLDB/codes_tables.dbf'
size 10M
extent_management local uniform size 256K;
```

Assuming that the block size for the database in which this tablespace is created is 4KB, in this example, the tablespace is created with the extent management declared as **local** and with a uniform size of 256KB. Each bit in the bitmap describes 64 blocks (256/4). If the **uniform size** clause is omitted, the default is **autoallocate**. The default **size** for **uniform** is 1MB.

NOTE
*If you specify **local** in a **create tablespace** command, you can not specify a **default storage** clause, **minextents**, or **temporary**. If you use the **create temporary tablespace** command to create the tablespace, you can specify **extent_management local**.*

In the case of the SYSTEM tablespace, you can declare the extent management as **local** in the **create database** statement. If you create the SYSTEM tablespace as locally managed, all of the rollback segments must be created in a locally managed tablespace. However, any of the other tablespaces in the database can have dictionary-managed extents. The use of local extent management with a specification for **local size** can ensure that space within the tablespace is reused effectively.

As your database objects grow in extents, locally managed tablespaces become more important. As noted in Chapter 4, DDL space management operations on tables with thousands of extents perform poorly due to the data dictionary management involved. If you use locally managed tablespaces, that performance penalty is significantly reduced.

PART III

Networked Oracle

CHAPTER
13

SQL*Net V2 and Net8

t's hard to find a computer these days that isn't tied into a network. Distributing computing power across servers and sharing information across networks greatly enhances the value of the computing resources available. Instead of being a stand-alone server, the server becomes an entry point for the information superhighway.

Databases can also be distributed; the ORACLE tool *SQL*Net* functions as the on-ramp to the database information highway. As of ORACLE8, SQL*Net has been modified and is referred to as Net8; Net8 and SQL*Net V2 share many common architectural components, and both can be used to connect to ORACLE databases. SQL*Net V2 and Net8 facilitate the sharing of data between databases, even if those databases are on different types of servers running different operating systems and communications protocols. They also allow for *client/server* applications to be created; the server can then function primarily for database I/O, while the data presentation requirements of an application can be moved to the front-end client machines.

SQL*Net V2 and Net8 support both ORACLE7 and ORACLE8. Thus, you could use SQL*Net V2 to access your ORACLE8 databases while you migrate your applications from ORACLE7 to ORACLE8. The major differences between SQL*Net V2 and Net8 are in their administrative tools and in the area of connection management. Once the migration to ORACLE8 is completed, the NET8 tool set should be used. In this chapter, you will see how to administer both SQL*Net V2 and Net8.

The installation and configuration instructions for SQL*Net V2 and Net8 depend on the particular hardware, operating system, and communications software you are using. The material provided here will help you get the most out of your database networking, regardless of your configuration.

Overview of SQL*Net V2 and Net8

Using SQL*Net V2 or Net8 distributes the workload associated with database applications. Since many database queries are performed via applications, a server-based application forces the server to support both the CPU requirements of the application and the I/O requirements of the database (see Figure 13-1a). Using a client/server configuration (also referred to as a *two-tier architecture*) allows this load to be distributed between two machines. The first, called the *client*, supports the application that initiates the request from the database. The back-end machine on which the database resides is called the *server*. The client bears the burden of presenting the data, while the database server is dedicated to supporting queries, not applications. This distribution of resource requirements is shown in Figure 13-1b.

When the client sends a database request to the server, the server receives and executes the SQL statement that is passed to it. The results of the SQL statement, plus any error conditions that are returned, are then sent back to the client. The

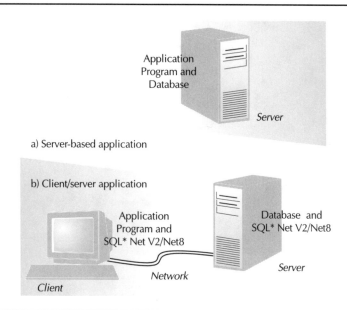

a) Server-based application

b) Client/server application

FIGURE 13-1.   *Client/server architecture*

client/server configuration needs a fairly robust workstation with a large hard drive (2GB or more) and large memory requirements (usually over 64MB of RAM). The resources required have caused the client/server configuration to sometimes be dubbed *fat client* architecture. Although workstation costs have dropped appreciably over recent years, the cost impact to a company can still be substantial.

A newer, more cost-effective architecture used with SQL*Net V2 and Net8 is a *thin-client* configuration (also referred to as a *three-tier* architecture). The application code is housed and executed using Java scripts on a separate server from the database server. The client resource requirements become very low and the cost is reduced dramatically. The application code becomes isolated from the database. Figure 13-2 shows the thin client configuration.

The client connects to the application server. Once the client is validated, display management code is downloaded to the client in the form of Java applets. A database request is sent from the client through the application server to the database server; the database server then receives and executes the SQL statement that is passed to it. The results of the SQL statement, plus any error conditions that are returned, are then sent back to the client through the application server. In some versions of the three-tier architecture, some of the application processing is performed on the application server and the rest is performed on the database

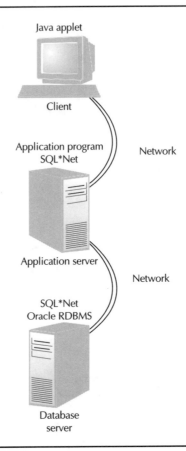

Java applet

Client

Application program
SQL*Net

Network

Application server

Network

SQL*Net
Oracle RDBMS

Database
server

FIGURE 13-2. *Thin-client architecture*

server. The advantage of a thin-client architecture is that you have low resource requirements and maintenance on the client side, medium resource requirements and central maintenance on the application server, and high resource but lower maintenance requirements on one or two back-end database servers.

In addition to client/server and thin-client implementations, *server/server* configurations are often needed. In this type of environment, databases on separate servers share data with each other. You can then physically isolate each server from every other server without logically isolating the servers. A typical implementation of this type involves corporate headquarters servers that communicate with departmental servers in various locations. Each server supports client applications, but it also has the ability to communicate with other servers in the network. This architecture is shown in Figure 13-3.

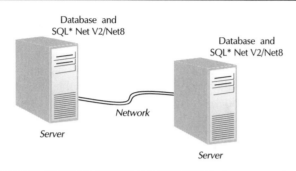

FIGURE 13-3.   *Server/server architecture*

When one of the servers sends a database request to another server, the sending server acts like a client. The receiving server executes the SQL statement that is passed to it, and returns the results plus error conditions to the sender.

SQL*Net V2 and Net8 allow these architectures to become reality. When run on the clients and the servers, they allow database requests made from one database (or application) to be passed to another database on a separate server. In most cases, machines can function both as clients and servers; the only exceptions are operating systems with single-user architectures, such as MS-DOS. In such cases, those machines can only function as clients.

The end result of a SQL*Net V2 or Net8 implementation is the ability to communicate with all databases that are accessible via the network. You can then create synonyms that give applications true network transparency; the user who submits the query will not know the location of the data that is used to resolve it. In this chapter, you will see the main configuration methods and files used to manage the interdatabase communications, along with usage examples. You will see more detailed examples of distributed database management in Chapter 16.

Each object in a database is uniquely identified by its owner and name. For example, there will only be one table named EMPLOYEE owned by the user HR; there cannot be two objects of the same name and type within the same schema.

Within distributed databases, two additional layers of object identification must be added. First, the name of the instance that accesses the database must be identified. Next, the name of the server on which that instance resides must be identified. Putting together these four parts of the object's name—its server, its instance, its owner, and its name—results in a *Fully Qualified Object Name* (*FQON*). In order to access a remote table, the table's FQON must be known. DBAs and application administrators can set up access paths to automate the selection of all four parts of the FQON. In the following sections, you will see how to set up the access paths used by SQL*Net V2 and Net8.

The foundation of SQL*Net V2 is the Transparent Network Substrate (TNS), which resolves all server-level connectivity issues. SQL*Net V2 relies on configuration files on the client and the server to manage the database connectivity. If the client and server use different communications protocols, the MultiProtocol Interchange (described in a later section of this chapter) manages the connections. The combination of the MultiProtocol Interchange and the TNS allows SQL*Net V2 connections to be made independent of the operating system and communications protocol run by each server.

SQL*Net V2 also has the capability to send and receive data requests in an asynchronous manner; this allows it to support the multithreaded server (MTS) architecture. The Net8 Connection Manager replaces the MultiProtocol Interchange and further expands ORACLE's support of the MTS architecture. Net8 for version 8.1.5 supports connections to databases running version 7.3.4 or higher.

Connect Descriptors

The server and instance portions of an object's FQON in SQL*Net V2 are identified by means of a *connect descriptor*. A connect descriptor specifies the communications protocol, server name, and instance name to use when performing the query. Because of the protocol-independence of SQL*Net V2, the descriptor also includes hardware connectivity information. The format for a SQL*Net V2 connect descriptor is shown in the following listing. The example shown here uses the TCP/IP protocol, and specifies a connection to an instance named LOC on a server named HQ. The keywords are protocol-specific.

```
(DESCRIPTION=
        (ADDRESS=
                (PROTOCOL=TCP)
                (HOST=HQ)
                (PORT=1521))
        (CONNECT DATA=
                (SID=loc)))
```

In this connect descriptor, the protocol is set to TCP/IP, the server (HOST) is set to HQ, and the port on that host that should be used for the connection is port 1521 (which is the recommended port assignment for SQL*Net V2 in UNIX installations). The instance name is specified in a separate part of the descriptor as the SID assignment.

The structure for this descriptor is consistent across all protocols. Also, the descriptors can be automatically generated via the Network Manager tool for ORACLE7 instances or the Net8 Assistant tool for ORACLE8 and ORACLE8i. As previously noted, the keywords used by the connect descriptors are protocol-specific. The keywords to use and the values to give them are provided in the operating-system-specific documentation for SQL*Net V2.

Service Names

Users are not expected to type in a connect descriptor each time they want to access remote data. Instead, the DBA can set up *service names* (aliases), which refer to these connect descriptors. Service names are stored in a file called tnsnames.ora. This file should be copied to all servers on the database network. Every client and application server should have a copy of this file.

On the server, the tnsnames.ora file should be located in the directory specified by the TNS_ADMIN environment variable. The file is usually stored in a common directory, such as the /etc directory on UNIX systems. On the client, the file should be located in the /network/admin subdirectory under your ORACLE software home directory.

A sample entry in the tnsnames.ora file is shown in the following listing. This example assigns a service name of LOC to the connect descriptor given above:

```
LOC =(DESCRIPTION=
        (ADDRESS=
                (PROTOCOL=TCP)
                (HOST=HQ)
                (PORT=1521))
        (CONNECT DATA=
                (SID=loc)))
```

A user wishing to connect to the LOC instance on the HQ server can now use the LOC service name, as shown in this example:

```
sqlplus hr/puffinstuff@LOC;
```

The @ sign tells the database to use the service name that follows it to determine which database to log in to. If the username and password are correct for that database, then a session is opened there and the user can begin using the database.

Service names create aliases for connect descriptors, so you do not need to give the service name the same name as the instance. For example, you could give the LOC instance the service name PROD or TEST, depending on its use within your environment. The use of synonyms to further enhance location transparency will be described in the "Usage Example: Database Links" section of this chapter.

Additional tnsnames.ora Parameters and Issues

In addition to the parameters shown in the preceding tnsnames.ora example, there are other configuration options. For example, you can specify the buffer sizes for SQL*Net to use (see the "Tuning SQL*Net and Net8" section later in this chapter for details). In SQL*Net V2, you can specify a COMMUNITY setting, for use by the MultiProtocol Interchange. The MultiProtocol Interchange is obsolete as of Net8, so Net8 simply ignores the COMMUNITY parameter if it exists. See "The MultiProtocol Interchange" section later in this chapter for a description of that service.

The MultiProtocol Interchange is replaced by the Connection Manager in Net8. If you set the SOURCE_ROUTE parameter in tnsnames.ora to YES, then Net8 will create a source route of addresses through the Connection Managers to the destination database. See the "Using Connection Manager" section later in this chapter for further details.

Keep the tnsnames.ora file as short as possible, since it is fully read each time a service name is referenced. If the tnsnames.ora file contains extraneous data (such as instance specifications for instances that no longer exist), then you are adversely impacting the performance of every database connection. If you have a highly secure environment, you may need to create multiple tnsnames.ora files, each of which contains only those entries that the users need to know about. For example, you may create a tnsnames.ora file that lists only the databases used by the marketing department, so no marketing users will be aware of any non-marketing databases. While this approach enhances your security, it increases the difficulty of managing tnsnames.ora entries and file distribution.

Listeners

Each database server on the network must contain a listener.ora file. The listener.ora file lists the names and addresses of all of the listener processes on the machine and the instances they support. Listener processes receive connections from SQL*Net V2 and Net8 clients.

A listener.ora file has four parts:

- A header section
- The address list—an interprocess calls (IPC) address-definition section
- Instance definitions
- Operational parameters

The listener.ora file is automatically generated by the Network Manager (SQL*Net V2) and Net8 Assistant tools. You can edit the resulting file as long as you follow its syntax rules. The following listing shows sample sections of a listener.ora file—an address definition and an instance definition:

```
LISTENER =
    (ADDRESS_LIST =
        (ADDRESS=
          (PROTOCOL=IPC)
          (KEY= loc.world)
        )
    )
SID_LIST_LISTENER =
  (SID_LIST =
```

```
(SID_DESC =
  (SID_NAME = loc)
  (ORACLE_HOME = /orasw/app/oracle/product/8.1.5.1)
)
)
```

The first portion of this listing contains the address list—one entry per instance. In this case, the listener is listening for connections to the service identified as loc.world. The .world suffix is the default domain name for SQL*Net V2 connections. In Net8, the default domain name has been changed to be a NULL string.

The second portion of the listing, beginning with the SID_LIST_LISTENER clause, identifies the ORACLE software home directory for each instance the listener is servicing. If you change the ORACLE software home directory for an instance, you need to change the listener.ora file for the server.

Additional listener.ora Parameters

The listener.ora file supports a number of additional parameters. The parameters should each be suffixed with the listener name. For example, the default listener name is LISTENER, so the LOG_FILE parameter is named LOG_FILE_LISTENER. The additional listener.ora parameters are listed in Table 13-1.

You can modify the listener parameters after the listener has been started. If you use the SAVE_CONFIG_ON_STOP option (available as of Net8), then any changes you make to a running listener will be written to its listener.ora file. See Chapter 14 for examples of controlling the listener in a UNIX environment.

Parameter	Description
CONNECT_TIMEOUT	Time, in seconds, that the listener will wait for a valid connection request after the listener has started. Default is 10.
LOG_DIRECTORY	The directory for the listener log file.
LOG_FILE	The name of the listener log file.
LOGGING	A flag to set logging ON or OFF.
PASSWORDS	The password for the listener. Default is LISTENER.
PRESENTATION	Typical Net8 clients use a presentation of two-task communication (TTC). Java clients use General Inter-ORB Protocol (GIOP).

TABLE 13-1.   *Additional listener.ora Parameters*

Parameter	Description
PROTOCOL_STACK	The presentation and session layer information for a connection. New in 8i.
SAVE_CONFIG_ON_STOP	Available as of Net8. A flag to indicate if changes made to the listener while it is running should be saved to the listener.ora file.
SERVICE_LIST	The services list supported by the listener (more general than the SID_LIST shown in the example).
SESSION	A virtual pipe that carries data requests. Can be NS or RAW.
STARTUP_WAIT_TIME	The number of seconds the listener sleeps before responding to a startup command.
TRACE_DIRECTORY	The directory for the listener trace file.
TRACE_FILE	The name of the listener trace file.
TRACE_LEVEL	The level of tracing (ADMIN, USER, SUPPORT, or OFF).
USE_PLUG_AND_PLAY	A flag (ON or OFF) to instruct the listener to register with a Names server.

TABLE 13-1.   *Additional listener.ora Parameters* (continued)

Listeners in ORACLE8i

Prior to ORACLE8i, the listener has to be configured through manual entries in the listener.ora file. In ORACLE8i, the database instances register themselves with the listener upon database startup. The database instance registration consists of the following two types of information:

- Service information—The database service names and instance names

- Multi-threaded server (MTS) dispatcher registration—The dispatcher information

If an instance is unavailable, database instance registration provides automatic failover to another listener for a client connection. Database instance registration also provides connection load balancing by balancing the number of active connections among all of the available instances and dispatchers for the same service.

Prior to ORACLE8i, the tnsnames.ora file is mined for the SID, which ORACLE uses in the connection attempt. In ORACLE8i, ORACLE uses either the SID or the service names in tnsnames.ora to resolve its connection. The SID or service name and connection information is passed to the listener for verification. Once the listener verifies the information, the connection is either accepted or denied.

To support the new approach, the following new parameters have been added to the tnsnames.ora file:

SERVICE_NAME	Set to a service name value
INSTANCE_NAME	Set to the name of the instance
LOAD_BALANCE	Set to ON to activate load balancing
FAILOVER	Set to ON to activate listener failover

The SERVICE_NAME and INSTANCE_NAME parameters are also placed in the init.ora file for the database, and the values are established at database startup.

Using the Net8 Configuration Assistant

As of ORACLE8i, a new tool, the Net8 Configuration Assistant, has been added to the Net8 tool set. The Net8 Configuration Assistant performs the initial network configuration steps after the ORACLE software installation and automatically creates the default, basic configuration files. The tool has a graphical user interface for configuring the following elements:

- Listener
- Naming methods
- Net service names
- Lightweight Directory Access Protocol (LDAP) directory service

In the ORACLE8i Net8 version, net service names replace the use of service name aliases. For the net service name LOC on the HQ server, the net service name maps to a connect server using the following syntax:

```
LOC=
  (DESCRIPTION=
  (ADDRESS =
      (PROTOCOL = TCP)
      (HOST = HQ)
      (PORT = 1521))
```

```
  )
  (CONNECT_DATA =
    (SERVICE_NAME = loc)
    (INSTANCE_NAME = loc)
  )
)
```

In this example, the service name and the instance name match. However, they can be different names. The client will connect to a server using the net service name just as the client connected using the service name in earlier versions.

```
sqlplus hr/puffinstuff@LOC
```

Figure 13-4 shows the initial screen of the Net8 Configuration Assistant. As shown in Figure 13-4, "Listener configuration" is the default option.

Configuring the Listener

Using the Net8 Configuration Assistant, you can configure a listener easily and quickly. The first step is to select a listener name. Figure 13-5 shows the Listener Name screen with the default listener name, LISTENER, displayed.

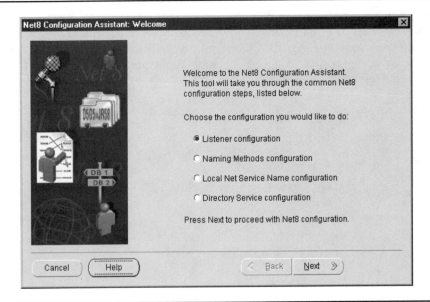

FIGURE 13-4. *The Net8 Configuration Assistant Welcome screen*

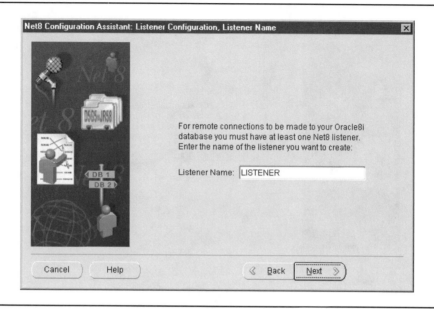

FIGURE 13-5. *The Listener Name screen*

After selecting a listener name, you must select a protocol. The default protocol selected is TCP. Figure 13-6 shows the protocol selection screen.

The next screen prompts for the connection client type. The options are as follows:

- Net8 clients

- Internet Inter-ORB Protocol (IIOP) clients

- Net8 clients + IIOP clients

Figure 13-7 shows the TCP Client Type selection screen.

Once the protocol is selected, you must designate the port number Net8 will use. Figure 13-8 shows the TCP/IP Protocol screen.

The next two screens, not shown here, are a prompt to configure another listener (response is No or Yes) and a confirmation that the listener configuration is completed for this listener.

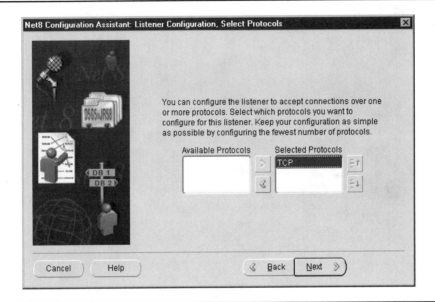

FIGURE 13-6. *The Protocol Selection screen*

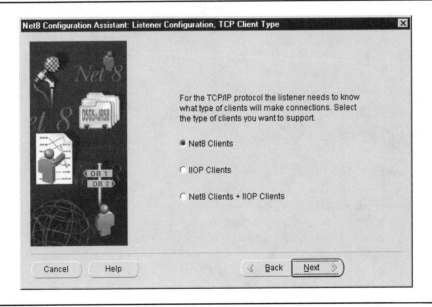

FIGURE 13-7. *The TCP Client Type selection screen*

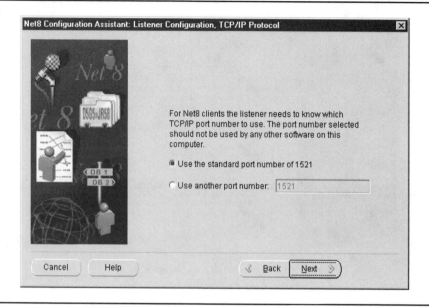

FIGURE 13-8.   *The TCP/IP Protocol screen*

Naming Methods Configuration

The naming methods configuration option of the Net8 Configuration Assistant configures net service names. There are many options available for naming methods. A few of them are listed here:

- **Local**   The tnsnames.ora file

- **Host name**   Uses a TCP naming service. Cannot use connection pooling or the ORACLE Connection Manager with this option

- **Names server**   An ORACLE Names server for use by ORACLE Names

- **Novell NDS, Sun NIS, DCE CDS**   External naming services

Figure 13-9 shows the Select Naming Methods screen. The Local and Host Name options are preselected.

If the Local option is chosen, the tool offers the option to create a net service name immediately or defer the creation of the name. If you accept the option to

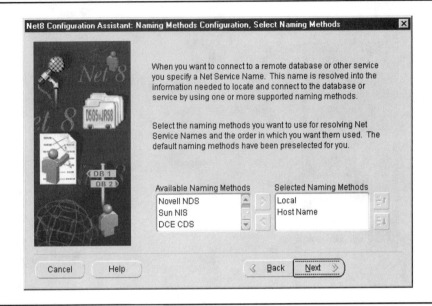

FIGURE 13-9. *The Select Naming Methods screen*

create a net service name immediately, the tool prompts for the database version using two options: ORACLE8i Release 8.1 (database or service) or ORACLE Release 8.0 (or previous version) database or service. The following screen prompts for a service name.

Having selected a naming convention, your next step is to select a connection protocol for the database you want to access. TCP/IP is the default. Figure 13-10 shows the Select Protocol screen.

The Net8 Configuration Assistant will prompt you to verify a database connection via a connection test. The default response is "No, do not test."

You are next prompted to supply a net service name. Figure 13-11 shows the Net Service Name screen. The service name selected is loc.

The next screen prompts for a host name for the database connection and a port specification. The value HQ has been used for the host name. The default port value is 1521. Figure 13-12 shows the TCP/IP Protocol host and port selection screen.

After entering the host name and selecting a port number, the configuration is complete. The Net8 Configuration Assistant will display a final Confirmation screen and will prompt for another net service name to be configured.

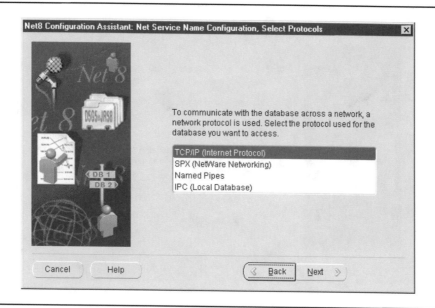

FIGURE 13-10. *The Select Protocol screen*

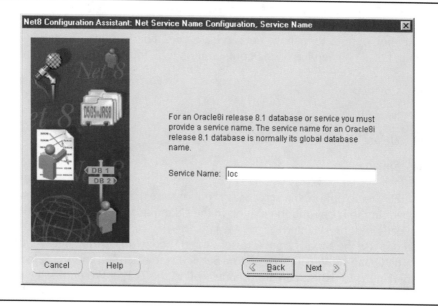

FIGURE 13-11. *The Net Service Name screen*

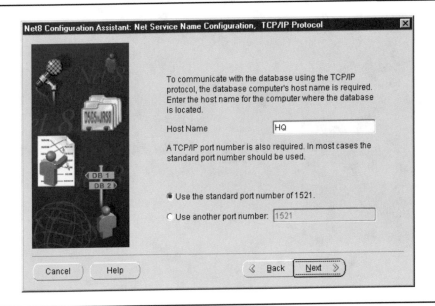

FIGURE 13-12. *The TCP/IP Protocol Host and Port Selection screen*

Local Net Service Name Configuration

You can use the Net8 Configuration Assistant's Local Net Service Name configuration options to manage net service names. For the Net8 Configuration Assistant, Local Net Service Name configuration tool, four options are available:

- Create

- Modify

- Delete

- Rename

For the Create option, the screens and options are the same as were described and shown in the Local option creation in the "Naming Methods Configuration" section earlier in this chapter.

You can use the Modify option to select and modify an existing net service name. The Database Version screen, the Service Name screen, and the Select Protocol (Figure 13-10) screen are used as well as the TCP/IP Protocol screen shown in Figure 13-11. The option to test the database connection is offered as well as the Net Service Name screen (Figure 13-12).

The Delete option displays the Select Net Service Name screen and, once a service name is selected, prompts with a Verification screen to confirm that the service name is to be deleted. A Deletion Confirmation screen and the general Net Service Name Completion screen complete the Delete option.

The Rename option displays the Select Net Service Name screen from which a service name is selected. The next screen prompts for a new name for the service. A Net Service Name Renamed Confirmation screen and the general Net Service Name Completion screen complete the Rename option.

Directory Service Configuration

A directory service provides a central repository of information for the network. Lightweight Directory Access Protocol (LDAP) directories and the LDAP server provide the following features:

- Store net service names

- Provide global database links and aliases

- Act as a clearinghouse for configuration information for clients across the entire network

- Aid in configuring other clients

- Update client configuration files automatically

This option requires the following network configuration components:

- An LDAP-compliant directory service to support enterprise security

- The host name of the server running the directory service

- The appropriate credentials to add information to that directory service

There are two primary screens used with the Directory Service Configuration tool. The first page prompts for an authorized username for an account that has access to the LDAP directory service, the account password, and the host name. If the directory service is already established, you only need to enter the host name. The second screen prompts for the *naming context* of the directory service. A naming context is a set of parameters that defines the particular set of service names that are being made available. The required parameters are country (c=) and organization or company (o=). A drop-down list of naming context options is provided and you select the context that has been defined for your organization.

The directory service is used to support global users and global roles for remote database administration from a single sign-on administration account.

Using the Net8 Assistant

When the Oracle Names Server was first introduced, a 16-bit application called the Configuration Manager was provided to use in generating the Names Server configuration. This application can still be used to configure the Oracle Names Server for version 7.

With Net8, you can use the Net8 Assistant to manage your configuration files. If you use the default values for your configuration (for example, using the default UNIX port for your UNIX listeners), then you will be able to use the default configuration created by the Net8 Assistant.

There is some overlap between the Net8 Assistant and the new Net8 Configuration Assistant functionality. Both tools can be used to configure a listener or a net service name. The Net8 Assistant is the only tool available to provide ease in configuring a Names server or local profile while the Net8 Configuration Assistant is the only tool provided to configure an LDAP-directory service. Which tool is better? The Net8 Configuration Assistant is a GUI tool that guides you through the configuration process step by step. The Net8 Assistant is not quite as user friendly but provides a more in-depth configuration alternative. The choice really is one of personal preference.

As shown in Figure 13-13, the opening screen of the Net8 Assistant lists the four areas it supports with a brief description of each: changing your local profile, managing the available net service names, managing the listeners, and managing the ORACLE Names servers. You can use the Net8 Assistant to manage your configuration files and test your connections.

For example, Figure 13-14 shows the different types of profile methods you can change and the naming types: either via tnsnames.ora files or via ORACLE Names. Options such as the ORACLE Security Server can be managed via the Net8 Assistant. The ORACLE Security Server and the Advanced Networking Option provide end-to-end encryption of data in a distributed environment. By default, your data will travel in clear text across your network unless you use ORACLE's encryption or a hardware-based encryption.

You can create a new net service name for your tnsnames.ora file via the ORACLE Net Service Names Wizard (see Figure 13-15). The Net8 Assistant will prompt you for each of the parameters required to establish a database connection and will modify your local tnsnames.ora file to reflect the information you provide. If you use the default connectivity information (for example, using port 1521 for UNIX connections), the wizard will be simplest to use. You can also use the Net8 Assistant to modify or test existing service names.

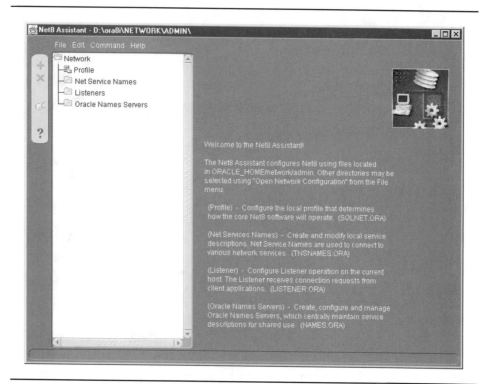

FIGURE 13-13. *The initial Net8 Assistant screen*

When you finish configuring a new service name, the Net8 Assistant will prompt you to test the service name. You can also test existing net service names by selecting the net service name from the displayed list of services and selecting the Test Connection option from the menu options.

When you test your connections, the Net8 Assistant will attempt to log in to the database using the default username SCOTT with the default password TIGER and will report the result of the connection attempt. The Net8 Assistant thus duplicates the functionality provided by the SQL*Net V2 TNSPING utility (see Chapter 14 for information on TNSPING).

The simpler you keep your client and server configurations, and the closer you adhere to the default values, the simpler the management of your configuration files will be. The Net8 Assistant simplifies your configuration file administration, but ideally you will accept the defaults for most of the prompted variables.

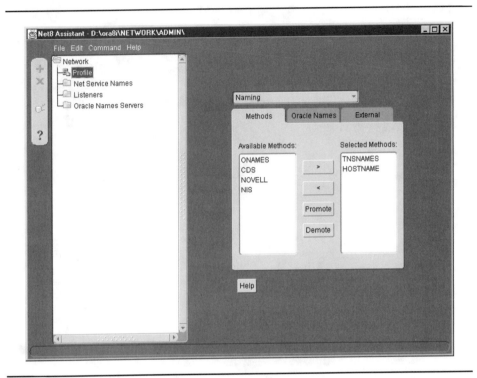

FIGURE 13-14. *The profile methods and naming types*

The MultiProtocol Interchange

The MultiProtocol Interchange portion of SQL*Net V2 is used to establish database communication links between otherwise incompatible network protocols. The concept of a network *community* is used to determine whether a MultiProtocol Interchange is necessary. The MultiProtocol Interchange is obsolete as of Net8, replaced by the Connection Manager.

A network community is a set of servers that communicate with each other via a single protocol. Examples of communities would include networks of UNIX servers using TCP/IP or of VAX servers using DECNet. To transfer database requests from one community to another in SQL*Net V2, you must use a MultiProtocol Interchange. An interchange is shown graphically in Figure 13-16.

The advantage of a MultiProtocol Interchange is that all servers do not have to be using the same communications protocol. Because of this, each server can use the communications protocol that is best suited to its environment, and can still be able to transfer data back and forth with other databases. This communication takes

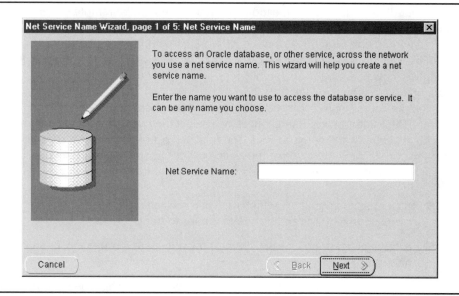

FIGURE 13-15.   *The ORACLE Net Service Names wizard*

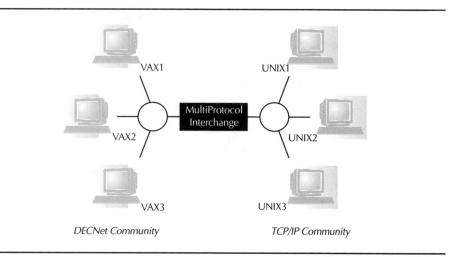

FIGURE 13-16.   *A sample MultiProtocol Interchange*

place regardless of the communications protocols used on the remote servers; the MultiProtocol Interchange takes care of the differences between the protocols.

In environments with three or more network communities, multiple MultiProtocol Interchanges are used. They may be physically configured so that multiple access paths are available between servers. A multiple interchange configuration is shown in Figure 13-17.

Multiple access paths can be used to transfer data from one community to another. The MultiProtocol Interchanges will select the most appropriate path based on path availability and network load. The relative cost of each path is specified via the Network Manager utility when the MultiProtocol Interchanges are set up.

Each MultiProtocol Interchange has three components:

■ A Connection Manager, which manages a listener process to detect connection requests and uses data pumps to transfer data

■ A Navigator, which chooses the best possible path through the TNS network

■ The Interchange Control Utility, which is used to manage the interchange's availability

You can use Network Manager to establish the configuration of each of these components when a new MultiProtocol Interchange is created.

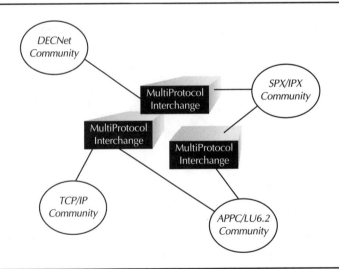

FIGURE 13-17.   *MultiProtocol Interchange configuration for four communities*

The network community in which a server exists should be added to the connect descriptors for its databases. A modified version of the connect descriptor shown earlier, with the COMMUNITY parameter added, is shown in the following listing. This is a modification to the tnsnames.ora files that are distributed throughout the network.

```
LOC =(DESCRIPTION=
        (ADDRESS=
                (COMMUNITY=TCP.HQ.COMPANY)
                (PROTOCOL=TCP)
                (HOST=HQ)
                (PORT=1521))
        (CONNECT DATA=
                (SID=loc)))
```

In this example, the host HQ is identified as being part of the TCP/IP community via the tnsnames.ora file. Other files that are generated from this tool for the MultiProtocol Interchanges are tnsnav.ora (community descriptions), tnsnet.ora (network overview), and intchg.ora (control parameters for the interchanges).

An additional file, sqlnet.ora, may be created to specify additional diagnostics beyond the default diagnostics provided.

Using Connection Manager

Net8 uses the Connection Manager in place of the MultiProtocol Interchange; it also supports connections within homogenous networks, reducing the number of physical connections maintained by the database. There are three main processes associated with the Connection Manager, as follows:

CMGW	The gateway process that acts as a hub for the Connection Manager
CMADMIN	A multithreaded process responsible for all administrative tasks and issues
CMCTL	The Connection Manager control process

The CMGW Process

The Connection Manager Gateway (CMGW) process registers itself with the CMADMIN process and listens for incoming connection requests. By default, this process listens on port 1630 using the TCP/IP protocol. The CMGW process initiates connection requests to listeners from clients and relays data between the client and server. The CMGW process also answers requests from the CMCTL process.

The CMADMIN Process

The multithreaded Connection Manager Administrative (CMADMIN) process performs many tasks and functions. The CMADMIN processes CMGW registrations and registers source route addressing information about the CMGW and listeners. Another function that the CMADMIN process performs is answering CMCTL requests. The CMADMIN process is tasked with identifying all listener processes that support at least one database. Using the Oracle Names servers, the CMADMIN performs the following tasks:

- Locates local Oracle Names servers

- Monitors registered listeners

- Maintains client address information

- Periodically updates the Connection Manager's cache of available services

The CMADMIN handles source route information about the CMGW and listeners.

The CMCTL Process

The Connection Manager control process provides administrative access to CMADMIN and CMGW. The Connection Manager is started via the **cmctl** command.

The command syntax is

 cmctl command process_type

The default startup command from an operating system prompt is

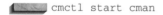 cmctl start cman

The available command options for the **cmctl** command are as follows:

exit	Disconnect from the CMCTL process
start	Start the CMCTL process (process must not be running)
stats	Provide statistic for total_relays, active_delays, most_relays, out_of_relay, and total_refused for the CMCTL process
stat	Provide basic status information about version, start time, and up time

stop	Stop a specific CMCTL process—either CMGW or CMADMIN
stop now	Stop all CMCTL processes (at least one process must be running)

There are three process_type options for the **cmctl** command:

cman	Controls both the CMGW and CMADMIN processes
adm	Controls just the CMADMIN process
cm	Controls just the CMGW process

If the Connection Manager has been started, any client that has SOURCE_ROUTE set to YES in its tnsnames.ora file can use the Connection Manager. The Connection Manager reduces system resource requirements by maintaining logical connections while reusing physical connections.

Using ORACLE Names

With ORACLE Names, all of the tasks of managing distributed databases are handled via a global naming service available to all servers in a network. The service is used to store information about the following:

- Connect descriptors
- Database links
- Object aliases

ORACLE Names changes the way in which database links are resolved. Before, when a database link was specified, the database first looked at the user's private database links. If none with the matching name was found, then the available public database links were checked.

ORACLE Names adds an additional level to this. Now, if the first two checks do not return a match for the database link name, the ORACLE Names server's list of global database link names is searched for the database link. If the link name is found there, ORACLE Names will return the link's specifications and resolve the query.

This greatly simplifies the administration of location transparency in a distributed environment. The information related to remote data access is now stored in a central location. The impact of this is felt every time a part of an FQON is modified. For example, if there were multiple links using specific connections to a single remote database, then a pre-Names modification to the user's password would require dropping and re-creating multiple database links. With Names, this change is made once.

ORACLE Names also supports the Domain Name Service (DNS) structure that ORACLE introduced with SQL*Net V2. ORACLE's DNS allows network hierarchies to be specified; thus, a server may be identified as HR.HQ.ACME.COM, which would be interpreted as the HR server in the HQ network of the ACME company.

If connect descriptors are also stored in ORACLE Names, the need for manually maintaining multiple copies of the tnsnames.ora file diminishes. The centralized ORACLE Names server defines the relationships among the network objects. The database network may be divided into administrative regions, and the management tasks may be likewise divided. A change to one region will be transparently propagated to the other regions.

You can control an ORACLE Names server via the **namesctl** utility, and you can configure it via the Net8 Assistant.

Usage Example: Client/Server Applications

There are several ad hoc query tools available that work in a client/server fashion. Consider the example of a query tool operating on a PC. The PC is connected via a network card to a TCP/IP network and is running a TCP/IP software package and SQL*Net V2 or Net8. The database that it will be accessing resides on a UNIX server on the same network. This configuration is depicted in Figure 13-18.

When the user runs the tool on the PC, a username, password, and service name for a database must be specified. When the user is connected to the database, he or she may then query from the tables available there. Every time a query is executed, the SQL statement for the query is sent to the server and executed. The data is then returned via SQL*Net V2 or Net8 and displayed on the client PC. See Chapter 17 for details of client/server implementation.

Usage Example: Database Links

For frequently used connections to remote databases, *database links* should be established. Database links specify the connect descriptor to be used for a connection, and may also specify the username to connect to in the remote database.

A database link is typically used to create local objects (such as views or synonyms) that access remote databases via server/server communications. The local synonyms for remote objects provide location transparency to the local users.

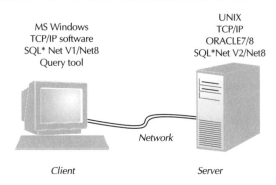

FIGURE 13-18. *Example client/server configuration*

When a database link is referenced by a SQL statement, it opens a session in the remote database and executes the SQL statement there. The data is then returned, and the remote session may stay open in case it is needed again. Database links can be created as **public** links (by DBAs, making the link available to all users in the local database) or as private links.

The following example creates a private database link called HR_LINK:

```
create database link HR_LINK
connect to HR identified by PUFFINSTUFF
using 'loc';
```

The **create database link** command, as shown in this example, has three parameters:

1. The name of the link (HR_LINK, in this example)

2. The account to connect to

3. The service name

A public database link can be created by adding the keyword **public** to the **create database link** command, as shown in the following example:

```
create public database link HR_LINK
connect to HR identified by PUFFINSTUFF
using 'loc';
```

If the LOC instance is moved to a different server, then the database links can be redirected to LOC's new location simply by distributing a tnsnames.ora file that contains the modification. You can generate the revised tnsnames.ora file by using either the Net8 Assistant or Net8 Configuration Assistant tool described previously in this chapter.

To use these links, simply add them as suffixes to table names in commands. The following example creates a local view of a remote table, using the HR_LINK database link:

```
create view LOCAL_EMPLOYEE_VIEW
as
select * from EMPLOYEE@HR_LINK
where Office='ANNAPOLIS';
```

The **from** clause in this example refers to EMPLOYEE@HR_LINK. Since the HR_LINK database link specifies the server name, instance name, and owner name, the FQON for the table is known. If no account name had been specified, the user's account name would have been used instead.

In this example, a view was created in order to limit the records that users could retrieve. If no such restriction is necessary, a synonym can be used instead. This is shown in the following example:

```
create public synonym EMPLOYEE for EMPLOYEE@HR_LINK;
```

Local users who query the local public synonym EMPLOYEE will automatically have their queries redirected to the EMPLOYEE table in the LOC instance on the HQ server. Location transparency has thus been achieved.

By default, a single SQL statement can use up to four database links. This limit can be increased via the OPEN_LINKS parameter in the database's init.ora file.

Usage Example: The copy Command

The SQL*Plus **copy** command is an underutilitized, underappreciated command. You can use the **copy** command to copy data between databases (or within the same database) via SQL*Plus. Although it allows the user to select which columns to **copy**, it works best when all of the columns of a table are being chosen. The greatest benefit of this command is its ability to **commit** after each array of data has been processed; this in turn generates transactions that are of a manageable size.

Consider the case of a large table (again, using EMPLOYEE as the example). What if the EMPLOYEE table has 100,000 rows that use a total of 100MB of space, and you need to make a copy of that table into a different database? The easiest option, using a database link, involves the following steps:

```
create database link HR_LINK
connect to HR identified by PUFFINSTUFF
using 'loc';

create table EMPLOYEE
as
select * from EMPLOYEE@HR_LINK;
```

The first command creates the database link, and the second command creates a new table based on all of the data in the remote table.

Unfortunately, this option places a heavy burden on your rollback segments. In order for this option to work, a transaction the size of the entire remote table (100MB) must be supported. This large transaction, in turn, requires a rollback segment that is at least that large.

To break the transaction into smaller entries, use the SQL*Plus **copy** command. The syntax for this command is

```
copy from
remote_username/remote_password@service_name
to
username/password@service_name
[append|create|insert|replace]
TABLE_NAME
using subquery;
```

If the current account is to be the destination of the copied data, then the local username, password, and service name are not necessary.

To set the transaction entry size, use the SQL*Plus **set** command to set a value for the **arraysize** parameter. This determines the number of records that will be retrieved in each "batch." The **copycommit** parameter tells SQL*Plus how many batches should be **commit**ted at one time. Thus, the following SQL*Plus script accomplishes the same data-copying goal that the **create table as** command met; however, it breaks up the single transaction into multiple transactions. In this example, the data is committed after every 1,000 records. This reduces the transaction's rollback segment entry size needed from 100MB to 1MB—a much more manageable transaction size.

```
set copycommit 1
set arraysize 1000
copy from HR/PUFFINSTUFF@loc -
create EMPLOYEE -
using -
select * from EMPLOYEE
```

Except for the last line, each line in the **copy** command must be terminated with a dash, since this is a SQL*Plus command.

The different data options within the **copy** command are described in Table 13-2.

The feedback provided by this command is confusing at first. After the final **commit** is complete, the database reports to the user the number of records that were **commit**ted in the *last* batch. The command feedback does not report the total number of records **commit**ted (unless they are all **commit**ted in a single batch).

Oracle Names Server Versus Client Configurations

The decision to use Oracle Names server or rely on distributing and maintaining the current SQL*Net2 or Net8 configuration for each client is a choice that every DBA faces. There are many considerations to weigh. Factors that will play a part in the decision are as follows:

- The number of clients on the system

- The number of servers on the system

- The number of different locations that are accessed

- The frequency at which databases are added or removed from the system

Each time a database is added or removed from the system, a new tnsnames.ora file should be generated to reflect the system change. In an environment where only

Option	Description
append	Inserts the rows into the destination table. Automatically creates the table if it does not exist.
create	Creates the table, then inserts the rows.
insert	Inserts the rows into the destination table if it exists; otherwise, returns an error. When using INSERT, all columns must be specified in the **using** subquery.
replace	Drops the existing destination table and replaces it with a new table containing the copied data.

TABLE 13-2. *Data Options for the **copy** Command*

a few clients are accessing only one or a few databases, it is easy to maintain the tnsnames.ora file and keep it current and disseminated to the clients. As the user base grows and the number of development, test, and production databases grows, tracking the specific clients who should receive connection information for specific databases becomes more complicated. Over time, the task of ensuring that each client's configuration is accurate for his or her needs becomes very complex. If there are servers in different locations across the country or around the world, ensuring that all of the correct connection information will get to all of the clients can be a daunting task.

If an Oracle Names server approach is chosen, you have one centralized place where changes to the connection configuration are made. Once the modifications are completed, the new configuration is sent to each Names server in the network, and the changes become available to clients without having to redistribute a tnsnames.ora file to each user.

Configuring the initial Oracle Names server can be a bit intimidating, but the reward of getting the Names server working is the ease of enabling all clients to access the correct connection information rapidly.

Tuning SQL*Net and Net8

Tuning SQL*Net applications is fairly straightforward: wherever possible, reduce the amount of data that is sent across the network, particularly for online transaction-processing applications. Also, reduce the number of times data is requested from the database. The basic procedures that should be applied include the following:

- The use of distributed objects, such as snapshots, to replicate static data to remote databases.

- The use of procedures to reduce the amount of data sent across the network. Rather than sending data back and forth, only the procedure's error status is returned.

- The use of the highest buffer size available for SQL*Net buffering.

- The use of homogenous servers wherever possible to eliminate the need for protocol interchange.

The first of these topics is discussed in detail in Chapters 8 and 16.

The buffer size used by SQL*Net V2 and Net8 should take advantage of the packet sizes used by the network protocols (such as TCP/IP). If you send large packets of data across the network, then the packets may be fragmented. Since each packet contains header information, reducing packet fragmentation reduces network traffic.

As of SQL*Net V2.3, you can tune the size of the service layer and transport layer buffer sizes. The specification for the service layer data buffer is called SDU; it may be specified in your tnsnames.ora and listener.ora files. For example, the following listing shows a section of tnsnames.ora file for the LOC service name. In this example, the service layer buffer size is set to 2KB via the SDU parameter. The transport layer buffer size, as defined by the TDU parameter, is also set to 2KB.

```
LOC =(DESCRIPTION=
        (SDU=2048)
        (TDU=2048)
        (ADDRESS=
            (PROTOCOL=TCP)
            (HOST=HQ)
            (PORT=1521))
        (CONNECT DATA=
            (SID=loc)))
```

The listener.ora file must contain matching entries.

```
LISTENER =
    (ADDRESS_LIST =
        (ADDRESS=
            (PROTOCOL=IPC)
            (KEY= loc.world)
        )
    )
SID_LIST_LISTENER =
    (SID_LIST =
        (SID_DESC =
            (SDU=2048)
            (TDU=2048)
            (SID_NAME = loc)
            (ORACLE_HOME = /orasw/app/oracle/product/8.0.3.1)
        )
    )
```

The listener.ora and tnsnames.ora SDU settings do not have to be identical; if they are different, the lower of the two will be used for the communications. The default size of the SDU setting is 2KB, as shown in the preceding listings.

The impact of changing the SDU and TDU settings is a reduction in network traffic and a shortening of the time required to connect to the database. However, you will need to know the size of the data being transferred in order to know whether increasing the SDU and TDU parameters can affect your performance. The buffer size for TCP/IP is 1,500 bytes; if your data exceeds this value, you will be using multiple network packets no matter what the values are for the other parameters. The amount of data transferred at a time is determined by your **arraysize** setting and the size of the rows being read.

For example, if you **set arraysize 100** in SQL*Plus, and query rows that are 100 bytes each, then your data will require 10,000 bytes—so you will be using multiple packets. If you use an array size of 10 instead, you will be transferring 1,000 bytes each time. Given the smaller array size, you can eliminate or reduce packet fragmentation by setting the SDU and TDU parameters to 2KB, as shown in the previous examples. Setting SDU to higher values will not have a noticeable effect on your network traffic, since you will be limited by the buffer size supported by the underlying network protocol. If you regularly query tables with large row sizes, you may not be able to reduce the network traffic generated.

CHAPTER
14

ORACLE Networking
in UNIX

NIX is the operating system of choice for many ORACLE installations; it supports small ORACLE databases as well as extremely large databases. The combination of operating system flexibility, tuning options, and scalability make UNIX a solid foundation for an ORACLE installation. In this chapter, you will see instructions for implementing SQL*Net V2 and Net8 in UNIX. You can use both SQL*Net V2 and Net8 to access ORACLE8 databases (both work for ORACLE7 databases as well). For ORACLE8i, Net8 will work with versions from 7.3.4 forward. Since the TCP/IP communications protocol is commonly used for UNIX servers, that protocol will be featured in the examples in this chapter.

Before a process can connect to a database on a server, there are several steps that the DBA must take in conjunction with the UNIX system administrator. The following sections describe each of these steps.

Identification of Hosts

A *host*, for the purposes of this chapter, will be defined as a server that is capable of communicating with another server via a network. Each host maintains a list of the hosts with which it can communicate. This list is maintained in a file called /etc/hosts. The "/etc" portion of the filename signifies that it is located in the /etc directory. This file contains the Internet address for the hosts, plus the host names. It may optionally include an alias for each host name. A sample portion of an /etc/hosts file is shown in the following listing:

```
127.0.0.1 localhost
130.110.238.109 nmhost
130.110.238.101 txhost
130.110.238.102 azhost   arizona
```

Your UNIX implementation may use a domain name server (DNS), in which case the host IP addresses may not all be listed in the /etc/hosts file. If DNS is in use, you can use the **nslookup** command to query the IP address of a known host name (or vice versa). The following listing shows a sample lookup of an IP address from DNS:

```
> nslookup txhost
Server:  txhost.company.com
Address: 130.110.238.101
```

In this example, there are four hosts listed. The first entry is the "loopback" entry for the server. The next two entries assign host names (nmhost and txhost) to Internet addresses. The last entry assigns both a host name (azhost) and an alias (arizona) to an Internet address.

Most networking software for PC clients uses a similar file, either located on the PC or on a shared network drive. Within the network software directory structure, a hosts file is maintained. This file lists the IP address and host name for each host that the client can directly reach. The file is identical in structure to the UNIX /etc/hosts file shown in the preceding listing.

Whenever possible, use the host names rather than IP addresses in the SQL*Net/Net8 configuration files. UNIX servers may use DHCP, a protocol that assigns IP addresses to hosts during each server startup. Servers that use DHCP may have different IP addresses each time they start up, so any connection based on a hard-coded IP address would fail.

Identification of Databases

All databases that are run on a host and are accessible to the network must be listed in a file, usually named /etc/oratab. The "/etc" portion of the file name signifies that it is located in the /etc directory. This file is maintained by the DBA.

NOTE
Depending on the version of UNIX in use, the name and location of the /etc/oratab file may vary. See your operating system–specific ORACLE installation guide for details.

The components of an entry in this file are listed in Table 14-1.

Component	Description
ORACLE_SID	Instance name (server ID).
ORACLE_HOME	Full path name of the root directory of the ORACLE software used by the database.
STARTUP_FLAG	Flag to indicate whether the instance should be started when the host is started. If set to Y, then it will be started. If set to N, then it will not be started. This flag is used by the db_startup command file provided by ORACLE.

TABLE 14-1. *Entry Components for /etc/oratab*

The Startup_Flag component doesn't seem to fit; after all, why should a network connection care about the startup schedule for an instance? This flag is part of the entry because this file is also used (by default; it can be changed) during system startup to start the server's ORACLE databases.

The three components are listed all on one line, separated only by colons (:). A sample /etc/oratab file is shown in the following listing:

```
loc:/orasw/app/oracle/product/8.1.5.1:Y
cc1:/orasw/app/oracle/product/8.1.5.1:N
old:/orasw/app/oracle/product/8.1.5.0:Y
```

This example shows entries for three instances, named loc, cc1, and old. The first two instances have the same ORACLE_HOME; the third uses an older version of the ORACLE kernel. Both loc and old will be automatically started when the server starts; cc1 will have to be manually started. To access the instances, you will first need to start the listener process; the next section describes the configuration of the listener process in UNIX.

Identification of Services

A *server process* listens for connection requests from clients. The server process directs those requests to the proper UNIX socket, and the connection can then take place. The method of managing the Listener server process—the server process for SQL*Net V2 and Net8—changed little between SQL*Net V2 and Net8.

The information needed by the listener process (such as the port specifications and the host names) is stored in files that are distributed throughout the network. The tnsnames.ora file on each host will include listings of *service names*, with their associated connect descriptors. These descriptors contain the information needed to establish a connection with a UNIX listener process. A sample entry for tnsnames.ora is shown in the following listing:

```
HQ =(DESCRIPTION=
        (ADDRESS=
            (PROTOCOL=TCP)
            (HOST=HQ)
            (PORT=1521))
        (CONNECT DATA=
            (SID=loc)))
```

In this example, the service name HQ is given to a specific connect descriptor. That descriptor specifies the host (HQ), the protocol (TCP), the port (1521), and the instance ID (loc).

In order for a client to connect to a database on a remote server, the remote server must be running a listener process. This process, called TNSLSNR (TNS listener—TNS stands for transparent network substrate), waits for connection attempts to the databases listed in the listener.ora file. The listener.ora file lists all of the listeners on the server. The listener.ora file thus plays an important role in the server's ability to "listen" to outside connection requests. A sample portion of a listener.ora file is shown in the following listing:

```
LISTENER =
    (ADDRESS_LIST =
        (ADDRESS=
            (PROTOCOL=IPC)
            (KEY= loc)
        )
    )
SID_LIST_LISTENER =
    (SID_LIST =
      (SID_DESC =
        (SID_NAME = loc)
        (ORACLE_HOME = /orasw/app/oracle/product/8.1.5.1)
      )
    )
```

This listener.ora segment shows the instance that the listener will service (in this case, the loc instance). The ORACLE software home directory for each instance must be listed in this file, as shown in the listing. As of ORACLE8, you can use the Net8 Configuration Assistant to manage your configuration files (see Chapter 13).

Alternately, in ORACLE8i, net service names can be defined in the tnsnames.ora file to enable connections to a database (see Chapter 13). The net service names approach will work for any ORACLE8 connection, but may cause some confusion for an ORACLE7 listener because the ORACLE7 listener will be expecting a SID value and may not recognize the service name option. For example, the version 8i entry in a tnsnames.ora file would be as follows:

```
LOC=
    (DESCRIPTION=
    (ADDRESS =
        (PROTOCOL = TCP)
        (HOST = HQ)
        (PORT = 1521))
    )
    (CONNECT_DATA =
      (SERVICE_NAME = loc)
      (INSTANCE_NAME = loc)
    )
)
```

When the connection data is passed to a version 7.3.4 listener, the SERVICE_NAME and INSTANCE_NAME init.ora parameters may not be understood. If you are going to interact with a version 7 listener, use the older-style connection data as follows:

```
(CONNECT_DATA =
      (SID = loc)
   )
```

When you attempt to use either the tnsnames.ora or listener.ora files, ORACLE will look in the directory identified by the TNS_ADMIN environment variable. In most cases, the /etc directory is used as the TNS_ADMIN directory for these two files.

Starting the listener process is described in the next section. When you migrate from SQL*Net V2 to Net8, there are several changes in the parameters of the listener control options.

Starting the Listener Server Process

The listener process is controlled by the Listener Control Utility, executed via the **lsnrctl** command. The options available for the **lsnrctl** command are described in the next section, "Controlling the Listener Server Process." To start the listener, use the command:

```
> lsnrctl start
```

This command will start the default listener (named LISTENER). If you wish to start a listener with a different name, include that listener's name as the second parameter in the **lsnrctl** command. For example, if you created a listener called MY_LSNR, then you could start it via the following command:

```
> lsnrctl start my_lsnr
```

In the next section you will find descriptions of the other parameters available for the Listener Control Utility.

After starting a listener, you can check that it is running by using the **status** option of the Listener Control Utility. The following command can be used to perform this check:

```
> lsnrctl status
```

Sample output for this command is shown in the following listing:

```
LSNRCTL for Solaris: Version 8.1.5.0.0 - Production on 25-JUN-99 16:53:20
(c) Copyright 1998 Oracle Corporation.  All rights reserved.
Connecting to (DESCRIPTION=(ADDRESS=(PROTOCOL=IPC)(KEY=EXTPROC0)))

STATUS of the LISTENER
----------------------
Alias                      LISTENER
Version                    TNSLSNR for Solaris: Version 8.1.5.0.0 - Production
Start Date                 25-JUN-99 13:36:53
Uptime                     0 days 3 hr. 16 min. 27 sec
Trace Level                off
Security                   OFF
SNMP                       OFF
Listener Parameter File    /oracle/products/815/network/admin/listener.ora
Listener Log File          /oracle/products/815/network/log/listener.log
Services Summary...
   loc          has 1 service handler(s)
```

The status output in the preceding listing shows that the listener has been started, and that it is currently supporting only one service (loc), as defined by its listener.ora file. The listener parameter file is identified as /etc/listener.ora and its log file location is shown.

If you wish to see the operating system–level processes that are involved, use the following command. This example uses the UNIX **ps -ef** command to list the system's active processes. The **grep tnslsnr** command then eliminates those rows that do not contain the term "tnslsnr".

```
> ps -ef | grep tnslsnr
```

Sample output for this command:

```
oracle   4022     1  0 13:36:53 ?        0:00 /oracle/products/815/bin/tnslsnr
                                          LISTENER -inherit
oracle   5469  2419  1 13:56:23 ttypc    0:00 grep tnslsnr
```

This output shows two processes: the listener process and the process that is checking for it. The first line of output is wrapped to the second line and may be truncated by the operating system.

Controlling the Listener Server Process

You may need to modify the listener server processes periodically. Since you don't want to have to shut down and restart the server just to change the listener parameters, you can use the **lsnrctl** utility to manage them.

You can use the Listener Control Utility, **lsnrctl**, to start, stop, and modify the listener process on the server. Its command options are listed in Table 14-2. Each of these commands may be accompanied by a value; for all except the **set password** command, that value will be a listener name. If no listener name is specified, then the default (LISTENER) will be used. Once within **lsnrctl**, you can change the listener being modified via the **set current_listener** command.

Command	Description
CHANGE_PASSWORD	Sets a new password for the listener. You will be prompted for the old password for the listener.
DBSNMP_START	Starts the DBSNMP subagent for a database on the server.
DBSNMP_STATUS	Provides status information on the DBSNMP subagent.
DBSNMP_STOP	Stops the DBSNMP subagent on the server.
EXIT	Exits **lsnrctl**.
HELP	Displays a list of the **lsnrctl** command options. You can also see additional options via the **help set** and **help show** commands.
QUIT	Exits **lsnrctl**.
RELOAD	Allows you to modify the listener services after the listener has been started. It forces SQL*Net to read and use the most current listener.ora file.
SAVE_CONFIG	New as of Net8. Creates a backup of your existing listener.ora file, then updates your listener.ora with parameters you have changed via **lsnrctl**.

TABLE 14-2.   *Listener Control Utility Commands*

Command	Description
SERVICES	Displays services available, along with its connection history. It also lists whether each service is enabled for remote DBA or autologin access.
SET	Sets parameter values. Options are **connect_timeout** time, in seconds, the listener will wait for a valid connection request after the listener has been started. **current_listener** changes the listener process whose parameters are being set or shown. **log_directory** the directory for the listener log file. **log_file** the name of the listener log file. **log_status** whether logging is ON or OFF. **password** listener password **save_config_on_stop** new as of Net8. Saves your configuration changes to your listener.ora file when you exit **lsnrctl**. **startup_waittime** the number of seconds the listener sleeps before responding to a **lsnrctl start** command. **trc_directory** the directory for the listener trace file. **trc_file** the name for the listener trace file. **trc_level** the trace level (ADMIN, USER, SUPPORT, or OFF). See **lsnrctl trace**.
SHOW	Shows current parameter settings. Options are the same as the **set** options with the sole omission of the **password** command.
SPAWN	Spawns a program that runs with an alias in the listener.ora file.
START	Starts the listener.
STATUS	Provides status information about the listener, including the time it was started, its parameter filename, its log file, and the services it supports. This can be used to query the status of a listener on a remote server.
STOP	Stops the listener.

TABLE 14-2. *Listener Control Utility Commands* (continued)

Command	Description
TRACE	Sets the trace level of the listener to one of four choices: OFF; USER (limited tracing); ADMIN (high level of tracing); and SUPPORT (for ORACLE Support).
VERSION	Displays version information for the listener, TNS, and the protocol adapters.

TABLE 14-2. *Listener Control Utility Commands* (continued)

NOTE
New options for **lsnrctl** *may be introduced with each new version of Net8.*

· You can enter the **lsnrctl** command by itself and enter the **lsnrctl** utility shell, from which all other commands can then be executed.

The command options listed in Table 14-2 give you a great deal of control over the listener process, as shown in the following examples. In most of these examples, the **lsnrctl** command is first entered by itself. This places the user in the **lsnrctl** utility (as indicated by the LSNRCTL prompt). The rest of the commands are entered from within this utility. The following examples show the use of the **lsnrctl** utility to stop, start, and generate diagnostic information about the listener.

To stop the listener:

```
> lsnrctl
LSNRCTL> set password lsnr_password
LSNRCTL> stop
```

To list status information for the listener:

```
> lsnrctl status
```

To list the status of a listener on another host, add a service name from that host
as a parameter to the **status** command. The following example uses the HQ service
name shown earlier in this chapter:

```
> lsnrctl status hq
```

To list version information about the listener:

```
> lsnrctl version
```

To list information about the services supported by the listener:

```
> lsnrctl
LSNRCTL> set password lsnr_password
LSNRCTL> services
```

To reload the services from the listener.ora file:

```
> lsnrctl
LSNRCTL> set password lsnr_password
LSNRCTL> reload
```

To save modified configuration parameters to the listener.ora file (available as
of Net8):

```
> lsnrctl
LSNRCTL> set password lsnr_password
LSNRCTL> save_config
```

To change the level of tracing performed:

```
> lsnrctl
LSNRCTL> set password lsnr_password
LSNRCTL> trace user
```

To start the listener process:

```
> lsnrctl
LSNRCTL> set password lsnr_password
LSNRCTL> start
```

Most of these commands require passwords. Therefore, it is not advisable to run them via batch commands, since that would involve either storing the password in a file or passing it as a parameter to a batch program.

Debugging Connection Problems

As described in this chapter, SQL*Net/Net8 connections in UNIX require that a number of communication mechanisms be properly configured. The connections involve host-to-host communication, proper identification of services and databases, and proper configuration of the listener server processes. In the event of connection problems when using SQL*Net V2 or Net8, it is important to eliminate as many of these components as possible.

Start by making sure that the host the connection is trying to reach is accessible via the network. This can be checked via the following command:

 > telnet *host_name*

If this command is successful, you will be prompted for a username and password on the remote host. If the **ping** command is available to you, then you may use it instead. This command, shown in the following listing, will check to see if the remote host is available and will return a status message:

 > ping *host_name*

If the host is available on the network, the next step is to check if the listener is running. At the same time, you can check to see what parameters it is currently using; this is important if you are attempting a remote autologin access. The **lsnrctl status** command will provide this information:

 > lsnrctl status *net_service_name*

The ***net_service_name*** clause should refer to the name of a service on the remote server. If the ***net_service_name*** clause is not used, then the command will return the status of the listener on the local server.

These two checks—of host availability and listener availability—will resolve over 95 percent of SQL*Net and Net8 connection problems in server/server communications. The rest of the problems will result from difficulties with the database specification that is being used. These problems include invalid username/password combinations, down databases, and databases in need of recovery.

In client/server communications, the same principles for debugging connection problems apply. First, verify that the remote host is accessible; most communications software for clients includes a **telnet** or **ping** command. If it is not accessible, the problem may be on the client side. Verify that *other* clients are able to access the host on which the database resides. If they can, the problem is isolated to the client. If they cannot, the problem lies on the server side, and the server, its listener processes, and its databases should be checked.

From the client, you can use the **tnsping** command to test connection to a listener. Execute the **tnsping** command with two parameters: the name of the service name to check and the number of connections to attempt. For example, if you run the command **tnsping hq 20**, then ORACLE will attempt to connect to the hq service 20 consecutive times. The multiple connections are used because the output of the **tnsping** command may be displayed very quickly, and forcing it through multiple tests gives you time to read the output. The **tnsping** command is provided as part of the Windows client SQL*Net and Net8 connectivity software. The Net8 Assistant contains a connection test component that performs the same function as **tnsping**.

CHAPTER
15

Networking in
Windows NT

he Windows NT operating system (referred to here as NT) is gaining popularity in the business environment. NT is a 32-bit operating system and supports both CISC and RISC architectures. Like UNIX and OpenVMS, NT has adopted the global networking standards such as TCP/IP and SNMP. ORACLE recommends that NT users use the TCP/IP communications protocol. Net8 on TCP/IP performs well because after the initial contact, no header data is forwarded and the data packets thus shrink in size. As with any platform, the response time for NT networking will be only as good as the speed of the slowest network segment involved. Therefore, the network itself must be tuned to perform at its maximum for Net8 to perform well.

To understand networking on an NT system, you must first understand how ORACLE and Net8 work in this environment. This chapter will examine the way network processing is handled on an NT system.

ORACLE and Windows NT

If you look at a UNIX system, you will see that there are several identifiable processes. In the example shown in the following listing, the **–v** clause tells UNIX to select everything that does not match the following string. The command says to look for all processes that contain the phrase ora but exclude the word LOCAL and grep. In the output, shown following the command, there are nine detached ORACLE processes and the listener running on this UNIX system.

```
ps -ef|grep ora|grep -v LOCAL|grep -v grep

oracle 221 1 0 Jun 15 ? 37:03
/opt/oracle/product/8.1.5/bin/tnslsnr LISTENER -inherit
oracle 258 1 0 Jun 15 ? 307:15 ora_dbw0_cc1
oracle 254 1 0 Jun 15 ? 0:01 ora_pmon_cc1
oracle 260 1 0 Jun 15 ? 0:40 ora_arch_cc1
oracle 262 1 0 Jun 15 ? 26:32 ora_lgwr_cc1
oracle 264 1 0 Jun 15 ? 1:43 ora_ckpt_cc1
oracle 266 1 0 Jun 15 ? 0:10 ora_smon_cc1
oracle 268 1 0 Jun 15 ? 0:02 ora_reco_cc1
oracle 272 1 2 Jun 15 ? 1991:58 ora_d000_cc1
oracle 19971 1 1 Jul 28 ? 197:17 ora_s000_cc1
```

The output shows the background processes for the CC1 instance. The NT architecture provides a built-in multithreading capability so a single executable can perform many different tasks at essentially the same time. In an NT environment for ORACLE8i, each detached process runs as a concurrently running *thread* within a single executable called ORACLE.EXE. (In ORACLE8.0, the executable is named ORACLE80.EXE.) Using the same executable with several threads, the threads all share the same code, memory space, and other structures. In other operating systems, each separate process requires its own separate code implementation. By having multiple threads within one executable, ORACLE reduces the number of code and data segments and stacks required for processing, reducing the amount of memory required. However, any memory operations that are performed affect all of the threads.

The Windows NT Task Manager is shown next, with the ORACLE8i executable (ORACLE.EXE) highlighted and the ORACLE8i listener (TNSLSNR.EXE), the ORACLE8.0 listener (TNSLSNR80.EXE), and the ORACLE8.0 executable (ORACLE80.EXE) running. You can access the Windows NT Task Manager by depressing the CTRL-ALT-DELETE keys at the same time and then selecting the Task Manager option from the displayed box.

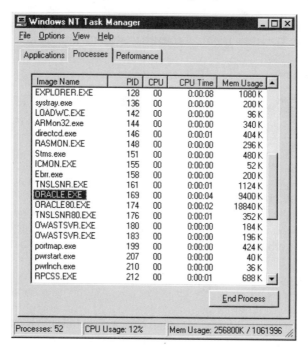

Each ORACLE instance on an NT system runs as a separate *service* or executable program that NT can keep track of and start up whenever NT is started. A service can run in the background or be configured for foreground interaction with users. A service can be started and remain running even when no users are logged on to the system. This is an important feature because you do not want your database server to rely on a specific process being logged on to the machine to keep the database or listener running.

To access the Services window, choose the Control Panel option from the Settings menu off the Start menu. Within the Control Panel, select the Services option (the icon is two gears and is labeled Services). In ORACLE8.0, two separate service entries are displayed in the Services window, while in ORACLE8i only one entry is displayed. The Services window with the ORACLE8i service ORC1 highlighted is shown here:

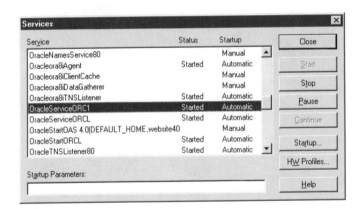

In the illustration, the ORACLE8.0 services that you can start and stop are identifiable by the nomenclature ORCL. Notice the service entries for the listeners for both 8.0 (OracleTNSListener80) and 8i (Oracleora8iTNSListener). The 8i Listener service includes the ORACLE_HOME (ora8i) in its name for easier identification. Also notice that both the 8.0 and 8i listeners and databases are started and available for use.

When working with ORACLE on an NT system, remember that ORACLE uses a single process with multiple threads. As of ORACLE8.0.4, you can have multiple ORACLE homes with different versions of the RDBMS running at the same time (as shown in both illustrations above). Since there are multiple threads for each process, this means that you will not be able to easily recognize what threads belong to which ORACLE process. You will, therefore, need to rely on either using the Services window or commands issued at the DOS prompt to start and stop the listener(s) on your system. The Performance Monitor window, with some of the ORACLE threads displayed, is shown here:

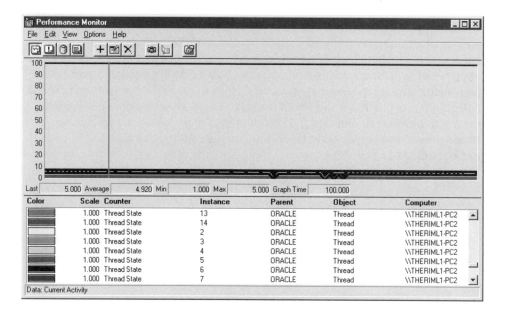

As shown in the illustration, sequential thread numbers are used to identify each thread, but no thread names are supplied. The ORACLE threads are assigned in the following order. Thread 0 is the dispatcher thread. It handles input from the Listener process (started through the services). Thread 1 is the worker or execution thread that handles the processing as requested by the dispatcher thread. The worker or execution thread usually handles launching another thread on behalf of the incoming connection on dedicated servers. Table 15-1 reflects the basic thread assignments used commonly in both ORACLE8.0 and ORACLE8i.

Thread Name	Thread#
PMON	2
DBW0	3
LGWR	4
CKPT	5
SMON	6
RECO	7

TABLE 15-1. *Basic ORACLE Thread Assignments*

If archive logging is enabled, the ARCH process will be assigned as thread 4 and the other threads will move down a number with LGWR becoming 5, CKPT becoming 6, etc. In ORACLE8i, the heterogeneous service agents have been multithreaded in an approach similar to the ORACLE Multithreaded Server (MTS) architecture and there is now a set of dispatchers to receive requests from ORACLE database server processes and return results to them. There is also a pool of task threads to process the requests and compute results. In this way, a greater number of concurrent user sessions can be accommodated. Although individual thread names of ORACLE processes are not visible from the operating system (Task Manager or Services window), they are obtainable through SQL*Plus via the following query:

```
select b.Name bkpr, s.Username spid, p.Pid
  from V$BGPROCESS b, V$SESSION s, V$PROCESS p
 where p.Addr = b.Paddr(+)
   and p.Addr = s.Paddr;


BKPR   SPID                                    PID
-----  ------------------------------  ---------
PMON                                           2
DBW0                                           3
LGWR                                           4
CKPT                                           5
SMON                                           6
RECO                                           7
SNP0                                           8
SNP1                                           9
       DBSNMP                                 12
       SYS                                    13
```

NOTE
The listener and the dispatcher threads do not show up in this list.

ORACLE and Net8

As you have seen in Chapters 13 and 14, there are many different components involved with configuring and using Net8. You need to install the Net8 software and configure various files (listener.ora, tnsnames.ora, and sqlnet.ora). If you use the Intelligent Agent for ORACLE Enterprise Manager, you also need to configure snmp_ro.ora (which you do not ever modify) and snmp_rw.ora (which you can modify).

When one computer communicates with another, the request is sent through a set of individual communications layers called a *stack*. Each layer of the stack performs a different function in translating a message into a series of electronic impulses to the underlying physical hardware. Each different type of network-specific protocol will have a different but similar stack since the basic job at hand is to get the message from one computer through a wire to another computer.

Net8 is a stack of layers that sit on top of a network protocol. Each machine that communicates with a database must have Net8 installed on it. Table 15-2 shows the Net8 layers that apply to the client computer.

Stack Layer	Description
ORACLE Call Interface (OCI)	Consists of a number of function calls that can be embedded in programs to enable sending and receiving calls to and from a database.
The Two-Task Common	Resolves character set differences between the sender and receiver.
Net8 (consists of three layers)	Network Interface (NI) hides the underlying network protocol and media from the client application. Network Routing (NR)/Network Naming (NN)/Network Authentication (NA) takes care of routing the data to its final destination. Transparent Network Substrate (TNS) takes care of generic communications like sending and receiving data.
ORACLE Protocol Adapter	A thin layer of code that insulates Net8 from the underlying network protocol.
Network-Specific Protocol	Usually another stack of layers that translate the SQL statement into packets to transmit across the network.

TABLE 15-2. *Net8 Client Components*

On the server side, the Net8 layers are the same with the exception of the top level. Instead of an ORACLE Call Interface, there is an ORACLE-side Programmatic Interface (OPI). If you are using the Internet Inter-ORB Protocol (IIOP) or ORACLE's Java Database Connectivity drivers (JDBC), the protocol stack will be slightly different from the one shown in Table 15-2.

Net8 Listener

The Net8 listener on an NT machine is a service that is usually started automatically when the machine is booted. There are three different ways to start the listener manually:

1. From the Start | Settings | Control Panel | Services window, you can choose the Oracle<oracle_home>TNSListener option and select the Start button.

2. Select the DOS window option from the Start | Programs menu. In the DOS window, issue the command:
   lsnrctl start <listener_name> (The default is LISTENER.)

3. You can create a .bat file and, within that file, issue the command:
   net start Oracle<oracle_home>TNSListener

Once the Net8 listener starts, it listens for connection requests coming from clients on the network. Once a request is received, Net8 is responsible for making the connection between the client and the database. Based on how you have configured Net8, the connection will be made as follows:

■ As a dedicated thread for that client's exclusive use until the client's processing has been totally completed

■ By transferring the connection to a prespawned thread

■ Via the Multithreaded Server (MTS) or Connection Manager (CM)

Once the connection is handed off from the listener to the thread, the listener's involvement completes and there is no further interaction between the listener and that particular client connection. If you must shut down and restart the listener for any reason, the current client connections to the database will not be affected by your action.

Using the Multithreaded Server

Although the Multithreaded Server (MTS) has been available on other platforms for years, it has only been available on NT since the release of ORACLE8.0 with NT version 4.0. In NT version 4.0, Windows sockets version 2 (WINSOCK2) was revised to contain much broader networking capabilities. The dispatchers and shared servers are now implemented as very lightweight threads so the whole system becomes much faster and more efficient. Note, however, that MTS only works with TCP/IP; no other protocol is supported. Also, MTS works best in environments where clients have some amount of "think" time involved with their processing (like decision support systems and online analytical processing). A large, batch load environment or one with heavy, rapid data entry would not be suited for MTS.

To configure MTS on NT, set values for MTS parameters in your init.ora file. Those parameters, such as MTS_MAX_DISPATCHERS and MTS_MAX_SERVERS, tell ORACLE how many dispatcher threads and shared server threads you want to enable. These threads enable a large number of users to be supported by a small number of actual, physical database connections.

When using MTS, the order in which you start the listener and databases becomes critical. You must perform the following tasks in the specific order:

1. First, you must start the listener.

2. Once the listener is started, the databases are started.

3. Based on the configuration parameters that have been set in the init.ora file, dispatchers are started and begin to listen on the address to which they have been assigned.

Each dispatcher registers its address with the Net8 listener. The default listener addresses are 1521 and 1526. If the listener is not listening on a default address, the listener's network name may be placed in the init.ora file using the LOCAL_LISTENER parameter to declare one or more listeners in the following form:

```
local_listener = "(ADDRESS_LIST = (Address = (Protocol = TCP) (Host=HQ1)
(Port=1524)) (Address=(Protocol = IPC)(Key= HQ)))"
```

Since the LOCAL_LISTENER parameter is a string value, quotation marks are used. In this example, the listener is located on the HQ1 machine and is listening on port 1524 (a nondefault port number). The key value (HQ) is the database name. The listener and database must be on the same machine to use the LOCAL_LISTENER parameter in your init.ora file.

After the dispatcher has registered with the listener, connections can be made between the client and the dispatcher via the listener. To see the dispatches that have been registered with a listener, you can issue the following command from the DOS command line:

```
lsnrctl
LSNRCTL> services
```

A DOS command window with the results of the command is shown next. In this example, only dedicated server processes are available. Dedicated connections are the Net8 default.

```
Command Prompt - lsnrctl                                          _ □ X
C:\>lsnrctl

LSNRCTL for 32-bit Windows: Version 8.1.5.0.0 - Production on 05-AUG-99 10:25:28


(c) Copyright 1998 Oracle Corporation.  All rights reserved.

Welcome to LSNRCTL, type "help" for information.

LSNRCTL> services
Connecting to (DESCRIPTION=(ADDRESS=(PROTOCOL=IPC)(KEY=EXTPROC0)))
Services Summary...
  PLSExtProc            has 1 service handler(s)
    DEDICATED SERVER established:0 refused:0
      LOCAL SERVER
  ORC1             has 3 service handler(s)
    DEDICATED SERVER established:0 refused:0
      LOCAL SERVER
    DEDICATED SERVER established:0 refused:0
      LOCAL SERVER
    DISPATCHER established:0 refused:0 current:0 max:254 state:ready
      D000 (machine: THERIML1-PC2, pid: 206)
      (ADDRESS=(PROTOCOL=tcp)(HOST=theriml1-pc2.jhuapl.edu)(PORT=1037))
      Presentation: oracle.aurora.server.SGiopServer
The command completed successfully
```

You can use the Oracle Net8 Configuration Assistant and Net8 Easy Config tools
to configure your listener.ora and tnsnames.ora files. See Chapter 13 for details on
how to use these tools.

Configuring Windows NT as a Back-End Server[1]

In the preceding sections, you have seen the networking capabilities and configuration
options for general client/server support on NT. In this section, you will see how to
configure the NT machine as a more efficient and effective database server.

On an NT system, there is a potential 4GB of memory space available for
addressing. Half of the addressable space is dedicated to the system services and
the file cache. User programs, such as ORACLE8i, can use the rest of the available
space. Because most Windows NT systems do not actually have 4GB of real memory
installed, the systems use a mechanism called *virtual memory* to balance the use of
real memory among applications. The Windows NT system will use a Virtual Memory
paging file to dynamically swap memory pages between physical RAM and the virtual
paging area. Since ORACLE8i is a memory-intensive application, the memory
requirements can exceed the actual physical memory capacity of the machine.

There are several steps that you can take to configure Windows NT as a back-end
server. The first of these steps is to ensure that the machine is not used for any other
activities like a primary or backup domain controller, a file or print server, a remote
access server, or a router or firewall server. In the following sections, you will see
descriptions of the other steps you can take to optimize NT server performance.

---

[1]This section references information from "Tuning the Windows NT Server Operating System," Oracle Corporation,
Oracle8i: ISV Development Kit Release1.5 for Windows NT, Part Number A67761-01.

Reduce the Priority of Interactive Foreground Applications

The next action that you can take is to reduce the priority of interactive foreground applications on the server console since they are given priority over background processes. To reduce the priority of interactive foreground applications, and thus increase the resources available for ORACLE8i, perform the following steps:

1. Choose the System option from the Control Panel under the Settings menu.

2. Click the Performance tab.

3. Move the Application Performance Boost slider to None.

4. Ensure that the Virtual Memory paging file size is set to at least 300MB.

5. Click OK on the dialog box.

6. Exit the Control Panel.

If you have more than one physical disk installed on your system, you can span your Virtual Memory paging file across the physical volumes. If you have logical, instead of physical, disks on your system, spanning your Virtual Memory paging file across them will not be worthwhile. If you have changed the Virtual Memory page file size, you must reboot your system for the change to take effect.

Reduce the Windows NT Server File Cache

Normally, Windows NT reserves 41 percent of the available memory for file cache activities on the system. While this is a good use of resources for a machine acting as a file server, it is unnecessary for the ORACLE8i database, which does its own caching via the SGA. The goal of reducing the file cache allocation is to provide more actual memory for the ORACLE8i application. To reduce the file cache, perform the following steps:

1. Choose the Network option from the Control Panel under the Settings menu.

2. Click the Services tab.

3. Select the Server service and click on the Properties option.

4. Select the button for the network applications configuration and click OK.

5. Click OK on the Network dialog box.

6. Exit the Control Panel.

In order for the new setting to take effect, you must reboot your system.

Disable Unnecessary Services

To retrieve additional memory for the ORACLE8i database, you can disable services that are not needed for core operating system functionality or ORACLE8i. Remember that the recommendation for unnecessary services to disable is based on the assumption that the Windows NT box is not being used for any other functions besides ORACLE8i. If this is the case, you can disable the following services: Plug and Play, Remote Access Autodial Manager, Remote Access Connection Manager, Remote Access Server, and Telephony Service. To disable these services, perform the following steps:

1. Choose the Services option from the Control Panel under the Settings menu.

2. Select each of the above-listed options in turn and select Startup.

3. Under Startup Type, select Disable and then click OK.

4. After resetting each of the options, click Close to exit the Control Panel.

Remove Unused Network Protocols and Reset Bind Order

Since not all of the protocols that may have been configured or allocated on the Windows NT machine are being used, processing time that could be used by critical protocols may be wasted. Therefore, you want to remove any network protocols that are not being used by the back-end server. To remove unused network protocols, identify the protocol(s) that you are using and then follow these steps:

1. Choose the Network option of the Control Panel under the Settings menu.

2. Click on the Protocols tab.

3. Select each unneeded protocol in turn and click the Remove option.

4. Click Yes to confirm your choices.

5. Once you have eliminated all unneeded protocols, click OK to exit.

   You will need to reboot your machine to enable the new settings to take effect.

If you are using more than one protocol, you can reset the network protocol bind order so that the protocol that is used most often by the ORACLE8i database is given the highest priority. To reset the bind order, perform the following steps:

1. Choose the Network option of the Control Panel under the Settings menu.

2. Click the Bindings tab.

3. Select All Services from the "Show Bindings for" display area.

4. Double click on the Server list to expand it.

5. Select the protocol that is used most by ORACLE8i (if it is not at the top of the list already) and click on Move Up until it is at the top of the list. You will want to do this for each network interface card that is installed on your system.

6. Click OK and exit the Control Panel.

You will need to reboot your machine to enable the new settings to take effect.

Other Available Configuration Options

Although the actions listed in the preceding sections will yield the most resource return for your back-end server, there are other actions that you can consider taking to help provide some (though not as much) benefit.

Periodically, Microsoft releases service packs with patches to provide bug fixes and product enhancements. Before applying any new service packs to your system, be sure to check with ORACLE Support to ensure that the new service pack has been certified with your current hardware configuration. If it has been approved and no major bugs have been reported within the service pack, applying the pack may help improve your system's performance.

If you are using the Windows NT system as a back-end server, you can close unnecessary foreground applications from the startup folder. Look in the Winnt\ Profiles\All Users\Start Menu\Programs\Startup directory for applications that are unnecessary. Programs like the FindFast indexing and MS Office Shortcut Toolbar can be removed.

Complex screen savers can quickly saturate the CPU. If a screen saver must be used for long-running processes, use a blank or limited-text screen saver to reduce the CPU impact. By eliminating programs and features that are unnecessary for ORACLE, you can improve the performance of any database or database networking on the server.

As an additional NT tuning option, you can ensure that all SGA pages are held in memory. To enable this option, set the PRE_PAGE_SGA init.ora parameter to TRUE prior to database startup. You should only use this option if your NT server has enough memory to hold the entire SGA in memory. Using the PRE_PAGE_SGA option will impact the time required for database startups and user logins, but the performance of other database activities involving the SGA will improve.

CHAPTER

16

Managing Distributed Databases

he distributed database architecture is based on the server/server configurations described in Chapter 13. In a distributed environment, databases on separate servers (hosts) share data with each other. Each server can be physically isolated without being logically isolated from other servers.

A typical distributed implementation involves corporate headquarters servers that communicate with departmental servers in various locations. Each server supports client applications, but it also has the ability to communicate with other servers in the network. This architecture is shown in Figure 16-1.

When one of the servers sends a database request to another server, the sending server acts like a client. The receiving server executes the SQL statement that is passed to it and returns the results plus error conditions to the sender.

SQL*Net V2 and Net8 allow this architecture to become reality. When run on all of the servers, SQL*Net and Net8 allow database requests made from one database (or application) to be passed to another database on a separate server. Both distributed queries and distributed updates are supported.

With this functionality, you can communicate with all of the databases that are accessible via your network. You can then create synonyms that give applications true network transparency; the user who submits a query will not know the location of the data that is used to resolve it.

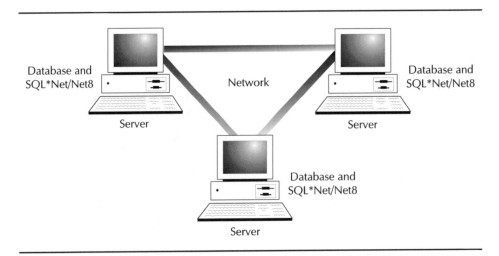

FIGURE 16-1. *Server/server architecture*

Remote Queries

The ability to perform remote queries is only one capability of a distributed database, and its usefulness is limited. Remote queries will only serve your needs if your data is isolated both logically and physically; that is, the "ownership" of the data can be assigned to a single database, and there are no data dependencies between databases.

To query a remote database, you must create a database link. The database link specifies the service name to use and may also specify the username to connect to in the remote database. When a database link is referenced by an SQL statement, ORACLE opens a session in the remote database and executes the SQL statement there. The data is then returned, and the remote session stays open in case it is needed again. You can create database links as public links (created by DBAs, making the link available to all users in the local database) or as private links.

The following example creates a public database link called HR_LINK:

```
create public database link HR_LINK
connect to HR identified by PUFFINSTUFF
using 'hq';
```

The **create database link** command, as shown in this example, has several parameters:

- The optional keyword **public**, which allows DBAs to create links for all users in a database. An additional optional keyword, **shared**, is described later in this chapter.

- The name of the link (HR_LINK, in this example)

- The account to connect to. You can configure the database link to use the local username and password in the remote database.

- The service name (hq)

To use the newly created link, simply add it as a suffix to table names in commands. The following example queries a remote table by using the HR_LINK database link:

```
select * from EMPLOYEE@HR_LINK
 where Office='ANNAPOLIS';
```

When you execute this query, ORACLE will establish a session via the HR_LINK database link and query the EMPLOYEE table in that database. The **where** clause will be applied to the EMPLOYEE rows, and the matching records will be returned. The execution of the query is shown graphically in Figure 16-2.

NOTE
Database links cannot be used to return values from columns with LONG datatypes.

The **from** clause in this example refers to EMPLOYEE@HR_LINK. Since the HR_LINK database link specifies the server name, instance name, and owner name, the full name of the table is known. If no account name had been specified in the database link, the user's account name and password in the local database would have been used when attempting to log in to the remote database.

The detailed management of database links is described in the "Managing Distributed Data" section later in this chapter.

Remote Data Manipulation: Two-Phase Commit

To achieve remote data manipulation, you'll need to use *Two-Phase Commit (2PC)*—and that's where ORACLE's distributed database capabilities come into play. 2PC allows groups of transactions across several nodes to be treated as a unit; either the transactions all **commit** or they all get rolled back. A set of distributed transactions is shown in Figure 16-3. In that figure, two **update** transactions are performed. The first **update** goes against a local table (EMPLOYEE); the second,

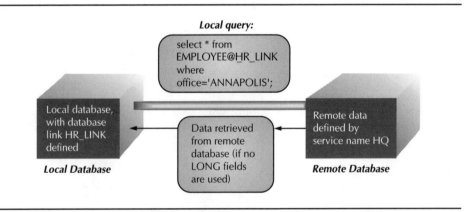

FIGURE 16-2. *Sample remote query*

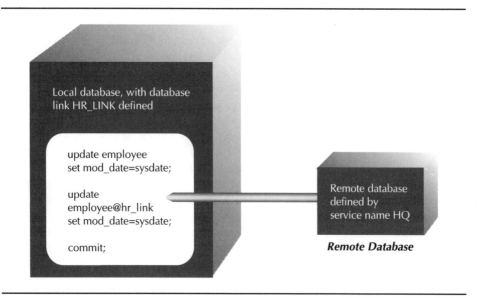

Local database, with database
link HR_LINK defined

update employee
set mod_date=sysdate;

update
employee@hr_link
set mod_date=sysdate;

commit;

Remote database
defined by
service name HQ

Remote Database

FIGURE 16-3. *Sample distributed transaction*

against a remote table (EMPLOYEE@HR_LINK). After the two transactions are performed, a single **commit** is then executed. If either transaction cannot **commit**, both transactions will be rolled back.

Distributed transactions yield two important benefits: databases on other servers can be **update**d, and those transactions can be grouped together with others in a logical unit. This second benefit occurs because of the database's use of 2PC. Its two phases are

- **The prepare phase** An initiating node called the *global coordinator* notifies all sites involved in the transaction to be ready to either **commit** or roll back the transaction.

- **The commit phase** If there is no problem with the Prepare phase, then all sites **commit** their transactions. If a network or node failure occurs, then all sites roll back their transactions.

The use of 2PC is transparent to the users. The detailed management of distributed transactions is discussed in the "Managing Distributed Transactions" section later in this chapter.

Dynamic Data Replication

To improve the performance of queries that use data from remote databases, you may wish to replicate that data on the local server. There are several options for accomplishing this, depending on which ORACLE features you are using.

You can use *database triggers* to replicate data from one table into another. For example, after every **insert** into a table, a trigger may fire to **insert** that same record into another table—and that table may be in a remote database. Thus, you can use triggers to enforce data replication in simple configurations. If the types of transactions against the base table cannot be controlled, then the trigger code needed to perform the replication will be unacceptably complicated.

When using ORACLE's distributed features, you can use *snapshots* to replicate data between databases. You do not have to replicate an entire table or limit yourself to data from just one table. When replicating a single table, you may use a **where** clause to restrict which records are replicated, and you may perform **group by** operations on the data. You can also join the table with other tables and replicate the result of the queries.

NOTE
You cannot use snapshots to replicate data using LONG, LONG RAW, BFILE, or abstract datatypes.

The data in the local snapshot of the remote table(s) will need to be refreshed. You can specify the refresh interval for the snapshot and the database will automatically take care of the replication procedures. If the snapshot is a one-to-one replication of records in a remote table (called a *simple snapshot*), then the database can use a *snapshot log* to send over only transaction data; otherwise, it is a *complex snapshot* and the database will usually perform complete refreshes on the local snapshot table. The dynamic replication of data via snapshots is shown in Figure 16-4.

Other methods may be used to replicate data, but they are not dynamically maintained by the database. For example, you can use the SQL*Plus **copy** command (see the "Usage Example: The **copy** Command" section of Chapter 13) to create copies of remote tables in local databases. However, the **copy** command would need to be repeated every time the data is changed; therefore, its use is limited to those situations in which large, static tables are replicated. Dynamic data requires dynamic replication.

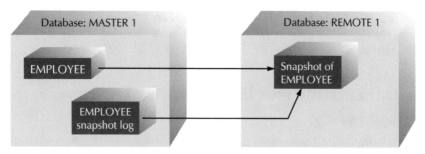

(a) A simple snapshot; snapshot logs can be used.

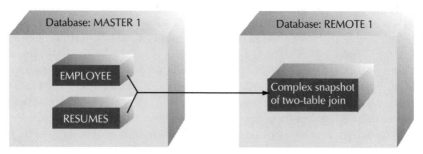

(b) A complex snapshot; the result of the join is replicated.

FIGURE 16-4. *Simple and complex snapshots*

Managing Distributed Data

Before you can worry about managing transactions against remote databases, you have to get the data there—and make it globally accessible to other databases. The following sections describe the requisite management tasks: enforcing location transparency, and managing the database links, triggers, and snapshots that are used to access the data.

NOTE
*The examples in this chapter assume that you are
using tnsnames.ora files for your database service
name resolution.*

The Infrastructure: Enforcing Location Transparency

To properly design your distributed databases for long-term use, you must start by
making the physical location of the data transparent to the application. The name of
a table within a database is unique within the schema that owns it. Thus, within any
single database, the combination of owner and table name will uniquely identify a
table. However, a remote database may have an account with the same name,
which may own a table with the same name. How can the table name be properly
qualified?

Within distributed databases, two additional layers of object identification must
be added. First, the name of the instance that accesses the database must be
identified. Next, the name of the host on which that instance resides must be
identified. Putting together these four parts of the object's name—its host, its
instance, its owner, and its name—results in a *fully qualified object name (FQON)*.
The FQON is sometimes referred to as the *global object name*. To access a remote
table, that table's FQON must be known. A sample is shown in Figure 16-5.

The goal of location transparency is to make the first three parts of the
FQON—the host, the instance, and the schema—transparent to the user. It is even
possible to make the object name itself transparent to the user (it may, for example,
point to a view that joins two tables), but this chapter will keep that portion of the
FQON intact as a point of reference.

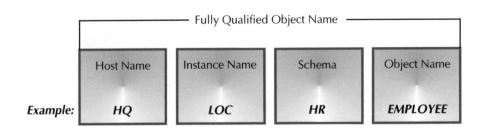

FIGURE 16-5. *Fully qualified object name*

The first three parts of the FQON are all specified via database links, so any effort at achieving location transparency should start there. First, consider a typical database link:

```
create public database link HR_LINK
connect to HR identified by PUFFINSTUFF
using 'hq';
```

NOTE
If the GLOBAL_NAMES init.ora parameter is set to TRUE, the database link name must be the same as the name of the remote database.

By using a service name (hq), the host and instance names are kept transparent. They are translated into their actual values via the local host's tnsnames.ora file. A partial entry in this file, for this service name, is shown in the following listing:

```
hq =(DESCRIPTION=
        (ADDRESS=
                (PROTOCOL=TCP)
                (HOST=HQ)
                (PORT=1521))
        (CONNECT DATA=
                (SID=loc))))
```

The two lines in bold in this listing fill in the two missing pieces of the FQON: when the HQ service name is used, the host name is HQ, and the instance name is LOC. This tnsnames.ora file shows the parameters for the TCP/IP protocol; other protocols may use different keywords, but their usage is the same. The tnsnames.ora entries provide transparency for the server and instance names.

The HR_LINK database link, if created via the code given earlier in this section, will thus provide transparency for the first two parts of the FQON. But what if the data moves from the HR schema, or the HR account's password changes? The database link would have to be dropped and re-created. The same would be true if account-level security was required; you may need to create and maintain multiple database links.

To resolve the transparency of the schema portion of the FQON, you can modify the database link syntax. Consider the database link in the following listing:

```
create public database link HR_LINK
connect to current_user
using 'hq';
```

This database link uses the **connect to current_user** clause. It will use what is known as a *default connection*. An example of this link being used is shown in the following listing:

```
select * from EMPLOYEE@HR_LINK;
```

When HR_LINK is used, the database will resolve the FQON in the following manner:

1. It will search the local tnsnames.ora file to determine the proper host name and port.

2. It will search the local tnsnames.ora file to determine the proper instance name.

3. It will search the database link for a **connect to** specification. If the **connect to current_user** clause is found, it will attempt to connect to the specified database using the *current user's* username and password.

4. It will search the **from** clause of the query for the object name.

Default connections are often used to access tables whose rows can be restricted based on the username that is accessing the table. For example, if the remote database had a table named HR.EMPLOYEE, and every employee was allowed to see his or her own record, then a database link with a specific connection, such as

```
create public database link HR_LINK
connect to HR identified by PUFFINSTUFF
using 'hq';
```

would log in as the HR account (the owner of the table). If this specific connection is used, you cannot restrict the user's view of the records on the remote host. However, if a default connection is used, and a view is created on the remote host using the User pseudocolumn, then only that user's data would be returned from the remote host. A sample database link and view of this type is shown in the following listing:

```
create public database link HR_LINK
connect to current_user
using 'hq';

create view REMOTE_EMP
as select * from EMPLOYEE@HR_LINK
where Ename=User;
```

The User pseudocolumn's value is the current ORACLE username. If you query the REMOTE_EMP view, you are using the HR_LINK database link. Since that link uses a default connection, your username and password will be used to connect to the hq service name's database. You will therefore retrieve only those records from EMPLOYEE@HR_LINK for which your username is equal to the value of the Ename column in that table.

Either way, the data being retrieved can be restricted. The difference is that when a default connection is used, the data can be restricted based on the username in the remote database; if a specific connection is used, then the data can be restricted after it has been returned to the local database. The default connection method thus reduces the amount of network traffic needed to resolve the query and adds an additional level of location transparency to the data.

Using default connections in database links raises a different set of maintenance issues. The tnsnames.ora files must be synchronized across the servers, and the username/password combinations in multiple databases must be synchronized. These issues are addressed in the next sections.

Using Shared Database Links

If you use the Multithreaded Server option for your database connections, and your application will employ many concurrent database link connections, then you may benefit from using shared database links. A shared database link uses shared server connections to support the database link connections. If you have multiple concurrent database link accesses into a remote database, you can use shared database links to reduce the number of server connections required.

To create a shared database link, use the **shared** keyword of the **create database link** command. As shown in the following listing, you will also need to specify a schema and password for the remote database:

```
create shared database link HR_LINK_SHARED
connect to current_user
authenticated by HR identified by puffinstuff
using 'hq';
```

The HR_LINK_SHARED database link uses default connections, as specified via the **connect to current_user** clause. In order to prevent unauthorized attempts to use the shared link, shared links require the **authenticated by** clause. In this example, the account used for authentication is an application account, but you can also use an empty schema for authentication. The authentication account must have the CREATE SESSION system privilege. During usage of the HR_LINK_SHARED link, connection attempts will include authentication against the HR link account.

If you change the password on the authentication account, you will need to drop and re-create each database link that references it. Thus, you should create an account that is only used for authentication of shared database link connections. The account should have only the CREATE SESSION system privilege, and should not have any privileges on any of the application tables.

If your application uses database links infrequently, you should use traditional database links without the **shared** clause. Without the **shared** clause, each database link connection requires a separate connection to the remote database.

Managing Database Links

You can retrieve information about public database links via the DBA_DB_LINKS data dictionary view. You can view private database links via the USER_DB_LINKS data dictionary view. Whenever possible, separate your users among databases by application so that they may all share the same public database links. As a side benefit, these users will usually also be able to share public grants and synonyms.

The columns of the DBA_DB_LINKS data dictionary view are listed in the following table. The password for the link to use is not viewable via DBA_DB_LINKS; it is stored unencrypted in the SYS.LINK$ table.

Column Name	Description
OWNER	Owner of the database link
DB_LINK	Name of the database link (such as HR_LINK in this chapter's examples)
USERNAME	The name of the account to use to open a session in the remote database, if a specific connection is used
HOST	The SQL*Net connect string that will be used to connect to the remote database
CREATED	A timestamp that marks the creation date for the database link

NOTE
The number of database links that can be used by a single query is limited by the OPEN_LINKS parameter in the database's init.ora file. Its default value is 4.

The managerial tasks involved for database links depend on the level to which you have implemented location transparency in your databases. They also depend on the version of SQL*Net you are using—users of Net8 should see Chapter 13 for details on the use of the Net8 Assistant.

In the best-case scenario, default connections are used along with service names or aliases. In that scenario, the only requirements for successful maintenance are that the tnsnames.ora file be consistent across hosts and that user account/password combinations be maintained globally. The file synchronization can be accomplished via the operating system—for example, by use of the UNIX **rcp** (remote copy) command to copy files to remote hosts.

Synchronizing account/password combinations is more difficult, but there are several alternatives. First, you may force all changes to user account passwords to go through a central authority. This central authority would have the responsibility for updating the password for the account in all databases in the network—a time-consuming task, but a valuable one.

Second, you may audit all user password changes by auditing all **alter user** commands. If a user's password changes in one database, then it is changed on all databases available in the network that are accessed via default connections. Synchronizing database password changes is more difficult if you use the password management features available as of ORACLE8, since you can force passwords to expire and force frequent password changes.

If any part of the FQON—such as a username—is embedded in the database link, a change affecting that part of the FQON requires that the database link be dropped and re-created. For example, if the HR user's password were changed, the HR_LINK database link with a specific connection defined earlier would be dropped with

```
drop database link HR_LINK;
```

and the link would then be re-created, using the new account specification:

```
create public database link HR_LINK
connect to HR identified by NEWPASSWORD
using 'hq';
```

You cannot create a database link in another user's account. If you attempt to create a database link in SCOTT's account, as shown here,

```
create database link SCOTT.HR_LINK
connect to HR identified by PUFFINSTUFF
using 'hq';
```

then ORACLE will not create the HR_LINK database link in SCOTT's account. Instead, ORACLE will create a database link named SCOTT.HR_LINK in the account that executed the **create database link** command. To create private database links, you must be logged in to the database in the account that will own the link.

Managing Database Triggers

If your data replication needs are fairly limited, you can use database triggers to replicate data from one table into another. In general, this method is used when the only type of data being sent to the remote database is either an **insert** or a **delete**. The code necessary to support **update** transactions is usually much more complex than a comparable snapshot; see the following sections for details on implementing snapshots.

Database triggers are executed when specific actions happen to specific tables. They can be executed for each row of a transaction, or for an entire transaction as a unit. When dealing with data replication, you will usually be concerned with each row of data.

Before creating the trigger, you must create a database link for the trigger to use. In this case, the link is created in the database that *owns* the data, accessible to the owner of the table being replicated.

```
create public database link TRIGGER_LINK
using 'remote1';
```

This link, named TRIGGER_LINK, uses a service name (remote1) to specify the connection to a remote database. Since no specific **connect** clause is specified, a default connection will be attempted instead. The default connection will attempt to log in to the remote1 database using the same username and password as the account that calls the link.

The trigger shown in the following listing uses this link. The trigger is fired after every row is **insert**ed into the EMPLOYEE table. Since the trigger executes after the row has been **insert**ed, the row's data has already been validated. The trigger **insert**s the same row into a remote table with the same structure, using the TRIGGER_LINK database link just defined. The remote table must already exist.

```
create trigger COPY_DATA
after insert on EMPLOYEE
for each row
begin
    insert into EMPLOYEE@TRIGGER_LINK
    values
    (:new.Empno, :new.Ename, :new.Deptno,
    :new.Salary, :new.Birth_Date, :new.Soc_Sec_Num);
end;
/
```

This trigger uses the **new** keyword to reference the values from the row that was just **insert**ed into the local EMPLOYEE table.

NOTE
*If you use trigger-based replication, your trigger
code must account for potential error conditions at
the remote site, such as duplicate key values, space
management problems, or a down database.*

To list information about triggers, use the DBA_TRIGGERS data dictionary view.
The following query will list the "header" information about the trigger—its type,
the statement that calls it, and the table on which it calls. This example shows the
header information for the COPY_DATA trigger just created:

```
select Trigger_Type,
       Triggering_Event,
       Table_Name
  from DBA_TRIGGERS
 where Trigger_Name = 'COPY_DATA';
```

Sample output from this query is shown here:

```
TYPE                 TRIGGERING_EVENT        TABLE_NAME
---------------     ----------------------   ------------
AFTER EACH ROW       INSERT                   EMPLOYEE
```

You can query the text of the trigger from DBA_TRIGGERS, as shown in the
following listing:

```
select Trigger_Body
  from DBA_TRIGGERS
 where Trigger_Name = 'COPY_DATA';
```

Sample output from this query is shown in the following listing:

```
TRIGGER_BODY
-------------------------------------------------------
begin
    insert into EMPLOYEE@TRIGGER_LINK
    values
    (:new.Empno, :new.Ename, :new.Deptno,
    :new.Salary, :new.Birth_Date, :new.Soc_Sec_Num);
end;
```

It is theoretically possible to create a trigger to replicate all possible
permutations of data manipulation actions on the local database, but this quickly
becomes difficult to manage. For a complex environment, you should consider the

use of snapshots or manual data copies. However, for the limited circumstances described earlier, triggers are a very easy solution to implement.

> **NOTE**
> *If you use triggers for your data replication, the success of a transaction in the master database is dependent on the success of the remote transaction.*

Managing Snapshots

You can use snapshots to dynamically replicate data between distributed databases. The master table will be updatable, but the snapshots will be either read-only or updatable. Read-only snapshots are the most common types of snapshots implemented. There are two types of snapshots available: *complex snapshots* and *simple snapshots.*

In a simple snapshot, each row is based on a single row in a single remote table. A row in a complex snapshot may be based on more than one row in a remote table—such as via a **group by** operation—or on the result of a multitable join. Simple snapshots are thus a specific subset of the snapshots that can be created.

Since the snapshot will create several objects in the local database, the user creating the snapshot must have the CREATE SNAPSHOT privilege and either the UNLIMITED TABLESPACE privilege or quota on the tablespace in which the snapshot's objects will be stored. Snapshots are created in the local database, and pull data from the remote master database.

Before creating a snapshot, you must first create a database link to the source database in the local database. The following example creates a private database link called HR_LINK (which has been used as an example throughout this chapter):

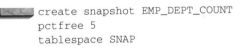

```
create database link HR_LINK
connect to HR identified by PUFFINSTUFF
using 'hq';
```

The syntax used to create the snapshot on the local server is shown in the following listing. In this example, the snapshot is given a name (EMP_DEPT_COUNT) and its storage parameters are specified. The tablespace and storage parameters apply to the local base table that will store the snapshot's data.

Its base query is given, as well as its refresh interval. In this case, the snapshot is told to immediately retrieve the master data, then to perform the snapshot operation again in seven days (SysDate+7).

```
create snapshot EMP_DEPT_COUNT
pctfree 5
tablespace SNAP
```

```
storage (initial 100K next 100K pctincrease 0)
refresh complete
      start with SysDate
      next SysDate+7
as select Deptno, COUNT(*) Dept_Count
    from HR.EMPLOYEE@HR_LINK
    group by Deptno;
```

NOTE
Because ORACLE uses the name of the snapshot in the names of the database objects that support it, the snapshot's name should be kept to fewer than 19 characters.

NOTE
A snapshot query cannot reference tables or views owned by the user SYS.

See Appendix A for the full syntax options for the **create snapshot** command. Because the records in this snapshot will not correspond one to one with the records in the master table (since the query contains a **group by** clause), this is a complex snapshot. Because the snapshot is a complex snapshot, the snapshot will need to be completely re-created every time it is refreshed.

NOTE
When you create a snapshot, reference the full object name in the remote database—in the preceding example, HR.EMPLOYEE.

When this snapshot is created, a table is created in the local database. ORACLE will create a table—the local base table for the snapshot—called SNAP$_*snapshotname* to store the records from the snapshot's query. This table should not be altered in any way, although it may be indexed. A read-only view of this table, named after the snapshot, will be created as well. A second view, named MVIEW$_*snapshotname*, will be created as a view of the remote master table(s). This view will be used during refreshes.

You can use the Oracle Enterprise Manager Schema Manager to create and administer database links and snapshots and monitor snapshot logs. Figure 16-6 shows the **create snapshot** screen with information filled in to create the EMP_DEPT_COUNT snapshot.

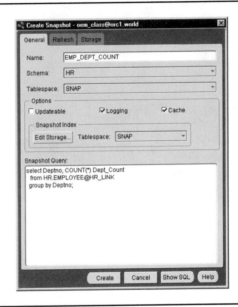

FIGURE 16-6. *Create Snapshot using OEM*

To drop a snapshot, use the **drop snapshot** command. An example of this is shown in the following listing:

```
drop snapshot EMP_DEPT_COUNT;
```

You can alter the snapshot's storage parameters via the **alter snapshot** command, as shown in the following listing:

```
alter snapshot EMP_DEPT_COUNT pctfree 5;
```

To improve the snapshot's performance, you may wish to add an index to its local base table. To do this, create the appropriate index on the underlying SNAP$_*snapshotname* table via the **create index** command.

NOTE
Do not create constraints on the local base table for the snapshot.

To view data about snapshots, query the DBA_SNAPSHOTS data dictionary view. A sample query against this view is shown in the following listing:

```
select
  Name,              /*Name of the view used for the snapshot*/
  Last_Refresh,      /*Timestamp for the last refresh*/
  Type,              /*Type of refresh used for automatic refreshes*/
  Query              /*Query used to create the snapshot*/
from DBA_SNAPSHOTS;
```

This query will return the most-used information for the snapshot. Other information, such as the master table name and the name of the database link used, can also be retrieved via the DBA_SNAPSHOTS view.

Dealing with Media Failures

Once you create a snapshot, its data is linked (logically, not physically) to the master data. If there is a problem with the server on which their master data resides, you may need to re-create or completely refresh the snapshot.

For example, the EMP_DEPT_COUNT snapshot described in the previous section of this chapter is based on data in the remote EMPLOYEE table. If there is a media failure on the server that is used by the EMPLOYEE table, you may need to perform database recovery on that server. Unless you can recover all of the lost data, your master EMPLOYEE table may not contain all of the records it contained when the snapshot was created. As a result, the data in the base (EMPLOYEE) table and its snapshot may be out of sync.

If the snapshot is a simple snapshot, you can create it using the **with rowid** clause. The **with rowid** clause tells ORACLE to use the RowIDs of the master table records as the means of correlating rows in the master table with rows in the snapshot (during fast refreshes). If you have to perform a recovery on the master table, then its RowID values may change—even if you perform a full recovery. If you have to perform recovery on the master table's database, you should completely refresh the snapshot. If you have to perform recovery on the snapshot's database, you should perform a complete refresh of the snapshot after the recovery has completed.

Enforcing Referential Integrity in Snapshots

The referential integrity between two related tables, both of which have simple snapshots to a remote database, may not be enforced in their snapshots. If the tables are refreshed at different times, or if transactions are occurring on the master tables during the refresh, it is possible for the snapshots of those tables to not reflect the referential integrity of the master tables.

If, for example, EMPLOYEE and DEPT are related to each other via a primary key/foreign key relationship, then simple snapshots of these tables may contain violations of this relationship. These violations may include foreign keys without matching primary keys. In this example, that could mean employees in the EMPLOYEE snapshot with DEPTNO values that do not exist in the DEPT snapshot.

There are a number of potential solutions to this problem. First, time the refreshes to occur when the master tables are not in use. Second, perform the refreshes manually (see the following section for information on this) immediately after locking the master tables. Third, you may join the tables in the snapshot, creating a complex snapshot that will be based on the master tables (which will be properly related to each other).

Using refresh groups is a fourth solution to the snapshot referential integrity problem. You can collect related snapshots into *refresh groups*. The purpose of a refresh group is to coordinate the refresh schedules of its members. Snapshots whose master tables have relationships with other snapshot master tables are good candidates for membership in refresh groups. Coordinating the refresh schedules of the snapshots will maintain the master tables' referential integrity in the snapshots as well. If refresh groups are not used, the data in the snapshots may be inconsistent with regard to the master tables' referential integrity.

All manipulation of refresh groups is achieved via the DBMS_REFRESH package. The procedures within that package are MAKE, ADD, SUBTRACT, CHANGE, DESTROY, and REFRESH, as shown in the following examples. Information about existing refresh groups can be queried from the USER_REFRESH and USER_REFRESH_CHILDREN data dictionary views.

NOTE
Snapshots that belong to a refresh group do not have to belong to the same schema, but they do have to be all stored within the same database.

Create a refresh group by executing the MAKE procedure in the DBMS_REFRESH package, whose structure is shown in the following listing:

```
DBMS_REFRESH.MAKE
(name IN VARCHAR2
{ list IN VARCHAR2, |
  tab IN DBMS_UTILITY.UNCL_ARRAY,}
next_date IN DATE,
interval IN VARCHAR2,
implicit_destroy IN BOOLEAN := FALSE,
lax IN BOOLEAN := FALSE,
job IN BINARY INTEGER := 0,
```

```
rollback_seg IN VARCHAR2 := NULL,
push_deferred_rpc IN BOOLEAN := TRUE,
refresh_after_errors IN BOOLEAN := FALSE,
purge_option IN BINARY_INTEGER := NULL,
parallelism IN BINARY_INTEGER := NULL,
heap_size IN BINARY_INTEGER := NULL);
```

All but the first four of the parameters for this procedure have default values that are usually acceptable. The *list* and *tab* parameters are mutually exclusive. You can use the following command to create a refresh group for snapshots named LOCAL_EMP and LOCAL_DEPT:

```
execute DBMS_REFRESH.MAKE
(name => 'emp_group',
 list => 'local_emp, local_dept',
 next_date => SysDate,
 interval => 'SysDate+7');
```

NOTE
The snapshot list parameter, which is the second parameter in the listing, has a single quote at its beginning and at its end, with none between. In this example, two snapshots—LOCAL_EMP and LOCAL_DEPT—are passed to the procedure via a single parameter.

The preceding command will create a refresh group named EMP_GROUP, with two snapshots as its members. The refresh group name is enclosed in single quotes, as is the *list* of snapshot members—but not each member.

If the refresh group is going to contain a snapshot that is already a member of another refresh group (for example, during a move of a snapshot from an old refresh group to a newly created refresh group), then you must set the lax parameter to TRUE. A snapshot can only belong to one refresh group at a time.

To add snapshots to an existing refresh group, use the ADD procedure of the DBMS_REFRESH package, whose structure is

```
DBMS_REFRESH.ADD
(name IN VARCHAR2,
{ list IN VARCHAR2, |
  tab IN DBMS_UTILITY.UNCL_ARRAY, }
 lax IN BOOLEAN := FALSE);
```

As with the MAKE procedure, the ADD procedure's lax parameter does not have to be specified unless a snapshot is being moved between two refresh groups. When this procedure is executed with the lax parameter set to TRUE, the snapshot is moved to the new refresh group and is automatically deleted from the old refresh group.

To remove snapshots from an existing refresh group, use the SUBTRACT procedure of the DBMS_REFRESH package, as in the following:

```
DBMS_REFRESH.SUBTRACT
(name IN VARCHAR2,
{ list IN VARCHAR2, |
  tab IN DBMS_UTILITY.UNCL_ARRAY, }
 lax IN BOOLEAN := FALSE);
```

As with the MAKE and ADD procedures, a single snapshot or a list of snapshots (separated by commas) may serve as input to the SUBTRACT procedure. You can alter the refresh schedule for a refresh group via the CHANGE procedure of the DBMS_REFRESH package.

```
DBMS_REFRESH.CHANGE
(name IN VARCHAR2,
 next_date IN DATE := NULL,
 interval IN VARCHAR2 := NULL,
 implicit_destroy IN BOOLEAN := NULL,
 rollback_seg IN VARCHAR2 := NULL,
 push_deferred_rpc IN BOOLEAN := NULL,
 refresh_after_errors IN BOOLEAN := NULL,
 purge_option IN BINARY_INTEGER := NULL,
 parallelism IN BINARY_INTEGER := NULL,
 heap_size IN BINARY_INTEGER := NULL);
```

The *next_date* parameter is analogous to the **start with** clause in the **create snapshot** command. The *interval* parameter is analogous to the **next** clause in the **create snapshot** command. For example, to change the EMP_GROUP's schedule so that it will be replicated every three days, you can execute the following command (which specifies a **NULL** value for the *next_date* parameter, leaving that value unchanged):

```
execute DBMS_REFRESH.CHANGE
(name => 'emp_group',
 next_date => null,
 interval => 'SysDate+3');
```

After this command is executed, the refresh cycle for the EMP_GROUP refresh group will be changed to every three days.

To delete a refresh group, use the DESTROY procedure of the DBMS_REFRESH package, as shown in the following example. Its only parameter is the name of the refresh group.

```
execute DBMS_REFRESH.DESTROY(name => 'emp_group');
```

You may also implicitly destroy the refresh group. If you set the *implicit_destroy* parameter to TRUE when you create the group with the MAKE procedure, the refresh group will be deleted (destroyed) when its last member is removed from the group (usually via the SUBTRACT procedure).

NOTE
Refresh operations on snapshot groups may take longer than comparable snapshot refreshes. Snapshot group refreshes may also require significant rollback segment space to maintain data consistency during the refresh.

Sizing and Storing Snapshots

The appropriate storage parameters for snapshots are derived from the data being selected. Since the data is being replicated, the source data is known and can be sized. Use the space calculations in Chapter 5 to size the snapshot's local base table.

If a complex snapshot is used, the storage needs will vary. For example, the EMP_DEPT_COUNT snapshot shown in the previous section should use less space than its master table since it performs a **group by** on the table and only returns two columns. For other complex snapshots—such as those involving joins and returning columns from multiple tables—the space needs for the snapshot may exceed those of any of the master tables involved. Therefore, always calculate the space for the local snapshot rather than relying on the storage parameters for the master tables.

Because of the nature of the snapshot data and objects, you may wish to create a tablespace that is dedicated to supporting them. The emphasis should be on providing enough contiguous space so that no snapshot refresh attempt will ever fail due to space availability problems.

Automatic and Manual Snapshot Refreshes

The EMP_DEPT_COUNT snapshot defined earlier contained the following specifications about its refresh interval:

```
refresh complete
    start with SysDate
    next SysDate+7
```

The **refresh complete** clause indicates that each time the snapshot is refreshed, it should be completely re-created. The available **refresh** options are listed in the following table:

Refresh Option	Description
COMPLETE	The snapshot tables are completely regenerated using the snapshot's query and the master tables every time the snapshot is refreshed.
FAST	If a simple snapshot is used, then a snapshot log can be used to send only the changes to the snapshot table.
FORCE	The default value. If possible, it performs a FAST refresh; otherwise, it will perform a COMPLETE refresh.

The **start with** clause tells the database when the snapshot should be refreshed. In this example, that is specified as SysDate so the database will replicate the data when the snapshot is created.

The **next** clause sets the interval for the refreshes. This period will be measured from the time of the last refresh, whether it was done automatically by the database or manually by the DBA. In this example, a refresh will occur seven days after the most recent snapshot.

For automatic snapshot refreshes to occur, you must tell ORACLE to create the SNP background processes that perform the snapshot refreshes. The number of SNP processes to create is determined by the JOB_QUEUE_PROCESSES init.ora parameter. If you do not set a value for this parameter, it will default to 0 and no automatic refreshes will ever occur. You will not typically need more than one background process (called SNP0) unless you have many snapshots being refreshed simultaneously. You can, however, create up to 36 SNP processes.

The interval, in seconds, between "wake-up calls" to the SNP*n* processes is set by the JOB_QUEUE_INTERVAL parameter in the init.ora parameter file. The default interval is 60 seconds.

NOTE
The JOB_QUEUE_PROCESSES and JOB_QUEUE_INTERVAL parameters create background processes that are used for job queue management as well as snapshot refreshes. Job queue management is described later in this chapter.

You may manually refresh the snapshot via the DBMS_SNAPSHOT package provided by ORACLE. You can use the REFRESH procedure of the DBMS_SNAPSHOT package to refresh a single snapshot. An example of the command's usage is shown in the following listing. In this example, the user uses the **execute** command to execute the procedure. The parameters passed to the procedure are described following the example.

```
execute DBMS_SNAPSHOT.REFRESH('emp_dept_count','?');
```

The REFRESH procedure of the DBMS_SNAPSHOT package, as shown in this listing, takes two parameters. The first is the name of the snapshot, which should be prefixed by the name of the snapshot's owner (if other than the user executing this command). The second parameter is the manual refresh option. The available values for the manual refresh option parameter are listed in the following table.

Manual Refresh Option	Description
F	Fast refresh
f	Fast refresh
C	Complete refresh
c	Complete refresh
?	Indicates that the default refresh option for the snapshot should be used

You can use another procedure in the DBMS_SNAPSHOT package to refresh all of the snapshots that are scheduled to be automatically refreshed. This procedure, named REFRESH_ALL, will refresh each snapshot separately. It does not accept any parameters. The following listing shows an example of its execution:

```
execute DBMS_SNAPSHOT.REFRESH_ALL;
```

Since the snapshots will be refreshed via REFRESH_ALL consecutively, they are not all refreshed at the same time. Therefore, a database or server failure during the execution of this procedure may cause the local snapshots to be out of sync with each other. If that happens, simply rerun this procedure after the database has been recovered.

You may manually refresh a refresh group via the REFRESH procedure of the DBMS_REFRESH package. The REFRESH procedure accepts the name of the refresh group as its only parameter. The command shown in the following listing will refresh the refresh group named EMP_GROUP:

```
execute DBMS_REFRESH.REFRESH('emp_group');
```

Managing Snapshot Logs

A snapshot log is a table that maintains a record of modifications to the master table in a snapshot. It is stored in the same database as the master table and is only used by simple snapshots. The data in the snapshot log is used during fast refreshes of the table's snapshots. If you are going to use this method, create the snapshot log before creating the snapshot.

To create a snapshot log, you must be able to create an AFTER ROW trigger on the table. This implies that you have CREATE TRIGGER and CREATE TABLE privileges. You cannot specify a name for the snapshot log.

NOTE
Because ORACLE uses the name of the master table in the names of the database objects that support its snapshot log, the master table's name should be kept to fewer than 19 characters.

Since the snapshot log is a table, it has the full set of table storage clauses available to it. The example in the following listing shows the creation of a snapshot log on a table named EMPLOYEE. The log will be placed in the DATA_2 tablespace, with the specified storage parameters.

```
create snapshot log on EMPLOYEE
tablespace DATA_2
storage(initial 100K next 50K pctincrease 0)
pctfree 5 pctused 90;
```

The **pctfree** value for this table can be set very low, and the **pctused** value should be set very high, as shown in this example. The size of the snapshot log depends on the number of changes that will be processed during each refresh. The more frequently the snapshot is refreshed, the less space that is needed for the snapshot log.

Just as snapshots create underlying tables, snapshot logs create a set of database structures. In the master table's database, the snapshot log creates a table named

MLOG$_*tablename* to store the RowID and a timestamp for the rows in the master table. This table will be used to identify the rows that have changed since the last refresh. An internal trigger will populate the MLOG$_*tablename* table. Do not alter the snapshot log table. If the snapshot is based on primary keys instead of RowIDs, then the snapshot log will contain the primary key values instead of the RowID values.

You can modify the storage parameters for the snapshot log via the **alter snapshot log** command. When using this command, specify the name of the master table, not its snapshot log table name. An example of altering the EMPLOYEE table's snapshot log is shown in the following listing:

```
alter snapshot log EMPLOYEE
pctfree 10;
```

You can query information about snapshot logs via the DBA_SNAPSHOT_LOGS data dictionary view. This view lists the owner of the snapshot log, its master table, its snapshot log table, and the trigger used. Since the snapshot log table is a segment in the database, and its name is known (MLOG$_*tablename*), its space usage can be tracked via the extent monitoring scripts provided in Chapter 6.

To drop a snapshot log, use the **drop snapshot log** command, as shown in the following example:

```
drop snapshot log on EMPLOYEE;
```

This command will drop the snapshot log and its associated objects from the database.

Choosing the Refresh Type

Which type of refresh is best for your snapshots? The correct answer may change from snapshot to snapshot within your database. The deciding factors should be

- **The network traffic**   Complete refreshes send a large volume of data across the network.

- **The transaction size**   A complete refresh generates a very large transaction (an **insert as select** command based on the base query for the snapshot). Fast refreshes typically generate smaller transaction sizes.

- **The volatility of the data**   If more than 25 percent of the rows have changed, a complete refresh will typically perform better than a fast refresh.

■ **The number of indexes on the local base table for the snapshot**   A
   complete refresh **truncate**s the local base table and then performs an **insert
   as select** into the local base table. All of the local base table's indexes are
   left in place during the complete refresh. If there are many indexes on the
   local base table, the refresh performance will be adversely affected.

■ **The storage requirements for the snapshot log**   In order to use fast
   refreshes, you have to create and maintain a snapshot log. The snapshot log
   will grow in size and will not automatically release freed space.

For low-volatility data, fast refreshes may be the most appropriate method to
use. Since multiple snapshots can use the same snapshot log, the space
requirements for the snapshot log data may be shared by many snapshots. If you use
fast refreshes, see the "Purging the Snapshot Log" section later in this chapter for
details on snapshot log space management.

Offline Instantiation of Snapshots

When you create a snapshot, ORACLE issues a single **create table as select**
command to create and populate the snapshot. If you have a great deal of data to
replicate, this may be an unacceptable solution since it generates a very large
transaction and a great deal of network traffic. If the transaction does not fit within
one of your rollback segments (see Chapter 7), the snapshot creation will fail.

To work around this problem, you can use the Import utility to bring the data into
the snapshot's database. In order to use this method (called *offline instantiation*), you
need to trick ORACLE by creating the proper objects in the master database first, and
then exporting them. This method requires that the rollback segments of the master
database be large enough to support the snapshot creation.

First, create an account at the master site that has privileges on the master table,
the ability to create database links, and the ability to create snapshots. Within that
account, create a database link with the same name as you will use in the remote
database when accessing the master database. Next, create the snapshot within this
new master database account, using the database link you just created.

For example, the following commands create the HR_LINK database link and
the EMP_DEPT_COUNT snapshot within an account in the master database:

```
create database link HR_LINK
connect to HR identified by PUFFINSTUFF
using 'hq';

create snapshot EMP_DEPT_COUNT
refresh complete
      start with SYSDATE
      next SYSDATE+7
```

```
as select Deptno, COUNT(*) Dept_Count
    from HR.EMPLOYEE@HR_LINK
   group by Deptno;
```

When these commands complete, you will have an account that has the
HR_LINK database link, the EMP_DEPT_COUNT snapshot (with its related objects),
and the data for the snapshot.

Next, export the user who owns the snapshot in the master database. You can
now transfer the Export dump file to the remote server and import that file's data
into the remote database. During the import, the database link will be created, the
snapshot will be created, and the snapshot's local base table will be populated. You
can control the size of the transactions created during the import (and thus the size
of the rollback segments required) via the COMMIT and BUFFER parameters of the
Import utility. See Chapter 10 for details on the use of Import and Export.

Purging the Snapshot Log

The snapshot log contains transient data; records are **insert**ed into the snapshot log,
used during refreshes, and then **delete**d. Therefore, you should encourage reuse of
the snapshot log's blocks by setting a high value for **pctused** when creating the
snapshot log.

If multiple snapshots use the same master table, then they share the same
snapshot log. If one of the snapshots is not refreshed for a long period, the snapshot
log may never delete any of its records. As a result, the space requirements of the
snapshot log will grow.

To reduce the space used by snapshot log entries, you can use the PURGE_LOG
procedure of the DBMS_SNAPSHOT package. PURGE_LOG takes three parameters:
the name of the master table, a num variable, and a DELETE flag. The num variable
specifies the number of least recently refreshed snapshots whose rows will be
removed from the snapshot log. For example, if you have three snapshots that use
the snapshot log and one of them has not been refreshed for a very long time, you
would use a num value of 1.

The following listing shows an example of the PURGE_LOG procedure. In this
example, the EMPLOYEE table's snapshot log will be purged of the entries required
by the least recently used snapshot:

```
execute DBMS_SNAPSHOT.PURGE_LOG
(master => 'EMPLOYEE',
   num => 1,
   flag => 'DELETE');
```

You can manage the rows within the snapshot log the same way you manage
the rows in any other table, as long as you can guarantee that rows are not being
written to the master table while you manage the snapshot log. For example, you

can export the snapshot log's data, **truncate** the log's table, and then import the data back into the snapshot log in order to reduce its space requirements.

To further support snapshot maintenance, ORACLE provides two snapshot-specific options for the **truncate** command. If you want to **truncate** the master table without losing its snapshot log entries, you can enter the command

```
truncate table EMPLOYEE preserve snapshot log;
```

If the EMPLOYEE table's snapshots are based on primary key values, the snapshot log values will still be valid following an export/import of the EMPLOYEE tables. However, if the EMPLOYEE table's snapshots are based on RowID values, the snapshot log would be invalid following an export/import of the base table (since different RowIDs may be assigned during the import). In that case, you should **truncate** the snapshot log when you **truncate** the base table.

```
truncate table EMPLOYEE purge snapshot log;
```

Managing Distributed Transactions

A single logical unit of work may include transactions against multiple databases. The example shown earlier in Figure 16-3 illustrates this: a **commit** is submitted after two tables in separate databases have been **update**d. ORACLE will transparently maintain the integrity between the two databases by ensuring that all of the transactions involved either **commit** or roll back as a group. This is accomplished automatically via ORACLE's Two-Phase Commit (2PC) mechanism.

The first phase of the 2PC is the prepare phase. In this phase, each node involved in a transaction prepares the data that it will need to either **commit** or roll back the data. Once prepared, a node is said to be *in doubt*. The nodes notify the initiating node for the transaction (known as the *global coordinator*) of their status.

Once all nodes are prepared, the transaction enters the commit phase, and all nodes are instructed to **commit** their portion of the logical transaction. The databases all **commit** the data at the same logical time, preserving the integrity of the distributed data.

Resolving In-Doubt Transactions

Transactions against stand-alone databases may fail due to problems with the database server; for example, there may be a media failure. Working with distributed databases increases the number of potential failure causes. For example, a transaction against a remote database requires that the network used to access that database and the remote host be available.

When a distributed transaction is pending, an entry for that transaction will appear in the DBA_2PC_PENDING data dictionary view. When the transaction completes, its DBA_2PC_PENDING record is removed. If the transaction is pending, but is not able to complete, then its record stays in DBA_2PC_PENDING.

The RECO (Recoverer) background process periodically checks the DBA_2PC_PENDING view for distributed transactions that failed to complete. Using the information there, the RECO process on a node will automatically attempt to recover the local portion of an in-doubt transaction. It then attempts to establish connections to any other databases involved in the transaction and resolves the distributed portions of the transaction. The related rows in the DBA_2PC_PENDING views in each database are then removed.

NOTE
The RECO background process will not be started unless the DISTRIBUTED_TRANSACTIONS parameter in your instance's init.ora file is set to a nonzero value prior to startup. This parameter should be set to the anticipated maximum number of concurrent distributed transactions.

The recovery of distributed transactions is performed automatically by the RECO process. You can manually recover the local portions of a distributed transaction, but this will usually result in inconsistent data between the distributed databases. Data inconsistency is counter to the purpose of distributed transactions, since they serve to enforce relationships between local and remote data. If a local recovery is performed, the remote data will be out of sync.

To minimize the number of distributed recoveries necessary, you can influence the way that the distributed transaction is processed. The transaction processing is influenced via the use of *commit point strengths* to tell the database how to structure the transaction.

Commit Point Strength

Each set of distributed transactions, by its nature, references multiple hosts and databases. Of those, one host and database can normally be singled out as being the most reliable, or as owning the most critical data. This database is known as the *commit point site*; if data is committed there, it is committed for all databases. If the transaction against the commit point site fails, the transactions against the other nodes are rolled back. This site also stores information about the status of the distributed transaction.

The commit point site will be selected by ORACLE based on each database's *commit point strength*. This is set via the init.ora file, as shown in the following listing:

```
COMMIT_POINT_STRENGTH=100
```

The values set for the COMMIT_POINT_STRENGTH parameter are set on a relative scale, not on an absolute scale. In the preceding example, it was set to 100. If another database has a commit point strength of 200, then that database would be the commit point site for a distributed transaction involving those two databases. The COMMIT_POINT_STRENGTH value cannot exceed 255.

Since the scale is relative, set up a site-specific scale. Set the commit point on your most reliable database to 200. Then, grade the other servers and databases relative to that one. If, for example, another database is only 80 percent as reliable as the most reliable database, then assign it a commit point strength of 160 (80 percent of 200). Fixing a single database at a definite point (in this case, 200) allows the rest of the databases to be graded on an even scale. This scale should result in the proper commit point site being used for each transaction.

Database Domains and Communities

All of the examples in this chapter have used the standard method for evaluating an object's FQON—using the object name in the query and resolving the rest of the object name via a database link. This method will work across all platforms and networking options. However, networks that use a domain name service (DNS) to name their hosts can take advantage of additional networking features within ORACLE.

A *domain name service* allows hosts within a network to be hierarchically organized. Each node within the organization is called a *domain*, and each domain is labeled by its function. These functions may include COM for companies and EDU for schools. Each domain may have many subdomains. Therefore, each host will be given a unique name within the network; its name contains information about how it fits into the network hierarchy. Host names within a network typically have up to four parts; the leftmost portion of the name is the host's name, and the rest of the name shows the domain to which the host belongs.

For example, a host may be named HQ.MYCORP.COM. In this example, the host is named HQ. It is identified as being part of the MYCORP subdomain of the COM domain.

The domain structure is significant for two reasons. First, the host name is part of the FQON. Second, ORACLE allows you to specify the DNS version of the host name in database link names, thus simplifying the management of distributed database connections.

To use DNS names in database links, you first need to add two parameters to your init.ora file for the database. The first of these, DB_NAME, may already be there; it should be set to the instance name. The second parameter, DB_DOMAIN, is set to the DNS name of the database's host. DB_DOMAIN specifies the network

domain in which the host resides. If a database named LOC is created on the
HQ.MYCORP.COM server, its init.ora entries will be

```
DB_NAME = loc
DB_DOMAIN = hq.mycorp.com
```

To enable the usage of the database domain name, the GLOBAL_NAMES
parameter must be set to TRUE in your init.ora file, as shown in the following listing:

```
GLOBAL_NAMES = true
```

Once these parameters have been set, the database must be shut down and
restarted using this init.ora file for the settings to take effect.

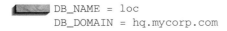

NOTE
*If you set GLOBAL_NAMES to TRUE, then all of
your database link names must follow the rules
described in this section.*

When using this method of creating global database names, the names of the
database links that are created are the same as the databases to which they point.
Thus, a database link that pointed to the LOC database listed earlier would be
named LOC.HQ.MYCORP.COM. This is shown in the following listing:

```
CREATE PUBLIC DATABASE LINK loc.hq.mycorp.com
USING 'service name';
```

In this configuration, it is still possible to create database links that do not
contain the global database name of the database to which they point. In those
cases, ORACLE appends the local database's DB_DOMAIN value to the name of
the database link. For example, if the database was within the HQ.MYCORP.COM
domain and the database link was named LOC, the database link name, when used,
would be automatically expanded to LOC.HQ.MYCORP.COM.
Using global database names thus establishes a link between the database
name, database domain, and database link names. This, in turn, makes it easier to
identify and manage database links. For example, you can create a public database
link (with no connect string, as shown in the preceding example) in each database
that points to every other database. Users within a database no longer need to guess
at the proper database link to use; if they know the global database name, they
know the database link name. If a table is moved from one database to another, or if
a database is moved from one host to another, it is easy to determine which of the
old database links must be dropped and re-created. Using global database names is
part of migrating from stand-alone databases to true networks of databases.

Database domains are often confused with communities. *Communities* are used by SQL*Net V2 to identify a group of servers that communicate via the same communications protocol. For example, a community may be named TCP.HQ.MYCORP.COM. That name would identify the community as being the community of servers using the TCP/IP protocol to communicate within the HQ.MYCORP.COM network domain. Thus, the network domain serves to help enforce the uniqueness of the SQL*Net community's name. The TCP portion of the community's name refers not to a host or database name, but to the communication protocol that the hosts share.

Since it is common for hosts in the same domain to share the same communications protocol, it is useful to make the network domain part of the SQL*Net community name. The .COM portion of the network domain name is usually left off the community name since communities usually do not span that level of the network hierarchy. Thus, the TCP/IP community in this example would be named TCP.HQ.MYCORP. Using a three-part community name also helps to reduce potential confusion between community names and network domain names.

Monitoring Distributed Databases

Most database-level monitoring systems, such as the Command Center database described in Chapter 6, analyze the performance of databases without taking their environments into account. However, there are several other key performance measures that must be taken into account for databases:

- The performance of the host

- The distribution of I/O across disks and controllers

- The usage of available memory

For distributed databases, you must also consider the following:

- The capacity of the network and its hardware

- The load on the network segments

- The usage of different physical access paths between hosts

None of these can be measured from within the database. The focus of monitoring efforts for distributed databases shifts from being database-centric to network-centric. The database becomes one part of the monitored environment, rather than the only part that is checked.

You still need to monitor those aspects of the database that are critical to its success—such as the extensions of its segments and the free space in tablespaces. However, the *performance* of distributed databases cannot be measured except as part of the performance of the network that supports them. Therefore, all performance-related tests, such as stress tests, must be coordinated with the network management staff. That staff may also be able to verify the effectiveness of your attempts to reduce the database load on the network.

The performance of the individual hosts can usually be monitored via a network monitoring package. This monitoring is thus performed in a top-down fashion—network to host to database. Use the monitoring system described in Chapter 6 as an extension to the network and host monitors.

Tuning Distributed Databases

When tuning a stand-alone database, the goal is to reduce the amount of time it takes to find data. As described in Chapter 8, you can use a number of database structures and options to increase the likelihood that the data will be found in memory or in the first place that the database looks.

When working with distributed databases, there is an additional consideration. Since data is now not only being found but also being shipped across the network, the performance of a query is made up of the performance of these two steps. You must therefore consider the ways in which data is being transferred across the network, with a goal of reducing the network traffic.

A simple way to reduce network traffic is to replicate data from one node to another. You can do this manually (via the SQL*Plus **copy** command) or automatically by the database (via snapshots). Replicating data improves the performance of queries against remote databases by bringing the data across the network once—usually during a slow period on the local host. Local queries can use the local copy of the data, eliminating the network traffic that would otherwise be required.

There are two problems with this solution: first, the local data may become out of sync with the remote data. This is an historic problem with derived data; it limits the usefulness of this option to tables whose data is fairly static. Even if a simple snapshot is used with a snapshot log, the data will not be refreshed continuously—only when scheduled.

The second problem with the replicated data solution is that the copy of the table may not be able to pass **update**s back to the master table. That is, if a read-only snapshot is used to make a local copy of a remote table, then the snapshot cannot be **update**d. The same must hold true for tables created with the SQL*Plus **copy** command; they are not the master tables and should be treated as read-only tables.

Thus, any **update**s against those tables must be performed against the master tables. If the table is frequently **update**d, then replicating the data will not improve your performance unless you are using ORACLE's Advanced Replication Option. This option supports multisite ownership of data, and users can make changes in any database designated as an owner of the data. The management of ORACLE's Advanced Replication Option is very involved, and requires creating a database environment (with database links, etc.) specifically geared toward supporting the two-way replication of data. See the ORACLE manuals for the Advanced Replication Option for details.

The type of snapshot to use depends on the nature of the application. Simple snapshots do not involve any data manipulation with the query—they are simply copies of rows from remote tables. Complex snapshots perform operations such as **group by**, **connect by**, or joins on the remote tables. Knowing which to use requires that you know the way in which the data is to be used by the local database.

If you use simple snapshots, you can use snapshot logs. When it is time to refresh that table's snapshots, only the transactions from the snapshot log are sent across the network. Therefore, if the remote table is frequently modified, and you need frequent refreshes of less than 25 percent of the table's rows, then using a simple snapshot will improve the performance of the snapshot refresh process.

When a complex snapshot is refreshed, it has to completely rebuild the snapshot tables. This seems at first like a tremendous burden to put on the system—why not find a way to use simple snapshots instead? However, there are a number of advantages to complex snapshots:

- Tables chosen for replication are typically modified infrequently. Therefore, the refreshes can normally be scheduled for low-usage times in the local database, lessening the impact of full refreshes.

- Complex snapshots may replicate less data than simple snapshots.

The second point seems a little cryptic. After all, a complex snapshot involves more processing than a simple snapshot, so shouldn't it require more work for the network? Actually, it may require *less* work for the network, because more work is being done by the database.

Consider the case of two tables being replicated via snapshots. The users on the local database will always query the two tables together, via a join. As shown in Figure 16-7, there are two options. You can either use two simple snapshots (Figure 16-7a), or you can perform the join via a complex snapshot (Figure 16-7b). What is the difference in performance between the two?

If the tables are joined properly, then the complex snapshot—even if it returns all columns from both tables—should not send any more data across the network than the two simple snapshots will when they are first created. In fact, it will most

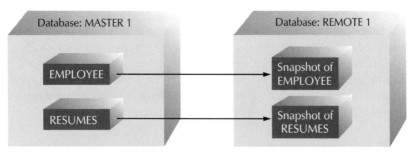

(a) Multiple simple snapshots; snapshot logs and REFRESH FAST can be used.

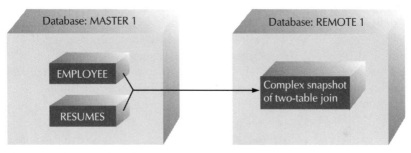

(b) A complex snapshot; the join is already performed.

FIGURE 16-7. *Data replication options for joins*

likely send less data during its creation. When choosing between these two alternatives on the basis of performance, you need to consider two factors:

- The performance of the refreshes
- The performance of queries against the snapshots

The second of these criteria is usually the more important of the two. After all, the data is being replicated to improve query performance. If the users only access the tables via a specific join, then the complex snapshot has already performed the join for them. Performing the join against two simple snapshots will take longer. You cannot determine which of these options is preferable until the access paths that the users will use have been fully defined. If the tables are sometimes queried separately, or via a different join path, then you will need to use simple snapshots or multiple complex snapshots.

The performance of the refreshes won't concern your users. What may concern them is the validity of the data. If the remote tables are frequently modified, and are of considerable size, you are almost forced to use simple snapshots with snapshot logs. Performing complete refreshes in the middle of a workday is generally unacceptable. Thus, it is the *frequency* of the refreshes, rather than the size of them, that determines which type of snapshot will have the better performance for the users. After all, users are most concerned about the performance of the system while they are using it; refreshes performed late at night do not directly affect them. If the tables need to be frequently synchronized, use simple snapshots with snapshot logs. Otherwise, custom complex snapshots should be used.

As was noted previously in this chapter, you may index the underlying SNAP$_*tablename* tables that are created by the snapshot in the local database. Indexing should also help to improve query performance, at the expense of slowing down the refreshes.

Another means of reducing network traffic, via remote procedure calls, is described in Chapter 8. That chapter also includes information on tuning SQL and the application design. If the database was properly structured, tuning the way the application processes data will yield the most significant performance improvements.

Using the Job Queues

In order to support snapshot refreshes and other replication functions, ORACLE manages a set of internal job queues. If you have enabled job queues within your database (via the JOB_QUEUE_PROCESSES and JOB_QUEUE_INTERVAL parameters described previously in this chapter), you can submit jobs of your own to the queues. You can use these queues in place of operating system job queues.

To manage the internal job queue, you can use the SUBMIT, REMOVE, CHANGE, WHAT, NEXT_DATE, INTERVAL, BROKEN, and RUN procedures of the DBMS_JOB package. The most important are the SUBMIT, REMOVE, and RUN procedures.

The SUBMIT procedure has five parameters, as follows:

```
PROCEDURE SUBMIT
   ( job        OUT BINARY_INTEGER,
     what       IN  VARCHAR2,
     next_date  IN  DATE DEFAULT sysdate,
     interval   IN  VARCHAR2 DEFAULT 'null',
     no_parse   IN  BOOLEAN DEFAULT FALSE);
```

The *job* parameter is an output parameter; ORACLE generates a job number for the job via the SYS.JOBSEQ sequence. When you submit a job, you should first define a variable that will accept the job number as the output. For example, the following listing defines a variable and submits a job to execute 'myproc' every day:

```
variable jobno number;
begin
  DBMS_JOB.SUBMIT(:jobno,'myproc',SysDate,SysDate+1);
  commit;
end;
/

print jobno

JOBNO
-----------
      8791
```

The submitter of a job can later alter the job (via the BROKEN, CHANGE, INTERVAL, NEXT_DATE and WHAT procedures), remove it from the queue (the REMOVE procedure), or force it to run (the RUN procedure). For each of these procedures, you will need to know the job number.

If you did not record the job number when you submitted your job, you can query DBMS_JOBS to see the jobs submitted in your database.

Managing Jobs

You can alter a job to "broken" state via the BROKEN procedure. If you mark a job as being broken, it will not be run the next time it is scheduled to run. The structure of the BROKEN procedure is

```
PROCEDURE BROKEN
( job       IN  BINARY_INTEGER,
  broken    IN  BOOLEAN,
  next_date IN  DATE DEFAULT SYSDATE );
```

If you have previously set a job to be broken (by setting the *broken* variable to TRUE), then you can set it to be not broken by setting the *broken* variable to FALSE.

The CHANGE procedure lets you change the code you want to have executed via the *what* parameter, the next date on which the job will be run, and the interval between job runs. Its structure is

```
PROCEDURE CHANGE
( job       IN  BINARY_INTEGER,
  what      IN  VARCHAR2,
  next_date IN  DATE,
  interval  IN  VARCHAR2);
```

If you do not specify a value for the CHANGE variables (or set them to **NULL**), they will be left at their former settings. Thus, you can change part of the job specification via the CHANGE procedure without having to reset all of the job's settings.

If you only want to change the interval between job executions, you can use the INTERVAL procedure, whose two parameters are the job number and the new interval function. You can use the NEXT_DATE procedure to change the next date on which the job is to be run; its two parameters are the job number and the date on which the job should be run.

If you want to change the PL/SQL code that is executed, you can use the WHAT procedure. Its two parameters are the job number and the PL/SQL code to be executed. The INTERVAL, NEXT_DATE, and WHAT procedures do not provide any capabilities that are not already provided via the CHANGE procedure described previously. When using CHANGE, just set to **NULL** the variables you don't want to change.

You can remove a job from the job queue via the REMOVE procedure. This procedure has the job number as its sole parameter. If you have many features of the job to change, you may wish to completely remove the job from the job queue and resubmit it.

To force a job to run at any time, use the RUN procedure. The RUN procedure, which takes the job number as its input variable, is the only way you can run a broken job.

Job queues are typically used to manage internal database functions (such as analyzing database objects). If the jobs are to be part of the regular production maintenance of the database, they should be run via the normal scheduling mechanism for the system on which the database resides. Even though you can run these jobs via the ORACLE job queues, it may be more appropriate to run them via a centrally controlled job management facility that is maintained outside of the database. Use the internal ORACLE job queues for small jobs that are not part of the production control of the database.

For further details on the DBMS_JOB procedures, see the dbmsjob.sql file, which is located in the /rdbms/admin subdirectory under the ORACLE software home directory.

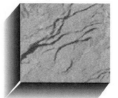

CHAPTER
17

Configuring Client/Server and Web Environments

ince ORACLE supports so many different configurations and platforms, there is no single set of specifications that will be valid for every client/server or thin-client environment. However, there are a number of general procedures that apply to the configuration of networked environments. For details on basic network configuration and UNIX configurations, see Chapters 13 and 14. In this chapter, you will see the network configuration guidelines for client/server and thin-client environments.

Overview of Client/Server Processing

Using a *client/server* configuration allows the CPU and processing load of an application to be distributed between two machines. The first, called the *client,* supports the application that initiates the request from the database. The back-end machine on which the database resides is called the *server.* The client may bear most of the CPU load, while the database server is dedicated to supporting queries, not applications. This distribution of resource requirements is shown in Figure 17-1.

A slight deviation from the architecture shown in Figure 17-1 involves moving the application's logic into PL/SQL packages stored in the database. In that configuration, the database server bears the CPU load for the application processing and the data access while the client is dedicated to the graphical presentation of the data. The network configuration for this type of environment is the same as in Figure 17-1, but the application performs calls to PL/SQL packages instead of executing **insert**, **update**, and **delete** commands.

When the client sends a database request to the server (via SQL*Net or Net8), the server receives and executes the SQL statement that is passed to it. The results of the SQL statement, plus any error conditions that are returned, are then sent back to the client.

To use a client/server architecture, the client and server machines must be capable of communicating with each other. This implies that there is a hardware connection between the two machines. Each machine must support a communications protocol that enables them to interchange data. You can use the SQL*Net V2 MultiProtocol Interchange or the Net8 Connection Manager to resolve compatibility problems between various protocol communities (see Chapter 13).

In this chapter, you will see client/server and Web-based (thin-client) configurations. First, consider a client that is running Microsoft Windows and SQL*Net V2. It is connected via a *network interface card (NIC)* to an Ethernet network. The server with which it hopes to communicate is also located on that network. To make this example generic, assume that the server is running UNIX and both machines are running the TCP/IP protocol. This generic configuration will be used as an illustration throughout the client/server portion of this chapter.

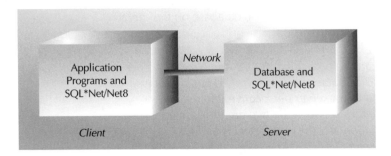

FIGURE 17-1. *Client/server architecture*

This configuration is shown graphically in Figure 17-2.
For the client and server to communicate, you must take several steps:

- The server must be configured to accept communications via the network.

- The server must identify which databases are available for network logins.

- The server must be running SQL*Net/Net8.

- The client must be configured to communicate via the network.

- The client must have adequate memory and disk resources available.

- The client must have SQL*Net/Net8 installed and specify a connect string.

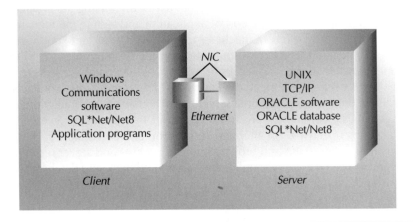

FIGURE 17-2. *Sample client/server configuration*

If any of these requirements is skipped, then the client application will be unable to communicate with the database on the server.

NOTE
You can use both SQL*Net V2 and Net8 to access ORACLE8 databases in networked environments. From a client/server perspective, the major differences between the two are the ease of installation and the parameters used in parameter files.

Overview of Thin-Client Configuration

The thin-client concept is an extension of the client/server architecture. Traditionally, a two-tier, client/server architecture tends to lead to high maintenance costs for the client. For the most part, the high cost of client machine maintenance is based on the complexity of the client's operating system. If you remove the requirement for the client to serve applications and focus on the networking capabilities of the client, then you can create a much "thinner," less expensive, and simpler-to-maintain client. Any machine that can connect to the network can be used as a client. The client no longer needs to be a resource-intensive machine. More recently, because more companies are placing emphasis on the Internet or on intranets, the requirements for a thin client can now include an Internet browser like Microsoft's Internet Explorer or Netscape Communicator.

If the client is much simpler, some of its former tasks must be performed somewhere else. Normally, the tasks are performed by an application server elsewhere on the network. Thus, a thin-client architecture will usually have three machines involved (three tiers) instead of two. Centralizing the application tasks may also help to reduce the cost of application and system maintenance. Figure 17-3 shows a set of client machines using a Web browser to connect to a middle-tier application server. The application server uses communication threads to present queries to and obtain results from the back-end database server.

In a client/server environment, the client, via SQL*Net or Net8, connects directly to the database located on a server and maintains that connection until all transactions are completed. The client maintains the connection even if there is no processing occurring. An alternate, less resource-intensive approach is to use an application server to act as a broker for client requests and server responses. Interaction between the client, application server, and back-end database are written using PL/SQL packages that generate HTML pages. The application server

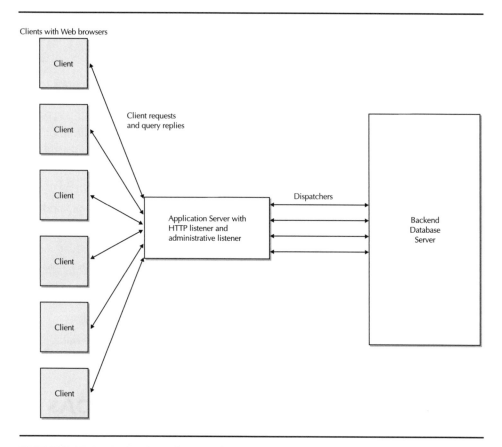

FIGURE 17-3.   *The thin-client architecture*

receives requests for information from the client through a Web browser or other interface software and makes a connection to the server. The request is processed and the information is returned from the server. The application server then disconnects from the server and returns the requested information to the client. Figure 17-3 reflects this activity.

Using this approach, the client does not stay connected to the database and the application server only stays connected for the time it takes to make a request and receive the results from that request. Idle processes do not take up network resources, network traffic is substantially reduced, queries can be processed more quickly, and response time is improved. If many clients are making frequent requests, you can change this configuration to enable the application server to prespawn connections to the database to reduce the amount of overhead time taken to create the connection each time a client query requires processing. Multithreaded servers and connection managers are used to maintain constant prespawned connections to the server; thus, the connections are reused.

Three-tier applications commonly use a transaction processing monitor (TPM) utility. The TPM, running on the Application Server, supports a high volume of transactions against the database. TPM features generally include the following:

- **Atomicity** All transactions are either entirely committed or rolled back.

- **Consistency** Multiple transactions (such as a credit and an associated debit) can be committed or rolled back as a set.

- **Isolation** Multiple related transactions appear to execute serially, even if their end result is a consistent change. Intermediate stages are not visible.

- **Durability** Once a transaction is committed, the change must persist within the database.

In a three-tier environment, your transaction may reference multiple databases. ORACLE supports such distributed transactions; see Chapter 16 for details on the management of distributed transactions.

Using the **ORACLE** Application Server (OAS)

ORACLE supplies an additional-cost application server called the ORACLE Application Server (OAS). The OAS uses a central object request broker (ORB) to handle interaction between the clients and servers. Requests for objects are handled using an industry standard for cross-platform communications between executable programs called the Common Object Request Broker Architecture (CORBA).

Just as in the client/server technology, there are several components that are required to use the OAS. Some of these components are supplied by ORACLE corporation, while others are not [as indicated by an asterisk (*)].

- An Internet browser*.

- An HTTP listener listening for requests (ORACLE provides the Spyglass HTTP listener).

- Cartridges to execute applications and return HTML content. Cartridges are ORACLE-supplied or third-party vendor software that communicate with the database using either ORACLE Call Interface (OCI) calls or PL/SQL.

- A dispatcher for requests that require cartridges

- The Web Request Broker (WRB)

- An ORACLE database (you build the database yourself)

Installing and Configuring the OAS

At the time of this writing, there is no OAS version released for ORACLE8i. The current OAS version must be installed using an ORACLE8.0.5 database. Once the OAS is installed and configured, you can use it to serve ORACLE8i applications.

You can either license the basic ORACLE Application Server version or the OAS Enterprise Edition version (the default); the latter provides more features and functionality. The example in this section is based on the OAS Enterprise Edition version 4.0.7. To install the OAS, you must make several decisions. The decision areas are as follows:

- The version to be installed

- The installation type

- The installation site name and boot port number

- The Node Manager Listener port number

- A username and password for the Node Manager

- The Administration Utility Listener port number

- The ORACLE Web Listener name and port number

After designating the version of the OAS that you are installing, you will be prompted for the type of installation you are going to perform: Typical, Complete, or Custom. The Typical option will install all of the components on a single node with the following cartridges: Jweb, JCORBA, LiveHTML, and PLSQL. The OAS components that will be installed are the Web Request Broker, the Oracle Web Listener, and the OAS Options. You can use the Complete option to install all cartridges and all components on one or more machines. With the Custom option, you can install one or more components on one or more machines to provide load balancing in the following combinations: OAS options, OAS listener, or OAS options and OAS listener. To add components, a previous installation must exist on the machine. For this example, a Typical installation was selected.

The installation process will then request information about the installation site. You will be prompted for a site name and boot port number. The default site name is website40 with the boot port default of 2649. The following screen asks for Node

Manager Listener information and requests a port number (8888 is the default), a username (admin), and a user password with no default given.

The Administration Utility Listener information is the next information requested. There is an informational note on the screen that tells you this is the TCP port number for the Administration Utility Listener and that the username and password which you entered for the Node Manager Listener will also be used for this listener. The default port is 8889.

The final requested information is the Oracle Web Listener name (www) and port number (80). Once all of this information is gathered, the product is installed. You must reboot your machine when the installation is completed and then complete the configuration. Shown next are the services that are created when you install the OAS.

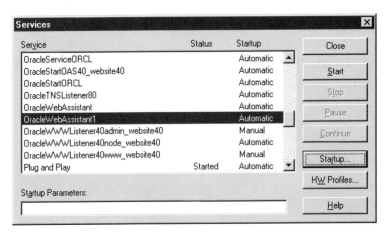

Once the machine has been rebooted, you will use your Web browser to connect to the Welcome page using the following form of Web address:

```
http://<your_machine_name>:8888
```

Once the connection is made, you will be prompted for the username and password for the site. This is the Node Manager username and password that you supplied during the installation. (Admin was the default value.) Figure 17-4 shows the Welcome screen that will be displayed once the correct username and password are entered.

To complete the configuration, bring up the OAS Manager page by clicking on the OAS Manager option on the OAS Welcome screen. The OAS Manager page has

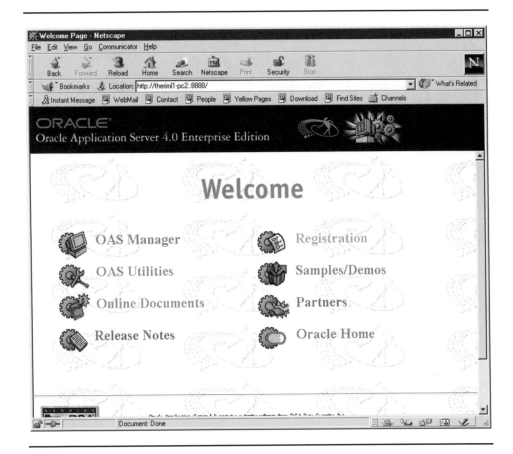

FIGURE 17-4. *The OAS Welcome screen*

two columns. Your Web site name will be on the left and a table showing the Web site status will be displayed on the right. Select All from the right frame and click the green Start button. Figure 17-5 shows the expanded Web site map with the status of the Application Server after the Start option has completed.

In the following sections of this chapter, you will see a description of traditional client/server computing, followed by examples of thin-client extensions to the client/server architecture.

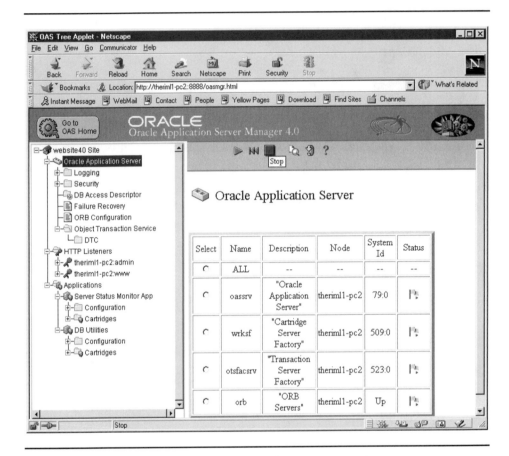

FIGURE 17-5. *The OAS Manager page with options started*

Configuring the Server

Server configurations are described in Chapter 14. The server must identify which hosts it can communicate with, specify which databases are available, and run the SQL*Net/Net8 listener process.

Identifying Available Hosts

A host is a server that is capable of communicating with another server via a network. Each host may maintain a list of the hosts with which it can communicate.

This list is usually maintained in a file called /etc/hosts. The /etc portion of the filename signifies that it is located in the /etc directory. This file contains the Internet address for the hosts, plus the host names. It may optionally include an alias for each host name. A sample portion of an /etc/hosts file is shown in the following listing:

```
130.110.238.109 nmhost
130.110.238.101 txhost
130.110.238.102 azhost   arizona
```

In this example, there are three hosts listed. The first two entries assign host names (nmhost and txhost) to Internet addresses. The last entry assigns both a host name (azhost) and an alias (arizona) to an Internet address.

Your UNIX implementation may use a domain name server (DNS), in which case the host IP addresses may not all be listed in the /etc/hosts file. If DNS is in use, you can use the **nslookup** command to query the IP address of a known host name (or vice versa). The following listing shows a sample lookup of an IP address from DNS:

```
> nslookup txhost
Server:  txhost.company.com
Address: 130.110.238.101
```

Identifying Available Services

A *server process* listens for connection requests from clients. The server process directs those requests to the proper UNIX socket, and the connection can then take place. The services for both SQL*Net V2 and Net8 are described in Chapters 13 and 14. The examples in this chapter will focus on the Net8 installation.

Services on a UNIX server are usually listed in a file called /etc/services. The /etc portion of the filename signifies that it is located in the /etc directory. Like the /etc/hosts file, this file is typically maintained by a UNIX systems administrator. You do not have to list all services in the /etc/services file, but doing so helps prevent conflicts for communications ports.

The Net8 service is called the listener for Net8, although you can use any name you want. If you are configuring more than one listener on a server, you will have to use different service names and different port numbers for each listener. In Net8, the standard port number assigned is port 1521. However, port 1526 is also commonly used. If you need to define more than two services, you can choose port numbers, but be sure to check the services file on your host to make sure that you do not choose port numbers that have been assigned to other processes or programs.

You can use more than one listener to load-balance the incoming requests. A Net8 entry in the /etc/services file is shown in the following listing. As shown, there are two parts to the entry: the service name and the port number. Once a connection is made via the listener's port, the operating system will move the communications for that session to a different port, removing a potential cause of resource contention.

```
listener  1521
```

Identifying Available Databases

All databases that are run on a UNIX host and are accessible to the network must be listed in a file named /etc/oratab. The /etc portion of the filename signifies that it is located in the /etc directory. This file is maintained by the DBA. Each database used in a client/server application must be listed in the /etc/oratab file.

A sample /etc/oratab file is shown in the following listing:

```
loc:/orasw/app/oracle/product/8.1.5.1:Y
cc1:/orasw/app/oracle/product/8.1.5.1:N
old:/orasw/app/oracle/product/8.1.5.0:Y
```

NOTE
The location of the oratab file is platform-dependent. For example, on some UNIX platforms the oratab file is located in /var/opt/oracle.

There are three components to each entry in the /etc/oratab file, separated only by colons (:). The entries' components, which are fully described in Chapter 14, are the instance name (ORACLE_SID), ORACLE software root directory (ORACLE_HOME), and a flag to indicate if the instance should be started on host startup (which is a necessary flag, but irrelevant to SQL*Net communications).

This example shows entries for three instances: LOC, CC1, and OLD (the first components in each entry). The first two instances have the same ORACLE_HOME; the third uses an older version of the ORACLE kernel (as shown in the second component of the entries). Both LOC and OLD will be automatically started when the server starts; CC1 will have to be manually started (by virtue of the Y and N flags in the third component of each entry).

On Windows NT Server, the databases will be listed in the registry under HKEY_LOCAL_MACHINE\SOFTWARE\ORACLE\ALL_HOMES\IDx. The illustration below shows the registry with the ALL_HOMES entry highlighted. The ALL_HOMES values will include the number of ORACLE homes using the parameter HOME_COUNTER and the last ORACLE_HOME will be identified by the parameter LAST_HOME with a number. In the following illustration, the value for ALL_HOMES is 3 while the LAST_HOME value is 2.

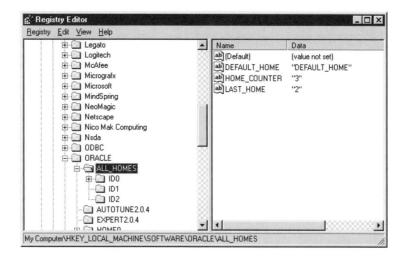

Each separate ORACLE_HOME will have an ID with a different number such as ID0 and ID1. In the illustration, the entries are ID0, ID1, and ID2. In each ID*x* listing, there will be a PATH parameter with a directory location. For example, Figure 17-6 shows ID1 selected with the PATH value of D:\ora8i. The NAME for this entry is ora8i.

Starting Net8

In the Windows-to-UNIX example, if the database application will be using Net8, the listener process must be started on the server. All of the available parameters for this process are listed in Chapter 14.

The following command starts the listener process for a listener called list1:

```
> lsnrctl start list1
```

To verify the status of the listener, execute the **lsnrctl status *service_name***
command, as shown in the following listing for the list1 service:

```
> lsnrctl status list1
```

For a full description of the options for the **lsnrctl** command, see Chapter 14. For Windows NT, you can start and stop the listener one of three ways:

1. Start or stop the listener from the Services screen.

2. Use an MS DOS window and issue the commands just as you would for UNIX.

3. Issue the appropriate command either interactively from the MS DOS prompt or from a batch file.

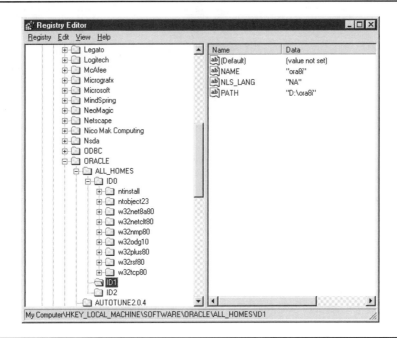

FIGURE 17-6. *A Windows NT Registry with ID1 selected*

The following listing shows an example of the third option, executing the **net start** command interactively:

```
net start Oracle<version_name>TNSListener
net stop Oracle<version_name>TNSListener
```

The *version_name* variable is the value stored in the NAME parameter of the ID section in the Registry (see Figure 17-6).

Configuring the Client

Before any communications can begin, the client machine must be physically connected to a network, and must have network communications software installed on it. The NIC in your client machine must be supported by the communications software. See the Net8 Administrator's Guide for your client operating system for a list of the supported communications packages. Be sure to check this listing every time you upgrade either the communications package or the client's Net8 version.

Identifying Available Hosts

Just as the server machine must identify its available hosts, the client machine must also specify the hosts to which it can connect. This is typically done via a domain name server (DNS) through the use of a file identical in structure to the server's /etc/hosts file.

The hosts file contains the Internet address for the hosts, plus the host names. It may optionally include an alias for each host name. A sample portion of a hosts file is shown in the following listing:

```
130.110.238.109 nmhost
130.110.238.101 txhost
130.110.238.102 azhost   arizona
```

In this example, there are three hosts listed. The first two entries assign host names (nmhost and txhost) to Internet addresses. The last entry assigns both a host name (azhost) and an alias (arizona) to an Internet address. If your network implementation uses DNS, you may not have a local hosts file listing the host IP addresses. If you are using a thin-client architecture and not using DNS, the name of the application server and its IP address will be in this file. In reality, any one of the servers defined in this sample could be an application server. Therefore, to make identification easier, you can add a comment to the end of the entry if you precede the comment with a pound sign (#) as follows:

```
130.110.238.101 txhost     # HR Application Server
```

Client Machine Specifications

Can your Windows client support these requirements? To do so, it will have to meet the following minimum specifications.

Hardware

- IBM, Compaq, or 100-percent compatible PC with an 80286 processor (or higher)

- Enough hard-disk space to store the files for your operating system, Net8, your communications software, and your applications software

- A disk drive to use during installations

- A NIC for network communications

Memory

- Enough memory to run your network software, Net8, and your application software; a minimum of 16MB is recommended

Software

- Microsoft Windows
- Net8 for Windows, with the TCP/IP protocol adapter
- Network communications software

The Net8 TCP/IP for Windows software takes 100KB of disk space, and approximately 120KB of memory. When sizing your client machine, keep in mind that the application front-end programs, operating system, and communications software will require far greater resources than Net8 will.

If your processor is slow, programs will usually run (just more slowly than you'd like). If not enough memory is available, applications may not run at all. For that reason, be sure that you have at least 16MB of memory on the PC—the more, the better.

The Middle-Tier Application Server

The Application Server houses the executable code for one or more applications. If you are not using the ORACLE Application Server extra-cost option described earlier in this chapter, you need a program that runs when a client makes a connection request to connect that client to the application and a second program within the application that connects the application to the database. Some third-party vendors supply software to perform these tasks. The vendor-supplied software may provide individual usernames and passwords for each client connecting to the application and only one single username and password to perform the connection to the database.

As the client, you would authenticate yourself to the application using the individual username and password that have been supplied to you, and the application would, in turn, connect to the database using a completely different username and password and a separate Net8 connection to perform your requested work.

Running Net8

Now that the machines are set up and ready to communicate, all you have to do is make sure that the tool you will be using to communicate with the remote database is properly configured. As noted in Chapter 11, there are often changes required to tools when you migrate from one version of ORACLE to another. There may also be differences between tools in the syntax of the database service name. For example, some tools require that the entire service name be entered in lowercase and enclosed in double quotes (though this is an isolated case). Be sure to test the connections thoroughly each time the network hardware, communications software, operating system, or Net8 version is changed.

ORACLE and Firewalls

Many organizations are implementing firewalls to protect their sites from both intentional and unintentional compromise of their business information. A firewall is a software program that runs on a server and accepts or refuses connections based on some form of preestablished security criteria. A correct username and password might be enough to successfully access a database through a firewall; in other configurations, a safeword card or other synchronized pass key challenge and response may be required. Once you have successfully responded to a firewall challenge, you are permitted access to either information on the firewall machine or, in most cases, a second machine that resides behind the firewall.

To access an ORACLE database behind a firewall, you will need to fulfill the following criteria:

- The tnsnames.ora file has to fully specify the remote host unless an alias has been set up for that host by your network administrator.

- The underlying network configuration must be in place. The servers have to be able to ping each other, the firewall has to allow that form of traffic, and the remote listener must be running and available.

- You must know the listener port number for the remote site. You'll put this port number in your tnsnames.ora file.

If you worked at the company headquarters and had to access the database behind a firewall at the field office designated as the machine name server1 at the location fld.com, the entry in the HOST file might look like:

```
server1.fld.com
```

In your tnsnames.ora file for the instance called FLD1, you would have an entry like the following:

```
fld1 =
  (DESCRIPTION =
    (ADDRESS_LIST =
      (ADDRESS = (PROTOCOL = TCP)
      (HOST = server1.fld.com)(PORT = 1521))
    )
    (CONNECT_DATA =
      (SID = fld1)
    )
  )
```

If the server name or port number or instance name changes, you will need to ensure that coordination between your site and the remote site is maintained.

PART
IV

Appendices

APPENDIX A

SQL Reference for DBA Commands

ALTER DATABASE

Syntax

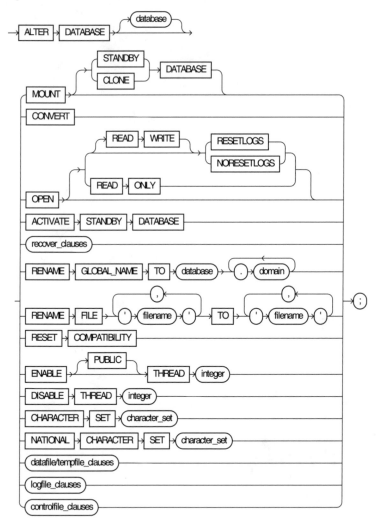

recover_clauses::=

general_recovery_clause::=

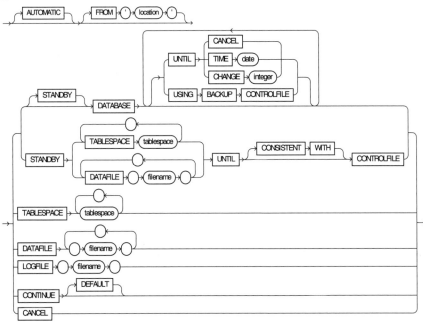

managed_recovery_clause::=

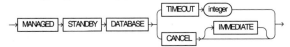

datafile/tempfile_clauses::=

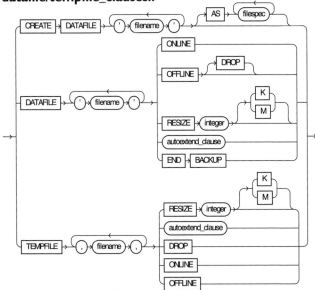

controlfile_clauses::=

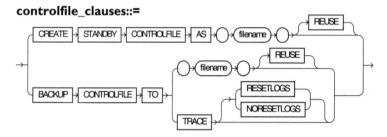

logfile_clauses::=

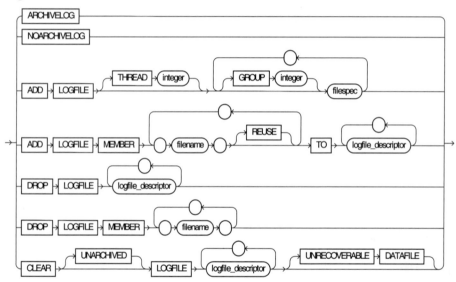

logfile_descriptor::=

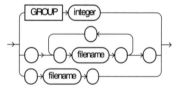

autoextend_clauses::=

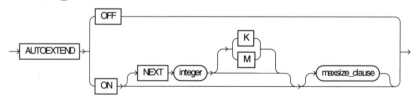

maxsize_clause::=

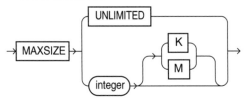

parallel_clause::=

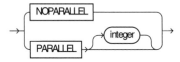

Purpose

To modify, maintain, or recover an existing database. For more information on using the ALTER DATABASE statement for database maintenance, see the *Oracle8i Administrator's Guide*. For examples of performing media recovery, see *Oracle8i Administrator's Guide* and *Oracle8i Backup and Recovery Guide*.

Prerequisites

You must have ALTER DATABASE system privilege. To specify the RECOVER clause, you must also have the OSDBA role enabled.

Keywords and Parameters

database identifies the database to be altered. The database name can contain only ASCII characters. If you omit database, Oracle alters the database identified by the value of the initialization parameter DB_NAME. You can alter only the database whose control files are specified by the initialization parameter CONTROL_FILES. The database identifier is not related to the Net8 database specification.

You can use the following clauses only when the database is not mounted by your instance:

- MOUNT mounts the database.

- STANDBY DATABASE mounts the standby database. For more information, see the *Oracle8i Backup and Recovery Guide*.

- CLONE DATABASE mounts the clone database. For more information, see the *Oracle8i Backup and Recovery Guide*.

- CONVERT completes the conversion of the Oracle7 data dictionary. After you use this clause, the Oracle7 data dictionary no longer exists in the Oracle database. Use this clause only when you are migrating to Oracle8i. For more information, see *Oracle8i Migration*.

- ACTIVATE STANDBY DATABASE changes the state of a standby database to an active database. For more information, see *Oracle8i Backup and Recovery Guide*.

- OPEN opens the database, making it available for normal use. You must mount the database before you can open it. You must activate a standby database before you can open it.

■ READ ONLY restricts users to read-only transactions, preventing them from generating redo logs. You can use this clause to make a standby database available for queries even while archive logs are being copied from the primary database site.
Restrictions:
You cannot open a database READ ONLY if it is currently opened READ WRITE by an other instance.
You cannot open a database READ ONLY if it requires recovery.
You cannot take tablespaces offline while the database is open READ ONLY. However, you can take datafiles offline and online, and you can recover offline datafiles and tablespaces while the database is open READ ONLY.

■ READ WRITE opens the database in read-write mode, allowing users to generate redo logs. This is the default.

■ RESETLOGS resets the current log sequence number to 1 and discards any redo information that was not applied during recovery, ensuring that it will never be applied. This effectively discards all changes that are in the redo log, but not in the database. You must use this clause to open the database after performing media recovery with an incomplete recovery using the RECOVER clause or with a backup control file. After opening the database with this clause, you should perform a complete database backup.

■ NORESETLOGS leaves the log sequence number and redo log files in their current state.
Restriction: You can specify RESETLOGS and NORESETLOGS only after performing incomplete media recovery or complete media recovery with a backup control file. In any other case, Oracle uses the NORESETLOGS automatically.

You can use any of the following clauses when your instance has the database mounted, open or closed, and the files involved are not in use:

■ *general_recovery_clause* lets you design media recovery for the database or standby database, or for specified tablespaces or files. For more information on media recovery, see *Oracle8i Backup and Recovery Guide*.

NOTE
If you do not have special media requirements, Oracle Corporation recommends that you use the SQL*Plus RECOVER statement. For more information, see SQL*Plus User's Guide and Reference.

Restrictions:
You can recover the entire database only when the database is closed.
Your instance must have the database mounted in exclusive mode.
You can recover tablespaces or datafiles when the database is open or closed, provided that the tablespaces or datafiles to be recovered are offline.
You cannot perform media recovery if you are connected to Oracle through the multi-threaded server architecture.

■ AUTOMATIC automatically generates the name of the next archived redo log file needed to continue the recovery operation. Oracle uses the LOG_ARCHIVE_DEST (or LOG_ARCHIVE_DEST_1) and LOG_ARCHIVE_FORMAT parameters (or their defaults) to generate the target redo log filename. If the file is found, the redo contained in that file is applied. If the file is not found, Oracle prompts you for a filename, displaying the generated filename as a suggestion. If you specify neither AUTOMATIC nor LOGFILE, Oracle prompts you for a filename, displaying the generated filename as a suggestion. You can then accept the generated filename or replace it with a fully qualified filename. If you know the archived filename differs from what Oracle would generate, you can save time by using the LOGFILE clause.

- ■ FROM *'location'* specifies the location from which the archived redo log file group is read. The value of *location* must be a fully specified file location following the conventions of your operating system. If you omit this parameter, Oracle assumes the archived redo log file group is in the location specified by the initialization parameter LOG_ARCHIVE_DEST or LOG_ ARCHIVE_DEST_1.

- ■ STANDBY DATABASE recovers the standby database using the control file and archived redo log files copied from the primary database. The standby database must be mounted but not open.

- ■ DATABASE recovers the entire database. This is the default. You can use this clause only when the database is closed.

NOTE

This clause recovers only online datafiles.

- ■ UNTIL specifies the duration of the recovery operation.

  - ■ CANCEL performs cancel-based recovery. This clause recovers the database until you issue the ALTER DATABASE RECOVER statement with the RECOVER CANCEL clause.

  - ■ TIME performs time-based recovery. This parameter recovers the database to the time specified by the date. The date must be a character literal in the format 'YYYY-MM-DD:HH24:MI:SS'.

  - ■ CHANGE performs change-based recovery. This parameter recovers the database to a transaction-consistent state immediately before the system change number (SCN) specified by *integer*.

- ■ USING BACKUP CONTROLFILE specifies that a backup control file is being used instead of the current control file.

- ■ TABLESPACE recovers only the specified tablespaces. You can use this clause if the database is open or closed, provided the tablespaces to be recovered are offline.

- ■ DATAFILE recovers the specified datafiles. You can use this clause when the database is open or closed, provided the datafiles to be recovered are offline.

- ■ STANDBY TABLESPACE | DATAFILE reconstructs a lost or damaged datafile or tablespace in the standby database using archived redo log files copied from the primary database and a control file.

  - ■ UNTIL [CONSISTENT WITH] CONTROLFILE specifies that the recovery of an old standby datafile or tablespace uses the current standby database control file. However, any redo in advance of the standby controlfile will not be applied. The keywords CONSISTENT WITH are optional and are provided for semantic clarity.

- ■ LOGFILE continues media recovery by applying the specified redo log file.

- ■ CONTINUE continues multi-instance recovery after it has been interrupted to disable a thread.

- ■ CONTINUE DEFAULT continues recovery using the redo log file that Oracle would automatically generate if no other logfile were specified. This clause is equivalent to specifying AUTOMATIC, except that Oracle does not prompt for a filename.

- CANCEL terminates cancel-based recovery.

- ***managed_recovery_clause*** specifies sustained standby recovery mode. This mode assumes that the standby database is an active component of an overall standby database architecture. A primary database actively archives its redo log files to the standby site. As these archived redo logs arrive at the standby site, they become available for use by a managed standby recovery operation. Sustained standby recovery is restricted to media recovery. For more information on the parameters of this clause, see *Oracle8i Backup and Recovery Guide*.
  Restrictions: The same restrictions apply as are listed under *general_recovery_clause*.

- TIMEOUT *integer* specifies in minutes the wait period of the sustained recovery operation. The recovery process waits for *integer* minutes for a requested archived log redo to be available for writing to the standby database. If the redo log file does not become available within that time, the recovery process terminates with an error message. You can then issue the statement again to return to sustained standby recovery mode. If you do not specify this clause, the database remains in sustained standby recovery mode until you reissue the statement with the RECOVER CANCEL clause or until instance shutdown or failure.

- CANCEL terminates the sustained recovery operation after applying all the redo in the current archived redo file.

- CANCEL IMMEDIATE terminates the sustained recovery operation after applying all the redo in the current archived redo file or after the next redo log file read, whichever comes first.
  Restriction: This clause cannot be issued from the same session that issued the RECOVER MANAGED STANDBY DATABASE statement.

- ***parallel_clause*** specifies whether the recovery of media will be parallelized.

  - NOPARALLEL specifies serial execution. This is the default.

  - PARALLEL causes Oracle to select a degree of parallelism equal to the number of CPUs available on all participating instances times the value of the PARALLEL_THREADS_PER_CPU initialization parameter.

  - PARALLEL *integer* specifies the *degree of parallelism*, which is the number of parallel threads used in the parallel operation. Each parallel thread may use one or two parallel execution processes. Normally Oracle calculates the optimum degree of parallelism, so it is not necessary for you to specify *integer*.

- RENAME GLOBAL_NAME changes the global name of the database. The *database* is the new database name and can be as long as eight bytes. The optional *domain* specifies where the database is effectively located in the network hierarchy. For more information on global names, see *Oracle8i Distributed Database System*s.

NOTE
Renaming your database does not change global references to your database from existing database links, synonyms, and stored procedures and functions on remote databases. Changing such references is the responsibility of the administrator of the remote databases.

- RENAME FILE renames datafiles, tempfiles, or redo log file members. This clause renames only files in the control file. It does not actually rename them on your operating system. You must specify each filename using the conventions for filenames on your operating system before specifying this clause.

- RESET COMPATIBILITY marks the database to be reset to an earlier version of Oracle when the database is next restarted.

NOTE
RESET COMPATIBILITY works only if you have successfully disabled Oracle features that affect backward compatibility. For more information on downgrading to an earlier version of Oracle, see Oracle8i Migration.

You can use the following clauses only when your instance has the database open:

- ENABLE THREAD in a parallel server, enables the specified thread of redo log file groups. The thread must have at least two redo log file groups before you can enable it.

  - PUBLIC makes the enabled thread available to any instance that does not explicitly request a specific thread with the initialization parameter THREAD. If you omit PUBLIC, the thread is available only to the instance that explicitly requests it with the initialization parameter THREAD.

- DISABLE THREAD disables the specified thread, making it unavailable to all instances. You cannot disable a thread if an instance using it has the database mounted.

- CHARACTER SET/NATIONAL CHARACTER SET   CHARACTER SET changes the character set the database uses to store data. NATIONAL CHARACTER SET changes the national character set used to store data in columns specifically defined as NCHAR, NCLOB, or NVARCHAR2. Specify *character_set* without quotation marks.

CAUTION
You cannot roll back an ALTER DATABASE CHARACTER SET or ALTER DATABASE NATIONAL CHARACTER SET statement. Therefore, you should perform a full backup before issuing either of these statements.

Restrictions:
You must have SYSDBA system privilege, and you must start up the database in restricted mode (for example, with the SQL*Plus STARTUP RESTRICT command).
The current character set must be a strict subset of the character set to which you change. That is, each character represented by a codepoint value in the source character set must be represented by the same codepoint value in the target character set. For a list of valid character sets, see *Oracle8i National Language Support Guide.*

- ***datafile/tempfile_clauses*** let you modify datafiles and tempfiles.

You can use any of the following clauses when your instance has the database mounted, open or closed, and the files involved are not in use:

- CREATE DATAFILE creates a new empty datafile in place of an old one. You can use this clause to re-create a datafile that was lost with no backup. The '*filename*' must identify a file that is or was once part of the database. The *filespec* specifies the name and size of the new datafile. If you omit the AS clause, Oracle creates the new file with the name and size as the file specified by '*filename*'. During recovery, all archived redo logs written to since the original datafile was created must be applied to the new, empty version of the lost datafile. Oracle creates the new file in the same state as the old file when it was created. You must perform media recovery on the new file to return it to the state of the old file at the time it was lost.

Restriction: You cannot create a new file based on the first datafile of the SYSTEM tablespace.

- DATAFILE affects your database files as follows:

  - ONLINE brings the datafile online.

  - OFFLINE takes the datafile offline. If the database is open, you must perform media recovery on the datafile before bringing it back online, because a checkpoint is not performed on the datafile before it is taken offline.

  - DROP takes a datafile offline when the database is in NOARCHIVELOG mode.

  - RESIZE attempts to increase or decrease the size of the datafile to the specified absolute size in bytes. Use K or M to specify this size in kilobytes or megabytes. There is no default, so you must specify a size. If sufficient disk space is not available for the increased size, or if the file contains data beyond the specified decreased size, Oracle returns an error.

  - *autoextend_clause* enables or disables the automatic extension of a datafile. If you do not specify this clause, datafiles are not automatically extended.

    - OFF disables autoextend if it is turned on. NEXT and MAXSIZE are set to zero. Values for NEXT and MAXSIZE must be respecified in further ALTER DATABASE AUTOEXTEND statements.

    - ON enables autoextend.

    - NEXT specifies in bytes the size of the next increment of disk space to be automatically allocated to the datafile when more extents are required. Use K or M to specify this size in kilobytes or megabytes. The default is one data block.

    - MAXSIZE specifies the maximum disk space allowed for automatic extension of the datafile.

    - UNLIMITED sets no limit on allocating disk space to the datafile.

  - END BACKUP avoids media recovery on database startup after an online tablespace backup was interrupted by a system failure or instance failure or SHUTDOWN ABORT.

CAUTION
Do not use ALTER TABLESPACE ... END BACKUP if you have restored any of the files affected from a backup. Media recovery is fully described in Oracle8i Backup and Recovery Guide.

- TEMPFILE lets you resize your temporary datafile or specify the *autoextend_clause*, with the same effect as with a permanent datafile.

  Restriction: You cannot specify TEMPFILE unless the database is open.

  - DROP drops *tempfile* from the database. The tablespace remains.

- *logfile_clauses* lets you add, drop, or modify log files.

- ARCHIVELOG specifies that the contents of a redo log file group must be archived before the group can be reused. This mode prepares for the possibility of media recovery. Use this clause only after shutting down your instance normally or immediately with no errors and then restarting it, mounting the database in parallel server disabled mode.

■ NOARCHIVELOG specifies that the contents of a redo log file group need not be archived so that the group can be reused. This mode does not prepare for recovery after media failure.

Use the ARCHIVELOG clause and NOARCHIVELOG clause only if your instance has the database mounted in parallel server disabled mode, but not open.

■ ADD LOGFILE adds one or more redo log file groups to the specified thread, making them available to the instance assigned the thread.

  ■ THREAD *integer* is applicable only if you are using Oracle with the Parallel Server option in parallel mode. If you omit THREAD, the redo log file group is added to the thread assigned to your instance.

  ■ GROUP *integer* uniquely identifies the redo log file group among all groups in all threads and can range from 1 to the MAXLOGFILES value. You cannot add multiple redo log file groups having the same GROUP value. If you omit this parameter, Oracle generates its value automatically. You can examine the GROUP value for a redo log file group through the dynamic performance view V$LOG.

  ■ *filespec* Each *filespec* specifies a redo log file group containing one or more members, or copies.

■ ADD LOGFILE MEMBER adds new members to existing redo log file groups. Each new member is specified by *'filename'*. If the file already exists, it must be the same size as the other group members, and you must specify REUSE. If the file does not exist, Oracle creates a file of the correct size. You cannot add a member to a group if all of the group's members have been lost through media failure.

You can specify an existing redo log file group in one of these ways:

■ GROUP *integer* Specify the value of the GROUP parameter that identifies the redo log file group.

■ *list of filenames* List all members of the redo log file group. You must fully specify each filename according to the conventions of your operating system.

■ DROP LOGFILE drops all members of a redo log file group. Specify a redo log file group as indicated for the ADD LOGFILE MEMBER clause.

  ■ To drop the current log file group, you must first issue an ALTER SYSTEM SWITCH LOGFILE statement.

  ■ You cannot drop a redo log file group if it needs archiving.

  ■ You cannot drop a redo log file group if doing so would cause the redo thread to contain less than two redo log file groups.

■ DROP LOGFILE MEMBER drops one or more redo log file members. Each 'filename' must fully specify a member using the conventions for filenames on your operating system.

  ■ To drop a log file in the current log, you must first issue an ALTER SYSTEM SWITCH LOGFILE statement.

  ■ You cannot use this clause to drop all members of a redo log file group that contains valid data. To perform this operation, use the DROP LOGFILE clause.

■ CLEAR LOGFILE reinitializes an online redo log, optionally without archiving the redo log. CLEAR LOGFILE is similar to adding and dropping a redo log, except that the statement may be issued even if there are only two logs for the thread and also may be issued for the current redo log of a closed thread.

- UNARCHIVED You must specify UNARCHIVED if you want to reuse a redo log that was not archived.

CAUTION
Specifying UNARCHIVED makes backups unusable if the redo log is needed for recovery.

Do not use CLEAR LOGFILE to clear a log needed for media recovery. If it is necessary to clear a log containing redo after the database checkpoint, you must first perform incomplete media recovery. The current redo log of an open thread can be cleared. The current log of a closed thread can be cleared by switching logs in the closed thread.

If the CLEAR LOGFILE statement is interrupted by a system or instance failure, then the database may hang. If this occurs, reissue the statement after the database is restarted. If the failure occurred because of I/O errors accessing one member of a log group, then that member can be dropped and other members added.

- UNRECOVERABLE DATAFILE   You must specify UNRECOVERABLE DATAFILE if you have taken the datafile offline with the database in ARCHIVELOG mode (that is, you specified ALTER DATABSE ... DATAFILE OFFLINE without the DROP keyword), and if the unarchived log to be cleared is needed to recover the datafile before bringing it back online. In this case, you must drop the datafile and the entire tablespace once the CLEAR LOGFILE statement completes.

controlfile_clauses

- CREATE STANDBY CONTROLFILE creates a control file to be used to maintain a standby database. For more information, see *Oracle8i Backup and Recovery Guide*. If the file already exists, you must specify REUSE.

- BACKUP CONTROLFILE backs up the current control file.

  - TO '*filename*' specifies the file to which the control file is backed up. You must fully specify the *filename* using the conventions for your operating system. If the specified file already exists, you must specify REUSE.

  - TO TRACE writes SQL statements to the database's trace file rather than making a physical backup of the control file. The SQL statements can start up the database, re-create the control file, and recover and open the database appropriately, based on the created control file.

    You can copy the statements from the trace file into a script file, edit the statements as necessary, and use the database if all copies of the control file are lost (or to change the size of the control file).

  - RESETLOGS specifies that the SQL statement written to the trace file for starting the database is ALTER DATABASE OPEN RESETLOGS.

  - NORESETLOGS specifies that the SQL statement written to the trace file for starting the database is ALTER DATABASE OPEN NORESETLOGS.

ALTER INDEX

Syntax

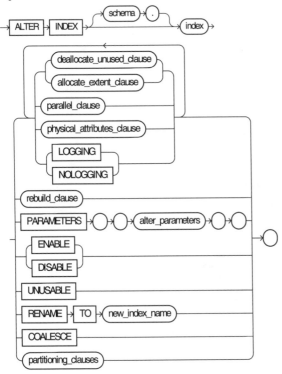

deallocate_unused_clause::=

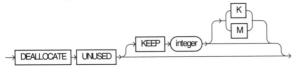

allocate_extent_clause::=

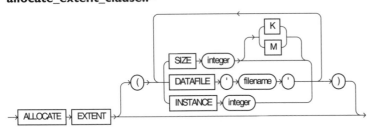

parallel_clause::=

physical_attributes_clause::=

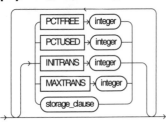

rebuild_clause::=

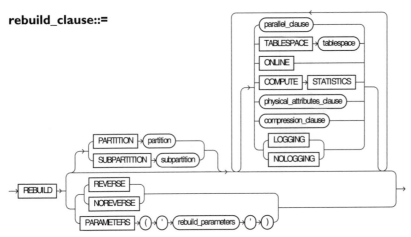

compression_clause::=

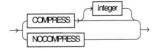

partitioning_clauses::=

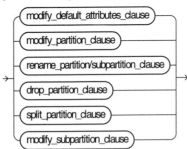

modify_default_attributes_clause::=

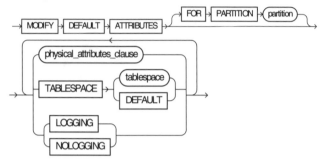

modify_partition_clause::=

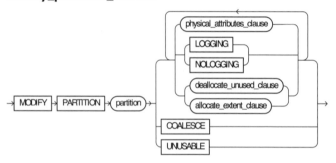

rename_partition/subpartition_clause::=

drop_partition_clause::=

split_partition_clause::=

partition_description::=

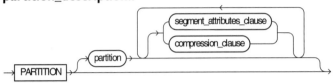

modify_subpartition_clause::=

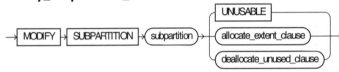

Purpose

To change or rebuild an existing index.

Prerequisites

The index must be in your own schema or you must have ALTER ANY INDEX system privilege. Schema object privileges are granted on the parent index, not on individual index partitions or subpartitions. You must have tablespace quota to modify, rebuild, or split an index partition or to modify or rebuild an index subpartition.

Keywords and Parameters

- *schema* is the schema containing the index. If you omit *schema*, Oracle assumes the index is in your own schema.

- *index* is the name of the index to be altered.
  Restrictions:
  If *index* is a domain index, you can specify only the PARAMETERS clause, the RENAME clause, or the *rebuild_clause* (with or without the PARAMETERS clause). No other clauses are valid. You cannot alter or rename a domain index that is marked LOADING or FAILED. If an index is marked FAILED, the only clause you can specify is REBUILD. For information on the LOADING and FAILED states of domain indexes, see *Oracle8i Data Cartridge Developer's Guide.*

- *deallocate_unused_clause* explicitly deallocates unused space at the end of the index and makes the freed space available for other segments in the tablespace. Only unused space above the high water mark can be freed.

  If *index* is range-partitioned or hash-partitioned, Oracle deallocates unused space from each index partition. If *index* is a local index on a composite-partitioned table, Oracle deallocates unused space from each index subpartition.
  Restrictions:
  You cannot specify this clause for an index on a temporary table.
  You cannot specify this clause and also specify the *rebuild_clause.*

- KEEP specifies the number of bytes above the high water mark that the index will have after deallocation. If the number of remaining extents are less than MINEXTENTS, then MINEXTENTS is set to the current number of extents. If the initial extent becomes smaller than INITIAL, then INITIAL is set to the value of the current initial extent. If you omit KEEP, all unused space is freed.

- *allocate_extent_clause* explicitly allocates a new extent for the index. For a local index on a hash-partitioned table, Oracle allocates a new extent for each partition of the index. **Restriction:** You cannot specify this clause for an index on a temporary table or for a range-partitioned or composite-partitioned index.

  - SIZE specifies the size of the extent in bytes. Use K or M to specify the extent size in kilobytes or megabytes. If you omit SIZE, Oracle determines the size based on the values of the index's storage parameters.

  - DATAFILE specifies one of the datafiles in the index's tablespace to contain the new extent. If you omit DATAFILE, Oracle chooses the datafile.

  - INSTANCE makes the new extent available to the specified instance. An instance is identified by the value of its initialization parameter INSTANCE_NUMBER. If you omit this parameter, the extent is available to all instances. Use this parameter only if you are using Oracle with the Parallel Server option in parallel mode.

    Explicitly allocating an extent with this clause does not change the values of the NEXT and PCTINCREASE storage parameters, so does not affect the size of the next extent to be allocated.

- *parallel_clause* changes the default degree of parallelism for queries and DML on the index.

  - NOPARALLEL specifies serial execution. This is the default.

  - PARALLEL causes Oracle to select a degree of parallelism equal to the number of CPUs available on all participating instances multiplied by the value of the PARALLEL_THREADS_PER_CPU initialization parameter.

  - PARALLEL *integer* specifies the *degree of parallelism*, which is the number of parallel threads used in the parallel operation. Each parallel thread may use one or two parallel execution processes. Normally Oracle calculates the optimum degree of parallelism, so it is not necessary for you to specify *integer*. **Restriction:** You cannot specify this clause for an index on a temporary table.

- *physical_attributes_clause* lets you change the values of parameters for a nonpartitioned index, all partitions and subpartitions of a partitioned index, a specified partition, or all subpartitions of a specified partition. **Restrictions:** You cannot specify this clause for an index on a temporary table. You cannot specify the PCTUSED parameter when altering an index. You cannot change the value of the PCTFREE parameter for the index as a whole (ALTER INDEX) or for a partition (ALTER INDEX ... MODIFY PARTITION). You can specify PCTFREE in all other forms of the ALTER INDEX statement.

  - *storage_clause* changes the storage parameters for a nonpartitioned index, index partition, or all partitions of a partitioned index, or default values of these parameters for a partitioned index.

- LOGGING | NOLOGGING specifies that subsequent Direct Loader (SQL*Loader) and direct-load INSERT operations against a nonpartitioned index, a range or hash index partition, or all partitions or subpartitions of a composite-partitioned index will be logged (LOGGING) or not logged (NOLOGGING) in the redo log file.

  In NOLOGGING mode, data is modified with minimal logging (to mark new extents invalid and to record dictionary changes). When applied during media recovery, the extent invalidation records mark a range of blocks as logically corrupt, because the redo data is not logged. Therefore, if you cannot afford to lose this index, you must take a backup after the operation in NOLOGGING mode.

  If the database is run in ARCHIVELOG mode, media recovery from a backup taken before an operation in LOGGING mode will re-create the index. However, media recovery from a backup taken before an operation in NOLOGGING mode will not re-create the index.

  An index segment can have logging attributes different from those of the base table and different from those of other index segments for the same base table.

  For more information about LOGGING and parallel DML, see *Oracle8i Concepts* and the *Oracle8i Parallel Server Concepts and Administration*.

  Restriction: You cannot specify this clause for an index on a temporary table.

- RECOVERABLE | UNRECOVERABLE   These keywords are deprecated and have been replaced with LOGGING and NOLOGGING, respectively. Although RECOVERABLE and UNRECOVERABLE are supported for backward compatibility, Oracle Corporation strongly recommends that you use the LOGGING and NOLOGGING keywords.

  RECOVERBLE is not a valid keyword for creating partitioned tables or LOB storage characteristics. UNRECOVERABLE is not a valid keyword for creating partitioned or index-organized tables. Also, it can be specified only with the AS subquery clause of CREATE INDEX.

- *rebuild_clause* re-creates an existing index or one of its partitions or subpartitions. For a function-based index, this clause also enables the index. If the function on which the index is based does not exist, the rebuild statement will fail.

  Restrictions:

  You cannot rebuild an index on a temporary table.

  You cannot rebuild an entire partitioned index. You must rebuild each partition or subpartition, as described below.

  You cannot also specify the *deallocate_unused_clause* in this statement.

  You cannot change the value of the PCTFREE parameter for the index as a whole (ALTER INDEX) or for a partition (ALTER INDEX ... MODIFY PARTITION). You can specify PCTFREE in all other forms of the ALTER INDEX statement.

  - PARTITION *partition* rebuilds one partition of an index. You can also use this clause to move an index partition to another tablespace or to change a create-time physical attribute. For more information about partition maintenance operations, see the *Oracle8i Administrator's Guide*.

    Restriction: You cannot specify this clause for a local index on a composite-partitioned table. Instead, use the REBUILD SUBPARTITION clause.

  - SUBPARTITION *subpartition* rebuilds one subpartition of an index. You can also use this clause to move an index subpartition to another tablespace. If you do not specify TABLESPACE, the subpartition is rebuilt in the same tablespace.

Restrictions: The only parameters you can specify for a subpartition are TABLESPACE and the *parallel_clause*.

■ REVERSE | NOREVERSE specifies whether the bytes of the index block are stored in reverse order.

■ REVERSE stores the bytes of the index block in reverse order and excludes the rowid when the index is rebuilt.

■ NOREVERSE stores the bytes of the index block without reversing the order when the index is rebuilt. Rebuilding a REVERSE index without the NOREVERSE keyword produces a rebuilt, reverse-keyed index.
Restrictions:
You cannot reverse a bitmap index or an index-organized table.
You cannot specify REVERSE or NOREVERSE for a partition or subpartition.

■ TABLESPACE specifies the tablespace where the rebuilt index, index partition, or index subpartition will be stored. The default is the default tablespace where the index or partition resided before you rebuilt it.

■ COMPRESS enables key compression, which eliminates repeated occurrence of key column values. Use *integer* to specify the prefix length (number of prefix columns to compress).

■ For unique indexes, the range of valid prefix length values is from 1 to the number of key columns minus 1. The default prefix length is the number of key columns minus 1.

■ For nonunique indexes, the range of valid prefix length values is from 1 to the number of key columns. The default prefix length is number of key columns.

Oracle compresses only nonpartitioned indexes that are nonunique or unique indexes of at least two columns.
Restriction: You cannot specify COMPRESS for a bitmapped index.

■ NOCOMPRESS disables key compression. This is the default.

■ ONLINE specifies that DML operations on the table or partition are allowed during rebuilding of the index.
Restriction: Parallel DML is not supported during online index building. If you specify ONLINE and then issue parallel DML statements, Oracle returns an error.

■ COMPUTE STATISTICS enables you to collect statistics at relatively little cost during the rebuilding of an index. These statistics are stored in the data dictionary for ongoing use by the optimizer in choosing a plan of execution for SQL statements. The types of statistics collected depend on the type of index you are rebuilding.

NOTE

If you create an index using another index (instead of a table), the original index might not provide adequate statistical information. Therefore, Oracle generally uses the base table to compute the statistics, which will improve the statistics but may negatively affect performance. Additional methods of collecting statistics are available in PL/SQL packages and procedures. See Oracle8i Supplied Packages Reference.

■ LOGGING | NOLOGGING specifies whether the ALTER INDEX...REBUILD operation will be logged.

■ PARAMETERS applies only to domain indexes. This clause specifies the parameter string for altering the index (or, in the *rebuild_clause*, rebuilding the index). The maximum length of the parameter string is 1000 characters. This string is passed uninterpreted to the appropriate indextype routine. For more information on these routines, see *Oracle8i Data Cartridge Developer's Guide*.
Restrictions:
You cannot specify this clause for any indexes other than domain indexes.
The parameter string is passed to the appropriate routine only if *index* is not marked UNUSABLE.

■ ENABLE applies only to a **function-based index** that has been disabled because a user-defined function used by the index was dropped or replaced. This clause enables such an index if

   ■ the function is currently valid

   ■ the signature of the current function matches the signature of the function when the index was created, and

   ■ the function is currently marked as DETERMINISTIC.
   Restriction: You cannot specify any other clauses of ALTER INDEX in the same statement with ENABLE.

■ DISABLE applies only to a **function-based index**. This clause enables you to disable the use of a function-based index. You might want to do so, for example, while working on the body of the function. Afterward you can either rebuild the index or specify another ALTER INDEX statement with the ENABLE keyword.

■ UNUSABLE marks the index or index partition(s) or index subpartition(s) UNUSABLE. An unusable index must be rebuilt, or dropped and re-created, before it can be used. While one partition is marked UNUSABLE, the other partitions of the index are still valid. You can execute statements that require the index if the statements do not access the unusable partition. You can also split or rename the unusable partition before rebuilding it.
Restriction: You cannot specify this clause for an index on a temporary table.

■ RENAME TO renames *index* to *new_index_name*. The *new_index_name* is a single identifier and does not include the schema name.

■ COALESCE instructs Oracle to merge the contents of index blocks where possible to free blocks for reuse. For more information on space management and coalescing indexes, see *Oracle8i Administrator's Guide*.
Restriction: You cannot specify this clause for an index on a temporary table.

■ *partitioning_clauses*: The remainder of the clauses of the ALTER INDEX statement are valid only for partitioned indexes.
Restrictions:
You cannot specify any of these clauses for an index on a temporary table.
You can combine several operations on the base index into one ALTER INDEX statement (except RENAME and REBUILD), but you cannot combine partition operations with other partition operations or with operations on the base index.

- *modify_default_attributes_clause* specifies new values for the default attributes of a partitioned index.
  Restriction: The only attribute you can specify for an index on a hash-partitioned or composite-partitioned table is TABLESPACE.

  - TABLESPACE specifies the default tablespace for new partitions of an index or subpartitions of an index partition.

  - LOGGING | NOLOGGING specifies the default logging attribute of a partitioned index or an index partition.

  - FOR PARTITION *partition* specifies the default attributes for the subpartitions of a partition of a local index on a composite-partitioned table.

- *modify_partition_clause* modifies the real physical attributes, logging attribute, or storage characteristics of index partition *partition* or its subpartitions.
  Restriction: You cannot specify the *physical_attributes_clause* for an index on a hash-partitioned table.

NOTE
If the index is a local index on a composite-partitioned table, the changes you specify here will override any attributes specified earlier for the subpartitions of index, as well as establish default values of attributes for future subpartitions of that partition. To change the default attributes of the partition without overriding the attributes of subpartitions, use ALTER TABLE ... MODIFY DEFAULT ATTRIBUTES OF PARTITION.

- *rename_partition/subpartition_clause* renames index partition or subpartition to *new_name*.

- *drop_partition_clause* removes a partition and the data in it from a partitioned global index. When you drop a partition of a global index, Oracle marks the index's next partition UNUSABLE. You cannot drop the highest partition of a global index.

- *split_partition_clause* splits a partition of a global partitioned index into two partitions, adding a new partition to the index.
  Splitting a partition marked UNUSABLE results in two partitions, both marked UNUSABLE. You must rebuild the partitions before you can use them. Splitting a usable partition results in two partitions populated with index data. Both new partitions are usable.

  - AT (*value_list*) specifies the new noninclusive upper bound for *split_partition_1*. The *value_list* must evaluate to less than the presplit partition bound for *partition_name_old* and greater than the partition bound for the next lowest partition (if there is one).

  - INTO describes the two partitions resulting from the split.

- *partition_description* specifies (optionally) the name and physical attributes of each of two partitions resulting from a split.

- *modify_subpartition_clause* lets you mark UNUSABLE or allocate or deallocate storage for a subpartition of a local index on a composite-partitioned table. All other attributes of such a subpartition are inherited from partition-level default attributes.

ALTER MATERIALIZED VIEW / SNAPSHOT

Syntax

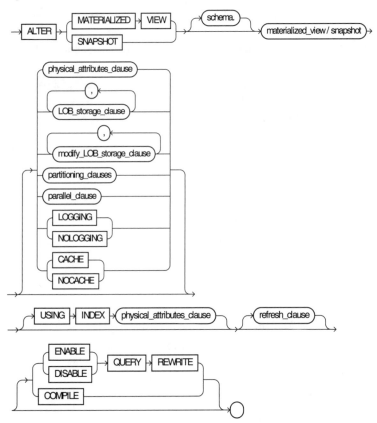

parallel_clause::=

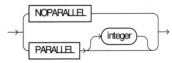

refresh_clause::=

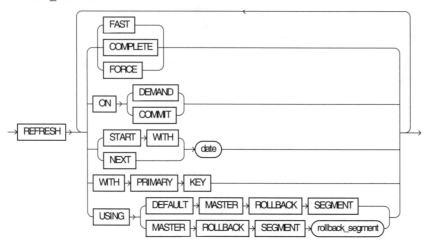

physical_attributes_clause::=

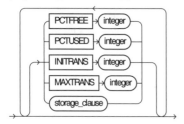

Purpose

To change the storage characteristics, refresh mode or time, or type of an existing materialized view. To enable or disable query rewrite. The terms "snapshot" and "materialized view" are synonymous. Both refer to a table that contains the results of a query of one or more tables, each of which may be located on the same or on a remote database. Replication and warehouse environments sometimes use different terms to describe the same thing. In this reference, **master tables** (a replication term) and **detail tables** (a warehouse term) both refer to the tables referenced by a materialized view.

For information on materialized views in a replication environment, see *Oracle8i Replication*. For information on materialized views in a data warehousing environment, see *Oracle8i Tuning*.

Prerequisites

To alter a materialized view's storage parameters, the materialized view must be contained in your own schema, or you must have the ALTER ANY SNAPSHOT or ALTER ANY MATERIALIZED VIEW system privilege. To enable a materialized view for query rewrite:

- If all the master tables in the materialized view are in your schema, you must have the QUERY REWRITE privilege.

- If any of the master tables are in another schema, you must have the GLOBAL QUERY REWRITE privilege.

- If the materialized view is in another user's schema, *both you and the owner of that schema* must have the appropriate QUERY REWRITE privilege described in the preceding two items.

For detailed information about the prerequisites for ALTER MATERIALIZED VIEW, see *Oracle8i Replication*.

Keywords and Parameters

- *schema* is the schema containing the materialized view. If you omit *schema*, Oracle assumes the materialized view is in your own schema.

- *materialized view / snapshot* is the name of the materialized view to be altered.

- *physical_attributes_clause* change the values of the PCTFREE, PCTUSED, INITRANS, and MAXTRANS parameters and the storage characteristics for the internal table that Oracle uses to maintain the materialized view's data.

- LOGGING | NOLOGGING specifies the logging attribute.

- CACHE | NOCACHE   For data that will be accessed frequently, specifies whether the blocks retrieved for this table are placed at the most recently used end of the LRU list in the buffer cache when a full table scan is performed. This attribute is useful for small lookup tables.

- *LOB_storage_clause* specifies the LOB storage characteristics.

- *modify_LOB_storage_clause* modifies the physical attributes of the LOB attribute *lob_item* or LOB object attribute.

- *partitioning_clauses*   The syntax and general functioning of the following partitioning clauses is the same as for the ALTER TABLE statement.
  Restrictions: You cannot use the *LOB_storage_clause* or *modify_LOB_storage_clause* when modifying a materialized view.
  If you attempt to drop, truncate, or exchange a materialized view partition, Oracle raises an error.

NOTE
After dropping or truncating a table partition, all materialized views on the table must be refreshed manually. A fast refresh will probably produce incorrect results, but Oracle will not raise an error.

- *parallel_clause* specifies the degree of parallelism for the materialized view. When this clause is set for master tables, performance for materialized view creation and refresh may improve (depending on the materialized view definition query).

  - NOPARALLEL specifies serial execution. This is the default.

  - PARALLEL causes Oracle to select a degree of parallelism equal to the number of CPUs available on all participating instances times the value of the PARALLEL_THREADS_PER_CPU initialization parameter.

  - PARALLEL *integer* specifies the *degree of parallelism*, which is number of parallel threads used in the parallel operation. Each parallel thread may use one or two parallel execution processes. Normally Oracle calculates the optimum degree of parallelism, so it is not necessary for you to specify *integer*.

- MODIFY PARTITION UNUSABLE LOCAL INDEXES marks UNUSABLE all the local index partitions associated with *partition*.

- MODIFY PARTITION REBUILD UNUSABLE LOCAL INDEXES rebuilds the unusable local index partitions associated with *partition*.

- USING INDEX changes the value of INITRANS, MAXTRANS, and STORAGE parameters for the index Oracle uses to maintain the materialized view's data. If USING INDEX is not specified, then default values are used for the index.
  Restriction: You cannot specify the PCTUSED or PCTFREE parameters in this clause.

- *refresh_clause* changes the mode and times for automatic refreshes.

  - FAST specifies a fast refresh. A fast refresh uses the materialized view log associated with the detail table or, if you also specify ON DEMAND, with the direct loader log. Oracle creates the direct loader log automatically. No user intervention is needed.
    Several restrictions exist on the types of materialized views that you can fast refresh. For a complete explanation of when you can fast refresh a materialized view used for replication, see *Oracle8i Replication*. For a complete explanation of when you can fast refresh a materialized view used for data warehousing, see *Oracle8i Tuning*.

  - COMPLETE specifies a complete refresh, or a refresh that re-creates the materialized view during each refresh.

  - FORCE specifies a fast refresh if one is possible or a complete refresh if a fast refresh is not possible. Oracle decides whether a fast refresh is possible at refresh time.

  - ON COMMIT specifies that the refresh is to occur automatically at the next COMMIT operation.
    Restriction: This clause is supported only for materialized views that either include no aggregations or that include no joins. For more information, see *Oracle8i Tuning*.

  - ON DEMAND specifies that a refresh will occur when you explicitly invoke a refresh procedure. This method is also called "warehouse refresh", and you can also specify it by calling the DBMS_MVIEW.REFRESH procedure.
    The types of materialized views you can create by specifying refresh on demand are described in *Oracle8i Tuning*. Alternatively, this clause specifies that a fast refresh will

occur only if you add data using a direct-path method. If you specify ON COMMIT or ON DEMAND, you cannot also specify START WITH or NEXT.

- START WITH specifies a date expression for the next automatic refresh time.

- NEXT specifies a new date expression for calculating the interval between automatic refreshes.

- START WITH and NEXT values must evaluate to times in the future.

- WITH PRIMARY KEY changes a rowid materialized view to a primary key materialized view. Primary key materialized views allow materialized view master tables to be reorganized without affecting the materialized view's ability to continue to fast refresh. The master table must contain an enabled primary key constraint. For detailed information about primary key materialized views, see *Oracle8i Replication*.

- USING ROLLBACK SEGMENT changes the remote rollback segment to be used during materialized view refresh; *rollback_segment* is the name of the rollback segment to be used.

  - DEFAULT specifies that Oracle will choose automatically which rollback segment to use. If you specify DEFAULT, you cannot specify rollback_segment.

  - MASTER specifies the remote rollback segment to be used at the remote master for the individual materialized view. (To change the local materialized view rollback segment, use the DBMS_REFRESH package, described in Oracle8i Replication.) The master rollback segment is stored on a per-materialized-view basis and is validated during materialized view creation and refresh. If the materialized view is complex, the master rollback segment, if specified, is ignored.

- QUERY REWRITE specifies whether the materialized view is eligible to be used for query rewrite.

  - ENABLE enables the materialized view for query rewrite. For more information on query rewrite, see *Oracle8i Concepts*.
    Restrictions: If the materialized view is in an invalid or unusable state, the ENABLE mode will not take effect until the materialized view is valid and usable.
    You can enable query rewrite only if all user-defined functions in the materialized view are DETERMINISTIC.
    If you use bind variables in a query, the query will not be rewritten to use materialized views even if you enable query rewrite.
    You can enable query rewrite only if the statement contains only repeatable expressions. For example, you cannot include CURRENT_TIME or USER. For more information, see *Oracle8i Tuning*.

  - DISABLE specifies that the materialized view is not eligible for use by query rewrite. (If a materialized view is in invalid state, it is not eligible for use by query rewrite, whether or not it is disabled.) However, a disabled materialized view can be refreshed.

- COMPILE explicitly revalidates a materialized view. If an object upon which the materialized view depends is dropped or altered, the materialized view remains accessible, but it is invalidated for purposes of query rewrite. You can use this clause to explicitly revalidate the materialized view to make it eligible for query rewrite.
  If the materialized view fails to revalidate, it cannot be either fast refreshed ON DEMAND or used for query rewrite.

ALTER MATERIALIZED VIEW LOG / SNAPSHOT LOG

Syntax

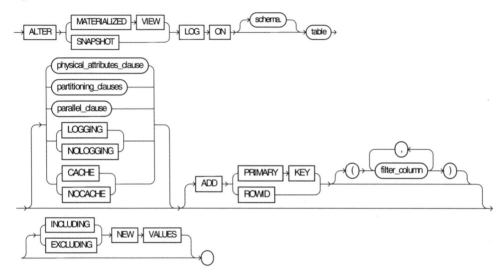

physical_attributes_clause::=

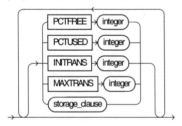

parallel_clause::=

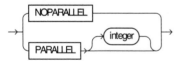

Purpose

To alter the storage characteristics, refresh mode or time, or type of an existing materialized view log. The terms "snapshot" and "materialized view" are synonymous. Both refer to a table that contains the results of a query of one or more tables, each of which may be located on the same or on a remote database.

Prerequisites

Only the owner of the master table or a user with the SELECT privilege for the master table can alter a materialized view log. For detailed information about the Prerequisites for ALTER SNAPSHOT LOG, see *Oracle8i Replication*.

Keywords and Parameters

- *schema* is the schema containing the master table. If you omit *schema*, Oracle assumes the materialized view log is in your own schema.

- *table* is the name of the master table associated with the materialized view log to be altered.

- *physical_attributes_clause* changes the value of PCTFREE, PCTUSED, INITRANS, and MAXTRANS parameters for the table, partition, the overflow data segment, or the default characteristics of a partitioned table.

- *partitioning_clauses*　The syntax and general functioning of the partitioning clauses is the same as for the ALTER TABLE statement.
  Restrictions: You cannot use the *LOB_storage_clause* or *modify_LOB_storage_clause* when modifying a materialized view log.
  If you attempt to drop, truncate, or exchange a materialized view log partition, Oracle raises an error.

- *parallel_clause* specifies the degree of parallelism for the materialized view. When this clause is set for master tables, performance for materialized view creation and refresh may improve (depending on the materialized view definition query).

  - NOPARALLEL specifies serial execution. This is the default.

  - PARALLEL causes Oracle to select a degree of parallelism equal to the number of CPUs available on all participating instances times the value of the PARALLEL_THREADS_PER_CPU initialization parameter.

  - PARALLEL *integer* specifies the *degree of parallelism*, which is number of parallel threads used in the parallel operation. Each parallel thread may use one or two parallel execution processes. Normally Oracle calculates the optimum degree of parallelism, so it is not necessary for you to specify *integer*.

- LOGGING | NOLOGGING specifies the logging attribute.

- CACHE | NOCACHE　For data that will be accessed frequently, specifies whether the blocks retrieved for this table are placed at the most recently used end of the LRU list in the buffer cache when a full table scan is performed. This attribute is useful for small lookup tables.

- ADD changes the materialized view log so that it records the primary key values or rowid values when rows in the materialized view master table are updated. This clause can also be used to record additional filter columns. To stop recording any of this information, you must first drop the materialized view log and then re-create it. Dropping the materialized view log and then re-creating it forces all existing materialized views on the master table to complete refresh.

  - PRIMARY KEY specifies that the primary-key values of all rows updated should be recorded in the materialized view log.

  - ROWID specifies that the rowid values of all rows updated should be recorded in the materialized view log.

- *filter_column(s)* are non-primary-key columns referenced by materialized views. For information about filter columns, see *Oracle8i Replication*.

- NEW VALUES specifies whether Oracle saves both old and new values in the materialized view log.

  - INCLUDING saves old as well as new values in the log. If you are creating a log for a materialized aggregate view with only one master table, and if you want the materialized view to be eligible for fast refresh, you must specify INCLUDING.

  - EXCLUDING saves only new values in the log. This is the default. To save overhead, use this clause for materialized join views and for materialized aggregate views with more than one master table. Such views do not require the old values.

ALTER OUTLINE

Syntax

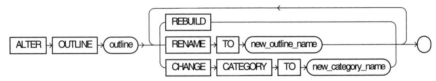

Purpose

To rename a stored outline, reassign it to a different category, or regenerate it by compiling the outline's SQL statement and replacing the old outline data with the outline created under current conditions. For more information on outlines, see *Oracle8i Tuning*.

Prerequisites

To modify an outline, you must have the ALTER ANY OUTLINE system privilege.

Keywords and Parameters

- REBUILD regenerates the execution plan for *outline* using current conditions.

- RENAME TO *new_outline_name* specifies an outline name to replace *outline*.

- CHANGE CATEGORY TO *new_category_name* specifies the name of the category into which the *outline* will be moved.

ALTER PROFILE

Syntax

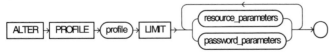

resource_parameters::=

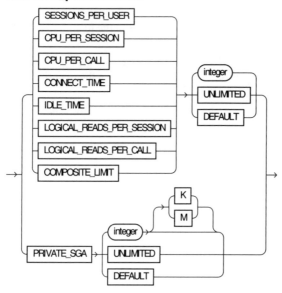

password_parameters::=

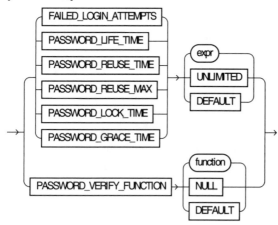

Purpose

To add, modify, or remove a resource limit or password management parameter in a profile. Changes made to a profile with an ALTER PROFILE statement affect users only in their subsequent sessions, not in their current sessions.

Prerequisites

You must have ALTER PROFILE system privilege to change profile resource limits. To modify password limits and protection, you must have ALTER PROFILE and ALTER USER system privileges.

Keywords and Parameters

The Keywords and Parameters in the ALTER PROFILE statement all have the same meaning as in the CREATE PROFILE statement.

> **NOTE**
> *You cannot remove a limit from the DEFAULT profile.*

ALTER ROLE

Syntax

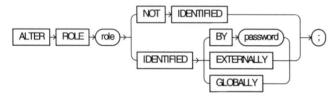

Purpose

To change the authorization needed to enable a role.

Prerequisites

You must either have been granted the role with the ADMIN OPTION or have ALTER ANY ROLE system privilege. Before you alter a role to IDENTIFIED GLOBALLY, you must

- Revoke all grants of roles identified externally to the role and
- Revoke the grant of the role from all users, roles, and PUBLIC.

The one exception to this rule is that you should not revoke the role from the user who is currently altering the role.

Keywords and Parameters

The Keywords and Parameters in the ALTER ROLE statement all have the same meaning as in the CREATE ROLE statement.

> **NOTE**
> *If you have the ALTER ANY ROLE system privilege and you change a role that is IDENTIFIED GLOBALLY to IDENTIFIED BY password, IDENTIFIED EXTERNALLY, or NOT IDENTIFIED, then Oracle grants you the altered role with the ADMIN OPTION, as it would have if you had created the role identified nonglobally.*

ALTER ROLLBACK SEGMENT

Syntax

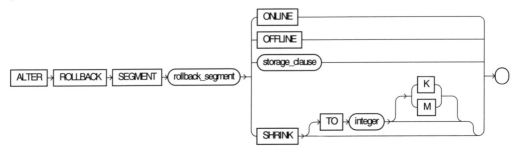

Purpose

To bring a rollback segment online or offline, to change its storage characteristics, or to shrink it to an optimal or specified size.

Prerequisites

You must have ALTER ROLLBACK SEGMENT system privilege.

Keywords and Parameters

- *rollback_segment* specifies the name of an existing rollback segment.

- ONLINE brings the rollback segment online. When you create a rollback segment, it is initially offline and not available for transactions. This clause brings the rollback segment online, making it available for transactions by your instance. You can also bring a rollback segment online when you start your instance with the initialization parameter ROLLBACK_SEGMENTS.

- OFFLINE takes the rollback segment offline.

  - If the rollback segment does not contain any information needed to roll back an active transactions, Oracle takes it offline immediately.

  - If the rollback segment does contain information for active transactions, Oracle makes the rollback segment unavailable for future transactions and takes it offline after all the active transactions are committed or rolled back.

  Once the rollback segment is offline, it can be brought online by any instance. To see whether a rollback segment is online or offline, query the data dictionary view DBA_ROLLBACK_SEGS. Online rollback segments have a STATUS value of IN_USE.
  Offline rollback segments have a STATUS value of AVAILABLE. For more information on making rollback segments available and unavailable, see *Oracle8i Administrator's Guide.*
  Restriction: You cannot take the SYSTEM rollback segment offline.

- *storage_clause* changes the rollback segment's storage characteristics.
  Restriction: You cannot change the values of the INITIAL and MINEXTENTS for an existing rollback segment.

- SHRINK attempts to shrink the rollback segment to an optimal or specified size. The success and amount of shrinkage depend on the available free space in the rollback segment and how active transactions are holding space in the rollback segment.

The value of *integer* is in bytes, unless you specify K or M for kilobytes or megabytes.

If you do not specify TO *integer*, then the size defaults to the OPTIMAL value of the *storage_clause* of the CREATE ROLLBACK SEGMENT statement that created the rollback segment. If OPTIMAL was not specified, then the size defaults to the MINEXTENTS value of the *storage_clause* of the CREATE ROLLBACK SEGMENT statement.

Regardless of whether you specify TO *integer*:

- The value to which Oracle shrinks the rollback segment is valid for the execution of the statement. Thereafter, the size reverts to the OPTIMAL value of the CREATE ROLLBACK SEGMENT statement.

- The rollback segment cannot shrink to less than two extents.

To determine the actual size of a rollback segment after attempting to shrink it, query the BYTES, BLOCKS, and EXTENTS columns of the DBA_SEGMENTS view.

Restriction: For a parallel server, you can shrink only rollback segments that are online to your instance.

ALTER SYSTEM

Syntax

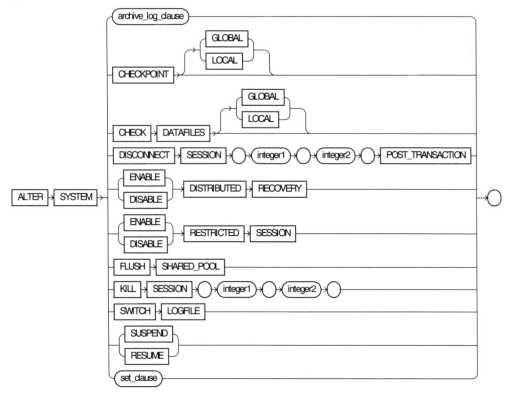

archive_log_clause::=

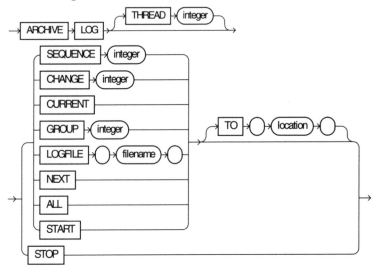

set_clause::=

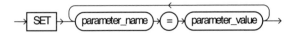

Purpose

To dynamically alter your Oracle instance. The settings stay in effect as long as the database is mounted.

Prerequisites

You must have ALTER SYSTEM system privilege. To specify the *archive_log_clause*, you must have the OSDBA or OSOPER role enabled.

Keywords and Parameters

- *archive_log_clause* manually archives redo log files or enables or disables automatic archiving. To use this clause, your instance must have the database mounted. The database can be either open or closed unless otherwise noted.

NOTE
You can also manually archive redo log file groups with the ARCHIVE LOG SQL*Plus statement. For information on this statement, see the SQL*Plus User's Guide and Reference.
You can also have Oracle archive redo log files groups automatically. For information on automatic archiving, see Oracle8i Administrator's Guide. *You can always manually archive redo log file groups regardless of whether automatic archiving is enabled.*

- THREAD specifies the thread containing the redo log file group to be archived. Set this parameter only if you are using Oracle with the Parallel Server option in parallel mode.

- SEQUENCE manually archives the online redo log file group identified by the log sequence number *integer* in the specified thread. If you omit the THREAD parameter, Oracle archives the specified group from the thread assigned to your instance.

- CHANGE manually archives the online redo log file group containing the redo log entry with the system change number (SCN) specified by *integer* in the specified thread. If the SCN is in the current redo log file group, Oracle performs a log switch. If you omit the THREAD parameter, Oracle archives the groups containing this SCN from all enabled threads. You can use this clause only when your instance has the database open.

- CURRENT manually archives the current redo log file group of the specified thread, forcing a log switch. If you omit the THREAD parameter, Oracle archives all redo log file groups from all enabled threads, including logs previous to current logs. You can use this clause only when your instance has the database open.

NOTE
If you specify a redo log file group for archiving with the CHANGE or CURRENT clause, and earlier redo log file groups are not yet archived, Oracle archives all unarchived groups up to and including the specified group.

- GROUP manually archives the online redo log file group with the GROUP value specified by *integer*. You can determine the GROUP value for a redo log file group by examining the data dictionary view DBA_LOG_FILES. If you specify both the THREAD and GROUP parameters, the specified redo log file group must be in the specified thread.

- LOGFILE manually archives the online redo log file group containing the redo log file member identified by *'filename'*. If you specify both the THREAD and LOGFILE parameters, the specified redo log file group must be in the specified thread.

- **Restriction:** You must archive redo log file groups in the order in which they are filled. If you specify a redo log file group for archiving with the LOGFILE parameter, and earlier redo log file groups are not yet archived, Oracle returns an error.

- NEXT manually archives the next online redo log file group from the specified thread that is full but has not yet been archived. If you omit the THREAD parameter, Oracle archives the earliest unarchived redo log file group from any enabled thread.

- ALL manually archives all online redo log file groups from the specified thread that are full but have not been archived. If you omit the THREAD parameter, Oracle archives all full unarchived redo log file groups from all enabled threads.

- START enables automatic archiving of redo log file groups.

- **Restriction:** You can enable automatic archiving only for the thread assigned to your instance.

- TO *'location'* specifies the primary location to which the redo log file groups are archived. The value of this parameter must be a fully specified file location following the conventions of your operating system. If you omit this parameter, Oracle archives the redo log file group to the location specified by the initialization parameters LOG_ARCHIVE_DEST or LOG_ARCHIVE_DEST_ n.

NOTE
You can enhance recovery reliability by setting the related archive parameters LOG_ARCHIVE_DEST_DUPLEX and LOG_ARCHIVE_MIN_SUCCEED_DEST.

- STOP disables automatic archiving of redo log file groups. You can disable automatic archiving only for the thread assigned to your instance.

- CHECKPOINT explicitly forces Oracle to perform a checkpoint, ensuring that all changes made by committed transactions are written to datafiles on disk. You can specify this clause only when your instance has the database open. Oracle does not return control to you until the checkpoint is complete.

  - GLOBAL in an Oracle Parallel Server environment, performs a checkpoint for all instances that have opened the database. This is the default.

  - LOCAL in an Oracle Parallel Server environment, performs a checkpoint only for the thread of redo log file groups for your instance. For more information on checkpoints, see *Oracle8i Concepts*.

- CHECK DATAFILES in a distributed database system, such as an Oracle Parallel Server environment, updates an instance's SGA from the database control file to reflect information on all online datafiles.

  - GLOBAL performs this synchronization for all instances that have opened the database. This is the default.

  - LOCAL performs this synchronization only for the local instance.

  Your instance should have the database open. For more information, see *Oracle8i Parallel Server Concepts and Administration*.

- DISCONNECT SESSION ... POST_TRANSACTION disconnects the current session by destroying the dedicated server process (or virtual circuit if the connection was made by way of a multi-threaded server). This clause allows ongoing transactions to complete before the session is disconnected, in contrast to the KILL SESSION clause.To use this clause, your instance must have the database open.
  If system parameters are appropriately configured, application failover will take effect. For more information about application failover see *Oracle8i Tuning* and *Oracle8i Parallel Server Concepts and Administration*. You must identify the session with both of the following values from the V$SESSION view:

  - *integer1* is the value of the SID column.

  - *integer2* is the value of the SERIAL# column.

- DISTRIBUTED RECOVERY specifies whether or not distributed recovery is enabled. To use this clause, your instance must have the database open.

- ENABLE enables distributed recovery. In a single-process environment, you must use this clause to initiate distributed recovery.
  You may need to issue the ENABLE DISTRIBUTED RECOVERY statement more than once to recover an in-doubt transaction if the remote node involved in the transaction is not accessible. In-doubt transactions appear in the data dictionary view DBA_2PC_PENDING. For more information about distributed transactions and distributed recovery, see *Oracle8i Distributed Database Systems*.

- DISABLE disables distributed recovery.

- RESTRICTED SESSION specifies whether logon to Oracle is restricted.

  - ENABLE allows only users with RESTRICTED SESSION system privilege to log on to Oracle. Existing sessions are not terminated.

  - DISABLE reverses the effect of the ENABLE RESTRICTED SESSION clause, allowing all users with CREATE SESSION system privilege to log on to Oracle. This is the default.
    You can use this clause regardless of whether your instance has the database dismounted or mounted, open or closed.

- FLUSH SHARED_POOL clears all data from the shared pool in the system global area (SGA). The shared pool stores cached data dictionary information and shared SQL and PL/SQL areas for SQL statements, stored procedures, function, packages, and triggers.

  This statement does not clear shared SQL and PL/SQL areas for items that are currently being executed. You can use this clause regardless of whether your instance has the database dismounted or mounted, open or closed.

- KILL SESSION terminates a session, rolls back ongoing transactions, releases all session locks, and frees all session resources. To use this clause, your instance must have the database open. You must identify the session with both of the following values from the V$SESSION view:

  - *integer1* is the value of the SID column.
  - *integer2* is the value of the SERIAL# column.

  If the session is performing some activity that must be completed, such as waiting for a reply from a remote database or rolling back a transaction, Oracle waits for this activity to complete, kills the session, and then returns control to you. If the waiting lasts a minute, Oracle marks the session to be killed and returns control to you with a message that the session is marked to be killed. Oracle then kills the session when the activity is complete.
  Restriction: You can kill a session only on the same instance as your current session.

- SWITCH LOGFILE explicitly forces Oracle to begin writing to a new redo log file group, regardless of whether the files in the current redo log file group are full. When you force a log switch, Oracle begins to perform a checkpoint. Oracle returns control to you immediately rather than when the checkpoint is complete. To use this clause, your instance must have the database open.

- SUSPEND suspends all I/O (datafile, control file, and file header) as well as queries, in all instances, enabling you to make copies of the database without having to handle ongoing transactions.

Restrictions:
Do not use this clause unless you have put the database tablespaces in hot backup mode.
If you start a new instance while the system is suspended, that new instance will not be suspended.

■ RESUME makes the database available once again for queries and I/O. For more information on the SUSPEND clause and RESUME clause, refer to *Oracle8i Backup and Recovery Guide*.

■ *set_clause* sets the system parameters that follow. You can set values for multiple parameters in the same *set_clause*.

The DEFERRED keyword sets or modifies the value of the parameter for future sessions that connect to the database.

CAUTION
Unless otherwise noted, these parameters are initialization parameters, and the descriptions provided here indicate only the general nature of the parameters. Before changing the values of initialization parameters, please refer to their full description in Oracle8i Reference *and* Oracle8i National Language Support Guide.

```
AQ_TM_PROCESSES = integer
```

is an Advanced Queuing parameter that specifies whether a time manager process is created. Accepted values are 1 (creates one time manager process to monitor messages) and 0 (does not create a time manager process).

```
BACKGROUND_DUMP_DEST = 'text'
```

specifies the pathname for a directory where debugging trace files for the background processes are written during Oracle operations.

```
BACKUP_TAPE_IO_SLAVES = {TRUE | FALSE} [DEFERRED]
```

specifies whether I/O slaves are used by the Recovery Manager to back up, copy, or restore data to tape.

```
CONTROL_FILE_RECORD_KEEP_TIME = integer [DEFERRED]
```

specifies (in days) the minimum age of a record in a reusable control file section at which the record can be reused.

```
CREATE_STORED_OUTLINES = { TRUE | FALSE | 'category_name' } [NOOVERRIDE]
```

determines whether Oracle should automatically create and store an outline for each query submitted on the system. CREATE_STORED_OUTLINES is not an initialization parameter.

■ TRUE enables automatic outline creation for subsequent queries in the system. These outlines receive a unique system-generated name and are stored in the DEFAULT category. If a particular query already has an outline defined for it in the DEFAULT category, that outline will remain and a new outline will not be created.

■ FALSE disables automatic outline creation for the system. This is the default.

- *category_name* has the same behavior as TRUE except that any outline created in the system is stored in the *category_name* category.

- NOOVERRIDE specifies that this system setting will not override the setting for any session in which this parameter was explicitly set. If you do not specify NOOVERRIDE, this setting takes effect in all sessions.

DB_BLOCK_CHECKING = {TRUE | FALSE} DEFERRED

controls whether data block checking is done. The default is FALSE, for compatibility with earlier releases where block checking is disabled as a default.

DB_BLOCK_CHECKSUM = {TRUE | FALSE}

specifies whether the database writer background process and the direct loader will calculate a checksum and store it in the cache header of every data lock when writing to disk.

DB_BLOCK_MAX_DIRTY_TARGET = integer

limits to *integer* the number of dirty buffers in the cache and the number of buffers that will need to be read during crash or instance recovery. This parameter does *not* relate to media recovery. A value of 0 disables this parameter. The minimum accepted value to enable the parameter is 1000.

DB_FILE_MULTIBLOCK_READ_COUNT = integer

specifies the maximum number of blocks read in one I/O operation during a sequential scan.

FAST_START_IO_TARGET

specifies the target number of IOs (reads and writes) to and from buffer cache that Oracle should perform upon crash or instance recovery. Oracle continuously calculates the actual number of IOs that would be needed for recovery and compares that number against the target. If the actual number is greater than the target, Oracle attempts to write additional dirty buffers to advance the checkpoint, while minimizing the affect on performance.
For information on how to tune this parameter, see *Oracle8i Tuning*.

FAST_START_PARALLEL_ROLLBACK = { FALSE | LOW | HIGH}

specifies the number of processes spawned to perform parallel recovery.

- FALSE specifies no parallel recovery. SMON will serially recover dead transactions.

- LOW specifies that the number of recovery servers may not exceed twice the value of the CPU_COUNT parameter.

- HIGH specifies that the number of recovery servers may not exceed four times the value of the CPU_COUNT parameter.

FIXED_DATE = { 'DD_MM_YY' | 'YYYY_MI_DD_HH24_MI-SS' }

specifies a constant date for SYSDATE instead of the current date.

GC_DEFER_TIME = integer

specifies the time (in hundredths of seconds) that Oracle waits before responding to forced-write requests from other instances.

```
GLOBAL_NAMES = {TRUE | FALSE}
```

When you start an instance, Oracle determines whether to enforce global name resolution for remote objects accessed in SQL statements based on the value of the initialization parameter GLOBAL_NAMES. This system parameter enables or disables global name resolution while your instance is running. TRUE enables the enforcement of global names. FALSE disables the enforcement of global names. You can also enable or disable global name resolution for your session with the GLOBAL_NAMES parameter of the ALTER SESSION statement. Oracle recommends that you enable global name resolution if you use or plan to use distributed processing. For more information on global name resolution and how Oracle enforces it, see *Oracle8i Distributed Database Systems*.

```
HASH_MULTIBLOCK_IO_COUNT = integer
```

specifies the number of data blocks to read and write during a hash join operation. The value multiplied by the DB_BLOCK_SIZE initialization parameter should not exceed 64K. The default value for this parameter is 1. If the multi-threaded server is used, the value is always 1, and any value given here is ignored.

```
HS_AUTOREGISTER = {TRUE | FALSE}
```

enables or disables automatic self-registration of non-Oracle system characteristics in the Oracle server's data dictionary by Heterogeneous Services agents. For more information on accessing non-Oracle systems through Heterogeneous Services, see *Oracle8i Distributed Database Systems*.

```
JOB_QUEUE_PROCESSES = integer
```

specifies the number of job queue processes per instance (SN*Pn*, where *n* is 0 to 9 followed by A to Z). Set this parameter to 1 or higher if you wish to have your snapshots updated automatically. One job queue process is usually sufficient unless you have many snapshots that refresh simultaneously.

Oracle also uses job queue processes to process requests created by the DBMS_JOB package. For more information on managing table snapshots, see *Oracle8i Replication*.

```
LICENSE_MAX_SESSIONS = integer
```

resets (for the current instance) the value of the initialization parameter LICENSE_MAX_SESSIONS, which establishes the concurrent usage licensing limit, or the limit for concurrent sessions. Once this limit is reached, only users with RESTRICTED SESSION system privilege can connect. A value of 0 disables the limit.

If you reduce the limit on sessions below the current number of sessions, Oracle does not end existing sessions to enforce the new limit. However, users without RESTRICTED SESSION system privilege can begin new sessions only when the number of sessions falls below the new limit.

CAUTION
Do not disable or raise session limits unless you have appropriately upgraded your Oracle license. For more information, contact your Oracle sales representative.

```
LICENSE_MAX_USERS = integer
```

resets (for the current instance) the value of the initialization parameter LICENSE_MAX_USERS, which establishes the limit for users connected to your database. Once this limit is reached, more users cannot connect. A value of 0 disables the limit.

Restriction: You cannot reduce the limit on users below the current number of users created for the database.

CAUTION

Do not disable or raise user limits unless you have appropriately upgraded your Oracle license. For more information, contact your Oracle sales representative.

```
LICENSE_SESSIONS_WARNING = integer
```

resets (for the current instance) the value of the initialization parameter LICENSE_SESSIONS_WARNING, which establishes a warning threshold for concurrent usage. Once this threshold is reached, Oracle writes warning messages to the database ALERT file for each subsequent session. Also, users with RESTICTED SESSION system privilege receive warning messages when they begin subsequent sessions. A value of 0 disables the warning threshold. If you reduce the warning threshold for sessions below the current number of sessions, Oracle writes a message to the ALERT file for all subsequent sessions.

```
LOG_ARCHIVE_DEST = string
```

specifies a valid operating system pathname as the primary destination for all archive redo log file groups.

Restrictions: If you set a value for this parameter:
You cannot have a value for LOG_ARCHIVE_DEST_ n in your initialization parameter file, nor can you set a value for that parameter using the ALTER SESSION or ALTER SYSTEM statement. You cannot set a value for the parameter LOG_ARCHIVE_MIN_SUCCEED_DEST using the ALTER SESSION statement.

```
LOG_ARCHIVE_DEST_n = null_string
|{LOCATION=pathname | SERVICE=servicename}
[MANDATORY | OPTIONAL]
[REOPEN[=retry_time_in_seconds]]
```

Restrictions: If you set a value for this parameter:
You cannot have definitions for the parameters LOG_ARCHIVE_DEST or LOG_ARCHIVE_DUPLEX_DEST in your initialization parameter file, nor can you set values for those parameters using the ALTER SYSTEM statement. You cannot start archiving to a specific location using the ALTER SYSTEM ARCHIVE LOG TO location statement.

```
LOG_ARCHIVE_DEST_STATE_n = {ENABLE | DEFER}
```

specifies the state associated with the corresponding LOG_ARCHIVE_DEST_n parameter.

■   ENABLE specifies that any associated valid destination can be used for archiving. This is the default.

■   DEFER specifies that Oracle will not consider for archiving any destination associated with the corresponding LOG_ARCHIVE_DEST_n parameter.

```
LOG_ARCHIVE_DUPLEX_DEST = string
```

specifies a valid operating system pathname as the secondary destination for all archive redo log file groups.

Restriction: If you set a value for this parameter:

You must have a definition for LOG_ARCHIVE_DEST.

You cannot have a value for the parameter LOG_ARCHIVE_DEST_n in your initialization parameter file, nor can you set a value for that parameter using the ALTER SYSTEM or ALTER SESSION statement.

You cannot set a value for the parameter LOG_ARCHIVE_MIN_SUCCEED_DEST using the ALTER SESSION statement.

`LOG_ARCHIVE_MAX_PROCESSES = integer`

specifies the number of archiver processes that are invoked. Permitted values are integers 1 through 10, inclusive. The default is 1.

`LOG_ARCHIVE_MIN_SUCCEED_DEST = integer`

specifies the minimum number of destinations that must succeed in order for the online log file to be available for reuse.

`LOG_CHECKPOINT_INTERVAL = integer`

limits to *integer* the number of redo blocks that can exist between an incremental checkpoint and the last block written to the redo log.

`LOG_CHECKPOINT_TIMEOUT = integer`

limits the incremental checkpoint to be at the position where the last write to the redo log (sometimes called the "tail of the log") was *integer* seconds ago, and signifies that no buffer will remain dirty (in the cache) for more than *integer* seconds. The default is 1800 seconds.

`MAX_DUMP_FILE_SIZE = { size | 'UNLIMITED'} [DEFERRED]`

specifies the trace dump file size upper limit for all user sessions. Specify the maximum *size* as either a nonnegative integer that represents the number of blocks, or as 'UNLIMITED'. If you specify 'UNLIMITED', no upper limit is imposed.

■ **Multi-Threaded Server Parameters:** When you start your instance, Oracle creates shared server processes and dispatcher processes for the multi-threaded server architecture based on the values of the MTS_SERVERS and MTS_DISPATCHERS initialization parameters. You can set the MTS_SERVERS and MTS_DISPATCHERS session parameters to perform one of the following operations while the instance is running:

■ Create additional shared server processes by increasing the minimum number of shared server processes.

■ Terminate existing shared server processes after their current calls finish processing.

■ Create more dispatcher processes for a specific protocol, up to a maximum across all protocols specified by the initialization parameter MTS_MAX_DISPATCHERS.

■ Terminate existing dispatcher processes for a specific protocol after their current user processes disconnect from the instance.

For more information on multi-threaded server architecture, see *Oracle8i Concepts, Oracle8i Tuning,* and *Oracle8i Parallel Server Concepts and Administration*.

```
MTS_DISPATCHERS = 'dispatch_clause'
```
   dispatch_clause::=
```
(PROTOCOL = protocol) |
( ADDRESS = address) |
(DESCRIPTION = description )
[options_clause]
```
   options_clause::=
```
(DISPATCHERS = integer |
SESSIONS = integer |
CONNECTIONS = integer |
TICKS = seconds |
POOL = { 1 | ON | YES | TRUE | BOTH | ({IN|OUT} = ticks) |
0 | OFF | NO | FALSE | ticks} |
MULTIPLEX = {1 | ON | YES | TRUE | 0 | OFF | NO |
FALSE | BOTH | IN | OUT} |
LISTENER = tnsname |
SERVICE = service |
PRESENTATION = { TTC | RO | GIOP | ejb_presentation_class } |
INDEX = integer)
```

modifies or creates the configuration of dispatcher processes. You can specify multiple MTS_DISPATCHERS parameters in a single statement for multiple network protocols. For more information on this parameter, see *Net8 Administrator's Guide* and *Oracle8i Administrator's Guide*.

```
MTS_SERVERS = integer
```

specifies a new minimum number of shared server processes.

```
QUERY_REWRITE_ENABLED = { TRUE | FALSE } [DEFERRED | NOOVERRIDE]
```

enables or disables query rewrite on all materialized views that have not been explicitly disabled. By default, TRUE enables query rewrite for all sessions immediately. Query rewrite is superseded and disabled by rule-based optimization (that is, if the OPTIMIZER_MODE parameter is set to RULE). Also enables or disables use of any function-based indexes defined on the materialized view.

- ■ DEFERRED specifies that query rewrite is enabled or disabled only for future sessions.
- ■ NOOVERRIDE specifies that query rewrite is enabled or disabled for all sessions that have not explicitly set this parameter using ALTER SESSION.

NOTE
Enabling or disabling query rewrite does not affect queries that have already been compiled, even if they are reissued. Enabling or disabling query rewrite does not affect descending indexes. For more information on query rewrite, see Oracle8i Tuning.

```
OBJECT_CACHE_MAX_SIZE_PERCENT = integer [DEFERRED]
```

specifies the percentage of the optimal cache size that the session object cache can grow past the optimal size.

`OBJECT_CACHE_OPTIMAL_SIZE = integer [DEFERRED]`

specifies (in kilobytes) the size to which the session object cache is reduced if it exceeds the maximum size.

`PARALLEL_ADAPTIVE_MULTI_USER = {TRUE | FALSE}`

specifies that Oracle should vary the degree of parallelism based on the total perceived load on the system.

`PARALLEL_INSTANCE_GROUP = 'text'`

specifies the name of the Oracle Parallel Server instance group to be used for spawning parallel query slaves.

`PARALLEL_THREADS_PER_CPU = integer`

used to compute the degree of parallelism for parallel operations where the degree of parallelism is unset. The default is operating system dependent.

`PLSQL_V2_COMPATIBILITY = {TRUE | FALSE} [DEFERRED]`

modifies the compile-time behavior of PL/SQL programs to allow language constructs that are illegal in Oracle8 and Oracle*8i* (PL/SQL V3), but were legal in Oracle7 (PL/SQL V2). See *PL/SQL User's Guide and Reference* and *Oracle8i Reference* for more information about this system parameter.

- `TRUE` enables Oracle8i PL/SQL V3 programs to execute Oracle7 PL/SQL V2 constructs.

- `FALSE disallows illegal Oracle7 PL/SQL V2 constructs. This is the default.`

`REMOTE_DEPENDENCIES_MODE = {TIMESTAMP | SIGNATURE}`

specifies how dependencies of remote stored procedures are handled by the server. For more information, see *Oracle8i Application Developer's Guide - Fundamentals*.

`RESOURCE_LIMIT = {TRUE | FALSE}`

When you start an instance, Oracle enforces resource limits assigned to users based on the value of the RESOURCE_LIMIT initialization parameter. This system parameter enables or disables resource limits for subsequent sessions. TRUE enables resource limits. FALSE disables resource limits.

Enabling resource limits only causes Oracle to enforce the resource limits already assigned to users. To choose resource limit values for a user, you must create a profile and assign that profile to the user.

`RESOURCE_MANAGER_PLAN = plan_name`

specifies the name of the resource plan Oracle should use to allocate system resources among resource consumer groups. For information on resource consumer groups and resource plans, refer to *Oracle8i Administrator's Guide*.

`SORT_AREA_RETAINED_SIZE = integer DEFERRED`

specifies (in bytes) the maximum amount of memory that each sort operation will retain after the first fetch is done, until the cursor ends. The default is the value of the SORT_AREA_SIZE parameter.

`SORT_AREA_SIZE = integer DEFERRED`

specifies (in bytes) the maximum amount of memory to use for each sort operation. The default is operating system dependent.

`SORT_MULTIBLOCK_READ_COUNT = integer DEFERRED`

specifies the number of database blocks to read each time a sort performs a read from temporary segments. The default is 2.

`STANDBY_ARCHIVE_DEST = string`

specifies a valid operating system pathname as the standby database destination for the archive redo log files.

`TIMED_STATISTICS = {TRUE | FALSE}`

specifies whether the server requests the time from the operating system when generating time-related statistics. The default is FALSE.

`TIMED_OS_STATISTICS = integer`

specifies that operating system statistics will be collected when a request is made from a client to the server or when a request completes.

`TRANSACTION_AUDITING = {TRUE | FALSE} DEFERRED`

specifies whether the transaction layer generates a special redo record containing session and user information.

`USE_STORED_OUTLINES = { TRUE | FALSE | 'category_name' } [NOOVERRIDE]`

determines whether the optimizer will use stored outlines to generate execution plans. `USE_STORED_OUTLINES` is not an initialization parameter.

- ■ TRUE causes the optimizer to use outlines stored in the DEFAULT category when compiling requests.

- ■ FALSE specifies that the optimizer should not use stored outlines. This is the default.

- ■ *category_name* causes the optimizer to use outlines stored in the *category_name* category when compiling requests.

- ■ NOOVERRIDE specifies that this system setting will not override the setting for any session in which this parameter was explicitly set. If you do not specify NOOVERRIDE, this setting takes effect in all sessions.

`USER_DUMP_DEST = 'directory_name'`

specifies the pathname where Oracle will write debugging trace files on behalf of a user process.

ALTER TABLE

Syntax

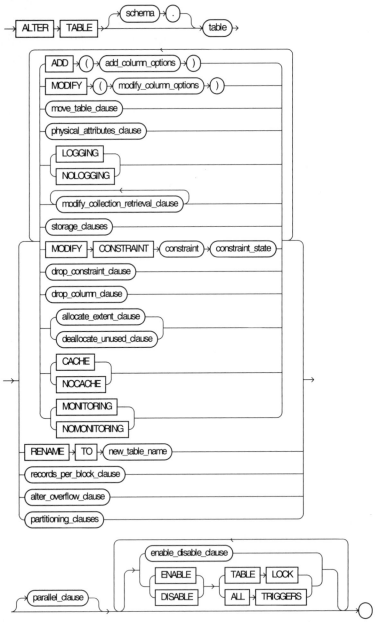

add_column_options::=

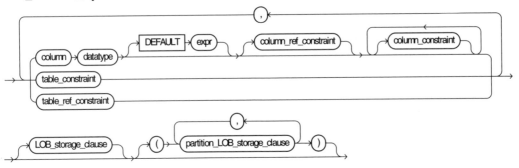

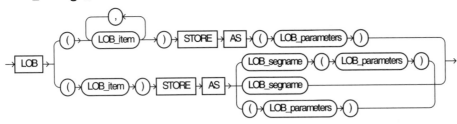

LOB_storage_clause::=

LOB_parameters::=

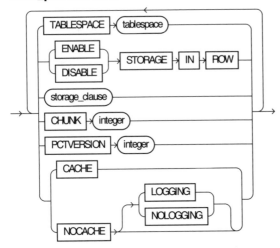

partition_LOB_storage_clause::=

modify_column_options::=

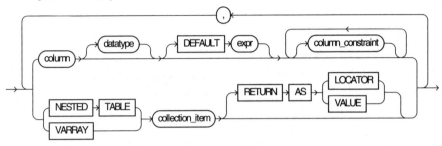

move_table_clause::=

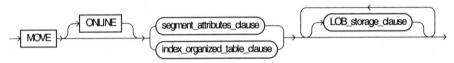

segment_attributes_clause::=

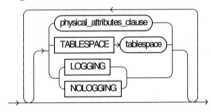

physical_attributes_clause::=

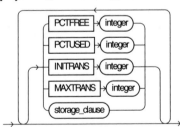

index_organized_table_clause::=

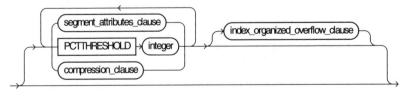

compression_clause::=

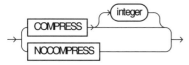

index_organized_overflow_clause::=

modify_collection_retrieval_clause::=

storage_clauses::=

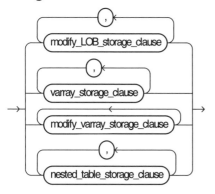

modify_LOB_storage_clause::=

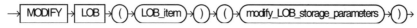

modify_LOB_storage_parameters::=

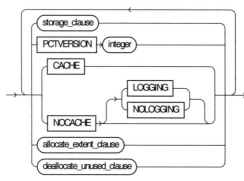

allocate_extent_clause::=

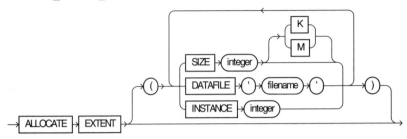

deallocate_unused_clause::=

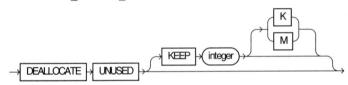

varray_storage_clause::=

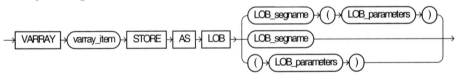

modify_varray_storage_clause::=

nested_table_storage_clause::=

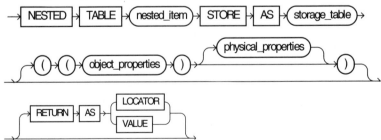

object_properties::=

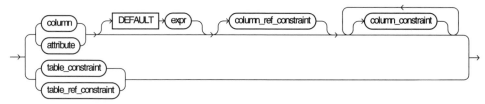

physical_properties::=

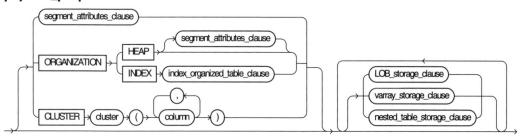

drop_constraint_clause::=

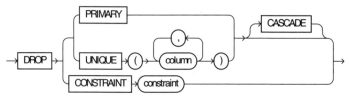

drop_column_clause::=

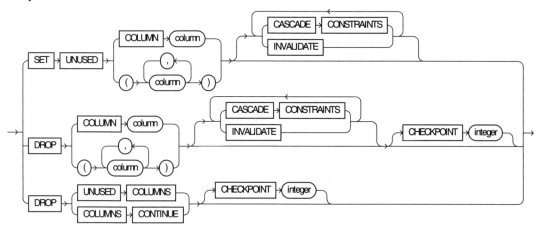

records_per_block_clause::=

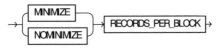

alter_overflow_clause::=

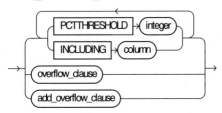

overflow_clause::=

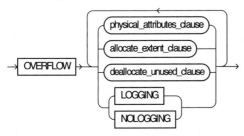

add_overflow_clause::=

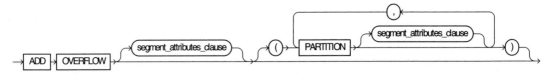

partitioning_clauses::=

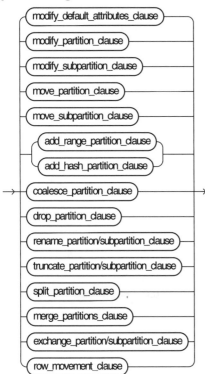

modify_default_attributes_clause::=

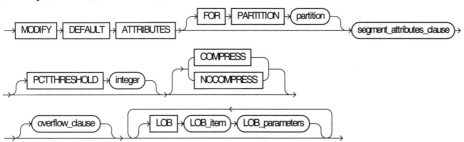

modify_partition_clause::=

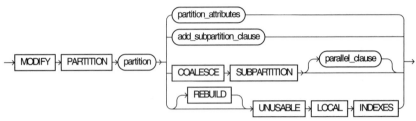

partition_attributes::=

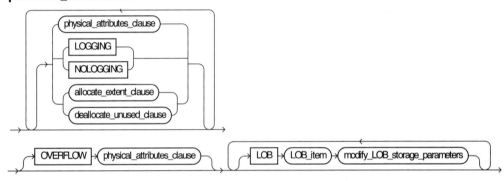

add_subpartition_clause::=

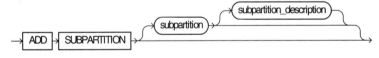

subpartition_description::=

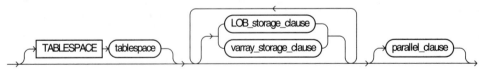

modify_subpartition_clause::=

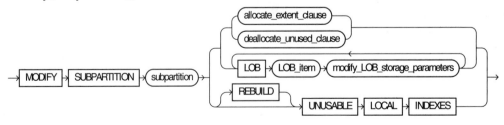

move_partition_clause::=

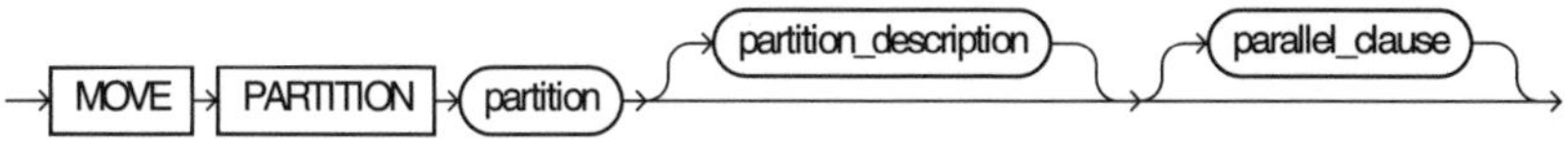

partition_description::=

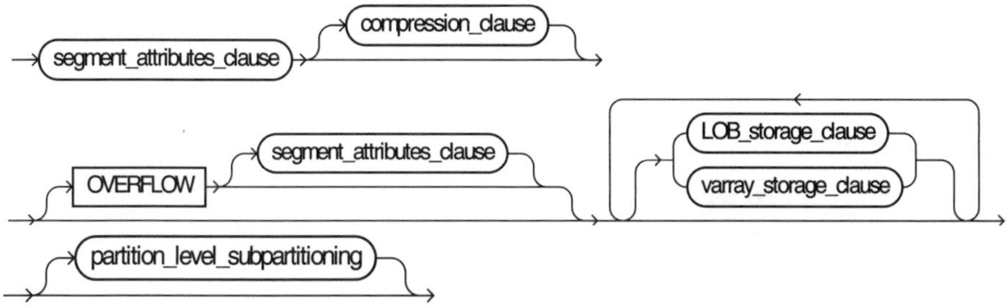

partition_level_subpartitioning::=

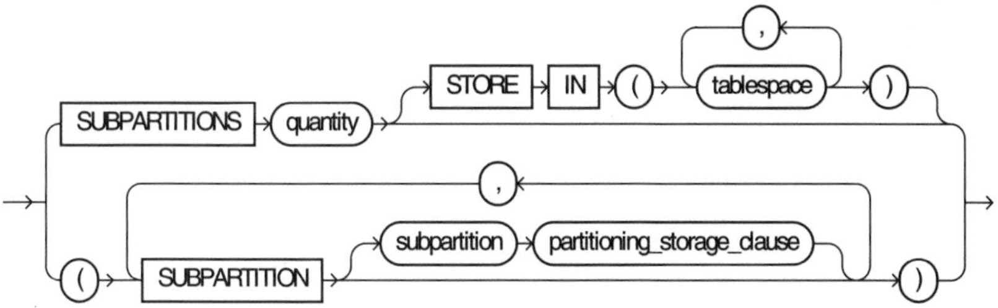

partitioning_storage_clause::=

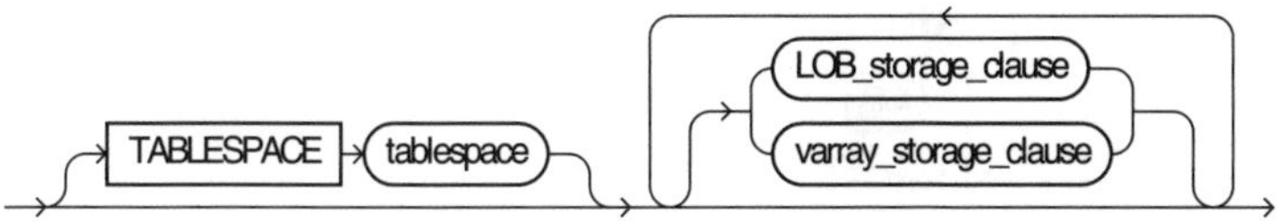

move_subpartition_clause::=

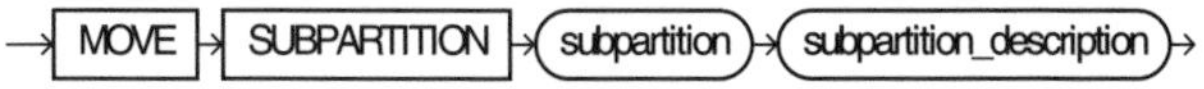

add_range_partition_clause::=

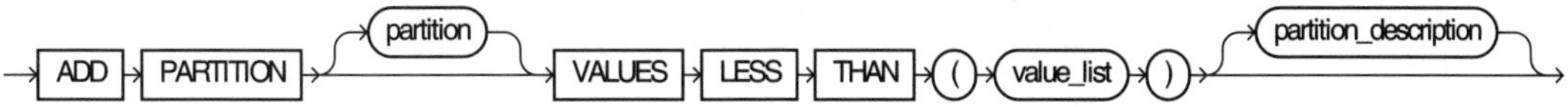

add_hash_partition_clause::=

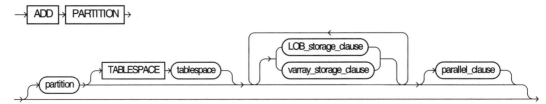

coalesce_partition_clause::=

drop_partition_clause::=

rename_partition/subpartition_clause::=

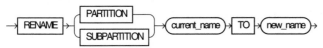

truncate_partition_clause/truncate_subpartition_clause::=

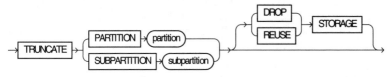

split_partition_clause::=

merge_partitions_clause::=

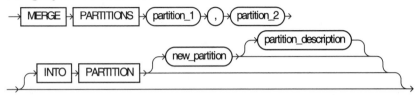

exchange_partition_clause/exchange_subpartition_clause::=

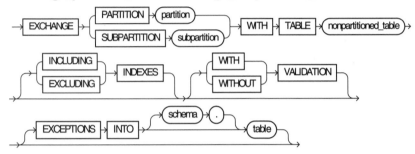

row_movement_clause::=

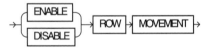

parallel_clause::=

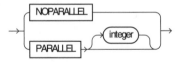

enable_disable_clause::=

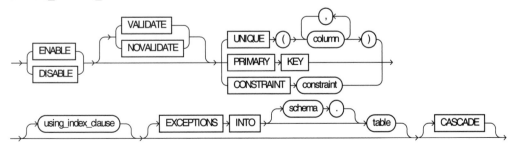

using_index_clause::=

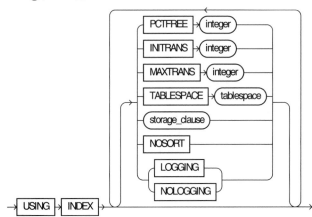

Purpose

To alter the definition of a nonpartitioned table, a partitioned table, a table partition, or a table subpartition.

Prerequisites

The table must be in your own schema, or you must have ALTER privilege on the table, or you must have ALTER ANY TABLE system privilege. For some operations you may also need the CREATE ANY INDEX privilege. In addition, if you are not the owner of the table, you need the DROP ANY TABLE privilege in order to use the *drop_partition_clause* or *truncate_partition_clause*. You must also have space quota in the tablespace in which space is to be acquired in order to use the *add_partition_clause*, *modify_ partition_clause*, *move_partition_clause*, and *split_partition_clause*. To enable a UNIQUE or PRIMARY KEY constraint, you must have the privileges necessary to create an index on the table. You need these privileges because Oracle creates an index on the columns of the unique or primary key in the schema containing the table. To enable or disable triggers, the triggers must be in your schema or you must have the ALTER ANY TRIGGER system privilege. To use an object type in a column definition when modifying a table, either that object must belong to the same schema as the table being altered, or you must have either the EXECUTE ANY TYPE system privilege or the EXECUTE schema object privilege for the object type.

Keywords and Parameters

The clauses described below have specialized meaning in the ALTER TABLE statement.

NOTE
Operations performed by the ALTER TABLE statement can cause Oracle to invalidate procedures and stored functions that access the table. For information on how and when Oracle invalidates such objects, see Oracle8i Concepts.

- *schema* is the schema containing the table. If you omit *schema*, Oracle assumes the table is in your own schema.

- *table* is the name of the table to be altered.

You can modify, or drop columns from, or rename a temporary table. However, for a temporary table, you cannot:

- Add columns of nested-table or varray type. You can add columns of other types.
- Specify referential integrity (foreign key) constraints for an added or modified column
- Specify the following clauses of the *LOB_storage_clause* for an added or modified LOB column: TABLESPACE, *storage_clause*, LOGGING|NOLOGGING, or the *LOB_index_clause*.
- Specify the *physical_attribute_clause*, *nested_table_storage_clause*, *parallel_clause*, *allocate_extent_clause*, *deallocate_unused_clause*, or any of the *index-organized table* clauses
- Exchange partitions between a partition and a temporary table
- Specify LOGGING or NOLOGGING
- Specify MOVE

NOTE
If you alter a table that is a master table for one or more materialized views, the materialized views are marked INVALID. Invalid materialized views cannot be used by query rewrite and cannot be refreshed. For more information on materialized views in general, see Oracle8i Tuning.

ADD

- ***add_column_options*** adds a column or integrity constraint. If you add a column, the initial value of each row for the new column is null.
  You can add an overflow data segment to each partition of a partitioned index-organized table. You can add LOB columns to nonpartitioned and partitioned tables. You can specify LOB storage at the table and at the partition or subpartition level.
  If you previously created a view with a query that used the "SELECT *" syntax to select all columns from table, and you now add a column to *table*, Oracle does not automatically add the new column to the view. To add the new column to the view, re-create the view using the CREATE VIEW statement with the OR REPLACE clause.
  Restrictions:
  You cannot add a LOB column to a partitioned index-organized table. (This restriction does not apply to nonpartitioned index-organized tables.)
  You cannot add a column with a NOT NULL constraint if *table* has any rows.
  If you specify this clause for an index-organized table, you cannot specify any other clauses in the same statement.

  - ***table_ref_constraint*, *column_ref_constraint*** These clauses let you further describe a column of type REF. The only difference between these clauses is that you specify *table_ref* from the table level, so you must identify the REF column or attribute you are defining. You specify *column_ref* after you have already identified the REF column or attribute.

  - *column_constraint* adds or removes a NOT NULL constraint to or from an existing column. You cannot use this clause to modify any other type of constraint using ALTER TABLE.

  - *table_constraint* adds or modifies an integrity constraint on the table.

■ **LOB_storage_clause** specifies the LOB storage characteristics for the newly added LOB column. You cannot use this clause to modify an existing LOB column. Instead, you must use the *modify_LOB_storage_clause*.

■ *lob_item* is the LOB column name or LOB object attribute for which you are explicitly defining tablespace and storage characteristics that are different from those of the table.

■ *lob_segname* specifies the name of the LOB data segment. You cannot use *lob_segname* if more than one *lob_item* is specified.

■ ENABLE | DISABLE STORAGE IN ROW specifies whether the LOB value is stored in the row (inline) or outside of the row. (The LOB locator is always stored in the row regardless of where the LOB value is stored.)

■ ENABLE specifies that the LOB value is stored inline if its length is less than approximately 4000 bytes minus system control information. This is the default.

■ DISABLE specifies that the LOB value is stored outside of the row regardless of the length of the LOB value.

Restriction: You cannot change STORAGE IN ROW once it is set. Therefore, you can specify this clause only as part of the *add_column_options* clause, not as part of the *modify_column_options* clause.

■ CHUNK *integer* specifies the number of bytes to be allocated for LOB manipulation. If *integer* is not a multiple of the database block size, Oracle rounds up (in bytes) to the next multiple. For example, if the database block size is 2048 and *integer* is 2050, Oracle allocates 4096 bytes (2 blocks).The maximum value is 32768 (32 K), which is the largest Oracle block size allowed. The default CHUNK size is one Oracle database block. You cannot change the value of CHUNK once it is set.

NOTE
The value of CHUNK must be less than or equal to the value of NEXT (either the default value or that specified in the storage clause). If CHUNK exceeds the value of NEXT, Oracle returns an error.

■ PCTVERSION *integer* is the maximum percentage of overall LOB storage space used for creating new versions of the LOB. The default value is 10, meaning that older versions of the LOB data are not overwritten until 10% of the overall LOB storage space is used.

■ **LOB_index_clause** This clause is deprecated as of Oracle8i. Oracle generates an index for each LOB column. The LOB indexes are system named and system managed, and reside in the same tablespace as the LOB data segments. Although it is still possible for you to specify this clause, Oracle Corporation strongly recommends that you no longer do so. For information on how Oracle manages LOB indexes in tables migrated from earlier versions, see *Oracle8i Migration*.

■ **partition_LOB_storage_clause** lets you specify a separate *LOB_storage_clause* for each partition. You must specify the partitions in the order of partition position. If you do not specify a *LOB_storage_clause* for a particular partition, the storage characteristics are those specified for the LOB item at the table level. If you also did not specify any storage characteristics at the table level for the LOB item, Oracle stores the LOB data partition in the same tablespace as the table partition to which it corresponds.

Restriction: You can specify only one list of *partition_LOB_storage_clauses* per ALTER TABLE statement, and all *LOB_storage_clauses* must precede the list of *partition_LOB_storage_clauses*.

■ MODIFY *modify_column_options* modifies the definition of an existing column. If you omit any of the optional parts of the column definition (datatype, default value, or column constraint), these parts remain unchanged.

You can change a CHAR column to VARCHAR2 (or VARCHAR) and a VARCHAR2 (or VARCHAR) to CHAR only if the column contains nulls in all rows or if you do not attempt to change the column size.

You can change any column's datatype or decrease any column's size if all rows for the column contain nulls.

You can always increase the size of a character or raw column or the precision of a numeric column, whether or not all the columns contain nulls.

Restrictions: You cannot modify the datatype or length of a column that is part of a table or index partitioning or subpartitioning key.

You cannot modify the definition of a column on which a domain index has been built.

If you specify this clause for an index-organized table, you cannot specify any other clauses in the same statement.

■ *column* is the name of the column to be added or modified. The only type of integrity constraint that you can add to an existing column using the MODIFY clause with the column constraint syntax is a NOT NULL constraint, and only if the column contains no nulls. To define other types of integrity constraints (UNIQUE, PRIMARY KEY, referential integrity, and CHECK constraints) on existing columns, using the ADD clause and the table constraint syntax.

■ *datatype* specifies a new datatype for an existing column. You can omit the datatype only if the statement also designates the column as part of the foreign key of a referential integrity constraint. Oracle automatically assigns the column the same datatype as the corresponding column of the referenced key of the referential integrity constraint. If you change the datatype of a column in a materialized view container table, the corresponding materialized view is invalidated.

Restrictions: You cannot specify a column of datatype ROWID for an index-organized table, but you can specify a column of type UROWID.

You cannot change a column's datatype to LOB or REF.

■ DEFAULT specifies a new default for an existing column. Oracle assigns this value to the column if a subsequent INSERT statement omits a value for the column. If you are adding a new column to the table and specify the default value, Oracle inserts the default column value into all rows of the table. The datatype of the default value must match the datatype specified for the column. The column must also be long enough to hold the default value. A DEFAULT expression cannot contain references to other columns, the pseudocolumns CURRVAL, NEXTVAL, LEVEL, and ROWNUM, or date constants that are not fully specified.

■ MODIFY CONSTRAINT *constraint* modifies the state of an existing constraint named *constraint*.

■ *move_table_clause*   For a **heap-organized table**, use the *segment_attributes_clause* of the syntax. The *move_table_clause* lets you relocate data of a nonpartitioned table into a new segment, optionally in a different tablespace, and optionally modify any of its storage attributes. You can also move any LOB data segments associated with the table using the *LOB_storage_clause*. (LOB items not specified in this clause are not moved.)

For an **index-organized table**, use the *index_organized_table_clause* of the syntax. The *move_* *table_clause* rebuilds the index-organized table's primary key index B*-tree. The overflow data segment is not rebuilt unless the OVERFLOW keyword is explicitly stated, with two exceptions:

- If you alter the values of PCTTHRESHOLD or the INCLUDING column as part of this ALTER TABLE statement, the overflow data segment is rebuilt.

- If any of out-of-line columns (LOBs, varrays, nested table columns) in the index-organized table are moved explicitly, then the overflow data segment is also rebuilt.

The index and data segments of LOB columns are not rebuilt unless you specify the LOB columns explicitly as part of this ALTER TABLE statement.

- ONLINE specifies that DML operations on the index-organized table are allowed during rebuilding of the table's primary key index B*-tree.
  Restrictions: You can specify this clause only for a nonpartitioned index-organized table. Parallel DML is not supported during online MOVE. If you specify ONLINE and then issue parallel DML statements, Oracle returns an error.

- *compression_clause* enables and disables key compression in an index-organized table.

    - COMPRESS enables key compression, which eliminates repeated occurrence of primary key column values in index-organized tables. Use *integer* to specify the prefix length (number of prefix columns to compress).
      The valid range of prefix length values is from 1 to the number of primary key columns minus 1. The default prefix length is the number of primary key columns minus 1.
      Restrictions: You can specify this clause only for an index-organized table. You can specify compression for a partition of an index-organized table only if compression has been specified at the table level.

    - NOCOMPRESS disables key compression in index-organized tables. This is the default.

- TABLESPACE specifies the tablespace into which the rebuilt index-organized table is stored.
  Restrictions: If you specify MOVE, it must be the first clause. For an index-organized table, the only clauses outside this clause that are allowed are the *physical_attribute_clause* and the *parallel_clause*. For heap-organized tables, you can specify those two clauses and the *LOB_storage_clauses*.
  You cannot MOVE an entire partitioned table (either heap or index organized). You must move individual partitions or subpartitions.

NOTE
For any LOB columns you specify in this clause:
Oracle drops the old LOB data segment and corresponding index segment and creates new segments, even if you do not specify a new tablespace.
If the LOB index in table resided in a different tablespace from the LOB data, Oracle collocates the LOB index with the LOB data in the LOB data's tablespace after the move.

- *physical_attributes_clause* changes the value of PCTFREE, PCTUSED, INITRANS, and MAXTRANS parameters and storage characteristics.
  Restriction: You cannot specify the PCTUSED parameter for the index segment of an index-organized table.

CAUTION
For a nonpartitioned table, the values you specify override any values specified for the table at create time.
For a range- or hash-partitioned table, the values you specify are the default values for the table and the actual values for every existing partition, overriding any values already set for the partitions. To change default table attributes without overriding existing partition values, use the modify_default_attributes_clause.
For a composite-partitioned table, the values you specify are the default values for the table and all partitions of the table and the actual values for all subpartitions of the table, overriding any values already set for the subpartitions. To change default partition attributes without overriding existing subpartition values, use the modify_default_attributes_clause with the FOR PARTITION clause.

- ■ ***modify_collection_retrieval_clause*** changes what is returned when a collection item is retrieved from the database.

    - ■ *collection_item* is the name of a column-qualified attribute whose type is nested table or varray.

    - ■ RETURN AS specifies what Oracle returns as the result of a query.

        - ■ LOCATOR specifies that a unique locator for the nested table is returned.

        - ■ VALUE specifies that a copy of the nested table itself is returned.

storage_clauses:

- ■ ***modify_LOB_storage_clause*** modifies the physical attributes of the LOB *lob_item*. You can specify only one *lob_item* for each *modify_LOB_storage_clause*.
    Restriction: You cannot modify the value of the INITIAL parameter in the *storage_clause* when modifying the LOB storage attributes.

- ■ ***varray_storage_clause*** lets you specify separate storage characteristics for the LOB in which a varray will be stored. In addition, if you specify this clause, Oracle will always store the varray in a LOB, even if it is small enough to be stored inline.
    Restriction: You cannot specify the TABLESPACE clause of *LOB_parameters* as part of this clause. The LOB tablespace for a varray defaults to the containing table's tablespace.

- ■ ***modify_varray_storage_clause*** lets you change the storage characteristics of an existing LOB in which a varray is stored.
    Restriction: You cannot specify the TABLESPACE clause of *LOB_parameters* as part of this clause. The LOB tablespace for a varray defaults to the containing table's tablespace.

- ■ ***nested_table_storage_clause*** enables you to specify separate storage characteristics for a nested table, which in turn enables you to define the nested table as an index-organized table. You must include this clause when creating a table with columns or column attributes whose type is a nested table. (Clauses within this clause that function the same way they function for parent object tables are not repeated here.)
    Restrictions: You cannot specify the *parallel_clause*.
    You cannot specify TABLESPACE (as part of the *segment_attributes_clause*) for a nested table. The tablespace is always that of the parent table.

- *nested_item* is the name of a column (or a top-level attribute of the table's object type) whose type is a nested table.

- *storage_table* is the name of the table where the rows of *nested_item* reside. The storage table is created in the same schema and the same tablespace as the parent table.

■ ***drop_constraint_clause*** drops an integrity constraint from the database. Oracle stops enforcing the constraint and removes it from the data dictionary. You can specify only one constraint for each *drop_constraint_clause*, but you can specify multiple *drop_constraint_clauses* in one statement.

- PRIMARY KEY drops the table's PRIMARY KEY constraint.

- UNIQUE drops the UNIQUE constraint on the specified columns.

- CONSTRAINT drops the integrity constraint named *constraint*.

- CASCADE drops all other integrity constraints that depend on the dropped integrity constraint. **Restrictions:** You cannot drop a UNIQUE or PRIMARY KEY constraint that is part of a referential integrity constraint without also dropping the foreign key. To drop the referenced key and the foreign key together, use the CASCADE clause. If you omit CASCADE, Oracle does not drop the PRIMARY KEY or UNIQUE constraint if any foreign key references it. You cannot drop a primary key constraint (even with the CASCADE clause) on a table that uses the primary key as its object identifier (OID).
  If you drop a referential integrity constraint on a REF column, the REF column remains scoped to the referenced table.
  You cannot drop the scope of the column.

■ ***drop_column_clause*** lets you free space in the database by dropping columns you no longer need, or by marking them to be dropped at a future time when the demand on system resources is less.

- SET UNUSED marks one or more columns as unused. Specifying this clause does not actually remove the target columns from each row in the table (that is, it does not restore the disk space used by these columns). Therefore, the response time is faster than it would be if you execute the DROP clause.
  You can view all tables with columns marked as unused in the data dictionary views USER_UNUSED_COL_TABS, DBA_UNUSED_COL_TABS, and ALL_UNUSED_COL_TABS. For information on these views, see *Oracle8i Reference*.
  Unused columns are treated as if they were dropped, even though their column data remains in the table's rows. After a column has been marked as unused, you have no access to that column. A "SELECT *" query will not retrieve data from unused columns. In addition, the names and types of columns marked unused will not be displayed during a DESCRIBE, and you can add to the table a new column with the same name as an unused column.

NOTE
Until you actually drop these columns, they continue to count toward the absolute limit of 1000 columns per table. Also, if you mark a column of datatype LONG as UNUSED, you cannot add another LONG column to the table until you actually drop the unused LONG column.

- DROP removes the column descriptor and the data associated with the target column from each row in the table. If you explicitly drop a particular column, all columns currently marked as unused in the target table are dropped at the same time.
  When the column data is dropped:

- All indexes defined on any of the target columns are also dropped.

- All constraints that reference a target column are removed.

- If any statistics types are associated with the target columns, Oracle disassociates the statistics from the column with the FORCE option and drops any statistics collected using the statistics type.

NOTE
If a constraint also references a nontarget column, Oracle returns an error and does not drop the column unless you have specified the CASCADE CONSTRAINTS clause. If you have specified that clause, Oracle removes all constraints that reference any of the target columns.

- DROP UNUSED COLUMNS removes from the table all columns currently marked as unused. Use this statement when you want to reclaim the extra disk space from unused columns in the table. If the table contains no unused columns, the statement returns with no errors.

- *column* specifies one or more columns to be set as unused or dropped. Use the COLUMN keyword only if you are specifying only one column. If you specify a column list, it cannot contain duplicates.

- CASCADE CONSTRAINTS drops all referential integrity constraints that refer to the primary and unique keys defined on the dropped columns, and drops all multicolumn constraints defined on the dropped columns. If any constraint is referenced by columns from other tables or remaining columns in the target table, then you must specify CASCADE CONSTRAINTS. Otherwise, the statement aborts and an error is returned.

- INVALIDATE   Note: Currently, Oracle executes this clause regardless of whether you specify the keyword INVALIDATE. Oracle invalidates all dependent objects, such as views, triggers, and stored program units. Object invalidation is a recursive process. Therefore, all directly dependent *and* indirectly dependent objects are invalidated. However, only local dependencies are invalidated, because Oracle manages remote dependencies differently from local dependencies. For more information on dependencies, refer to *Oracle8i Concepts*. An object invalidated by this statement is automatically revalidated when next referenced. You must then correct any errors that exist in that object before referencing it.

- CHECKPOINT specifies that a checkpoint for the drop column operation will be applied after processing *integer* rows; *integer* is optional and must be greater than zero. If *integer* is greater than the number of rows in the table, Oracle applies a checkpoint after all the rows have been processed. If you do not specify *integer*, Oracle sets the default of 512. Checkpointing cuts down the amount of undo logs accumulated during the drop column operation to avoid running out of rollback segment space. However, if this statement is interrupted after a checkpoint has been applied, the table remains in an unusable state. While the table is unusable, the only operations allowed on it are DROP TABLE, TRUNCATE TABLE, and ALTER TABLE DROP COLUMNS CONTINUE (described below). You cannot use this clause with SET UNUSED, because that clause does not remove column data.

- DROP COLUMNS CONTINUE continues the drop column operation from the point at which it was interrupted. Submitting this statement while the table is in a valid state results in an error.

Restrictions: Each of the parts of the *drop_column_clause* can be specified only once in the statement and cannot be mixed with any other ALTER TABLE clauses. For example, the following statements are not allowed:

```
ALTER TABLE t1 DROP COLUMN f1 DROP (f2);
ALTER TABLE t1 DROP COLUMN f1 SET UNUSED (f2);
ALTER TABLE t1 DROP (f1) ADD (f2 NUMBER);
ALTER TABLE t1 SET UNUSED (f3)
ADD (CONSTRAINT ck1 CHECK (f2 > 0));
```

You can drop an object type column only as an entity. Dropping an attribute from an object type column is not allowed.
If you drop a nested table column, its storage table is removed.
If you drop a LOB column, the LOB data and its corresponding LOB index segment are removed.
If you drop a BFILE column, only the locators stored in that column are removed, not the files referenced by the locators.
You can drop a column from an index-organized table only if it is not a primary key column. The primary key constraint of an index-organized table can never be dropped, so you cannot drop a primary key column even if you have specified CASCADE CONSTRAINTS.
You can export tables with dropped or unused columns. However, you can import a table only if all the columns specified in the export files are present in the table (that is, none of those columns has been dropped or marked unused). Otherwise, Oracle returns an error.
You cannot drop a column on which a domain index has been built.

You cannot use this clause to drop:

A pseudocolumn, clustered column, or partitioning column. (You can drop nonpartitioning columns from a partitioned table if all the tablespaces where the partitions were created are online and in read-write mode.)

A column from a nested table, an object table, or a table owned by SYS.

- *allocate_extent_clause* explicitly allocates a new extent for the table, the partition or subpartition, the overflow data segment, the LOB data segment, or the LOB index.
  Restriction: You cannot allocate an extent for a composite-partitioned table.

  - SIZE specifies the size of the extent in bytes. Use K or M to specify the extent size in kilobytes or megabytes. If you omit this parameter, Oracle determines the size based on the values of the STORAGE parameters of the table's overflow data segment or of the LOB index.

  - DATAFILE specifies one of the datafiles in the tablespace of the table, overflow data segment, LOB data tablespace, or LOB index to contain the new extent. If you omit this parameter, Oracle chooses the datafile.

  - INSTANCE makes the new extent available to the freelist group associated with the specified instance. If the instance number exceeds the maximum number of freelist groups, the former is divided by the latter, and the remainder is used to identify the freelist group to be used. An instance is identified by the value of its initialization parameter INSTANCE_NUMBER. If you omit this parameter, the space is allocated to the table, but is not drawn from any particular freelist group. Rather, the master freelist is used, and space is allocated as needed. For more information, see *Oracle8i Concepts*. **Use this parameter only if you are using Oracle with the Parallel Server option in parallel mode.**

Explicitly allocating an extent with this clause does affect the size for the next extent to be allocated as specified by the NEXT and PCTINCREASE storage parameters.

- *deallocate_unused_clause* explicitly deallocates unused space at the end of the table, partition or subpartition, overflow data segment, LOB data segment, or LOB index and makes the space available for other segments in the tablespace. You can free only unused space above the high water mark (that is, the point beyond which database blocks have not yet been formatted to receive data).

  Oracle credits the amount of the released space to the user quota for the tablespace in which the deallocation occurs.

  Oracle deallocates unused space from the end of the object toward the high water mark at the beginning of the object. If an extent is completely contained in the deallocation, then the whole extent is freed for reuse. If an extent is partially contained in the deallocation, then the used part up to the high water mark becomes the extent, and the remaining unused space is freed for reuse. The exact amount of space freed depends on the values of the INITIAL, MINEXTENTS, and NEXT parameters.

  - KEEP specifies the number of bytes above the high water mark that the table, overflow data segment, LOB data segment, or LOB index will have after deallocation.

    If you omit KEEP and the high water mark is above the size of INITIAL and MINEXTENTS, then all unused space above the high water mark is freed. When the high water mark is less than the size of INITIAL or MINEXTENTS, then all unused space above MINEXTENTS is freed.

    If you specify KEEP, then the specified amount of space is kept and the remaining space is freed. When the remaining number of extents is less than MINEXTENTS, then MINEXTENTS is adjusted to the new number of extents. If the initial extent becomes smaller than INITIAL, then INITIAL is adjusted to the new size.

    In either case, NEXT is set to the size of the last extent that was deallocated.

- CACHE   For data that is accessed frequently, specifies that the blocks retrieved for this table are placed at the most recently used end of the LRU list in the buffer cache when a full table scan is performed. This attribute is useful for small lookup tables.
  Restriction: You cannot specify CACHE for index-organized tables.

- NOCACHE for data that is not accessed frequently, specifies that the blocks retrieved for this table are placed at the least recently used end of the LRU list in the buffer cache when a full table scan is performed.
  For LOBs, the LOB value is either not brought into the buffer cache or brought into the buffer cache and placed at the least recently used end of the LRU list. (The latter is the default behavior.)
  Restriction: You cannot specify NOCACHE for index-organized tables.

- MONITORING specifies that Oracle can collect modification statistics on *table*. These statistics are estimates of the number of rows affected by DML statements over a particular period of time. They are available for use by the optimizer or for analysis by the user. For more information on using this clause, see *Oracle8i Tuning*.

- NOMONITORING specifies that Oracle will not collect modification statistics on *table*.
  Restriction: You cannot specify MONITORING or NOMONITORING for a temporary table.

- LOGGING | NOLOGGING specifies whether subsequent Direct Loader (SQL*Loader) and direct-load INSERT operations against a nonpartitioned table, table partition, all partitions of a partitioned table, or all subpartitions of a partition will be logged (LOGGING) or not logged (NOLOGGING) in the redo log file.

When used with the *modify_default_attributes_clause*, this clause affects the logging attribute of a partitioned table.

LOGGING | NOLOGGING also specifies whether ALTER TABLE...MOVE and ALTER TABLE...SPLIT operations will be logged or not logged.

In NOLOGGING mode, data is modified with minimal logging (to mark new extents invalid and to record dictionary changes). When applied during media recovery, the extent invalidation records mark a range of blocks as logically corrupt, because the redo data is not logged. Therefore, if you cannot afford to lose this table, it is important to take a backup after the NOLOGGING operation.

If the database is run in ARCHIVELOG mode, media recovery from a backup taken before the LOGGING operation will restore the table. However, media recovery from a backup taken before the NOLOGGING operation will not restore the table.

The logging attribute of the base table is independent of that of its indexes. For more information about the *logging_clause* and parallel DML, *see Oracle8i Parallel Server Concepts and Administration.*

- RENAME TO renames *table* to *new_table_name*.

NOTE
Using this clause will invalidate any dependent materialized views.
For more information on materialized views, see Oracle8i Tuning.

- ***records_per_block_clause*** determines whether Oracle restricts the number of records that can be stored in a block.
  This clause ensures that any bitmap indexes subsequently created on the table will be as small (compressed) as possible.
  Restrictions: You cannot specify either MINIMIZE or NOMINIMIZE if a bitmap index has already been defined on *table*. You must first drop the bitmap index.
  You cannot specify this clause for an index-organized table or nested table.

  - MINIMIZE instructs Oracle to calculate the largest number of records in any block in the table, and limit future inserts so that no block can contain more than that number of records.
    Restriction: You cannot specify MINIMIZE for an empty table.

  - NOMINIMIZE disables the MINIMIZE feature. This is the default.

- ***alter_overflow_clause*** modifies the definition of an index-organized table. Index-organized tables keep data sorted on the primary key and are therefore best suited for primary-key-based access and manipulation.

NOTE
When you alter an index-organized table, Oracle evaluates the maximum size of each column to estimate the largest possible row. If an overflow segment is needed but you have not specified OVERFLOW, Oracle raises an error and does not execute the ALTER TABLE statement. This checking function guarantees that subsequent DML operations on the index-organized table will not fail because an overflow segment is lacking.

  - PCTTHRESHOLD *integer* specifies the percentage of space reserved in the index block for an index-organized table row. Any portion of the row that exceeds the specified threshold

is stored in the overflow area. PCTTHRESHOLD must be a value from 1 to 50.
Restrictions: You cannot reduce the value of PCTTHRESHOLD so much that the primary key will not fit.
You cannot specify PCTTHRESHOLD for individual partitions of an index-organized table.

■ INCLUDING *column_name* specifies the column at which to divide an index-organized table row into index and overflow portions. All non-primary-key columns that follow *column_name* are stored in the overflow data segment. The *column_name* is either the name of the last primary key column or any subsequent non-primary-key column.
If you use the *drop_column_clause* to drop (or mark unused) a column defined as an INCLUDING column, the column stored immediately before this column will become the new INCLUDING column.

■ *overflow_clause* specifies the overflow data segment physical storage and logging attributes to be modified for the index-organized table. Parameters specified in this clause are applicable only to the overflow data segment.
Restriction: You cannot specify OVERFLOW for a partition of a partitioned index-organized table unless the table already has an overflow segment.

■ *add_overflow_clause* adds an overflow data segment to the specified index-organized table. For a partitioned index-organized table:

■ If you do not specify PARTITION, Oracle automatically allocates an overflow segment for each partition. The physical attributes of these segments are inherited from the table level.

■ If you wish to specify separate physical attributes for one or more partitions, you must specify such attributes for **every** partition in the table. You do not specify the name of the partitions, but you must specify their attributes in the order in which they were created.
You can find the order of the partitions by querying the PARTITION_NAME and PARTITION_POSITION columns of the USER_IND_PARTITIONS view.

■ If you do not specify TABLESPACE for a particular partition, Oracle uses the tablespace specified for the table. If you do not specify TABLESPACE at the table level, Oracle uses the tablespace of the partition's primary key index segment.

■ *partitioning_clauses*   The following clauses apply only to partitioned tables. You cannot combine partition operations with other partition operations or with operations on the base table in one ALTER TABLE statement.

NOTE
If you drop, exchange, truncate, move, modify, or split a partition on a table that is a master table for one or more materialized views, existing bulk load information about the table will be deleted. Therefore, be sure to refresh all dependent materialized views before performing any of these operations.

■ *modify_default_attributes_clause* specifies new default values for the attributes of *table*. Partitions and LOB partitions you create subsequently will inherit these values unless you override them explicitly when creating the partition or LOB partition. Existing partitions and LOB partitions are not affected by this clause.
Only attributes named in the statement are affected, and the default values specified are overridden by any attributes specified at the individual partition level.

- FOR PARTITION applies only to composite-partitioned tables. This clause specifies new default values for the attributes of *partition*. Subpartitions and LOB subpartitions of *partition* that you create subsequently will inherit these values, unless you override them explicitly when creating the subpartition or LOB subpartition. Existing subpartitions are not affected by this clause.

  Restrictions: The PCTTHRESHOLD, COMPRESS, *physical_attributes_clause*, and *overflow_clause* are valid only for partitioned index-organized tables.

  You cannot specify the PCTUSED parameter for the index segment of an index-organized table.

  You can specify COMPRESS only if compression is already specified at the table level.

- *modify_partition_clause* modifies the real physical attributes of the *partition* table partition. Optionally modifies the storage attributes of one or more LOB items for the partition. You can specify new values for any of the following physical attributes for the partition: the logging attribute; PCTFREE, PCTUSED, INITRANS, or MAXTRANS parameter; or storage parameters. If *table* is composite-partitioned:

  - If you specify the *allocate_extent_clause*, Oracle will allocate an extent for each subpartition of *partition*.

  - If you specify *deallocate_unused_clause*, Oracle will deallocate unused storage from each subpartition of *partition*.

  - Any other attributes changed in this clause will be changed in subpartitions of *partition* as well, overriding existing values. To avoid changing the attributes of existing subpartitions, use the FOR PARTITION clause of the *modify_default_attributes_clause*.

    Restriction: If *table* is hash partitioned, you can specify only the *allocate_extent* and *deallocate_unused* clauses. All other attributes of the partition are inherited from the table-level defaults except TABLESPACE, which stays the same as it was at create time.

  - *add_subpartition_clause* adds a hash subpartition to *partition*. Oracle populates the new subpartition with rows rehashed from the other subpartition(s) of *partition* as determined by the hash function.

    Oracle marks UNUSABLE, and you must rebuild, the local index subpartitions corresponding to the added and to the rehashed subpartitions.

    If you do not specify *subpartition*, Oracle assigns a name in the form SYS_SUB*Pnnnn*. If you do not specify TABLESPACE, the new subpartition will reside in the default tablespace of *partition*.

  - COALESCE SUBPARTITION specifies that Oracle should select a hash subpartition, distribute its contents into one or more remaining subpartitions (determined by the hash function), and then drop the selected subpartition.

    Local index subpartitions corresponding to the selected subpartition are also dropped. Oracle marks UNUSABLE, and you must rebuild, the index subpartitions corresponding to one or more absorbing subpartitions.

  - UNUSABLE LOCAL INDEXES clause

    The next two clauses modify the attributes of local **index partitions** corresponding to *partition*.

    - UNUSABLE LOCAL INDEXES marks UNUSABLE all the local index partitions associated with *partition*.

    - REBUILD UNUSABLE LOCAL INDEXES rebuilds the unusable local index partitions associated with *partition*.

Restrictions: You cannot specify this clause with any other clauses of the *modify_partition_clause*.
You cannot specify this clause for partitions that are subpartitioned.

■ ***modify_subpartition_clause*** lets you allocate or deallocate storage for an individual subpartition of *table*.
Restriction: The only *modify_LOB_storage_parameters* you can specify for subpartition are the *allocate_extent_clause* and *deallocate_unused_clause*.

  ■ UNUSABLE LOCAL INDEXES marks UNUSABLE all the local index subpartitions associated with *subpartition*.

  ■ REBUILD UNUSABLE LOCAL INDEXES rebuilds the unusable local index subpartitions associated with su*bpartition*.

■ ***rename_partition/subpartition_clause*** renames a table partition or subpartition *current_name* to *new_name*. For both partitions and subpartitions, *new_name* must be different from all existing partitions and subpartitions of the same table.

■ ***move_partition_clause*** moves table partition *partition* to another segment. You can move partition data to another tablespace, recluster data to reduce fragmentation, or change create-time physical attributes.
If the table contains LOB columns, you can use the *LOB_storage_clause* to move the LOB data and LOB index segments associated with this partition. Only the LOBs named are affected. If you do not specify the *LOB_storage_clause* for a particular LOB column, its LOB data and LOB index segments are not moved.
If *partition* is not empty, MOVE PARTITION marks UNUSABLE all corresponding local index partitions and all global nonpartitioned indexes, and all the partitions of global partitioned indexes. When you move a LOB data segment, Oracle drops the old data segment and corresponding index segment and creates new segments even if you do not specify a new tablespace.
The move operation obtains its parallel attribute from the *parallel_clause*, if specified. If not specified, the default parallel attributes of the table, if any, are used. If neither is specified, Oracle performs the move without using parallelism.
The *parallel_clause* on MOVE PARTITION does not change the default parallel attributes of *table*.

NOTE
For index-organized tables, Oracle uses the address of the primary key, as well as its value, to construct logical rowids. The logical rowids are stored in the secondary index of the table. If you move a partition of an index-organized table, the address portion of the rowids will change, which can hamper performance. To ensure optimal performance, rebuild the secondary index(es) on the moved partition to update the rowids. For more information on logical rowids, see Oracle8i Concepts.

Restrictions: If *partition* is a hash partition, the only attribute you can specify in this clause is TABLESPACE.
You cannot move a partition of a composite-partitioned table. You must move each subpartition separately with the *move_subpartition_clause*.
You cannot specify this clause for a partition containing subpartitions. However, you can move subpartitions using the *move_subpartition_clause*.

■ **move_subpartition_clause** moves the table subpartition *subpartition* to another segment. If you do not specify TABLESPACE, the subpartition will remain in the same tablespace.

Unless the subpartition is empty, Oracle marks UNUSABLE all local index subpartitions corresponding to the subpartition being moved, as well as global nonpartitioned indexes and partitions of global indexes.

If the table contains LOB columns, you can use the *LOB_storage_clause* to move the LOB data and LOB index segments associated with this subpartition. Only the LOBs named are affected. If you do not specify the *LOB_storage_clause* for a particular LOB column, its LOB data and LOB index segments are not moved.

When you move a LOB data segment, Oracle drops the old data segment and corresponding index segment and creates new segments even if you do not specify a new tablespace.

■ **add_range_partition_clause** adds a new range partition *partition* to the "high" end of a partitioned table (after the last existing partition). You can specify any create-time physical attributes for the new partition. If the table contains LOB columns, you can also specify partition-level attributes for one or more LOB items.

You can specify up to 64K-1 partitions. For a discussion of factors that might impose practical limits less than this number, refer to *Oracle8i Administrator's Guide.*

Restrictions: If the first element of the partition bound of the high partition is MAXVALUE, you cannot add a partition to the table. Instead, use the *split_partition_clause* to add a partition at the beginning or the middle of the table.

The *compression_clause*, *physical_attributes_clause*, and OVERFLOW are valid only for a partitioned index-organized table.

You cannot specify the PCTUSED parameter for the index segment of an index-organized table. You can specify OVERFLOW only if the partitioned table already has an overflow segment. You can specify compression only if compression is enabled at the table level.

■ VALUES LESS THAN *(value_list)* specifies the upper bound for the new partition. The *value_list* is a comma-separated, ordered list of literal values corresponding to *column_list.* The *value_list* must collate greater than the partition bound for the highest existing partition in the table.

■ *partition_level_subpartitioning* is permitted only for a composite-partitioned table. This clause lets you specify particular hash subpartitions for *partition.* You specify composite partitioning in one of two ways:

You can specify individual subpartitions by name, and optionally the tablespace where each should be stored, or

You can specify the number of subpartitions (and optionally one or more tablespaces where they are to be stored). In this case, Oracle assigns partition names of the form SYS_SUB*Pnn*n. The number of tablespaces does not have to equal the number of subpartitions. If the number of subpartitions is greater than the number of tablespaces, Oracle cycles through the names of the tablespaces.

The subpartitions inherit all their attributes from any attributes specified for *new_partition,* except for TABLESPACE, which you can specify at the subpartition level. Any attributes not specified at the subpartition or partition level are inherited from table-level defaults.

This clause overrides any subpartitioning specified at the table level. If you do not specify this clause but you specified default subpartitioning at the table level, *new_partition_name* will inherit the table-level default subpartitioning.

■ **add_hash_partition_clause** adds a new hash partition to the "high" end of a partitioned table. Oracle will populate the new partition with rows rehashed from other partitions of *table* as determined by the hash function.

You can specify a name for the partition, and optionally a tablespace where it should be stored. If you do not specify *new_partition_name*, Oracle assigns a partition name of the form SYS_*Pnnn*. If you do not specify TABLESPACE, the new partition is stored in the table's default tablespace. Other attributes are always inherited from table-level defaults.

For more information on hash partitioning, see and *Oracle8i Concepts*.

   ■ *parallel_clause* lets you specify whether to parallelize the creation of the new partition.

■ **coalesce_partition_clause** applies only to hash-partitioned tables. This clause specifies that Oracle should select a hash partition, distribute its contents into one or more remaining partitions (determined by the hash function), and then drop the selected partition. Local index partitions corresponding to the selected partition are also dropped. Oracle marks UNUSABLE, and you must rebuild, the local index partitions corresponding to one or more absorbing partitions.

■ **drop_partition_clause** applies only to tables partitioned using the range or composite method. This clause removes partition *partition*, and the data in that partition, from a partitioned table. If you want to drop a partition but keep its data in the table, you must merge the partition into one of the adjacent partitions. See the *merge_partitions_clause* of this statement.

If the table has LOB columns, the LOB data and LOB index partitions (and their subpartitions, if any) corresponding to *partition* are also dropped:

   ■ Oracle drops local index partitions and subpartitions corresponding to *partition*, even if they are marked UNUSABLE.

   ■ Oracle marks UNUSABLE all global nonpartitioned indexes defined on the table and all partitions of global partitioned indexes, unless the partition being dropped or all of its subpartitions are empty.

   ■ If you drop a partition and later insert a row that would have belonged to the dropped partition, Oracle stores the row in the next higher partition. However, if that partition is the highest partition, the insert will fail because the range of values represented by the dropped partition is no longer valid for the table.

   Restriction: If *table* contains only one partition, you cannot drop the partition. You must drop the table.

truncate_partition_clause, truncate_subpartition_clause

■ PARTITION removes all rows from *partition* or, if the table is composite-partitioned, all rows from *partition*'s subpartitions. SUBPARTITION removes all rows from *subpartition*.

If the table contains any LOB columns, the LOB data and LOB index segments for this partition are also truncated. If the table is composite-partitioned, the LOB data and LOB index segments for this partition's subpartitions are truncated.

If the partition or subpartition to be truncated contains data, you must first disable any referential integrity constraints on the table. Alternatively, you can delete the rows and then truncate the partition.

For each partition or subpartition truncated, Oracle also truncates corresponding local index partitions and subpartitions. If those index partitions or subpartitions are marked UNUSABLE, Oracle truncates them and resets the UNUSABLE marker to VALID. In addition, if the truncated partition or subpartition, or any of the subpartitions of the truncated partition are not empty, Oracle marks as UNUSABLE *all* global nonpartitioned indexes and partitions of global indexes defined on the table.

■ DROP STORAGE deallocates space from the deleted rows and makes it available for use by other schema objects in the tablespace.

■ REUSE STORAGE keeps space from the deleted rows allocated to the partition or subpartition. The space is subsequently available only for inserts and updates to the same partition or subpartition.

■ *split_partition_clause* from an original partition *partition_name_old*, creates two new partitions, each with a new segment and new physical attributes, and new initial extents. The segment associated with *partition_name_old* is discarded.
Restriction: You cannot specify this clause for a hash-partitioned table.

   ■ AT (*value_list*) specifies the new noninclusive upper bound for *split_partition_*1. The *value_list* must compare less than the original partition bound for *partition_name_old* and greater than the partition bound for the next lowest partition (if there is one).

   ■ INTO describes the two partitions resulting from the split.

   ■ *partition_description, partition_description* specifies optional names and physical attributes of the two partitions resulting from the split. If you do not specify new partition names, Oracle assigns names of the form SYS_P*n*. Any attributes you do not specify are inherited from *partition_name_old*.
   Restriction: You can specify the *compression_clause, physical_attributes_clause*, and OVERFLOW only for a partitioned index-organized table.
   You cannot specify the PCTUSED parameter for the index segment of an index-organized table.

   ■ *parallel_clause* parallelizes the split operation, but does not change the default parallel attributes of the table.
   If you specify subpartitioning for the new partitions, you can specify only TABLESPACE for the subpartitions. All other attributes will be inherited from the containing new partition.
   If *partition_name_old* is subpartitioned, and you do not specify any subpartitioning for the new partitions, the new partitions will inherit the number and tablespaces of the subpartitions in *partition_name_old*.
   Oracle also splits corresponding local index partitions, even if they are marked UNUSABLE. The resulting local index partitions inherit all their partition-level default attributes from the local index partition being split.
   If *partition_name_old* was not empty, Oracle marks UNUSABLE *all* global nonpartitioned indexes and all partitions of global indexes on the table. (This action on global indexes does not apply to index-organized tables.) In addition, if any partitions or subpartitions resulting from the split are not empty, Oracle marks as UNUSABLE all corresponding local index partitions and subpartitions.
   If *table* contains LOB columns, you can use the *LOB_storage_clause* to specify separate LOB storage attributes for the LOB data segments resulting from the split. Oracle drops the LOB data and LOB index segments of *partition_name_old* and creates new segments for each LOB column, for each partition, even if you do not specify a new tablespace.

■ *merge_partitions_clause* merges the contents of two adjacent partitions of *table* into one new partition, and then drops the original two partitions.
The new partition inherits the partition-bound of the higher of the two original partitions. Any attributes not specified in the *segment_attributes_clause* are inherited from table-level defaults. If you do not specify *new_partition_name*, Oracle assigns a name of the form SYS_P*nnn*. If the new partition has subpartitions, Oracle assigns subpartition names of the form SYS_SUB*Pnnn*n.

If either or both of the original partitions was not empty, Oracle marks UNUSABLE *all* global nonpartitioned global indexes and all partitions of global indexes on the table. In addition, if the partition or any of its subpartitions resulting from the merge is not empty, Oracle marks UNUSABLE all corresponding local index partitions and subpartitions.

Restriction: You cannot specify this clause for an index-organized table or for a table partitioned using the hash method.

- ■ *partition_level_partitioning* specifies hash subpartitioning attributes for the new partition. Any attributes not specified in this clause are inherited from table-level defaults.
  If you do not specify this clause, the new merged partition inherits subpartitioning attributes from table-level defaults.

- ■ *parallel_clause* specifies that the merging operation is to be parallelized.

- ■ **exchange_partition_clause, exchange_subpartition_clause** converts a partition (or subpartition) into a nonpartitioned table, and a nonpartitioned table into a partition (or subpartition) of a partitioned table by exchanging their data (and index) segments. The default behavior is EXCLUDING INDEXES WITH VALIDATION.
  You must have ALTER TABLE privileges on **both** tables to perform this operation.
  This clause facilitates high-speed data loading when used with transportable tablespaces.
  For information on this topic, see *Oracle8i Administrator's Guide*.
  If *table* contains LOB columns, for each LOB column Oracle exchanges LOB data and LOB index partition or subpartition segments with corresponding LOB data and LOB index segments of *table*.
  All statistics of the table and partition are exchanged, including table, column, index statistics, and histograms. The aggregate statistics of the partitioned table are recalculated.
  The logging attribute of the table and partition is also exchanged.

  - ■ WITH TABLE *table* specifies the table with which the partition will be exchanged.

  - ■ INCLUDING INDEXES specifies that the local index partitions or subpartitions should be exchanged with the corresponding regular indexes.

  - ■ EXCLUDING INDEXES specifies that all the local index partitions or subpartitions corresponding to the partition and all the regular indexes on the exchanged table are marked UNUSABLE.

  - ■ WITH VALIDATION specifies that if any rows in the exchanged table do not map into partitions or subpartitions being exchanged, Oracle should return an error.

  - ■ WITHOUT VALIDATION specifies that the proper mapping of rows in the exchanged table is not checked.

  - ■ EXCEPTIONS INTO   This clause applies only to loading a nonpartitioned table into a partitioned table. It lets you specify a table into which Oracle places the rowids of all rows violating the partitioned table's UNIQUE constraint. The script used to create such a table is UTLEXCPT1.SQL.

NOTE
You can use the UTLEXCPT1.SQL script with index-organized tables.
You could not use earlier versions of the script for this purpose. See
Oracle8i Migration *for compatibility information.*

Restrictions: This clause is not valid with subpartitions.
The partitioned table must have been defined with a UNIQUE constraint, and that constraint must be in DISABLE VALIDATE state.
If these conditions are not true, Oracle ignores this clause.

Restrictions: For partitioned index-organized tables, the following restrictions apply:
The source and target table/partition must have their primary key set on the same columns, in the same order.
If compression is enabled, it must be enabled for both the source and the target, and with the same prefix length.
An index-organized table partition cannot be exchanged with a regular table or vice versa.
Both the source and target must have overflow segments, or neither can have overflow segments.

- ■ *row_movement_clause* determines whether a row can be moved to a different partition or subpartition because of a change to one or more of its key values.
  Restriction: You can specify this clause only for a partitioned table.

  - ■ ENABLE allows Oracle to move a row to a different partition or subpartition as the result of an update to the partitioning or subpartitioning key.
    Restriction: You cannot specify this clause if a domain index has been built on any column of the table.

CAUTION
Moving a row in the course of an UPDATE operation changes that row's ROWID.

  - ■ DISABLE returns an error if an update to a partitioning or subpartitioning key would result in a row moving to a different partition or subpartition. This is the default.

- ■ *parallel_clause* changes the default degree of parallelism for queries and DML on the table.

  - ■ NOPARALLEL specifies serial execution. This is the default.

  - ■ PARALLEL causes Oracle to select a degree of parallelism equal to the number of CPUs available on all participating instances times the value of the PARALLEL_THREADS_PER_CPU initialization parameter.

  - ■ PARALLEL *integer* specifies the **degree of parallelism**, which is the number of parallel threads used in the parallel operation. Each parallel thread may use one or two parallel execution processes. Normally Oracle calculates the optimum degree of parallelism, so it is not necessary for you to specify *integer*.
    Restriction: If *table* contains any columns of LOB or user-defined object type, subsequent INSERT, UPDATE, and DELETE operations on *table* are executed serially without notification. Subsequent queries, however, will be executed in parallel.

NOTE
If you specify the parallel_clause in conjunction with the move_table_clause, the parallelism applies only to the move, not to subsequent DML and query operations on the table.

- ■ *enable_disable_clause* lets you specify whether Oracle should apply an integrity constraint.

- ENABLE TABLE LOCK enables DML and DDL locks on a table in a parallel server environment. For more information, see *Oracle8i Parallel Server Concepts and Administration*.

NOTE
DML table locks are not acquired on temporary tables.

- DISABLE TABLE LOCK disables DML and DDL locks on a table to improve performance in a parallel server environment. For more information, see *Oracle8i Parallel Server Concepts and Administration*.

- ENABLE ALL TRIGGERS enables all triggers associated with the table. Oracle fires the triggers whenever their triggering condition is satisfied.
  To enable a single trigger, use the *enable_clause* of ALTER TRIGGER.

- DISABLE ALL TRIGGERS disables all triggers associated with the table. Oracle will not fire a disabled trigger even if the triggering condition is satisfied.

ALTER TABLESPACE

Syntax

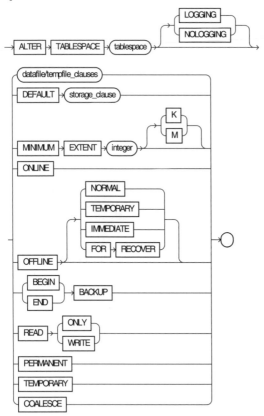

datafile/tempfile_clauses::=

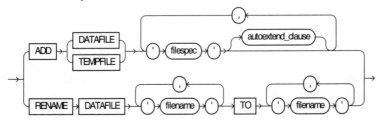

autoextend_clause::=

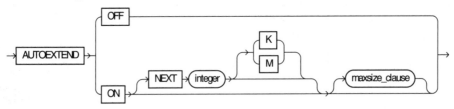

maxsize_clause::=

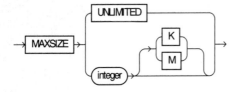

Purpose

To alter an existing tablespace or one or more of its datafiles or tempfiles.

Prerequisites

If you have ALTER TABLESPACE system privilege, you can perform any of this statement's operations. If you have MANAGE TABLESPACE system privilege, you can only perform the following operations:

- Take the tablespace online or offline.
- Begin or end a backup.
- Make the tablespace read-only or read-write.

Before you can make a tablespace read-only, the following conditions must be met:

- The tablespace must be online.

- The tablespace must not contain any active rollback segments. For this reason, the SYSTEM tablespace can never be made read-only, because it contains the SYSTEM rollback segment. Additionally, because the rollback segments of a read-only tablespace are not accessible, Oracle recommends that you drop the rollback segments before you make a tablespace read-only.

- The tablespace must not be involved in an open backup, because the end of a backup updates the header file of all datafiles in the tablespace.

Performing this function in restricted mode may help you meet these restrictions, because only users with RESTRICTED SESSION system privilege can be logged on.

Keywords and Parameters

- *tablespace* is the name of the tablespace to be altered.

- LOGGING | NOLOGGING specifies the default logging attribute of all tables, indexes, and partitions within the tablespace. The tablespace-level logging attribute can be overridden by logging specifications at the table, index, and partition levels.
  When an existing tablespace logging attribute is changed by an ALTER TABLESPACE statement, all tables, indexes, and partitions created *after* the statement will have the new default logging attribute (which you can still subsequently override). The logging attributes of existing objects are not changed.
  Only the following operations support NOLOGGING mode:
  DML: direct-load INSERT (serial or parallel); Direct Loader (SQL*Loader)
  DDL: CREATE TABLE... AS SELECT, CREATE INDEX, ALTER INDEX... REBUILD, ALTER INDEX... REBUILD PARTITION, ALTER INDEX... SPLIT PARTITION, ALTER TABLE... SPLIT PARTITION, ALTER TABLE... MOVE PARTITION.
  In NOLOGGING mode, data is modified with minimal logging (to mark new extents invalid and to record dictionary changes). When applied during media recovery, the extent invalidation records mark a range of blocks as logically corrupt, because the redo data is not logged. Therefore, if you cannot afford to lose the object, it is important to take a backup after the NOLOGGING operation.

- *datafile/tempfile_clauses* adds or modifies a datafile or tempfile.

  - ADD DATAFILE | TEMPFILE adds to the tablespace a datafile or tempfile specified by *filespec*. You can add a datafile or tempfile to a locally managed tablespace that is online or to a dictionary managed tablespace that is online or offline. Be sure the file is not in use by another database.

NOTE
As the syntax shows, you cannot combine an ADD clause with any other clauses in the same ALTER TABLESPACE statement. In addition, for a locally managed temporary tablespace, you cannot specify any of the other clauses for this tablespace at any time.

■ RENAME DATAFILE renames one or more of the tablespace's datafiles. Take the tablespace offline before renaming the datafile. Each '*filename*' must fully specify a datafile using the conventions for filenames on your operating system. This clause merely associates the tablespace with the new file rather than the old one. This clause does not actually change the name of the operating system file. You must change the name of the file through your operating system.

■ ***autoextend_clause*** enables or disables the autoextending of the size of the datafile in the tablespace.

   ■ OFF disables autoextend if it is turned on. NEXT and MAXSIZE are set to zero. Values for NEXT and MAXSIZE must be respecified in further ALTER TABLESPACE AUTOEXTEND statements.

   ■ ON enables autoextend.

   ■ NEXT specifies the size in bytes of the next increment of disk space to be allocated automatically to the datafile when more extents are required. Use K or M to specify this size in kilobytes or megabytes. The default is one data block.

   ■ *maxsize_clause* specifies maximum disk space allowed for automatic extension of the datafile.

      ■ UNLIMITED sets no limit on allocating disk space to the datafile.

■ DEFAULT ***storage_clause*** specifies the new default storage parameters for objects subsequently created in the tablespace. For a dictionary-managed temporary table, Oracle considers only the NEXT parameter of the *storage_clause*.
   Restriction: You cannot specify this clause for a locally managed tablespace.

■ MINIMUM EXTENT *integer* controls free space fragmentation in the tablespace by ensuring that every used or free extent size in a tablespace is at least as large as, and is a multiple of, *integer*. This clause is not relevant for a dictionary-managed temporary tablespace. For more information about using MINIMUM EXTENT to control space fragmentation, see *Oracle8i Administrator's Guide*.
   Restriction: You cannot specify this clause for a locally managed tablespace.

■ ONLINE brings the tablespace online.

■ OFFLINE takes the tablespace offline and prevents further access to its segments.

   ■ NORMAL flushes all blocks in all datafiles in the tablespace out of the SGA. You need not perform media recovery on this tablespace before bringing it back online. This is the default.

   ■ TEMPORARY performs a checkpoint for all online datafiles in the tablespace but does not ensure that all files can be written. Any offline files may require media recovery before you bring the tablespace back online.

   ■ IMMEDIATE does not ensure that tablespace files are available and does not perform a checkpoint. You must perform media recovery on the tablespace before bringing it back online.

■ FOR RECOVER takes the production database tablespaces in the recovery set offline for tablespace point-in-time recovery. For additional information see *Oracle8i Backup and Recovery Guide.*

TIP
Before taking a tablespace offline for a long time, you may want to alter the tablespace allocation of any users who have been assigned the tablespace as either a default or temporary tablespace. When the tablespace is offline, these users cannot allocate space for objects or sort areas in the tablespace.

■ BEGIN BACKUP signifies that an open backup is to be performed on the datafiles that make up this tablespace. This clause does not prevent users from accessing the tablespace. You must use this clause before beginning an open backup. You cannot use this clause on a read-only tablespace.

NOTE
While the backup is in progress, you cannot take the tablespace offline normally, shut down the instance, or begin another backup of the tablespace.

■ END BACKUP signifies that an open backup of the tablespace is complete. Use this clause as soon as possible after completing an open backup. You cannot use this clause on a read-only tablespace. If you forget to indicate the end of an online tablespace backup, and an instance failure or SHUTDOWN ABORT occurs, Oracle assumes that media recovery (possibly requiring archived redo log) is necessary at the next instance start up. To restart the database without media recovery, see *Oracle8i Administrator's Guide.*

■ READ ONLY signifies that no further write operations are allowed on the tablespace. (This clause waits for all existing transactions either to commit or roll back before taking effect.) The tablespace becomes read only.
Once a tablespace is read only, you can copy its files to read-only media. You must then rename the datafiles in the control file to point to the new location by using the SQL statement ALTER DATABASE ... RENAME. For more information on read-only tablespaces, see *Oracle8i Concepts.*

■ READ WRITE signifies that write operations are allowed on a previously read-only tablespace.

■ PERMANENT specifies that the tablespace is to be converted from a temporary to a permanent one. A permanent tablespace is one in which permanent database objects can be stored. This is the default when a tablespace is created.

■ TEMPORARY specifies that the tablespace is to be converted from a permanent to a temporary one. A temporary tablespace is one in which no permanent database objects can be stored. Objects in a temporary tablespace persist only for the duration of the session.

■ COALESCE   For each datafile in the tablespace, coalesces all contiguous free extents into larger contiguous extents.
Restriction: COALESCE cannot be specified with any other statement clause.

ALTER USER

Syntax

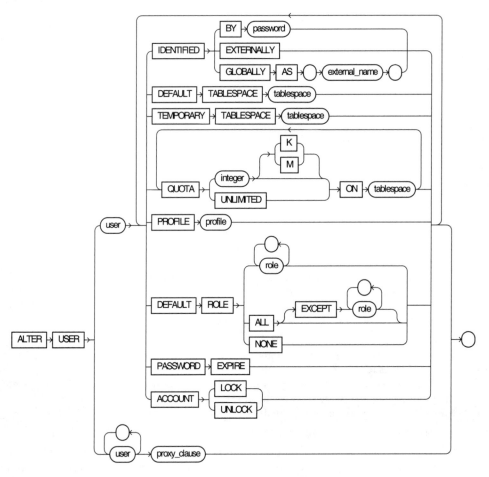

proxy_clause::=

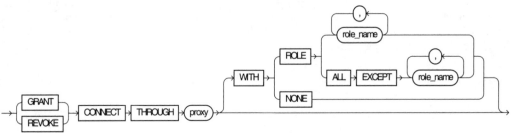

Purpose

To change the authentication or database resource characteristics of a database user. To permit a proxy server to connect as a client without authentication.

Prerequisites

You must have the ALTER USER system privilege. However, you can change your own password without this privilege.

Keywords and Parameters

The Keywords and Parameters shown below are unique to ALTER USER or have different functionality than they have in CREATE USER. All the remaining Keywords and Parameters in the ALTER USER statement have the same meaning as in the CREATE USER statement.

> **NOTE**
> *ALTER USER syntax does not accept the old password.*

Therefore it neither authenticates using the old password nor checks the new password against the old before setting the new password. If these checks against the old password are important, use the OCIPasswordChange() call instead of ALTER USER. For more information, see *Oracle Call Interface Programmer's Guide.*

- IDENTIFIED GLOBALLY AS indicates that a user must be authenticated by way of an LDAP V3 compliant directory service such as Oracle Internet Directory.
  You can change a user's access verification method to IDENTIFIED GLOBALLY AS *'external_name'* only if all external roles granted directly to the user are revoked.
  You can change a user created as IDENTIFIED GLOBALLY AS *'external_name'* to IDENTIFIED BY *password* or IDENTIFIED EXTERNALLY.

- DEFAULT ROLE can contain only roles that have been granted directly to the user with a GRANT statement. You cannot use the DEFAULT ROLE clause to enable:
  roles not granted to the user
  roles granted through other roles
  roles managed by an external service (such as the operating system), or by the Oracle Internet Directory. Oracle enables default roles at logon without requiring the user to specify their passwords.

- *proxy_clause* controls the ability of a **proxy** (an application or application server) to connect as the specified user and to activate all, some, or none of the user's roles. For more information on proxies and their use of the database, see *Oracle8i Concepts.*

  - GRANT allows the connection.

  - REVOKE prohibits the connection.

  - *proxy* identifies the proxy connecting to Oracle.

  - WITH ROLE specifies the roles that the application is permitted to activate after it connects as the user. If you do not include this clause, Oracle activates all roles granted to the specified user automatically.

    - *role_name* permits the proxy to connect as the specified user and to activate only the roles that are specified by *role_name.*

- ALL EXCEPT *role_name* permits the proxy to connect as the specified user and to activate all roles associated with that user except those specified by *role_name*.
- NONE permits the proxy to connect as the specified user, but prohibits the proxy from activating any of that user's roles after connecting.

ANALYZE

Syntax

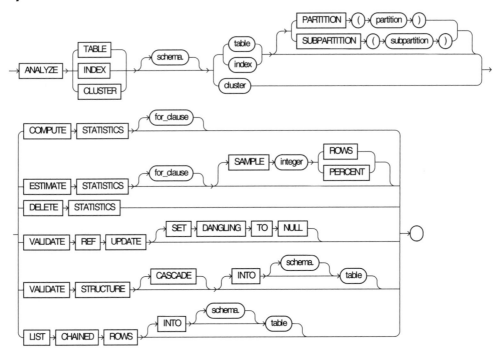

for_clause::=

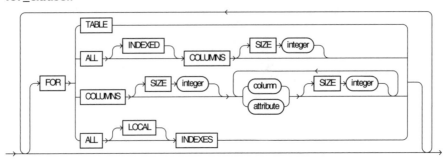

Purpose

To collect or delete statistics about an index or index partition, table or table partition, index-organized table, cluster, or scalar object attribute. To validate the structure of an index or index partition, table or table partition, index-organized table, cluster, or object reference (REF). To identify migrated and chained rows of a table or cluster.

Prerequisites

The schema object to be analyzed must be in your own schema or you must have the ANALYZE ANY system privilege. If you want to list chained rows of a table or cluster into a list table, the list table must be in your own schema, or you must have INSERT privilege on the list table, or you must have INSERT ANY TABLE system privilege. If you want to validate a partitioned table, you must have INSERT privilege on the table into which you list analyzed rowids, or you must have INSERT ANY TABLE system privilege.

Keywords and Parameters

- *schema* is the schema containing the index, table, or cluster. If you omit *schema*, Oracle assumes the index, table, or cluster is in your own schema.

- INDEX *index* identifies an index to be analyzed (if no *for_clause* is used).
  Oracle collects the following statistics for an index (statistics marked with an asterisk are always computed exactly):
  Depth of the index from its root block to its leaf blocks*
  Number of leaf blocks
  Number of distinct index values
  Average number of leaf blocks per index value
  Average number of data blocks per index value (for an index on a table)
  Clustering factor (how well ordered the rows are about the indexed values)

  Index statistics appear in the data dictionary views USER_INDEXES, ALL_INDEXES, and DBA_INDEXES.
  For a **domain inde**x, this statement invokes the user-defined statistics collection function specified in the statistics type associated with the index. If no statistics type is associated with the domain index, the statistics type associated with its indextype is used. If no statistics type exists for either the index or its indextype, no user-defined statistics are collected. User-defined index statistics appear in the data dictionary views USER_USTATS, ALL_USTATS, and DBA_USTATS.
  Restriction: You cannot analyze a domain index that is marked LOADING or FAILED.

- TABLE *table* identifies a table to be analyzed. When you collect statistics for a table, Oracle also automatically collects the statistics for each of the table's indexes and domain indexes, provided that no *for_clauses* are used.
  When you analyze a table, Oracle collects statistics about expressions occurring in any function-based indexes as well. Therefore, be sure to create function-based indexes on the table before analyzing the table.
  When analyzing a table, Oracle skips all domain indexes marked LOADING or FAILED.

  Table statistics, including the status of domain indexes, appear in the data dictionary views USER_TABLES, ALL_TABLES, and DBA_TABLES.
  Oracle collects the following statistics for a table (statistics marked with an asterisk are always computed exactly):
  - Number of rows

- Number of data blocks below the high water mark (that is, the number of data blocks formatted to receive data, regardless whether they currently contain data or are empty)

- Number of data blocks allocated to the table that have never been used

- Average available free space in each data block in bytes

- Number of chained rows

- Average row length, including the row's overhead, in bytes
  Restrictions: You cannot use ANALYZE to collect statistics on data dictionary tables. You cannot use ANALYZE to collect default statistics on a temporary table. However, if you have created an association between one or more columns of a temporary table and a user-defined statistics type, you can use ANALYZE to collect the user-defined statistics on the temporary table.
  You cannot compute or estimate statistics for the following column types: REFs, varrays, nested tables, LOBs (LOBs are not analyzed, they are skipped), LONGs, or object types. However, if a statistics type is associated with such a column, user-defined statistics are collected.

■ PARTITION | SUBPARTITION specifies that statistics will be gathered for *partition* or *subpartition*. You cannot use this clause when analyzing clusters.
If you specify PARTITION and *table* is composite-partitioned, Oracle analyzes all the subpartitions within the specified partition.

■ CLUSTER *cluster* identifies a cluster to be analyzed. When you collect statistics for a cluster, Oracle also automatically collects the statistics for all the cluster's tables and all their indexes, including the cluster index.

- For an indexed cluster, Oracle collects the average number of data blocks taken up by a single cluster key value and all of its rows.

- For a hash cluster, Oracle collects the average number of data blocks taken up by a single hash key value and all of its rows.

These statistics appear in the data dictionary views USER_CLUSTERS and DBA_CLUSTERS.

■ COMPUTE STATISTICS computes exact statistics about the analyzed object and stores them in the data dictionary.
When you analyze a table, both table and column statistics are collected.

■ ESTIMATE STATISTICS estimates statistics about the analyzed object and stores them in the data dictionary.
Both computed and estimated statistics are used by the Oracle optimizer to choose the execution plan for SQL statements that access analyzed objects. These statistics may also be useful to application developers who write such statements. For information on how these statistics are used, see *Oracle8i Tuning*.

- SAMPLE *integer* specifies the amount of data from the analyzed object Oracle samples to estimate statistics. If you omit this parameter, Oracle samples 1064 rows.
  The default sample value is adequate for tables up to a few thousand rows. If your tables are larger, specify a higher value for SAMPLE. If you specify more than half of the data, Oracle reads all the data and computes the statistics.

- ROWS causes Oracle to sample *integer* rows of the table or cluster or *integer* entries from the index. The integer must be at least 1.

- PERCENT causes Oracle to sample *integer* percent of the rows from the table or cluster or *integer* percent of the index entries. The integer can range from 1 to 99.

- **for_clause** specifies whether an entire table or index, or just particular columns, will be analyzed. The following clauses apply only to the ANALYZE TABLE version of this statement:

  - FOR TABLE restricts the statistics collected to only table statistics rather than table and column statistics.

  - FOR COLUMNS restricts the statistics collected to only column statistics for the specified columns and scalar object attributes, rather than for all columns and attributes.

  - FOR ALL COLUMNS collects column statistics for all columns and scalar object attributes.

  - FOR ALL INDEXED COLUMNS collects column statistics for all indexed columns in the table.

  Column statistics can be based on the entire column or can use a histogram by specifying SIZE (see below). For more information on histograms, see *Oracle8i Tuning*.

  Oracle collects the following column statistics:

  - Number of distinct values in the column as a whole

  - Maximum and minimum values in each band

  Column statistics appear in the data dictionary views USER_TAB_COLUMNS, ALL_TAB_COLUMNS, and DBA_TAB_COLUMNS. Histograms appear in the data dictionary views USER_HISTOGRAMS, DBA_HISTOGRAMS, and ALL_HISTOGRAMS.

NOTE
The MAXVALUE and MINVALUE columns of USER_, DBA_, and ALL_TAB_COLUMNS have a length of 32 bytes. If you analyze columns with a length >32 bytes, and if the columns are padded with leading blanks, Oracle may take into account only the leading blanks and return unexpected statistics.

If a user-defined statistics type has been associated with any columns, the *for_clause* collects user-defined statistics using that statistics type. If no statistics type is associated with a column, Oracle checks to see if any statistics type has been associated with the type of the column, and uses that statistics type. If no statistics type has been associated with either the column or its user-defined type, no user-defined statistics are collected. User-defined column statistics appear in the data dictionary views USER_USTATS, ALL_USTATS, and DBA_USTATS.

NOTE
If you want to collect statistics on both the table as a whole and on one or more columns, be sure to generate the statistics for the table first, and then for the columns. Otherwise, the table-only ANALYZE will overwrite the histograms generated by the column ANALYZE. For example, issue the following statements:

```
ANALYZE TABLE emp ESTIMATE STATISTICS;
ANALYZE TABLE emp ESTIMATE STATISTICS FOR ALL COLUMNS;
```

- *attribute* specifies the qualified column name of an item in an object.

- FOR ALL INDEXES specifies that all indexes associated with the table will be analyzed.

- FOR ALL LOCAL INDEXES specifies that all local index partitions are analyzed. You must specify the keyword LOCAL if the PARTITION clause and INDEX are specified.

- SIZE specifies the maximum number of partitions in the histogram. The default value is 75, minimum value is 1, and maximum value is 254.

- DELETE STATISTICS deletes any statistics about the analyzed object that are currently stored in the data dictionary. Use this statement when you no longer want Oracle to use the statistics.

  When you use this clause on a table, Oracle also automatically removes statistics for all the table's indexes. When you use this clause on a cluster, Oracle also automatically removes statistics for all the cluster's tables and all their indexes, including the cluster index.

  If user-defined column or index statistics were collected for an object, Oracle also removes the user-defined statistics by invoking the statistics deletion function specified in the statistics type that was used to collect the statistics.

- VALIDATE REF UPDATE validates the REFs in the specified table, checks the rowid portion in each REF, compares it with the true rowid, and corrects, if necessary. You can use this clause only when analyzing a table.

  - SET DANGLING TO NULL sets to NULL any REFs (whether or not scoped) in the specified table that are found to point to an invalid or nonexistent object.

NOTE
If the owner of the table does not have SELECT object privilege on the referenced objects, Oracle will consider them invalid and set them to NULL. Subsequently these REFs will not be available in a query, even if it is issued by user with appropriate privileges on the objects.

- VALIDATE STRUCTURE validates the structure of the analyzed object. The statistics collected by this clause are not used by the Oracle optimizer, as are statistics collected by the COMPUTE STATISTICS and ESTIMATE STATISTICS clauses.

  - For a table, Oracle verifies the integrity of each of the table's data blocks and rows.

  - For a cluster, Oracle automatically validates the structure of the cluster's tables.

  - For a partitioned table, Oracle also verifies that the row belongs to the correct partition. If the row does not collate correctly, the rowid is inserted into the INVALID_ROWS table.

  - For a temporary table, Oracle validates the structure of the table and its indexes during the current session.

  - For an index, Oracle verifies the integrity of each data block in the index and checks for block corruption. This clause does not confirm that each row in the table has an index entry or that each index entry points to a row in the table. You can perform these operations by validating the structure of the table with the CASCADE clause.

  Oracle stores statistics about the index in the data dictionary views INDEX_STATS and INDEX_HISTOGRAM, which are described in Oracle8i Reference.

  Validating the structure of an object prevents SELECT, INSERT, UPDATE, and DELETE statements from concurrently accessing the object. Therefore, do not use this clause on the tables, clusters, and indexes of your production applications during periods of high database activity.

If Oracle encounters corruption in the structure of the object, an error message is returned to you. In this case, drop and re-create the object.

- INTO specifies a table into which Oracle lists the rowids of the partitions whose rows do not collate correctly. If you omit *schema,* Oracle assumes the list is in your own schema. If you omit this clause altogether, Oracle assumes that the table is named INVALID_ROWS. The SQL script used to create this table is UTLVALID.SQL.

- CASCADE validates the structure of the indexes associated with the table or cluster. If you use this clause when validating a table, Oracle also validates the table's indexes. If you use this clause when validating a cluster, Oracle also validates all the clustered tables' indexes, including the cluster index.
  If you use this clause to validate an enabled (but previously disabled) function-based index, validation errors may result. In this case, you must rebuild the index.

- LIST CHAINED ROWS identifies migrated and chained rows of the analyzed table or cluster. You cannot use this clause when analyzing an index.

  - INTO specifies a table into which Oracle lists the migrated and chained rows. If you omit *schema*, Oracle assumes the list table is in your own schema. If you omit this clause altogether, Oracle assumes that the table is named CHAINED_ROWS. The script used to create this table is UTLCHAIN1.SQL. The list table must be on your local database.

NOTE
You can use the UTLCHAIN1.SQL script with index-organized tables.
You could not use earlier versions of the script for this purpose.

See *Oracle8i Migration* for compatibility information.

To analyze index-organized tables, you must create a separate chained-rows table for each index-organized table to accommodate the primary-key storage of index-organized tables. Use the SQL scripts DBMSIOTC.SQL and PRVTIOTC.PLB to define the BUILD_CHAIN_ROWS_TABLE procedure, and then execute this procedure to create an IOT_CHAINED_ROWS table for an index-organized table.
For information on the SQL scripts, see the DBMS_IOT package in *Oracle8i Supplied Packages Reference.* For information on eliminating migrated and chained rows, see *Oracle8i Tuning.*

ASSOCIATE STATISTICS

Syntax

column_association::=

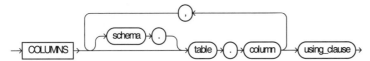

function_association::=

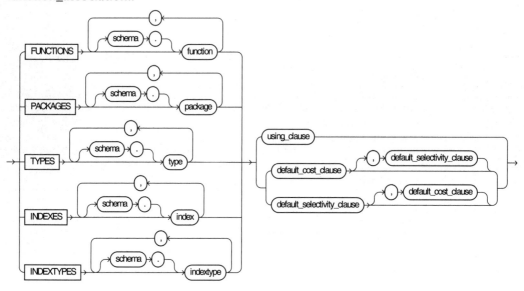

using_clause::=

default_cost_clause::=

default_selectivity_clause::=

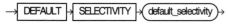

Purpose

To associate a statistics type (or default statistics) containing functions relevant to statistics collection, selectivity, or cost with one or more columns, standalone functions, packages, types, domain indexes, or indextypes. For a listing of all current statistics type associations, refer to the USER_ASSOCIATIONS table. If you analyze the object with which you are associating statistics, you can also view the associations in the USER_USTATS table.

Prerequisites

To issue this statement, you must have the appropriate privileges to alter the base object (table, function, package, type, domain index, or indextype). In addition, unless you are associating only default statistics, you must have execute privilege on the statistics type. The statistics type must already have been defined.

Keywords and Parameters

- ***column_association*** specifies a list of one or more table columns. If you do not specify *schema*, Oracle assumes the table is in your own schema.

- ***function_association*** specifies a list of one or more standalone functions, packages, user-defined datatypes, domain indexes, or indextypes. If you do not specify *schema*, Oracle assumes the object is in your own schema.

  - FUNCTIONS refers only to standalone functions, not to method types or to built-in functions.

  - TYPES refers only to user-defined types, not to internal SQL datatypes.
    Restriction: You cannot specify an object for which you have already defined an association. You must first disassociate the statistics from this object.

- ***using_clause*** specifies the statistics type being associated with columns, functions, packages, types, domain indexes, or indextypes. The *statistics_type* must already have been created.

- ***default_cost_clause*** specifies default costs for standalone functions, packages, types, domain indexes, or indextypes. If you specify this clause, you must include one number each for CPU cost, I/O cost, and network cost, in that order. Each cost is for a single execution of the function or method or for a single domain index access. Accepted values are integers of zero or greater.

- ***default_selectivity_clause*** specifies as a percent the default selectivity for predicates with standalone functions, types, packages, or user-defined operators. The *default_selectivity* must be a whole number between 0 and 100. Values outside this range are ignored.
  Restriction: You cannot specify DEFAULT SELECTIVITY for domain indexes or indextypes.

AUDIT sql_statements

Syntax

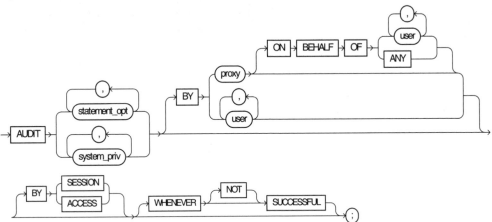

Purpose

To track the occurrence of specific SQL statements in subsequent user sessions. Auditing options specified by the AUDIT *sql_statements* statement apply only to subsequent sessions, not to current sessions.

Prerequisites

You must have AUDIT SYSTEM system privilege. You must enable auditing by setting the initialization parameter AUDIT_TRAIL to DB. You can specify auditing options regardless of whether auditing is enabled. However, Oracle does not generate audit records until you enable auditing.

Keywords and Parameters

- *statement_opt* chooses specific SQL statements for auditing. For a list of these statement options and the SQL statements they audit, see Table A-1 and Table A-2. For each audited operation, Oracle produces an audit record containing this information:

  - user performing the operation

  - type of operation

  - object involved in the operation

  - date and time of the operation

  Oracle writes audit records to the audit trail, which is a database table containing audit records. You can review database activity by examining the audit trail through data dictionary views. For information on these views, see the *Oracle8i Reference*.

- *system_priv* chooses SQL statements that are authorized by the specified system privilege for auditing.

  Oracle provides shortcuts for specifying groups of system privileges and statement options at once. However, Oracle encourages you to choose individual system privileges and statement options for auditing, because these shortcuts may not be supported in future versions of Oracle. The shortcuts are:

  - CONNECT is equivalent to specifying the CREATE SESSION system privilege

  - RESOURCE is equivalent to specifying the following system privileges:

    - ALTER SESSION

    - CREATE CLUSTER

    - CREATE DATABASE LINK

    - CREATE PROCEDURE

    - CREATE ROLLBACK SEGMENT

    - CREATE SEQUENCE

    - CREATE SYNONYM

    - CREATE TABLE

    - CREATE TABLESPACE

    - CREATE VIEW

- DBA is equivalent to the SYSTEM GRANT statement option and the following system privileges:
  - AUDIT SYSTEM
  - CREATE PUBLIC DATABASE LINK
  - CREATE PUBLIC SYNONYMN
  - CREATE ROLE
  - CREATE USER
- ALL is equivalent to specifying all statements options shown in Table A–1 but not the additional statement options shown in Table A–2.
- ALL PRIVILEGES is equivalent to specifying all system privileges.
- BY *user* chooses only SQL statements issued by specified users for auditing. If you omit this clause, Oracle audits all users' statements.
- BY *proxy* chooses for auditing only SQL statements issued by the specified proxy. For more information on proxies and their use of the database, see *Oracle8i Concepts*.
  - ON BEHALF OF specifies the user or users on whose behalf the proxy executes the specified statement.
    - *user* specifies auditing of statements executed on behalf of a particular user.
    - ANY specifies auditing of statements executed on behalf of any user.
- BY SESSION causes Oracle to write a single record for all SQL statements of the same type issued in the same session.
- BY ACCESS causes Oracle to write one record for each audited statement.

Statement Option SQL	Statements and Operations
CLUSTER	CREATE CLUSTER
	AUDIT CLUSTER
	DROP CLUSTER
	TRUNCATE CLUSTER
CONTEXT	CREATE CONTEXT
DROP	CONTEXT
DATABASE LINK	CREATE DATABASE LINK
DROP	DATABASE LINK

TABLE A-1.   *Statement Auditing Options for Database Objects*

Statement Option SQL	Statements and Operations
DIMENSION	CREATE DIMENSION
	ALTER DIMENSION
	DROP DIMENSION
DIRECTORY	CREATE DIRECTORY
	DROP DIRECTORY
INDEX	CREATE INDEX
	ALTER INDEX
	DROP INDEX
NOT EXISTS	All SQL statements that fail because a specified object does not exist.
PROCEDURE[1]	CREATE FUNCTION
	CREATE LIBRARY
	CREATE PACKAGE
	CREATE PACKAGE BODY
	CREATE PROCEDURE
	DROP FUNCTION
	DROP LIBRARY
	DROP PACKAGE
	DROP PROCEDURE
	PROFILE CREATE PROFILE
	ALTER PROFILE
	DROP PROFILE
PUBLIC DATABASE LINK	CREATE PUBLIC DATABASE LINK
	DROP PUBLIC DATABASE LINK
PUBLIC SYNONYM	CREATE PUBLIC SYNONYM
	DROP PUBLIC SYNONYM
ROLE	CREATE ROLE
	ALTER ROLE
	DROP ROLE
	SET ROLE
ROLLBACK STATEMENT	CREATE ROLLBACK SEGMENT
	ALTER ROLLBACK SEGMENT
	DROP ROLLBACK SEGMENT
SEQUENCE	CREATE SEQUENCE
	DROP SEQUENCE

TABLE A-I. *Statement Auditing Options for Database Objects* (continued)

Statement Option SQL	Statements and Operations
SESSION	Logons
SYNONYM	CREATE SYNONYM
	DROP SYNONYM
SYSTEM AUDIT	AUDIT sql_statements
	NOAUDIT sql_statements
SYSTEM GRANT	GRANT system_privileges_and_roles
	REVOKE system_privileges_and_roles
TABLE	CREATE TABLE
	DROP TABLE
	TRUNCATE TABLE
	COMMENT ON TABLE
	DELETE [FROM] table
TABLESPACE	CREATE TABLESPACE
	ALTER TABLESPACE
	DROP TABLESPACE
TRIGGER	CREATE TRIGGER
	ALTER TRIGGER
	with ENABLE and DISABLE clauses
	DROP TRIGGER
	ALTER TABLE
	with ENABLE ALL TRIGGERS clause
	and DISABLE ALL TRIGGERS clause
TYPE	CREATE TYPE
	CREATE TYPE BODY
	ALTER TYPE
	DROP TYPE
	DROP TYPE BODY
USER	CREATE USER
	ALTER USER
	DROP USER
VIEW	CREATE VIEW
	DROP VIEW

[1] Java schema objects (sources, classes, and resources) are considered the same as procedures for purposes of auditing SQL statements.

TABLE A-1. *Statement Auditing Options for Database Objects* (continued)

Statement Option SQL	Statements and Operations
ALTER SEQUENCE	ALTER SEQUENCE
ALTER TABLE	ALTER TABLE
COMMENT TABLE	COMMENT ON TABLE table, view, snapshot
	COMMENT ON COLUMN table.column, view.column, snapshot.column
DELETE TABLE	DELETE FROM table, view
EXECUTE PROCEDURE	CALL
	Execution of any procedure or function or access to any variable, library, or cursor inside a package.
GRANT DIRECTORY	GRANT privilege ON directory
	REVOKE privilege ON directory
GRANT PROCEDURE	GRANT privilege ON procedure, function, package
	REVOKE privilege ON procedure, function, package
GRANT SEQUENCE	GRANT privilege ON sequence
	REVOKE privilege ON sequence
GRANT TABLE	GRANT privilege ON table, view, snapshot.
	REVOKE privilege ON table, view, snapshot
GRANT TYPE	GRANT privilege ON TYPE
	REVOKE privilege ON TYPE
INSERT TABLE	INSERT INTO table, view
LOCK TABLE	LOCK TABLE table, view
SELECT SEQUENCE	Any statement containing sequence.CURRVAL or sequence.NEXTVAL
SELECT TABLE	SELECT FROM table, view, snapshot
UPDATE TABLE	UPDATE table, view

TABLE A-2. *Additional Statement Auditing Options for SQL Statements*

If you specify statement options or system privileges that audit data definition language (DDL) statements, Oracle automatically audits by access regardless of whether you specify the BY SESSION clause or BY ACCESS clause.

For statement options and system privileges that audit SQL statements other than DDL, you can specify either BY SESSION or BY ACCESS. BY SESSION is the default.

■ WHENEVER SUCCESSFUL chooses auditing only for statements that succeed.

■ NOT chooses auditing only for statements that fail or result in errors.

If you omit the WHENEVER SUCCESSFUL clause, Oracle audits SQL statements regardless of success or failure.

AUDIT schema_objects

Syntax

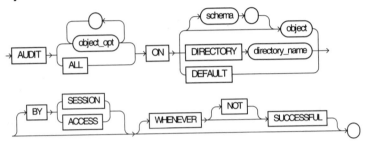

Purpose
To track operations on a specific schema object. Auditing keeps track of operations performed by database users. Auditing options established by the AUDIT *schema_objects* statement apply to current sessions as well as to subsequent sessions.

Prerequisites
The object you choose for auditing must be in your own schema or you must have AUDIT ANY system privilege. In addition, if the object you choose for auditing is a directory object, even if you created it, you must have AUDIT ANY system privilege.

Keywords and Parameters

- *object_opt* specifies a particular operation for auditing. Table A-3 shows each object option and the types of objects to which it applies. The name of each object option specifies a SQL statement to be audited. For example, if you choose to audit a table with the ALTER option, Oracle audits all ALTER TABLE statements issued against the table. If you choose to audit a sequence with the SELECT option, Oracle audits all statements that use any of the sequence's values.

- ALL is a shortcut equivalent to specifying all object options applicable for the type of object. You can use this shortcut rather than explicitly specifying all options for an object.

- *schema* is the schema containing the object chosen for auditing. If you omit *schema*, Oracle assumes the object is in your own schema.

- *object* identifies the object chosen for auditing. The object must be a table, view, sequence, stored procedure, function, package, snapshot, or library.

  You can also specify a synonym for a table, view, sequence, procedure, stored function, package, or snapshot.

- ON DEFAULT establishes the specified object options as default object options for subsequently created objects. Once you have established these default auditing options, any subsequently created object is automatically audited with those options. The default auditing options for a view are always the union of the auditing options for the view's base tables.

Object Option	Table	View	Sequence	Procedure Function Package[2]	Material- ized View / Snapshot	Directory	Library	Object Type	Context
ALTER	X		X		X			X	
AUDIT	X	X	X	X	X	X		X	X
COMMENT	X	X			X				
DELETE	X	X			X				
EXECUTE				X			X		
GRANT	X	X	X	X	X	X	X	X	X
INDEX	X				X				
INSERT	X	X			X				
LOCK	X	X			X				
READ						X			
RENAME	X	X		X	X				
SELECT	X	X	X		X				
UPDATE	X	X			X				

2 Java schema objects (sources, classes, and resources) are considered the same as procedures, functions, and packages for purposes of auditing options.

TABLE A-3. *Object Auditing Options*

If you change the default auditing options, the auditing options for previously created objects remain the same. You can change the auditing options for an existing object only by specifying the object in the ON clause of the AUDIT statement.

■ ON DIRECTORY *directory_name* identifies the name of the directory chosen for auditing.

■ BY SESSION causes Oracle to write a single record for all operations of the same type on the same object issued in the same session. This is the default.

■ BY ACCESS causes Oracle to write one record for each audited operation.

■ WHENEVER SUCCESSFUL chooses auditing only for SQL statements that complete successfully.

■ NOT chooses auditing only for statements that fail, or result in errors.

If you omit the WHENEVER SUCCESSFUL clause entirely, Oracle audits all SQL statements, regardless of success or failure.

CREATE CONTROLFILE

Syntax

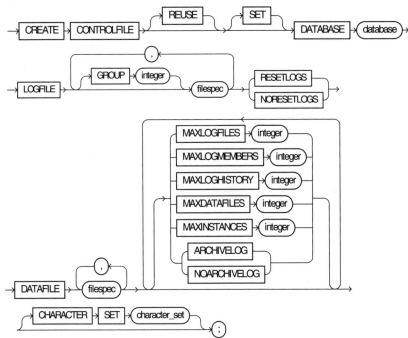

CAUTION

Oracle recommends that you perform a full backup of all files in the database before using this statement. For more information, see Oracle8i Backup and Recovery Guide.

Purpose

To re-create a control file in one of the following cases:

- All copies of your existing control files have been lost through media failure.

- You want to change the name of the database.

- You want to change the maximum number of redo log file groups, redo log file members, archived redo log files, datafiles, or instances that can concurrently have the database mounted and open.

When you issue a CREATE CONTROLFILE statement, Oracle creates a new control file based on the information you specify in the statement. If you omit any clauses, Oracle uses the default values rather than the values for the previous control file. After successfully creating the control file, Oracle mounts the database in the mode specified by the initialization parameter PARALLEL_SERVER. You then must perform media recovery before opening the database. It is recommended that you then shut down the instance and take a full backup of all files in the database. For more information about using this statement, see *Oracle8i Backup and Recovery Guide*.

Prerequisites

You must have the OSDBA role enabled. The database must not be mounted by any instance. If the REMOTE_LOGIN_PASSWORDFILE initialization parameter is set to EXCLUSIVE, Oracle returns an error when you attempt to re-create the control file. To avoid this message, either set the parameter to SHARED, or re-create your password file before re-creating the control file. For more information about the REMOTE_LOGIN_PASSWORDFILE parameter, see *Oracle8i Reference*.

Keywords and Parameters

- REUSE specifies that existing control files identified by the initialization parameter CONTROL_FILES can be reused, thus ignoring and overwriting any information they may currently contain. If you omit this clause and any of these control files already exists, Oracle returns an error.

- DATABASE *database* specifies the name of the database. The value of this parameter must be the existing database name established by the previous CREATE DATABASE statement or CREATE CONTROLFILE statement.

- SET DATABASE *database* changes the name of the database. The name of a database can be as long as eight bytes.

- LOGFILE specifies the redo log files for your database. You must list all members of all redo log file groups.

  - GROUP *integer* specifies logfile group. If you specify GROUP values, Oracle verifies these values with the GROUP values when the database was last open.

- RESETLOGS ignores the contents of the files listed in the LOGFILE clause. These files do not have to exist. Each filespec in the LOGFILE clause must specify the SIZE parameter. Oracle assigns all online redo log file groups to thread 1 and enables this thread for public use by any instance. After using this clause, you must open the database using the RESETLOGS clause of the ALTER DATABASE statement.

- NORESETLOGS specifies that all files in the LOGFILE clause should be used as they were when the database was last open. These files must exist and must be the current online redo log files rather than restored backups. Oracle reassigns the redo log file groups to the threads to which they were previously assigned and reenables the threads as they were previously enabled.

- DATAFILE specifies the datafiles of the database. You must list all datafiles. These files must all exist, although they may be restored backups that require media recovery.

- MAXLOGFILES *integer* specifies the maximum number of online redo log file groups that can ever be created for the database. Oracle uses this value to determine how much space in the control file to allocate for the names of redo log files. The default and maximum values depend on your operating system. The value that you specify should not be less than the greatest GROUP value for any redo log file group.

■ MAXLOGMEMBERS *integer* specifies the maximum number of members, or identical copies, for a redo log file group. Oracle uses this value to determine how much space in the control file to allocate for the names of redo log files. The minimum value is 1. The maximum and default values depend on your operating system.

■ MAXLOGHISTORY *integer* specifies the maximum number of archived redo log file groups for automatic media recovery of the Oracle Parallel Server. Oracle uses this value to determine how much space in the control file to allocate for the names of archived redo log files. The minimum value is 0. The default value is a multiple of the MAXINSTANCES value and depends on your operating system. The maximum value is limited only by the maximum size of the control file. This parameter is useful only if you are using Oracle with the Parallel Server option in both parallel mode and archivelog mode.

■ MAXDATAFILES *integer* specifies the initial sizing of the datafiles section of the control file at CREATE DATABASE or CREATE CONTROLFILE time. An attempt to add a file whose number is greater than MAXDATAFILES, but less than or equal to DB_FILES, causes the Oracle control file to expand automatically so that the datafiles section can accommodate more files.

The number of datafiles accessible to your instance is also limited by the initialization parameter DB_FILES.

■ MAXINSTANCES *integer* specifies the maximum number of instances that can simultaneously have the database mounted and open. This value takes precedence over the value of the initialization parameter INSTANCES. The minimum value is 1. The maximum and default values depend on your operating system.

■ ARCHIVELOG establishes the mode of archiving the contents of redo log files before reusing them. This clause prepares for the possibility of media recovery as well as instance or crash recovery.

■ NOARCHIVELOG If you omit both the ARCHIVELOG clause and NOARCHIVELOG clause, Oracle chooses NOARCHIVELOG mode by default. After creating the control file, you can change between ARCHIVELOG mode and NOARCHIVELOG mode with the ALTER DATABASE statement.

■ CHARACTER SET *character_set* optionally reconstructs character set information in the control file. In case media recovery of the database is required, this information will be available before the database is open, so that tablespace names can be correctly interpreted during recovery.

This clause is useful only if you are using a character set other than the default US7ASCII.

If you are re-creating your control file and you are using Recovery Manager for tablespace recovery, and if you specify a different character set from the one stored in the data dictionary, then tablespace recovery will not succeed. (However, at database open, the control file character set will be updated with the correct character set from the data dictionary.) For more information on tablespace recovery, see *Oracle8i Backup and Recovery Guide*.

NOTE
You cannot modify the character set of the database with this clause.

CREATE DATABASE

Syntax

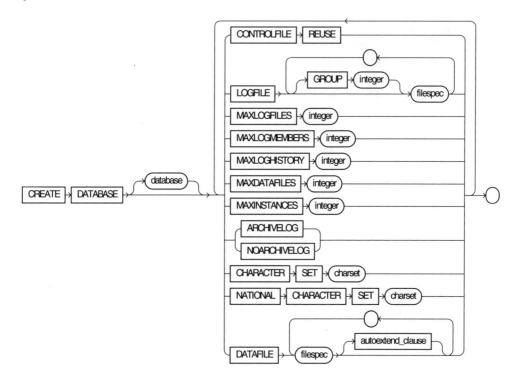

autoextend_clause::=

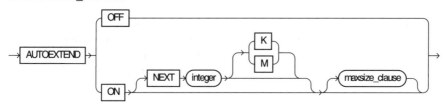

maxsize_clause::=

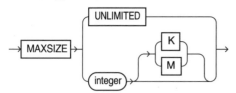

CAUTION
This statement prepares a database for initial use and erases any data currently in the specified files. Use this statement only when you understand its ramifications.

Purpose

To create a database, making it available for general use. This statement erases all data in any specified datafiles that already exist in order to prepare them for initial database use. If you use the statement on an existing database, all data in the datafiles is lost. After creating the database, this statement mounts it in either exclusive or parallel mode (depending on the value of the PARALLEL_SERVER initialization parameter) and opens it, making it available for normal use. You can then create tablespaces and rollback segments for the database.

Prerequisites

You must have the OSDBA role enabled. If the REMOTE_LOGIN_PASSWORDFILE initialization parameter is set to EXCLUSIVE, Oracle returns an error when you attempt to re-create the database. To avoid this message, either set the parameter to SHARED, or re-create your password file before re-creating the database. For more information about the REMOTE_LOGIN_PASSWORDFILE parameter, see *Oracle8i Reference*.

Keyword and Parameters

- *database* is the name of the database to be created and can be up to 8 bytes long. The database name can contain only ASCII characters. Oracle writes this name into the control file. If you subsequently issue an ALTER DATABASE statement that explicitly specifies a database name, Oracle verifies that name with the name in the control file.

NOTE
You cannot use special characters from European or Asian character sets in a database name. For example, characters with umlauts are not allowed.

If you omit the database name from a CREATE DATABASE statement, Oracle uses the name specified by the initialization parameter DB_NAME. If the DB_NAME initialization parameter has been set, and you specify a different name from the value of that parameter, Oracle returns an error.

- CONTROLFILE REUSE reuses existing control files identified by the initialization parameter CONTROL_FILES, thus ignoring and overwriting any information they currently contain. Normally you use this clause only when you are re-creating a database, rather than creating one for the first time. You cannot use this clause if you also specify a parameter value that requires that the control file be larger than the existing files.

  These parameters are MAXLOGFILES, MAXLOGMEMBERS, MAXLOGHISTORY, MAXDATAFILES, and MAXINSTANCES.

  If you omit this clause and any of the files specified by CONTROL_FILES already exist, Oracle returns an error.

- LOGFILE specifies one or more files to be used as redo log files. Each *filespec* specifies a redo log file group containing one or more redo log file members (copies). All redo log files specified in a CREATE DATABASE statement are added to redo log thread number 1.

- GROUP *integer* uniquely identifies a redo log file group and can range from 1 to the value of the MAXLOGFILES parameter. A database must have at least two redo log file groups. You cannot specify multiple redo log file groups having the same GROUP value. If you omit this parameter, Oracle generates its value automatically. You can examine the GROUP value for a redo log file group through the dynamic performance table V$LOG.

    If you omit the LOGFILE clause, Oracle creates two redo log file groups by default. The names and sizes of the default files depend on your operating system.

- MAXLOGFILES *integer* specifies the maximum number of redo log file groups that can ever be created for the database. Oracle uses this value to determine how much space in the control file to allocate for the names of redo log files. The default, minimum, and maximum values depend on your operating system.

- MAXLOGMEMBERS *integer* specifies the maximum number of members, or copies, for a redo log file group. Oracle uses this value to determine how much space in the control file to allocate for the names of redo log files. The minimum value is 1. The maximum and default values depend on your operating system.

- MAXLOGHISTORY *integer* specifies the maximum number of archived redo log files for automatic media recovery with Oracle Parallel Server. Oracle uses this value to determine how much space in the control file to allocate for the names of archived redo log files. The minimum value is 0. The default value is a multiple of the MAXINSTANCES value and depends on your operating system. The maximum value is limited only by the maximum size of the control file.

NOTE
This parameter is useful only if you are using Oracle with the Parallel Server option in parallel mode, and archivelog mode enabled.

- MAXDATAFILES *integer* specifies the initial sizing of the datafiles section of the control file at CREATE DATABASE or CREATE CONTROLFILE time. An attempt to add a file whose number is greater than MAXDATAFILES, but less than or equal to DB_FILES, causes the Oracle control file to expand automatically so that the datafiles section can accommodate more files.

    The number of datafiles accessible to your instance is also limited by the initialization parameter DB_FILES.

- MAXINSTANCES *integer* specifies the maximum number of instances that can simultaneously have this database mounted and open. This value takes precedence over the value of initialization parameter INSTANCES. The minimum value is 1. The maximum and default values depend on your operating system.

- ARCHIVELOG specifies that the contents of a redo log file group must be archived before the group can be reused. This clause prepares for the possibility of media recovery.

- NOARCHIVELOG specifies that the contents of a redo log file group need not be archived before the group can be reused. This clause does not allow for the possibility of media recovery. The default is NOARCHIVELOG mode. After creating the database, you can change between ARCHIVELOG mode and NOARCHIVELOG mode with the ALTER DATABASE statement.

- CHARACTER SET specifies the character set the database uses to store data. You cannot change the database character set after creating the database. The supported character sets and default value of this parameter depend on your operating system.
    Restriction: You cannot specify any fixed-width multibyte character sets as the database character set. For more information about character sets, see *Oracle8i National Language Support Guide.*

- NATIONAL CHARACTER SET specifies the national character set used to store data in columns specifically defined as NCHAR, NCLOB, or NVARCHAR2. If not specified, the national character set defaults to the database character set. See Oracle8i National Language Support Guide for valid character set names.

- DATAFILE specifies one or more files to be used as datafiles. All these files become part of the SYSTEM tablespace. If you omit this clause, Oracle creates one datafile by default. The name and size of this default file depend on your operating system.

NOTE
Oracle recommends that the total initial space allocated for the
SYSTEM tablespace be a minimum of 5 megabytes.

- *autoextend_clause* enables or disables the automatic extension of a datafile. If you do not specify this clause, datafiles are not automatically extended.

    - OFF disables autoextend if it is turned on. NEXT and MAXSIZE are set to zero. Values for NEXT and MAXSIZE must be respecified in ALTER DATABASE AUTOEXTEND or ALTER TABLESPACE AUTOEXTEND statements.

    - ON enables autoextend.

    - NEXT specifies the size in bytes of the next increment of disk space to be allocated to the datafile automatically when more extents are required. Use K or M to specify this size in kilobytes or megabytes. The default is the size of one data block.

    - MAXSIZE specifies the maximum disk space allowed for automatic extension of the datafile.

    - UNLIMITED sets no limit on the allocation of disk space to the datafile.

CREATE DATABASE LINK

Syntax

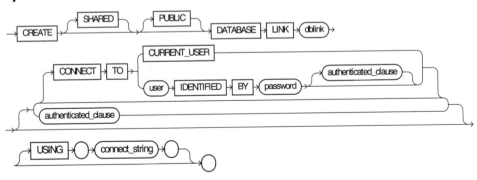

authenticated_clause::=

Purpose

To create a database link. A *database link* is a schema object in the local database that allows you to access objects on a remote database. The remote database need not be an Oracle system. Once you have created a database link, you can use it to refer to tables and views on the remote database. You can refer to a remote table or view in a SQL statement by appending *@dblink* to the table or view name. You can query a remote table or view with the SELECT statement. For information about accessing remote tables or views with PL/SQL functions, procedures, packages, and datatypes, see *Oracle8i Application Developer's Guide -Fundamentals*. For information on distributed database systems, see *Oracle8i Distributed Database Systems*.

Prerequisites

To create a private database link, you must have CREATE DATABASE LINK system privilege. To create a public database link, you must have CREATE PUBLIC DATABASE LINK system privilege. You must have CREATE SESSION privilege on the remote Oracle database. Net8 must be installed on both the local and remote Oracle databases. To access non-Oracle systems you must use the Oracle Heterogeneous Services.

Keyword and Parameters

- SHARED uses a single network connection to create a public database link that can be shared between multiple users. This clause is available only with the multi-threaded server configuration. For more information about shared database links, see *Oracle8i Distributed Database Systems*.

- PUBLIC creates a public database link available to all users. If you omit this clause, the database link is private and is available only to you.

- dblink is the complete or partial name of the database link.
  Restrictions: You cannot create a database link in another user's schema, and you cannot qualify dblink with the name of a schema. (Periods are permitted in names of database links, so Oracle interprets the entire name, such as RALPH.LINKTOSALES, as the name of a database link in your schema rather than as a database link named LINKTOSALES in the schema RALPH.) The number of different database links that can appear in a single statement is limited to the value of the initialization parameter OPEN_LINKS.

- CONNECT TO enables a connection to the remote database.

- CURRENT_USER creates a **current user database link**. The current user must be a global user with a valid account on the remote database for the link to succeed.

  If the database link is used directly, that is, not from within a stored object, then the current user is the same as the connected user.

  When executing a stored object (such as a procedure, view, or trigger) that initiates a database link, CURRENT_USER is the username that owns the stored object, and not the username that called the object. For example, if the database link appears inside procedure SCOTT.P (created by SCOTT), and user JANE calls procedure SCOTT.P, the current user is SCOTT. However, if the stored object is an invoker-rights function, procedure, or package, the invoker's authorization ID is used to connect as a remote user. For example, if the privileged database link appears inside procedure SCOTT.P (an invoker-rights procedure created by SCOTT), and user JANE calls procedure SCOTT.P, then CURRENT_USER is JANE and the procedure executes with JANE's privileges.

- *user* IDENTIFIED BY *password* is the username and password used to connect to the remote database (fixed user database link). If you omit this clause, the database link uses the username and password of each user who is connected to the database (connected user database link).

■ **authenticated_clause** specifies the username and password on the target instance. This clause authenticates the user to the remote server and is required for security. The specified username and password must be a valid username and password on the remote instance. The username and password are used only for authentication. No other operations are performed on behalf of this user. You must specify this clause when using the SHARED clause.

■ USING '*connect string*' specifies the service name of a remote database. For information on specifying remote databases, see *Net8 Administrator's Guide*.

CREATE DIRECTORY

Syntax

Purpose

To create a directory object. A directory object specifies an alias for a directory on the server's file system where external binary file LOBs (BFILEs) are located. You can use directory names when referring to BFILES in your PL/SQL code and OCI calls, rather than hard-coding the operating system pathname, thereby allowing greater file management flexibility. All directories are created in a single namespace and are not owned by an individual's schema. You can secure access to the BFILES stored within the directory structure by granting object privileges on the directories to specific users. When you create a directory, you are automatically granted the READ object privilege and can grant READ privileges to other users and roles. The DBA can also grant this privilege to other users and roles.

Prerequisites

You must have CREATE ANY DIRECTORY system privileges to create directories. You must also create a corresponding operating system directory for file storage. Your system or database administrator must ensure that the operating system directory has the correct read permissions for Oracle processes. Privileges granted for the directory are created independently of the permissions defined for the operating system directory. Therefore, the two may or may not correspond exactly. For example, an error occurs if user SCOTT is granted READ privilege on the directory schema object, but the corresponding operating system directory does not have READ permission defined for Oracle processes.

Keywords and Parameters

■ OR REPLACE re-creates the directory database object if it already exists. You can use this clause to change the definition of an existing directory without dropping, re-creating, and regranting database object privileges previously granted on the directory.

Users who had previously been granted privileges on a redefined directory can still access the directory without being regranted the privileges.

■ *directory* is the name of the directory object to be created. The maximum length of *directory* is 30 bytes. You cannot qualify a directory object with a schema name.

NOTE
Oracle does not verify that the directory you specify actually exists.
Therefore, take care that you specify a valid directory in your
operating system. In addition, if your operating system uses
case-sensitive pathnames, be sure you specify the directory in the
correct format. (However, you need not include a trailing slash at the
end of the pathname.)

- *'path_name'* is the full pathname of the operating system directory on the server where the files are located. The single quotes are required, with the result that the path name is case sensitive.

CREATE INDEX

Syntax

cluster_index_clause::=

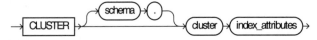

table_index_clause::=

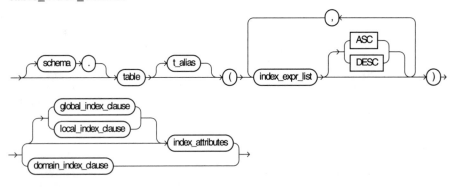

index_expr_list::=

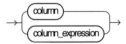

index_attributes::=

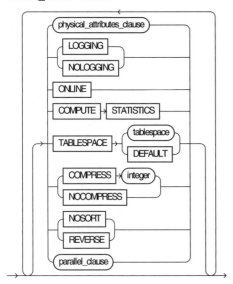

physical_attributes_clause::=

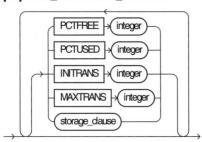

domain_index_clause::=

global_index_clause::=

local_index_clauses::=

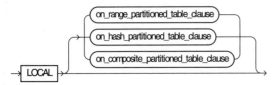

on_range_partitioned_table_clause::=

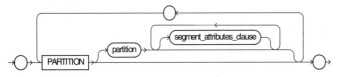

segment_attributes_clause::=

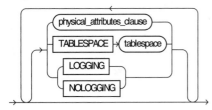

on_hash_partitioned_table_clause::=

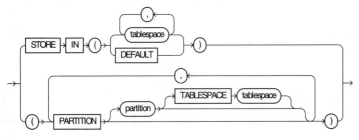

on_composite_partitioned_table_clause::=

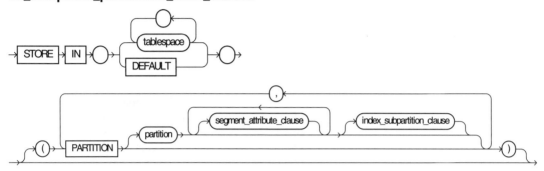

index_subpartitioned_clause::=

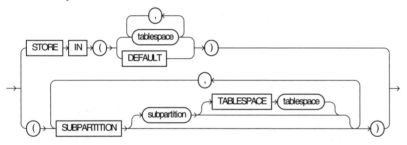

global_partition_clause::=

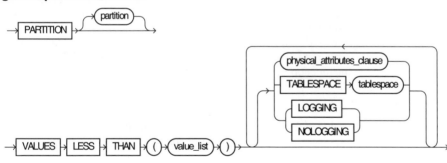

parallel_clause::=

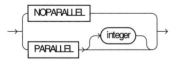

Purpose

To create an index on

- One or more columns of a table, a partitioned table, an index-organized table, or a cluster
- One or more scalar typed object attributes of a table or a cluster
- A nested table storage table for indexing a nested table column

To create a *domain index*, which is an instance of an application-specific index of type *indextype*. An *index* is a schema object that contains an entry for each value that appears in the indexed column(s) of the table or cluster and provides direct, fast access to rows. A *partitioned index* consists of partitions containing an entry for each value that appears in the indexed column(s) of the table. A *function-based index* is an index on expressions. It enables you to construct queries that evaluate the value returned by an expression, which in turn may include functions (built-in or user-defined).

Prerequisites

To create an index in your own schema, one of the following conditions must be true:

- The table or cluster to be indexed must be in your own schema.
- You must have INDEX privilege on the table to be indexed.
- You must have CREATE ANY INDEX system privilege.

To create an index in another schema, you must have CREATE ANY INDEX system privilege. Also, the owner of the schema to contain the index must have either space quota on the tablespaces to contain the index or index partitions, or UNLIMITED TABLESPACE system privilege. To create a domain index in your own schema, you must also have EXECUTE privilege on the indextype. If you are creating a domain index in another user's schema, the index owner also must have EXECUTE privilege on the indextype and its underlying implementation type. Before creating a domain index, you should first define the indextype. To create a function-based index in your own schema on your own table, you must have the QUERY REWRITE system privilege. To create the index in another schema or on another schema's table, you must have the GLOBAL QUERY REWRITE privilege. The table owner must also have the EXECUTE object privilege on the function(s) used in the function-based index.

Keywords and Parameters

- UNIQUE specifies that the value of the column (or columns) upon which the index is based must be unique. If the index is local nonprefixed (see *local_index_clause* below), then the index key must contain the partitioning key.

    Oracle recommends that you do not explicitly define UNIQUE indexes on tables.

    Uniqueness is strictly a logical concept and should be associated with the *definition* of a table.

    Therefore, define UNIQUE integrity constraints on the desired columns.
    Restrictions: You cannot specify both UNIQUE and BITMAP.
    You cannot specify UNIQUE for a domain index.

- BITMAP specifies that *index* is to be created as a bitmap, rather than as a B-tree. Bitmap indexes store the rowids associated with a key value as a bitmap. Each bit in the bitmap corresponds to a possible rowid, and if the bit is set, it means that the row with the corresponding rowid contains the key value. The internal representation of bitmaps is best suited for applications with low

levels of concurrent transactions, such as data warehousing. See *Oracle8i Concepts* and *Oracle8i Tuning* for more information about using bitmap indexes.
Restrictions: You cannot specify BITMAP when creating a global partitioned index or an index-organized table.
You cannot specify both UNIQUE and BITMAP.
You cannot specify BITMAP for a domain index.

- *schema* is the schema to contain the index. If you omit *schema*, Oracle creates the index in your own schema.

- *index* is the name of the index to be created. An *index* can contain several partitions.

- *cluster_index_clause* specifies the cluster for which a cluster index is to be created. If you do not qualify cluster with *schema*, Oracle assumes the cluster is in your current schema. You cannot create a cluster index for a hash cluster.

- *table_index_clause* specifies *table* (and its attributes) on which you are defining the index. If you do not qualify *table* with *schema*, Oracle assumes the table is contained in your own schema.

    You create an index on a nested table column by creating the index on the nested table storage table. Include the NESTED_TABLE_ID pseudocolumn of the storage table to create a UNIQUE index, which effectively ensures that the rows of a nested table value are distinct.
    Restrictions: If the index is local, then *table* must be partitioned.
    If the table is index-organized, this statement creates a secondary index. You cannot specify BITMAP or REVERSE for this secondary index, and the combined size of the index key and the logical rowid should be less than half the block size.
    If *table* is a temporary table, the index will also be temporary with the same scope (session or transaction) as *table*. The following restrictions apply to indexes on temporary table:

    - The index cannot be a partitioned index or a domain index.

    - You cannot specify the *physical_attributes_clause* or the *parallel_clause*.

    - You cannot specify LOGGING, NOLOGGING, or TABLESPACE.

    For more information on temporary tables, see *Oracle8i Concepts*.

- *t_alias* specifies a correlation name (alias) for the table upon which you are building the index.

NOTE
This alias is required if the index_expression_list references any object type attributes or object type methods.

- *index_expr_list* lets you specify the column or column expression upon which the index is based.

- *column* is the name of a column in the table. A bitmap index can have a maximum of 30 columns.

    Other indexes can have as many as 32 columns.
    Restriction: You cannot create an index on columns or attributes whose type is user-defined, LONG, LONG RAW, LOB, or REF, except that Oracle supports an index on REF type columns or attributes that have been defined with a SCOPE clause.

    You can create an index on a scalar object attribute column or on the system-defined NESTED_TABLE_ID column of the nested table storage table. If you specify an object attribute column, the column name must be qualified with the table name. If you specify a nested table column attribute, it must be qualified with the outermost table name, the containing column name, and all intermediate attribute names leading to the nested table column attribute.

■   *column_expression* is an expression built from columns of *table*, constants, SQL functions, and user-defined functions. When you specify *column_expression*, you create a **function-based index**.

Name resolution of the function is based on the schema of the index creator. User-defined functions used in *column_expression* are fully name resolved during the CREATE INDEX operation.

After creating a function-based index, collect statistics on both the index and its base table using the ANALYZE statement. Oracle cannot use the function-based index until these statistics have been generated.

When you subsequently query a table that uses a function-based index, you must ensure in the query that *column_expression* is not null.

If the function on which the index is based becomes invalid or is dropped, Oracle marks the index DISABLED. Queries on a DISABLED index fail if the optimizer chooses to use the index. DML operations on a DISABLED index fail unless

■   The index is also marked UNUSABLE *and*

■   Tthe parameter SKIP_UNUSABLE is set to true

Oracle's use of function-based indexes is also affected by the setting of the QUERY_REWRITE_ENABLED session parameter.

Restrictions: Any user-defined function referenced in *column_expression* must be DETERMINISTIC. For more information, see *PL/SQL User's Guide and Reference*.

For a function-based globally partitioned index, the *column_expression* cannot be the partitioning key.

All functions must be specified with parentheses, even if they have no parameters. Otherwise Oracle interprets them as column names.

Any function you specify in *column_expression* must return a repeatable value. For example, you cannot specify the SYSDATE or USER function or the ROWNUM pseudocolumn.

You cannot build a function-based index on LOB, REF, nested table, or varray columns. In addition, the function in *column_expression* cannot take as arguments any objects with attributes of type LOB, REF, nested table, or varray.

The *column_expression* cannot contain any aggregate functions.

NOTE
If a public synonym for a function, package, or type is used in column_expression, and later an actual object with the same name is created in the table owner's schema, then Oracle will disable the function-based index. When you subsequently enable the function-based index using ALTER INDEX ... ENABLE or ALTER INDEX ... REBUILD, the function, package, or type used in the column_expression will continue to resolve to the function, package, or type to which the public synonym originally pointed. It will not resolve to the new function, package, or type.

■   ASC | DESC specifies whether the index should be created in ascending or descending order. Indexes on character data are created in ascending or descending order of the character values in the database character set.

Oracle treats descending indexes as if they were function-based indexes. You do not need the QUERY REWRITE or GLOBAL QUERY REWRITE privileges to create them, as you do with other function-based indexes. However, as with other function-based indexes, Oracle does not use descending indexes until you first analyze the index and the table on which the index is defined. **Restriction:** You cannot specify either of these clauses for a domain index. You cannot specify DESC for a bitmapped index or a reverse index.

index_attributes

- *physical_attributes_clause* establishes values for physical and storage characteristics for the index. **Restriction:** You cannot specify the PCTUSED parameter for an index.

    - PCTFREE is the percentage of space to leave free for updates and insertions within each of the index's data blocks.

    - *storage_clause* establishes the storage characteristics for the index.

- TABLESPACE is the name of the tablespace to hold the index, index partition, or index subpartition. If you omit this clause, Oracle creates the index in the default tablespace of the owner of the schema containing the index.

    For a local index, you can specify the keyword DEFAULT in place of *tablespace*. New partitions or subpartitions added to the local index will be created in the same tablespace(s) as the corresponding partitions or subpartitions of the underlying table.

- COMPRESS enables key compression, which eliminates repeated occurrence of key column values and may substantially reduce storage. Use *integer* to specify the prefix length (number of prefix columns to compress).

    For unique indexes, the valid range of prefix length values is from 1 to the number of key columns minus 1. The default prefix length is the number of key columns minus 1.

    For nonunique indexes, the valid range of prefix length values is from 1 to the number of key columns. The default prefix length is number of key columns.

    Oracle compresses only nonpartitioned indexes that are nonunique or unique indexes of at least two columns. **Restriction:** You cannot specify COMPRESS for a bitmapped index.

- NOCOMPRESS disables key compression. This is the default.

- NOSORT indicates to Oracle that the rows are stored in the database in ascending order, so that Oracle does not have to sort the rows when creating the index. If the rows of the indexed column or columns are not stored in ascending order, Oracle returns an error. For greatest savings of sort time and space, use this clause immediately after the initial load of rows into a table. **Restrictions:** You cannot specify REVERSE with this clause. You cannot use this clause to create a cluster, partitioned, or bitmap index. You cannot specify this clause for a secondary index on an index-organized table.

- REVERSE stores the bytes of the index block in reverse order, excluding the rowid. You cannot specify NOSORT with this clause. You cannot reverse a bitmap index or an index-organized table.

- LOGGING | NOLOGGING specifies that the creation of the index will be logged (LOGGING) or not logged (NOLOGGING) in the redo log file. It also specifies that subsequent Direct Loader (SQL*Loader) and direct-load INSERT operations against the index are logged or not logged. LOGGING is the default.

    If *index* is nonpartitioned, this is the logging attribute of the index.

If *index* is partitioned, the logging attribute specified is

■ The default value of all partitions specified in the CREATE statement (unless you specify LOGGING|NOLOGGING in the PARTITION description clause)

■ The default value for the segments associated with the index partitions

■ The default value for local index partitions or subpartitions added implicitly during subsequent ALTER TABLE ... ADD PARTITION operations

In NOLOGGING mode, data is modified with minimal logging (to mark new extents INVALID and to record dictionary changes). When applied during media recovery, the extent invalidation records mark a range of blocks as logically corrupt, since the redo data is not logged. Thus if you cannot afford to lose this index, it is important to take a backup after the NOLOGGING operation.

If the database is run in ARCHIVELOG mode, media recovery from a backup taken before the LOGGING operation will re-create the index. However, media recovery from a backup taken before the NOLOGGING operation will not re-create the index.

The logging attribute of the index is independent of that of its base table.

If you omit this clause, the logging attribute is that of the tablespace in which it resides.

For more information about logging and parallel DML, see *Oracle8i Concepts* and *Oracle8i Parallel Server Concepts and Administration*.

■ ONLINE specifies that DML operations on the table will be allowed during creation of the index. For a description of online index building and rebuilding, see *Oracle8i Concepts*. **Restriction:** Parallel DML is not supported during online index building. If you specify ONLINE and then issue parallel DML statements, Oracle returns an error.

■ COMPUTE STATISTICS enables you to collect statistics at relatively little cost during the creation of an index. These statistics are stored in the data dictionary for ongoing use by the optimizer in choosing a plan of execution for SQL statements.

The types of statistics collected depend on the type of index you are creating.

NOTE
If you create an index using another index (instead of a table), the original index might not provide adequate statistical information. Therefore, Oracle generally uses the base table to compute the statistics, which will improve the statistics but may negatively affect performance.

Additional methods of collecting statistics are available in PL/SQL packages and procedures. For more information, refer to *Oracle8i Supplied Packages Reference*.

■ *global_index_clause* specifies that the partitioning of the index is user defined and is not equipartitioned with the underlying table. By default, nonpartitioned indexes are global indexes.

■ PARTITION BY RANGE specifies that the global index is partitioned on the ranges of values from the columns specified in *column_list*. You cannot specify this clause for a local index.

■ *(column_list)* is the name of the column(s) of a table on which the index is partitioned.

■ The *column_list* must specify a left prefix of the index column list.

You cannot specify more than 32 columns in *column_list,* and the columns cannot contain the ROWID pseudocolumn or a column of type ROWID.

■ PARTITION *partition* describes the individual partitions. The number of clauses determines the number of partitions. If you omit *partition*, Oracle generates a name with the form SYS_*Pn*.

■ VALUES LESS THAN *(value_list)* specifies the (noninclusive) upper bound for the current partition in a global index. The *value_list* is a comma-separated, ordered list of literal values corresponding to *column_list* in the *partition_by_range_clause*. Always specify MAXVALUE as the *value_list* of the last partition.

NOTE

If index is partitioned on a DATE column, and if the NLS date format does not specify the century with the year, you must use the TO_DATE function with a 4-character format mask for the year. The NLS date format is determined implicitly by NLS_TERRITORY or explicitly by NLS_DATE_FORMAT. For more information on these initialization parameters, see Oracle8i National Language Support Guide.

Restriction: You cannot specify this clause for a local index.

■ *local_index_clauses* specify that the index is partitioned on the same columns, with the same number of partitions and the same partition bounds as *table*. Oracle automatically maintains LOCAL index partitioning as the underlying table is repartitioned.

■ *on_range_partitioned_table_clause* describes an index on a range-partitioned table.

■ PARTITION *partition* describes the individual partitions. The number of clauses determines the number of partitions. For a local index, the number of index partitions must be equal to the number of the table partitions, and in the same order.

If you omit *partition*, Oracle generates a name that is consistent with the corresponding table partition. If the name conflicts with an existing index partition name, the form SYS_*Pn* is used.

■ *on_hash_partitioned_table_clause* describes an index on a hash-partitioned table. If you do not specify *partition*, Oracle uses the name of the corresponding base table partition, unless it conflicts with an explicitly specified name of another index partition. In this case, Oracle generates a name of the form SYS_*Pnn*n. You can optionally specify TABLESPACE for all index partitions or for one or more individual partitions. If you do not specify TABLESPACE at the index or partition level, Oracle stores each index partition in the same tablespace as the corresponding table partition.

■ *on_composite_partitioned_table_clause* describes an index on a composite-partitioned table. The first STORE IN clause specifies the default tablespace for the index subpartitions. You can override this storage by specifying a different tablespace in the *index_subpartitioning_clause.*

If you do not specify TABLESPACE for subpartitions either in this clause or in the *index_subpartitioning_clause*, Oracle uses the tablespace specified for *index.* If you also do not specify TABLESPACE for *index*, Oracle stores the subpartition in the same tablespace as the corresponding table subpartition.

■ STORE IN lets you specify how index hash partitions (for a hash-partitioned index) or index subpartitions (for a composite-partitioned index) are to be distributed across various tablespaces. The number of tablespaces does not have to equal the number of index partitions. If the number of index partitions is greater than the number of tablespaces, Oracle cycles through the names of the tablespaces.

■ DEFAULT is valid only for a local index on a hash or composite-partitioned table.

This clause overrides any tablespace specified at the index level for a partition or subpartition, and stores the index partition or subpartition in the same partition as the corresponding table partition or subpartition.

■ *index_subpartition_clause* specifies one or more tablespaces in which to store all subpartitions in *partition* or one or more individual subpartitions in *partition*. The subpartition inherits all other attributes from *partition*. Attributes not specified for *partition* are inherited from *index*.

■ **domain_index_clause** specifies that index is a domain index.
   Restrictions: The *index_expr_list* can specify only a single column.
   You can define only one domain index on a column.
   You cannot specify a BITMAP, UNIQUE, or function-based domain index.
   You cannot create a local domain index on a partitioned table.
   You cannot create a domain index on a partitioned table with row movement enabled.

   ■ *column* specifies the table columns or object attributes on which the index is defined. Each *column* can have only one domain index defined on it.
      Restrictions: You cannot create a domain index on a column of datatype REF, varray, nested table, LONG, or LONG RAW.
      You can create a domain index on a column of user-defined type, but not on an attribute of a column of user-defined type if that attribute itself is a user-defined type.

   ■ *indextype* specifies the name of the indextype. This name should be a valid schema object that you have already defined.

   ■ PARAMETERS '*string*' specifies the parameter string that is passed uninterrupted to the appropriate indextype routine. The maximum length of the parameter string is 1000 characters.

      Once the domain index is created, Oracle invokes this routine (see *Oracle8i Data Cartridge Developer's Guide* for information on these routines.) If the routine does not return successfully, the domain index is marked FAILED. The only operation supported on an failed domain index is DROP INDEX.

■ **parallel_clause** causes creation of the index to be parallelized.

   ■ NOPARALLEL specifies serial execution. This is the default.

   ■ PARALLEL causes Oracle to select a degree of parallelism equal to the number of CPUs available on all participating instances times the value of the PARALLEL_THREADS_PER_CPU initialization parameter.

   ■ PARALLEL *integer* specifies the **degree of parallelism**, which is the number of parallel threads used in the parallel operation. Each parallel thread may use one or two parallel execution servers. Normally Oracle calculates the optimum degree of parallelism, so it is not necessary for you to specify *integer*.

CREATE LIBRARY

Syntax

Purpose

To create a schema object associated with an operating-system shared library. The name of this schema object can then be used in the *call_spec* of CREATE FUNCTION or CREATE PROCEDURE statements, or when declaring a function or procedure in a package or type, so that SQL and PL/SQL can call to third-generation-language (3GL) functions and procedures. For more information on functions and procedures, see *PL/SQL User's Guide and Reference*.

Prerequisites

To create a library in your own schema, you must have the CREATE LIBRARY system privilege. To create a library in another user's schema, you must have the CREATE ANY LIBRARY system privilege. To use the procedures and functions stored in the library, you must have EXECUTE object privileges on the library. The CREATE LIBRARY statement is valid only on platforms that support shared libraries and dynamic linking.

Keywords and Parameters

- OR REPLACE re-creates the library if it already exists. Use this clause to change the definition of an existing library without dropping, re-creating, and regranting schema object privileges granted on it.

  Users who had previously been granted privileges on a redefined library can still access the library without being regranted the privileges.

- *libname* is the name you with to create to represent this library when declaring a function or procedure with a *call_spec*.

- *'filespec'* is a string literal, enclosed in single quotes. This string should be the path or filename your operating system recognizes as naming the shared library.

The *'filespec'* is not interpreted during execution of the CREATE LIBRARY statement. The existence of the library file is not checked until an attempt is made to execute a routine from it.

CREATE OUTLINE

Syntax

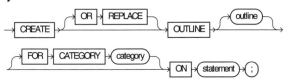

Purpose

To create a *stored outline*, which is a set of attributes used by the optimizer to generate an execution plan. You can then instruct the optimizer to use a set of outlines to influence the generation of execution plans whenever a particular SQL statement is issued, regardless of changes in factors that can affect optimization. You enable or disable the use of stored outlines dynamically for an individual session or for the system. For more information on outlines, see also *Oracle8i Tuning*.

Prerequisites

To create an outline, you must have the CREATE ANY OUTLINE system privilege.

Keywords and Parameters

- OR REPLACE replaces an existing outline with a new outline of the same name.

- *outline* is the unique name to be assigned to the stored outline. If you do not specify *outline*, the system generates an outline name.

- FOR CATEGORY *category* specifies an optional name used to group stored outlines. For example, you could specify a category of outlines for end-of-week use and another for end-of-quarter use. If you do not specify *category*, the outline is stored in the DEFAULT category.

- ON *statement* is the SQL statement for which Oracle will create an outline when the statement is compiled. You can specify any one of the following statements:

  - SELECT
  - DELETE
  - UPDATE
  - INSERT ... SELECT
  - CREATE TABLE ... AS SELECT

NOTE
You can specify multiple outlines for a single statement, but each outline for the same statement must be in a different category.

CREATE PROFILE

Syntax

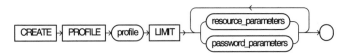

resource_parameters::=

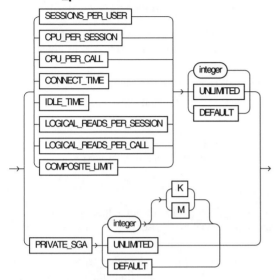

password_parameters::=

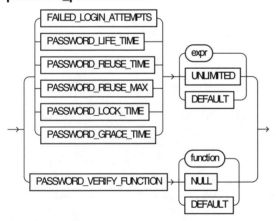

Purpose
To create a profile. A **profile** is a set of limits on database resources. If you assign the profile to a user, that user cannot exceed these limits.

Prerequisites

You must have CREATE PROFILE system privilege. To specify resource limits for a user, you must

- Enable resource limits dynamically with the ALTER SYSTEM statement or with the initialization parameter RESOURCE_LIMIT. (This parameter does not apply to password resources; these are always enabled.)

- Create a profile that defines the limits using the CREATE PROFILE statement.

- Assign the profile to the user using the CREATE USER or ALTER USER statement.

Keywords and Parameters

- *profile* is the name of the profile to be created. Use profiles to limit the database resources available to a user for a single call or a single session.

  Oracle enforces resource limits in the following ways:

  - If a user exceeds the CONNECT_TIME or IDLE_TIME session resource limit, Oracle rolls back the current transaction and ends the session. When the user process next issues a call, Oracle returns an error.

  - If a user attempts to perform an operation that exceeds the limit for other session resources, Oracle aborts the operation, rolls back the current statement, and immediately returns an error. The user can then commit or roll back the current transaction, and must then end the session.

  - If a user attempts to perform an operation that exceeds the limit for a single call, Oracle aborts the operation, rolls back the current statement, and returns an error, leaving the current transaction intact.

NOTE
You can use fractions of days for all parameters that limit time, with days as units. For example, 1 hour is 1/24 and 1 minute is 1/1440. You can specify resource limits for users regardless of whether the resource limits are enabled. However, Oracle does not enforce the limits until you enable them.

- UNLIMITED   When specified with a resource parameter, indicates that a user assigned this profile can use an unlimited amount of this resource. When specified with a password parameter, indicates that no limit has been set for the parameter.

- DEFAULT omits a limit for this resource in this profile. A user assigned this profile is subject to the limit for this resource specified in the DEFAULT profile. The DEFAULT profile initially defines unlimited resources. You can change those limits with the ALTER PROFILE statement.

  Any user who is not explicitly assigned a profile is subject to the limits defined in the DEFAULT profile. Also, if the profile that is explicitly assigned to a user omits limits for some resources or specifies DEFAULT for some limits, the user is subject to the limits on those resources defined by the DEFAULT profile.

resource_parameters

- SESSIONS_PER_USER limits a user to *integer* concurrent sessions.

- CPU_PER_SESSION limits the CPU time for a session, expressed in hundredth of seconds.

- CPU_PER_CALL limits the CPU time for a call (a parse, execute, or fetch), expressed in hundredths of seconds.

- CONNECT_TIME limits the total elapsed time of a session, expressed in minutes.

- IDLE_TIME limits periods of continuous inactive time during a session, expressed in minutes. Long-running queries and other operations are not subject to this limit.

- LOGICAL_READS_PER_SESSION specifies the number of data blocks read in a session, including blocks read from memory and disk.

- LOGICAL_READS_PER_CALL specifies the number of data blocks read for a call to process a SQL statement (a parse, execute, or fetch).

- PRIVATE_SGA specifies the amount of private space a session can allocate in the shared pool of the system global area (SGA), expressed in bytes. Use K or M to specify this limit in kilobytes or megabytes.

NOTE
This limit applies only if you are using multi-threaded server architecture. The private space for a session in the SGA includes private SQL and PL/SQL areas, but not shared SQL and PL/SQL areas.

- COMPOSITE_LIMIT specifies the total resources cost for a session, expressed in *service unit*s. Oracle calculates the total service units as a weighted sum of CPU_PER_SESSION, CONNECT_TIME, LOGICAL_READS_PER_SESSION, and PRIVATE_SGA.

password_parameters

For a detailed description and explanation of how to use password management and protection, see *Oracle8i Administrator's Guide*.

- FAILED_LOGIN_ATTEMPTS specifies the number of failed attempts to log in to the user account before the account is locked.

- PASSWORD_LIFE_TIME limits the number of days the same password can be used for authentication.

  The password expires if it is not changed within this period, and further connections are rejected.

- PASSWORD_REUSE_TIME specifies the number of days before which a password cannot be reused. If you set PASSWORD_REUSE_TIME to an integer value, then you must set PASSWORD_REUSE_MAX to UNLIMITED.

- PASSWORD_REUSE_MAX specifies the number of password changes required before the current password can be reused. If you set PASSWORD_REUSE_MAX to an integer value, then you must set PASSWORD_REUSE_TIME to UNLIMITED.

- PASSWORD_LOCK_TIME specifies the number of days an account will be locked after the specified number of consecutive failed login attempts.

- PASSWORD_GRACE_TIME specifies the number of days after the grace period begins during which a warning is issued and login is allowed. If the password is not changed during the grace period, the password expires.

- PASSWORD_VERIFY_FUNCTION allows a PL/SQL password complexity verification script to be passed as an argument to the CREATE PROFILE statement. Oracle provides a default script, but you can create your own routine or use third-party software instead.

■ *function* is the name of the password complexity verification routine.

■ NULL indicates that no password verification is performed.

Restrictions: If PASSWORD_REUSE_TIME is set to an integer value, PASSWORD_REUSE_MAX must be set to UNLIMITED. If PASSWORD_REUSE_MAX is set to an integer value, PASSWORD_REUSE_TIME must be set to UNLIMITED.
If both PASSWORD_REUSE_TIME and PASSWORD_REUSE_MAX are set to UNLIMITED, then Oracle uses neither of these password resources.
If PASSWORD_REUSE_MAX is set to DEFAULT and PASSWORD_REUSE_TIME is set to UNLIMITED, then Oracle uses the PASSWORD_REUSE_MAX value defined in the DEFAULT profile.
If PASSWORD_REUSE_TIME is set to DEFAULT and PASSWORD_REUSE_MAX is set to UNLIMITED, then Oracle uses the PASSWORD_REUSE_TIME value defined in the DEFAULT profile.
If both PASSWORD_REUSE_TIME and PASSWORD_REUSE_MAX are set to DEFAULT, then Oracle uses whichever value is defined in the DEFAULT profile.

CREATE ROLE

Syntax

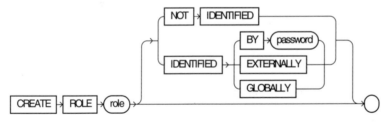

Purpose

To create a *role*, which is a set of privileges that can be granted to users or to other roles. You can use roles to administer database privileges. You can add privileges to a role and then grant the role to a user. The user can then enable the role and exercise the privileges granted by the role. A role contains all privileges granted to the role and all privileges of other roles granted to it. A new role is initially empty. You add privileges to a role with the GRANT statement. When you create a role that is NOT IDENTIFIED or is IDENTIFIED EXTERNALLY or BY *password*, Oracle grants you the role with ADMIN OPTION. However, when you create a role IDENTIFIED GLOBALLY, Oracle does not grant you the role. For a detailed description and explanation of using global roles, see *Oracle8i Distributed Database Systems*.

Prerequisites

You must have CREATE ROLE system privilege.

Keywords and Parameters

■ *role* is the name of the role to be created. Oracle recommends that the role contain at least one single-byte character regardless of whether the database character set also contains multibyte characters.

Some roles are defined by SQL scripts provided on your distribution media.

■ NOT IDENTIFIED indicates that this role is authorized by the database and that no password is required to enable the role.

■ IDENTIFIED indicates that a user must be authorized by the specified method before the role is enabled with the SET ROLE statement:

■ BY *password* creates a **local user** and indicates that the user must specify the password to Oracle when enabling the role. The password can contain only single-byte characters from your database character set regardless of whether this character set also contains multibyte characters.

■ EXTERNALLY creates an **external user** and indicates that a user must be authorized by an external service (such as an operating system or third-party service) before enabling the role.

Depending on the operating system, the user may have to specify a password to the operating system before the role is enabled.

■ GLOBALLY creates a **global user** and indicates that a user must be authorized to use the role by the enterprise directory service before the role is enabled with the SET ROLE statement, or at login.

If you omit both the NOT IDENTIFIED clause and the IDENTIFIED clause, the role defaults to NOT IDENTIFIED.

CREATE ROLLBACK SEGMENT

Syntax

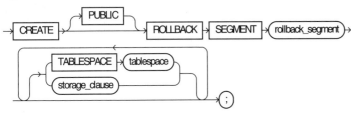

Purpose

To create a rollback segment. A **rollback segment** is an object that Oracle uses to store data necessary to reverse, or undo, changes made by transactions.

Prerequisites

You must have CREATE ROLLBACK SEGMENT system privilege.

Keyword and Parameters

- PUBLIC specifies that the rollback segment is public and is available to any instance. If you omit this clause, the rollback segment is private and is available only to the instance naming it in its initialization parameter ROLLBACK_SEGMENTS.

- *rollback_segment* is the name of the rollback segment to be created.

- TABLESPACE identifies the tablespace in which the rollback segment is created. If you omit this clause, Oracle creates the rollback segment in the SYSTEM tablespace.
  Restriction: You cannot create a rollback segment in a tablespace that is system managed (that is, during creation you specified EXTENT MANAGEMENT LOCAL AUTOALLOCATE).

NOTE
A tablespace can have multiple rollback segments. Generally, multiple rollback segments improve performance.
The tablespace must be online for you to add a rollback segment to it. When you create a rollback segment, it is initially offline. To make it available for transactions by your Oracle instance, bring it online using the ALTER ROLLBACK SEGMENT statement. To bring it online automatically whenever you start up the database, add the segment's name to the value of the ROLLBACK_SEGMENTS initialization parameter.

For more information on creating rollback segments and making them available, see *Oracle8i Administrator's Guide.*

- *storage_clause* specifies the characteristics for the rollback segment.

NOTE
The OPTIMAL parameter of the storage_clause is of particular interest, because it applies only to rollback segments.
You cannot specify the PCTINCREASE parameter of the storage_clause with CREATE ROLLBACK SEGMENT.

CREATE SYNONYM

Syntax

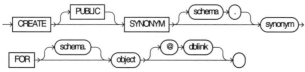

Purpose

To create a synonym. A *synonym* is an alternative name for a table, view, sequence, procedure, stored function, package, materialized view, Java class schema object, or another synonym. For general information on synonyms, see *Oracle8i Concepts*. Synonyms provide both data independence and location transparency. Synonyms permit applications to function without modification regardless of which user owns the table or view and regardless of which database holds the table or view.

Prerequisites

To create a private synonym in your own schema, you must have CREATE SYNONYM system privilege. To create a private synonym in another user's schema, you must have CREATE ANY SYNONYM system privilege. To create a PUBLIC synonym, you must have CREATE PUBLIC SYNONYM system privilege.

Keywords and Parameters

- PUBLIC creates a public synonym. Public synonyms are accessible to all users.

  Oracle uses a public synonym only when resolving references to an object if the object is not prefaced by a schema and the object is not followed by a database link.

  If you omit this clause, the synonym is private and is accessible only within its schema. A private synonym name must be unique in its schema.

- *schema* is the schema to contain the synonym. If you omit *schema*, Oracle creates the synonym in your own schema. You cannot specify schema if you have specified PUBLIC.

- *synonym* is the name of the synonym to be created.

- FOR identifies the object for which the synonym is created. If you do not qualify object with *schema*, Oracle assumes that the schema object is in your own schema. The schema object can be of the following types:

  - table or object table
  - view or object view
  - sequence
  - stored procedure, function, or package
  - materialized view
  - Java class schema object
  - synonym

  The schema object need not currently exist and you need not have privileges to access the object. **Restrictions:** The schema object cannot be contained in a package.

  You cannot create a synonym for an object type.

- *dblink*   You can use a complete or partial *dblink* to create a synonym for a schema object on a remote database where the object is located. If you specify *dblink* and omit *schema*, the synonym refers to an object in the schema specified by the database link. Oracle Corporation recommends that you specify the schema containing the object in the remote database.

  If you omit *dblink*, Oracle assumes the object is located on the local database. **Restriction:** You cannot specify *dblink* for a Java class synonym.

CREATE TABLE

Syntax

relational_table:

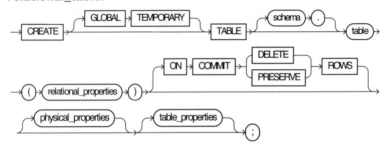

object_table:

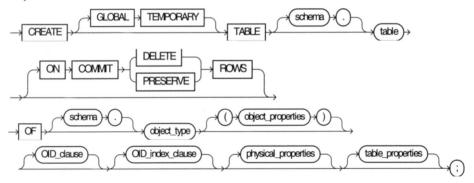

relational_properties::=

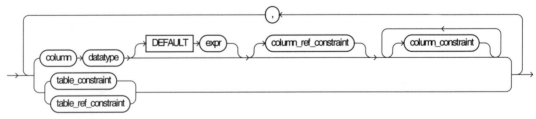

object_properties::=

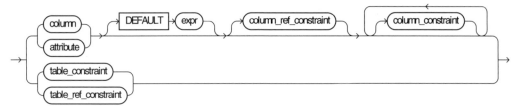

physical_properties::=

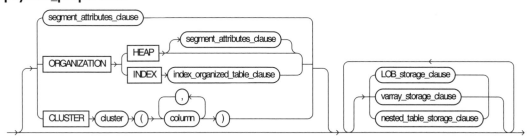

table_properties::=

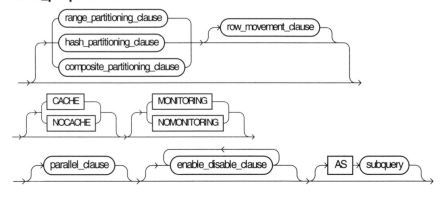

OID_clause::=

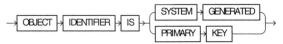

OID_index_clause::=

segment_attributes_clause::=

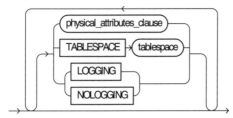

row_movement_clause::=

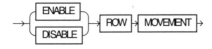

physical_attributes_clause::=

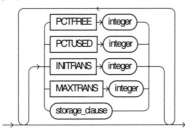

index_organized_table_clause::=

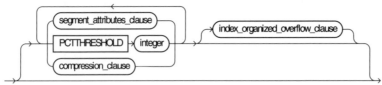

compression_clause::=

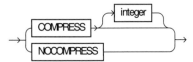

index_organized_overflow_clause::=

LOB_storage_clause::=

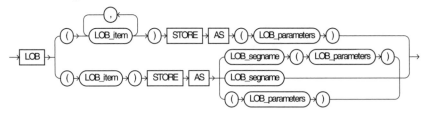

LOB_parameters::=

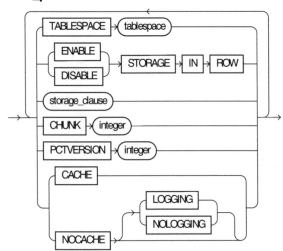

varray_storage_clause::=

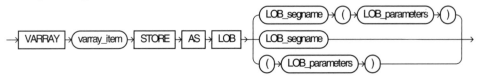

nested_table_storage_clause::=

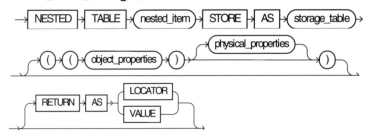

range_partitioning_clause::=

composite_partitioning_clause::=

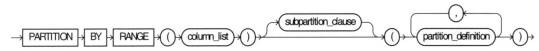

partition_definition::=

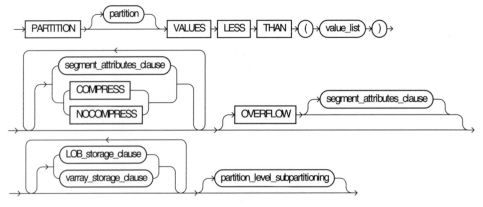

subpartition_clause::=

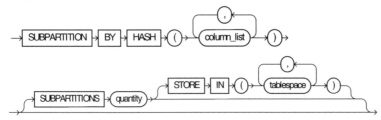

partition_level_subpartitioning::=

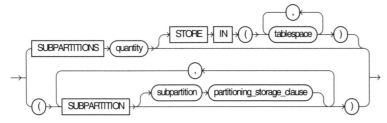

hash_partitioning_clause::=

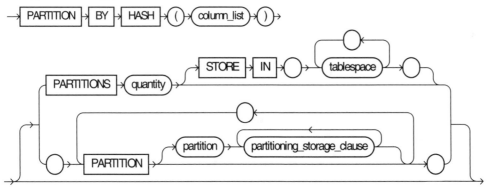

partitioning_storage_clause::=

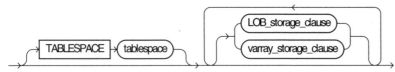

parallel_clause::=

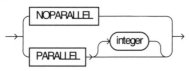

enable_disable_clause::=

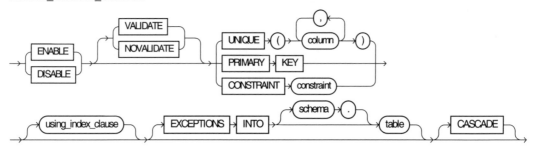

using_index_clause::=

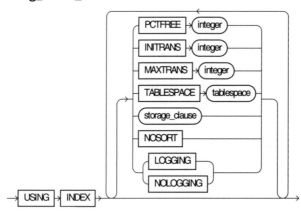

Purpose

To create a *relational table,* the basic structure to hold user data. To create an *object table* or a table that uses an object type for a column definition. An object table is a table explicitly defined to hold object instances of a particular type. You can also create an object type and then use it in a column when creating a relational table. For more information about creating objects, see *Oracle8i Application Developer's Guide – Fundamentals.* Tables are created with no data unless a query is specified. You can add rows to a table with the INSERT statement. After creating a table, you can define additional columns, partitions, and integrity constraints with the ADD clause of the ALTER TABLE statement. You can change the definition of an existing column or partition with the MODIFY clause of the ALTER TABLE statement.

Prerequisites

To create a relational table in your own schema, you must have CREATE TABLE system privilege. To create a table in another user's schema, you must have CREATE ANY TABLE system privilege. Also, the owner of the schema to contain the table must have either space quota on the tablespace to contain the table or UNLIMITED TABLESPACE system privilege. In addition to the table privileges above, to create a table that uses types, the owner of the table must have the EXECUTE object privilege in order to access all types referenced by the table, or you must have the EXECUTE ANY TYPE system privilege. These privileges must be granted explicitly and not acquired through a role. Additionally, if the table owner intends to grant access to the table to other users, the owner must have been granted the EXECUTE privileges to the referenced types with the GRANT OPTION, or have the EXECUTE ANY TYPE system privilege with the ADMIN OPTION. Without these privileges, the table owner has insufficient privileges to grant access on the table to other users. To enable a UNIQUE or PRIMARY KEY constraint, you must have the privileges necessary to create an index on the table. You need these privileges because Oracle creates an index on the columns of the unique or primary key in the schema containing the table. For more information about the privileges required to create tables using types, see *Oracle8i Application Developer's Guide – Fundamentals*.

Keywords and Parameters

- GLOBAL TEMPORARY specifies that the table is temporary and that its definition is visible to all sessions. The data in a temporary table is visible only to the session that inserts the data into the table.

  A temporary table has a definition that persists the same as the definitions of regular tables, but it contains either **session-specific** or **transaction-specific** data. You specify whether the data is session- or transaction-specific with the ON COMMIT keywords (below).

  For more information on temporary tables, please refer to *Oracle8i Concepts*.
  Restrictions: Temporary tables cannot be partitioned, index-organized, or clustered.
  You cannot specify any referential integrity (foreign key) constraints on temporary tables.
  Temporary tables cannot contain columns of nested table or varray type.
  You cannot specify the following clauses of the *LOB_storage_clause*: TABLESPACE, *storage_clause*, LOGGING or NOLOGGING, MONITORING or NOMONITORING, or *LOB_index_clause*.
  Parallel DML and parallel queries are not supported for temporary tables. (Parallel hints are ignored. Specification of the *parallel_clause* returns an error.)
  You cannot specify the *segment_attributes_clause, nested_table_storage_clause,* or *parallel_clause*.
  Distributed transactions are not supported for temporary tables.

- *schema* is the schema to contain the table. If you omit *schema*, Oracle creates the table in your own schema.

- *table* is the name of the table (or object table) to be created. A partitioned *table* cannot be a clustered table or an object table.

- OF *object_type* explicitly creates an object table of type *object_type*. The columns of an object table correspond to the top-level attributes of type *object_type*. Each row will contain an object instance, and each instance will be assigned a unique, system-generated object identifier (OID) when a row is inserted. If you omit schema, Oracle creates the object table in your own schema.

Objects residing in an object table are referenceable. For more information about using REFs, see *Oracle8i Administrator's Guide*.

■ *column* specifies the name of a column of the table.

If you also specify AS *subquery*, you can omit *column* and *datatype* unless you are creating an index-organized table (IOT). If you specify AS *subquery* when creating an IOT, you must specify *column*, and you must omit *datatype*.

The absolute maximum number of columns in a table is 1000. However, when you create an object table (or a relational table with columns of object, nested table, varray, or REF type), Oracle maps the columns of the user-defined types to relational columns, creating in effect "hidden columns" that count toward the 1000-column limit. For details on how Oracle calculates the total number of columns in such a table, please refer to *Oracle8i Administrator's Guide*.

■ *attribute* specifies the qualified column name of an item in an object.

■ *datatype* is the datatype of a column.
Restrictions: You cannot specify a LOB column or a column of type VARRAY for a partitioned index-organized table. The datatypes for nonpartitioned index-organized tables are not restricted. You can specify a column of type ROWID, but Oracle does not guarantee that the values in such columns are valid rowids.

You can omit *datatype*:

■ If you also specify AS *subquery*. (If you are creating an index-organized table and you specify AS *subquery*, you *must* omit the datatype.)

■ If the statement also designates the column as part of a foreign key in a referential integrity constraint. (Oracle automatically assigns to the column the datatype of the corresponding column of the referenced key of the referential integrity constraint.)

■ DEFAULT specifies a value to be assigned to the column if a subsequent INSERT statement omits a value for the column. The datatype of the expression must match the datatype of the column. The column must also be long enough to hold this expression. A DEFAULT expression cannot contain references to other columns, the pseudocolumns CURRVAL, NEXTVAL, LEVEL, and ROWNUM, or date constants that are not fully specified.

■ **table_ref_constraint** and **column_ref_constraint**   These clauses let you further describe a column of type REF. The only difference between these clauses is that you specify *table_ref* from the table level, so you must identify the REF column or attribute you are defining. You specify *column_ref* after you have already identified the REF column or attribute.

■ *column_constraint* defines an integrity constraint as part of the column definition.

You can create UNIQUE, PRIMARY KEY, and REFERENCES constraints on scalar attributes of object type columns. You can also create NOT NULL constraints on object type columns, and CHECK constraints that reference object type columns or any attribute of an object type column.

■ *table_constraint* defines an integrity constraint as part of the table definition.

NOTE
You must specify a PRIMARY KEY constraint for an index-organized table.

segment_attributes_clause:

- *physical_attributes_clause* specifies the value of the PCTFREE, PCTUSED, INITRANS, and MAXTRANS parameters and the storage characteristics of the table.

    For a nonpartitioned table, each parameter and storage characteristic you specify determines the actual physical attribute of the segment associated with the table.

    For partitioned tables, the value you specify for the parameter or storage characteristic is the default physical attribute of the segments associated with all partitions specified in this CREATE statement (and in subsequent ALTER TABLE ... ADD PARTITION statements), unless you explicitly override that value in the PARTITION clause of the statement that creates the partition.

- PCTFREE specifies the percentage of space in each data block of the table, object table OID index, or partition reserved for future updates to the table's rows. The value of PCTFREE must be a value from 0 to 99. A value of 0 allows the entire block to be filled by inserts of new rows.

    The default value is 10. This value reserves 10% of each block for updates to existing rows and allows inserts of new rows to fill a maximum of 90% of each block.

    PCTFREE has the same function in the PARTITION description and in the statements that create and alter clusters, indexes, snapshots, and snapshot logs. The combination of PCTFREE and PCTUSED determines whether new rows will be inserted into existing data blocks or into new blocks.

- PCTUSED specifies the minimum percentage of used space that Oracle maintains for each data block of the table, object table OID index, or index-organized table overflow data segment. A block becomes a candidate for row insertion when its used space falls below PCTUSED.

    PCTUSED is specified as a positive integer from 1 to 99 and defaults to 40.

    PCTUSED has the same function in the PARTITION description and in the statements that create and alter clusters, snapshots, and snapshot logs.

    PCTUSED is not a valid table storage characteristic for an index-organized table (ORGANIZATION INDEX).

    The sum of PCTFREE and PCTUSED must be less than 100. You can use PCTFREE and PCTUSED together to utilize space within a table more efficiently. For information on the performance effects of different values PCTUSED and PCTFREE, see *Oracle8i Tuning*.

- INITRANS specifies the initial number of transaction entries allocated within each data block allocated to the table, object table OID index, partition, LOB index segment, or overflow data segment. This value can range from 1 to 255 and defaults to 1. In general, you should not change the INITRANS value from its default.

    Each transaction that updates a block requires a transaction entry in the block. The size of a transaction entry depends on your operating system.

    This parameter ensures that a minimum number of concurrent transactions can update the block and helps avoid the overhead of dynamically allocating a transaction entry.

    The INITRANS parameter serves the same purpose in the PARTITION description, clusters, indexes, snapshots, and snapshot logs as in tables. The minimum and default INITRANS value for a cluster or index is 2, rather than 1.

- MAXTRANS specifies the maximum number of concurrent transactions that can update a data block allocated to the table, object table OID index, partition, LOB index segment, or index-organized overflow data segment. This limit does not apply to queries. This value can range from 1 to 255 and the default is a function of the data block size. You should not change the MAXTRANS value from its default.

  If the number of concurrent transactions updating a block exceeds the INITRANS value, Oracle dynamically allocates transaction entries in the block until either the MAXTRANS value is exceeded or the block has no more free space.

  The MAXTRANS parameter serves the same purpose in the PARTITION description, clusters, snapshots, and snapshot logs as in tables.

- *storage_clause* specifies the storage characteristics for the table, object table OID index, partition, LOB storage, LOB index segment, or index-organized table overflow data segment. This clause has performance ramifications for large tables. Storage should be allocated to minimize dynamic allocation of additional space.

- TABLESPACE specifies the tablespace in which Oracle creates the table, object table OID index, partition, LOB storage, LOB index segment, or index-organized table overflow data segment. If you omit TABLESPACE, then Oracle creates that item in the default tablespace of the owner of the schema containing the table.

  For heap-organized tables with one or more LOB columns, if you omit the TABLESPACE clause for LOB storage, Oracle creates the LOB data and index segments in the tablespace where the table is created.

  However, for an index-organized table with one or more LOB columns, if you omit TABLESPACE, the LOB data and index segments are created in the tablespace in which the primary key index segment of the index-organized table is created.

  For nonpartitioned tables, the value specified for TABLESPACE is the actual physical attribute of the segment associated with the table. For partitioned tables, the value specified for TABLESPACE is the default physical attribute of the segments associated with all partitions specified in the CREATE statement (and on subsequent ALTER TABLE ...ADD PARTITION statements), unless you specify TABLESPACE in the PARTITION description.

- LOGGING | NOLOGGING specifies whether the creation of the table (and any indexes required because of constraints), partition, or LOB storage characteristics will be logged in the redo log file. The logging attribute of the table is independent of that of its indexes. This attribute also specifies that subsequent Direct Loader (SQL*Loader) and direct-load INSERT operations against the table, partition, or LOB storage are logged (LOGGING) or not logged (NOLOGGING).

  If you omit LOGGING|NOLOGGING, the logging attribute of the table or table partition defaults to the logging attribute of the tablespace in which it resides. For LOBs, if you omit LOGGING|NOLOGGING,

  - If you specify CACHE, then LOGGING is used (because you cannot have CACHE NOLOGGING).

  - Otherwise, the logging attribute defaults to the logging attribute of the tablespace in which it resides.

  For nonpartitioned tables, the value specified for LOGGING is the actual physical attribute of the segment associated with the table. For partitioned tables, the logging attribute value specified is the default physical attribute of the segments associated with all partitions specified in the

CREATE statement (and in subsequent ALTER TABLE ... ADD PARTITION statements), unless you specify LOGGING|NOLOGGING in the PARTITION description.

In NOLOGGING mode, data is modified with minimal logging (to mark new extents INVALID and to record dictionary changes). When applied during media recovery, the extent invalidation records mark a range of blocks as logically corrupt, because the redo data is not fully logged. Therefore, if you cannot afford to lose this table, you should take a backup after the NOLOGGING operation.

The size of a redo log generated for an operation in NOLOGGING mode is significantly smaller than the log generated with the LOGGING attribute set.

If the database is run in ARCHIVELOG mode, media recovery from a backup taken before the LOGGING operation restores the table. However, media recovery from a backup taken before the NOLOGGING operation does not restore the table.

For more information about logging and parallel DML, see *Oracle8i Concepts* and *Oracle8i Administrator's Guide.*

■ RECOVERABLE | UNRECOVERABLE   These keywords are deprecated and have been replaced with LOGGING and NOLOGGING, respectively. Although RECOVERABLE and UNRECOVERABLE are supported for backward compatibility, Oracle Corporation strongly recommends that you use the LOGGING and NOLOGGING keywords.
Restrictions: You cannot specify RECOVERABLE for partitioned tables or LOB storage characteristics.
You cannot specify UNRECOVERABLE for a partitioned or index-organized tables.
You can specify UNRECOVERABLE only with AS *subquery.*

■ ORGANIZATION HEAP specifies that the data rows of *table* are stored in no particular order. This is the default.

■ ORGANIZATION INDEX specifies that *table* is created as an index-organized table. In an index-organized table, the data rows are held in an index defined on the primary key for the table.

■ ***index_organized_table_clause*** specifies that Oracle should maintain the table rows (both primary key column values and non-key column values) in a B*-tree index built on the primary key. Index-organized tables are therefore best suited for primary key-based access and manipulation. An index-organized table is an alternative to

   ■ A nonclustered table indexed on the primary key by using the CREATE INDEX statement

   ■ A clustered table stored in an indexed cluster that has been created using the CREATE CLUSTER statement that maps the primary key for the table to the cluster key
   Restrictions: You cannot specify a column of type ROWID for an index-organized table. A partitioned index-organized table cannot contain columns of LOB or varray type. (This restriction does not apply to nonpartitioned index-organized tables.)

NOTE
You must specify a primary key for an index-organized table, because the primary key uniquely identifies a row. Use the primary key instead of the rowid for directly accessing index-organized rows.

■ PCTTHRESHOLD *integer* specifies the percentage of space reserved in the index block for an index-organized table row. Any portion of the row that exceeds the specified threshold is stored

in the overflow segment. PCTTHRESHOLD must be a value from 1 to 50.
Restriction: PCTTHRESHOLD must be large enough to hold the primary key.
You cannot specify PCTTHRESHOLD for individual partitions of an index-organized table.

■ OVERFLOW specifies that index-organized table data rows exceeding the specified threshold are placed in the data segment listed in this clause.

When you create an index-organized table, Oracle evaluates the maximum size of each column to estimate the largest possible row. If an overflow segment is needed but you have not specified OVERFLOW, Oracle raises an error and does not execute the CREATE TABLE statement. This checking function guarantees that subsequent DML operations on the index-organized table will not fail because an overflow segment is lacking.

All physical attributes and storage characteristics you specify in this clause after the OVERFLOW keyword apply only to the overflow segment of the table. Physical attributes and storage characteristics for the index-organized table itself, default values for all its partitions, and values for individual partitions must be specified before this keyword.

If the index-organized table contains one or more LOB columns, the LOBs will be stored out-of-line unless you specify OVERFLOW, even if they would otherwise be small enough be to stored inline.

■ INCLUDING *column_name* specifies a column at which to divide an index-organized table row into index and overflow portions. All non-primary-key columns that follow *column_name* are stored in the overflow data segment. A *column_name* is either the name of the last primary-key column or any subsequent nonprimary-key column.
Restriction: You cannot specify this clause for individual partitions of an index-organized table.

■ *compression_clause* enables or disables key compression.

   ■ COMPRESS enables key compression, which eliminates repeated occurrence of primary key column values in index-organized tables. Use *integer* to specify the prefix length (number of prefix columns to compress).

   The valid range of prefix length values is from 1 to the number of primary key columns minus 1. The default prefix length is the number of primary key columns minus 1.
   Restriction: At the partition level, you can specify COMPRESS, but you cannot specify the prefix length with *integer*.

   ■ NOCOMPRESS disables key compression in index-organized tables. This is the default.

■ *LOB_storage_clause* specifies the storage attributes of LOB data segments.

   For a nonpartitioned table (that is, when specified in the *physical_properties* clause without any of the partitioning clauses), this clause specifies the table's storage attributes of LOB data segments.

   For a partitioned table specified at the table level (that is, when specified in the *physical_properties* clause along with one of the partitioning clauses), this clause specifies the default storage attributes for LOB data segments associated with each partition or subpartition. These storage attributes apply to all partitions or subpartitions unless overridden by a *LOB_storage_clause* at the partition or subpartition level.

   For an individual partition of a partitioned table (that is, when specified as part of a *partition_definition*), this clause specifies the storage attributes of the data segments of that partition or the default storage attributes of any subpartitions of this partition. A partition-level *LOB_storage_clause* overrides a table-level *LOB_storage_clause*.

For an individual subpartition of a partitioned table (that is, when specified as part of a *subpartition_claus*e), this clause specifies the storage attributes of the data segments of this subpartition. A subpartition-level *LOB_storage_clause* overrides both partition-level and table-level *LOB_storage_clauses.*
Restrictions: The only parameter of the *LOB_storage_clause* you can specify for a hash partition or hash subpartition is TABLESPACE.
You cannot specify the *LOB_index_clause* if *table* is partitioned.

For detailed information about LOBs, see Oracle8i Application Developer's Guide -Fundamentals.

- ■ *lob_item* is the LOB column name or LOB object attribute for which you are explicitly defining tablespace and storage characteristics that are different from those of the table. Oracle automatically creates a system-managed index for each *lob_item* you create.
Restriction: If table is partitioned, you cannot specify LOB storage for a LOB object attribute.

■ STORE AS *lob_segname* specifies the name of the LOB data segment. You cannot use *lob_segname* if you specify more than one *lob_item.*

■ *lob_parameters*

  - ■ ENABLE STORAGE IN ROW specifies that the LOB value is stored in the row (inline) if its length is less than approximately 4000 bytes minus system control information. This is the default.
  Restriction: For an index-organized table, you cannot specify this parameter unless you have specified an OVERFLOW segment in the *index_organized_table_clause.*

  - ■ DISABLE STORAGE IN ROW specifies that the LOB value is stored outside of the row regardless of the length of the LOB value.

  The LOB locator is always stored in the row regardless of where the LOB value is stored.

  You cannot change the value of STORAGE IN ROW once it is set.

  - ■ CHUNK *integer* specifies the number of bytes to be allocated for LOB manipulation. If *integer* is not a multiple of the database block size, Oracle rounds up (in bytes) to the next multiple. For example, if the database block size is 2048 and *integer* is 2050, Oracle allocates 4096 bytes (2 blocks). The maximum value is 32768 (32K), which is the largest Oracle block size allowed. The default CHUNK size is one Oracle database block.

    You cannot change the value of CHUNK once it is set.

NOTE
The value of CHUNK must be less than or equal to the value of NEXT
(either the default value or that specified in the storage_clause).

  If CHUNK exceeds the value of NEXT, Oracle returns an error.

  - ■ PCTVERSION *integer* is the maximum percentage of overall LOB storage space used for creating new versions of the LOB. The default value is 10, meaning that older versions of the LOB data are not overwritten until 10% of the overall LOB storage space is used.

  - ■ *LOB_index_clause*   This clause is deprecated as of Oracle8i. Oracle generates an index for each LOB column. The LOB indexes are system named and system managed.

    Although it is still possible for you to specify this clause, Oracle Corporation strongly recommends that you no longer do so.

For information on how Oracle manages LOB indexes in tables migrated from earlier versions, see *Oracle8i Migration*.

- *varray_storage_clause* lets you specify separate storage characteristics for the LOB in which a varray will be stored. In addition, if you specify this clause, Oracle will always store the varray in a LOB, even if it is small enough to be stored inline.

  - For a nonpartitioned table (that is, when specified in the *physical_properties* clause without any of the partitioning clauses), this clause specifies the storage attributes of the varray's LOB data segments.

  - For a partitioned table specified at the table level (that is, when specified in the *physical_properties* clause along with one of the partitioning clauses), this clause specifies the default storage attributes for the varray's LOB data segments associated with each partition (or its subpartitions, if any).

  - For an individual partition of a partitioned table (that is, when specified as part of a *partition_definition*), this clause specifies the storage attributes of the varray's LOB data segments of that partition or the default storage attributes of the varray's LOB data segments of any subpartitions of this partition. A partition-level *varray_storage_clause* overrides a table-level *varray_storage_clause*.

  - For an individual subpartition of a partitioned table (that is, when specified as part of a *subpartition_clause*), this clause specifies the storage attributes of the varray's data segments of this subpartition. A subpartition-level *varray_storage_clause* overrides both partition-level and table-level *varray_storage_clauses*.

    Restriction: You cannot specify the TABLESPACE parameter of *lob_parameters* as part of this clause. The LOB tablespace for a varray defaults to the containing table's tablespace.

- *nested_table_storage_clause* enables you to specify separate storage characteristics for a nested table, which in turn enables you to define the nested table as an index-organized table. The storage table is created in the same tablespace as its parent table (using the default storage characteristics) and stores the nested table values of the column for which it was created.

  You must include this clause when creating a table with columns or column attributes whose type is a nested table. (Clauses within this clause that function the same way they function for parent object tables are not repeated here.)

  Restrictions: You cannot specify this clause for a temporary table.

  You cannot specify the *parallel_clause* or the the *OID_clause*.

  You cannot specify TABLESPACE (as part of the *segment_attributes_clause*) for a nested table. The tablespace is always that of the parent table.

  At create time, you cannot specify (as part of *object_properties*) a *table_ref_constraint*, *column_ref_constraint*, or referential constraint for the attributes of a nested table. However, you can modify a nested table to add such constraints using ALTER TABLE.

  You cannot query or perform DML statements on the storage table directly, but you can modify the nested table column storage characteristics by using the name of storage table in an ALTER TABLE statement.

  - *nested_item* is the name of a column (or a top-level attribute of the table's object type) whose type is a nested table.

  - *storage_table* is the name of the table where the rows of *nested_item* reside. The storage table is created in the same schema and the same tablespace as the parent table.

You cannot query or perform DML statements on *storage_table* directly, but you can modify its storage characteristics by specifying its name in an ALTER TABLE statement.

■ RETURN AS specifies what Oracle returns as the result of a query.

    ■ VALUE returns a copy of the nested table itself.

    ■ LOCATOR returns a collection locator to the copy of the nested table.

NOTE
The locator is scoped to the session and cannot be used across sessions. Unlike a LOB locator, the collection locator cannot be used to modify the collection instance.

If you do not specify the *segment_attributes_clause* or the *LOB_storage_clause*, the nested table is heap organized and is created with default storage characteristics.

■ CLUSTER specifies that the table is to be part of *cluster*. The columns listed in this clause are the table columns that correspond to the cluster's columns. Generally, the cluster columns of a table are the column or columns that make up its primary key or a portion of its primary key.

Specify one column from the table for each column in the cluster key. The columns are matched by position, not by name.

A clustered table uses the cluster's space allocation. Therefore, do not use the PCTFREE, PCTUSED, INITRANS, or MAXTRANS parameters, the TABLESPACE clause, or the *storage_clause* with the CLUSTER clause.
Restriction: Object tables cannot be part of a cluster.

■ ON COMMIT can be specified only if you are creating a temporary table. This clause specifies whether the data in the temporary table persists for the duration of a transaction or a session.

    ■ DELETE ROWS specifies that the temporary table is transaction specific (this is the default). Oracle will truncate the table (delete all its rows) after each commit.

    ■ PRESERVE ROWS specifies that the temporary table is session specific. Oracle will truncate the table (delete all its rows) when you terminate the session.

■ *OID_clause* lets you specify whether the object identifier (OID) of the object table should be system generated or should be based on the primary key of the table. The default is SYSTEM GENERATED.
Restrictions: You cannot specify OBJECT IDENTIFIER IS PRIMARY KEY unless you have already specified a PRIMARY KEY constraint for the table.
You cannot specify this clause for a nested table.

NOTE
A primary key OID is locally (but not necessarily globally) unique. If you require a globally unique identifier, you must ensure that the primary key is globally unique.

■ *OID_index_clause* This clause is relevant only if you have specified the *OID_clause* as SYSTEM GENERATED.

It specifies an index, and optionally its storage characteristics, on the hidden object identifier column.

■ *index* is the name of the index on the hidden system-generated object identifier column. If not specified, Oracle generates a name.

■ *hash_partitioning_clause* specifies that the table is to be partitioned using the hash method. Oracle assigns rows to partitions using a hash function on values found in columns designated as the partitioning key. For more information on hash partitioning, see *Oracle8i Concept*s.

■ *column_list* is an ordered list of columns used to determine into which partition a row belongs (**the partitioning key**).
Restrictions: You cannot specify more than 16 columns in *column_list*.
The *column_list* cannot contain the ROWID or UROWID pseudocolumns.
The columns in *column_list* can be of any built-in datatype except ROWID, LONG, or LOB.

You can specify hash partitioning in one of two ways:

■ You can specify the number of partitions. In this case, Oracle assigns partition names of the form SYS_*P*n*nn*. The STORE IN clause specifies one or more tablespaces where the hash partitions are to be stored. The number of tablespaces does not have to equal the number of partitions. If the number of partitions is greater than the number of tablespaces, Oracle cycles through the names of the tablespaces.

■ Alternatively, you can specify individual partitions by name. The TABLESPACE clause specifies where the partition should be stored.

NOTE
The only attribute you can specify for hash partitions (or subpartitions) is TABLESPACE. Hash partitions inherit all other attributes from table-level defaults. Hash subpartitions inherit any attributes specified at the partition level, and inherit all other attributes from the table-level defaults.

Tablespace storage specified at the table level is overridden by tablespace storage specified at the partition level, which in turn is overridden by tablespace storage specified at the subpartition level.

■ *range_partitioning_clause*

■ PARTITION BY RANGE specifies that the table is partitioned on ranges of values from *column_list*. For an index-organized table, *column_list* must be a subset of the primary key columns of the table.

■ *column_list* is an ordered list of columns used to determine into which partition a row belongs (**the partitioning key**).

■ *composite_partitioning_clause* specifies that table is to be first range partitioned, and then the partitions further partitioned into hash subpartitions. This combination of range partitioning and hash subpartitioning is called **composite partitioning**.

■ *subpartition_clause* specifies that Oracle should subpartition by hash each partition in *tabl*e. The subpartitioning *column_list* is unrelated to the partitioning key.

■ SUBPARTITIONS *quantity* specifies the default number of subpartitions in each partition of *table*, and optionally one or more tablespaces in which they are to be stored.

The default value is 1. If you do not specify the *subpartition_clause* here, Oracle will create each partition with one hash subpartition unless you subsequently specify the *partition_level_hash_subpartitioning* clause.

- **■** *partition_definition* PARTITION *partition* specifies the physical partition attributes. If *partition* is omitted, Oracle generates a name with the form SYS_P*n* for the partition.

NOTES
You can specify up to 64K-1 partitions and 64K-1 subpartitions. For a discussion of factors that might impose practical limits less than this number, please refer to Oracle8i Administrator's Guide.
You can create a partitioned table with just one partition. Note, however, that a partitioned table with one partition is different from a nonpartitioned table. For instance, you cannot add a partition to a nonpartitioned table.

- **■** VALUES LESS THAN specifies the noninclusive upper bound for the current partition.

- **■** *value_list* is an ordered list of literal values corresponding to *column_list* in the *partition_by_range_clause*. You can substitute the keyword MAXVALUE for any literal in *value_list*. MAXVALUE specifies a maximum value that will always sort higher than any other value, including NULL.

  Specifying a value other than MAXVALUE for the highest partition bound imposes an implicit integrity constraint on the table. See *Oracle8i Concepts* for more information about partition bounds.

NOTE
If table is partitioned on a DATE column, and if the NLS date format does not specify the century with the year, you must use the TO_DATE function with a 4-character format mask for the year. The NLS date format is determined implicitly by NLS_TERRITORY or explicitly by NLS_DATE_FORMAT. For more information on these initialization parameters, see Oracle8i National Language Support Guide.

- **■** *LOB_storage_clause* lets you specify LOB storage characteristics for one or more LOB items in this partition. If you do not specify the *LOB_storage_clause* for a LOB item, Oracle generates a name for each LOB data partition. The system-generated names for LOB data and LOB index partitions take the form SYS_LOB_*Pn* and SYS_IL_*Pn*, respectively, where P stands for "partition" and *n* is a system-generated number.

- **■** *partition_level_subpartitioning* lets you specify hash subpartitions for *partition*. This clause overrides the default settings established in the *subpartition_clause*.
  Restriction: You can specify this clause only for a composite-partitioned table.
  You can specify individual subpartitions by name, and optionally the tablespace where each should be stored, or
  You can specify the number of subpartitions (and optionally one or more tablespaces where they are to be stored). In this case, Oracle assigns subpartition names of the form SYS_SUB*Pnn*n.

The number of tablespaces does not have to equal the number of subpartitions. If the number of partitions is greater than the number of tablespaces, Oracle cycles through the names of the tablespaces.

- **row_movement_clause** determines whether a row can be moved to a different partition or subpartition because of a change to one or more of its key values during an update operation. **Restriction:** You can specify this clause only for a partitioned table.

  - ENABLE allows Oracle to move a row to a different partition or subpartition as the result of an update to the partitioning or subpartitioning key.

CAUTION
Moving a row in the course of an UPDATE operation changes that row's ROWID.

  - DISABLE returns an error if an update to a partitioning or subpartitioning key would result in a row moving to a different partition or subpartition. This is the default.

- **parallel_clause** causes creation of the table to be parallelized, and sets the default degree of parallelism for queries and DML on the table after creation.

  - NOPARALLEL specifies serial execution. This is the default.

  - PARALLEL causes Oracle to select a degree of parallelism equal to the number of CPUs available on all participating instances times the value of the PARALLEL_THREADS_PER_CPU initialization parameter.

  - PARALLEL *integer* specifies the **degree of parallelism**, which is the number of parallel threads used in the parallel operation. Each parallel thread may use one or two parallel execution servers. Normally Oracle calculates the optimum degree of parallelism, so it is not necessary for you to specify *integer*.
    Restriction: If *table* contains any columns of LOB or user-defined object type, this statement as well as subsequent INSERT, UPDATE, or DELETE operations on *table* are executed serially without notification. Subsequent queries, however, will be executed in parallel.

NOTE
This syntax supersedes syntax appearing in earlier releases of Oracle. Superseded syntax is still supported for backward compatibility, but may result in slightly different behavior. For more information, see Oracle8i Migration.
A parallel hint overrides the effect of the parallel_clause.
If the query portion of a parallel DML statement (INSERT, UPDATE, or DELETE) or a parallel DDL statement (CREATE TABLE ... AS SELECT) statement references a remote object, the operation is executed serially without notification.

For more information on parallelized operations, see *Oracle8i Tuning*, *Oracle8i Concepts*, and *Oracle8i Parallel Server Concepts and Administration*.

- **enable_disable_clause** lets you specify whether Oracle should apply a constraint. By default, constraints are created in ENABLE VALIDATE state.
  Restrictions: To enable or disable any integrity constraint, you must have defined the constraint

in this or a previous statement.
You cannot enable a referential integrity constraint unless the referenced unique or primary key constraint is already enabled.

■ ENABLE specifies that the constraint will be applied to all new data in the table.

■ VALIDATE additionally specifies that all old data also complies with the constraint.

An enabled validated constraint guarantees that all data is and will continue to be valid.

If any row in the table violates the integrity constraint, the constraint remains disabled and Oracle returns an error. If all rows comply with the constraint, Oracle enables the constraint. Subsequently, if new data violates the constraint, Oracle does not execute the statement and returns an error indicating the integrity constraint violation.

If you place a primary key constraint in ENABLE VALIDATE mode, the validation process will verify that the primary key columns contain no nulls. To avoid this overhead, mark each column in the primary key NOT NULL before enabling the table's primary key constraint. (For optimal results, do this before entering data into the column.)

■ NOVALIDATE ensures that all new DML operations on the constrained data comply with the constraint. This clause does not ensure that existing data in the table complies with the constraint and therefore does not require a table lock.

If you specify neither VALIDATE nor NOVALIDATE, the default is VALIDATE.
If you enable a unique or primary key constraint, and if no index exists on the key, Oracle creates a unique index. This index is dropped if the constraint is subsequently disabled, so Oracle rebuilds the index every time the constraint is enabled.

To avoid rebuilding the index and eliminate redundant indexes, create new primary key and unique constraints initially disabled. Then create (or use existing) nonunique indexes to enforce the constraint. Oracle does not drop a nonunique index when the constraint is disabled, so subsequent ENABLE operations are facilitated.

If you change the state of any single constraint from ENABLE NOVALIDATE to ENABLE VALIDATE, the operation can be performed in parallel, and does not block reads, writes, or other DDL operations.
Restriction: You cannot enable a foreign key that references a unique or primary key that is disabled.

■ DISABLE disables the integrity constraint. Disabled integrity constraints appear in the data dictionary along with enabled constraints. If you do not specify this clause when creating a constraint, Oracle automatically enables the constraint.

■ DISABLE VALIDATE disables the constraint and drops the index on the constraint, but keeps the constraint valid. This feature is most useful in data warehousing situa-tions, where the need arises to load into a range-partitioned table a quantity of data with a distinct range of values in the unique key. In such situations, the disable validate state enables you to save space by not having an index. You can then load data from a nonpartitioned table into a partitioned table using the *exchange_partition_clause* of the ALTER TABLE statement. All other modifications to the table by other SQL state-ments are disallowed.

If the unique key coincides with the partitioning key of the partitioned table, disabling the constraint saves overhead and has no detrimental effects. If the unique key does not coincide with the partitioning key, Oracle performs automatic table scans during the exchange to validate the constraint, which might offset the benefit of loading without an index.

- DISABLE NOVALIDATE signifies that Oracle makes no effort to maintain the constraint (because it is disabled) and cannot guarantee that the constraint is true (because it is not being validated). For information on when to use this setting, see *Oracle8i Tuning.*

  You cannot drop a table whose primary key is being referenced by a foreign key even if the foreign key constraint is in DIASABLE NOVALIDATE state. Further, the optimizer can use constraints in DISABLE NOVALIDATE state.

  If you specify neither VALIDATE nor NOVALIDATE, the default is NOVALIDATE.

  If you disable a unique or primary key constraint that is using a unique index, Oracle drops the unique index.

- UNIQUE enables or disables the unique constraint defined on the specified column or combination of columns.

- PRIMARY KEY enables or disables the table's primary key constraint.

- CONSTRAINT enables or disables the integrity constraint named *constraint.*

- ***using_index_clause*** specifies parameters for the index Oracle creates to enforce a unique or primary key constraint. Oracle gives the index the same name as the constraint. You can choose the values of the INITRANS, MAXTRANS, TABLESPACE, STORAGE, and PCTFREE parameters for the index. These parameters are described earlier in this statement.
  Restriction: Use these parameters only when enabling unique and primary key constraints.

- EXCEPTIONS INTO specifies a table into which Oracle places information about rows that violate the integrity constraint. The table must exist on your local database before you use this clause. If you omit *schema*, Oracle assumes the exception table is in your own schema.

NOTE
You must create an appropriate exceptions report table to accept information from the EXCEPTIONS INTO clause of the enable_disable_clause before enabling the constraint.

You can create an exception table by submitting the script UTLEXCPT1.SQL, which creates a table named EXCEPTIONS. You can create additional exceptions tables with different names by modifying and resubmitting the script. (You can use the UTLEXCPT1.SQL script with index-organized tables. You could not use earlier versions of the script for this purpose. See *Oracle8i Migration* for compatibility information.)

For more information on identifying exceptions, see *Oracle8i Application Developer's Guide – Fundamentals.*

- CASCADE disables any integrity constraints that depend on the specified integrity constraint. To disable a primary or unique key that is part of a referential integrity constraint, you must specify this clause.
  Restriction: You can specify CASCADE only if you have specified DISABLE.

- CACHE For data that will be accessed frequently, specifies that the blocks retrieved for this table are placed at the most recently used end of the LRU list in the buffer cache when a full table scan is performed. This clause is useful for small lookup tables.

As a parameter in the *LOB_storage_clause*, CACHE specifies that Oracle preallocates and retains LOB data values in memory for faster access.
Restriction: You cannot specify CACHE for an index-organized table.

■   NOCACHE   For data that will not be accessed frequently, specifies that the blocks retrieved for this table are placed at the least recently used end of the LRU list in the buffer cache when a full table scan is performed. This is the default.

For LOBs, the LOB value either is not brought into the buffer cache or is brought into the buffer cache and placed at the least recently used end of the LRU list.

As a parameter in the *LOB_storage_clause*, NOCACHE specifies that LOB values are not preallocated in memory.
Restriction: You cannot specify NOCACHE for an index-organized table.

■   MONITORING specifies that modification statistics can be collected on this table. These statistics are estimates of the number of rows affected by DML statements over a particular period of time. They are available for use by the optimizer or for analysis by the user.
Restriction: You cannot specify MONITORING for a temporary table.

■   NOMONITORING specifies that the table will not have modification statistics collected. This is the default.
Restriction: You cannot specify NOMONITORING for a temporary table.

■   AS *subquery* inserts the rows returned by the subquery into the table upon its creation.
Restrictions: The number of columns in the table must equal the number of expressions in the subquery.
The column definitions can specify only column names, default values, and integrity constraints, not datatypes.
You cannot define a referential integrity constraint in a CREATE TABLE statement that contains AS *subquery*. Instead, you must create the table without the constraint and then add it later with an ALTER TABLE statement.

If you specify the *parallel_clause* in this statement, Oracle will ignore any value you specify for the INITIAL storage parameter, and will instead use the value of the NEXT parameter.

Oracle derives datatypes and lengths from the subquery. Oracle also follows the following rules for integrity constraints:

   ■   Oracle automatically defines any NOT NULL constraints on columns in the new table that existed on the corresponding columns of the selected table if the subquery selects the column rather than an expression containing the column.

   ■   If a CREATE TABLE statement contains both AS *subquery* and a CONSTRAINT clause or an ENABLE clause with the EXCEPTIONS INTO clause, Oracle ignores AS *subquery*.

If any rows violate the constraint, Oracle does not create the table and returns an error.

If all expressions in *subquery* are columns, rather than expressions, you can omit the columns from the table definition entirely. In this case, the names of the columns of table are the same as the columns in *subquery*.

You can use *subquery* in combination with the TO_LOB function to convert the values in a LONG column in another table to LOB values in a column of the table you are creating. For a discussion of why and when to copy LONGs to LOBs, see *Oracle8i Migration*.

NOTE
If subquery returns (in part or totally) the equivalent of an existing materialized view, Oracle may use the materialized view (for query rewrite) in place of one or more tables specified in subquery. For more information on materialized views and query rewrite, see Oracle8i Tuning.

- ***order_by_clause*** orders rows returned by the statements.

NOTE
When specified with CREATE TABLE, this clause does not necessarily order data cross the entire table. (For example, it does not order across partitions.) Specify this clause if you intend to create an index on the same key as the ORDER BY key column. Oracle will cluster data on the ORDER BY key so that it corresponds to the index key.

For object tables, *subquery* can contain either one expression corresponding to the table type, or the number of top-level attributes of the table type.

CREATE TABLESPACE

Syntax

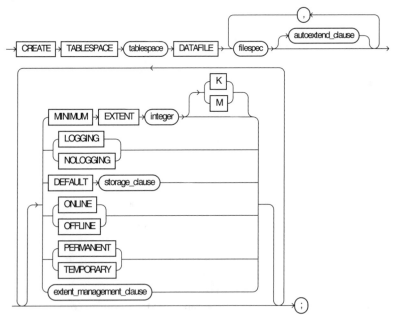

autoextend_clause::=

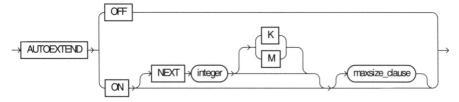

maxsize_clause::=

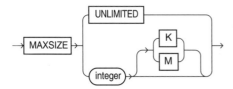

extent_management_clause::=

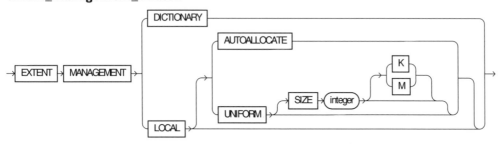

Purpose

To create a tablespace. A *tablespace* is an allocation of space in the database that can contain schema objects. For information on tablespaces, see *Oracle8i Concepts*. When you create a tablespace, it is initially a read-write tablespace. You can subsequently use the ALTER TABLESPACE statement to take the tablespace offline or online, add datafiles to it, or make it a read-only tablespace. You can also drop a tablespace from the database with the DROP TABLESPACE statement.

Prerequisites

You must have CREATE TABLESPACE system privilege. Also, the SYSTEM tablespace must contain at least two rollback segments including the SYSTEM rollback segment. Before you can create a tablespace you must create a database to contain it.

Keywords and Parameters

- *tablespace* is the name of the tablespace to be created.
- DATAFILE *filespec* specifies the datafile or files to make up the tablespace.

NOTE
For operating systems that support raw devices, the filespec REUSE keyword has no meaning when specifying a raw device as a datafile. Such a CREATE TABLESPACE statement will succeed whether or not you specify REUSE.

- ***autoextend_clause*** enables or disables the automatic extension of the datafile.

    - OFF disables autoextend if it is turned on. NEXT and MAXSIZE are set to zero. Values for NEXT and MAXSIZE must be respecified in further ALTER TABLESPACE AUTOEXTEND statements.

    - ON enables autoextend.

    - NEXT specifies the disk space to allocate to the datafile when more extents are required.

    - ***maxsize_clause*** specifies the maximum disk space allowed for allocation to the datafile.

    - UNLIMITED sets no limit on allocating disk space to the datafile.

- MINIMUM EXTENT *integer* controls free space fragmentation in the tablespace by ensuring that every used or free extent size in a tablespace is at least as large as, and is a multiple of, *integer*. For more information about using MINIMUM EXTENT to control fragmentation, see *Oracle8i Concepts*.

NOTE
This clause is not relevant for a dictionary-managed temporary tablespace.

- LOGGING | NOLOGGING specifies the default logging attributes of all tables, indexes, and partitions within the tablespace. LOGGING is the default.

    The tablespace-level logging attribute can be overridden by logging specifications at the table, index, and partition levels.

    Only the following operations support the NOLOGGING mode:

    - **DML**: direct-load INSERT (serial or parallel), Direct Loader (SQL*Loader)

    - **DDL**: CREATE TABLE ... AS SELECT, CREATE INDEX, ALTER INDEX ... REBUILD, ALTER INDEX ... REBUILD PARTITION, ALTER INDEX ... SPLIT PARTITION, ALTER TABLE ... SPLIT PARTITION, and ALTER TABLE ... MOVE PARTITION.

    In NOLOGGING mode, data is modified with minimal logging (to mark new extents INVALID and to record dictionary changes). When applied during media recovery, the extent invalidation records mark a range of blocks as logically corrupt, because the redo data is not logged. Therefore, if you cannot afford to lose the object, you should take a backup after the NOLOGGING operation.

- DEFAULT ***storage_clause*** specifies the default storage parameters for all objects created in the tablespace. For a dictionary-managed temporary tablespace, Oracle considers only the NEXT parameter of the *storage_clause*.

- ONLINE makes the tablespace available immediately after creation to users who have been granted access to the tablespace. This is the default.

- OFFLINE makes the tablespace unavailable immediately after creation.

- The data dictionary view DBA_TABLESPACES indicates whether each tablespace is online or offline.

- PERMANENT specifies that the tablespace will be used to hold permanent objects. This is the default.

- TEMPORARY specifies that the tablespace will be used only to hold temporary objects, for example, segments used by implicit sorts to handle ORDER BY clauses.

- *extent_management_clause* specifies how the extents of the tablespace will be managed.

  - DICTIONARY specifies that the tablespace is managed using dictionary tables. This is the default.

  - LOCAL specifies that tablespace is locally managed. Locally managed tablespaces have some part of the tablespace set aside for a bitmap. For a discussion of locally managed tablespaces, see *Oracle8i Concepts.*

- AUTOALLOCATE specifies that the tablespace is system man-aged. Users cannot specify an extent size.

- UNIFORM specifies that the tablespace is managed with uniform extents of SIZE bytes. Use K or M to specify the extent size in kilo-bytes or megabytes. The default SIZE is 1 megabyte.

  If you do not specify either AUTOALLOCATE or UNIFORM, then AUTOALLOCATE is the default.
  Restriction: If you specify LOCAL, you cannot specify DEFAULT *storage_clause,* MINIMUM EXTENT, or TEMPORARY.

CREATE TEMPORARY TABLESPACE

Syntax

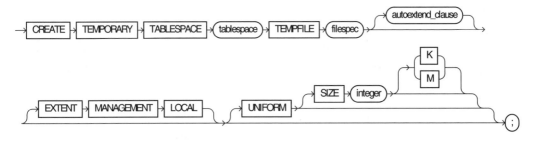

autoextend_clause::=

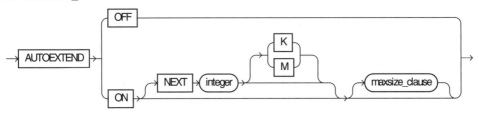

maxsize_clause::=

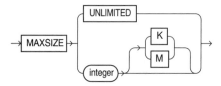

Purpose

To create a **temporary tablespace**, which is an allocation of space in the database that can contain schema objects for the duration of a session.

Prerequisites

You must have the CREATE TABLESPACE system privilege.

Keywords and Parameters

- *tablespace* is the name of the temporary tablespace.

- TEMPFILE *filespec* specifies the tempfiles that make up the tablespace.

NOTE
Media recovery does not recognize tempfiles.

- *autoextend_clause* enables or disables the automatic extension of the tempfile.

    - OFF disables autoextend if it is turned on. NEXT and MAXSIZE are set to zero. Values for NEXT and MAXSIZE must be respecified in further ALTER TABLESPACE AUTOEXTEND statements.

    - ON enables autoextend.

    - NEXT specifies the disk space to allocate to the tempfile when more extents are required.

    - *maxsize_clause* specifies the maximum disk space allowed for allocation to the tempfile.

    - *integer* specifies in bytes the maximum disk space allowed for allocation to the tempfile. Use K or M to specify this space in kilobytes or megabytes.

    - UNLIMITED sets no limit on allocating disk space to the tempfile.

- EXTENT MANAGEMENT LOCAL specifies that the tablespace is locally managed, meaning that some part of the tablespace is set aside for a bitmap. For a discussion of locally managed tablespaces, see *Oracle8i Concepts*.

    - UNIFORM determines the size of the extents of the temporary tablespace in bytes.

      All extents of temporary tablespaces are the same size (uniform). If you do not specify this clause, Oracle uses uniform extents of 1M.

    - SIZE specifies in bytes the size of the tablespace extents. Use K or M to specify the size in kilobytes or megabytes.

      If you do not specify SIZE, Oracle uses the default extent size of 1M.

CREATE USER

Syntax

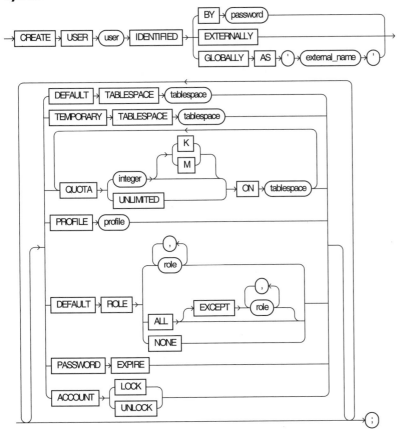

Purpose
To create and configure a database user, or an account through which you can log in to the database and establish the means by which Oracle permits access by the user.

Prerequisites
You must have CREATE USER system privilege. When you create a user with the CREATE USER statement, the user's privilege domain is empty. To log on to Oracle, a user must have CREATE SESSION system privilege. Therefore, after creating a user, you should grant the user at least the CREATE SESSION privilege.

NOTE
You can enable a user to connect to Oracle through a proxy (that is, an application or application server).

Keywords and Parameters

■ *user* is the name of the user to be created. This name can contain only characters from your database character set. Oracle recommends that the user name contain at least one single-byte character regardless of whether the database character set also contains multi-byte characters.

■ IDENTIFIED indicates how Oracle authenticates the user. See *Oracle8i Application Developer's Guide – Fundamentals* and your operating system specific documentation for more information.

   ■ BY *password* creates a **local user** and indicates that the user must specify *password* to log on. Passwords can contain only single-byte characters from your database character set regardless of whether this character set also contains multibyte characters.

   Also refer to *Oracle8i Administrator's Guide* for a detailed description and explanation of how to use password management and protection.

   ■ EXTERNALLY creates an **external user** and indicates that a user must be authenticated by an external service (such as an operating system or a third-party service). Doing so causes Oracle to rely on the login authentication of the operating system to ensure that a specific operating system user has access to a specific database user.

CAUTION
Oracle strongly recommends that you do not use IDENTIFIED EXTERNALLY with operating systems that have inherently weak login security. For more information, see Oracle8i Administrator's Guide.

   ■ GLOBALLY AS '*external_name*' creates a **global user** and indicates that a user must be authenticated by the enterprise directory service. The '*external_name*' string is the X.509 name at the enterprise directory service that identifies this user.

   It should be of the form 'CN=*username,other_attributes*', where *other_attributes* is the rest of the user's distinguished name (DN) in the directory.

NOTE
You can control the ability of an application server to connect as the specified user and to activate that user's roles using the ALTER USER statement.

■ DEFAULT TABLESPACE identifies the default tablespace for objects that the user creates. If you omit this clause, objects default to the SYSTEM tablespace.

■ TEMPORARY TABLESPACE identifies the tablespace for the user's temporary segments. If you omit this clause, temporary segments default to the SYSTEM tablespace.

■ QUOTA allows the user to allocate space in the tablespace and optionally establishes a quota of *integer* bytes. Use K or M to specify the quota in kilobytes or megabytes. This quota is the maximum space in the tablespace the user can allocate.

   ■ A CREATE USER statement can have multiple QUOTA clauses for multiple tablespaces.

   ■ UNLIMITED allows the user to allocate space in the tablespace without bound.

■ PROFILE reassigns the profile named to the user. The profile limits the amount of database resources the user can use. If you omit this clause, Oracle assigns the DEFAULT profile to the user.

- ■ DEFAULT ROLE lets you assign and enable a default role or roles to the user.
  - ■ *role* assigns one or more predefined roles
  - ■ ALL [EXCEPT] *role* assigns all predefined roles to the user, or all except those specified.
  - ■ NONE assigns no roles to the user.
- ■ PASSWORD EXPIRE causes the user's *password* to expire. This setting forces the user (or the DBA) to change the password before the user can log in to the database.
- ■ ACCOUNT LOCK locks the user's account and disables access.
- ■ ACCOUNT UNLOCK unlocks the user's account and enables access to the account.

EXPLAIN PLAN

Syntax

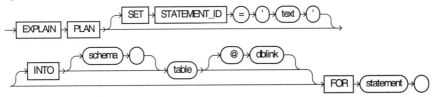

Purpose

To determine the execution plan Oracle follows to execute a specified SQL statement. This statement inserts a row describing each step of the execution plan into a specified table. If you are using cost-based optimization, this statement also determines the cost of executing the statement. If any domain indexes are defined on the table, user-defined CPU and I/O costs will also be inserted. See *Oracle8i Tuning* for information on the output of EXPLAIN PLAN. The definition of a sample output table PLAN_TABLE is available in a SQL script on your distribution media. Your output table must have the same column names and datatypes as this table. The common name of this script is UTLXPLAN.SQL. The exact name and location depend on your operating system. You can also issue the EXPLAIN PLAN statement as part of the SQL trace facility. For information on how to use the SQL trace facility, as well as a detailed discussion of how to generate and interpret execution plans, see *Oracle8i Tuning*.

Prerequisites

To issue an EXPLAIN PLAN statement, you must have the privileges necessary to insert rows into an existing output table that you specify to hold the execution plan.

NOTE
Do not use the EXPLAIN PLAN statement to determine the execution plans of SQL statements that access data dictionary views or dynamic performance tables.

You must also have the privileges necessary to execute the SQL statement for which you are determining the execution plan. If the SQL statement accesses a view, you must have privileges to access any tables and views on which the view is based. If the view is based on another view that is based on a table, you must have privileges to access both the other view and its underlying table. To examine the execution plan produced by an EXPLAIN PLAN statement, you must have the privileges necessary to query the output table. The EXPLAIN PLAN statement is a data manipulation language (DML) statement, rather than a data definition language (DDL) statement. Therefore, Oracle does not implicitly commit the changes made by an EXPLAIN PLAN statement. If you want to keep the rows generated by an EXPLAIN PLAN statement in the output table, you must commit the transaction containing the statement.

Keywords and Parameters

- SET STATEMENT_ID specifies the value of the STATEMENT_ID column for the rows of the execution plan in the output table. You can then use this value to identify these rows among others in the output table. Be sure to specify a STATEMENT_ID value if your output table contains rows from many execution plans. If you omit this clause, the STATEMENT_ID value defaults to null.

- INTO specifies name of the output table, and optionally its schema and database. This table must exist before you use the EXPLAIN PLAN statement.

  If you omit *schema*, Oracle assumes the table is in your own schema.

  The *dblink* can be a complete or partial name of a database link to a remote Oracle database where the output table is located. You can specify a remote output table only if you are using Oracle's distributed functionality. If you omit *dblink*, Oracle assumes the table is on your local database.

  If you omit INTO altogether, Oracle assumes an output table named PLAN_TABLE in your own schema on your local database.

- FOR *statement* specifies a SELECT, INSERT, UPDATE, DELETE, CREATE TABLE, or CREATE INDEX statement for which the execution plan is generated.

NOTE
If statement includes the parallel_clause, the resulting execution plan will indicate parallel execution. However, EXPLAIN PLAN actually inserts the statement into the plan table, so that the parallel DML statement you submit is no longer the first DML statement in the transaction. This violates the Oracle restriction of one parallel DML statement per transaction, and the statement will be executed serially. To maintain parallel execution of the statements, you must commit or roll back the EXPLAIN PLAN statement, and then submit the parallel DML statement.

filespec

Syntax

filespec_datafiles & filespec_tempfiles::=

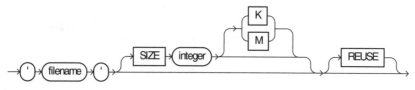

filespec_redo_log_file_groups::=

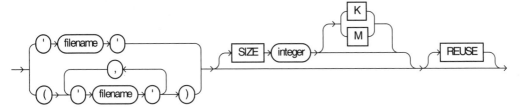

Purpose
To specify a file as a datafile or tempfile To specify a group of one or more files as a redo log file group.

Prerequisites
A *filespec* can appear in the following statements:

- CREATE DATABASE
- ALTER DATABASE
- CREATE TABLESPACE
- ALTER TABLESPACE
- CREATE CONTROLFILE
- CREATE LIBRARY
- CREATE TEMPORARY TABLESPACE

You must have the privileges necessary to issue one of these statements.

Keywords and Parameters

- *'filename'* is the name of either a datafile, tempfile, or a redo log file member. A *'filename'* can contain only single-byte characters from 7-bit ASCII or EBCDIC character sets. Multibyte characters are not valid.

  A redo log file group can have one or more members (copies). Each *'filename'* must be fully specified according to the conventions for your operating system.

- SIZE *integer* specifies the size of the file. Use K or M to specify the size in kilobytes or megabytes.
  - You can omit this parameter **only** if the file already exists.
  - The size of a tablespace must be one block greater than the sum of the sizes of the objects contained in it.
- REUSE allows Oracle to reuse an existing file.
  - If the file already exists, Oracle verifies that its size matches the value of the SIZE parameter (if you specify SIZE).
  - If the file does not exist, Oracle ignores this clause and creates the file.
  - You can omit this clause only if the file does not already exist. If you omit this clause, Oracle creates the file.

NOTE
*Whenever Oracle uses an existing file, the file's previous contents
are lost.*

GRANT system_privileges_and_roles

Syntax

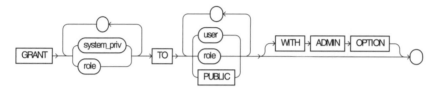

Purpose

To grant system privileges and roles to users and roles. Both privileges and roles are either local, global, or external. You can authorize database users to use roles through means other than the database and the GRANT statement. For example, some operating systems have facilities that grant operating system privileges to operating system users. You can use such facilities to grant roles to Oracle users with the initialization parameter OS_ROLES. If you choose to grant roles to users through operating system facilities, you cannot also grant roles to users with the GRANT statement, although you can use the GRANT statement to grant system privileges to users and system privileges and roles to other roles. For information about other authorization methods, see *Oracle8i Administrator's Guide.*

Prerequisites

To grant a system privilege, you must either have been granted the system privilege with the ADMIN OPTION or have been granted the GRANT ANY PRIVILEGE system privilege. To grant a role, you must either have been granted the role with the ADMIN OPTION or have been granted the GRANT ANY ROLE system privilege, or you must have created the role.

Keywords and Parameters

- *system_priv* is a system privilege to be granted. Table A-4 lists the system privileges (organized by the database object operated upon).

  - If you grant a privilege to a *user*, Oracle adds the privilege to the user's privilege domain. The user can immediately exercise the privilege.

  - If you grant a privilege to a *role*, Oracle adds the privilege to the role's privilege domain. Users who have been granted and have enabled the role can immediately exercise the privilege. Other users who have been granted the role can enable the role and exercise the privilege.

  - If you grant a privilege to *PUBLIC*, Oracle adds the privilege to the privilege domains of each user. All users can immediately perform operations authorized by the privilege. **Restrictions:** A privilege or role cannot appear more than once in the list of privileges and roles to be granted.
    You cannot grant a role to itself.

System Privilege	Allows grantee to . . .
CLUSTERS	
CREATE CLUSTER	Create clusters in grantee's schema
CREATE ANY CLUSTER	Create a cluster in any schema except SYS. Behaves similarly to CREATE ANY TABLE.
ALTER ANY CLUSTER	Alter clusters in any schema except SYS
DROP ANY CLUSTER	Drop clusters in any schema except SYS
CONTEXTS	
CREATE ANY CONTEXT	Create any context namespace
DROP ANY CONTEXT	Drop any context namespace
DATABASE	
ALTER DATABASE	Alter the database
ALTER SYSTEM	Issue ALTER SYSTEM statements
AUDIT SYSTEM	Issue AUDIT *sql_statements* statements
DATABASE LINKS	
CREATE DATABASE LINK	Create private database links in grantee's schema
CREATE PUBLIC DATABASE LINK	Create public database links
DROP PUBLIC DATABASE LINK	Drop public database links
DIMENSIONS	
CREATE DIMENSION	Create dimensions in the grantee's schema
CREATE ANY DIMENSION	Create dimensions in any schema except SYS
ALTER ANY DIMENSION	Alter dimensions in any schema except SYS
DROP ANY DIMENSION	Drop dimensions in any schema except SYS
DIRECTORIES	
CREATE ANY DIRECTORY	Create directory database objects
DROP ANY DIRECTORY	Drop directory database objects
INDEXTYPES	
CREATE INDEXTYPE	Create an indextype in the grantee's schema
CREATE ANY INDEXTYPE	Create an indextype in any schema except SYS
DROP ANY INDEXTYPE	Drop an indextype in any schema except SYS
EXECUTE ANY INDEXTYPE	Reference an indextype in any schema except SYS
INDEXES	
CREATE INDEX	Create in the grantee's schema an index on any table in the grantee's schema or a domain index
CREATE ANY INDEX	Create in any schema except SYS a domain index or an index on any table in any schema except SYS
ALTER ANY INDEX	Alter indexes in any schema except SYS
DROP ANY INDEX	Drop indexes in any schema except SYS
QUERY REWRITE	Enable rewrite using a materialized view, or create a function-based index, when that materialized view or index references tables and views that are in the grantee's own schema

TABLE A-4.   *System Privileges*

System Privilege	Allows grantee to . . .
GLOBAL QUERY REWRITE	Enable rewrite using a materialized view, or create a function-based index, when that materialized view or index references tables or views in any schema except SYS
LIBRARIES	
CREATE LIBRARY	Create external procedure/function libraries in grantee's schema
CREATE ANY LIBRARY	Create external procedure/function libraries in any schema except SYS
DROP LIBRARY	Drop external procedure/function libraries in the grantee's schema
DROP ANY LIBRARY	Drop external procedure/function libraries in any schema except SYS
MATERIALIZED VIEWS (which are identical to SNAPSHOTS)	
CREATE MATERIALIZED VIEW	Create a materialized view in the grantee's schema
CREATE ANY MATERIALIZED VIEW	Create materialized views in any schema except SYS
ALTER ANY MATERIALIZED VIEW	Alter materialized views in any schema except SYS
DROP ANY MATERIALIZED VIEW	Drop materialized views in any schema except SYS
QUERY REWRITE	Enable rewrite using a materialized view, or create a function based index, when that materialized view or index references tables and views that are in the grantee's own schema
GLOBAL QUERY REWRITE	Enable rewrite using a materialized view, or create a function based index, when that materialized view or index references tables or views in any schema except SYS
OPERATORS	
CREATE OPERATOR	Create an operator and its bindings in the grantee's schema
CREATE ANY OPERATOR	Create an operator and its bindings in any schema except SYS
DROP ANY OPERATOR	Drop an operator in any schema except SYS
EXECUTE ANY OPERATOR	Reference an operator in any schema except SYS
OUTLINES	
CREATE ANY OUTLINE	Create outlines that can be used in any schema that uses outlines
ALTER ANY OUTLINE	Modify outlines
DROP ANY OUTLINE	Drop outlines
PROCEDURES	
CREATE PROCEDURE	Create stored procedures, functions, and packages in grantee's schema
CREATE ANY PROCEDURE	Create stored procedures, functions, and packages in any schema except SYS
ALTER ANY PROCEDURE	Alter stored procedures, functions, or packages in any schema except SYS
DROP ANY PROCEDURE	Drop stored procedures, functions, or packages in any schema except SYS
EXECUTE ANY PROCEDURE	Execute procedures or functions (standalone or packaged) Reference public package variables in any schema except SYS
PROFILES	
CREATE PROFILE	Create profiles

TABLE A-4. *System Privileges* (continued)

System Privilege	Allows grantee to . . .
ALTER PROFILE	Alter profiles
DROP PROFILE	Drop profiles
ROLES	
CREATE ROLE	Create roles
ALTER ANY ROLE	Alter any role in the database
DROP ANY ROLE	Drop roles
GRANT ANY ROLE	Grant any role in the database
ROLLBACK SEGMENTS	
CREATE ROLLBACK SEGMENT	Create rollback segments
ALTER ROLLBACK SEGMENT	Alter rollback segments
DROP ROLLBACK SEGMENT	Drop rollback segments
SEQUENCES	
CREATE SEQUENCE	Create sequences in grantee's schema
CREATE ANY SEQUENCE	Create sequences in any schema except SYS
ALTER ANY SEQUENCE	Alter any sequence in the database
DROP ANY SEQUENCE	Drop sequences in any schema except SYS
SELECT ANY SEQUENCE	Reference sequences in any schema except SYS
SESSIONS	
CREATE SESSION	Connect to the database
ALTER RESOURCE COST	Set costs for session resources
ALTER SESSION	Issue ALTER SESSION statements
RESTRICTED SESSION	Logon after the instance is started using the SQL*Plus STARTUP RESTRICT statement
SNAPSHOTS (which are identical to MATERIALIZED VIEWS)	
CREATE SNAPSHOT	Create snapshots in grantee's schema
CREATE ANY SNAPSHOT	Create snapshots in any schema except SYS
ALTER ANY SNAPSHOT	Alter any snapshot in the database
DROP ANY SNAPSHOT	Drop snapshots in any schema except SYS
GLOBAL QUERY REWRITE	Enable rewrite using a snapshot, or create a function based index, when that snapshot or index references tables or views in any schema except SYS.
QUERY REWRITE	Enable rewrite using a snapshot, or create a function based index, when that snapshot or index references tables and views that are in the grantee's own schema
SYNONYMS	
CREATE SYNONYM	Create synonyms in grantee's schema
CREATE ANY SYNONYM	Create private synonyms in any schema except SYS
CREATE PUBLIC SYNONYM	Create public synonyms
DROP ANY SYNONYM	Drop private synonyms in any schema except SYS
DROP PUBLIC SYNONYM	Drop public synonyms

TABLE A-4.   *System Privileges* (continued)

System Privilege	Allows grantee to . . .
TABLES	
CREATE ANY TABLE	Create tables in any schema except SYS. The owner of the schema containing the table must have space quota on the tablespace to contain the table.
ALTER ANY TABLE	Alter any table or view in the schema
BACKUP ANY TABLE	Use the Export utility to incrementally export objects from the schema of other users
DELETE ANY TABLE	Delete rows from tables, table partitions, or views in any schema except SYS
DROP ANY TABLE	Drop or truncate tables or table partitions in any schema except SYS
INSERT ANY TABLE	Insert rows into tables and views in any schema except SYS
LOCK ANY TABLE	Lock tables and views in any schema except SYS
UPDATE ANY TABLE	Update rows in tables and views in any schema except SYS
SELECT ANY TABLE	Query tables, views, or snapshots in any schema except SYS
TABLESPACES	
CREATE TABLESPACE	Create tablespaces
ALTER TABLESPACE	Alter tablespaces
DROP TABLESPACE	Drop tablespaces
MANAGE TABLESPACE	Take tablespaces offline and online and begin and end tablespace backups
UNLIMITED TABLESPACE	Use an unlimited amount of any tablespace. This privilege overrides any specific quotas assigned. If you revoke this privilege from a user, the user's schema objects remain but further tablespace allocation is denied unless authorized by specific tablespace quotas. You cannot grant this system privilege to roles.
TRIGGERS	
CREATE TRIGGER	Create a database trigger in grantee's schema
CREATE ANY TRIGGER	Create database triggers in any schema except SYS
ALTER ANY TRIGGER	Enable, disable, or compile database triggers in any schema except SYS
DROP ANY TRIGGER	Drop database triggers in any schema except SYS
ADMINISTER DATABASE TRIGGER	Create a trigger on DATABASE. (You must also have the CREATE TRIGGER or CREATE ANY TRIGGER privilege.)
TYPES	
CREATE TYPE	Create object types and object type bodies in grantee's schema
CREATE ANY TYPE	Create object types and object type bodies in any schema except SYS
ALTER ANY TYPE	Alter object types in any schema except SYS
DROP ANY TYPE	Drop object types and object type bodies in any schema except SYS
EXECUTE ANY TYPE	Use and reference object types and collection types in any schema except SYS, and invoke methods of an object type in any schema *if you make the grant to a specific user*. If you grant EXECUTE ANY TYPE to a role, users holding the enabled role will not be able to invoke methods of an object type in any schema.
USERS	
CREATE USER	Create users. This privilege also allows the creator to Assign quotas on *any* tablespace Set default and temporary tablespaces Assign a profile as part of a CREATE USER statement

TABLE A-4. *System Privileges* (continued)

System Privilege	Allows grantee to . . .
`ALTER USER` Alter any user.	This privilege authorizes the grantee to Change another user's password or authentication method, Assign quotas on *any* tablespace, Set default and temporary tablespaces, and Assign a profile and default roles
`BECOME USER`	Become another user. (Required by any user performing a full database import.)
`DROP USER`	Drop users
VIEWS	
`CREATE VIEW`	Create views in grantee's schema
`CREATE ANY VIEW`	Create views in any schema except SYS
`DROP ANY VIEW`	Drop views in any schema except SYS
MISCELLANEOUS	
`ANALYZE ANY`	Analyze any table, cluster, or index in any schema except SYS
`AUDIT ANY`	Audit any object in any schema except SYS using AUDIT *schema_objects* statements
`COMMENT ANY TABLE`	Comment on any table, view, or column in any schema except SYS
`FORCE ANY TRANSACTION`	Force the commit or rollback of any in-doubt distributed transaction in the local database Induce the failure of a distributed transaction
`FORCE TRANSACTION`	Force the commit or rollback of grantee's in-doubt distributed transactions in the local database
`GRANT ANY PRIVILEGE`	Grant any system privilege
`SYSDBA`	Perform `STARTUP` and `SHUTDOWN` operations `ALTER DATABASE`: open, mount, back up, or change character set `CREATE DATABASE ARCHIVELOG` and `RECOVERY` Includes the `RESTRICTED SESSION` privilege

`SYSOPER`	Perform `STARTUP and SHUTDOWN` operations
	`ALTER DATABASE OPEN/MOUNT/BACKUP`
	`ARCHIVELOG and RECOVERY`
	Includes the `RESTRICTED SESSION` privilege

TABLE A-4.   *System Privileges* (continued)

You cannot grant a role IDENTIFIED GLOBALLY to anything.
cannot grant a role IDENTIFIED EXTERNALLY to a global user or global role.

You cannot grant roles circularly. For example, if you grant the role BANKER to the role TELLER, you cannot subsequently grant TELLER to BANKER.

■ *role* is a role to be granted. You can grant an Oracle predefined role or a user-defined role.

Table 7-5 lists the predefined roles.

■ If you grant a role to a *user*, Oracle makes the role available to the user. The user can immediately enable the role and exercise the privileges in the role's privilege domain.

■ If you grant a role to another *role*, Oracle adds the granted role's privilege domain to the grantee role's privilege domain. Users who have been granted the grantee role can enable it and exercise the privileges in the granted role's privilege domain.

Predefined Role	Purpose
CONNECT, RESOURCE, and DBA	These roles are provided for compatibility with previous versions of Oracle. You should not rely on these roles, because they may not be created automatically by future versions of Oracle. Rather, Oracle recommends that you to design your own roles for database security.
DELETE_CATALOG_ROLE EXECUTE_CATALOG_ROLE SELECT_CATALOG_ROLE	These roles are provided for accessing exported data dictionary views and packages. For more information on these roles, see *Oracle8i Application Developer's Guide – Fundamentals*.
EXP_FULL_DATABASE IMP_FULL_DATABASE	These roles are provided for convenience in using the Import and Export utilities. For more information on these roles, see *Oracle8i Utilities*.
AQ_USER_ROLE AQ_ADMINISTRATOR_ROLE	You need these roles to use Oracle's Advanced Queuing functionality. For more information on these roles, see *Oracle8i Application Developer's Guide – Advanced Queuing*.
SNMPAGENT	This role is used by Enterprise Manager/Intelligent Agent. For more information, see *Oracle Enterprise Manager Administrator's Guide*.
RECOVERY_CATALOG_OWNER	You need this role to create a user who owns a recovery catalog. For more information on recovery catalogs, see *Oracle8i Backup and Recovery Guide*.
HS_ADMIN_ROLE	A DBA using Oracle's heterogeneous services feature needs this role to access appropriate tables in the data dictionary and to manipulate them with the DBMS_HS package. For more information, refer to *Oracle8i Distributed Database Systems* and *Oracle8i Supplied Packages Reference*.

TABLE A-5.   *Oracle Predefined Roles*

- If you grant a role to *PUBLIC*, Oracle makes the role available to all users. All users can immediately enable the role and exercise the privileges in the roles privilege domain.

- TO identifies users or roles to which system privileges and roles are granted.
  Restriction: A user, role, or PUBLIC cannot appear more than once in the TO clause.

- PUBLIC grants system privileges or roles to all users.

- WITH ADMIN OPTION enables the grantee to

  - Grant the role to another user or role, unless the role is a GLOBAL role Revoke the role from another user or role

  - Alter the role to change the authorization needed to access it

  - Drop the role

  If you grant a system privilege or role to a user without specifying WITH ADMIN OPTION, and then subsequently grant the privilege or role to the user WITH ADMIN OPTION, the user has the ADMIN OPTION on the privilege or role.

  To revoke the admin option on a system privilege or role from a user, you must revoke the privilege or role from the user altogether and then grant the privilege or role to the user without the admin option.

  Oracle also creates other roles that authorize you to administer the database. On many operating systems, these roles are called OSOPER and OSDBA. Their names may be different on your operating system.

GRANT object_privileges

Syntax

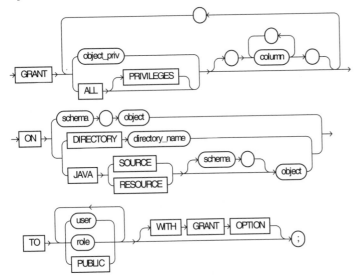

Purpose
To grant privileges for a particular object to users, roles, and PUBLIC. To grant system privileges and roles, use the GRANT *system_privileges_and_roles* statement described in the previous section of this chapter. Table A-6 summarizes the object privileges that you can grant on each type of object. If you grant a privilege to a *user*, Oracle adds the privilege to the user's privilege domain. The user can immediately exercise the privilege. If you grant a privilege to a *role*, Oracle adds the privilege to the role's privilege domain. Users who have been granted and have enabled the role can immediately exercise the privilege. Other users who have been granted the role can enable the role and exercise the privilege. If you grant a privilege to *PUBLIC*, Oracle adds the privilege to the privilege domain of each user. All users can immediately exercise the privilege. Table A-7 lists object privileges and the operations that they authorize. You can grant any of these system privileges with the GRANT statement.

Prerequisites
You must own the object or the owner of the object must have granted you the object privileges with the GRANT OPTION. This rule applies to users with the DBA role.

Keywords and Parameters
- *object_priv* is an object privilege to be granted. You can substitute any of the values shown in Table A-6. See also Table A-7.
  Restriction: A privilege cannot appear more than once in the list of privileges to be granted.

- ALL [PRIVILEGES] grants all the privileges for the object that you have been granted with the GRANT OPTION. The user who owns the schema containing an object automatically has all privileges on the object with the GRANT OPTION. (The keyword PRIVILEGES is optional.)

Object Privilege	Table	View	Sequence	Procedures, Functions, Packages[1]	Material-ized View / Snapshot	Direc-tory	Library	User-defined Type	Oper-ator	Index-type
ALTER	X		X							
DELETE[2]	X	X			X[2]					
EXECUTE				X			X	X	X	X
INDEX	X									
INSERT[2]	X	X			X[2]					
READ						X				
REFERENCES	X									
SELECT	X	X	X		X					
UPDATE[2]	X	X			X[2]					

[1] Oracle treats a Java class, source, or resource as if it were a procedure for purposes of granting object privileges.
[2] The DELETE, INSERT, and UPDATE privileges can be granted only to *updatable* materialized views.

TABLE A-6. *Object Privileges*

Object Privilege	Allows Grantee to . . .
The following **table privileges** authorize operations on a table. Any one of following object privileges allows the grantee to lock the table in any lock mode with the LOCK TABLE statement.	
ALTER	Change the table definition with the ALTER TABLE statement.
DELETE	Remove rows from the table with the DELETE statement.
Note: You must grant the SELECT privilege on the table along with the DELETE privilege.	
INDEX	Create an index on the table with the CREATE INDEX statement.
INSERT	Add new rows to the table with the INSERT statement.
REFERENCES	Create a constraint that refers to the table. You cannot grant this privilege to a role.
SELECT	Query the table with the SELECT statement.
UPDATE	Change data in the table with the UPDATE statement.
Note: You must grant the SELECT privilege on the table along with the UPDATE privilege.	
The following **view privileges** authorize operations on a view. Any one of the following object privileges allows the grantee to lock the view in any lock mode with the LOCK TABLE statement.	

TABLE A-7. *Object Privileges and the Operations They Authorize*

Object Privilege	**Allows Grantee to . . .**
To grant a privilege on a view, you must have that privilege with the GRANT OPTION on all of the view's base tables.	
DELETE	Remove rows from the view with the DELETE statement.
INSERT	Add new rows to the view with the INSERT statement.
SELECT	Query the view with the SELECT statement.
UPDATE	Change data in the view with the UPDATE statement.
The following **sequence privileges** authorize operations on a sequence.	
ALTER	Change the sequence definition with the ALTER SEQUENCE statement.
SELECT	Examine and increment values of the sequence with the CURRVAL and NEXTVAL pseudocolumns.
The following **procedure, function, and package privilege** authorizes operations on procedures, functions, or packages. This privilege also applies to **Java sources, classes, and resources**, which Oracle treats as though they were procedures for purposes of granting object privileges.	
EXECUTE	Compile the procedure or function or execute it directly, or access any program object declared in the specification of a package.
Note: Users do not need this privilege to execute a procedure, function, or package indirectly. For more information, refer to *Oracle8i Concepts* and *Oracle8i Application Developer's Guide – Fundamentals*.	
The following **snapshot privilege** authorizes operations on a snapshot.	
SELECT	Query the snapshot with the SELECT statement.
Synonym privileges are the same as the privileges for the base object. Granting a privilege on a synonym is equivalent to granting the privilege on the base object. Similarly, granting a privilege on a base object is equivalent to granting the privilege on all synonyms for the object. If you grant a user a privilege on a synonym, the user can use either the synonym name or the base object name in the SQL statement that exercises the privilege.	
The following **directory privilege** provides secured access to the files stored in the operating system directory to which the directory object serves as a pointer. The directory object contains the full pathname of the operating system directory where the files reside. Because the files are actually stored outside the database, Oracle server processes also need to have appropriate file permissions on the file system server. Granting object privileges on the directory database object to individual database users, rather than on the operating system, allows Oracle to enforce security during file operations.	

TABLE A-7.   *Object Privileges and the Operations They Authorize* (continued)

Object Privilege	Allows Grantee to . . .
READ	Read files in the directory.
The following **object type privilege** authorizes operations on an object type.	
EXECUTE	Use and reference the specified object and to invoke its methods.
The following **indextype privilege** authorizes operations on indextypes.	
EXECUTE	Reference an indextype.
The following **operator privilege** authorizes operations on user-defined operators	
EXECUTE	Reference an operator.

TABLE A-7. *Object Privileges and the Operations They Authorize* (continued)

- *column* specifies a table or view column on which privileges are granted. You can specify columns only when granting the INSERT, REFERENCES, or UPDATE privilege. If you do not list columns, the grantee has the specified privilege on all columns in the table or view.

- ON identifies the object on which the privileges are granted. Directory schema objects and Java source and resource schema objects are identified separately because they reside in separate namespaces.

  - *object* identifies the schema object on which the privileges are granted. If you do not qualify object with *schema*, Oracle assumes the object is in your own schema. The object can be one of the following types (see Table A-6):

    - table, view, or materialized view / snapshot
    - sequence
    - procedure, function, or package
    - user-defined type
    - synonym for any of the above items
    - directory, library, operator, or indextype
    - a Java source, class, or resource

NOTE
You cannot grant privileges directly to a single partition of a partitioned table. For information on how to grant privileges to a single partition indirectly, refer to Oracle8i Concepts.

  - DIRECTORY identifies a directory schema object on which privileges are granted by the DBA. You cannot qualify *directory_name* with a schema name.

  - JAVA SOURCE | RESOURCE identifies a Java source or resource schema object on which privileges are granted.

- TO identifies users or roles to which the object privilege is granted.
  Restriction: A user or role cannot appear more than once in the TO clause.

  - PUBLIC grants object privileges to all users.

- WITH GRANT OPTION allows the grantee to grant the object privileges to other users and roles. The grantee must be a user or PUBLIC, rather than a role.

NOAUDIT sql_statements

Syntax

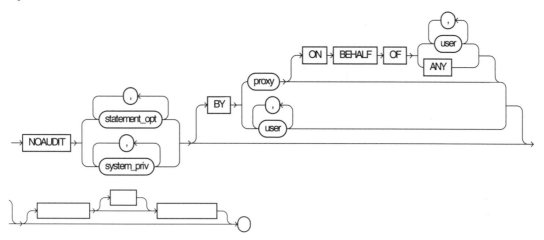

Purpose

To stop auditing previously enabled by the AUDIT *sql_statements* statement. The NOAUDIT statement must have the same syntax as the previous AUDIT statement. Further, it reverses the effects only of that particular statement. Therefore, if one AUDIT statement (statement A) enables auditing for a specific user, and a second (statement B) enables auditing for all users, then a NOAUDIT statement to disable auditing for all users (statement C) reverses statement B, but leaves statement A in effect and continues to audit the user that statement A specified.

Prerequisites

You must have the AUDIT SYSTEM system privilege.

Keywords and Parameters

- *statement_opt* is a statement option for which auditing is stopped. For a list of the statement options and the SQL statements they audit, see Table A-1 and Table A-2.

- *system_priv* is a system privilege for which auditing is stopped. For a list of the system privileges and the statements they authorize, see Table A-4.

- BY *user* stops auditing only for SQL statements issued by specified users in their subsequent sessions. If you omit this clause, Oracle stops auditing for all users' statements, except for the situation described for WHENEVER SUCCESSFUL.

- BY *proxy* stops auditing only for the SQL statements issued by the specified proxy, on behalf of a specific user or any user.
- WHENEVER SUCCESSFUL stops auditing only for SQL statements that complete successfully.

  - NOT stops auditing only for statements that result in Oracle errors.

  If you omit the WHENEVER SUCCESSFUL clause entirely, Oracle stops auditing for all statements, regardless of success or failure.

NOAUDIT schema_objects

Syntax

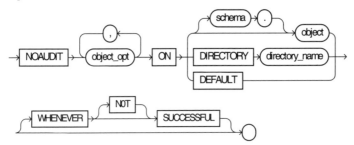

Purpose

To stop auditing previously enabled by the AUDIT *schema_objects* statement.

Prerequisites

The object on which you stop auditing must be in your own schema or you must have the AUDIT ANY system privilege. In addition, if the object you chose for auditing is a directory, even if you created it, you must have the AUDIT ANY system privilege.

Keywords and Parameters

- *object_opt* stops auditing for particular operations on the object. For a list of these options, see Table A-3.
- ON identifies the object on which auditing is stopped. If you do not qualify object with *schema*, Oracle assumes the object is in your own schema.
- *object* must a table, view, sequence, stored procedure, function, or package, snapshot, or library.
- DIRECTORY *directory_name* identifies the name of the directory on which auditing is being stopped.
- DEFAULT removes the specified object options as default object options for subsequently created objects.
- WHENEVER SUCCESSFUL stops auditing only for SQL statements that complete successfully.

  - NOT stops auditing only for statements that result in Oracle errors.

  If you omit the WHENEVER SUCCESSFUL clause entirely, Oracle stops auditing for all statements, regardless of success or failure.

RENAME

Syntax

Purpose

To rename a table, view, sequence, or private synonym for a table, view, or sequence:

- Oracle automatically transfers integrity constraints, indexes, and grants on the old object to the new object.

- Oracle invalidates all objects that depend on the renamed object, such as views, synonyms, and stored procedures and functions that refer to a renamed table. Do not use this statement to rename public synonyms. Instead, drop the public synonym and then create another public synonym with the new name.

Prerequisites

The object must be in your own schema.

Keywords and Parameters

- *old* is the name of an existing table, view, sequence, or private synonym.

- *new* is the new name to be given to the existing object. The new name must not already be used by another schema object in the same namespace.

SET TRANSACTION

Syntax

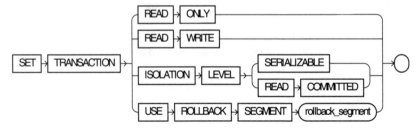

Purpose

To establish the current transaction as a read-only or read-write, establish its isolation level, or assign it to a specified rollback segment. The operations performed by a SET TRANSACTION statement affect only your current transaction, not other users or other transactions. Your transaction ends whenever you issue a COMMIT or ROLLBACK statement. Oracle implicitly commits the current transaction before and after executing a data definition language (DDL) statement.

Prerequisites

If you use a SET TRANSACTION statement, it must be the first statement in your transaction. However, a transaction need not have a SET TRANSACTION statement.

Keywords and Parameters

- READ ONLY establishes the current transaction as a read-only transaction. This clause established **transaction-level read consistency**. For more information on this topic, see *Oracle8i Concepts*.

    All subsequent queries in that transaction only see changes committed before the transaction began. Read-only transactions are useful for reports that run multiple queries against one or more tables while other users update these same tables.
    Restriction: Only the following statements are permitted in a read-only transaction:
    subqueries (that is, SELECT statements without the *for_update_clause*)
    LOCK TABLE
    SET ROLE
    ALTER SESSION
    ALTER SYSTEM

- READ WRITE establishes the current transaction as a read-write transaction. This clause established **statement-level read consistency**, which is the default.
    Restriction: You cannot toggle between transaction-level and statement-level read consistency in the same transaction.

- ISOLATION LEVEL specifies how transactions containing database modifications are handled.

    - SERIALIZABLE specifies serializable transaction isolation mode as defined in SQL92.

        If a serializable transaction contains data manipulation language (DML) that attempts to update any resource that may have been updated in a transaction uncommitted at the start of the serializable transaction, then the DML statement fails.

NOTE
The COMPATIBLE initialization parameter must be set to 7.3.0 or higher for SERIALIZABLE mode to work.

    - READ COMMITTED is the default Oracle transaction behavior. If the transaction contains DML that requires row locks held by another transaction, then the DML statement waits until the row locks are released.

- USE ROLLBACK SEGMENT assigns the current transaction to the specified rollback segment. This clause also implicitly establishes the transaction as a read-write transaction.

    This clause lets you to assign transactions of different types to rollback segments of different sizes. For example:

    - If no long-running queries are concurrently reading the same tables, you can assign small transactions to small rollback segments, which are more likely to remain in memory.

    - You can assign transactions that modify tables that are concurrently being read by long-running queries to large rollback segments, so that the rollback information needed for the read-consistent queries is not overwritten.

    - You can assign transactions that insert, update, or delete large amounts of data to rollback segments large enough to hold the rollback information for the transaction.

You cannot use the READ ONLY clause and the USE ROLLBACK SEGMENT clause in a single SET TRANSACTION statement or in different statements in the same transaction.

Read-only transactions do not generate rollback information and therefore are not assigned rollback segments.

storage_clause

Syntax

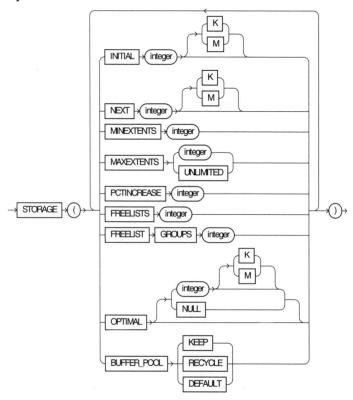

Purpose
To specify storage characteristics for any of the following schema objects:

- clusters
- indexes
- rollback segments
- materialized views / snapshots
- materialized view logs / snapshot logs
- tables

- tablespaces
- partitions

Storage parameters affect both how long it takes to access data stored in the database and how efficiently space in the database is used. For a discussion of the effects of these parameters, see *Oracle8i Tuning*. When you create a tablespace, you can specify values for the storage parameters. These values serve as default values for segments allocated in the tablespace. When you alter a tablespace, you can change the values of storage parameters. The new values serve as default values only for subsequently allocated segments (or subsequently created objects). When you create a cluster, index, rollback segment, snapshot, snapshot log, table, or partition, you can specify values for the storage parameters for the segments allocated to these objects. If you omit any storage parameter, Oracle uses the value of that parameter specified for the tablespace. When you alter a cluster, index, rollback segment, snapshot, snapshot log, table, or partition, you can change the values of storage parameters. The new values affect only future extent allocations.

Prerequisites
To change the value of a STORAGE parameter, you must have the privileges necessary to use the appropriate CREATE or ALTER statement.

NOTE
The storage_clause is interpreted differently for locally managed tablespaces. At creation, Oracle ignores MAXEXTENTS and uses the remaining parameter values to calculate the initial size of the segment.

Keywords and Parameters

- INITIAL specifies in bytes the size of the object's first extent. Oracle allocates space for this extent when you create the schema object. Use K or M to specify this size in kilobytes or megabytes.

  The default value is the size of 5 data blocks. The minimum value is the size of 2 data blocks for nonbitmapped segments or 3 data blocks for bitmapped segments, plus one data block for each free list group you specify.

  The maximum value depends on your operating system. Oracle rounds values up to the next multiple of the data block size for values less than 5 data blocks, and rounds up to the next multiple of 5 data blocks for values greater than 5 data blocks.
  Restriction: You cannot specify INITIAL in an ALTER statement.

- NEXT specifies in bytes the size of the next extent to be allocated to the object. Use K or M to specify the size in kilobytes or megabytes. The default value is the size of 5 data blocks.

  The minimum value is the size of 1 data block. The maximum value depends on your operating system. Oracle rounds values up to the next multiple of the data block size for values less than 5 data blocks. For values greater than 5 data blocks, Oracle rounds up to a value that minimizes fragmentation, as described in *Oracle8i Concepts*.

  If you change the value of the NEXT parameter (that is, if you specify it in an ALTER statement), the next allocated extent will have the specified size, regardless of the size of the most recently allocated extent and the value of the PCTINCREASE parameter.

■ PCTINCREASE specifies the percent by which the third and subsequent extents grow over the preceding extent. The default value is 50, meaning that each subsequent extent is 50% larger than the preceding extent. The minimum value is 0, meaning all extents after the first are the same size. The maximum value depends on your operating system.

Oracle rounds the calculated size of each new extent to the nearest multiple of the data block size.

If you change the value of the PCTINCREASE parameter (that is, if you specify it in an ALTER statement), Oracle calculates the size of the next extent using this new value and the size of the most recently allocated extent.

TIP

If you wish to keep all extents the same size, you can prevent SMON from coalescing extents by setting the value of PCTINCREASE to 0. In general, Oracle Corporation recommends a setting of 0 as a way to minimize fragmentation and avoid the possibility of very large temporary segments during processing.

RESTRICTION

You cannot specify PCTINCREASE for rollback segments. Rollback segments always have a PCTINCREASE value of 0.

■ MINEXTENTS specifies the total number of extents to allocate when the object is created. This parameter enables you to allocate a large amount of space when you create an object, even if the space available is not contiguous. The default and minimum value is 1, meaning that Oracle allocates only the initial extent, except for rollback segments, for which the default and minimum value is 2. The maximum value depends on your operating system.

If the MINEXTENTS value is greater than 1, then Oracle calculates the size of subsequent extents based on the values of the INITIAL, NEXT, and PCTINCREASE parameters.
Restriction: You cannot specify MINEXTENTS in an ALTER statement.

■ MAXEXTENTS specifies the total number of extents, including the first, that Oracle can allocate for the object. The minimum value is 1 (except for rollback segments, which always have a minimum value of 2). The default value depends on your data block size.

   ■ UNLIMITED specifies that extents should be allocated automatically as needed.

Oracle Corporation recommends this setting as a way to minimize fragmentation.

However, do not use this clause for rollback segments. Rogue transactions containing inserts, updates, or deletes, that continue for a long time will continue to create new extents until a disk is full.

CAUTION

A rollback segment that you create without specifying the storage_clause has the same storage parameters as the tablespace that the rollback segment is created in. Thus, if you create the tablespace with MAXEXTENTS UNLIMITED, then the rollback segment will also have the same default.

- FREELIST GROUPS for schema objects other than tablespace, specifies the number of groups of free lists for a table, partition, cluster, or index. The default and minimum value for this parameter is 1.

  Use this parameter only if you are using Oracle with the Parallel Server option in parallel mode.

  Oracle uses one data block for each free list group. If you do not specify a large enough value for INITIAL to cover the minimum value plus one data block for each free list group, Oracle increases the value of INITIAL the necessary amount.

- FREELISTS for objects other than tablespace, specifies the number of free lists for each of the free list groups for the table, partition, cluster, or index. The default and minimum value for this parameter is 1, meaning that each free list group contains one free list. The maximum value of this parameter depends on the data block size. If you specify a FREELISTS value that is too large, Oracle returns an error indicating the maximum value.

  Restriction: You can specify the FREELISTS and the FREELIST GROUPS parameters only in CREATE TABLE, CREATE CLUSTER, and CREATE INDEX statements.

- OPTIMAL is relevant only to rollback segments. It specifies an optimal size in bytes for a rollback segment. Use K or M to specify this size in kilobytes or megabytes. Oracle tries to maintain this size for the rollback segment by dynamically deallocating extents when their data is no longer needed for active transactions. Oracle deallocates as many extents as possible without reducing the total size of the rollback segment below the OPTIMAL value.

  - NULL specifies no optimal size for the rollback segment, meaning that Oracle never deallocates the rollback segment's extents. This is the default behavior.

  The value of OPTIMAL cannot be less than the space initially allocated for the rollback segment specified by the MINEXTENTS, INITIAL, NEXT, and PCTINCREASE parameters. The maximum value depends on your operating system. Oracle rounds values up to the next multiple of the data block size.

- BUFFER_POOL defines a default buffer pool (cache) for a schema object. All blocks for the object are stored in the specified cache. If a buffer pool is defined for a partitioned table or index, then the partitions inherit the buffer pool from the table or index definition, unless overridden by a partition-level definition.

NOTE
BUFFER_POOL is not a valid clause for creating or altering tablespaces or rollback segments. For more information about using multiple buffer pools, see Oracle8i Tuning.

- KEEP retains the schema object in memory to avoid I/O operations.
- RECYCLE eliminates blocks from memory as soon as they are no longer needed, thus preventing an object from taking up unnecessary cache space.
- DEFAULT always exists for objects not assigned to KEEP or RECYCLE.

TRUNCATE

Syntax

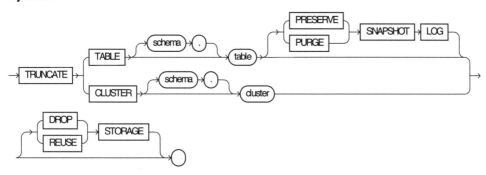

WARNING
You cannot roll back a TRUNCATE statement.

Purpose

To remove all rows from a table or cluster and reset the STORAGE parameters to the values when the table or cluster was created. Deleting rows with the TRUNCATE statement can be more efficient than dropping and re-creating a table. Dropping and re-creating a table invalidates the table's dependent objects, requires you to regrant object privileges on the table, and requires you to re-create the table's indexes, integrity constraint, and triggers and respecify its storage parameters. Truncating has none of these effects.

Prerequisites

The table or cluster must be in your schema or you must have DROP ANY TABLE system privilege.

Keywords and Parameters

■   TABLE specifies the schema and name of the table to be truncated. This table cannot be part of a cluster. If you omit *schema*, Oracle assumes the table is in your own cluster.

You can truncate index-organized tables and temporary tables. When you truncate a temporary table, only the rows created during the current session are truncated.

The table's storage parameter NEXT is changed to be the size of the last extent deleted from the segment in the process of truncation.

Oracle also automatically truncates and resets any existing UNUSABLE indicators for the following indexes on *table*: range and hash partitions of local indexes and subpartitions of local indexes.

If *table* is not empty, Oracle marks UNUSABLE all nonpartitioned indexes and all partitions of global partitioned indexes on the table.

For a domain index, this statement invokes the appropriate truncate routine to truncate the domain index data. For more information, see *Oracle8i Data Cartridge Developer's Guide.*

If *table* (whether it is a regular or index-organized table) contains LOB columns, all LOB data and LOB index segments will be truncated.

If *table* is partitioned, all partitions or subpartitions, as well as the LOB data and LOB index segments for each partition or subpartition, will be truncated.

NOTE
When you truncate a table, Oracle automatically deletes all data in the table's indexes and any materialized view direct-load INSERT information held in association with the table. (This information is independent of any materialized view/snapshot log.) If this direct-load INSERT information is deleted, an incremental refresh of the materialized view may lose data.

RESTRICTIONS
You cannot individually truncate a table that is part of a cluster. You must either truncate the cluster, delete all rows from the table, or drop and re-create the table.
You cannot truncate the parent table of an enabled referential integrity constraint. You must disable the constraint before truncating the table. (An exception is that you may truncate the table if the integrity constraint is self-referential.)
You cannot truncate a table if any domain indexes defined on any of its columns are marked LOADING or FAILED.

■ SNAPSHOT LOG specifies whether a snapshot log defined on the table is to be preserved or purged when the table is truncated. This clause allows snapshot master tables to be reorganized through export/import without affecting the ability of primary-key snapshots defined on the master to be fast refreshed. To support continued fast refresh of primary-key snapshots, the snapshot log must record primary-key information. For more information about snapshot logs and the TRUNCATE statement, see *Oracle8i Replication.*

   ■ PRESERVE specifies that any snapshot log should be preserved when the master table is truncated. This is the default.

   ■ PURGE specifies that any snapshot log should be purged when the master table is truncated.

■ CLUSTER specifies the schema and name of the cluster to be truncated. You can truncate only an indexed cluster, not a hash cluster. If you omit *schema*, Oracle assumes the table is in your own cluster.

When you truncate a cluster, Oracle also automatically deletes all data in the cluster's tables' indexes.

- DROP STORAGE deallocates all space from the deleted rows from the table or cluster except the space allocated by the table's or cluster's MINEXTENTS parameter. This space can subsequently be used by other objects in the tablespace. This is the default.

- REUSE STORAGE retains the space from the deleted rows allocated to the table or cluster. Storage values are not reset to the values when the table or cluster was created. This space can subsequently be used only by new data in the table or cluster resulting from inserts or updates.

- The DROP STORAGE clause and REUSE STORAGE clause also apply to the space freed by the data deleted from associated indexes.

NOTE
If you have specified more than one free list for the object you are truncating, the REUSE STORAGE clause also removes any mapping of free lists to instances, and resets the high-water mark to the beginning of the first extent.

APPENDIX B

init.ora Parameter Changes in ORACLE8.0 and ORACLE8i

The available init.ora parameters change with each version of ORACLE. In this appendix, you will see the parameters from three different versions of the database: 7.3.4, 8.0.5, and 8.1.5. In Figure B-1, the three sets of parameters are presented side by side to ease comparisons between the parameter sets in the different versions. You can use the parameter list in Figure B-1 to anticipate changes in your init.ora files as you upgrade ORACLE versions.

If a parameter is not supported in a version of the database, then there will be a blank in that row in that version's column in Figure B-1. For example, the first parameter, O7_DICTIONARY_ACCESSIBILITY, is not valid in ORACLE7.3.4, so there is no entry for the O7_DICTIONARY_ACCESSIBILITY parameter's row in the 7.3.4 column. Similarly, the ASYNC_READ parameter is valid in ORACLE7.3.4 but not in any version of ORACLE8, so that parameter's entries are blank in the columns for 8.0.5 and 8.1.5.

Although a parameter is listed, it may not be fully supported by ORACLE. For example, the ARCH_IO_SLAVES parameter was introduced in ORACLE8.0, and is still allowed as a parameter in ORACLE8.1.5, but it is officially an obsolete parameter as of 8.1.3. If a parameter is obsolete in ORACLE8i but is still allowed in the init.ora file, its entry in Figure B-1 is shown in bold. Following the listing of parameters in Figure B-1, you will see explanations of the changes, including those changes that primarily affect the support level of the parameter.

NOTE
In some cases, the parameter names in the database do not match the documentation. In the case of such discrepancies, the values in V$PARAMETER are used to assign a starting version for the parameter.

ORACLE7.3.4	ORACLE8.0.5	ORACLE8.1.5
	O7_DICTIONARY_ACCESSIBILITY	O7_DICTIONARY_ACCESSIBILITY
	ALLOW_PARTIAL_SN_RESULTS	**ALLOW_PARTIAL_SN_RESULTS**
ALWAYS_ANTI_JOIN	ALWAYS_ANTI_JOIN	ALWAYS_ANTI_JOIN
	ALWAYS_SEMI_JOIN	ALWAYS_SEMI_JOIN
	AQ_TM_PROCESSES	AQ_TM_PROCESSES
	ARCH_IO_SLAVES	**ARCH_IO_SLAVES**
ASYNC_READ		
ASYNC_WRITE		
AUDIT_FILE_DEST	AUDIT_FILE_DEST	AUDIT_FILE_DEST
AUDIT_TRAIL	AUDIT_TRAIL	AUDIT_TRAIL
B_TREE_BITMAP_PLANS	B_TREE_BITMAP_PLANS	**B_TREE_BITMAP_PLANS**
BACKGROUND_CORE_DUMP	BACKGROUND_CORE_DUMP	BACKGROUND_CORE_DUMP
BACKGROUND_DUMP_DEST	BACKGROUND_DUMP_DEST	BACKGROUND_DUMP_DEST
	BACKUP_DISK_IO_SLAVES	**BACKUP_DISK_IO_SLAVES**
	BACKUP_TAPE_IO_SLAVES	BACKUP_TAPE_IO_SLAVES
BITMAP_MERGE_AREA_SIZE	BITMAP_MERGE_AREA_SIZE	BITMAP_MERGE_AREA_SIZE
BLANK_TRIMMING	BLANK_TRIMMING	BLANK_TRIMMING
	BUFFER_POOL_KEEP	BUFFER_POOL_KEEP
	BUFFER_POOL_RECYCLE	BUFFER_POOL_RECYCLE
CACHE_SIZE_THRESHOLD	CACHE_SIZE_THRESHOLD	**CACHE_SIZE_THRESHOLD**
CCF_IO_SIZE		
CHECKPOINT_PROCESS		
CLEANUP_ROLLBACK_ENTRIES	CLEANUP_ROLLBACK_ENTRIES	**CLEANUP_ROLLBACK_ENTRIES**
CLOSE_CACHED_OPEN_CURSORS	CLOSE_CACHED_OPEN_CURSORS	**CLOSE_CACHED_OPEN_CURSORS**
COMMIT_POINT_STRENGTH	COMMIT_POINT_STRENGTH	COMMIT_POINT_STRENGTH
COMPATIBLE	COMPATIBLE	COMPATIBLE

FIGURE B-1. *init.ora parameters for ORACLE7.3.4, 8.0.5, and 8.1.5*

ORACLE7.3.4	ORACLE8.0.5	ORACLE8.1.5
COMPATIBLE_NO_RECOVERY	COMPATIBLE_NO_RECOVERY	**COMPATIBLE_NO_RECOVERY**
	COMPLEX_VIEW_MERGING	**COMPLEX_VIEW_MERGING**
	CONTROL_FILE_RECORD_KEEP_TIME	CONTROL_FILE_RECORD_KEEP_TIME
CONTROL_FILES	CONTROL_FILES	CONTROL_FILES
CORE_DUMP_DEST	CORE_DUMP_DEST	CORE_DUMP_DEST
CPU_COUNT	CPU_COUNT	CPU_COUNT
CREATE_BITMAP_AREA_SIZE	CREATE_BITMAP_AREA_SIZE	CREATE_BITMAP_AREA_SIZE
CURSOR_SPACE_FOR_TIME	CURSOR_SPACE_FOR_TIME	CURSOR_SPACE_FOR_TIME
DB_BLOCK_BUFFERS	DB_BLOCK_BUFFERS	DB_BLOCK_BUFFERS
DB_BLOCK_CHECKPOINT_BATCH	DB_BLOCK_CHECKPOINT_BATCH	**DB_BLOCK_CHECKPOINT_BATCH**
		DB_BLOCK_CHECKING
DB_BLOCK_CHECKSUM	DB_BLOCK_CHECKSUM	DB_BLOCK_CHECKSUM
DB_BLOCK_LRU_EXTENDED_STATISTICS	DB_BLOCK_LRU_EXTENDED_STATISTICS	**DB_BLOCK_LRU_EXTENDED_STATISTICS**
DB_BLOCK_LRU_LATCHES	DB_BLOCK_LRU_LATCHES	DB_BLOCK_LRU_LATCHES
DB_BLOCK_LRU_STATISTICS	DB_BLOCK_LRU_STATISTICS	**DB_BLOCK_LRU_STATISTICS**
	DB_BLOCK_MAX_DIRTY_TARGET	DB_BLOCK_MAX_DIRTY_TARGET
DB_BLOCK_SIZE	DB_BLOCK_SIZE	DB_BLOCK_SIZE
DB_DOMAIN	DB_DOMAIN	DB_DOMAIN
	DB_FILE_DIRECT_IO_COUNT	DB_FILE_DIRECT_IO_COUNT
DB_FILE_MULTIBLOCK_READ_COUNT	DB_FILE_MULTIBLOCK_READ_COUNT	DB_FILE_MULTIBLOCK_READ_COUNT
	DB_FILE_NAME_CONVERT	DB_FILE_NAME_CONVERT
DB_FILE_SIMULTANEOUS_WRITES	DB_FILE_SIMULTANEOUS_WRITES	**DB_FILE_SIMULTANEOUS_WRITES**
DB_FILE_STANDBY_NAME_CONVERT		
DB_FILES	DB_FILES	DB_FILES
DB_NAME	DB_NAME	DB_NAME
DB_WRITERS		

FIGURE B-1. *init.ora parameters for ORACLE7.3.4, 8.0.5, and 8.1.5 (continued)*

ORACLE7.3.4	ORACLE8.0.5	ORACLE8.1.5
	DB_WRITER_PROCESSES	DB_WRITER_PROCESSES
DBLINK_ENCRYPT_LOGIN	DBLINK_ENCRYPT_LOGIN	DBLINK_ENCRYPT_LOGIN
	DBWR_IO_SLAVES	DBWR_IO_SLAVES
DELAYED_LOGGING_BLOCK_CLEANOUTS	DELAYED_LOGGING_BLOCK_CLEANOUTS	DELAYED_LOGGING_BLOCK_CLEANOUTS
DISCRETE_TRANSACTIONS_ENABLED	DISCRETE_TRANSACTIONS_ENABLED	**DISCRETE_TRANSACTIONS_ENABLED**
	DISK_ASYNCH_IO	DISK_ASYNCH_IO
DISTRIBUTED_LOCK_TIMEOUT	DISTRIBUTED_LOCK_TIMEOUT	**DISTRIBUTED_LOCK_TIMEOUT**
DISTRIBUTED_RECOVERY_CONNECTION_HOLD_TIME	DISTRIBUTED_RECOVERY_CONNECTION_HOLD_TIME	**DISTRIBUTED_RECOVERY_CONNECTION_HOLD_TIME**
DISTRIBUTED_TRANSACTIONS	DISTRIBUTED_TRANSACTIONS	DISTRIBUTED_TRANSACTIONS
DML_LOCKS	DML_LOCKS	DML_LOCKS
ENQUEUE_RESOURCES	ENQUEUE_RESOURCES	ENQUEUE_RESOURCES
EVENT	EVENT	EVENT
FAST_CACHE_FLUSH	FAST_FULL_SCAN_ENABLED	**FAST_FULL_SCAN_ENABLED**
FIXED_DATE	FIXED_DATE	FIXED_DATE
	FREEZE_DB_FOR_FAST_INSTANCE_RECOVERY	FREEZE_DB_FOR_FAST_INSTANCE_RECOVERY
GC_DB_LOCKS		
	GC_DEFER_TIME	GC_DEFER_TIME
GC_FILES_TO_LOCKS	GC_FILES_TO_LOCKS	GC_FILES_TO_LOCKS
GC_FREELIST_GROUPS		
	GC_LATCHES	**GC_LATCHES**
GC_LCK_PROCS	GC_LCK_PROCS	**GC_LCK_PROCS**
GC_RELEASABLE_LOCKS	GC_RELEASABLE_LOCKS	GC_RELEASABLE_LOCKS
GC_ROLLBACK_LOCKS	GC_ROLLBACK_LOCKS	GC_ROLLBACK_LOCKS
GC_ROLLBACK_SEGMENTS		
GC_SAVE_ROLLBACK_LOCKS		

FIGURE B-1. *init.ora parameters for ORACLE7.3.4, 8.0.5, and 8.1.5 (continued)*

ORACLE7.3.4	ORACLE8.0.5	ORACLE8.1.5
GC_SEGMENTS		
GC_TABLESPACES		
GLOBAL_NAMES	GLOBAL_NAMES	GLOBAL_NAMES
HASH_AREA_SIZE	HASH_AREA_SIZE	HASH_AREA_SIZE
HASH_JOIN_ENABLED	HASH_JOIN_ENABLED	HASH_JOIN_ENABLED
HASH_MULTIBLOCK_IO_COUNT	HASH_MULTIBLOCK_IO_COUNT	HASH_MULTIBLOCK_IO_COUNT
	HI_SHARED_MEMORY_ADDRESS	HI_SHARED_MEMORY_ADDRESS
		HS_AUTOREGISTER
IFILE	IFILE	IFILE
	INSTANCE_GROUPS	INSTANCE_GROUPS
		INSTANCE_NAME
INSTANCE_NUMBER	INSTANCE_NUMBER	INSTANCE_NUMBER
		JAVA_POOL_SIZE
JOB_QUEUE_INTERVAL	JOB_QUEUE_INTERVAL	JOB_QUEUE_INTERVAL
JOB_QUEUE_KEEP_CONNECTIONS		
JOB_QUEUE_PROCESSES	JOB_QUEUE_PROCESSES	JOB_QUEUE_PROCESSES
	LARGE_POOL_MIN_ALLOC	**LARGE_POOL_MIN_ALLOC**
	LARGE_POOL_SIZE	LARGE_POOL_SIZE
	LGWR_IO_SLAVES	**LGWR_IO_SLAVES**
LICENSE_MAX_SESSIONS	LICENSE_MAX_SESSIONS	LICENSE_MAX_SESSIONS
LICENSE_MAX_USERS	LICENSE_MAX_USERS	LICENSE_MAX_USERS
LICENSE_SESSIONS_WARNING	LICENSE_SESSIONS_WARNING	LICENSE_SESSIONS_WARNING
	LM_LOCKS	LM_LOCKS
	LM_PROCS	LM_PROCS
	LM_RESS	LM_RESS
	LOCAL_LISTENER	LOCAL_LISTENER

FIGURE B-1. *init.ora parameters for ORACLE7.3.4, 8.0.5, and 8.1.5 (continued)*

ORACLE7.3.4	ORACLE8.0.5	ORACLE8.1.5
	LOCK_NAME_SPACE	LOCK_NAME_SPACE
	LOCK_SGA	LOCK_SGA
	LOCK_SGA_AREAS	**LOCK_SGA_AREAS**
LOG_ARCHIVE_BUFFER_SIZE	LOG_ARCHIVE_BUFFER_SIZE	**LOG_ARCHIVE_BUFFER_SIZE**
LOG_ARCHIVE_BUFFERS	LOG_ARCHIVE_BUFFERS	**LOG_ARCHIVE_BUFFERS**
LOG_ARCHIVE_DEST	LOG_ARCHIVE_DEST	**LOG_ARCHIVE_DEST**
		LOG_ARCHIVE_DEST_n
		LOG_ARCHIVE_DEST_STATE_n
	LOG_ARCHIVE_DUPLEX_DEST	LOG_ARCHIVE_DUPLEX_DEST
LOG_ARCHIVE_FORMAT	LOG_ARCHIVE_FORMAT	LOG_ARCHIVE_FORMAT
		LOG_ARCHIVE_MAX_PROCESSES
LOG_ARCHIVE_MIN_SUCCEED_DEST	LOG_ARCHIVE_MIN_SUCCEED_DEST	LOG_ARCHIVE_MIN_SUCCEED_DEST
LOG_ARCHIVE_START	LOG_ARCHIVE_START	LOG_ARCHIVE_START
LOG_BLOCK_CHECKSUM	LOG_BLOCK_CHECKSUM	**LOG_BLOCK_CHECKSUM**
LOG_BUFFER	LOG_BUFFER	LOG_BUFFER
LOG_CHECKPOINT_INTERVAL	LOG_CHECKPOINT_INTERVAL	LOG_CHECKPOINT_INTERVAL
LOG_CHECKPOINT_TIMEOUT	LOG_CHECKPOINT_TIMEOUT	LOG_CHECKPOINT_TIMEOUT
LOG_CHECKPOINTS_TO_ALERT	LOG_CHECKPOINTS_TO_ALERT	LOG_CHECKPOINTS_TO_ALERT
LOG_FILE_STANDBY_NAME_CONVERT	LOG_FILE_NAME_CONVERT	LOG_FILE_NAME_CONVERT
LOG_FILES	LOG_FILES	**LOG_FILES**
LOG_SIMULTANEOUS_COPIES	LOG_SIMULTANEOUS_COPIES	**LOG_SIMULTANEOUS_COPIES**
LOG_SMALL_ENTRY_MAX_SIZE	LOG_SMALL_ENTRY_MAX_SIZE	**LOG_SMALL_ENTRY_MAX_SIZE**
MAX_COMMIT_PROPAGATION_DELAY	MAX_COMMIT_PROPAGATION_DELAY	MAX_COMMIT_PROPAGATION_DELAY
MAX_DUMP_FILE_SIZE	MAX_DUMP_FILE_SIZE	MAX_DUMP_FILE_SIZE
MAX_ENABLED_ROLES	MAX_ENABLED_ROLES	MAX_ENABLED_ROLES

FIGURE B-1. init.ora parameters for ORACLE7.3.4, 8.0.5, and 8.1.5 (continued)

ORACLE7.3.4	ORACLE8.0.5	ORACLE8.1.5
MAX_ROLLBACK_SEGMENTS	MAX_ROLLBACK_SEGMENTS	MAX_ROLLBACK_SEGMENTS
MAX_TRANSACTION_BRANCHES	MAX_TRANSACTION_BRANCHES	**MAX_TRANSACTION_BRANCHES**
MTS_DISPATCHERS	MTS_DISPATCHERS	MTS_DISPATCHERS
MTS_LISTENER_ADDRESS	MTS_LISTENER_ADDRESS	**MTS_LISTENER_ADDRESS**
MTS_MAX_DISPATCHERS	MTS_MAX_DISPATCHERS	MTS_MAX_DISPATCHERS
MTS_MAX_SERVERS	MTS_MAX_SERVERS	MTS_MAX_SERVERS
MTS_MULTIPLE_LISTENERS	MTS_MULTIPLE_LISTENERS	**MTS_MULTIPLE_LISTENERS**
	MTS_RATE_LOG_SIZE	**MTS_RATE_LOG_SIZE**
	MTS_RATE_SCALE	**MTS_RATE_SCALE**
MTS_SERVERS	MTS_SERVERS	MTS_SERVERS
MTS_SERVICE	MTS_SERVICE	**MTS_SERVICE**
		MVIEW_REWRITE_ENABLED
	NLS_CALENDAR	NLS_CALENDAR
		NLS_COMP
NLS_CURRENCY	NLS_CURRENCY	NLS_CURRENCY
NLS_DATE_FORMAT	NLS_DATE_FORMAT	NLS_DATE_FORMAT
NLS_DATE_LANGUAGE	NLS_DATE_LANGUAGE	NLS_DATE_LANGUAGE
NLS_ISO_CURRENCY	NLS_ISO_CURRENCY	NLS_ISO_CURRENCY
NLS_LANGUAGE	NLS_LANGUAGE	NLS_LANGUAGE
NLS_NUMERIC_CHARACTERS	NLS_NUMERIC_CHARACTERS	NLS_NUMERIC_CHARACTERS
NLS_SORT	NLS_SORT	NLS_SORT
NLS_TERRITORY	NLS_TERRITORY	NLS_TERRITORY
		NLS_UNION_CURRENCY
	OBJECT_CACHE_MAX_SIZE_PERCENT	OBJECT_CACHE_MAX_SIZE_PERCENT
	OBJECT_CACHE_OPTIMAL_SIZE	OBJECT_CACHE_OPTIMAL_SIZE
	OGMS_HOME	**OGMS_HOME**

FIGURE B-1. *init.ora parameters for ORACLE7.3.4, 8.0.5, and 8.1.5 (continued)*

ORACLE7.3.4	ORACLE8.0.5	ORACLE8.1.5
OPEN_CURSORS	OPEN_CURSORS	OPEN_CURSORS
OPEN_LINKS	OPEN_LINKS	OPEN_LINKS
	OPEN_LINKS_PER_INSTANCE	OPEN_LINKS_PER_INSTANCE
	OPS_ADMIN_GROUP	**OPS_ADMIN_GROUP**
	OPTIMIZER_FEATURES_ENABLE	OPTIMIZER_FEATURES_ENABLE
		OPTIMIZER_INDEX_CACHING
		OPTIMIZER_INDEX_COST_ADJ
		OPTIMIZER_MAX_PERMUTATIONS
OPTIMIZER_MODE	OPTIMIZER_MODE	OPTIMIZER_MODE
OPTIMIZER_PARALLEL_PASS		
OPTIMIZER_PERCENT_PARALLEL	OPTIMIZER_PERCENT_PARALLEL	OPTIMIZER_PERCENT_PARALLEL
OPTIMIZER_SEARCH_LIMIT	OPTIMIZER_SEARCH_LIMIT	OPTIMIZER_SEARCH_LIMIT
ORACLE_TRACE_COLLECTION_NAME	ORACLE_TRACE_COLLECTION_NAME	ORACLE_TRACE_COLLECTION_NAME
ORACLE_TRACE_COLLECTION_PATH	ORACLE_TRACE_COLLECTION_PATH	ORACLE_TRACE_COLLECTION_PATH
ORACLE_TRACE_COLLECTION_SIZE	ORACLE_TRACE_COLLECTION_SIZE	ORACLE_TRACE_COLLECTION_SIZE
ORACLE_TRACE_ENABLE	ORACLE_TRACE_ENABLE	ORACLE_TRACE_ENABLE
ORACLE_TRACE_FACILITY_NAME	ORACLE_TRACE_FACILITY_NAME	ORACLE_TRACE_FACILITY_NAME
ORACLE_TRACE_FACILITY_PATH	ORACLE_TRACE_FACILITY_PATH	ORACLE_TRACE_FACILITY_PATH
OS_AUTHENT_PREFIX	OS_AUTHENT_PREFIX	OS_AUTHENT_PREFIX
OS_ROLES	OS_ROLES	OS_ROLES
PARALLEL_ADAPTIVE_MULTI_USER	PARALLEL_ADAPTIVE_MULTI_USER	PARALLEL_ADAPTIVE_MULTI_USER
		PARALLEL_AUTOMATIC_TUNING
	PARALLEL_BROADCAST_ENABLED	PARALLEL_BROADCAST_ENABLED
PARALLEL_DEFAULT_MAX_INSTANCES	PARALLEL_DEFAULT_MAX_INSTANCES	**PARALLEL_DEFAULT_MAX_INSTANCES**
	PARALLEL_EXECUTION_MESSAGE_SIZE	PARALLEL_EXECUTION_MESSAGE_SIZE
	PARALLEL_INSTANCE_GROUP	PARALLEL_INSTANCE_GROUP

FIGURE B-1. *init.ora parameters for ORACLE7.3.4, 8.0.5, and 8.1.5* (continued)

ORACLE7.3.4	ORACLE8.0.5	ORACLE8.1.5
PARALLEL_MAX_SERVERS	PARALLEL_MAX_SERVERS	PARALLEL_MAX_SERVERS
	PARALLEL_MIN_MESSAGE_POOL	**PARALLEL_MIN_MESSAGE_POOL**
PARALLEL_MIN_PERCENT	PARALLEL_MIN_PERCENT	PARALLEL_MIN_PERCENT
PARALLEL_MIN_SERVERS	PARALLEL_MIN_SERVERS	PARALLEL_MIN_SERVERS
	PARALLEL_SERVER	PARALLEL_SERVER
PARALLEL_SERVER_IDLE_TIME	PARALLEL_SERVER_IDLE_TIME	**PARALLEL_SERVER_IDLE_TIME**
		PARALLEL_SERVER_INSTANCES
		PARALLEL_THREADS_PER_CPU
		PARALLEL_TRANSACTION_RECOVERY
	PARALLEL_TRANSACTION_RESOURCE_TIMEOUT	**PARALLEL_TRANSACTION_RESOURCE_TIMEOUT**
PARTITION_VIEW_ENABLED	PARTITION_VIEW_ENABLED	PARTITION_VIEW_ENABLED
	PLSQL_V2_COMPATIBILITY	PLSQL_V2_COMPATIBILITY
POST_WAIT_DEVICE		
PRE_PAGE_SGA	PRE_PAGE_SGA	PRE_PAGE_SGA
PROCESSES	PROCESSES	PROCESSES
	PUSH_JOIN_PREDICATE	**PUSH_JOIN_PREDICATE**
	READ_ONLY_OPEN_DELAYED	READ_ONLY_OPEN_DELAYED
RECOVERY_PARALLELISM	RECOVERY_PARALLELISM	RECOVERY_PARALLELISM
REDUCE_ALARM	REDUCE_ALARM	**REDUCE_ALARM**
REMOTE_DEPENDENCIES_MODE	REMOTE_DEPENDENCIES_MODE	REMOTE_DEPENDENCIES_MODE
REMOTE_LOGIN_PASSWORDFILE	REMOTE_LOGIN_PASSWORDFILE	REMOTE_LOGIN_PASSWORDFILE
REMOTE_OS_AUTHENT	REMOTE_OS_AUTHENT	REMOTE_OS_AUTHENT
REMOTE_OS_ROLES	REMOTE_OS_ROLES	REMOTE_OS_ROLES
	REPLICATION_DEPENDENCY_TRACKING	REPLICATION_DEPENDENCY_TRACKING
RESOURCE_LIMIT	RESOURCE_LIMIT	RESOURCE_LIMIT
		RESOURCE_MANAGER_PLAN

FIGURE B-I.   *init.ora parameters for ORACLE7.3.4, 8.0.5, and 8.1.5 (continued)*

ORACLE7.3.4	ORACLE8.0.5	ORACLE8.1.5
		REWRITE_INTEGRITY
ROLLBACK_SEGMENTS	ROLLBACK_SEGMENTS	ROLLBACK_SEGMENTS
ROW_CACHE_CURSORS	ROW_CACHE_CURSORS	**ROW_CACHE_CURSORS**
ROW_LOCKING	ROW_LOCKING	ROW_LOCKING
SEQUENCE_CACHE_ENTRIES	SEQUENCE_CACHE_ENTRIES	**SEQUENCE_CACHE_ENTRIES**
SEQUENCE_CACHE_HASH_BUCKETS	SEQUENCE_CACHE_HASH_BUCKETS	**SEQUENCE_CACHE_HASH_BUCKETS**
SERIALIZABLE	SERIAL_REUSE	SERIAL_REUSE
		SERVICE_NAMES
SESSION_CACHED_CURSORS	SESSION_CACHED_CURSORS	SESSION_CACHED_CURSORS
	SESSION_MAX_OPEN_FILES	SESSION_MAX_OPEN_FILES
SESSIONS	SESSIONS	SESSIONS
SHADOW_CORE_DUMP	SHADOW_CORE_DUMP	SHADOW_CORE_DUMP
	SHARED_MEMORY_ADDRESS	SHARED_MEMORY_ADDRESS
SHARED_POOL_RESERVED_MIN_ALLOC	SHARED_POOL_RESERVED_MIN_ALLOC	**SHARED_POOL_RESERVED_MIN_ALLOC**
SHARED_POOL_RESERVED_SIZE	SHARED_POOL_RESERVED_SIZE	SHARED_POOL_RESERVED_SIZE
SHARED_POOL_SIZE	SHARED_POOL_SIZE	SHARED_POOL_SIZE
SNAPSHOT_REFRESH_INTERVAL		
SNAPSHOT_REFRESH_KEEP_CONNECTIONS		
SNAPSHOT_REFRESH_PROCESSES		
SORT_AREA_RETAINED_SIZE	SORT_AREA_RETAINED_SIZE	SORT_AREA_RETAINED_SIZE
SORT_AREA_SIZE	SORT_AREA_SIZE	SORT_AREA_SIZE
SORT_DIRECT_WRITES	SORT_DIRECT_WRITES	**SORT_DIRECT_WRITES**
		SORT_MULTIBLOCK_READ_COUNT
SORT_READ_FAC	SORT_READ_FAC	**SORT_READ_FAC**
SORT_SPACEMAP_SIZE	SORT_SPACEMAP_SIZE	**SORT_SPACEMAP_SIZE**

FIGURE B-1. init.ora parameters for ORACLE7.3.4, 8.0.5, and 8.1.5 (continued)

ORACLE7.3.4	ORACLE8.0.5	ORACLE8.1.5
SORT_WRITE_BUFFER_SIZE	SORT_WRITE_BUFFER_SIZE	**SORT_WRITE_BUFFER_SIZE**
SORT_WRITE_BUFFERS	SORT_WRITE_BUFFERS	**SORT_WRITE_BUFFERS**
SPIN_COUNT	SPIN_COUNT	**SPIN_COUNT**
SQL92_SECURITY	SQL92_SECURITY	SQL92_SECURITY
SQL_TRACE	SQL_TRACE	SQL_TRACE
		STANDBY_ARCHIVE_DEST
	STAR_TRANSFORMATION_ENABLED	STAR_TRANSFORMATION_ENABLED
	TAPE_ASYNCH_IO	TAPE_ASYNCH_IO
TEMPORARY_TABLE_LOCKS	TEMPORARY_TABLE_LOCKS	**TEMPORARY_TABLE_LOCKS**
TEXT_ENABLE	TEXT_ENABLE	TEXT_ENABLE
THREAD	THREAD	THREAD
	TIMED_OS_STATISTICS	TIMED_OS_STATISTICS
TIMED_STATISTICS	TIMED_STATISTICS	TIMED_STATISTICS
	TRANSACTION_AUDITING	TRANSACTION_AUDITING
TRANSACTIONS	TRANSACTIONS	TRANSACTIONS
TRANSACTIONS_PER_ROLLBACK_SEGMENT	TRANSACTIONS_PER_ROLLBACK_SEGMENT	TRANSACTIONS_PER_ROLLBACK_SEGMENT
UNLIMITED_ROLLBACK_SEGMENTS		
	USE_INDIRECT_DATA_BUFFERS	USE_INDIRECT_DATA_BUFFERS
USE_ISM	USE_ISM	**USE_ISM**
USE_POST_WAIT_DRIVER		
USE_READV		
USER_DUMP_DEST	USER_DUMP_DEST	USER_DUMP_DEST
UTL_FILE_DIR	UTL_FILE_DIR	UTL_FILE_DIR
V733_PLANS_ENABLED		

FIGURE B-1. *init.ora parameters for ORACLE7.3.4, 8.0.5, and 8.1.5 (continued)*

Obsolete Parameters in **ORACLE8.0**

The following table lists the parameters that were acceptable in ORACLE7.3.4 but are obsolete as of ORACLE8.0.5.

Parameter	Comments/Related ORACLE8 Parameters
ASYNC_READ	DISK_ASYNCH_IO
ASYNC_WRITE	DISK_ASYNCH_IO
CCF_IO_SIZE	DB_FILE_DIRECT_IO_COUNT
CHECKPOINT_PROCESS	CKPT process is automatically created
DB_FILE_STANDBY_NAME_CONVERT	DB_FILE_NAME_CONVERT
DB_WRITERS	DBWR_PROCESSES, DBWR_IO_SLAVES
FAST_CACHE_FLUSH	
GC_DB_LOCKS	
GC_FREELIST_GROUPS	
GC_SAVE_ROLLBACK_SEGMENTS	
GC_SEGMENTS	
GC_TABLESPACES	
JOB_QUEUE_KEEP_CONNECTIONS	
LOG_FILE_STANDBY_NAME_CONVERT	LOG_FILE_NAME_CONVERT
OPTIMIZER_PARALLEL_PASS	
POST_WAIT_DEVICE	
SERIALIZABLE	
SNAPSHOT_REFRESH_INTERVAL	JOB_QUEUE_REFRESH_INTERVAL
SNAPSHOT_REFRESH_KEEP_CONNECTIONS	JOB_QUEUE_KEEP_CONNECTIONS (also desupported as of ORACLE8.0)
SNAPSHOT_REFRESH_PROCESSES	JOB_QUEUE_PROCESSES
UNLIMITED_ROLLBACK_SEGMENTS	Used during upgrades to 7.3
USE_POST_WAIT_DRIVER	
USE_READV	
V733_PLANS_ENABLED	Enabled 7.3 features such as partition views

New Parameters in ORACLE8.0

The following table lists the parameters that are new as of ORACLE8 Release 8.0.5. For each parameter, you will see the default value where applicable, along with comments regarding the parameter's usage. Please see the ORACLE documentation for the full description of each parameter.

Parameter	Default Setting and Comments
O7_DICTIONARY_ACCESSIBILITY	Defaults to TRUE, allowing access to SYS tables via SYSTEM-level privileges such as SELECT ANY TABLE.
ALLOW_PARTIAL_SN_RESULTS	Defaults to FALSE; ORACLE Parallel Server parameter that allows partial results to be returned from queries of global dynamic performance views. Obsolete in ORACLE8i.
ALWAYS_SEMI_JOIN	No default; set to NESTED LOOPS, MERGE, or HASH_SJ to set the type of join used during EXISTS queries.
AQ_TM_PROCESSES	Defaults to 0; if greater than 0, then a queue monitor process is started.
ARCH_IO_SLAVES	Defaults to 0; allows multiple I/O slaves to support the ARCH process; obsolete in ORACLE8i.
BACKUP_DISK_IO_SLAVES	Defaults to 0; if greater than 0, then multiple I/O slaves are used by RMAN during backup and restore operations. Obsolete in ORACLE8i.
BACKUP_TAPE_IO_SLAVES	Defaults to FALSE; if TRUE, then RMAN used multiple I/O slaves during tape I/O.
BUFFER_POOL_KEEP	No default; allows you to keep an object in the buffer cache.
BUFFER_POOL_RECYCLE	No default; allows you to limit the size of an object in the buffer cache.
COMPLEX_VIEW_MERGING	Defaults to OFF; when set to TRUE, complex views may be merged with other parts of a SQL statement; when OFF or FALSE, the complex view is processed without prior merging. Obsolete in ORACLE8i.
CONTROL_FILE_RECORD_KEEP_TIME	Defaults to 7 days, the number of days' worth of backup records (created via RMAN) stored in the control file.
DB_BLOCK_MAX_DIRTY_TARGET	Defaults to the number of buffers in the cache; specifies the number of buffers that can be modified before DBWR initiates a write operation.
DB_FILE_DIRECT_IO_COUNT	Default to 64; specifies the number of blocks to be used for I/O operations done by backup, restore, or direct path read and write functions.
DB_FILE_NAME_CONVERT	No default; replaces DB_FILE_STANDBY_NAME_CONVERT.
DB_WRITER_PROCESSES	Default value is 1; replaces DB_WRITERS parameter. If you set DBWR_IO_SLAVES > 1, then your setting for DB_WRITER_PROCESSES will be ignored.
DBWR_IO_SLAVES	Default is 0; values > 0 enable multiple I/O slaves for the DBWR process.
DISK_ASYNCH_IO	Defaults to TRUE, enabling asynchronous I/O.
FAST_FULL_SCAN_ENABLED	Defaults to FALSE; setting to TRUE enables full index scans to replace full table scans where appropriate. Obsolete in ORACLE8i.
FREEZE_DB_FOR_FAST_INSTANCE_RECOVERY	ORACLE Parallel Server parameter that controls whether a database is frozen during recovery operations.
GC_DEFER_TIME	Defaults to 10; ORACLE Parallel Server parameter controlling server wait time for forced writes.

Parameter	Default Setting and Comments
GC_LATCHES	ORACLE Parallel Server parameter controlling the number of lock element latches available to the LCK process.
HI_SHARED_MEMORY_ADDRESS	If specified, gives the starting high-memory address for the SGA.
INSTANCE_GROUPS	ORACLE Parallel Server parameter assigning an instance to an instance group.
LARGE_POOL_MIN_ALLOC	Defaults to 16KB; sets the minimum allocation size for an object in the large pool. Obsolete in ORACLE8i.
LARGE_POOL_SIZE	Defaults to 0; if > 0, then large objects are stored in the large pool section of the shared pool.
LGWR_IO_SLAVES	Defaults to 0; allows multiple I/O slaves to support the LGWR process. Obsolete in ORACLE8i.
LM_LOCKS	ORACLE Parallel Server parameter; sets the number of locks configured for the lock manager.
LM_PROCS	ORACLE Parallel Server parameter, setting the number of processes per lock manager.
LM_RESS	ORACLE Parallel Server parameter, limits the number of resources each lock manager can lock.
LOCAL_LISTENER	No default; defines local listeners for Net8.
LOCK_NAME_SPACE	ORACLE Parallel Server parameter; specifies name space used by the distributed lock manager.
LOCK_SGA	Defaults to FALSE; if TRUE, then SGA may be locked in physical memory.
LOCK_SGA_AREAS	Lock individual components of the SGA into memory; setting uses binary values for the different memory areas, see the Reference Guide. Obsolete in ORACLE8i.
LOG_ARCHIVE_DUPLEX_DEST	No default; specifies a second destination device for archived redo logs. ARCH must successfully write to the primary location specified in LOG_ARCHIVE_DEST. Obsolete in ORACLE8i, replaced by LOG_ARCHIVE_DEST_N.
LOG_ARCHIVE_MIN_SUCCEED_DEST	Defaults to 1; specifies the number of archived redo log destinations that must be successful. Obsolete in ORACLE8i.
LOG_FILE_NAME_CONVERT	Replaces LOG_FILE_STANDBY_NAME_CONVERT.
MTS_RATE_LOG_SIZE	Specifies the size for each type of statistic being gathered for an MTS configuration. Obsolete in ORACLE8i.
MTS_RATE_SCALE	Specifies the rate at which MTS statistics are reported, in hundredths of seconds. Obsolete in ORACLE8i.
NLS_CALENDAR	Defaults to Gregorian; can be set to other calendars, such as Arabic Hijrah and Thai Buddha.
OBJECT_CACHE_MAX_SIZE_PERCENT	Defaults to 10; specifies percent above its optimal size that the object cache can grow to.
OBJECT_CACHE_OPTIMAL_SIZE	Defaults to 100 KB; specifies the optimal size of the object cache.
OGMS_HOME	Specifies the directory where background files can find the GMS key file. Obsolete in ORACLE8i.
OPEN_LINKS_PER_INSTANCE	Defaults to 4; sets the maximum number of migratable open connections.
OPS_ADMIN_GROUP	ORACLE Parallel Server parameter; sets the administrative group for an instance. Obsolete in ORACLE8i.
OPTIMIZER_FEATURES_ENABLE	Defaults to 8.0.0; set to 8.0.4 to enable optimizer features introduced in ORACLE8.

Parameter	Default Setting and Comments
PARALLEL_ADAPTIVE_MULTI_USER	Defaults to FALSE. Set to TRUE to balance the parallel query option requirements of multiple users.
PARALLEL_BROADCAST_ENABLED	Defaults to FALSE. Set to TRUE to optimize parallelized joins involving very large tables joined to small tables.
PARALLEL_EXECUTION_MESSAGE_SIZE	Default value is operating system dependent; controls the amount of shared pool space used by PQO queries.
PARALLEL_INSTANCE_GROUP	ORACLE Parallel Server parameter; defines the instance group used for query server processes.
PARALLEL_MIN_MESSAGE_POOL	Default value is environment specific; sets the size of the shared pool portion devoted to PQO messages. Obsolete in ORACLE8i.
PARALLEL_SERVER	Defaults to FALSE; set to TRUE to enable the ORACLE Parallel Server.
PARALLEL_TRANSACTION_RESOURCE_TIMEOUT	ORACLE Parallel Server parameter. Defaults to 300 seconds; sets the maximum time for a timeout of a parallel transaction. Obsolete in ORACLE8i.
PLSQL_V2_COMPATIBILITY	Default is FALSE; set to TRUE to enable PL/SQL V2 compatibility.
PUSH_JOIN_PREDICATE	Default is FALSE; set to TRUE to enable optimizer changes that push join predicates into views. Obsolete in ORACLE8i.
READ_ONLY_OPEN_DELAYED	Default is FALSE. If set to TRUE, then read-only tablespaces are not accessed when the database is opened, improving the performance of database startups in databases with many read-only tablespaces.
REPLICATION_DEPENDENCY_TRACKING	Default is TRUE; use the default setting to enable dependency tracking for read/write operations in a replicated environment.
SERIAL_REUSE	Default is **NULL**; setting the value to cursor types (such as SELECT or DML) enables those cursor types to move their cursors from private areas of memory to the shared pool.
SESSION_MAX_OPEN_FILES	Default is 10; sets the maximum number of BFILE files a session can open.
SHARED_MEMORY_ADDRESS	Default is 0; specifies the shared memory address of the SGA.
STAR_TRANSFORMATION_ENABLED	Default is FALSE; set to TRUE to enable star query transforms (common in data warehouses) to be applied to queries.
TAPE_ASYNCH_IO	Default is TRUE; enables asynchronous I/O to tape devices.
TIMED_OS_STATISTICS	Default is 0; if set to CALL, operating system statistics are gathered for every user call operation; if set to LOGOFF, statistics are gathered at user logoff time.
USE_INDIRECT_DATA_BUFFERS	Defaults to FALSE; controls the database's ability to use an extended buffer cache in environments with >4GB of memory available.

Desupported and Obsolete init.ora parameters in ORACLE8i

All of the parameters that are supported in ORACLE8.0.5 are also supported in ORACLE8.1.5. However, a large number of the supported parameters in 8.1.5 are officially obsolete, and you should no longer use them. Those obsolete parameters are listed here:

Parameter

ALLOW_PARTIAL_SN_RESULTS

ARCH_IO_SLAVES

B_TREE_BITMAP_PLANS

BACKUP_DISK_IO_SLAVES

CACHE_SIZE_THRESHOLD

CLEANUP_ROLLBACK_ENTRIES

CLOSE_CACHED_OPEN_CURSORS

COMPATIBLE_NO_RECOVERY

COMPLEX_VIEW_MERGING

DB_BLOCK_CHECKPOINT_BATCH

DB_BLOCK_LRU_EXTENDED_STATISTICS

DB_BLOCK_LRU_STATISTICS

DB_FILE_SIMULTANEOUS_WRITES

DISCRETE_TRANSACTIONS_ENABLED

DISTRIBUTED_LOCK_TIMEOUT

DISTRIBUTED_RECOVERY_CONNECTION_HOLD_TIME

FAST_FULL_SCAN_ENABLED

GC_LATCHES

GC_LCK_PROCS

LARGE_POOL_MIN_ALLOC

LGWR_IO_SLAVES

LOCK_SGA_AREAS

LOG_ARCHIVE_BUFFER_SIZE

LOG_ARCHIVE_BUFFERS

LOG_ARCHIVE_DEST

LOG_BLOCK_CHECKSUM

LOG_FILES

LOG_SIMULTANEOUS_COPIES

LOG_SMALL_ENTRY_MAX_SIZE

MAX_TRANSACTION_BRANCHES

Parameter

MTS_LISTENER_ADDRESS

MTS_MULTIPLE_LISTENERS

MTS_RATE_LOG_SIZE

MTS_RATE_SCALE

MTS_SERVICE

OGMS_HOME

OPS_ADMIN_GROUP

PARALLEL_DEFAULT_MAX_INSTANCES

PARALLEL_MIN_MESSAGE_POOL

PARALLEL_SERVER_IDLE_TIME

PARALLEL_TRANSACTION_RESOURCE_TIMEOUT

PUSH_JOIN_PREDICATE

REDUCE_ALARM

ROW_CACHE_CURSORS

SEQUENCE_CACHE_ENTRIES

SEQUENCE_CACHE_HASH_BUCKETS

SHARED_POOL_RESERVED_MIN_ALLOC

SORT_DIRECT_WRITES

SORT_READ_FAC

SORT_SPACEMAP_SIZE

SORT_WRITE_BUFFER_SIZE

SORT_WRITE_BUFFERS

SPIN_COUNT

TEMPORARY_TABLE_LOCKS

USE_ISM

New init.ora Parameters in ORACLE8i

The following table lists the parameters that are new as of ORACLE8i Release 8.1.5. For each parameter, you will see the default value where applicable, along with comments regarding the parameter's usage. Please see the ORACLE documentation for the full description of each parameter.

NOTE
The available parameters may change with each new version of ORACLE8i.

Parameter	Default Setting and Comments
DB_BLOCK_CHECKING	Defaults to TRUE; enables block checking at transaction time, replacing user-set events 10210 and 10211.
HS_AUTOREGISTER	Defaults to TRUE; controls automatic registration of HS agents.
INSTANCE_NAME	No default. Specifies the name of an instance on a server when multiple instances share the same Net8 service name.
JAVA_POOL_SIZE	Default is 10 MB; specifies the size of the Java pool.
LOG_ARCHIVE_DEST_N	Replaces LOG_ARCHIVE_DEST; specifies up to 5 destination locations for archived redo log files. The destination locations are written to concurrently, not sequentially.
LOG_ARCHIVE_DEST_STATE_N	Default is ENABLE, other value is DEFER; specifies whether corresponding LOG_ARCHIVE_DEST_N location is enabled as a destination site for archived redo logs.
LOG_ARCHIVE_MAX_PROCESSES	Default is 1; specifies the number of ARCH processes to start.
MVIEW_REWRITE_ENABLED	Default is FALSE; set to TRUE to enable the cost-based optimizer to rewrite queries used as the basis for materialized views.
NLS_COMP	Default is BINARY; simplifies NLS comparison operations, eliminating the need for NLS_SORT in **where** clauses.
NLS_UNION_CURRENCY	Overrides the default dual currency symbol for the NLS setting.
OPTIMIZER_INDEX_CACHING	Default is 0; sets the percentage (0 to 100) of an index that the optimizer should assume is in the data block buffer cache. Setting a high value makes NESTED LOOPS joins more likely than HASH JOINs or MERGE JOINs.
OPTIMIZER_INDEX_COST_ADJ	Default is 100; sets a percentage multiplier (0 to 10,000) by which the optimizer should adjust the cost of index-based accesses. Setting a value below 100 will cause index accesses to have a lower estimated cost, and therefore be more likely to be chosen.
OPTIMIZER_MAX_PERMUTATIONS	Default value is 80,000; limits the number of permutations the optimizer can evaluate before selecting an execution path.
PARALLEL_SERVER_INSTANCES	ORACLE Parallel Server parameter; default value is 1. Specifies the number of instances configured.
PARALLEL_THREADS_PER_CPU	Default is operating system dependent. Specifies the number of PQO threads executed per CPU; this parameter is set via PARALLEL_AUTOMATIC_TUNING.
PARALLEL_TRANSACTION_RECOVERY	Default is 'false'. If set to 'low' or 'high', then a low or high degree of parallelism is in effect during parallel recoveries.
RESOURCE_MANAGER_PLAN	Default is **NULL**; specifies the top resource plan in the database.
REWRITE_INTEGRITY	Default is ENFORCE; other values are USE_STALE and NO_ENFORCE. Specifies the degree of integrity checking that must be in place for queries to be rewritten by the optimizer; mostly a factor for materialized views.

Parameter	Default Setting and Comments
SERVICE_NAMES	Default is DB_NAME.DB_DOMAIN values; specifies the service name for the instance.
SORT_MULTIBLOCK_READ_COUNT	Default is 2; specifies the number of blocks to read from temporary segments during a multiblock read.
STANDBY_ARCHIVE_DEST	No default; specifies the archive log destination directory for a standby database.

In addition to the parameters just listed, users of Trusted Oracle have several new init.ora parameters available as of ORACLE8i: AUTOMOUNTING, DB_MOUNT_MODE, LABEL_CACHE_SIZE, MLS_LABEL_FORMAT, and OPEN_MOUNTS. See the Trusted ORACLE documentation for details on the use of these parameters.

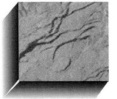

APPENDIX C

Redesigning for 24x7 Availability

As systems are modified to support larger user communities, the availability requirements for the systems may increase. For example, if your company merges with a global corporation, your financials system may have to be available 24 hours a day—a requirement that may not have been part of your original technical requirements. Another common source for increased availability requirements is an Internet-based user community. Once you enable users to execute transactions in your database via the Internet, users will expect the database to be available around the clock, with very few interruptions.

Twenty-four-hour-a-day, seven-day-a-week availability (24x7) is a significant technical requirement. Often, it is considered only after an application has been moved into the production environment. Improving the availability of an existing application is difficult and may require redesign of the system. In this appendix, you will see a brief overview of approaches to follow when dealing with a 24x7 requirement. For best results, you should approach 24x7 as a business-process requirement rather than a technical requirement. Once you focus on the business process being served, the number of technical solutions available expands dramatically.

In the first section of this appendix, you will see a set of technical approaches for high-availability database applications. Following the approaches, you will see a set of technical solutions for high availability.

Technical Approaches

Depending on your application life cycle, you may not be able to influence the technical approach used by the application. If you can influence the technical design of the application, you should follow these guidelines:

- Limit database accesses
- Limit database size
- Eliminate points of failure

In the following sections, you will see examples of each of these approaches.

Limit Database Accesses

At some point, your database will need to be unavailable—during an upgrade, or a cold backup, or due to a power failure. During that time, you should minimize the impact that the database outage has on the business process. To minimize the downtime impact, you should minimize the number of times the database is accessed by the application.

For example, if your application writes to the database via ODBC in batch transactions, you could have those ODBC transactions write to files instead, followed by loading those files into ORACLE via SQL*Loader. If the database is down, the SQL*Loader portion of the transaction cannot complete, but the ODBC portion of the application could still be successfully executed.

If your users repeatedly execute the same reports, you can pregenerate reports and distribute them (or publish them via the Internet or local network). Users would be able to view their most-used data without directly accessing the database. If the database is seldom directly accessed for ad hoc queries not served by your pregenerated reports, then the impact of a database outage on the business processes is minimized.

These two approaches address the availability issue by using batch transactions for data input and data viewing. In each case, you would need to determine the allowable data latency—how old can the data be before it impacts your business practices? If users can make effective business decisions with data that is eight hours old, then you may be able to use that window of time to manage your database without interrupting the business.

If your users enter data interactively, then you should limit the number of times you query the database during data entry. Many traditional OLTP applications query the database to perform lookups of code values. For example, you may validate a purchase requisition number, as it is entered, against a set of valid purchase requisition numbers. However, if you want to limit the database accesses, you can use different approaches to data validation during interactive inserts. For example, you can assume that the users will do their job correctly, avoiding the need for data validation steps for each field inserted; instead, you could let the defined referential integrity in the database validate the data. You can help users via training and by customizing the data entry screens with drop-down lists of valid values.

These changes involve changing the way the data is entered, accepted, processed, and displayed. Such significant changes are difficult to make unless the application is reengineered to account for the 24x7 requirement. If you cannot make these changes, you will need to pursue other technical approaches and solutions.

Limit Database Size

If a database has to be available 24x7, you should make the database as small as possible. Any data that is not directly related to the business process served should be removed from the database. If only a small transactional system needs to be available 24x7, don't put a large data warehouse in the same instance. The smaller the database is, the easier it will be to achieve a high-availability requirement.

Separating data among instances may help—the data may have significantly different growth and usage characteristics. However, separating data among instances may make the administration of the overall database environment more complex. In a more distributed environment, you will have more issues with managing database links, tuning remote queries, and keeping replicated data in sync.

Again, as you implement your database for 24x7, keep it as small as possible. Once the application has been created in your database, it will be more difficult to split its objects among instances. If the application has already been implemented and has no obvious divisions, you will need to pursue other technical approaches and solutions.

Eliminate Points of Failure

Within the database environment, you should eliminate any known areas that can cause the database or hardware to become unavailable. Eliminating points of failure may include the following:

- Implementing RAID and mirroring systems for the hardware. As described in Chapter 4, these systems guard your availability against the loss of a single disk.

- Implement fault-tolerant and redundant hardware. Many manufacturers provide solutions that have redundant hardware components, allowing for immediate failover in the event of a disruption. Some manufacturers provide solutions that automatically copy data from one set of disks to another set, providing disk-level replication.

- Use autoextendable datafiles. You will need to make sure the disks used have adequate space available to support extensions of your datafiles.

- Set the MAXDATAFILES parameter setting to its maximum value for your operating system. Increasing MAXDATAFILES requires you to shut down the database and re-create the control files (see Chapter 1), a situation you need to avoid in 24x7 environment.

- Use unlimited extents. Having too many extents will impact the performance of your DDL operations, but if your goal is high availability then you should avoid failures caused by objects reaching their maximum number of extents. You should size your objects properly (see Chapter 5) to avoid acquiring a large number of extents.

- Create a large SGA. If you cannot shut down the database, you cannot increase the size of the data block buffer cache or the Shared SQL Pool. Estimate your future requirements and create a large SGA when the application is first in production.

■ If you use ARCHIVELOG mode (see Chapter 10), leave a large space available for archived redo log files. Monitor the size of the redo log destination areas and manage those areas as necessary to maintain adequate free space. If the ARCH process cannot write new archived redo log files to the destination areas, the database will stop until space is made available.

■ Within the database, allocate extra space for rollback segments, temporary segments, and the data dictionary.

These approaches will eliminate many of the most common points of failure in the database. If your application is particularly susceptible to a point of failure, you should attempt to minimize its impact. For example, if your application data changes frequently, you will need to schedule times when you can **analyze** the tables without impacting the users. You can minimize the impact of the **analyze** commands by using the **estimate** option, by analyzing partitions rather than tables, and by scheduling the **analyze** actions to avoid conflicts with user actions on those tables.

These technical approaches may dramatically improve your ability to support a 24x7 business process. As noted in these approaches, you need to be able to control the size of the data, the way it is accessed, and the points of failure in its environment. In the following sections, you will see technical solutions for administration and recovery in 24x7 environments.

Technical Solutions

To effectively administer a high-availability database, you need to be able to perform database administration actions quickly, with minimal interference to the business process. The technical approaches in the preceding sections focused on application redesign in an attempt to reduce the availability requirements on the database. If you are not able to modify the application design, you may need to implement a technical solution to your business problem. It is unlikely that any technical solution will fully achieve 24x7 availability for a system that was implemented without 24x7 as a technical design requirement.

Any technical solution for achieving high availability should include the following components:

■ Extensive testing of database administration actions

■ Very fast administration procedures

■ Very short recovery time requirements

In addition to these solutions, you will need a mechanism to automate fast notification of failures. For example, you can configure an SNMP-enabled monitor to page a DBA in the event of a database problem. Quick notification of failure conditions reduces the time required to react following a problem occurrence. You can also configure the monitor program to automatically perform actions, such as attempting to restart a database.

In the following sections, you will see descriptions of each solution.

Testing of Database Administration Activities

If you are not able to redesign your application and database according to the technical approaches described in the first half of this appendix, then you will need to perform periodic administration activities on the database. For example, you may need to add datafiles, resize tables, or move objects among tablespaces.

Before making these changes, you must be able to effectively test them in an environment that mimics the production environment. You can use the test results to determine the best procedures to follow for upgrades and modifications. Based on those results, you can evaluate the impact of your changes on the application and schedule the changes appropriately. Testing may not identify every problem, but it will allow you to anticipate major issues. If you discover problems during testing, you can reduce the number of errors introduced into the production environment, thereby improving your database availability.

Administer Quickly

Your choice of database administration procedures will be influenced by a high-availability requirement for an existing database. Consider three DBA activities: database software upgrades, data movement among databases, and database backups.

Database Software Upgrades

If the database cannot be unavailable for long, your database upgrades will probably not involve using Export and Import to move data between separate instances. Instead, you will likely use the incremental upgrade technique described in Chapter 2. If your operating system can support multiple versions of the ORACLE software, the process for upgrading your ORACLE database may involve only a short shutdown of the database. The database will be pointed to its new ORACLE software home directory, and its listener.ora and /etc/oratab entries can be updated quickly. After the new listener is started for the instance and the database is opened, you can quickly execute the data dictionary catalog scripts provided in the /rdbms/admin directory under the ORACLE software home directory.

Version-specific upgrade details are provided in the README.doc file in the /rdbms/doc directory under the ORACLE software home directory.

Before performing an upgrade of the database software, you should perform a backup of the current database and its software. In a 24x7 environment, you may need to implement technical solutions specifically designed with your backup needs in mind. See the "Database Backups" section later in this appendix for further details on database backups.

While the catalog upgrade method for database upgrades is valid for most version upgrades, upgrades between major releases will involve more complex procedures. To assist in the upgrades between major releases such as from ORACLE7 to ORACLE8, ORACLE provides migration utilities. Upgrades that use the migration utilities should be thoroughly tested in your DBA testing environment prior to being implemented in the production environment. You will also need to evaluate if the migration utility has additional performance or availability costs incurred following the upgrade.

Data Movement Among Databases

If you need to move a large quantity of data among databases, you have a number of options. With each of its recent releases, ORACLE has introduced new features designed to improve the performance of large data loads. For example, you can use the **nologging** parameter, SQL*Loader Direct Path loading, the **parallel** options, and the APPEND hint to improve data loading operations.

If the data is in one database and needs to be moved quickly to another database, you should investigate the use of transportable tablespaces. As described in Chapter 12, you can use transportable tablespaces to move a self-contained set of tablespaces from one database to another. In the target database, you only import the tablespace's metadata, not its data. As a result, the performance of the data move will be significantly better than a full import of all of the tables.

NOTE
You should minimize the amount of data and the number of tables moved in order to improve the performance of data movement operations.

You can only use the transportable tablespaces option if the source and target databases are both using ORACLE8i, and if the operating environments are identical. As a further restriction, the tablespaces in the transport set must be self-contained, with no dependencies on objects in other tablespaces. To take advantage of transportable tablespaces, you may need to redesign the tablespace layout for your database objects.

Database Backups

The only kind of database backup that directly impacts availability is an offline file system backup. To perform offline backups quickly, you will need to configure the operating environment with this requirement in mind. Ideally, you should build the operating environment to have three copies of your production data: the database, a mirror set, and a second mirror set. To perform offline backups, you would follow these steps:

1. Shut down the database.

2. Break the second mirror set from the configuration.

3. Start up the database.

4. Back up the files on the second mirror set to your backup media.

5. Resync the second mirror set.

During this process, the database is only unavailable for as long as it takes you to break the second mirror set from the configuration. The resync process in step 5 is performed at the operating system level; many hardware vendors support a resync process that sends only the changes since the mirror set was broken. If your configuration requires complete re-creation of the mirror set, you will need to factor the performance impact of the mirror set re-creation into your design.

If you use Export to back up your data, you should minimize the impact the export has on the production system. To improve the performance of your exports, you should use the DIRECT=Y option. Direct exports perform dramatically faster than traditional exports. You should also evaluate your need for the CONSISTENT parameter for your exports. A consistent export performs much slower than a CONSISTENT=N export. If you use CONSISTENT=N for your exports, your export performance will improve but the data in the export file may violate the referential integrity rules defined for the database. See Chapter 10 for further details on these parameters.

Recover Quickly

In addition to designing a backup method that minimizes downtime, a 24x7 database must have a recovery strategy that minimizes the mean time to recovery (MTTR). While planning your backup and recovery strategy, you will need your users' input in order to give the backup and recovery requirements proper weight. Your users may choose to purchase redundant hardware to limit the likelihood of a hardware failure impacting database availability. If the hardware environment is not a source of failures, and all changes are properly tested before being implemented in production, then you may not perform many recoveries. If that is the case, you may alter your backup and recovery plans to lengthen the MTTR while performing backups faster. The decisions you make regarding the backup and recovery procedures will directly impact the business processes, so you must work with your users to determine the proper direction.

There are four common methods for reducing MTTR:

- Mirrored environments

- Standby databases

- Replication

- ORACLE Parallel Server

Regardless of the method you choose, you must be sure it does not significantly impact the performance and availability of the application. In the following sections, you will see descriptions of each of these solutions.

Mirrored Environments

As described in the "Database Backups" section earlier in this appendix, you can use mirrored environments to significantly reduce the time required to perform backups. You can also use mirrored environments to reduce the time required to perform recoveries. You can use the previous night's mirror set as an online copy of the database files, available instantly during a recovery. For example, assume you have two mirror sets of a set of datafiles. During an offline backup, your backup process may be as in the following:

1. Shut down the database.

2. Break the second mirror set from the configuration.

3. Start up the database.

4. Back up the files on the second mirror set to your backup media.

Instead of resyncing the second mirror set, leave the set broken. The mirror set thus serves as a disk copy of the database from the last backup, immediately available during a recovery. During the next night's offline backup, the backup process may be as in the following:

1. Resync the second mirror.

2. Shut down the database.

3. Break the second mirror set from the configuration.

4. Start up the database.

5. Back up the files on the second mirror set to your backup media.

The second mirror set thus serves as a permanent backup set. Because it is configured as a backup set, you can resync it as the primary mirror set if you experience a media failure with your primary mirror set.

If you use online backups, the backup methods are slightly different. In an online backup approach, you can use the second set of disks as a detached set, not a mirror set. During your backups, perform disk-to-disk backups of the datafiles from the primary disks to the second set of disks. You will then have a set of mirror disks in the event of a media failure and an online copy of your backups in the event of a major failure.

Standby Databases

As described in Chapter 10, you can maintain a standby database for quick disaster recovery. A standby database maintains a copy of the production database in a permanent state of recovery. In the event of a disaster in the production database, you can open the standby database with a minimal amount of recovery necessary. A standby database offers a short MTTR, at the expense of the potential loss of the contents of the online redo log files in your production database.

The potential loss may be greater than just the online redo log files. If there is a large distance between the primary database and the standby database, then the time required to transfer the archived redo log files from the primary to the standby server may be significant. If the primary system has a disaster during the archived redo log file transfer, then the data loss will include the online redo log files and at least one archived redo log file. Depending on the time interval between redo log switches, the potential data loss may have an adverse impact on the ongoing business processes. During a recovery, you need to open the standby database, effectively breaking its connection to the production instance. A standby database may be appropriate if you can re-create the transactions that would be lost during a failover operation. Also, note that once the standby database is activated, you no longer have a standby database. Once you activate the standby database as your new primary database, you will need to create a new standby database in order to maintain the recoverability of your data. You will need to perform more database administration activities, but the MTTR will be reduced.

Replication

You can replicate your data at the database level and at the operating system level. At the database level, you can use ORACLE's replication methods (see Chapter 16) to create read-only copies of your master tables. During a recovery situation, you could have the users connect to the replica instance and perform transactions there.

Quick recovery via a replication solution requires careful planning. As soon as you allow users to enter data into the replica environment, you create possible conflicts with the primary production environment. You will need to decide whether to use read-only replication or the more difficult to administer multimaster replication offerings. Lastly, you will need to schedule and monitor the replication schedule to support your MTTR needs.

A successful replication solution typically replicates as little data as possible. If you cannot limit the database size, you should limit the number of tables and rows replicated. The replica does not have to be a full copy of the production instance—it may only need to be large enough to process the entry of new rows during the recovery of the primary database. You will need to work with the application maintenance team to understand the minimum requirements for the replica environment.

When planning your replication environment, you should also consider operating system–level replication. Several vendors offer replication services that replicate data at the operating system level. If you **insert** a new record into a table, the operating system replication will replicate the changes to the datafiles that the **insert** affects. Since this replication occurs at the operating system level, it may be much more efficient than replication at the database level. Operating system–level replication, combined with a small database to support transactions during a failure, provides for a very short MTTR with (potentially) no data loss.

ORACLE Parallel Server

ORACLE Parallel Server (OPS), as described in Chapter 2, supports multiple instances on a single cluster accessing the same set of datafiles. If one of the servers in the cluster fails, users can access the datafiles from the second instance. In such a situation, there is no recovery time needed—the database is still available.

Before choosing an OPS solution, you should evaluate the causes of service outages in your environment. OPS is an effective solution if you have a clustered environment in which the disks are not prone to failure. In an OPS environment, a disk failure results in a service outage, because the instances access the same set of datafiles. If your disks fail more frequently than your servers fail, you should either improve your disk redundancy methods or choose a different recovery strategy.

When using a two-instance OPS strategy for quick recoveries, you should not allow users to access the second instance unless the primary instance fails. If you allow users to access both instances, you will encounter performance problems caused by contention for the same database blocks in the separate instances. Managing an OPS environment is not trivial, but requires careful planning of the lock distribution and init.ora parameters—settings that cannot be changed postimplementation without impacting availability. To effectively implement OPS, you may need to redesign the application's table layout and data access patterns.

Establish Business Contingency Plans

Designing for 24x7 availability requires you to make trade-offs, such as time required for backups against the cost of additional disks for mirror sets. You should establish a test environment that is robust enough to support tests that can justify the technical decisions you need to make. Based on the test results, you may choose to use different database administration and data movement procedures than you use in your non-24x7 databases. In the worst-case scenario, you may prove that the application needs to be significantly altered in order to be supported 24x7. You may need to segment the application, allowing some components to fail with a longer MTTR than the rest of the application.

If the application cannot be altered, then it may fail. You should keep in mind that there are always components of an application architecture that are beyond your control. If your users access the database via the Internet, their connection is as reliable as their client, their phone lines, their ISP, and their ISP's connection to your service. The goal in 24x7 design is to minimize the impact of any outage on the effective execution of the business process. Thus, your design must account for the total failure of all these components—potentially even taking orders on paper until the system is available again. You will need to work closely with your users to implement a technical approach and solution that meets their needs for high availability.

For each business process, there should be a matching contingency plan describing the actions required during a failure of the process's technical components. You can use the approaches and solutions presented in this appendix as components of a contingency plan for the database environment. Your database contingency plans and technical solutions must be part of a larger plan for the overall technical architecture contingency. Once you have implemented a technical approach, you can establish service-level agreements with your users, and you can get closer to achieving 24x7 availability.

Index

B

F

G

Think you're
smart?

**You're an Oracle DBA.
You're implementing a
backup and recovery plan.
Which component stores
the synchronization
information needed for
database recovery?**

a. redo log files

b. control file

c. parameter file

d. trace file

Think you're ready to wear this badge?

Get Your **FREE** Subscription to Oracle Magazine

Stay informed and increase your productivity with every issue of *Oracle Magazine*. Inside each FREE, bimonthly issue you'll get:

- Up-to-date information on Oracle Data Server, Oracle Applications, Network Computing Architecture, and tools
- Third-party news and announcements
- Technical articles on Oracle products and operating environments
- Software tuning tips
- Oracle customer application stories

Three easy ways to subscribe:

1 MAIL Cut out this page, complete the questionnaire on the back, and mail it to: *Oracle Magazine*, P.O. Box 1263, Skokie, IL 60076-8263.

2 FAX Cut out this page, complete the questionnaire on the back, and fax it to **+ 847.647.9735.**

3 WEB Visit our Web site at **www.oramag.com.** You'll find a subscription form there, plus much more!

If there are other Oracle users at your location who would like to receive their own subscription to *Oracle Magazine,* please photocopy the form and pass it along.

You must answer all eight questions below.

1 What is the primary business activity of your firm at this location?
(circle only one)
- ○ 01 Agriculture, Mining, Natural Resources
- ○ 02 Architecture, Construction
- ○ 03 Communications
- ○ 04 Consulting, Training
- ○ 05 Consumer Packaged Goods
- ○ 06 Data Processing
- ○ 07 Education
- ○ 08 Engineering
- ○ 09 Financial Services
- ○ 10 Government—Federal, Local, State, Other
- ○ 11 Government—Military
- ○ 12 Health Care
- ○ 13 Manufacturing—Aerospace, Defense
- ○ 14 Manufacturing—Computer Hardware
- ○ 15 Manufacturing—Noncomputer Products
- ○ 16 Real Estate, Insurance
- ○ 17 Research & Development
- ○ 18 Human Resources
- ○ 19 Retailing, Wholesaling, Distribution
- ○ 20 Software Development
- ○ 21 Systems Integration, VAR, VAD, OEM
- ○ 22 Transportation
- ○ 23 Utilities (Electric, Gas, Sanitation)
- ○ 24 Other Business and Services _____

2 Which of the following best describes your job function? *(circle only one)*
CORPORATE MANAGEMENT/STAFF
- ○ 01 Executive Management (President, Chair, CEO, CFO, Owner, Partner, Principal)
- ○ 02 Finance/Administrative Management (VP/Director/ Manager/Controller, Purchasing, Administration)
- ○ 03 Sales/Marketing Management (VP/Director/Manager)
- ○ 04 Computer Systems/Operations Management (CIO/VP/Director/ Manager MIS, Operations)
- ○ 05 Other Finance/Administration Staff
- ○ 06 Other Sales/Marketing Staff

IS/IT Staff
- ○ 07 Systems Development/ Programming Management
- ○ 08 Systems Development/ Programming Staff
- ○ 09 Consulting
- ○ 10 DBA/Systems Administrator
- ○ 11 Education/Training
- ○ 12 Engineering/R&D/Science Management
- ○ 13 Engineering/R&D/Science Staff
- ○ 14 Technical Support Director/ Manager
- ○ 15 Webmaster/Internet Specialist
- ○ 16 Other Technical Management/ Staff

3 What is your current primary operating platform? *(circle all that apply)*
- ○ 01 DEC UNIX
- ○ 02 DEC VAX VMS
- ○ 03 Java
- ○ 04 HP UNIX
- ○ 05 IBM AIX
- ○ 06 IBM UNIX
- ○ 07 Macintosh
- ○ 08 MPE-ix
- ○ 09 MS-DOS
- ○ 10 MVS
- ○ 11 NetWare
- ○ 12 Network Computing
- ○ 13 OpenVMS
- ○ 14 SCO UNIX
- ○ 15 Sun Solaris/ SunOS
- ○ 16 SVR4
- ○ 17 Ultrix
- ○ 18 UnixWare
- ○ 19 VM
- ○ 20 Windows
- ○ 21 Windows NT
- ○ 22 Other _____
- ○ 23 Other UNIX _____

4 Do you evaluate, specify, recommend, or authorize the purchase of any of the following? *(circle all that apply)*
- ○ 01 Hardware
- ○ 02 Software
- ○ 03 Application Development Tools
- ○ 04 Database Products
- ○ 05 Internet or Intranet Products

5 In your job, do you use or plan to purchase any of the following products or services?
(check all that apply)

SOFTWARE

	Use	Plan to buy
01 Business Graphics	☐	☐
02 CAD/CAE/CAM	☐	☐
03 CASE	☐	☐
04 CIM	☐	☐
05 Communications	☐	☐
06 Database Management	☐	☐
07 File Management	☐	☐
08 Finance	☐	☐
09 Java	☐	☐
10 Materials Resource Planning	☐	☐
11 Multimedia Authoring	☐	☐
12 Networking	☐	☐
13 Office Automation	☐	☐
14 Order Entry/ Inventory Control	☐	☐
15 Programming	☐	☐
16 Project Management	☐	☐
17 Scientific and Engineering	☐	☐
18 Spreadsheets	☐	☐
19 Systems Management	☐	☐
20 Workflow	☐	☐

HARDWARE

	Use	Plan to buy
21 Macintosh	☐	☐
22 Mainframe	☐	☐
23 Massively Parallel Processing	☐	☐
24 Minicomputer	☐	☐
25 PC	☐	☐
26 Network Computer	☐	☐
27 Supercomputer	☐	☐
28 Symmetric Multiprocessing	☐	☐
29 Workstation	☐	☐

PERIPHERALS

	Use	Plan to buy
30 Bridges/Routers/Hubs/ Gateways	☐	☐
31 CD-ROM Drives	☐	☐
32 Disk Drives/Subsystems	☐	☐
33 Modems	☐	☐
34 Tape Drives/Subsystems	☐	☐
35 Video Boards/Multimedia	☐	☐

SERVICES

	Use	Plan to buy
36 Computer-Based Training	☐	☐
37 Consulting	☐	☐
38 Education/Training	☐	☐
39 Maintenance	☐	☐
40 Online Database Services	☐	☐
41 Support	☐	☐
42 **None of the above**	☐	☐

6 What Oracle products are in use at your site? *(circle all that apply)*
SERVER/SOFTWARE
- ○ 01 Oracle8
- ○ 02 Oracle7
- ○ 03 Oracle Application Server
- ○ 04 Oracle Data Mart Suites
- ○ 05 Oracle Internet Commerce Server
- ○ 06 Oracle InterOffice
- ○ 07 Oracle Lite
- ○ 08 Oracle Payment Server
- ○ 09 Oracle Rdb
- ○ 10 Oracle Security Server
- ○ 11 Oracle Video Server
- ○ 12 Oracle Workgroup Server

TOOLS
- ○ 13 Designer/2000
- ○ 14 Developer/2000 (Forms, Reports, Graphics)
- ○ 15 Oracle OLAP Tools
- ○ 16 Oracle Power Object

ORACLE APPLICATIONS
- ○ 17 Oracle Automotive
- ○ 18 Oracle Energy
- ○ 19 Oracle Consumer Packaged Goods
- ○ 20 Oracle Financials
- ○ 21 Oracle Human Resources
- ○ 22 Oracle Manufacturing
- ○ 23 Oracle Projects
- ○ 24 Oracle Sales Force Automat▮
- ○ 25 Oracle Supply Chain Management
- ○ 26 Other _____
- ○ 27 **None of the above**

7 What other database products are in at your site? *(circle all that apply)*
- ○ 01 Access
- ○ 02 BAAN
- ○ 03 dbase
- ○ 04 Gupta
- ○ 05 IBM DB2
- ○ 06 Informix
- ○ 07 Ingres
- ○ 08 Microsoft Access
- ○ 09 Microsoft SQL Serve▮
- ○ 10 Peoplesof▮
- ○ 11 Progress
- ○ 12 SAP
- ○ 13 Sybase
- ○ 14 VSAM
- ○ 15 **None of th▮ above**

8 During the next 12 months, how much you anticipate your organization will spend on computer hardware, softwar peripherals, and services for your location? *(circle only one)*
- ○ 01 Less than $10,000
- ○ 02 $10,000 to $49,999
- ○ 03 $50,000 to $99,999
- ○ 04 $100,000 to $499,999
- ○ 05 $500,000 to $999,999
- ○ 06 $1,000,000 and over

OM

About the CD-ROM

The CD-ROM that comes with this book includes the scripts featured in this book. The scripts are all available as plain ASCII text files so you can easily copy them to the operating platform of your choice. The scripts are compiled into files on a chapter-by-chapter basis. There is one file per chapter. The scripts are shown in the order in which they occur in the chapter. There are no scripts associated with any of the appendixes.

For details on the use of the scripts and interpretation of the output, see the appropriate chapter of this book.

The scripts are shown out of context, with none of the accompanying text. The scripts are provided here to simplify your testing and development process. Some of the scripts contain variables whose values you will need to change prior to running the commands.

The online versions of these files will be updated as the book is updated, and as corrections are implemented. Errata will be posted at http://www.kevinloney.com and will be fixed in later printings.

Copyright Information